THE GENERALISSIMO'S SON

Chiang Ching-kuo as an officer in the Chinese Army
(c. 1938). *KMT Central Committee Archives*

The
Generalissimo's Son

CHIANG CHING-KUO AND THE REVOLUTIONS

IN CHINA AND TAIWAN

Jay Taylor

HARVARD UNIVERSITY PRESS

CAMBRIDGE, MASSACHUSETTS

LONDON, ENGLAND

2000

LIBRARY OF CONGRESS CATALOGING-IN-PUBLICATION DATA

Taylor, Jay.
    The Generalissimo's son : Chiang Ching-kuo and the revolutions in
China and Taiwan / Jay Taylor.
      p.   cm.
    Includes index.
    ISBN 0-674-00287-3 (alk. paper)
    1. Chiang, Ching-kuo, 1910–1988. 2. Presidents—Taiwan—
Biography. 3. China—History—1912–1949. 4. Taiwan—History—
1945– I. Title: Chiang Ching-kuo and the revolutions in China and
Taiwan. II. Title.

DS799.82.C437 T39 2000
951.24'905'092—dc21
[B]   00-035053

FOR THE GOLDEN HORDE

John, Laurie, Amy, Cynthia, Maureen, Jeff, Jim,
David, Jeanette, Taylor, Myles, Jessica, Emily, Jack,
Savannah, Nathaniel, Gabrielle, Ayston,
and those to come

Other books by the author:

China and Southeast Asia: Peking's Relations with Revolutionary Movements

The Dragon and the Wild Goose: China and India

The Rise and Fall of Totalitarianism in the Twentieth Century

Acknowledgments

IN 1995 I SIGNED AN AGREEMENT with the China Times Publishing Company in Taipei to write a biography of Chiang Ching-kuo. Central to the arrangement was the written stipulation—purposefully redundant—that I would have "complete and total editorial control" of both the English and Chinese language editions. In a meeting with the Chairman of the China Times, Mr. Yu Chi-chung, I underscored my intention to write the story of Chiang Ching-kuo in as objective a manner as I could, describing the favorable, the controversial, and the unfavorable. There would probably be, I warned, many warts or worse in the portrait that emerged. Mr. Yu, a long-time friend and supporter of Chiang Ching-kuo, replied that he fully understood and accepted my condition. Mr. Yu and the China Times Publishing Company never sought to influence my research or even to suggest changes in the manuscript as it developed through various drafts.

Subsequently, Harvard University Press undertook to publish the English edition of *The Generalissimo's Son,* and in an agreement between the Press and the China Times Publishing Company, it was stipulated that the latter would publish an unaltered Chinese translation of the Harvard book.

FOR CHIANG CHING-KUO'S RUSSIAN YEARS, I enjoyed the valuable assistance of Professor Alexander Larin of the Institute of Far Eastern Studies in Moscow and Ambassador (ret.) Andrei Ledovsky. I also benefited from many meetings with Dr. Yu Min-ling of Taipei's Academia Sinica, who kindly shared the fruit of her prolonged research in the Moscow archives. During my trips to China, and via frequent e-mail communications, I received the invaluable support of Professor Yang Tianshi and the Institute of Modern Chinese History in Peking, which he then headed. I am indebted to Professor Yang for the material from Chiang Kai-shek's diaries in the Nanking Number Two National Archives. I also wish to acknowledge support from the archivist at the Nanking Archives, Ma Ch'en-tu, and the archivist at the Shanghai Municipal Archives, Ch'en Cheng-ch'ing. Special mention must also be made of Wang Hsun-ch'i, a Fenghua researcher and writer on Chiang Ching-kuo's early life, who assisted on trips to Fenghua and Hsikou and provided unique material.

A group meeting with other local researchers in Fenghua was also extremely helpful. These included: Wang Yueh-hsi, Deputy Secretary General of the Fenghua Federation of Literary and Arts Circles; the Mayor of Fenghua, Szu Tuan-lu; Hu Yuan-fu, Chu Chia-hui and Hsia Ming-hsi, cadre of the Fenghua Taiwan Affairs Office; and Mao Ping-yueh and other distant relatives of Chiang Ching-kuo. During my travels on the mainland I was ably assisted by Jia Wei and Xiao Tonghua.

My associate on Taiwan during my first visit in pursuit of this project was the very efficient Ms. Halima Dick. Since that time, Ms. Shen Shiau-chi has been my key and invaluable associate on the island; Ms. Andrea Cheng ably filled in when Ms. Shen was not available. Tsu Sung-chiu and Wang Shao-yu, old Chiang Ching-kuo comrades, and Dr. Thomas Chang of Suchow University were also very helpful and kind during my trips to Taiwan. In the United States, a number of graduate students at the University of Virginia provided vital research assistance. These associates included Liu Debin, He Songbei, and Karen Zeng. From early on, Tu Chih-ping was an enthusiastic and productive associate.

Cornelia Levin ably boiled down the 1,200-page first draft to a more manageable version. My son John then undertook the final editing project. I am grateful to a number of friends and scholars for reading various drafts and providing candid criticisms and suggestions. These include

Parris Chang, Ralph Clough, David Dean, Norman Fu, Harvey Feldman, Hsu Cho-yun, William Kirby, Leng Shao-chuan, James Lilley, Mark Pratt, Tsu Sung-chiu, Tu Chih-ping, and Wei Xing-li. Sometimes, of course, sources and readers differed on details and interpretation. As always, the author is solely responsible for the contents as they appear. A final note of thanks to Betsy, who provided love and support through the long march and was companion, adviser, and administrator on my travels.

Note on Romanization of Chinese Names

THE THREE MOST COMMON WAYS to romanize Chinese names into English are: (1) the Wade-Giles system used on Taiwan; (2) the pinyin system used on the mainland; and (3) idiosyncratic spellings and English-Chinese name combinations adopted by individuals themselves (for example, Wellington Koo, John Chang, or Y. S. Tsiang). In this text Chinese names are written in the Wade-Giles system, except for idiosyncratic spellings and the universally used pinyin form for names of the best-known leaders of the Peoples Republic of China, Mao Zedong, Zhou Enlai, and Deng Xiaoping.

The Romanization Table in the Appendix provides the name of each Chinese as used in the text; the same name in Wade-Giles; and the name in pinyin.

In the text Chinese places, rivers, and mountains are given their historic or traditional names in English: for example, Yangtze, Peking, Amoy, Tibet, Chekiang, and for that matter, China. The Chinese, incidentally, have shown the good sense not to change their traditional names for American or other foreign places. In Chinese usage, San Francisco remains "Old Gold Mountain." In the text, aside from those places and geographic features with peculiar but traditional English-language names, other places and features are romanized in the Wade-Giles system.

Contents

NOTE ON ROMANIZATION OF CHINESE NAMES   /x

ABBREVIATIONS   /xiii

Part One   Revolution

1   Upright Stone   /3

2   A Teachable Son   /14

3   Dreams of the Red Chamber   /27

4   Socialist Man   /49

5   Reunion and War   /74

6   The Kannan Model   /96

7   Dean and General   /116

8   Manchurian Candidate   /129

9   Defeat   /144

10   End Game   /165

Part Two   The Island

11   An Unintended Consequence   /191

12   Secret Wars   /206

13   Family, Friends, Enemies   /223

14   Managing the Great Patron   /236

15   China Leaps Backward   /255

16   The Minister   /272

17   The Golden Cudgel   /284

18   The Premier   /303

19   Old Orders Passing   /320

20   The Divorce   /331

21   Riot and Trials   /346

22   Island and Mainland   /361

23   Successors, Brokers, Killers   /377

24   Building Consensus   /395

25   Breakthrough   /405

26   A Chinese Democracy   /421

EPILOGUE   /431
APPENDIX: ROMANIZATION TABLE   /437
NOTES   /447
INDEX   /513

ILLUSTRATIONS FOLLOW P. 187

Abbreviations

ACNSC—Anti-Communist National Salvation Corps
AID—Agency for International Development
AIT—American Institute in Taiwan
AFP—Anti-Communist Patriotic Front
BBC—British Broadcasting Corporation
CAT—Civil Air Transport
CC Clique—Political clique of Ch'en Kuo-fu and Ch'en Li-fu
CCNAA—Coordination Council for North American Affairs
CCP—Chinese Communist Party
CEPD—Council for Economic Planning and Development
CIA—Central Intelligence Agency
CIEC—Council for International Economic Cooperation
Comintern—Communist International
CPSU—Communist Party of the Soviet Union
DDI—Deputy (CIA) Director for Intelligence
DPP—Democratic Progressive Party
FBIS—Foreign Broadcast Information Service
FBI—Federal Bureau of Investigation
FEER—Far Eastern Economic Review
FEMC—Financial, Economic, and Monetary Conference
FX—advanced fighter aircraft

GIO—Government Information Office
GPWD—General Political Warfare Department
GRC—Government of the Republic of China
IBMND—Intelligence Bureau of the Ministry of National Defense
ICA—International Cooperation Agency
ITRI—Industrial Technology Research Institute
JCRR—Joint Commission on Rural Reconstruction
KGB—Committee of State Security
KMT—Kuomintang (Nationalist Party)
KOMSOMOL—Communist Youth League
LSK—Liu Hsiao-k'ang Office
MAAG—Military Assistance Advisory Group
NACC—Naval Auxiliary Communications Center
NCO—non-commissioned officers
NIE—National Intelligence Estimate
NKVD—Ministry of State Security
NSA—National Security Agency
NSB—National Security Bureau
NSC—National Security Council
NT—New Taiwan dollar
NTU—National Taiwan University
OGPU—Unified States Political Administration (Soviet internal security)
OPC—Office of Policy Coordination
OSS—Office of Strategic Services
PKI—Communist Party of Indonesia
PLA—Peoples Liberation Army
POW—prisoner of war
PRC—-Peoples Republic of China.
PS—China Patriotic Society
ROC—Republic of China
Sunovka—Sun Yat-sen University
TRA—Taiwan Relations Act
USSR—Union of Soviet Socialist Republics
VACRS—Vocational Assistance Commission for Retired Servicemen
VOA—Voice of America

PART ONE

Revolution

1

Upright Stone

FOR SUCH A HISTORY-STRUCK CULTURE AS CHINA, the end of the nineteenth and the beginning of the twentieth century was the most demoralizing period in four thousand years of recorded civilization. In 1636 two million Manchus from beyond the Great Wall defeated the 120 million Han Chinese under the reign of the Ming dynasty. But this "barbarian" conqueror dynasty, like the Mongols and others in the more distant past, recognized the superiority of Chinese culture, adopted its language and most of its trappings, and relied on and maintained traditional society, including its scholar gentry and rural elite. The land was conquered, but Chinese civilization triumphed.

Western nineteenth-century intrusions into China were different. These "foreign devils" not only were militarily superior; they did not accept the benevolent supremacy of Chinese culture. After five decades of denial, sporadic resistance, and humiliating defeats at the hands of Europeans and Japanese, Chinese confidence was shattered. It is difficult to portray fully the intensity of the sense of loss and confusion that pervaded the country. A civilization of great power, subtlety, and refinement—civilization itself in the minds of the Chinese—had collapsed.

By the end of the nineteenth century, the Chiang clan had lived in and around the mountain hamlet of Hsikou for hundreds of years, perhaps a thousand or more. Ching-kuo's paternal great grandfather, Chiang Yu-piao, farmed about five acres of hillside bamboo and a small plot of paddy. His family's status changed when he obtained a license to sell salt and wine. Under his son Su-an, the small Chiang Salt Shop in Hsikou prospered, and the family moved into the category of "non-gentry elite." Chiang Su-an was determined that his own children would climb further up the ladder in the Chinese way—through education.[1]

Hsikou (Brook Mouth) is located in the coastal province of Chekiang. It was a full day's walk or ride by sedan chair to the county seat of Fenghua. One could also pole down connecting streams to the Yung River and the city of Ningbo, one of the Treaty Ports opened to foreigners after the Opium War. Wildflowers, exotic birds, terraces of rice, and rows of Chekiang tea festooned the hills around the hamlet. Misty ridges rose steeply in the near distance. Six miles by trail and 3,000 feet up Hole-in-the-Snow Mountain stood an ancient and famous monastery of the same name.

The Chiangs lived above the salt store, which had its own inner court and white-washed walls. Su-an's first wife bore him a son and a daughter before she died; his childless second spouse also died. In 1886 he married for the third time, a young woman named Wang Ts'ai-yu. Ts'ai-yu came from a very poor village—its only crop was bamboo. But she was shrewd, intelligent, and ambitious. Like most Chinese women of the day, she hobbled about on bound feet.[2] Even two generations later, Chiang Ching-kuo would still see peasants carrying their crippled wives to the fields where they worked through the day on their hands and knees.[3]

In 1887, a year after her marriage, Ts'ai-yu bore a son in one of the small upstairs rooms above the salt store. Yu-piao named the boy Jui-yuan. Later in life he received the honorific name of Chieh-shih, or Kai-shek in Cantonese, literally Upright Stone. Ts'ai-yu was a strict mother but, in the Chinese tradition, would prove to be an indulgent grandmother.[4]

As the Chiang salt outlet developed into a general store, the family's savings increased. In 1889 the two generations moved into a middle-class, two-story house a hundred feet down Wuling Street. Most of the surrounding households in the new neighborhood—and in fact in Hsikou itself—belonged to the Chiang clan. Two daughters soon came into the world, but only one survived infancy. Kai-shek's older half-brother, Hsu-hou, was the prize student of the family and thus his father's pride and joy. Kai-shek also plunged early on into a classical education. In 1894 Ts'ai-yu gave birth to a second son, Jui-ch'ing, a beautiful child with a lovable disposition.[5] In 1896 father Su-an died suddenly at age fifty. Following this unexpected tragedy, an uncle adopted Kai-shek's older half-brother, the scholarly Hsu-hou, who received the salt shop for his inheritance. Since women did not own property, the nine-year-old Kai-shek inherited the house, a bamboo grove that produced 40 to 50 silver dollars a year, and the rice paddy.[6]

When Kai-shek was fourteen, his mother decided it was time for her son to have a wife. Ts'ai-yu chose a young, rather plain nineteen-year-old named Mao Fu-mei, who came from the nearby village of Yenta along with a young woman servant of about the same age called Ah Wang. Fu-mei was stout and strong with an amiable personality. She had only partially bound feet and was thus a better worker, an attribute that appealed to Ts'ai-yu. The young woman may have learned a few characters at home, but, like Ts'ai-yu, she was basically illiterate. In later life she would have to ask others to read her son's letters to her.[7]

The wedding took place in the winter of 1901–1902. Fu-mei claimed later that she and Kai-shek had been happy the first two months of their marriage, until her mother-in-law chastised her for abetting her son in idleness, going on walks together, and laughing and carrying on in their room. Fu-mei dutifully became more distant, and the young couple drifted apart.[8]

In 1899 a fanatical anti-foreign secret society called the Patriotic Harmonious Fists spread across China, ripping up railroad tracks and killing missionaries. An international force that included the Japanese seized Peking again, and in retribution for the depredations of the Boxers, as foreigners jokingly called the Fists, burned down the summer palace. In Fenghua county, as elsewhere in China, the traumas of 1900 further eroded what remained of the prestige of the Ch'ing Court.

Revolution was stirring in China and in Chinese communities outside the country. The conservative nineteenth-century concept of reform through "self-strengthening" was giving way to more radical formulas for saving China. While young Chiang Kai-shek was still plowing through the classics, a Hong Kong-trained medical doctor named Sun Yat-sen was traveling around the world seeking support for his revolutionary goals—transforming China into a quasi socialist republic that would redistribute land and take democracy as its long term objective but begin with an indefinite period of "tutelage."

By means of force and "unequal treaties," the Russian empire had gained extensive rights in China's northeast region of Manchuria. In January 1905 Japanese troops drove the Russians out of two Chinese cities in Manchuria—Port Arthur and Mukden. Most dramatic of all, in May the Japanese fleet under Admiral Togo Heihachiro annihilated a large Russian fleet that had sailed from the Baltic Sea to do battle. Only forty years earlier, Japan had been as traditional a society as China, yet in little more than a generation it possessed an industrial base and a navy capable of defeating one of the European powers. These events confirmed Chiang Kai-shek's desire to follow a military career, beginning with training in Japan.

In 1907, after failing to gain admission to a Japanese military school, Chiang entered the highly competitive National Army School near Peking, later known as the Paoting Military Academy. Soon he was selected as one of the few Chinese cadets to go to Shimbu Gakko, a preparatory school in Japan for the Japanese Military Academy. During weekend leaves in Tokyo Chiang became involved with the Chinese exile community and joined Sun Yat-sen's movement, the Revolutionary Alliance.[9]

During his summer vacations Chiang went to Shanghai and worked at the alliance's secret headquarters in the French Concession area. He did not return to Hsikou. Fu-mei almost certainly had remained dutiful and amiable, but by this time Chiang had become embarrassed by his illiterate, old-fashioned spouse. Fu-mei complained to her friends that Kai-shek frequently beat her.[10] Twenty years later, in a letter to his mother, Chiang Ching-kuo recalled how his father had dragged her by the hair down a flight of stairs.[11] In the summer of 1909, therefore, it seemed Fu Mei would have no children. But Kai-shek's mother learned from a fortuneteller that her son's first wife would bear a baby boy who would become a high-ranking official. This was good news, but some conjugal business had to be attended to if the prophecy was to be realized. Ts'ai-yu escorted her daughter-in-law to Shanghai. When they arrived in the city, Kai-shek initially refused to go along with his mother's plans, but after she threatened to kill herself, he agreed to do his duty. Fu-mei spent some time with Kai-shek over the hot summer months and did her part by becoming pregnant before returning to Hsikou.[12]

On April 27, 1910, Fu-mei went into labor. By the lunar calendar it was March 18. Ts'ai-yu called the local midwife. Ah Wang, the servant girl, was also there to help. While Fu-mei lay in the middle room upstairs in the Chiang home, Ts'ai-yu sat downstairs with relatives, drinking tea and waiting for developments. In the traditional birthing techniques of the day, when the baby was in the birth canal, Fu-mei knelt on the bed or on a footstool while one of the midwives held her around the waist from behind, helping her push.[13]

When the baby boy emerged, the midwife severed the umbilical cord and washed him in warm water in a red basin. She then bound him in swaddling clothes and presented him to the exhausted but proud Fu-mei. Ts'ai-yu, hearing the baby crying, rushed in to greet the newborn. That day she dictated a letter to Kai-shek to inform him that he was father of a healthy boy—the best possible news a Chinese could receive. She also asked Kai-shek for permission to register the infant in the ancestral tablets as the son of Jui-ch'ing, Kai-shek's brother and her favorite child, who had died at age four. Kai-shek readily agreed. Thus, according to the ancestral tablets and the civil records in Fenghua, Ching-kuo is not the son of Chiang Kai-shek.[14]

Kai-shek had graduated from Shimbu Gakko and was serving as a private in the Japanese army prior to entering the academy. He did not record his feelings on learning that he was a father. Nor did he take the trouble to visit Hsikou even briefly in the summer of 1910, although he was again in Shanghai assisting the Revolutionary Alliance in its underground work.

⎯

CHING-KUO'S FIRST BIRTHDAY (in the Chinese reckoning it would have been his second) happened to be on the day that the Revolutionary Alliance launched its largest military venture thus far—the Canton Uprising of April 27, 1911. Although it turned out to be another defeat, the scale and audacity of the effort was a psychological boost for the movement.

To follow up, the revolutionaries planned a late October uprising in the tri-city of Wuhan. On October 9 a bomb exploded accidentally in one of the rebels' secret bomb factories in that Yangtze River metropolis, alerting the Ch'ing authorities to the plot. Sergeants in the Imperial Army shot their officers, and the revolution was under way. Within a month of the uprising in Wuhan, assemblies met in thirteen provinces and passed resolutions of secession from the rule of the Ch'ing dynasty. In many provinces senior military officers of the Imperial Army became the *de facto* government leaders. In some cases, bandit chiefs in alliance with army units seized control. The warlord period had begun.[15]

When Chiang Kai-shek, still in Japan, heard about the events in Wuhan, he left his army base and rushed off to Tokyo. Stopping only to return his uniform by parcel post, he caught a steamer to Shanghai. Upon arrival he was directed to lead an assault on the headquarters of the governor general in the city of Hangchow, 150 kilometers away in his native province of Chekiang. Chiang took command of a "dare-to-die" shock force, composed of secret society members from the Green Gang in Shanghai and men recruited from a fishing village in Fenghua county. The twenty-four-year old soldier wrote to his mother, telling her, "I have sworn to give my life for the revolution" and asking her to forgive him for "neglecting my filial duties." The seizure of Hangchow was not a major event in the rebellion, but it was boldly and successfully carried out. Afterwards, Chiang turned down the position of governor of Chekiang and returned to Shanghai as a ranking military officer in the revolutionary ranks.[16]

Over the next ten years Kai-shek was repeatedly engaged in combat of one sort or another—conventional assaults, guerrilla attacks, or terrorist strikes. Usually he lived undercover, with a price on his head. As a soldier and revolutionary he would display courage, dedication, loyalty, and self-discipline—the traits of his own heroes and ones that he intensely and consciously cultivated. But when not fighting, planning, or reading, he was a frequent patron of Shanghai's "sing-song girls," of whom there were thousands. He contracted venereal disease several times and became sterile, a condition he did not suspect for some years.[17] In 1912 Chiang met Yao Yeh-ch'eng, a parlormaid in a Shanghai brothel. Yao became his concubine or "live-in girl friend" and stayed with him off and on for the next eight years.[18]

During this period Chiang cemented a number of key relationships, including one with Wu Chih-hui, a modern scholar who had spent many years in France and England. On a more personal level he formed a sworn brotherhood with Tai Chi-tao, whom he had known in Japan, and with Ch'en Kuo-fu, who with his younger brother Ch'en Li-fu would later constitute the powerful CC Clique in the KMT.[19] The young revolutionary officer from Hsikou also solidified his ties to secret societies, primarily the Green Gang. Like the European authorities in Shanghai, Sun Yat-sen, and later the Communist party leaders, Chiang sought to use the secret societies and gangs to serve the purposes of his party as well as his own ends.[20] Similarly, in the late 1920s Mao Zedong would make alliances with bandit gangs in the Chingkang Mountains of Kiangsi province. Whether in Shanghai or the mountains, the gangs linked up with rebel groups because they too were traditionally anti-Manchu, and also because they hoped eventually to turn revolutionary connections to their advantage.

DURING THESE HECTIC YEARS Ching-kuo grew up in a tranquil home full of women who doted on him. In addition to his mother, grandmother (who was head of the household), and the servant Ah Wang, his maternal great grandmother was also present for part of this time. Ching-kuo was a happy and obedient child, small for his age and not as robust as most of his friends.[21] Vaccinations were unheard of in Hsikou. To ward off evil spirits, Fu-mei and Ts'ai-yu prayed more than usual and had the baby wear a sword made of copper coins. Despite these precautions, at age three Ching-kuo came down with the dreaded smallpox. Several times a day his mother and grandmother hobbled down Wuling Street to the temple. After many prayers and the burning of much incense, the boy recovered. To express their thanks, the women built a small pavilion near the Hole-in-the-Snow Monastery and paid to have a path leading to the monastery's main temple paved with cobblestones. Ching-kuo's face would show small signs of his early bout with the evil spirit.[22]

With a devout mother and grandmother, Ching-kuo's childhood was full of religious observance. The young boy often accompanied his grandmother to the temple, one hand supporting the old lady and the other carrying her Buddhist basket. In those years he walked many times up the path to the Hole-in-the-Snow Monastery and spent some summer days living with the monks and hiking in the mountains.[23]

The great political events of 1911 and 1912 meant that small communities like Hsikou were more than ever on their own. In many parts of China, law and order broke down, rural bandits grew in number and audacity, and local militias were formed to combat them. Remote and mountainous Hsikou largely escaped these tribulations, and its most notable changes involved certain social customs. The pigtail—the 300-year-old tonsorial symbol of subservience to the Manchus—disappeared overnight. Foot bindings were also coming off, and *corvee* (compulsory) labor was officially abolished, although "voluntary" work was still expected on community projects.[24]

Shortly after the revolution, clan associations in Hsikou opened the Wushan Grammar School on the grounds of the local temple. In March 1916, Ching-kuo, then not quite six years old, entered the first grade. Wushan was not a modern institution. The boy's first teacher was a gentleman named Chou Tung, who taught in the old-fashioned manner, using excerpts from ancient writings to pound characters into the heads of his first graders. Ching-kuo remained at the Wushan school for two or three years.[25]

⸺

THIS WAS THE PERIOD of the First World War in Europe, an intra-European conflict that would destroy imperial rule in both Germany and Russia and eventually provide new revolutionary models for China—fascism and communism. The immediate result of the war, however, was a sharp decline in the attention and resources that Europe could devote to China, and, as a consequence, a freer hand for Japan. In November the Bolsheviks seized power in St. Petersburg and then in Moscow. Few grasped the significance of these events for China. But Dr. Sun, as one revolutionary to another, cabled his congratulations to Lenin. In 1919 international developments again shook China. In the Versailles Peace Treaty that ended World War I, the Great Powers agreed to assign defeated Germany's rights in the province of Shantung to Japan, rather than return full sovereignty to China. On May 4, 1919, students in

Peking marched to the foreign legations area in the city to protest the treaty. Police broke up the demonstration and arrested a number of students, but the incident sparked protests around the country. In Shanghai and other cities thousands of workers went on strike.

FOREIGNERS SIPPING GIN AND TONICS at the Cercle Sportif in Shanghai did not view the agitation as any more threatening than recurrent demonstrations and disorders over the previous eight years. But both the international and the local environments had changed. There were now other options for China. In July 1919 the Communist regime in Moscow proclaimed it would return to China all territory wrongfully taken by the Czarist empire, give up control of the Chinese Eastern Railway in Manchuria, waive Russia's share of the Boxer indemnity, and end extraterritorial rights for Russians living in China. In return, it asked only that Peking recognize the revolutionary government in Moscow.

Inspired by Marxist writings in Europe, small socialist study groups had been active in Shanghai for several years before the Bolshevik Revolution. After the Russian revolution, Peking University overnight became a hotbed of revolutionary thought. The leading leftists were Ch'en Tu-hsiu, dean of the College of Letters, and Li Ta-chao, head librarian. Their vision of a new, dynamic, independent, and Marxist China also inspired a young clerk in the university library, Mao Zedong. Likewise, the great revolution in Russia fascinated many in the KMT, including Sun Yat-sen. Chiang Kai-shek's friend Tai Chi-tao grew close to the group around Ch'en Tu-hsiu and supported Ch'en's decision to organize a Communist nucleus in Shanghai. In the same year, among the hundreds of leftist Chinese students leaving for work-study experiences in France were Zhou Enlai and Deng Xiaoping.

THE FIRST DECADE OF CHINA'S MODERN REVOLUTION ended as it began: with division, violence, and betrayal. These traumatic years in which China was free of the Manchus but not free of the past etched into the minds of young revolutionaries like Chiang Kai-shek and Mao

Zedong the truism that as long as China was splintered by warlords, political parties, secret societies, and others fighting for power and spoils, foreign powers would continue to victimize it. The question was, who would be the great unifier?

In 1920 the only area in which the KMT controlled sizable armed forces was the southern city of Canton and parts of the surrounding province of Kwangtung. At this time—whether living undercover in Shanghai, working in exile in Japan, or going on secret missions—Chiang Kai-shek strengthened his reputation as a headstrong and often erratic officer. Yet Sun Yat-sen clearly thought the soldier from Hsikou was invaluable. The aspects of Chiang's temperament that irritated his friends and outraged his enemies were the same features that made him the most capable military leader in the KMT. He was unmatched in self-assurance, willpower, and decisiveness. He had proved himself personally courageous if often foolhardy. For the revolution he had been a soldier, a clandestine agent, an organizer, a writer, a stockbroker, and perhaps once or twice an assassin. Like Sun Yat-sen, he appeared incorruptible. His ties to secret societies and his reported but unconfirmed involvement in at least one robbery were on behalf of the revolution.

But Chiang's impetuousness and frequent abuse of colleagues and subordinates continued to cause him problems. Sun remarked in a letter that his "fiery temper" and "hatred of mediocrity" often led to quarrels and made cooperation difficult. Sun was also well aware of Chiang's reputation for hard living, whoring, and drinking.[26]

Around the time of Ching-kuo's tenth birthday, however, Kai-shek began to change in some respects. For one thing he began to show some interest in the boy, who, he now suspected, would be his sole biological heir. From this point on Chiang viewed his fatherhood with detached earnestness. He would seek to reinforce his personal model of rigorous discipline with ponderous advice and moral injunctions. During a visit to Fenghua in early 1920 Chiang looked up his old tutor, a Confucian scholar with modern ideas named Ku Ch'ing-lien, and asked him to help with Ching-kuo's education. Ku went to Hsikou and spent some time studying the lad's potential, setting out a course of study for him, and perhaps for some period acting as his tutor. In his first letter to Ching-kuo, dated February 9, 1920, Chiang told his son that Ku had reported to him that "you are not brilliant, but like to study very much." Chiang said he was "somewhat comforted after learning this."[27] He then arranged for another Fenghua scholar named Wang Ou-sheng to tutor his son in the classics and *The Four Books.*[28]

Whatever the tutors' merits, Chiang soon decided that his son should not be stuck in Hsikou as he (the senior Chiang) had been until his early teens. When Ching-kuo was nine or ten, his father sent him off to Fenghua to a school he had once attended, the Phoenix Mountain Academy. In separate entries in his diary in February and March of 1920, Chiang Kai-shek noted that he had worked on Ching-kuo's "school timetable."[29] In April Chiang wrote a didactic list of injunctions to his son: "obey the instructions of your grandmother and mother. In talking and walking your manner must be serious." The second letter commanded, "never conduct yourself with levity . . . don't be frivolous and make sure to be serious."[30] During a visit to Hsikou in November, Chiang discussed Ching-kuo's education with Mao Fu-mei and noted in his diary that her ideas could do harm to the boy. On one occasion Fu-mei took Ching-kuo home to Hsikou without her husband's consent. This incident greatly annoyed Kai-shek and contributed to his decision to bring his son to Shanghai the following year to continue his studies.[31]

Sometime in 1920 Chiang's concubine, Yao Yeh-ch'eng, arrived in Hsikou with a four-year-old boy in tow. The lad was Kai-shek's adopted son, Wei-kuo. The real father was Chiang's friend Tai Chi-tao, and the mother was a Japanese woman he had met during a period of exile in Tokyo. Since Tai already had a family, Kai-shek had agreed to adopt the boy.[32] Wei-kuo and the woman he thought was his mother, Mama Yao, took up residence in the Chiang family home. At the time the grandmother, Wang Ts'ai-yu, was seriously ill, and Kai-shek and Mao Fu-mei were still formally married. According to local stories and Wei-kuo's own account, Fu-mei and Yao Yeh-ch'eng did not get along. Fu-mei assigned to the newcomers a little room behind the family home that was normally full of firewood and hay. Fleas tormented little Wei-kuo, and eventually his uncle moved the young woman and the boy to his own house.[33] Since Ching-kuo was at school in Fenghua, the two step-brothers did not see much of each other. To the younger boy, however, ten-year-old Ching-kuo was even then an imposing figure.[34]

2

A Teachable Son

CHING-KUO WAS CLOSE TO HIS GRANDMOTHER, and her death on June 4 was a emotional blow to the eleven-year-old. Her passing, however, would provide the occasion for his longest and most intimate contact with his father, who went through all the Confucian rituals prescribed for mourning a departed parent. Despite the ongoing, intense maneuvering within the KMT and the critical military situation in the south, Chiang Kai-shek remained for several months in Hsikou. Many days spent in meditation in a cabin on the mountain brought him to a new stage in his personal life, in which he would seek to practice what he had long professed to believe—the principles of neo-Confucian idealism, including rectitude, serenity, and constancy. "He began to withdraw from the pleasures of the world" and showed signs of "greater stability in his behavior and an integration of his personality and his social environment." The transformation was like the rebirth of a devout soul, in this case that of a man filled with an unbounded faith in himself and his mission. Kai-shek now had no doubt—he was to be China's "man of destiny."[1]

One day, after going for a walk with his two sons, Chiang Kai-shek noted that "Ching-kuo is teachable and Wei-kuo is lovable."[2] Several 1922 letters to Wei-kuo could be from an indulgent modern-day father: "Recently I ride horses every day and I enjoy it a lot. When I return home, I will definitely buy a little horse for you and teach you to ride. I will also buy a big horse and we can ride together."[3]

Wei-kuo was only five and six years old when Chiang wrote these letters. The boy's youth and the fact that it was not long since he had been adopted may account for his father's show of affection. But clearly Wei-kuo found a warmer spot in Chiang's heart than did his eldest and only biological son. Yet on most days when he was at home in Hsikou, Chiang did spend some time with Ching-kuo. Sometimes father and son took late afternoon outings, sitting in bamboo chairs on a bamboo raft poled along the tranquil Shan Creek, watching trained cormorants catch fish, and listening to the summer symphony of cicadas.[4] Most of the time, however, the visiting parent kept to himself, mourning, meditating, reading, and working on military planning. He certainly had little to do with Fu-mei. Ching-kuo was accustomed to the distant and strained relationship between his parents.

After the burial of his mother, Kai-shek made a monetary settlement with Miss Yao and also with Ching-kuo's mother, whom he formally divorced. At first Chiang told Fu-mei she could no longer live at the family home, but when she wept and pleaded, he relented. The son observed this exchange.[5] In a letter to his brother-in-law, Mao Mao-ching, Chiang Kai-shek described his feelings toward his wife of twenty years: "for the past ten years. I have not been able to bear hearing the sound of her footsteps or seeing her shadow . . ."[6]

CHIANG'S DECISION TO DIVORCE—perfunctory as the act was in those days—was also part of another drama: his passionate desire to take up with a young girl named Ch'en Chieh-ju, the daughter of a Sun Yat-sen supporter in Shanghai. Chiang had met Chieh-ju in 1919 when she was just thirteen—although by her own testimony her friends said she looked eighteen—and he became infatuated with her pubescent innocence. On a pretext he lured her to a hotel room, but she ran away.[7]

In early September 1921, Chiang was temporarily back in Shanghai and again met Chieh-ju. This time he was determined to marry her or have her as a concubine, depending on what story one believes. After initial resistance, the girl's mother agreed. The wedding, Chieh-ju tells us, took place on December 5, 1921. She was fifteen. Her new stepson, Ching-kuo, was only four years younger.[8]

On her honeymoon she contracted a venereal disease. In repentance, Kai-shek swore never to drink alcohol, coffee, or tea again. From that time on, he abstained from liquor most of the time and usually drank boiled water rather than tea. Chieh-ju says that doctors cured them both of what appears to have been a case of gonorrhea.[9]

———

AT THE AGE OF TWELVE, Ching-kuo enrolled in the fourth grade at the Ten Thousand Bamboo Grammar School in Shanghai. He lived for a time with Chieh-ju at number 9, 3rd Lane Ch'ing Shunli, Notre Dame Road in the French Concession. Kai-shek was away most of the time, and she and Ching-kuo established a warm relationship. He called his sixteen-year-old stepmother Shanghai Mother.[10] She was both a sister to the dutiful and eager boy and a teen-age, sensual, second mother, who contributed to his life-long romantic idealization of women.

As an adolescent, young Chiang had close-cropped hair, a square face that resembled his mother's, a high forehead (like his father), a large mouth, and prominent teeth.[11] The son was very courteous but highly nervous in the presence of his father. The elder Chiang expected Ching-kuo to write a letter to him every Sunday containing "about two to three hundred characters" with a report on his studies and the books he had read. He upbraided the boy if he fell behind in his correspondence.[12] The father suggested that his son save his letters and reread them during his free time. Often, however, he himself did not have time to write a letter but would simply dispatch reading assignments.[13] He continued to emphasize *The Four Books,* most particularly Mencius, the *Letters* and *Family Teaching of Tseng Kuo-fan,* and the collected works of Wang Yang-ming. Sun Yat-sen's *Three Peoples Principles* were on the required reading list, but seemed to have less priority. On occasion, Chiang would send Ching-kuo books he had read that included his own annotations.[14] He suggested that Ching-kuo read each of the classical works "more than one hundred times."[15]

Ching-kuo's character writing also received repeated attention. "Your calligraphy has not yet improved," the father remonstrated, "You should copy one to two hundred characters every other day."[16] Chiang apparently recognized that his own ideographs were not especially elegant, and he hoped his son would learn the flowing, stylistic script more in keeping with the tradition of a scholar-statesman. At the same time, he constantly emphasized the study of English. Today, he said, "those who don't speak English are like being mute."[17]

IN 1922 CHIANG SET OFF on one of the escapades that marked his and Sun Yat-sen's careers. He returned to duty in Canton, but when Sun rejected his warnings about the treachery of one of his commanders (Chen Chiung-ming, called the Hakka General), he resigned and returned to Hsikou. On June 16 the Hakka General attacked Sun's presidential headquarters in Canton, intending to kill him. Sun escaped to the gunboat *Yungfeng* in the Pearl River and sent a cable to Fenghua addressed to the little boy Wei-kuo in Hsikou. The message, of course, was intended for the eyes of Chiang Kai-shek. "Hope you come quickly," it said.[18]

Chiang immediately caught a steamer to Hong Kong and there rented a motor launch to take him up the Pearl River. On June 29 he joined Dr. Sun on the *Yungfeng*, which lay at anchor off the island of Whampoa. Sun and his entourage reached Shanghai on August 14, and there they held talks with a Comintern (Communist International) agent named Maring. Five months later, Sun Yat-sen and a new Soviet envoy, Adolph Joffe, issued a joint communiqué to the effect that conditions did not exist in China for communism, and that national unification and full independence were China's paramount goals. Moscow promised support for the Chinese revolution, including help in reorganizing Sun's political organization, the Kuomintang (KMT) or Nationalist Party. The agreement greatly alarmed conservatives in the Party, but Chiang Kai-shek was in the forefront of those who enthusiastically endorsed the pro-Soviet line.

Sun and Joffe agreed that the KMT would send representatives to Moscow to study military, government, and political organization and to obtain arms. Sun asked Chiang to lead the delegation. Kai-shek and three compatriots arrived in Moscow on September 2, 1923, and spent almost three months in the USSR. Much of what Chiang saw impressed him, including the political commissar system and the work of Komsomol, the youth organization of the CPSU: "This [the Komsomol] is the best policy of the CPSU."

Thirty years later Chiang claimed that while in Moscow, he became convinced that Soviet political institutions were "instruments of tyranny and terror," and that the objective of the CPSU was to turn the Chinese Communist Party into "an instrument for its own use."[19] In his letters to Ching-kuo during and after his visit to Russia, however, there is no criticism of the USSR, much less any stern warning about nefarious Communists. At the time, everyone knew that the newly formed Chinese Communist Party (CCP) was rapidly expanding its recruitment among students and workers in Shanghai. But Chiang did not display any concern about his son being exposed to such activity.

Dr. Sun was also increasingly enthusiastic not only about Soviet aid that was beginning to flow into the KMT, but about the Soviet Union itself. While Chiang was in the USSR, the new Comintern advisor, Michael Borodin, arrived in Canton and immediately set about reshaping the KMT's political and military organization along Leninist lines. Borodin himself drafted (in English) the new Party constitution and manifesto. The First National KMT Congress, held January 20–24, 1924, approved this fundamental makeover of the Party and agreed that Communist delegates could simultaneously belong to the KMT and the CCP.

News of Lenin's death came while the Congress was being held. Sun in his eulogy praised Lenin as a "great man."[20] In the midst of this sharp turn to the left, the Congress appointed Chiang Kai-shek to the Party's Military Council and to a committee charged with setting up a military academy at Whampoa. After Chiang was appointed commandant of the new academy, he personally requested that Soviet General Vasili K. Blyucher, Commander-in-Chief of the Soviet Siberian Army, whom he had met during his travels in Russia, serve as his chief of staff. Chiang was clearly not resisting ties with the Communists.

On May 3, 1924, he became Commandant of the Whampoa Academy and presided over its opening. He gave the elder of the Chen brothers, Ch'en Kuo-fu, the responsibility of recruiting most of the cadets, a task for which Ch'en solicited the help of the Green Gang.[21] Ching-kuo had been a frequent visitor at the Ch'en house in the French Quarter, but now he spent less time there because Kuo-fu was usually away and the younger Ch'en brother, Li-fu, had gone to the United States the year before.[22]

By giving its cadets three-month intensive courses, Whampoa graduated 2,000 new officers in one year. The CCP selected a certain number of the cadets, among whom in the first class was an enthusiastic young man named Lin Piao. The majority of the officer candidates, however, were to prove fiercely loyal to Chiang Kai-shek. They were for the most part sons of landowning rural families or relatively well-off urban households. This "Whampoa clique" would provide the Generalissimo's core supporters over the next twenty-five and in some cases fifty years.

A little earlier, on March 20, Ching-kuo sent his father an interesting letter proposing that the Wushan grammar school in Hsikou set up a free night school for the "common people."

> I have a suggestion to make about the Wushan School, though I am not sure whether you can agree to it or not. My suggestion is that the school establish a night school for the common people who cannot afford to go to school. My school has established a night school with great success. I can tell you something about the night school:
>
> 1. Name: Wushan School for the Common People.
> 2. Tuition fee: Free of charge with stationery supplied.
> 3. Class hours: 7 PM to 9 PM.
> 4. Age limit: 14 or older.
> 5. Schooling Period: 16 or 20 weeks.
>
> At the time of graduation, the trainees will be able to write simple letters and keep simple accounts. They will be issued a diploma if they pass the examinations. The textbooks they use were published by the Commercial Press and are entitled "One Thousand Characters for the Common People." I do not know whether you will accept my suggestion. If a night school is established at Wushan, it will greatly benefit the local people.[23]

The tone of Ching-kuo's letter to his father was respectful but strikingly straightforward, lacking the traditional language of filial obeisance and humbleness. Chiang Kai-shek, however, dryly rejected Ching-kuo's proposal, noting that Hsikou did not have electricity, the peasants in Hsikou went to bed early, and besides, they did not yet appreciate education.[24]

In June, a few months after the Congress, KMT conservatives submitted their first petition for an order of censure against Communist members of the Party. According to a friendly biographer, "Chiang was one of the very few who realized that at this critical moment their ranks must be closed and that members of the KMT must fight hand-in-hand with Communists against their common enemy," the warlords who controlled most of China. On June 29, in a public speech at Whampoa, Chiang praised the Communist Party of the Soviet Union: "Members of the Russian Communist Party are willing to work for the welfare of their country and the common people, not solely for their private interest."[25]

In January 1925, the mutinous Hakka General launched another effort to seize control of Canton. Leading his Whampoa cadets, Chiang rode to the rescue. With only a few months of training and armed with Soviet weapons, including artillery, Chiang's young officer candidates crushed the rebellious army. By the end of March Chiang occupied all of eastern Kwangtung province. In the midst of this success, news arrived from the north that Sun Yat-sen had died of liver cancer.

At this time Chiang was still not part of the KMT's Central Standing Committee. While his reputation had risen dramatically, most observers and insiders did not consider him among the contenders for the top leadership. He seemed dedicated to serving the Party and the country as a military officer. His repeated "resignations" over matters of principle had given him an unusual reputation for rectitude. He soon became garrison commander at Canton while continuing as commandant at Whampoa.

AFTER FINISHING ELEMENTARY SCHOOL, Ching-kuo entered Shanghai's Pudong High School in early 1925. That spring, two months after the death of Sun Yat-sen, a wave of demonstrations and bloody police action ripped through Shanghai. On May 30 a crowd of 3,000 gathered outside a police substation on Nanking Road, demanding the release of detained students.[26] Screaming "kill the foreigners!" the crowd surged toward the building. A British officer ordered the Chinese and Sikh police on duty to open fire. Eleven demonstrators died, and twenty received serious wounds. According to *The New York Times*, the police attributed the disorders to "Chinese Bolshevik activities, particularly the radical branch of the Kuomintang,"[27] a clear reference to Ching-kuo's father, whom the Western press now called "the Red General." Protests continued the following week.

During this time, Ching-kuo's fellow students selected him to lead them in four "mass uprisings."[28] Although some writers repeat the story that Ching-kuo was among those arrested at the police station riot, there is no record of this in the Shanghai archives.[29] General strikes protesting the May 30 incident broke out in Shanghai, Hong Kong, and elsewhere. The *Times* correspondent warned that "the radical party" (the KMT) was determined to terminate "all special foreign positions, privileges, and extraterritorial treaties." Even Japan, he warned, might "side with the position of the yellow world against the West."[30] In Wuhan British volunteers turned a machine gun on "thousands of rioting coolies."[31] In Canton, on June 23, a huge parade of Chinese protesters, including boy scouts and Whampoa cadets, passed by the foreign concession area on Shameen Island. British troops on the island fired on the crowd, killing 52 and wounding over 100.[32] KMT and CCP recruiters had a field day. CCP membership tripled to about 3,000.

The wave of political activism swept into rural areas of interior provinces like Hunan. Mao Zedong was in his home province at the time of the May 30 incident, caring for his dying mother. He and his colleagues quickly went into the countryside and organized peasant unions. The Hunan military overlord sent troops to arrest Mao, and the young Communist fled to Canton. He became editor of the *Political Weekly*, a publication of the KMT's political department, and also chief of the unit training peasant organizers.[33] On July 1, 1925, the KMT proclaimed a National government at Canton and elected Wang Ching-wei, also known to be pro-Soviet, as chairman of a new ruling political committee. Wang seemed to be the likely successor to Sun Yat-sen. The Kuomintang now geared up for its greatest challenge—bringing the whole of China under its control.

MOVING INTO ACTION ON HIS OWN DOMESTIC FRONT, Chiang decided to send Ching-kuo to a school that his friend, Wu Chih-hui, the renowned scholar and linguist, had just opened in Peking. It was a small academy on South School Street, combining classical and modern approaches to education. Although the city was ruled by warlord Feng Yu-hsiang, security for the students seemed not to be a problem. Presumably Wu Chih-hui had received the warlord's assurances that the KMT students would not be in any danger. In fact, Feng had entered at least one of his own children in the school. Feng, a large and garrulous man, professed a social conscience and sympathy for the KMT. After his marriage to an educated Christian lady, he had become know as the Christian General, reputedly baptizing his troops with a fire hose. But it was Feng's children by his first wife—a son, Hung-kuo, and his sister, Fu-neng—who would play an important role in Ching-kuo's early life.

Ching-kuo by this time thought of himself as a "progressive revolutionary." Shortly after his arrival in Peking, a prominent Kuomintang journalist and former deputy director of Shanghai University, Shao Li-tzu, introduced him to a number of leading Communists, including Li Ta-chao, who was on the standing committees of both the CCP and the KMT.[34] Shao, apparently a clandestine Communist, then left for Whampoa to become Chiang Kai-shek's chief secretary. Ching-kuo naturally fell in with a leftist group of students, who regularly attended movies at the Soviet mission and met frequently with Soviet embassy officers.[35] The idea of studying in Moscow now seized his imagination.[36]

Since the 1917 Revolution, the Soviet Union had provided military training and education for revolutionaries from China and other Far Eastern countries. Various training schools eventually combined to become the University of the Toilers of the East. Then, in 1925, the Soviet party decided to establish a separate institution for Chinese students—the Sun Yat-sen University of the Toilers of China (Sunovka). The selection of applicants for this institution lay with the central executive committees of the CPSU and the KMT, with participation of the CCP's Central Committee.[37] The KMT and the CCP each nominated a certain number of students for the first class.[38]

Ching-kuo and several of his friends decided to apply. Ching-kuo asked Wu Chih-hui to name him as a KMT candidate. When Wu asked why Ching-kuo wanted to go, the boy replied that it was for the revolution. Wu laughed. "Revolution means rebellion . . . Are you not afraid?" Ching-kuo said he was not. "It's not that simple," Wu told him. "You should reconsider." Two weeks later, Ching-kuo returned and said he was still determined to go. "It might be good for you to have a try," Wu said. "It is always good for young people to try more."[39] Within the year, Wu would become an important member of the arch anti-Communist Western Hills Group in the KMT, which would help to bring about the purge of the Communists and the break with Moscow. But in the summer of 1925 the political and intellectual atmosphere was quite different from what it would be only a few months later. Wu did not try to dissuade the son of Chiang Kai-shek from his plans or warn him of the dangers of communism.

THE LEADERSHIP PICTURE WITHIN THE KMT changed swiftly and dramatically. On August 20 gunmen burst into a meeting of the Executive Committee and assassinated Liao Chung-k'ai, a leading leftist. Suspicion fell on the conservatives. Chiang Kai-shek headed a three-person panel to investigate the assassination. Although not charged with involvement, the leading right-winger, Hu Han-min, was forced to resign. With the death of Liao and the departure of Hu, Chiang was not only the senior military leader of the Revolutionary Army but also one of the two most powerful political figures in the KMT. The other was Wang Ching-wei. Chiang seemed to confirm his radical bent by appointing Zhou Enlai to replace Liao as head of the political department of the First Army, the KMT's original Revolutionary Army. Prominent KMT supporters in Canton—large landowners, industrialists, rich merchants, and intellectual conservatives—were alarmed. Many packed up and hastened back to Shanghai and Peking.

The political situation in China was suddenly more chaotic and complex than ever. The number of actors and subplots in the national drama had multiplied. Now they included the KMT left, which supported cooperation with the Soviets and the CCP; the KMT right, which strongly opposed such an alliance; the CCP, which accepted orders from Moscow;

some Communists, both Soviet and Chinese, who warned that catastrophe would follow alliance with the KMT; Soviet advisers committed to working with the Revolutionary Army (and thus with Chiang Kai-shek); warlords like Feng Yu-hsiang who accepted aid from the Soviets and flew the white-sun KMT flag; militarists like Chang Tso-lin and Wu P'ei-fu who now and again worked with the Japanese; other provincial and regional satraps, like those in Ningpo and Fenghua, who nominally swore allegiance to whatever force seemed strongest; and radical militarists who were gaining power in Japan and asserting greater authority in Manchuria. As a participant in this rapidly churning scene, the Soviet Union had many, sometimes conflicting interests: a strong, united China to counter the imperialists; an eventual Bolshevik revolution in China; avoidance of a provocation to Japan; and advancement of its own economic interests in Manchuria. Conversely, the Western powers feared the Soviets, the Japanese, the local Communists, and the leftist-dominated KMT.

CHIANG KAI-SHEK DID NOT TRUST THE COMMUNISTS, but he trusted few others. Although his traditional values inclined him to reject class war and other extreme aspects of communism, it was not the policies of the Communists that most disturbed him. Most important was the stark political dynamic: the CCP, despite its alliance with the KMT, was an upstart and rival organization committed like the Kuomintang not only to restoring China's unity and dignity but to achieving total power for itself. Most disturbing, it was also a rival supported by the big neighbor to the north.

But in the summer of 1925, Chiang was not planning to purge the Communists from the KMT or to break with the Soviets. Likewise, Stalin's policy toward the KMT at this time was also theoretically but not operationally duplicitous. The Marxists considered Chiang and the KMT part of the "petty national bourgeoisie" and thus ultimately viewed them as class enemies. The new, post-1924 Kuomintang, however, was a distinctly unique bourgeois party, one clearly dominated by pro-Soviet and leftist leaders. Moscow, after all, had designed the KMT's organizational structure and revised its ideology. KMT, CCP, and Soviet personnel called each other "comrade." Both the CCP and the CPSU felt that there was a strong possibility that the KMT leadership could eventually be taken over by the Communists and the Kuomintang right wing would split away. Sun Yat-sen's increasingly pro-Soviet and Leninist positions before his death encouraged them to think that this was possible. With Chiang Kai-shek they were less certain, but he also seemed in the summer of 1925 to be a good friend of the Soviet Union and a firm leftist. Did Chiang not work well with Borodin and General Blyucher? Had he not publicly praised the CPSU? Had he not appointed Zhou Enlai head of the First Army's political department? Was he not about to send his son to study in Moscow?

Moreover, at this moment in history, Stalin's primary concern was to promote the emergence of a united China that would be anti-imperialist and friendly toward the USSR and also a buffer against Japan and Britain. Since the possibility of the CCP leading the movement to unify China was at best uncertain, working with the dominant and increasingly leftist KMT seemed the most feasible way for Moscow to achieve its objectives.

———

THAT SAME SUMMER OF 1925, Ching-kuo traveled to Whampoa to discuss his Moscow plans with his father. Before facing him, the youth told Ch'en Chieh-ju, his "Shanghai mother," now a fully flowered young woman of twenty, of his intention to go to Moscow and asked if she would inform his father and seek his consent.[40]

In her version, Chiang Kai-shek at first rejected the idea offhand. "That block of wood is useless," he said, referring to his son. Besides, Chiang added, he could not afford it. Ch'en argued Ching-kuo's case and at last persuaded her husband to agree.[41] If Chiang Kai-shek had at that time harbored strong feelings against the Soviet Union and communism, the one person with whom he would have discussed his son's plans would have been his friend and sworn brother Ch'en Kuo-fu. Yet Kuo-fu, who would soon be one of the KMT's most vigorous anti-Communists, displayed no alarm on hearing of Ching-kuo's plans. Instead, he promised to provide warm clothing for the boy's trip. Ch'en's brother, Li-fu, who was then studying in America, said in a 1996 interview that he understood why Chiang Kai-shek permitted his son to go to Russia—"he needed Soviet support at that time." [42] Chiang Kai-shek's diary entry of October 1, 1925, noted simply, "Again, I gave Ching-kuo some instructions. I decided to allow him to pursue studies in Russia."[43] Sending his son to Moscow served Chiang's political and professional interests and was quite consistent with his ideological bent at the time. But Chiang did suggest to Ching-kuo that although he was only fifteen, before departing he should become a full member of the KMT.

3

Dreams of the Red Chamber

IN LATE OCTOBER 1925 Ching-kuo and his friends boarded a Soviet cargo ship anchored at the Bund in Shanghai. His berth was in a hold previously used for transporting cattle. Before the ship moved, he became sick to his stomach and thought of abandoning the enterprise. But on seeing his friends making the best of it, he knew that as "son of the Commandant of the Whampoa Academy" he could not back out. Soon the ship was steaming down the crowded Huangpu River, past the stretch of European buildings on the west bank, the stinky Suchow Creek, and the grimy factories and boat yards that ran on for miles. The students sang the *Song of National Revolution* and the *Internationale.* Within an hour the boat entered the great yawning mouth of the muddy Yangtze and finally broke into blue waters—the East China Sea. Ching-kuo would not put foot on Chinese soil again for over twelve years.[1]

Among the ninety student passengers was eighteen-year-old Chang Hsi-yuan (or Chang Hsi-chiung), who within a year would become the lover of Deng Xiaoping.[2] Also on board was Shao Chih-kang, son of Chiang Kai-shek's chief secretary (and secret Marxist) Shao Li-tzu, and another eighteen-year-old Anhui Communist, Ch'en Shao-yu. Ch'en, whose Chinese pseudonym in the CCP would be Wang Ming, later gained the distinction of becoming a key enemy of both Chiang Ching-kuo and Mao Zedong.[3]

The student passengers formed small groups that met, talked, studied, and ate together. This was Ching-kuo's first experience with a collective way of life, and he felt happy and fulfilled. Discussions lasted long into the night. He read Nikolai Bukharin's *ABC of Communism,* the first book he had ever seen on the subject.[4] A few days later the students landed at Vladivostok, and on October 31 boarded an "ordinary," non-express train for Moscow.

It had a wood-burning engine, unheated coaches, and no dining car. The water froze, both the drinking variety and that used for cleaning oneself after using the paperless, hole-in-the-floor toilet. The train stopped frequently at stations along the way to load new stacks of wood and to pick up passengers. On these occasions, the Chinese would run to the stalls for food and drink and more urgently to the latrines.[5] Despite the cold and the grimness of the setting, the fervor and the promise of the Soviet Union swept up Ching-kuo and most of his colleagues. At some depots, representatives of workers and peasants welcomed them with placards reading, "Long Live China's National Revolution!" and "Long Live Sino-Russian Cooperation." Often there would be a parade along the station platform. Marching arm and arm with the Chinese, the Russians would sing, "March Forward! Dawn Is Ahead!"

THE RUSSIAN REVOLUTION WAS ONLY EIGHT YEARS OLD, but it seemed like a lifetime. War, revolution, terror, and famine had swept relentlessly across the vast land. After Lenin's death, the question of whether the next epoch in building socialism required gradualist or radical means divided the Soviet leadership—or more accurately, provided the ideological ammunition with which the leaders battled for power. One fundamental issue framed the debate—could socialism realistically be built in a large peasant country surrounded by a hostile capitalist world? This conundrum led to arguments about a parallel question: in colonial and semi-colonial countries like China, should the Soviet Union support anti-imperialist, nationalist bourgeoisie revolutions like that of the KMT, or only those led by Communists?

If one believed that the Soviet Union could stand alone against capitalist encirclement and that the peasantry could provide the basis for building socialism, it followed that the priority for all progressive people, not just those in the USSR, was to solidify the revolution in the Soviet Union. The leader of the right-wing position in this debate, Nikolai I. Bukharin, who wrote the *ABC of Communism,* believed that socialism could and should be built gradually on the existing mixed economy, and that industrial growth and thus progress toward socialism depended on an expanding consumer market, which in turn led to private peasant accumulation. This process would provide the necessary capital for rapid industrialization. Agriculture and industry would thus progress hand-in-hand.

The left wing, led by Leon Trotsky, focused on the danger of creeping *embourgeoisement* of Soviet society—its corruption by material desires. Trotsky insisted that Russian peasants could not be good Communists. Thus the realization of full socialism in the USSR would require successful proletarian revolutions in more developed countries. Trotsky's policy came to be known as "permanent revolution."

Stalin, for his part, carved out a middle ground that would allow him to weaken Trotsky and then to align with the right in order to purge the leftists. In early 1924 Stalin had ousted Trotsky as War Commissar, a position which had given him control of the Red Army. Yet nearly two years later, when Ching-kuo arrived in Moscow, Trotsky and his supporters, known as the Left Opposition, believed their cause was still alive.

IN LATE NOVEMBER, the shivering but eager band of Chinese students arrived at the bleak central station in Moscow. Staff from the new university, including the rector, Karl Radek, greeted the new arrivals. The Chinese and their hosts rode a bus across the circular roads of the inner city to Sun Yat-sen University at 16 Volkhona Street. The four-story, nondescript building of almost a hundred rooms was fronted by a row of leafless trees. Not far away was the frozen Moscow River. From the main gate, Ching-kuo and his friends could see the six gilded domes of the Cathedral of the Redeemer (Christ the Savior). In the long months to come, the students would do morning exercises in the great square in front of the cathedral and during their leisure time walk in its beautiful gardens, talking politics.

Administrators handed the students a list of their Russian names. Ching-kuo would henceforth be Nikolai Vladimirovich Elizarov. Ch'en Shao-yu (Wang Ming) was comrade Golubev. A few days later, the students attended the university's official opening. Portraits of Lenin and Sun Yat-sen and the flags of the USSR and the KMT hung in the large auditorium. Leon Trotsky presided. After praising the ongoing Chinese revolution led by the KMT and Chiang Kai-shek, Trotsky added an interesting twist. "From now on," he said, "any Russian, be he a comrade or a citizen, who greets a Chinese student with an air of contempt is not entitled to be either a Russian Communist or a Soviet citizen."[6]

Trotsky was referring to traditional Russian racial prejudice against Mongols and Chinese. Ching-kuo and the other students, for example, were sometimes asked by Russians on the street, "Friend, do you want salt?" Eventually they discovered that this was a mocking reference to the custom of Chinese in Russia of packing the bodies of their dead in salt to be sent back to their old homes for burial.

The school, known by its Russian acronym Sunovka, divided the students into eleven groups of between 30 and 40 members each, depending upon their Party allegiance and age as well as educational attainment. Russian language study and introductory courses on communism and imperialism were the immediate priorities. Also taught were practical skills such as how to infiltrate a government and an army and how to create peasant and labor movements. On many evenings the students adjourned to art theaters to watch melodramatic plays depicting the humiliation British and American imperialists had inflicted on the Chinese people.[7]

Each student kept a diary of his political actions and thought, including criticism of himself and other students, and read these out at the meetings.[8] Ching-kuo took part enthusiastically in all of the school's political activities, including participation in criticism and self-criticism.

Conditions at the school were quite good, considering the scarcities that ravaged the economy. Breakfast consisted of eggs, bread and butter, milk, sausages, black tea, and occasionally even caviar. When the students grew tired of Russian fare, the school employed a Chinese chef and offered a choice of Russian or Chinese meals.[9]

Whenever Ching-kuo went to a movie theater he would see newsreels of his dashing father and troops of the KMT's Revolutionary Army on parade. *Pravda, Izvestia,* and Radio Moscow constantly hailed Chiang Kai-shek and the Kuomintang.[10] Ching-kuo was very proud of his father. Every Chinese student at Sun Yat-sen University knew that the youngest one among them was the son of the famous General Chiang.[11] Ching-kuo soon joined the Chinese Communist Youth Corps and in December also signed up with the Soviet Komsomol. He wrote an article entitled, "Reforming the Heart before Conducting Revolution," which appeared on Red Wall, the University bulletin board. It so impressed the staff that they made the 15-year old author editor of Red Wall.[12]

—

AT THIS TIME it was the Trotsky world view that dominated the CCP's Moscow Committee and also the Chinese Communist Youth Corps' Moscow branch.[13] Likewise, Trotskyites were prominent among the Sunovka European faculty. Rector Karl Radek (born Sobelsohn) was a Russo-Polish revolutionary who had been with Lenin on the sealed train that had carried the Bolshevik leader to the Finland Station in Saint Petersburg in 1917, and he now supported Trotsky and the Left Opposition.[14] Pavel Mif, a Stalin supporter, was vice-rector, presumably appointed to keep an eye on Radek.

Radek was a short, stocky man with a "simian face," high intellectual forehead, small jaw, thick-lensed glasses, and "a smile that completely filled the space between two enormous sideburns."[15] As a Chinese student described him, he resembled central casting's idea of a mad anarchist: "He was very near-sighted and if he did not wear his glasses, he could not even walk. His hair was often uncombed and his beard untrimmed. He never seemed to change the dark gray suit which he wore every day. He always clenched a pipe in his mouth, whether there was tobacco in it or not."[16]

Two years older than Chiang Kai-shek, Radek became a father figure to Ching-kuo. He taught Ching-kuo's class in Chinese history and had frequent private discussions with him. Consumed with the idea that the socialist revolution had to spread around the world if it was to survive at all, Radek saw in the son of Chiang Kai-shek a potential leader of the movement in China and thus of the world revolution. He urged his young student to display audacity and revolutionary daring. "As a young revolutionist, you must first be brave," he proclaimed. "Secondly, you must work hard and be aggressive. . . . Don't try to go up step by step, as it doesn't show the proper spirit which a revolutionist should have. Thirdly, you should never yield or retreat."[17]

Radek explained that surplus profits from exploitation of colonies and semi-colonies like China permitted Western capitalists to keep their own "wage slaves" above starvation level and thus to avoid proletarian revolution. It followed that national freedom for China depended upon the struggle of the workers in the capitalist countries, diverting and weakening the power of the imperialists.

A professor named Prigozhin supplied Ching-kuo and some of his friends with Trotskyite literature.[18] Ching-kuo was one of the first among the students to be persuaded of the correctness of the Trotsky position.[19] He and other young Chinese leftists agreed with Trotsky that the Communist International had to give the highest priority to promoting proletarian revolutions in the imperialist countries. Otherwise the powerful capitalist and imperial nations of Europe and Japan would suppress Marxist movements in backward societies like China and eventually destroy the socialist motherland itself.

Back in China, the long expected fighting between the northern warlords broke out with a new set of alignments. The young Chinese revolutionaries in Moscow rejoiced at the news that Feng Yu-hsiang was now arrayed against "the Old Marshal" from Manchuria, Chang Tso-lin, and the cruel Wu P'ei-fu. General Feng, however, overextended his forces in seizing Tientsin and was forced to abandon Peking.

ON JANUARY 12, 1926, a new CCP student checked into the dormitory at Sun Yat-sen University. Deng Xiaoping, then twenty-one years of age, had arrived directly from Paris where he had lived for five years and had edited a CCP mimeographed weekly entitled *Red Light*, thus earning the nickname "Mr. Mimeograph." Deng received his Russian pseudonym, Ivan Sergeevich, but within a few weeks his hard work and discipline earned him a new nickname—"Little Cannon."[20] After his rigorous life in Paris, Deng enjoyed the privileges as well as the challenges of Sunovka. He found a place to buy croissants and also time for the occasional hand of bridge in the club room.[21]

According to former students at Sunovka, Deng and Ching-kuo were assigned to the same classroom of twenty students. Deng was team leader of the Chinese Communist Youth Corps, which made him responsible for evaluating the performance and ideology of all its members.[22] Unfortunately, his report on Ching-kuo has not come to light, but the two apparently struck up a close relationship. Xiaoping, at barely five feet, was shorter than Ching-kuo, but their similar stature contributed to their rapport. During strolls along the Moscow River, Ching-kuo frequently asked Deng about his days in Paris. In response, the young man wrote several articles describing his work in France for Ching-kuo's bulletin board.[23] Deng became romantically involved with Chang Hsi-yuan, the railroad official's daughter who had been one of Ching-kuo's companions on the long trip from China. Xiaoping and Hsi-yuan "became very close."[24]

ALSO IN JANUARY, Ch'en Kuo-fu's little brother Li-fu, with an MS degree in engineering in his pocket and a year's work experience in the coal mines of Pennsylvania, arrived in Canton. Li-fu had agreed to become confidential secretary to "Third Uncle Kai-shek." The slim, handsome young man immediately experienced one of Chiang's violent temper tantrums. He told the General he would serve him loyally but would leave if he was ever "verbally abused" again. Chiang promised to be civil and for the next twenty-five years kept his word. In return Li-fu, like his brother, would become one of Chiang's most loyal supporters, and also a power in his own right.[25]

One of Li-fu's jobs was to screen intelligence reports. He was, he says, "well aware of what the Communists were doing." The materials originated in the network of informers that Ch'en Kuo-fu had established with the help of the Green Gang. The Ch'ens produced a flow of information to Chiang about his enemies and potential enemies in

Canton and elsewhere. On March 18, a member of the CCP executive committee warned Chiang that a plot against him was afoot.[26] Two days later, the Nationalist gunboat *Chungshan* moved mysteriously from Canton to Whampoa and uncovered its deck guns. Chiang struck quickly, arresting the captain and crew and detaining 25 Communists officials, including Zhou Enlai. Chiang now had the political as well as the military reins of the KMT firmly in his hands. He assured the Soviets that he did not desire to jeopardize cooperation with them or the Chinese Communists—he had simply acted against individuals who had erred. He asked for the early return of Borodin, who was in Moscow on consultations, and requested that his friend General Blyucher, who had been called home, come back and resume his position as the senior military adviser. In an open letter to the Whampoa cadets he wrote that, like Dr. Sun, he believed the revolutionary front would not be united without accommodation with the Communists. He released Zhou Enlai and other CCP members whom he had detained and, to demostrate balance, arrested some right-wing officers.

Chiang Kai-shek had assumed that the KMT could manage the alliance with the Communists without serious threat to its own supremacy. But even before the gunboat incident, reports provided to him by the Ch'en brothers had raised his concern, and he had moved to assert his authority in the coalition. At the same time, Chiang understood that Soviet material assistance was still critical to the success of the Northern Expedition. Consequently, when and how a break with the Communists might come would still depend upon events. In Chiang's mind, the odd coalition could even go on indefinitely, as long as neither the Soviets nor the CCP sought to challenge him.

In fact, Chiang Kai-shek's world view was still very much a leftist one. This outlook was reflected in the interesting exchange of letters between the KMT leader and his son just prior to the gunboat incident. On February 12, Ching-kuo expressed concern that a previous letter from his father had reflected "the prevailing thinking of traditional society." Ching-kuo then asked his father to explain the relationship between Sun Yat-sen's principle of "the people's livelihood" and communism. The elder Chiang replied that the old-fashioned thinking evident in his previous letter had been intended to test Ching-kuo, and he expressed pleasure that his son's own "thinking and language" were both "correct." He went on to explain that Sun Yat-sen's principle of "the people's livelihood" included communism. The Chinese Revolution becomes meaningful, he said, "only when it becomes part of the world revolution."

In a letter dated March 16, the elder Chiang supported his son's decision to join the Chinese Communist Youth Corps. The KMT and the CCP were "comrades in terms of the revolution." Chiang Kai-shek knew the Soviet secret police would intercept and read his letters to Ching-kuo and in part they were probably shaped with this in mind. But they also reflected the elder Chiang's continuing radical stance only four days before he reacted to the alleged gunboat plot.[27]

DESPITE THIS INCIDENT, the Comintern agreed to push ahead with the alliance with the Kuomintang. Although the CCP leaders wanted to sever the connection, they once more showed their obedience and accepted orders to continue the coalition.[28] Stalin (as well as Trotsky at this time) was mostly concerned with buying off the Japanese in Manchuria at China's expense.[29] The Soviet Politburo had accepted that "southern Manchuria would remain in Japanese hands in the period ahead," and that the USSR should seek "peaceful and stable relations" with Marshal Chang Tso-lin, the warlord who held northern Manchuria and parts of north China. Stalin made it clear that the KMT/CCP united front should for the time being emphatically reject any idea of an aggressive military campaign to unite China and, in general, any activity that might push the "imperialists onto the path of military intervention."[30]

In the summer of 1926 Chiang Kai-shek became Commander-in-Chief or (adopting the Italian title) Generalissimo of the National Revolutionary Army. Wu Chih-hui presented him the ceremonial flag on the occasion. Ch'en Kuo-fu now assumed the key position as head of the organization department of the Party. Working closely with his brother and others, Ch'en set off to reorganize the Party branches in Kwangtung and neighboring provinces, purging most CCP members from leadership positions and even the lower levels. Ch'en began to infiltrate his own clandestine "political units" into labor unions, peasant associations, and the CCP itself.[31] In July Chiang "persuaded" the Canton Chamber of Commerce to make a large cash contribution to the Revolutionary Army. With these funds in hand, the Generalissimo began the march north to bring all of China under one flag, that of the KMT. The various warlord forces Chiang meant to overcome were ten times larger than his army.

CHING-KUO CONTINUED TO SEE EVENTS in his homeland in a highly positive light. He understood that it had been necessary for his father to assert firm control and deal with the dissidents in Canton. Unlike CCP members who envisioned an eventual takeover of the Chinese revolution and the KMT by their vanguard party, Ching-kuo believed that the Kuomintang under the leadership of his father would achieve not only the defeat of imperialism and the unity of China but also a proletarian and Marxist revolution. In this scenario, the CCP would be a supporting party and eventually the KMT—the real vanguard party—would absorb it.[32]

Ching-kuo published in the university's Chinese-language journal an article entitled "China's National Revolution and the Chinese Communist Party." The author criticized the CCP for hampering the revolutionary cause, sowing seeds of dissension within the KMT, and rallying "tramps and loafers" to spark insurrections against the KMT forces. He accused the Communist Party of conducting infiltration activities to enlarge its scope of control and to build up its own power. The CCP, Ching-kuo believed, was causing problems for the true revolutionary force in China, the KMT led by his father.[33] Understandably, at this point his relations with the Chinese Communists began to deteriorate.

IN OCTOBER STALIN REMOVED TROTSKY from the Politburo and denounced him and his supporters as Social Democrat deviationists. Still, most Chinese students at the university, Radek, and others on the faculty persisted in favoring Trotsky's concept of "permanent revolution." Students began to call Ching-kuo "the organizer of the Trotsky school."[34]

Then news arrived that despite Soviet disapproval of the move, his father had led the relatively small Revolutionary Army out of Kwangtung and headed north. Chiang Kai-shek was a stirring example of the audacious revolutionary about whom Radek so often raved.

⎯

AROUND THIS TIME, at the precocious age of sixteen, Ching-kuo also discovered romance. He and fifteen-year-old Feng Fu-neng, the warlord's daughter, became sweethearts and then lovers. (She and her brother Hung-kuo had arrived in Moscow in May.) Fu-neng wrote love letters to her boyfriend, modestly expressing pleasure and wonder that such an outstanding student cared for her.[35] Male students greatly outnumbered females at the university, and most were older than Ching-kuo. His success in winning the favor of one of the most beautiful girls was a coup.

Ching-kuo's broad features and relatively short stature did not place him among the most handsome of the students, but he did have the rugged good looks of a robust peasant boy. Although still slim, he had, through exercise, grown rather muscular. His classmates attest to his good humor as well as his vigor and self-confidence. As in Shanghai, he was the natural leader who envisioned goals and harnessed his peers to the task of achieving them.

At first, the few married couples at the university had been compelled to live separately. The male students roomed in the university building; the female quarters were in the former residence of a dispossessed nobleman on Petrovka Street. After complaints, the school authorities established a "secret meeting room" for conjugal use while family dormitories were being built. Unmarried couples also made use of the room.[36]

Ching-kuo's "secret" meetings with Fu-neng constituted the beginning of a long and varied romantic career. He would, however, pursue women of equal status rather than sing-song girls like those with whom his father had consorted for many years. Raised by women who smothered him with love and, as an adolescent, infatuated with a sensual "Shanghai mother" young enough to be a girlfriend, Ching-kuo worshipped and romanticized women. Throughout his life he would be seeking the perfect love, often finding the pursuit more rewarding than the consummation.

Soon Ching-kuo and Fu-neng decided to marry. Marriage was a simple process in Moscow in those days. It was not even necessary to register such a union. Cohabitation was all that was required. An official university list of students from that period (1926) identifies Nezhdanova (Feng Fu-neng) as "wife of Elizarov" (Chiang Ching-kuo). Presumably they shared one of the new rooms for married couples. Because Fu-neng was not an activist, however, Ching-kuo's socialist friends disapproved of the match.[37]

As often as they could, Ching-kuo and Fu-neng went to the Chinese Workers Club in Moscow, which had the city's best collection of Chinese newspapers. Hunched over cups of tea or hot water, they kept up with the good news from China. Ching-kuo was called upon to address audiences on these exciting events. At one point, he spoke to 3,000 Muscovites on "The Aims of the [KMT's] Northern Expedition in China and Its Eventual Success." Later he delivered a similar speech to 3,500 railroad workers.[38]

SOVIET FEARS that a China united under the revolutionary Kuomintang would be a provocation to Japan or England had fallen away. With Soviet weapons and the help of General Blyucher, the Generalissimo was marching northward with surprising speed. The fighting was often fierce and casualties were high, but first Changsha and then the three Wuhan cities fell to the Revolutionary Army. By the time Chiang's forces reached the Yangtze, thirty-four warlords had seen the light and joined the KMT. This motley collection of latecomers to the revolution would prove to be a mixed blessing for the Kuomintang.[39]

In August 1926 Moscow papers reported the words of Chiang Kai-shek speaking in Changsha, after his forces had captured that important city in central China: "If we want our revolution to succeed, we must unite with Russia to overthrow imperialism . . . the Chinese revolution is part of the world revolution . . ."[40] Very possibly Chiang at this point believed that the USSR would continue indefinitely to support anti-imperialist struggles like that in China but not meddle in them. Most people in Moscow took his revolutionary words seriously. Ching-kuo, in particular, saw them as confirming his own idealized vision of his father as a true Leninist, even a Trotskyite.

In the field, however, the KMT military commanders were not acting like leftists. Ahead of the advancing Revolutionary Army, Communist agitators organized peasant and labor unions. But once KMT generals occupied a territory, they reversed land seizures and cracked down on the various CCP-organized associations and unions in the liberated areas. Political commissars trained by Zhou Enlai held posts at the regimental level and above in the Revolutionary Army. Theoretically, they had authority over line commanders. But the latter persistently ignored this statutory requirement, and after March 20, replaced many political commissars with men of their own choosing. The CCP decided to order its members who were local officials in KMT-controlled areas to resign from their government positions so as not to be seen as responsible for what was occurring. The Comintern, however, reversed this decision.[41]

Chiang Kai-shek could trust the bulk of the senior officer corps in the Revolutionary Army, but Communist and leftists were more influential at the KMT headquarters. After Chiang left Canton on August 12, their influence grew swiftly. The KMT liberals, including Sun Yat-sen's widow, Soong Ch'ing-ling, increasingly feared that Chiang intended to establish a military dictatorship. Borodin, as political adviser, stayed on in Canton and played an important role among the leftists. In October the Central Executive Committee, including Soong Ch'ing-ling, met in Canton and passed resolutions implicitly critical of Chiang's concentration of political power in his hands. In November, the committee voted to move the Party headquarters and the National government to the industrial and presumably more leftist city of Wuhan, rejecting Chiang's preference for Nanch'ang, which was then the site of his military headquarters.[42]

Pamphlets in Wuhan appeared comparing Chiang with Mussolini. But the Moscow press and Marxist journals in New York and elsewhere continued to heap praise on the Gimo's dramatic victories. At the Seventh Plenum of the Comintern in November, Stalin pointed to these successes as a vindication of his policies. The dictator had convinced himself that the Kuomintang would do anything he wanted, and that a China united under the KMT would be responsive to his interests. Moreover, he believed that "inevitably" leadership of the KMT would go to the working class, and the Chinese bourgeoisie would break away or be eliminated.[43] Geopolitics also argued for backing the increasingly powerful Kuomintang. Stalin still expected—correctly—that a united China would eventually excite the Japanese into asserting their hegemony over all of Manchuria. But as Chiang Kai-shek moved north, the Soviet leader came to view Japanese expansionism as equally or more likely under a weak and divided China. Thus a strong neighbor to the south was in the Soviet interest so long as it was friendly, a condition the KMT promised to fulfill. The KMT actually attended the November Soviet Party Plenum in Moscow as an "associate member." The delegate who reported to the "comrades" on behalf of Chiang Kai-shek was no other than Shao Li-tzu, Chiang Kai-shek's chief secretary.[44]

In January of 1927 Deng Xiaoping left Moscow to join the Christian General as a CCP adviser.[45] He was returning to China at an exciting moment. One column of the Generalissimo's forces consisting of the Kwangsi armies of Pai Ch'ung-hsi and Li Tsung-jen had liberated the Gimo's home province of Chekiang. The road to Shanghai now lay open. Initially, the Wuhan KMT, including the Communists, wanted to move north toward Peking. Chiang insisted on taking Shanghai first. If he could win control of the Chinese section of Shanghai, he would have access to large financial resources, could expect foreign recognition of his government, and would no longer need to depend upon the Soviets. With little fighting, Chiang occupied Shanghai on March 21.

Trotsky and Radek were alarmed at the reports from China describing the growing persecution of Communist organizers in the field and the continuing starboard drift of the Kuomintang. Trotsky for the first time openly called for the CCP to break completely with Chiang Kaishek and the right Kuomintang. He still assumed, however, that the CCP could not relinquish its support of the left KMT-dominated National government in Wuhan and the units of the Revolutionary Army apparently at its command.[46] Radek soon followed Trotsky's line, demanding that the CCP join with the left Kuomintang and seize control from the Generalissimo and the right wing. By the end of March, the rector was boldly predicting that Chiang would turn on the Communists and betray the revolution.[47]

For Ching-kuo it was a confusing time. His Soviet heroes, Trotsky and Radek, were now enemies of the father he worshipped, while Stalin and the official press continued to defend the alliance with the KMT and its leader. When news reached Moscow that the Northern Expedition had occupied Shanghai, newspapers in the Russian capital put out extra editions and "excited mobs" filled the streets.[48] The students at Sunovka held a jubilant meeting at the university and fired off a letter of congratulations to Ching-kuo's father. With Ching-kuo in the front row of marchers, the students led a rally of thousands of workers in front of the Comintern building. The demonstrations lasted until late in the evening. In the days that followed, the Chinese students were cheered wherever they went. Russian girls came to the university to offer themselves to the young revolutionaries.

At this time, the left-dominated KMT Executive Committee held a plenum in Wuhan and issued edicts subordinating Chiang's authority as Commander-in-Chief to a military council. It also transferred the key posts he held in the Party to his principal rival, Wang Ching-wei. The die was cast. Chiang probably did not make up his mind to suppress the CCP until sometime in late March. To the extent he consulted with anyone about this draconian move, it was with his small coterie of close associates including the Ch'en brothers, Tai Chi-tao, and Wu Chih-hui.

Wang Ching-wei arrived in Shanghai on April 1. The next day, the scholar Wu, no doubt acting with Chiang's knowledge, presented a letter to a secret meeting of the KMT's Central Supervisory Committee—formally just an advisory group but one in which the conservatives dominated. Not mincing words, the letter proposed a "purge" of the Communists. The committee unanimously agreed. The Party seal required to put the final requirement on the order was in Wuhan, but Ch'en Li-fu quickly arranged to have a copy made in Shanghai.

On April 5, in Peking, troops of the Manchurian warlord, Marshal Chang Tso-lin, broke into the Soviet Embassy, arrested the Chinese Communists hiding there, and confiscated safes full of secret documents. The files detailed extensive involvement of the USSR in the CCP's infiltration and clandestine operations and in recent street agitation. The old Marshal hanged twenty of the Communist prisoners, including the most prominent, Li Ta-chao. As a student in Peking, Ching-kuo had come to know and admire Li.

In Shanghai, the KMT's Supervisory Committee met again and set up a committee to carry out the purge. The "cleansing" began on April 12, 1927. According to Ch'en Li-fu, no formal plan of collaboration or alliance with the Green Gang existed, but "the major figure who organized and executed the purge was Yang Hu, a leader of the Gang." Yang passed "whatever we suggested to (the Green Gang leader) Tu Yueh-sheng, and . . . the Green Gang went into action." Army units took over the offices of the Labor Union Federation and shot down resisting workers there and in the streets. KMT troops disarmed "Communist pickets," seizing 3,000 rifles. The next day, the army opened fire on protesters in the streets. Numerous executions followed. Zhou Enlai was among the captives, but he managed to escape. Some say the Kwangsi militarist Pai Ch'ung-hsi let him go. Chiang ordered a similar sweep in Canton on April 15. Ch'en Li-fu concludes, "It was a bloodthirsty way to eliminate the enemy within. I must admit that many innocent people were killed. We paid a heavy price."[49]

In Moscow, students at Sun Yat-sen University had been preparing for the upcoming May Day celebrations. Portraits of Chiang Kai-shek and Feng Yu-hsiang were on display in and around the school.[50] Among the huge posters of Marx, Lenin, Stalin, and other socialist notables that the masses would parade across Red Square on the great holiday would be one of Chiang Kai-shek.[51] The Gimo was a hero of the world revolutionary movement. Communist papers around the world had joined in the praise of the Red Generalissimo.

But the Chinese students were unaware of Stalin's cynical explanation of his support of Chiang Kai-shek. On April 6, the Georgian had felt obliged to reply to the heavy carping from Trotsky and other critics and in an unpublicized speech to the Party workers of Moscow he raised the China issue. The KMT, he assured his listeners, was a "sort of revolutionary parliament" that included the right, the left, and the Communists. "Why drive away the right when it is of use to us," he asked. "When it is no more use we will drive it away." Then he offered his famous image of Chiang Kai-shek, to be "squeezed out like a lemon and thrown away."[52]

Six days later later, the news from China hit Moscow. The Gimo had squeezed first. The Sun Yat-sen students were incredulous. As the details came in, the reaction changed to outrage. The students quickly convened a meeting. Ching-kuo climbed to the stage and addressed the gathering, "not as the son of Chiang Kai-shek, but as the son of the Chinese Komsomol." His "eloquent" denunciation of his father as a "traitor and murderer" won a thunderous ovation.[53] Ching-kuo then issued a statement, which the Soviet press featured on its front pages:

> Chiang Kai-shek was my father and a revolutionary friend. He has now become my enemy. A few days ago he died as a revolutionary and arose as a counter-revolutionary. He used fine words about the revolution, but at the most convenient opportunity he betrayed it. . . . Down with Chiang Kai-shek. Down with the traitor![54]

Following up this denunciation, on April 21, *Izvestia* carried an article entitled "Father and Son," which contained excerpts from an open letter that Ching-kuo had written his father:

> Kai-shek, I do not believe you are going to listen to what I have to say. You probably would not want even to read it. But I am writing to you anyway and I do not care if you read it or not. Today, I would like to repeat your words which you once wrote to me, remember, "revolution is the only thing I know and I am willing to die for it. . . ." Now I would like to respond: revolution is the only thing I know, and I do not know you as my father anymore. [55]

STALIN QUICKLY BLAMED the CCP and Trotsky for the debacle. He claimed he had foreseen that the KMT right would turn on the revolution. But he now put his faith in the continuing alliance with the left Kuomintang in Wuhan and with Fu-neng's father, the supposedly leftist Christian General Feng Yu-hsiang.[56] In two articles in *Pravda,* Stalin's then ally, Bukharin, insisted that the revolutionary cause was not lost and that the left KMT remained a reliable force. The majority of the KMT Central Executive Committee were leftists, he pointed out, and they and the Communists controlled the Wuhan government now arrayed against the regime of Chiang Kai-shek.[57] Trotskyites, in contrast, called for a total break with all wings of the KMT and the establishment of worker and peasant *soviets* to take power throughout China.

At first, Ching-kuo intensified his support of the Trotsky line. Appearing at meetings where students could speak for five minutes, he talked like a machine gun while leafing through reference books to find the proper Trotsky quotation. One fellow student called him a "brilliantly organized" speaker who made maximum use of his five minutes. Ching-kuo also wrote essays touting Trotsky's position which were posted on Red Wall and other bulletin boards through out the school. At one point, he and several colleagues met with Trotsky himself.[58]

—

BACK IN SHANGHAI, the elder Chiang read the wire service reports on his son's statements. For a Chinese son to declare his father an enemy was almost beyond imagination. In nineteenth-century China, a father could kill his son for a much lesser insult and be considered within his rights. The Generalissimo's reaction to Ching-kuo's statement is unknown. He did not speak about it, probably because his anger was mixed heavily with guilt. If, as seems likely, Chiang consciously made the decision not to bring Ching-kuo back before the Shanghai coup for fear of revealing his hand, he would have felt an especially heavy responsibility for his son's predicament. On the surface and perhaps in his heart, Chiang accepted the official explanation that Ching-kuo had been forced to make the statements attributed to him, and neither in his diary nor elsewhere did he ever comment on the subject.

—

BEFORE THE EVENTS OF APRIL 12, the continued presence in Moscow of the son of Chiang Kai-shek had served as a confirmation that Stalin was correct in believing that his support for Chiang was expedient and wise. After Chiang "betrayed" Stalin, the Russian ruler would have heard of Ching-kuo's denunciation of his father and realized that the boy was potentially a useful asset. Ching-kuo states in his memoirs that at this time he asked to return to China. If so, it was in the context of joining the revolution against his father. To have suggested he wished to join Chiang Kai-shek in the new KMT headquarters in Nanking to help finish off the CCP would have marked him as an anti-Communist turncoat. Stalin would most likely have summarily rejected any such request.

In the event, a Comintern representative informed Ching-kuo that although he had completed only 17 months of the two-year university course at Sunovka, he would receive early graduation and then enter a military school in Moscow in preparation for admission into a military academy. No doubt he made it clear that Ching-kuo would have to abandon his pro-Trotsky activities and beliefs.

Within a matter of months, the seventeen-year-old Ching-kuo had to confront two critical decisions, both with profound personal and moral implications. In April he had to choose between his father and his revolutionary ideals. Now he had to decide whether or not to compromise his radical commitment to Trotsky or suffer a fruitless martyrdom.

Ching-kuo was attracted to grand designs that required heroic effort, but only to ones that had a fair chance of succeeding. That spring, he "suddenly abandoned the Trotsky movement."[59] This was the first important instance in his life in which instinctive pragmatism overcame his emotional and intellectual attraction to resounding ideals. The experience gave him an appreciation of the complexities and contingencies of life. It also began a life-long pattern in which empirical judgment would shape his pursuit of intuitive and visionary goals. Action would have to be justified by sound reason, not just emotional or political commitment.

DURING MAY various incidents highlighted the chasm that separated the KMT liberals in Wuhan from the Communists. The KMT leftists were modernizers and serious reformers, but they remained law-and-order moderates. On June 1, M. N. Roy, the Comintern agent in Wuhan, received a cable from Stalin to the effect that the vacillating "old leaders" (that is, the left bourgeoisie such as Wang Ching-wei) would either have to come around or "be discarded." Stalin's cable, which Roy inexplicably showed to the Kuomintang leftists in Wuhan, said the chief thing was to lay the foundation for new revolutionary regiments and divisions, that is, a CCP-led army.[60]

About this time, Deng Xiaoping sensed that a purge against the Communists in Feng Yu-hsiang's camp was brewing and quietly slipped away. A few days later, Feng held talks with Chiang Kai-shek in Hsuchow. The two generals reached complete agreement on getting rid of the Communists. On July 15, 1927, the left KMT Executive Council expelled the CCP from the Party and the government. Left KMT troops rounded up and executed CCP members. The Communist leaders again scattered, some into the foreign concession areas of Wuhan and others to Shanghai and CCP-controlled territories in Kiangsi. Mao and Deng were in the latter group. Borodin hastily departed for Russia, and the Soviet advisers in Feng's camp also packed up and headed off across the Gobi. There is no indication what if any thought General Feng gave to the fate of his children in Moscow. His son, Hung-kuo, immediately denounced his father and called Chiang Kai-shek a "butcher of workers and peasants."[61]

Stalin again claimed to have seen the break coming and blamed the CCP leadership for having failed to carry out an agrarian revolution and to arm the workers. He ordered the CCP to prepare for a revolutionary offensive. Ch'u Ch'iu-pai replaced Ch'en Tu-hsiu as Party leader and affirmed the new aggressive line from Moscow. Mao recruited an army of about 2,000 and launched attacks on various towns. Local forces put down this Autumn Harvest Uprising, and Mao fled with his surviving forces to the Chingkang Mountains in nearby Kiangsi province. There his approximately 1,000 troops were joined by two of the areas' bandit gangs affiliated with secret societies.[62]

AFTER THE APRIL 12 COUP, KMT headquarters in Nanking sent instructions to all KMT students in Moscow to leave the university. Many did not know what to do. The Russian archives contain a confession written by Ching-kuo in July announcing he was terminating the spousal relationship with Fu-neng. He charged that the KMT had used her to keep watch on him and to influence his political thinking. Yet the young couple continued to exchange letters into the fall of 1927. On 5 August, 239 students, nearly all KMT members, were allowed to return to China. The remaining 320 Chinese students were mostly CCP members. About 50, however, were KMT students who had elected to remain. These included Ching-kuo, Fu-neng, and her brother Hung-kuo.[63]

DURING THE NOVEMBER CELEBRATION of the tenth anniversary of the Bolshevik Revolution, Stalin and the other denizens of the Politburo stood on Lenin's tomb to view the masses and the weapons passing on parade. Among the prominent foreign guests on the VIP platform was the widow of Sun Yat-sen, Soong Ch'ing-ling, the left KMT adherent who had become a CCP sympathizer and a bitter foe of Chiang Kai-shek. Lacking the proper boots and clothing, she shivered for hours in the frigid cold.[64]

When one group of Russian marchers came abreast of Stalin, they suddenly waved hidden placards and shouted slogans in support of Trotsky. Fistfights broke out as security police and plainclothesmen waded into the group of protesters. Police pushed them out of sight just as the Sun Yat-sen University contingent marched by the tomb. The handful of militant pro-Trotsky students and teachers broke out their cloth banners hailing the Trotskyites and yelled anti-Stalin slogans. The much more numerous pro-Stalin marchers quickly restored order with the assistance of security personnel.

This embarrassing spectacle sealed the fate of the Trotskyites. In January of 1928 Stalin ordered Trotsky into exile in central Asia and Radek to western Siberia. Stalin also directed Pavel Mif to root out the Trotskyites at Sunovka, after which the Trotsky movement on the campus would be clandestine until it was completely suppressed in 1930 with the arrest of 36 Chinese students, most of whom perished.

The earlier events taught Hung-kuo to see discretion as the better part of politics; he pulled out of the pro-Trotsky group, but unlike his friend Ching-kuo, both he and his sister then opted to return to China and make peace with their father. But for months the Fengs remained in limbo. From morning to evening they sat in the library and read "weighty Russian tomes."[65]

DESPITE HIS MAJOR SUCCESSES in the first half of 1927, Chiang Kai-shek's leadership position was still far from secure. In July his forces suffered a defeat at Hsuchow at the hands of hostile warlord forces from the north. Wang Ching-wei and other left KMT members renewed their political maneuvering against Chiang's leadership. On the 13th of August

Chiang made another dramatic resignation, citing the deadlock between the KMT factions in Nanking and Wuhan, and set off on the familiar path to his home town. The Ch'en brothers stayed behind in Nanking, continuing their efforts to build a network of political and intelligence support.

Chiang and 200 bodyguards headed for Hole-in-the-Snow Monastery. Pacing the mountain paths in his flowing robe, the Gimo told visitors he was no longer interested in politics. In reality, Chiang knew that he was the KMT's indispensable man. The Nanking regime quickly found that without him it could not raise sufficient funds to maintain itself, much less renew the Northern Expedition. Over the next year, Chiang Kai-shek would consolidate his position as the leader of modern China and one of the most important statesmen on the world stage. He would also soon take a glamorous and rich wife. Chiang's only personal anguish was that his son had become his enemy.

4

Socialist Man

IN THE FALL OF 1927 Ching-kuo was among the top five trainees selected for advanced studies at the Central Tolmatchev Military and Political Institute in Leningrad, the premier academy of the Red Army. In his first year he studied military tactics, administration, transportation, topography, and principles of artillery. Guerrilla warfare was also a major subject.[1] Ching-kuo's instructor in military strategy was Marshal Mikhail Tukhachevsky, the Red Army's legendary Civil War hero.[2] The curriculum included numerous classes in Marxism-Leninism and the techniques of political commissar work in the armed forces.[3]

HE HAD HARDLY SETTLED IN at the academy when disturbing news from China arrived. A Communist uprising in Canton ordered by Stalin had ended in a bloody debacle for the Communists. And two weeks before that, Ching-kuo's father had married Soong Mei-ling, Sun Yat-sen's sister-in-law (Soong Ch'ing-ling's sister), in a lavish wedding at the Majestic Hotel in Shanghai. The sisters' American-educated father, Charlie Soong, had made a fortune publishing bibles and manufacturing dried noodles in Shanghai. He had been one of Sun Yat-sen's key financial backers, but had bitterly opposed Ch'ing-ling's marriage to the much older and just divorced Dr. Sun. (A third daughter was the wife of H. H. Kung, who was becoming even richer than his father-in-law.) Chiang Kai-shek announced that he and Ch'en Chieh-ju, Ching-kuo's affectionate young "Shanghai mother," had never been married, and that he had paid her off as he had his previous concubine.

The Soviet press charged that this was a political marriage, joining the military might of the "KMT dictator" to the wealth and influence of the new Chinese capitalist class. Certainly the union served a grand political purpose, not only in China but around the world. In addition to her wealth and connections, Chiang's bride had the high status he probably felt he deserved and required as the leader of modern China—and the beautiful, sophisticated, and American-educated Mei-ling fit the bill. But a romantic element was also clearly present. Even critical biographers cite letters and anecdotes suggesting that Chiang was in fact deeply in love with Mei-ling, whatever her other attractions.[4]

ALTHOUGH CHING-KUO had ceased active participation in the pro-left opposition group of Chinese students in the summer of 1927, the following January he wrote a formal statement renouncing his Trotskyite views. "Since I was not certain then myself of the truth of Trotsky's theories, I followed this advice [of his military colleagues] and ended my relations with the secret activities of this clique."[5] Evidently, this statement was a *quid pro quo* for his remaining at the academy. His files were purged of any reference to his involvement in the Trotsky movement.[6]

While at Tolmatchev, Ching-kuo tells us, he published several articles on "philosophy" in a "historical magazine." Like all published writings in the Soviet Union at the time, Ching-kuo's articles no doubt reflected a materialistic-dialectical interpretation of life and politics. During his first year, the institute staff named Ching-kuo cadet company commander. He also became a full member of the Komsomol, a reflection of good political, military, and academic standing. Still, the authorities kept a watch on him. According to colleagues, his roommate was an OGPU agent.[7]

On May 25, 1928, the Fengs received permission to return to China.[8] Since entering the academy, Ching-kuo had apparently stopped writing to Fu-neng. She and her brother and sister eventually made it home. Hung-kuo reconciled with his father, who sent him off to a Japanese military academy.[9]

SOMETIME IN EARLY 1928, a few students at Sunovka wrote Ching-kuo at the academy asking him to be president of a proposed Chekiang-Kiangsu association. His OGPU roommate discovered the letter and turned it in.[10] Wang Ming, who had become head of the CCP branch in the USSR, charged that the proposed association was a counter-revolutionary body.[11] An investigation by the Comintern, however, found no evidence of subversion.[12]

Ching-kuo did take special care to cultivate Chinese comrades from his own dialect group. This was a practice he had learned from his father, and indeed one which was traditional in China among aspiring national leaders. Ching-kuo had on occasions sold his own possessions to help out fellow students, especially if he or she hailed from Chekiang or neighboring Kiangsu. One classmate recalls Ching-kuo selling his radio for such a purpose.[13]

THE YEAR 1928 was the first time since 1911 that a Chinese government would become the recognized authority throughout 95 percent of the country. In January the Kuomintang appointed Chiang Kai-shek Commander-in-Chief. Chiang's new brother-in-law, T. V. Soong, became Finance Minister. With funding wrung from Shanghai capitalists, Chiang now firmed up his alliance with Feng Yu-hsiang and resumed the march north.

On June 4, 1928, as the Manchurian warlord Marshal Chang Tso-lin was traveling in a luxury rail car, Japanese officers, hoping to create a pretext for Japan's further expansion in the area, blew up the train, killing the old bandit-soldier. A more enlightened and nationalistic figure replaced the Marshal as chief of the Manchurian forces—his son, Chang Hsueh-liang. The "Young Marshal" had a reputation as a dandy and womanizer and since 1926 had been an opium addict. Nevertheless, he proved ruthless when he had to be. He was also more a nationalist than a warlord. As the Japanese demanded, he officially maintained the informal "autonomy" of Manchuria, but after formation of the new National government in Nanking on October 10, he became a member of the new State Council and his troops raised the KMT flag.

Now, at last, China seemed to be united from the Ussuri River in the far north to the border with Southeast Asia. Chiang Kai-shek was the leader of all China—save the parts under the control and administration of the Japanese and other imperialists, and the small CCP *soviets* in Kiangsi and neighboring provinces. In reality, however, Chiang's power extended only to the city of Shanghai and the provinces of Kiangsu, Chekiang, Anhui, and Kiangsi. Elsewhere, local and regional power holders gave formal obeisance to the KMT and the State Council but continued to act as separate kingdoms. Over the next few years, a number of warlords who had thrown in with the KMT would break away to form their own regimes. Feng Yu-hsiang would be the most prominent example. But none of the militarists, including Feng, could pose a serious challenge for national power. Chiang's only rivals on this scale were the Communists.

In 1928 the CCP held its Sixth Congress in Moscow, there being no safe place for such a gathering in China. Among the Politburo members attending was Zhou Enlai, who had arrived in the Russian capital early in the year. Only thirty years old, Zhou had survived a dangerous year. Having barely escaped with his life from Shanghai in April 1927, he fled Wuhan in July with the police on his tail, helped plan a failed uprising in Nanch'ang in August, retreated with the rebel army to Swatow, caught malaria, was evacuated to Hong Kong, and sneaked back into Shanghai in December.[14]

During his lengthy Moscow stay, Zhou met at least once with Chiang Ching-kuo. Zhou told the young man that his denunciation of Chiang Kai-shek had been a good thing, but that he should not forget to write his father from time to time.[15] In his memoirs, Ching-kuo tells us that in the period between June and August he did write numerous letters to his father but did not send them.[16] Wang Ming and other CCP Stalinists in Moscow distrusted Ching-kuo and saw him as a potential rival. Like Stalin, however, Zhou Enlai apparently thought the young Chiang could some day play a useful role and thus it was wise to keep open the door to the possibility that he might reconcile with his father and the KMT.

In the CCP hierarchy at this point, the two dominant leaders were Li Li-san and Wang Ming, both of whom toed the Stalinist line. The most important CCP activity, however, was going on in mountainous Kiangsi. General Chu Te joined forces with Mao, creating the Fourth Red Army, whose motto was, "The enemy advances, we retreat; the enemy camps, we harass; the enemy tires, we attack; the enemy retreats, we pursue." Similarly, in Kwangsi province Deng Xiaoping was putting into practice the principle he and Mao were to follow for the next sixty years—spilling blood was not only necessary to advance the revolution, it was essential.[17]

By 1930, most of the world's governments had recognized the Nanking-based Republic of China (ROC) as the legal government of all China. The Communist bands in their scattered mountain strongholds constituted a tiny problem, but given their international link, Chiang Kai-shek viewed their liquidation as a priority in achieving his top goal: consolidation of KMT power within China.

AT THE BEGINNING OF 1928, the cadets at Tolmatchev read in the newspapers that Stalin had deported Trotsky to Turkey. A few months later, Ching-kuo's mentor, Karl Radek, admitted his errors and embraced Stalin's benevolent leadership. Stalin accepted the *mea culpa,* and Radek came crawling back to Moscow. None of these developments shook Ching-kuo's commitment to the ideals of a new socialist world.[18] In the summer, Stalin called on Party workers to "liquidate the kulaks as a class."[19] At Tolmatchev, little was heard of the vast deportations in the countryside. During his second year at the school, Ching-kuo became a candidate member of the Communist Party of the Soviet Union (CPSU).[20]

By then a diplomatic crisis was fast developing in Manchuria. In January 1929 the Young Marshal, Chang Hsueh-liang, consolidated his hold on Manchuria's regional forces by inviting his two pro-Japanese rivals to dinner and having them shot while he excused himself for his regular injection of dope. In April Marshal Chang's police raided Soviet consulates in northern Manchuria, revealing more documents that detailed Moscow's use of its diplomatic missions and the Chinese Eastern Railway Company for subversion and espionage. In July, in the name of the National government, the Young Marshal took control of this railway, which had been under joint Sino-Russian management since a 1896 treaty, and evicted Russian officials from their offices.

The Soviet government held that these actions violated its treaty rights and international law. In mid-November Soviet troops crossed the border and, in a brief struggle, inflicted humiliating defeats on Chang Hsueh-liang's troops. In keeping with his doctrine of avoiding premature conflict with foreign powers, the Gimo ordered Chang to retreat. The subsequent Khabarovsk Protocol restored the *status quo ante*. The CCP dutifully supported the USSR's use of military force to restore its economic position in Manchuria.[21]

Meanwhile, instability was spreading throughout China. As a result of the collapse of international trade, China's budding exports in silk, tobacco, cotton, and soybeans sharply declined. In some rural areas, thousands died of famine. The hard times made it more difficult for the government in Nanking, a shaky coalition of KMT nationalists, capitalists, and various warlords, to institute the financial and rural reforms to which they gave lip service.[22] The political and psychological effects of world depression were even more important than the economic ones. The crisis convinced Stalin that an uneven but worldwide revolutionary upsurge was under way, and he decided to move faster with his own internal revolution and purges as well as with a more radical (ironically, Trotskyite) international policy, including with regard to China.

THE GREAT DEPRESSION thus added momentum to outbursts of right- and left-wing ideology around the world. It was a time of enormous social disintegration combined with continuing upheaval in everyday life. Ancient institutions were vanishing, and new dangers seemed to rise up at every turn. The specter of communism fed fascism, and the monster of Nazism seemed to excuse the extremes of the leftists.[23] Nazi Germany envisioned the conquest of Europe. Fascist Italy saw Africa and the Balkans as its prey. The spirit of the times—grandiose schemes of historic revision—found fertile ground in Japan. Resentful of the West's dominance of Asia and of the bans in America and elsewhere on Japanese immigration, right-wing nationalists in Japan used white racism as a target as well as a model of their own imperial movement and claims to racial ascendancy.[24] Having gained dominion over Taiwan in 1895 and Korea in 1910, the Japanese military began to look to Russia and China for further expansion. In November 1930, a young Japanese ultranationalist shot and killed the moderate prime minister. From this point on, political power in Japan flowed into the hands of radical imperialists.

Chiang Kai-shek also began to lean more to the right. This tendency grew as his reliance on German and Italian military advisers, trainers, and equipment increased. There was no alternative source of assistance for the ROC, and just as Chiang's previous reliance on Soviet aid brought out an ideological tinge of "redness," so it was inevitable that he would tend to cater to the views of the new supporting powers. But a distinct ideological affinity also developed. Though he had no use for racism, the tenets of fascism that preached loyalty and obedience to the state had a strong appeal to Chiang. Over the next few years he would exploit certain fascist as well as Communist techniques to try to establish a stronger intellectual and philosophical base for the Kuomintang and to reinvigorate its members with selfless idealism.

CHING-KUO GRADUATED from Tolmatchev in May 1930 with the highest grade point average in his class—a consistent score of "excellent."[25] His graduation thesis was on guerrilla war. His personnel file described him as "very talented . . . the best student at the Academy."[26] After graduation, Ching-kuo tells us, he once more asked to return home, but as a second choice, he requested permission to enter the Red Army as a commissioned officer. In fact he requested to remain in the USSR, very likely hoping for a military career.[27] Probably Stalin himself decided Ching-kuo should not become a Soviet officer as this would compromise his Chinese nationalist credentials and make him potentially less useful in the future.

Ching-kuo's military years had hardened his body. He seemed the picture of good health. When he returned to Moscow in 1930, however, he became seriously ill.[28] This was one of several more than routine illnesses that he suffered during his years in the USSR. These bouts of sickness were unquestionably connected to his diabetes, aggravated by heavy libations of vodka. The convivial Ching-kuo had taught his Russian friends the Chinese drinking game, *hua chuan* ("matching numbers"), a finger game at which he was a master.

IN OCTOBER HE RECOVERED and went on to his next assignment, an apprenticeship at the Dynamo Electrical Plant in Moscow—a key industrial facility. Ching-kuo's job at first involved strenuous manual labor eight hours a day as a machine tool operator. The pay was only 45 rubles a month. The Comintern wanted him "to learn about the life of the proletariat."[29] He rose at seven in the morning and in the evenings studied engineering at the Lenin International School until eleven. Food shortages caused by the chaotic situation in the villages were now felt in the cities, and Ching-kuo sometimes went to work on an empty stomach. Putting his studies to good use, he suggested a number of technical improvements at the plant. Within five months his pay was more than doubled. The increased wages reflected Stalin's sudden denunciation of "leveling," his introduction of piece work in the factories, and his encouragement of an elite class of technocrats. By Ching-kuo's own account, a "mounting zeal" for his work possessed him. In addition to factory labor and studies, he taught military science at the plant seven hours a week.[30]

Around this time, Ching-kuo criticized Wang Ming during a meeting at the International School, and as a result the Comintern asked him to leave Moscow and go to a mining plant in Altai in Siberia. Pleading poor health, Ching-kuo appealed to the headquarters of the CPSU, and the assignment was cancelled. In the summer of 1930, Wang Ming and a number of other pro-Stalinist graduates of Sun Yat-sen University returned secretly to Shanghai. This group of "28 Bolsheviks" constituted the Stalinist "returned students" faction that over the next few years would struggle with Mao for control of the CCP. Meanwhile, the Generalissimo took time off from battling his own intra-party enemies, and he and Mei-ling repeated their marriage vows in a Shanghai church, pledging to follow a life dedicated to Christian principles. After the ceremony, the Gimo launched his first "extermination campaign" against the "Communist bandits" in Kiangsi. Employing guerrilla tactics with daring and imagination, Mao and his military commander, Chu Te, evaded the government forces.

In South China, Deng Xiaoping learned that in Shanghai Chang Hsi-yuan had died in childbirth along with their baby.[31] Deng soon gave up the fight in Kwangsi and joined the Communists in the mountains of Kiangsi, where he became a key supporter of Mao against the 28 Bolsheviks. Mao and Chu Te defeated Chiang's second and third extermination campaigns in April and July of 1931, capturing thousands of weapons.

FOR THEIR PART, Japanese militarists both in China and at home were pressing Tokyo for decisive action. On September 18, 1931, following a staged incident outside of Mukden (Shenyang), Japanese troops overran the city and others moved across the Korean border into Manchuria. Believing Chang Hsueh-liang was not ready for a showdown, Chiang ordered him to pull back to positions south of Great Wall.

As a result of the Japanese aggression, the warring KMT factions nominally settled their differences. But anti-foreign sentiment and student protests against Chiang Kai-shek's failure to resist the Japanese swept the country. For the next fourteen years, Chiang would remain on the political defensive on this issue. For the Communists, Japanese aggression was a "win, win" situation. If Chiang fought the Japanese, this would remove pressure from the CCP. If he pulled back, he would be vulnerable to charges that he was refusing to defend Chinese sovereignty. The CCP denounced the "robber campaign of Japanese imperialism" and accused Chiang of "groveling before world imperialism."[32] On November 7, 1931, Mao formally declared the founding of the Chinese Soviet Republic in Kiangsi, with himself as chairman.

The Japanese takeover of Manchuria, although expected for some years, caused alarm in Moscow. Imperial Japan now faced the Red Army along one of the world's most extended continental frontiers. Stalin ordered a sharp increase in Russia's already enormous military spending and accelerated both the pace of industrialization and the removal of factories into the Urals. The Japanese move also nourished the idea in the Russian dictator's mind that the country needed a bloody and wrenching internal purge to steel itself for the wars to come. Given the new situation in the Far East, the geopolitical significance of China loomed larger than ever.

Shortly after the Japanese seizure of Manchuria, Ching-kuo received a surprising message—General Secretary Stalin, wanted to see him. Authorities in Moscow have not released the file of this meeting, and Ching-kuo does not refer to it in either the English or Chinese accounts of his Soviet experience.[33] It is safe to assume, however, that Stalin wanted to talk with young Chiang about the implications for the Soviet Union and China of the Japanese takeover of Manchuria. He must also have questioned Ching-kuo about his views on developments in China, in particular the political dynamics between the KMT and the CCP and within each of these two warring parties. Finally, he very likely asked whether it was possible that the CCP and the KMT could again form a united front—this time to resist the Japanese—and whether Ching-kuo would one day be willing to return to his father and work for such an alliance to save the country.

The supposition that Stalin stunned his young visitor with this possibility is suggested by the events that immediately followed. In early December, Madame Chiang's sister, the leftist Soong Ch'ing-ling, visited Chiang Kai-shek in Nanking to talk about a KMT prisoner named Hilaire Naulen. Before his arrest Naulen, a Polish national, had run the CCP's regional bureaus from Shanghai and was thought to be in charge of Communist parties in India, the Philippines, Malaya, Korea, Vietnam, and Japan.[34] Ch'ing-ling, undoubtedly acting for Moscow, proposed that Naulen and his attractive wife be released in return for Ching-kuo's repatriation.

As it turned out, this was a timely approach. The Gimo had begun to miss his son. On January 25, 1931, in his diary's first indirect reference to

Ching-kuo in six years, he wrote, "When I was young, I did not try my best to learn how to conduct myself. As a result I have not done anything good for my parents and I do not know how to be kind to my children. I regret that."[35] Then on November 28, a few days before Ch'ing-ling appeared in Nanking, Chiang jotted down a rare affectionate thought about Ching-kuo: "I miss Ching-kuo very much. I am bad because I am not taking good care of him. I am sorry about that."[36]

Still, the Gimo did not immediately reply to Ch'ing-ling's proposal, and when he discussed the subject with his wife, it was in terms of the question of an heir. He and Mei-ling had been married for four years; she was now thirty-five years old. Her failure to become pregnant (and before her, Yao Yeh-ch'eng's and Ch'en Chieh-ju's childlessness) had confirmed the Gimo's sterility. Two months before Ch'ing-ling's initiative, Mei-ling had coincidentally raised with her husband the question of Ching-kuo's status and the possibility of his return. Mei-ling now urged her husband to accept the trade-off.[37] Chiang refused, but he was torn by this decision.

"I have been unable to see my son since he went to Russia, and the Republic [of China] is only a small child," he wrote.

> Alas! I am neither loyal to the nation and the Party nor filial to my mother or kind to my children. I feel ashamed. . . . Madame Sun wanted me to release Naulen in return for the repatriation of Ching-kuo, [but] I would rather let Ching-kuo be exiled or killed in Soviet Russia than exchange a criminal for him. God decides whether you will have an heir and whether your nation will be subjugated. How dare I do anything about it. What I want is not to violate the law, betray my country, harm the reputation of my parents, or waste my life. It is not worth it to sacrifice the interest of the country for the sake of my son.[38]

On December 15 Chiang "resigned" all his posts once more, and he and his wife left Nanking for Hsikou. It has usually been assumed that continuing factionalism in the KMT and the criticism that Chiang was receiving for his failure to resist the Japanese provoked this move. While these political factors no doubt played a part, Chiang's concerns about his son strongly contributed to this decision.

THE CHIANGS DID NOT STAY at the family house in Hsikou. As Kai-shek had agreed in the divorce settlement, Mao Fu-mei and some of her relatives were entrenched there. Nevertheless, over the years, he had enlarged the old homestead. Workers had cleared out the surrounding 25 houses and built a new compound next to the original house in which Ching-kuo was born. The new complex included a two-story main house with a central reception area, which opened in the rear to a traditional compound, including an open hall for the family altar and ancestor tablets. A second-story bridge connected the new house to the original, more modest residence.[39] Above the outer gate of the new abode, the Generalissimo placed the carved characters "Feng Hao Fang" or "The House of Feng and Hao," referring to the infant names of Chiang Ching-kuo and the adopted Chiang Wei-kuo.

As usual Chiang spent several days at Hole-in-the-Snow Monastery, which at that time of year lived up to its name. About a mile further up the mountain he built an austere retreat on a sharp bluff looking down a thousand feet to a fertile valley below. The cabin, called High Terrace of Wonder (Miao Gao Tai), had two small rooms. Here and at the monastery, Chiang sat and reflected. On December 27, he wrote:

> A person will be remembered because he has moral integrity and achievements but not because he has an heir. Many of the heroes, martyrs and officials . . . in the history of China did not have children. but their spirit and achievements will always be remembered. I feel ashamed because I am worried that I will be left heirless if Ching-kuo is killed. If Ching-kuo is not killed by our Russian enemy, and even if I may not see him again, I am sure that he will be back after I die. If that is what will happen, I wish I would die soon so as to soothe my parents.[40]

FAILURE TO GIVE PRIORITY to his obligation to his ancestors pained Chiang most of all. Mencius said that there were three ways to be a bad son, of which the most serious was to fail to have an heir. As leader of the nation, however, the Gimo believed he could not make the small concession required to obtain a very personal goal. Four days later, he was still torn by his decision: "I am in an emotional turmoil . . . I cannot be utterly loyal to my country and fulfill my duty to my parents and children. My life is not worth living."[41]

But other matters clamored for his attention. As in the past, letters and telegrams poured in beseeching the Gimo to return to Nanking. After another reconciliation with Wang Ching-wei, Chiang again said good-bye to Hsikou, and he and Mei-ling flew back to Nanking. Shortly thereafter, Japanese forces attacked the Chinese garrison in Shanghai.

———

WHEN CH'ING-LING REPORTED to Moscow the results of her conversation with Chiang Kai-shek, Stalin decided that this was not after all the time for Ching-kuo to go back to China. Instead, he sent him to a collective farm in the village of Zhukova on the outskirts of the Moscow oblast in the Korovinsky region (now the Ryaza region).[42] The restructuring process, so wrenching in other parts of the country, had proceeded relatively well in the Moscow oblast. These farms supplied Moscow with food, and the existence of nearby "model collectives" was also useful for propaganda purposes.

It is strange that in his memoirs Ching-kuo makes only a passing reference to the collectivization process and none to the fate of the kulaks or to food shortages. Given the relative stability of Zhukova and the Orwellian world in which everyone in Russia lived at that time, Ching-kuo very likely believed that the rural reforms were necessary and proceeding with "dizzying success," as Stalin put it.

The peasants of Zhukova were mostly "uneducated and ill-mannered" and more than half were infested with lice and fleas. On his first evening, Ching-kuo slept in an outbuilding of a church. The next morning, when he went for breakfast, some peasants mocked him, saying, "Look, here comes a man who knows how to enjoy his bread without knowing how to plow." Ching-kuo immediately set about learning to till the soil. The first morning he worked until sundown and after a quick meal collapsed in his bed. The peasants were impressed. After ten days, they selected Ching-kuo as "their representative to negotiate with organizations in town concerning loans, taxes and the purchase of farming tools." They never asked him to do manual labor again.[43] In fact, within a few months he became chairman of the collective. But suddenly, in October 1932, he was again transferred. The appraisal of the Zhukova period in his Soviet personnel file reads: "He can be used as part of the leadership, even at the level of the regional Party office."[44]

Wang Ming was now back in Moscow as CCP representative to the Comintern, the organization that exercised principal control over Ching-kuo. Wang was not happy to find young Chiang also in the Soviet capital, where he had frequent contact with other Chinese exiles. Wang reputedly again suggested to the Comintern that assignment to a gold mine would be suitable for Ching-kuo—someplace in Siberia "thousands of miles from Moscow." Although Russian officials usually sided with Ching-kuo in the CCP's maneuverings against him, they were concerned that a "substantial number" of Chinese exiles in the city sided with him against Wang Ming, and they wished to dampen down factionalism among the Chinese in the capital. According to Ching-kuo, CPSU officials told him, "We want you to stay in Moscow to continue your study, but since you are at odds with the delegation of the Chinese Communist Party, you had better leave."[45] In October Ching-kuo traveled to the grimy industrial city of Sverdlovsk to begin a new job.

Immediately after his arrival in the Urals, he once again became seriously ill and went into a hospital for 25 days—his third prolonged illness in three years. When he recovered in January 1933, he was sent, for reasons he does not give, to the Altai region of Siberia. Although he does not say specifically that his destination was part of the Gulag, Ching-kuo describes his experience there as a "Siberian exile." He worked "side by side with professors, students, aristocrats, engineers, rich farmers and robbers." Each of them had "an unlooked-for, unexpected misfortune which had sent him into exile." Nine months later, as a reward for a "remarkable record of work," he was allowed to return to Sverdlovsk.[46]

Available Russian material, including the chronology in Ching-kuo's own official autobiographical statement of 1934, contains no reference to this Siberian episode. Russian scholars can find no evidence of it. Odd as it may seem, it is likely that following his illness on first arrival in Sverdlovsk, the authorities sent Ching-kuo to Altai not as punishment but for his health—to get him out of the terrible pollution of Sverdlovsk so that he might better recover from his mysterious sickness.

On his return, the Urals District Party Committee assigned him to an enormous machinery complex called Uralmash, which Soviet propaganda called "the factory of factories." He began as deputy supervisor of a machine shop that employed "several thousand workers."[47] Initially, Ching-kuo's appointment caused some grumbling. A woman worker named Maria Semyonovna Anikeyeva came home from the factory on Ching-kuo's first day at work and asked her husband why the plant could not find a Russian to be the deputy supervisor. But, she added grudgingly, "the Chinese . . . *is* very smart." Maria and her husband, Fyodor, became close friends of Ching-kuo.[48] "A smile never left his face," she said. "It always seemed that he was trying to open up to you completely. We never saw him unhappy."[49]

In the same year that Ching-kuo began work at Uralmash, a local technical institute assigned several young female graduates to the complex. Among them was a blond girl named Faina Epatcheva Vahaleva (or Vakhrina), a seventeen-year-old orphan who lived with her sister. Maria described her as "a good looking average girl" who made a big impression when she smiled and looked at you with her "slightly Japanese eyes." She was slim, quiet, and unassuming and about the same height as Ching-kuo. Ching-kuo immediately took to her, and Faina soon abandoned her blond Russian boy friend for the young Chinese.

In June Wang Ming cabled Ching-kuo to report to Moscow. When he arrived, Wang told him that his father had announced in Shanghai that he had heard his son was returning to China and if so, he would arrest him on the spot.[50] After a two-year lapse, Generalissimo Chiang had in fact started thinking again about his exiled son, but still in a sentimental, not, as Wang Ming supposedly suggested, a vengeful manner. In a February diary entry, the Gimo lamented his broken family "with my son gone away." Soong Mei-ling had apparently been talking with him again about Ching-kuo. "Anyone," Chiang wrote, "who recognizes me as father must recognize only my wife, Mei-ling, as mother."[51]

ON THE DIPLOMATIC FRONT, the chances of KMT China's advancing its political objectives vis-à-vis the Soviet Union were improving. A side effect of this dynamic, the Gimo thought, might be the return of Ching-kuo. In the summer of 1934, Chiang Kai-shek's gradual advances in his war against the Chinese Communists were also revising views in Moscow. Chang Hsueh-liang had returned from Europe and underwent a cold-turkey treatment in a Shanghai hospital that cured his drug addiction. Chiang assigned to him the task of wiping out the Communist *soviets* in the Hupei-Honan-Anhui border region, a mission which the Young Marshal promptly accomplished. The CCP leaders in Kiangsi, increasingly hard-pressed by the KMT Army assisted by German military advisers, debated breaking through the encirclement and retreating to a remote area closer to the USSR. They referred the question to Stalin.[52]

Shaken by the rise of Hitler, the Russian dictator had recently ordered the Comintern to abandon its ultra-leftist international line. Moscow was now looking fervently for allies among the bourgeois governments of Europe. The USSR joined the League of Nations, promised to help defend capitalist democracies against the fascists, and initialed pacts with France and Czechoslovakia. Ever since the Mukden Incident, Stalin had been anticipating a similar policy of *realpolitik* toward China. Now it was time to begin. For the foreseeable future, the CCP could not hope to lead a united China. Therefore the Soviet leader saw a fundamental advantage for the USSR in the CCP's immediately breaking off its military confrontation with the Kuomintang. With the Chinese Communists on the ropes in Kiangsi, there was little prospect the KMT would accept the idea of a CCP-KMT united front and Sino-Soviet cooperation against Japan. But if the Communists could break out of their present trap and make it to a safe haven in the north, Chinese public opinion might then pressure Chiang into accepting the idea of a new alliance. If, on the other hand, the Communists in retreat were wiped out, the USSR could still proceed to enhance its relations with Chiang Kai-shek.

———

SOMETIME AFTER CHING-KUO had returned to Sverdlovsk from Moscow, the Chinese government initiated "official talks with the Russians" on the resumption of Nanking-Moscow relations and also on "the repatriation of Chiang Ching-kuo."[53] The Naulens were still in jail in Nanking, but the elder Chiang did not revive the proposal for a swap that Ch'ing-ling had put forward in 1931. About this time, the Comintern, undoubtedly reflecting Stalin's decision, advised the Chinese Communists in Kiangsi to "pull out and seek safety somewhere—as far away as Outer Mongolia, if necessary."[54]

On October 16, 1934, several Communist columns totaling about 80,000 men, about one third with rifles, began their Long March out of Kiangsi. Zhou Enlai coordinated the breakout strategy. Lin Piao, a twenty-seven-year-old Whampoa graduate, led the First Army Corps, while P'eng Te-huai commanded the Third. Deng Xiaoping too marched out of Kiangsi, where he had been editor of the Party paper, *Red Star*, having survived a brief purge by the 28 Bolsheviks. A journey of 6,000 miles lay ahead.

For several months, Stalin chewed over the Generalissimo's request that Ching-kuo be sent home. In his memoirs, Ching-kuo reports that from August to November the NKVD suddenly put him under close watch; two men shadowed him every day. In the middle of this increased surveillance, Ching-kuo became the deputy editor of the Uralmash plant newspaper, *Tyazheloye Mashinostroyenie (Heavy Machinery)*. No one under serious suspicion would have come close to getting this agitprop job. Presumably, the agents were confirming Ching-kuo's loyalties.

Some weeks later, a comrade Lishtov, chief of the Urals Branch of the NKVD, summoned Ching-kuo to his office to inform him that the Chinese government had asked for his return. According to Ching-kuo, Lishtov said that the NKVD wanted him to write to the Ministry of Foreign Affairs in Moscow "telling them that you are unwilling to go back to China." Ching-kuo claims he refused to do so and that a few days later Lishtov told him a secretary from the Chinese embassy wished to see him. Ching-kuo met with the Chinese diplomat alone, but two other people sat in the next room. The implication was that Ching-kuo could not speak freely.[55] "I, of course, dared not say much or even disclose my wish to go back to China. We talked only about the progress made at home and how much my family wanted me back."[56]

The Chinese embassy reported to Nanking Ching-kuo's reaction to their approach. More than sixty years later, the Taipei government still will not release the cable traffic between Nanking and the Chinese embassy in Moscow on this subject, presumably fearing that Ching-kuo's strong pro-Soviet and anti-KMT language would be embarrassing. On

December 14, 1934, Chiang Kai-shek wrote in his diary: "When I was told that Ching-kuo was reluctant to come back from Russia, I knew that was invented by our Russian enemy. I took that calmly. I thought that I had made progress because I dismissed this family problem with a smile."[57]

IN JANUARY 1935 the Comintern asked Ching-kuo to come again to Moscow,[58] very likely to have him take part in discussions on developments in China and within the CCP. (Several months into the Long March, Mao Zedong had won out in a political contest with the 28 Bolsheviks. Deng was now one of his most valuable and committed supporters.) On this occasion Ching-kuo had dinner with Stalin: "a good thick soup, buckwheat kasha, and a fruit drink."[59] With the beginning of the Great Terror, Ching-kuo, like everyone else in Russia, had to be more careful than ever before to appear politically orthodox. All indications are that, in general, his thinking was in fact orthodox.

Ching-kuo returned to Sverdlovsk, and in March he and Faina were married by a simple registration process. Ching-kuo was now getting the handsome salary of 700 rubles a month.[60] The newlyweds received a new two-room apartment, which by the standards of the day was "considered very nice." Holiday parties thereafter were held in the Elizarov (the Chiang) apartment. Outdoing the Russians, Ching-kuo would entertain the guests with Caucasian dances and Russian songs. Among the regulars were regional Party Secretary Leopold Averbach, a former Trotskyite, and the plant's director, comrade Vladimirov. Ching-kuo and Faina took a holiday in the Crimea—a treat provided only to the most favored workers and cadres.

In addition to his two jobs, his engineering studies, and his socializing, Ching-kuo found time to begin writing a history of Uralmash.[61] He also gave lectures on international affairs. On these occasions, grandmothers would refuse to baby-sit and insist on going to hear Elizarov. After Averbach, Ching-kuo was considered the best analyst of international news.[62] "Oh my God," recalled Maria Anikeyeva, "He was so clever, so knowledgeable!"[63]

Ching-kuo gave no sign that he missed his country. A friend said he never talked about his parents or his homeland.[64] In December Faina, then nineteen, gave birth to their first child, a premature boy weighing only 3½ pounds. Ching-kuo named him Ai-lian (Love of virtue), from which later derived his English name Alan. During the first three months Faina and Ching-kuo took turns at night to feed him hourly with an eye-dropper.[65]

IN THE SPRING OF 1935 the Soviet Union formally concluded alliances with France and Czechoslovakia. Although the Chinese Communist forces were still undergoing the ordeal of their Long March, Stalin decided that it was time to move more decisively toward a united front strategy in China. Probably sometime in May or June the Comintern informed the CCP leaders that the Party should call for cooperation with Chiang Kai-shek, who up to that moment had been denounced as an evil brigand. The only condition was that Chiang should halt the KMT's "fight against its own people" and form a united front against Japanese imperialism. On August 1, the CCP formally called for an Anti-Japanese Peoples United Front.

Chiang rejected the proposal. In October Mao and about 9,000 of the original 80,000 who had left Kiangsi a year before arrived at a desolate place called Yenan in northern Shensi province. Together with local Communists and another column led by Chang Kuo-tao, the new CCP stronghold contained approximately 20,000 personnel, not all with rifles. The Gimo instructed the Young Marshal, Chang Hsueh-liang, to coordinate a round of attacks on these forces. In a bloody engagement, both the Red Army and the KMT Manchurian forces suffered heavy losses.

At the same time, the Japanese military, emboldened by its success in Manchuria, where it had established the puppet state of Manchukuo, seized more of Hopei province around Peking. Chinese police in Peking suppressed demonstrations by thousands of angry students protesting the Japanese aggression. Similar protests broke out in Nanking and other cities. The Young Marshal, who hated Japan, began to wonder if it was not time to reconsider the call for a united front. The Gimo, however, continued to believe it was essential to eliminate the Communists and build up China's military strength before confronting Japan.

He ordered Marshal Chang once again to step up pressures on the "bandits." The Communists, however, were pushing their public campaign for a united front, and they found eager listeners among the Young Marshal's troops, whose homes were in occupied Manchuria. A good number began to defect to the Communists. In February Marshal Chang for the first time met secretly with CCP officials.

As Nazi Germany formed closer ties to Tokyo, the chances increased that German aid to the Chinese armed forces would end. The Gimo nevertheless held on to his German connection as long as possible. In 1936, he sent his second son, Wei-kuo, to attend the Kriegshochschule, a military academy in Munich, a decision strikingly reminiscent of his decision eleven years earlier to allow Ching-kuo to go to Moscow for study.

Adding an item to this confused maneuvering, *Pravda* published a letter from Ching-kuo to his mother.[66] The tone was as hostile toward his father as the one he had used after the Shanghai purge. He denounced Chiang Kai-shek as "the enemy of the whole people and therefore the implacable enemy of his son." He asserted that he was "ashamed of such a father" and that he had no intention of returning to China. He reminded Fu-mei of the abuses she had suffered in the past: "Don't you remember, Mother, how he dragged you by the hair from the second floor? Whom did you implore on your knees not to throw you out of the house? Who drove my grandmother to the grave by beatings and insults? Wasn't it he? That was all done by the man who now babbles of filial affection and family morals." Ching-kuo also praised his experience in the Soviet Union: "Your son is wealthy in knowledge of human life and the methods of liberating exploited oppressed humanity . . . [he] will never go home to drag out there the miserable existence of a timid weapon in the hands of a mountebank father."[67]

According to Ching-kuo, the idea of the letter came from the unscrupulous Wang Ming, who said: "It is rumored in China that you have been arrested in Russia. You should write a letter to your mother saying that you are working and are completely free here."[68] Wang then gave him a draft letter, which Ching-kuo at first refused to sign. Friends advised him, however, that if he signed the letter he might have a chance of returning to China in the future. He supposedly gave in and accepted the draft, but insisted on adding a sentence telling his mother that if she wished to see him, "please come to Western Europe and let us meet there."[69]

The next day, writes Ching-kuo, he discussed the letter with the head of the NKVD, Genrikh Yagoda, a man responsible for the arrest and execution of hundreds of thousands. Yagoda not only took time to see Ching-kuo but sympathized with him and told Wang Ming to destroy the letter. Ching-kuo drafted his own letter, in which he did not mention his hope of going home but "tried to convey my longing for my family" in one sentence: "I have never stopped even for one day desiring to have some homemade dishes which I have missed for such a long time." Wang Ming accepted the new letter, but, according to Ching-kuo, sent the original to China and had the text published in *Pravda*. Given Stalin's demonstrated interest in Ching-kuo—underscored again by Yagoda's unusual attention to the affair of the letter—it is probable that the General Secretary himself saw some tactical advantage in such a painful reminder for the Gimo of his estrangement from his only natural son.

IN THE SUMMER OF 1936, in the midst of chilling developments in Europe and Japan, the first public trials of the Great Terror opened in Moscow. Prosecutors charged sixteen old Bolsheviks, mostly former Trotsky allies, with treason. Their "confessions" incriminated others. A vicious and rapidly widening campaign of terror began, bringing monstrous charges, abject confessions, sweeping incriminations, and finally execution or dispatch to the Gulag. The chief hatchet man himself, Genrikh Yagoda, lost his job in September and went abjectly to the same wall to which he had condemned countless others.

Many persons close to Ching-kuo faced such kangaroo trials or simply disappeared. Ching-kuo's guide and teacher, Karl Radek, made such an extravagant confession that he escaped with a long prison sentence and died miserably there in 1939.[70] Leopold Averbach, a former Trotsky supporter, was vulnerable, and soon he was starring in one of the show trials (in which he may have tried to incriminate Ching-kuo). Eventually, the NKVD arrested 3.8 million people for counter-revolutionary crimes and executed over 780,000. In 1937 Stalin turned on the military high command. Among the new victims were the hero Marshal Tukhachevsky, who had taught Ching-kuo military strategy, and the Marshal's wife and two brothers. General Blyucher, Chiang Kai-shek's friend, was a member of the tribunal that condemned Tukhachevsky. Shortly after, Blyucher himself went down before a firing squad. Michael Borodin somehow survived until the mid-1940s, when he disappeared.[71] In total, Stalin shot 30,000 Red Army officers, more than the Nazis would kill in the first two years of the coming war.[72] Almost all local and regional Party officials, including those in Sverdlovsk, whom Ching-kuo knew quite well, lost their lives or went by boxcar to Siberia. Ching-kuo's memoirs make no mention of the purges of his friends and teachers or his reaction to them. Probably, like almost everyone in the Soviet Union at the time, he did not dare think critically, much less voice skepticism. Moreover, the regime's suffocating propaganda rationalized the political trials as a necessity in light of the specters of terrible war that loomed in both east and west. This apparently convinced the majority of Russians, even the victims who went to their graves, that it was all somehow justified. It was the spirit of the age—the worship of ideology, war, and death.

Ching-kuo apparently also remained a believer. On November 16, 1936, he applied for full membership in the Communist Party of the Soviet Union.[73] The implication was clear—he felt that he was likely to spend the rest of his life in the USSR. About this time, the new ROC Ambassador to the Soviet Union, Tsiang T'ing-fu, arrived in Moscow. Shortly before the ambassador left China, Madame Chiang called him to a private meeting. The Generalissimo, she said, "wished very much that his son, Ching-kuo, would return to China." In one of his first interviews in the Soviet Foreign Ministry, Tsiang mentioned Ching-kuo and said he would appreciate any inquiries that could be made as to his whereabouts. The Deputy Commissar for Foreign Affairs, Stemenikov, thought this would be difficult, but promised to try.[74] Within a few weeks, however, events in China suddenly opened the door for a new KMT-CCP united front and for Ching-kuo's return.

THE PREVIOUS SPRING, the Young Marshal had traveled secretly to the Communist base area in Shensi and met with Zhou Enlai. Zhou convinced Chang of the CCP's sincere desire to give absolute priority to fighting the Japanese. Subsequently, Yen Hsi-shan, the anti-Communist warlord of Shansi province, who had played a critical role in the past in supporting Chiang Kai-shek, listened sympathetically to the Young Marshal's arguments for a united front. In the summer, leading generals in the south allied to Chiang Kai-shek led their troops into Honan and Kiangsi demanding that they be sent to fight the Japanese.

During the autumn the confrontation with Japan worsened. Puppet troops from Manchukuo, supported by Japanese planes and tanks, invaded the northern province of Suiyuan. But Chiang Kai-shek still believed he could and must eliminate the Communists before confronting Japan. Like Mao, however, Chiang also believed in *"ta, ta, tan, tan"* (fight, fight, talk, talk). While pressing for military action against the CCP, he authorized Ch'en Li-fu to hold secret talks with Zhou Enlai. Zhou traveled secretly to Nanking late in 1936 together with a Chinese representative from the Comintern, P'an Han-nien. The two sides tentatively agreed on the outline of a united front proclamation in which the CCP would agree to abolish all *soviets* in the countryside and disband the Red Army, placing the latter under the control of the government's military council. These were precisely the terms that would finally be agreed to in 1937. Zhou, however, wanted to report back to Yenan and in early December departed under a safe-conduct pass for Hsian, where he intended to brief the Young Marshal on his talks.[75]

Not heeding warnings that the trip would be dangerous, Chiang Kai-shek too flew to Hsian for discussions with his wavering commanders. On December 11 he held a tense meeting with the senior officers, stressing the need to finish off the Communists. At dawn the next morning, a contingent of the Young Marshal's soldiers descended on the hot springs resort of Lint'ung, ten miles outside of Hsian, where the Gimo and his entourage were staying. Chiang escaped through a window in the cabin where he was taking a sulfur bath, ran naked up a barren hill, and jumped over a wall, injuring his back. The troops found him in a nearby cave. "Shoot me, and finish it all"! the enraged Generalissimo shouted.

The young captain in charge replied, "We will not shoot you. We only ask you to lead our country."[76]

Confusion and uncertainty reigned in both Yenan and Nanking when news arrived that Chiang Kai-shek was being held by the Young Marshal's troops. The government prepared to deploy a vast array of forces to attack the rebels. Some in the CCP camp thought that Chiang Kai-shek should be killed and a united front formed with the Young Marshal. But in a telegram sent to all sides on December 12, Chang Hsueh-liang made it clear that he was not seeking to overthrow the Generalissimo but only demanding that he form a new popular front to save the nation.

When informed of the incident, Stalin understood both the danger and the opportunity. He also knew of the earlier discussions in Nanking. If the crisis in Hsian was not resolved quickly, it could lead to a new and much more violent civil war in China, possibly resulting in the KMT's turning to the Japanese for support. If the Communists could play the key role in bringing about Chiang's release, this could tip the scales toward the united front against Japan.

Izvestia and *Pravda* both published leading articles denouncing the kidnapping and proclaiming that China must be united, given its dangerous international position, and that a united China was only possible with the Generalissimo as its leader.[77] Stalin sent a long telegram to Yenan with the same message—Chiang remained the only man with the prestige to lead a national united front in China. Stalin suggested that the Japanese may have plotted the kidnapping in order to drive China deeper into civil war.[78]

Mao and Zhou also feared that the death of Chiang Kai-shek could bring about a pro-Japanese KMT regime in Nanking.[79] Mao dispatched Zhou back to Hsian to negotiate the Gimo's release. Meanwhile, Chang Hsueh-liang read the Gimo's diary and discovered the leader's secret plans to resist the Japanese after dispatching the Communists. Meanwhile, a wave of sympathy for the Gimo swept over the country.

On December 14, in Sverdlovsk, Ching-kuo read about the Hsian crisis. The same day, the Comintern discovered to its dismay that the Uralmash Party Committee was about to approve the elevation of the Generalissimo's son to full membership in the Communist Party of the Soviet Union![80] The Comintern urgently cabled that no action should be taken on the matter and instructed the young man to report urgently to Moscow. On December 16 Zhou Enlai arrived in Hsian and met with the Gimo. Chiang Kai-shek had steadfastly refused to negotiate with his kidnappers, asserting only that if he was unconditionally released, he would review the question of a united front. Zhou told him that the CCP was prepared to accept his leadership and assured him that as part of the rapprochement, Ching-kuo would return from Russia. As a patriot, the son undoubtedly also wished his father to resist the invaders of China.[81] With the CCP, the USSR, and most of China calling for the Gimo's release, the Young Marshal and his allies capitulated.

Now only one issue held up the Gimo's freedom—what to do with Chang Hsueh-liang. Chiang demanded that the Marshal return with him and face trial. Madame Chiang, however, had given Chang her word that if he freed the Generalissimo, he would not be punished. On Christmas Day the Chiangs flew back to the capital to a tumultuous welcome. Despite entreaties on his behalf by Madame Chiang, a military court sentenced Chang Hsueh-liang to ten years imprisonment. The Gimo then commuted the sentence to indefinite house arrest.[82]

Shortly after the Gimo's return, he called Ch'en Li-fu into his bedroom. "How was Zhou Enlai's attitude in Hsian?" Ch'en asked. "Very good," Chiang replied. Ch'en suggested that the vast government forces now deployed in and around Shansi province should attack Yenan and finish off Mao and the Communists. Chiang bent his head and did not answer. Seeing he was tired, Ch'en hurried off.[83]

5

Reunion and War

WHEN CHING-KUO ARRIVED IN MOSCOW in December 1936, Deputy Commissar for Foreign Affairs Stemenikov informed him that his father wished him to return home. The Soviet government, he said, considered the Chinese government a friendly regime and was prepared to accept the request. Stemenikov and others no doubt also told Ching-kuo that he could now best serve the revolution by returning to China and working for the united front against Japan. After a short stay in the capital, Ching-kuo went back to Sverdlovsk to await instructions. A few weeks later the Comintern ordered termination of his employment at the Uralmash factory and at the newspaper. Allegations of improper thinking that circulated against him at that time most likely came from people he knew well, like Radek and Averbach, then on trial for their lives.[1] Stalin obviously paid no heed to these desperate charges.

As 1937 began, the elder Chiang was still unsure whether he would ever see Ching-kuo again. "I deeply wish that my son could come back," he wrote in his diary. "However, . . . I would rather have no offspring than sacrifice our nation's interests."[2] The Gimo had made no commitment to cease the civil war. His popularity had been restored. His armies totaled more than a million and a half men, his air force, with 100 first-line aircraft, was tiny compared to that of Japan but 100 percent larger than Mao's nonexistent air force. Captain Claire Chennault, retired from the

American Army Air Force because of a hearing problem, was now on board as Chiang's air adviser. In February the KMT Central Committee refused to endorse a united front and reiterated the need for anti-Communist vigilance. Ch'en Li-fu and the dominant conservative wing of the Party wanted to cast aside the draft agreement with Zhou Enlai and pursue the civil war to an early victorious end. The Gimo, however, had made his decision.

In February Moscow again summoned Ching-kuo from Sverdlovsk; this time he was told to bring his family and what belongings they could take on the train. At the Sverdlovsk station many comrades from the factory showed up to bid the family they knew as the Elizarovs good-bye.[3] In the cold winter air, they all had a tea party on the platform and danced the foxtrot. As Ching-kuo told his friends, "the Central Committee [of the CPSU] is sending me to China so that I may win my father over to our side."[4]

Back in Moscow, over vodka and hearty meals, Red Army officer friends told Ching-kuo the Soviet Union would do everything possible to help China defeat Japan. Marshal Tukhachevsky, then still in good standing, was most probably one of those who talked with him. Stemenikov met with Ching-kuo again and expressed the hope that under the Generalissimo's leadership China and the USSR would become closer and closer.[5] Most intriguing, Ching-kuo saw Stalin for a final chat, the subject of which no doubt was the urgency of establishing the united front.[6]

One cold and blustery evening, apparently in early March, an embassy servant told Ambassador Tsiang that a Chinese visitor who would not give his name wanted to see him. The caller, a smiling, red-cheeked young man, was ushered in and immediately identified himself. Before Tsiang could ask a question, Ching-kuo inquired, "Do you think my father would like to have me back?" The ambassador assured him that his father was eager to have him come home.[7]

A few days later Faina accompanied her husband to dine with the ambassador. Tsiang described her as "a charming blonde, but extremely shy." During the dinner Ching-kuo talked enthusiastically about his plans for reforming China. This exposition irritated the ambassador, and he suggested that Ching-kuo try to learn as much as possible about the ills of China and their causes before pronouncing grand prescriptions.

Ching-kuo's mood was exuberant. The past was the past. If his father was willing to forget, so was he. Ching-kuo's pragmatism and optimism, combined with his Chinese patriotism and Marxist beliefs, caused him to embrace the future that had suddenly opened up. Later, the ambassador helped him select gifts—desk knickknacks made of Ural black marble for the Generalissimo, and a coat of Persian lamb for his wife. The embassy also provided a Western suit for Ching-kuo and a long, rather elegant dress and coat for Faina.[8]

The day before Ching-kuo departed Moscow, the Chairman of the Comintern, Georgi Dimitrov, told him that he should convince the Gimo that the CCP was most sincere in its decision to unite with the Kuomintang. Then Dimitrov summed up the Comintern's renewed admiration of Chiang Kai-shek: "We all know that the Generalissimo is the most capable strategist and outstanding statesman and the greatest leader of the Chinese people." At the suggestion of the Comintern, Ching-kuo wrote 13 articles describing each of the years (1925–1937) he had been in the Soviet Union. The collection, entitled "My Life in Russia," was a straightforward, positive account of his experiences and of Soviet achievements.[9]

Just prior to the family's departure for Vladivostok, a young Chinese named K'ang Sheng called on Ching-kuo. K'ang, a CCP delegate to the Comintern, specialized in internal security. In recent months, as part of the ongoing purge, he had fingered many Chinese in the USSR for execution as Trotsky followers. K'ang informed Ching-kuo that he would accompany the Chiangs on their long trans-Siberian trip.[10] Before boarding the train, Ching Kuo sent a telegram to his friends in Sverdlovsk saying that he, Faina, and son would be passing through on their way east. The Anikeyevs and others met them on the station platform and for the last time exchanged embraces with the young Chinese-Russian family they had come to love.[11] Then, stoked with a new supply of wood, the old steam engine chugged out of the grimy city, down the mountain range and onto the steppes. The couple would never again be the Elizarovs.

The train rolled for days across the vast frozen land, giving Ching-kuo a chance to reflect on his life in the Soviet Union. Few of his Russian contemporaries had had such a broad experience of Soviet society. Now, at a mature twenty-seven years of age, his destiny again lay in China and with the Chinese people. On arriving in cold and bleak Vladivostok, Ching-kuo sent his family on to the waiting steamer. Then he and K'ang Sheng went to the local NKVD office and dispatched a telegram, which both signed, to the CCP committee in Moscow: "Now, the Party sends me to China. This is an important task . . . tell the Comintern Executive Committee that I will strictly follow Party discipline . . . we send to you our most warm Communist greetings from the shores of the Soviet Union."[12]

The cable was the last thing Ching-kuo would do for the Communist Party of either China or Russia, whatever their hopes regarding him may have been.[13]

BEFORE CHING-KUO'S ARRIVAL IN CHINA, the CCP Central Committee accepted the draft principles of a new political agreement worked out by Zhou Enlai and Ch'en Li-fu. It placed the Red Army under the orders of the Nanking government, ceased the confiscation and redistribution of land, and ordered democratic elections in Communist areas. Chiang Kai-shek had not overnight become naive about the Communists' intentions. He would later assert that his failure in early 1937 to press on with the annihilation of the CCP's Red Army was a fatal mistake. But the depredations of the Japanese militarists would have made this a politically dangerous course. Besides, a united front again made possible the prospect of large-scale Soviet military assistance, which would not only help the National government resist Japan but could also further widen the Nationalist military advantage over the CCP. Moreover, as a result of the rapprochement, the Generalissimo's only natural son was on his way home—and with a grandson. The ancestors would be relieved.

Shortly after Ching-kuo's departure from Russia, the American ambassador in Moscow, Joseph E. Davies, reported to Washington that relations between China and the Soviet union had "within a few days" improved immeasurably. It was Davies' impression that a definite understanding had been reached, and that the USSR would lend no more support to independent (meaning Communist) political and military elements in China.[14]

As Stalin had anticipated, the prospect of a KMT-Communist united front excited the militarists in Japan into moving up their timetable for all-out military action against China. The Imperial Army saw Manchuria and large parts of northern China as rightfully belonging to Japan, but its real *Lebensraum,* like that of Germany, was in the vast reaches of Russia. The ultra-nationalists did not want to wait for a stronger and united China to emerge in their rear. It was necessary to bring China quickly to heel so that Japan could turn its main forces against the Soviet Union.

Civilian leaders in Japan, however, wanted to dominate China rather than occupy it. Some gave priority to the anti-Communist cause and sensed a quagmire in the enormous land from which Japan had derived its culture. Even in 1937, in their talks with the Japanese, KMT officials like Wang Ching-wei and Ch'en Li-fu were pushing the line that the shared anti-communism of the Nanking and Tokyo governments should make them allies, not enemies.[15] Wang—the former leftist—would, in fact, soon throw in his lot with the Japanese. But the impulse to roll over China could not be restrained. The Zeitgeist of war and expansion and the string of spectacular but easy military victories since 1895 had imbued the Imperial Army and Navy with unbounded ambition. Events in Europe seemed to confirm that the future lay with those races endowed with a martial, all-conquering spirit.

ON APRIL 19, 1937, Ching-kuo stood on the deck of the Soviet freighter as it slowly made its way up the Huangpu River. Faina stood beside him, holding an excited two-year-old Alan. There were many more factories and boatyards than Ching-kuo remembered. Traffic and pollution were heavier. Off the Bund, several warships from the Imperial Japanese Navy's Third Fleet lay quietly at anchor, gray canvas shrouding their gun barrels.

The director of the President's Confidential Department and the mayor of Hangchow greeted Ching-kuo and his family at the wharf.[16] Accompanied by a small contingent of bodyguards, the new arrivals went directly to the train station and in a few hours were in beautiful Hangchow. The Gimo recorded the event in his diary. "The spirit of my deceased mother could be comforted by Ching-kuo's return," he wrote.[17] But Chiang did not appear impatient to see his son. Several days after his arrival, Ching-kuo paid a call on Ch'en Li-fu in Nanking. After exchanging warm hugs, young Chiang complained that his father had put off receiving him and they had still not met. Ch'en replied, "Well, you are still a Communist. You denounced him in that letter. You must write him and tell him that you are no longer a Communist and that you want to join the Kuomintang."[18]

Indeed, Ching-kuo had never written his father asking forgiveness, renouncing Marxism, and expressing a desire to rejoin the KMT. It had simply never occurred to him, even after he was safely back in China. The elder Chiang had sought his return without conditions. No apology had been demanded and thus none had been offered. But now, respect and tradition required that Ching-kuo accept the role of the prodigal son and declare the error of his ways and undying fealty to his father.

Ching-kuo wrote the letter. In addition, he called on Wu Chih-hui, the first authority figure with whom he had talked about going to study in Moscow, over twelve years ago. As if it had only been a brief sojourn, the philosophical Wu asked, "Well, how was it?"[19] Wu was probably among those who talked to the Gimo stressing the ordeals that Ching-kuo had been through. Finally, Chiang agreed to receive his son.[20] The meeting was in the president's residence in Hangchow, the former mansion of the late head of the China Merchants' Steamship Navigation Company. After the door behind him closed, Ching-kuo approached his father, then knelt and touched his forehead three times on the floor.

———

AFTER THE FORMAL GREETINGS, the Gimo discussed with Ching-kuo his immediate future. Ching-kuo said he felt he was prepared for a career in either industry or politics.[21] And, as he told his father, "I have ideas—progressive ideas—and I want an opportunity to prove them." He added that he would like to try them out "under the worst possible conditions."[22] The elder Chiang stressed that before talking about possible assignments, there were certain basics to be dealt with. First of all, by now Ching-kuo could barely write Chinese characters. Secondly, he had neglected his classical and scholarly readings. An intense review course was required. Finally, the Gimo thought it would be a good idea for Ching-kuo to pen a brief memoir about his long experience in the Soviet Union. Then the Generalissimo took his son into the parlor to meet Madame Chiang. Ching-kuo addressed her as "mother," then he asked permission to introduce his own wife and son, who were sitting downstairs.[23]

For Faina it had been a nerve-wracking wait. The twenty-two-year-old Russian girl found herself transported to an utterly foreign and exotic culture, about to be introduced into a famous and powerful family whose language she could not speak. Faina was a poised but shy and relatively simple person with a technical school education. Her natural good looks were adorned with only a little touch of rouge. She had two or three simple dresses to her name, plus the fancy one given her in Moscow. Her new step-mother-in-law was a glamorous, rich, and sophisticated woman, already known and admired around the world.

The introduction went well. No doubt Madame Chiang, who was in good part responsible for the reunion taking place, tried to put Faina at ease. Perhaps it was on this occasion that Faina received from the Gimo her first Chinese name, Fang-niang, which means "fragrant mother." Ching-kuo did not take to this name for his young wife, and at some point revised it to Fang-liang, which was close enough and means "upright and good." As they said good-bye, Madame Chiang handed Ching-kuo an envelope of money. This, she whispered, was to buy clothes for himself and his family.[24]

Eventually, differences and a political rivalry developed between Ching-kuo and Soong Mei-ling. But he would always treat her with dignity, and despite the serious problems and tensions that arose, each retained a grudging respect for the other.[25] Faina also would maintain a proper and friendly although not close relationship with her mother-in-law. She would never try to compete with or emulate her. Instead, Fang-liang became, rather remarkably, a traditional Chinese wife, devoting her life to her family. Her ties to Russia and her relatives and friends were completely severed. She absorbed Chinese customs and became an excellent speaker of the Ningpo dialect.

AFTER THE MEETING IN HANGCHOW, the *New York Times* cited "persons close to the Generalissimo" rejecting as "Russian inventions" reports that the young Chiang had been "a thorough-going Communist" and had denounced his father.[26]

Ching-kuo's family and its small entourage traveled by boat to Ningpo and then by military cars along the new dirt road through the mountains around Hsikou. The lush green of a Chekiang spring welcomed the travelers. Small boys ran after the cars as they drove under the new Wuling gate that the Generalissimo had erected on the edge of town. Ching-kuo pointed out the sparkling Shan Creek and the verdant mountains rising up not a mile away. In a minute, they were before the old but now enlarged family house.[27]

Although for some time they used sign language, Faina and Fu-mei immediately hit it off. Fu-mei was not disturbed in the least that her daughter-in-law was not Chinese. She told her friends that Faina was in fact the most beautiful woman she had ever seen. Sometime after their arrival, the couple were remarried in a Chinese wedding, with Faina bedecked in traditional attire and bespangled head dress. According to custom, the bride cooked several dishes—presumably Russian ones—to demonstrate her skills, but village jokesters slipped in wet firewood, which caused the kitchen to fill with smoke.[28]

During the spring and summer months that followed, Faina enjoyed riding a bicycle about the village and sometimes went horseback riding. She even put on a bathing suit and went swimming in the deep ponds of the Shan Creek. These activities scandalized the townsfolk, but Fu-mei defended her daughter-in-law, explaining that Western women, however exalted, did these things.[29]

Ching-kuo often did not sleep at the Feng Hao Fang house but in the much smaller guesthouse or pavilion that his father had built on the banks of the stream just below the town gate. Ching-kuo's tutor selected by the Gimo, Hsu Tao-lin, moved in with him. The young Chiang began writing his memoir, "12 Years in the Land of Snow and Ice," in Russian, while re-memorizing and practicing characters. The elder Chiang resumed his practice of sending didactic instructions to guide the studies of his twenty-seven-year-old son. As Ching-kuo explained it, his father feared that he "lacked deep understanding of China's moral philosophy and national spirit."[30]

Not surprisingly, the Gimo insisted that Ching-kuo concentrate on reading Ts'eng Kuo-fan; especially Ts'eng's *Letters to His Children,* as well as Mencius, the Confucian *Analects,* and Wang Yang-ming. In a letter of May 12 he told Ching-kuo to read *The Political Theory of Sun Yat-sen* twice before proceeding to read the *Three Principles of the People.*[31]

Years later, Hsu Tao-lin recalled that Ching-kuo was particularly interested in the history of Wang Mang, the controversial Han dynasty figure (45 BC–AD 23) who experimented with certain rudimentary social reforms. Hsu also reported that the young Chiang continued to express admiration for the egalitarian and nonmaterialistic features of Soviet society and its emphasis on youth mobilization and development of mass support for government action. Ching-kuo, who saw no need to hide his views on these matters, showed Hsu a copy of the articles about his years in Russia that he had written before leaving Moscow.[32] He also sent the articles, together with his new recollections, to his father. The elder Chiang told his son he had been "deeply moved": "When you recall the difficulties and sufferings that you have been through, you could appreciate more being home in your mother country." But the Gimo wanted Ching-kuo himself to translate his memoirs: it would be "very embarrassing," the Gimo said, to ask someone to translate his memoirs into Chinese.[33]

Soon after his arrival in Hsikou, Ching-kuo visited the Hole-in-the-Snow Monastery. From there he hiked up to the small Western-style house that had been built for the detained former Young Marshal, Chang Hsueh-liang. He and Chang developed a friendship that would continue over the next fifty years. The detainee and the son of his jailer had much in common. Both their fathers were famous military figures and authoritarian personalities. The Young Marshal, like Ching-kuo, had been disloyal to Chiang Kai-shek out of belief that he was serving a higher cause. Both men were also romantics and idealists, with low-key, unassuming, but energetic personalities.

The two soon began taking walks together in the forest. Sometimes Hsu (the tutor) accompanied Ching-kuo up the mountain and gave his lectures on Confucius or Chinese history to both men. In their leisure time the Young Marshal and Ching-kuo enjoyed drinking and playing the finger game. The Marshal also devoted himself to his long-time girlfriend, known as Miss Chao, and to the study of the Ming dynasty, his collection of Chinese art, and mahjong.[34]

Chiang Kai-shek continued to send epistles directing Ching-kuo's study until July 24, when the last injunction arrived: "You should concentrate on studying Chinese [and] practicing Chinese calligraphy. . . . Don't be distracted by the Japanese invasion. I have the means to counter them."[35]

THE ALL-OUT WAR WITH JAPAN that Chiang Kai-shek had been trying to put off for so long began on July 7, 1937, at the Marco Polo Bridge outside Peking. Japanese and Chinese troops clashed during a confused and inconclusive night encounter. Two weeks later, the Japanese prime minister, Prince Konoye, called for "a fundamental solution of Sino-Japanese relations." The Generalissimo responded: "The only course open to us now is to lead the masses of the nation, under a single national plan, to struggle to the last."[36] The Imperial Army quickly occupied Peking. But the battle for Shanghai was a heroic disaster that dragged on for three months.

Initially, Chiang did not adopt a retreat and scorched-earth strategy. He committed his best German-trained divisions and almost all his artillery to the fight for Shanghai. These were the "means" he had confidently referred to in his July 24 letter to Ching-kuo. Chiang lost 60 percent of these elite forces.[37] After the fall of Shanghai, the Chinese retreated toward Nanking. In Geneva, China and the Soviet Union demanded action by the League of Nations. The League as well as individual democratic countries, including the United States, urged Japan to withdraw and expressed sympathy for China, but aside from contributions of food and medicine by missionary boards, the West offered no assistance. One could sympathize with Chinese who believed that the Soviet Union and China were the only nations in the world that were willing to stand up to a fascist aggressor.

On August 21, 1937, China and the USSR signed a nonaggression pact. Soviet ships, loading up at Odessa, began the long voyage bringing military equipment and supplies to the port of Canton. Hundreds of

Soviet aviators, instructors, and planes flew across the Gobi to Chinese bases in Kansu province. The scale of assistance Stalin provided to Chiang Kai-shek at a time when threats against the Soviet Union were escalating testified to the critical importance to Russia of China's successful resistance. Over the next two years the Soviet Union furnished the Gimo with approximately one thousand aircraft, two thousand pilots, and five hundred military advisers.[38] Total Russian aid between 1937 and 1945 would come to US $250 million, the great bulk of which arrived during the first four years, when no other nation considered the integrity of China a significant priority.[39]

In November one wing of the Japanese invasion force captured Hangchow and then began sweeping down the coast. In some areas the Chinese forces put up a courageous defense, but elsewhere they collapsed outright. On December 13 the seven-week rape of Nanking began, in which Japanese soldiers raped tens of thousands of women and beheaded or bayoneted captured Chinese soldiers and civilians, including infants and young children. While graphic photos of these atrocities moved the Western world, still no material help was forthcoming, and the surviving Nationalist troops withdrew up the Yangtze to Wuhan.

The CCP's Red Army, in keeping with its agreement with the central government, was officially reconstituted as the Eighth Route Army nominally under Nationalist command. Deng Xiaoping became political commissar in the 129th Division, whose commander was Liu Po-ch'eng. Scattered Communist forces that had been left behind south of the Yangtze during the Long March became the New Fourth Route Army. In January of 1938 Ching-kuo attended the founding ceremony of the New Fourth Army and gave a speech, saying that the KMT and CCP should proceed "hand in hand" to defeat the Japanese.[40]

WHILE CHIANG'S ARMIES were suffering enormous losses, Mao's forces avoided confronting the enemy head-on. This was in keeping with the Chairman's 1938 thesis "On Protracted War," which laid down a strategy of guerrilla conflict, political mobilization, and the build-up of base areas. The CCP also proved to be much more effective than the KMT in setting up clandestine administrative systems in occupied areas. The Communists profited from the outburst of patriotic fervor sparked by the devastating Japanese invasion, and the legitimacy they gained from the united front with the KMT. Communist membership swelled from 40,000 in 1937 to an estimated 800,000 in 1940.[41]

In the spring of 1938, at the suggestion of Hsiung Shih-hui, governor of Kiangsi, Chiang Kai-shek appointed Ching-kuo deputy director of the Provincial Peace Preservation Corps headquartered in the provincial capital of Nanch'ang. Ching-kuo received a commission as a major general in the PPC. This was a high rank for a young man of twenty-seven, but given the positions he had attained in the Soviet Union, his record at Tolmatchev, and the demands of the war, it was not as egregious as it might seem.

Nanch'ang, a grimy industrial and mining city on the Kan River, was a teeming and chaotic place, clogged with hundreds of thousands of refugees. Ching-kuo and Faina, who in February had given birth to their second child, Aimee or Amy, moved into a modest but comfortable house, and he immediately set to work. In April 1938, at the Generalissimo's behest, the KMT's Extraordinary National Congress adopted a resolution creating the Three Peoples Principles Youth Corps.[42] Ching-kuo persuaded his father that the new corps should replace the fascist Blue Shirts, an organization that had been established a few years earlier by the military intelligence chief Tai Li. Although officially disbanded, the Blue Shirts remained a potent force. Back from Russia little more than year, Ching-kuo became a member of the new Youth Corps central committee and director of its Kiangsi branch.[43]

Also as Ching-kuo proposed, Youth Corps members were made equal in status to full-time Party members. Moreover, after reaching age twenty-five, Corps members could indefinitely remain in the youth organization and need not join the KMT.[44] This unusual status greatly upset the Ch'en brothers, who controlled the Party structure. Ch'en Li-fu saw it as "strictly a political move" by the Gimo and as another example of the leader's divide-and-rule political strategy.[45] "People always accused us [the Ch'en brothers] of setting up small factions within the Party," he said in his memoirs. "[But] actually we were under orders to do so." The Ch'ens now maneuvered to get control of this new potential power center, which they knew was intended to be Ching-kuo's domain.

The Gimo, of course, added leadership of the Youth Corps to the list of his own official titles, but he appointed one of his most able generals, Ch'en Ch'eng, as director general. The slight, mild-mannered Ch'en (not related to the CC Clique brothers) was not only able and loyal, he was honest—and he was from Chekiang. General Stilwell would later call him "a joy."[46] The Gimo at this point saw Ch'en Ch'eng as a general with a political future, even possibly as a potential successor. Various KMT warlords and Ho Ying-ch'in, the Gimo's most senior general, perceived Ch'en as a comrade but also a political rival. Now Ching-kuo, only a year off the boat, was already marked as another political competitor.

Ch'en Ch'eng and Ching-kuo had much in common. Ch'en, for example, supported Ching-kuo's idea of keeping the Youth Corps separate from the corrupt Party structure. But in mid-1938 Ch'en Ch'eng was not going to have much time to devote to the Youth Corps. He was commander of the Ninth Military Area, dean of the Army's Central Training Corps, and governor of Hubei province.[47] His nominal appointment to the corps simply signaled that he was on course for high political office. The person who essentially ran the Youth Corps (as director of its organization department) was K'ang Tse, a former leading member of the officially disbanded Blue Shirts, with strong ties to Tai Li. K'ang sought to bring the Youth Corps into the sphere of the KMT military intelligence and related secret society wings; thus he was also a threat to the CC brothers. He was "a man of ambition," according to Ch'en Li-fu, but also the fascist type of official that Ching-kuo intensely disliked.[48] Soon after the formation of the Youth Corps, K'ang Tse sent a dozen people, most of them former members of the Blue Shirts, to "help" Ching-kuo organize the Kiangsi branch. According to one of the group, they tried without success to manipulate Ching-kuo and preempt his authority on Youth Corps matters. Ching-kuo hoped to shape the Kiangsi division of the corps into a model of what the national organization and eventually the Kuomintang should become. This set him at odds with Tai Li's former Blue Shirts as well as with the provincial and local KMT apparatus, which the CC Clique controlled.[49]

Ching-kuo's principal responsibility in Kiangsi was his government job. Hsiung had especially created the Deputy Peace Preservation (internal security) position in Nanch'ang for him, and he expected it would be a comfortable beginning for the young man and would not involve much real work. Ching-kuo, however, threw himself into the job. To the consternation of local Party and government chiefs, he started off by making unexpected visits around the province. Soon complaints were flowing into Hsiung's office that Ching-kuo's work style resembled that of the Communists.[50]

To keep Ching-kuo in town, Hsiung opened a political training institute in Nanch'ang and reassigned the young major general as commander of Military Education and deputy director of the Education and Training Department. In addition, he gave him the position of director of training for new draftees in the Peace Preservation command. In the latter position, Ching-kuo soon found himself approving the execution of a deserter, the first time he had taken responsibility for the death of a human being. He also introduced a number of new rules to help the mostly rural draftees, decreeing, for example, that new soldiers would have a three-year grace period before making payments on old loans and requiring landlords to continue leasing land to the families of soldiers.[51]

CHING-KUO ALSO RAISED SUSPICIONS by inviting Soviet military advisers to address anti-fascist rallies in Nanch'ang and by himself accepting invitations to speak at the New Fourth Army liaison headquarters in the city.[52] Accusations about Ching-kuo's over-eager and leftist approach reached the Generalissimo. At the Gimo's instructions, Tai Li called in Major General Wen Ch'ang, who headed the Loyal National Salvation Army, another Tai Li-controlled security organization in nearby Anhui province. Tai told Wen, a Whampoa graduate and a contemporary of Ching-kuo, that the Gimo wanted him to talk to Ching-kuo on a regular basis about China's domestic politics so that his son would not be influenced by the Communists. For the next year and a half, Wen met on a monthly basis with Ching-kuo.[53]

Ching-kuo took the sessions with Wen in good spirit, using the meetings to learn about factionalism and personalities in the KMT. But Marxist training still influenced his thinking. He often referred to the Soong family stalwarts, H. H. Kung and T. V. Soong, as "big bourgeoisie." Later, he accepted Wen's suggestion that he not employ this expression when talking about prominent people, particularly his relatives. But, according to Wen, Ching-kuo from the start never had any use for the rich kin he had acquired by his father's marriage. Wen also had to warn Ching-kuo about speaking too highly of the Soviet Union. Wen kept notes of his meetings and sent them to Tai, who forwarded them on to the Gimo.[54] Wen remained on the mainland in 1949, a decision that suggests that he may also have been sending his reports to Yenan.

When Ching-kuo returned to China, he was not surprised to find an extensive internal network of KMT spies. The two largest surveillance organizations were Tai Li's Military Bureau of Investigation and Statistics and the Ch'en brothers' Central Investigation and Statistical Bureau. In addition, the separate branches of the military, the central police, provincial governments, the Central Bank, and other bureaucratic structures all employed agents to spy on each other as well as on the Japanese and the Communists. Political commissars in the Nationalist army as in the Communist armed forces carried out surveillance of their own personnel along with targeted civilian populations.[55]

What disturbed Ching-kuo as he came to understand the KMT's intelligence and covert action system was not its mission but its connections with criminal elements—the traditional triads or gangs of China. In this they were not alone: Sun Yat-sen, Mao Zedong, and European officials in the foreign concessions all employed secret societies, criminal triads, and bandits to serve their respective ends.[56] Overall, Ching-kuo had no direct role in the national leadership of the KMT's major security agencies, but in areas of his jurisdiction he eliminated the ties to organized crime. He continued, however, to believe in the vital necessity of a secret police.

IN APRIL 1938 forces in Shantung under General Li Tsung-jen, the on-again-off-again ally of Chiang from Kwangsi province, inflicted the first defeat on the Japanese. This did little to halt their advance, however, and the Gimo ordered the destruction of the Yellow River dikes. The resulting floods delayed the invading army for several months, but also washed away 4,000 villages and shifted the mouth of the Yellow River from north of the Shantung Peninsula to the south. In late summer Japanese troops moved up the Yangtze valley and attacked Wuhan. Soviet airplanes pounded Japanese positions around the city, and the outgunned Nationalist army put up another courageous defense. In July Japan demanded that Soviet troops withdraw from the border region of Korea, the Soviet Union, and China, claiming the territory belonged to Manchukuo. The Imperial Army pushed into the contested area, but in a history-shifting victory, the Far Eastern Red Army beat back the invaders, inflicting heavy casualties.

On October 25 the Japanese finally occupied the destroyed city of Wuhan, and the Gimo established a new base at Chungking, far above the Yangtze gorges. Also in October, Japanese forces captured Canton and cut off the National government from the sea. Chiang Kai-shek continued to exercise command over his far-flung armies, but factionalism prevented any significant consolidation of Nationalist China's more than 300 under-strength divisions.[57] In the course of a year Japan had butchered two million Chinese, occupied 1.5 million square kilometers of Chinese territory from the far north to the Vietnamese border, destroyed whole cities, and devastated Chinese industry and infrastructure.

IN MID-MARCH 1939, the Japanese 101st Division moved within a few miles of Nanch'ang. Refugees and citizens associated with the government began evacuating the city and heading south. Hsiung transferred the draftee training center for the Peace Preservation Corps to Kanchow, a town in southern Kiangsi. A few days before Nanch'ang's defenses collapsed on March 27, Ching-kuo and his family rode an army truck down the dirt road headed south, past long lines of fleeing families. Faina held her baby and the three-year old, Alan.

The ochre-colored Kan River begins with the confluence of the Kung and the Chang rivers among the denuded hills of southern Kiangsi. Here at this riverine junction, on a rare expanse of level ground, sits the town that takes its name Kanchow (Kan City) from the two tributaries, as does the combined river. When Ching-kuo and his family arrived, Kanchow municipality had a population of about 100,000. The major avenue was South World Street (Nan shih chieh), an ancient winding lane lined with houses of gray, earth brick turned black by centuries of cooking fires. Rickshaw pullers padded along the cobbled road and a nine-layered pagoda hung over the street.

The Chiang family lived in a small Western-style house on a low hill overlooking the town. Ching-kuo was to be commissioner and Peace Preservation commander of the entire Fourth Administrative Region, an area known as Kannan that consisted of all of southern Kiangsi—11 counties (about the size of Massachusetts) with a population of some two million.[58] It was a poor area long under the control of neighboring Kwangsi warlords and local bandit gangs.[59]

CHING-KUO ASKED SEVERAL former Moscow classmates to join him in the Kannan regional office. One of these was Huang Chung-mei, who was thought to have been an OGPU informer among the students at Sun Yat-sen University. Huang became Ching-kuo's chief secretary and also was in charge of setting up an intelligence network. Two other Moscow students, Chou Pai-chieh and Yu Chi-yu, became section chiefs, while a third, Hsu Chi-yuan, headed the Department for the Suppression of Opium.[60] Ch'u Wu, an ex-Trotskyite who said he had been in a Siberian labor camp, also received a position in Kanchow.[61] Meanwhile, the Gimo asked a military officer named Hu Kui, who had been one of his favorite students at Whampoa, to go to Kanchow and work for Ching-kuo. Hu, whom Ching-kuo appointed secretary of the Kiangsi Youth Corps, became one of young Chiang's closest subordinates.[62]

Immediately after receiving his new appointment, Ching-kuo systematically visited every part of his domain. He walked as much as fifty miles a day and eventually covered 900 miles, talking to peasants, merchants, officials, artisans, and refugees.[63] Not everyone welcomed his arrival. "The arrogant landed gentry regarded him suspiciously with ill-concealed contempt. The merchants of vice ignored him and continued to operate gambling houses and opium dens, confident of the protection of corrupt officials. Highwaymen fattened on the countryside; bloody clan

feuds took their regular toll of life while the common people, long resigned to abuse, were indifferent."[64]

Ching-kuo decided that law and order was his first priority, and he
called for a year of "mopping up operations."[65] At his request, Governor
Hsiung increased the size of the 3,000-man Peace Preservation unit in
Kannan. In addition, Ching-kuo established a 600-man self-defense
team.[66] But he used conciliation as well as military force to bring the bandit problem under control. One day, with only a few unarmed colleagues
and several bottles of wine, he visited a bandit leader named Chou
Sheng-lien in the mountain area of Ch'ung Yi. Chou was known as a Chinese Robin Hood because he used funds collected from a road tax to
help the local people. The bandit chief told Ching-kuo that the corruption of local officials had driven him to banditry. After numerous toasts,
Ching-kuo asked Chou, in return for a pardon for any past misdeeds, to
cease his illegal activities and work with him for the common good.
Chou, impressed, agreed to behave so long as Ching-kuo was administrator. Thirty-four bandit leaders accepted similar offers.[67] By the end of the
year, 541 bandits had reportedly given themselves up, and Ching-kuo's
various police units had arrested 2,246 others and executed several.[68]

Eradicating vice, Ching-kuo decided, was the key to reducing crime
and banditry. In the summer he announced a "zero-tolerance" ban on
smoking opium and gambling. No one was exempt. Wives of two local
officials were caught playing mahjong for money and were required, like
other violators, to kneel for two days before a town monument to soldiers
who had died fighting the Japanese.[69]

Ching-kuo announced that after one year anyone convicted of opium
smoking would receive the death sentence. After the warning period
ended, police arrested the son of an important businessman for using the
drug. Ching-kuo was considering clemency when he received a cable
from Hsiung Shih-hui ordering him to transfer the prisoner to the provi-
sional provincial capital. Learning that the father of the convicted man
had used his influence for this purpose, Ching-kuo ordered the execution carried out and then told Hsiung that his cable had arrived too late.[70]

Banning prostitution was more difficult. There were 150 brothels in
the eleven counties, and 687 registered prostitutes. A prostitution tax had
traditionally provided an important part of county revenues. Nonetheless,

in 1941 Ching-kuo outlawed prostitution, provided factory jobs for the women involved, and eliminated the government offices that taxed the trade. According to a local researcher, the profession had virtually ceased to exist in Kannan by the end of the year.[71]

Ching-kuo also decreed a 25 percent reduction in land rent for all forms of tenancy and introduced a Land to the Tiller program, setting up demonstration farms on tenant land and giving uncultivated land to poor peasants.[72] They paid for this land, on average less than one hectare, in installments. Productivity reputedly rose by 20 percent within two years.[73] While instituting these reforms, the young Chiang "hardly had any relations with the local establishment—the landed gentry, the armed forces, and local Party bigwigs."[74] Instead, he tried to end the many abuses inflicted by landlords and "local tyrants" on the peasants. In Anyuan county a powerful landlord known as Tiger T'ang controlled a whole village and had an arsenal of over 100 guns. After hearing many complaints about the landlord's behavior, Ching-kuo seized T'ang, confiscated his guns, and had him carried away hanging from a pole like a captured tiger.[75]

Local tyrants such as T'ang ended up in Ching-kuo's re-education center called the New Man School. Most of the "students" belonged to one of the categories of "four ghosts": violators of the bans on opium smoking, gambling, prostitution, and drunkenness. According to the official who ran the school, Ching-kuo insisted that the staff treat the inmates humanely, with education first and punishment second. The purpose of the New Man School, Ching-kuo emphasized, was to help those who had misbehaved begin new lives.[76]

Ching-kuo held open court once a week, when any citizen with a problem could personally present his or her case. In 1942 he received 1,023 citizens.[77] Harrison Forman, an American journalist who visited Kanchow that year, described one such session:

> A shopkeeper appealed confiscation of twelve bolts of unregistered cloth he'd been hoarding. He pleaded the loss would mean hardship for his five children. Chiang ordered an investigation of his financial status and promised if his statement was true he would order him paid the cost price and have the merchandise given to the poor. A blind woman with three beggar children asked for food. He directed her to a relief kitchen.
> "Is there really food there?" she asked.

"Yes."

"Every day?"

"Yes, every day."

Her face beamed happily as Chiang detailed a smartly saluting Boy Scout to escort her and her children to the kitchen. A pregnant woman with a baby in her arms asked for money to pay debts since her husband was in jail. Chiang refused, saying that personal debts were not the government's responsibility, but he volunteered to give her free hospital service until the new baby was born.[78]

Forman also attended a group wedding of 34 couples with Ching-kuo officiating. Among his other social reforms Ching-kuo had forbidden the traditionally expensive weddings that often took the entire savings of the bridegroom's family. Now only group ceremonies were allowed in Kannan. During the ceremony "young Chiang clowned with each couple as they came forward to receive their license, while several thousand spectators crowding a new auditorium cheered and laughed."[79]

Ching-kuo had the ability to stir large crowds to other emotions. One night, during a big campfire for Kannan Boy Scouts, he mounted a rickety, improvised platform in the center of Kanchow's large parade ground. He led the crowd of thousands in shouting, "long live China! Long live the Generalissimo! Down with the Japanese dwarfs!"

> Then Young Chiang asked, "what shall we do with the traitor Wang Ching-wei?" [Wang had defected to the Japanese in 1939.]
>
> "Burn him! Burn him!" the crowd shouted.
>
> "Then let's do it now."
>
> An effigy was rolled onto the field and as the torch was applied, Chiang beat a gong and the crowd yelled, "Kill, kill, kill." Spontaneously, a huge snake dance began with thousands of youngsters stripped to the waist, leaping and whooping in the flickering light from three bonfires. Jumping from the platform, young Chiang brought up the tail of the wild dance. He shouted hoarsely and banged the tocsin, but the crowd drowned out these sounds in a roar of approval.[80]

LOOKING AT EVENTS ON A WORLD SCALE, what was happening in Europe would dictate the direction of the war in China. The year 1939 began with Hitler telling the Reichstag that the final solution of the Jewish problem was a war which would result in the "destruction of the Jewish race in Europe." In March the German leader carved off more slices of Czechoslovakia, and Mussolini invaded Albania. Britain and France gave guarantees to Poland that they would fight to retain its independence. Weighing his bargaining position vis-à-vis both Germany and the West, Stalin chose a deal with Hitler that would allow the Soviet Union to sit back and watch the capitalist powers—fascist and bourgeois-democratic—destroy each other. Such a war would permit Russia to husband its military resources and thus also discourage Japanese designs on Siberia. On August 23, 1939, Stalin formally reversed course in Europe, tore up the popular front idea—except in colonial or semi-colonial countries like China—and signed a nonaggression treaty with Nazi Germany. One week later German and Soviet forces invaded Poland, Britain and France declared war on the Third Reich, and the European phase of the earth's great civil war began.

Hitler's astounding accord with the Soviet Union took the Japanese utterly by surprise and shaped the final course of the shifting direction of Japanese imperial ambitions. Tokyo dropped the idea of grand conquest at the expense of Russia. Now it was the East Asian colonies of beleaguered Britain and France that looked ripe for the picking. The Japanese navy, which had long trained for all-out war against the Anglo-Saxons, would have its way. As Japan's war planning increasingly focused on Southeast Asia and the Pacific, the conflict in China fell into a set pattern. The Japanese army attacked Chinese forces that threatened them but rarely followed up with occupation of new territory. Instead, they followed a strategy of advance-fight-withdraw against Communist guerrillas and Nationalist regulars alike. Efforts by the Japanese to capture most of Kiangsi province ground to a halt. For the moment, Kanchow was safe.[81]

The Hitler-Stalin accord also came as a stunning surprise to Chingkuo. Since his return, young Chiang had seen no reason to question his belief that the Soviet Union was a force for peace in the world. The USSR had sent critical military assistance to China, thousands of Soviet personnel were participating directly in the war against Japan, and once again there was high praise of the Generalissimo in Soviet media. But suddenly the Soviet Union had made common cause with the Nazis and invaded Poland and Finland, giving Japan reason and leeway to concentrate on Asia.

Still, Ching-kuo's faith in the socialist motherland was not seriously shaken. After signing the pact with Berlin, Stalin assured the Generalissimo that Soviet relations with China, including the provision of military aid, would not change. One month after the signing of the Molotov-Ribbentrop Pact, Ching-kuo spoke to a youth seminar. He emphasized that the Soviet Union still was the only nation that was helping China fight the Japanese invaders; moreover, as a socialist country, the USSR would not commit acts of aggression. Helping the Soviet Union defend itself, he said, would be beneficial to others resisting aggression, most particularly China.

6

The Kannan Model

LATE IN 1939 the Japanese military intelligence, the Kempeitai, decided to target the Generalissimo's hometown, specifically his family home. One bright morning two dive bombers appeared in the sky over the little hamlet, and the air raid siren on Wuling Street sounded its shrill alarm. Mao Fu-mei and Ah Wang, who were on the second floor in Feng Hao Fang, hastened down the back stairs—built narrow for the convenience of ladies with bound feet—and ran toward the rear of the house. Ah Wang heard the scream of a bomb. Just as they opened the back gate, the missile smashed into the courtyard. The servant woman recovered, but Fu-mei died instantly.[1]

Within hours Ching-kuo heard the news by short-wave radio and immediately left for Hsikou. The trip involved a treacherous journey of 400 miles by dirt road across the mountains of Kiangsi and Chekiang. He drove for twenty hours, fording rivers where bridges were bombed out, and arrived the day after Fu-mei's death. After viewing his mother's torn body, he arranged a temporary burial and ordered a small three-foot-high memorial erected at the spot where she died. The stone slab, still in Hsikou, proclaims, "It takes blood to wash out blood."[2]

The Japanese bombed the little hamlet 13 times over the next four months. Finally, in April 1943, Imperial troops occupied the town and used Feng Hao Fang as their headquarters. Hoping perhaps to generate good will in the heart of the Generalissimo, the Japanese commander and representatives of Wang Ching-wei's puppet government swept the graves of the dead Chiangs, including those of Ching-kuo's mother and grandmother, then sent photos of these gestures to Chiang Kai-shek and Ching-kuo. They did not have the desired effect.[3]

For many weeks after he returned to Kanchow, Ching-kuo did not shave and did not smile.[4] To assuage his grief, he threw himself into his work. He had decided that to administer his territory and carry out his reforms, he needed trustworthy subordinates, specifically a corps of incorruptible inspectors to assure that local officials were implementing his programs. The best way to obtain such people was to open his own cadre school. His father agreed, and the Central Military Academy selected 72 of the 1,000 graduates of the political training classes of that year to attend the new Young Cadre School that Ching-kuo opened at Ch'ichuling, in the mountains several miles outside of Kanchow.[5] Another 72 students entered through a competitive examination. Ching-kuo regularly came to speak at the school, where some classes met in caves, and on occasion slept in the barracks with the students, rising at dawn and leading them in their oaths of allegiance to the Republic and the Generalissimo.

Ching-kuo enthusiastically promoted devotion to his father, but he drew the line well short of a personality cult.[6] One day, as he was addressing a group of Peace Preservation Corps soldiers, he noticed that everyone stood up whenever he mentioned "Generalissimo Chiang" or "Director General Chiang." He changed further references to his father to "the old man," which in Chinese as in the American navy is a slang term of respect for the skipper. Nevertheless, Ching-kuo's audience, when they heard these words, again jumped from their chairs and stood at attention. Ching-kuo once more interrupted his talk and said impatiently, "The reason I called the Generalissimo 'the old man' is to avoid the ritual of standing. This is fascist. Let's forget it!"[7]

One of the students at the school was a young man named Wang Sheng, born to a rich landowning family in Longnan county in Kannan. Decisive and full of energy, Wang finished the Kannan cadre course at the head of his class and received an appointment as chief inspector for three counties.[8] He performed so well in his assigned territory that in 1940 Ching-kuo called him back to the regional office in Kanchow and put him in control of seven townships.

Another student in the first class was a young woman named Chang Ya-juo, whose father was from a scholar family in Nanch'ang. At the age of seventeen she had wed a cousin in an arranged marriage. She was in her twenties and had two young children when her husband committed suicide. Ya-juo was a patriotic and determined woman who wanted to join the struggle against Japan. She heard about the Young Cadre School and, leaving her children with her late husband's parents, set off for Kanchow.[9]

Judging by her photos and the recollections of those who knew her, Ya-juo was an attractive, charming, and high-spirited woman. At the school, her best friends were Wang Sheng and a female student named Kui Hui.[10] On completing the cadre course, Ya-juo went to work in the Anti-Japanese Mobilization News Agency in the regional office, where she impressed Ching-kuo with her enthusiasm. Ya-juo also sang Peking opera at a professional level and sometimes took part in performances in Kanchow. One Saturday evening, after watching her sing, Ching-kuo went backstage and warmly greeted her. Ya-juo told Kui Hui that she did not sleep that night.[11]

Ching-kuo soon asked Ya-juo to be his private secretary. She also occasionally went to the Chiang house and tutored his two children. She and Faina obviously got to know each other. At some point, Ya-juo and Ching-kuo became intimately involved. Ya-juo, like Ching-kuo, was an incorrigible romantic. When they were alone, she would call him "wind" (hui feng) and he would call her "cloud" (hui yun).[12] Ching-kuo gave her only one small gift, one to reflect her beauty, he said—a European compact that he had found in a second-hand market in Chungking. Apparently Faina knew nothing about the relationship.[13]

⸺

BECAUSE OF HIS BACKGROUND, Ching-kuo paid special attention to the importance of psychological warfare, including propaganda. To counter the popular slogan "going to Yenan," referring to the trek of student volunteers to Mao's headquarters, Ching-kuo promoted the slogan "coming to Kannan." He set up his own newspaper, the *Cheng Ch'i* (Right Spirit), a news agency, the New Kannan Publishing Company, the New Kannan Bookstore, and the *Kiangsi Youth Monthly*.[14] Most of these media enterprises competed with established KMT-controlled counterparts in the province and in Kanchow itself. These moves outraged local KMT officials, who felt Ching-kuo was promoting himself at their expense. In a letter to his son, the Gimo warned: "You should focus on practical work at the local level. You don't need to propagate your activities to the outside world, because the more our family hides itself, the less we will invite jealousy from others."[15]

Indeed, agents of the Central Investigation and Statistical Bureau, which the Ch'en brothers controlled, and officers in Tai Li's Military Bureau of Investigation and Statistics began to send reports to Chungking charging that Communists worked in Ching-kuo's propaganda enterprises. Former Blue Shirts also sent in allegations of Communist infiltration in Ching-kuo's office itself. And the established gentry repeated the charge first heard in Nanch'ang that young Chiang's methods and slogans were similar to those of the Communists. In June 1940 Tai Li's men captured an undercover CCP member named Chu P'ing, who was in charge of youth affairs for the Communists in Kiangsi and Guangdong. Chu P'ing was soon persuaded to cooperate, and he identified several members of the CCP working in Kannan.[16]

The Gimo summoned Ching-kuo to Chungking and showed him the reports.[17] Ching-kuo vouched for the top five on the list of alleged CCP members, including his secretary and intelligence chief, Huang Chung-mei. After Ching-kuo returned to Kanchow, police arrested the other suspected Communists, and in December the Peace Preservation Corps took in more than 20 alleged CCP supporters during a raid on a clandestine Party meeting in Sannan county.[18]

For help in dealing with these and other security problems, Ching-kuo appointed Wang Sheng Chief of Police for the entire region. Wang was thereafter responsible for all intelligence as well as police work in Kannan.[19] Ching-kuo also appointed Wang to the concurrent position of Chief of Military Affairs, including conscription. The region had fallen behind in meeting its quota for army conscripts, and Ching-kuo "owed" the central government 3,000 able-bodied men. In his previous position Wang Sheng had dealt effectively with conscription, on one occasion arresting 200 young men who could not produce identification cards and sending them off to the army. Kannan thereafter met its quota.[20]

———

AFTER MOPPING UP THE BANDITS and other "bad elements," Ching-kuo set out a scheme to transform Kannan into a model economic area. In January 1940 he announced a "three-year plan" and, in a typical Chinese penchant for numbered slogans, a list of objectives called "the five haves": sufficient food, clothing, shelter, books, and work.

The commissioner's office established pilot economic development companies. Before Ching-kuo's arrival, Kannan's economy depended on mining and hardscrabble agriculture that met only half the area's food consumption needs. A few small factories, mills, kilns, and other rural enterprises began to appear. New rural agricultural officers encouraged farmers to raise silkworms and launched a program to assure that every hundred households, or "paos," had a fish pond that could also be used for watering vegetable gardens.[21]

Education was a central aspect of the plan, including compulsory schooling for young children. In the villages, clan ancestral temples became one-room schoolhouses, bringing "new Gods to old temples." Ching-kuo required adults who had no education to take literacy courses, grouping families into units of ten and compelling them to spend two hours daily on reading and writing as well as arithmetic and current events. His office printed simple texts on rough paper; a village might have to share one copy.

On his tours of the region, wearing common cotton clothes, "Hsiao Chiang" (Young Chiang) would stop at villages and ask to see the shared lesson book and to hear it read. He would also check the report cards that traveling teachers had written. One American reporter accompanying him on a walk through the countryside saw villagers kneeling before him, with Ching-kuo immediately pulling them up while commanding, "Don't kneel, don't kneel!"[22]

———

IN THE SUMMER OF 1939 Ching-kuo's brother, Wei-kuo, graduated from the Military Academy in Munich. The year before, wearing a German uniform with the rank of sergeant-officer candidate, Wei-kuo had been on a Mountain Division truck speeding into Austria.[23] There was no fighting in the course of the *Anschluss;* the invading Germans simply took over the Austrian military, and Wei-kuo and other officer candidates ended up commanding Austrian army units. In October German forces also occupied Sudetenland in Czechoslovakia. Wei-kuo did not take part in this exercise, although he admitted later he would have liked to.[24]

After his graduation, Wei-kuo received a commission in the Chinese army as a second lieutenant. The War Ministry in Chungking ordered him to join a German infantry division on the Oder River as an observer. But, to his regret, Wei-kuo missed the opportunity to ride along on the invasion of Poland. On his way to the border he traveled through Berlin and reported to the Chinese embassy. There he received new orders. He was to travel to the United States for training. He caught a ship in Amsterdam and arrived in America just as the conflict in Europe was exploding. After serving as escort officer for a visiting Chinese air force mission, he began training at the Army Air Corps School at Maxwell Field, Alabama. On learning that the young Chiang had experience in the German army, however, the U.S. military invited him to be a consultant at the new Armored Force Center at Fort Knox. For four months he participated in training and division-level war games, in the process developing an impressive fluency in English.[25]

In November 1940 Wei-kuo flew from Hawaii in a Pan American Clipper plane and after six stopovers landed on the calm waters of Hong Kong harbor. The Union Jack was still flying at the governor's residence above Central, and it was possible to travel from Nationalist-controlled areas to the colony. Meeting him at the wharf was an old boyhood friend and another young man. After greeting Wei-kuo, the friend asked, "do you know this guy?" "He looks very familiar," Wei-kuo replied. "This is your brother," said the friend. The stepbrothers, who had not seen each other for fifteen years, embraced, retired to the Repulse Bay Hotel, and stayed up all night talking and drinking beer.[26]

The next day Ching-kuo took his brother to introduce him to their stepmother. Although Soong Mei-ling had been married to Chiang Kai-shek for nine years before Wei-kuo left for Germany, he had never met her and she had not known of his existence. In 1927, prior to his marriage, Chiang had sent "Mama Yao" and Wei-kuo to live in her hometown, Suchow. From 1928 to 1936 Wei-kuo went to school and then university in that city. During this time he occasionally visited Nanking to stay a few days with his father, who saw to it that the boy on these occasions did not encounter Madame Chiang. At their meeting in Hong Kong, however, she greeted him warmly and regretted that her husband had kept them apart.[27] Mei-ling had gone to Hong Kong for medical treatment, and Ching-kuo had accompanied her at the Gimo's request. This was to be Ching-kuo's only look at the pearl of the British empire. The brothers Chiang stayed in Hong Kong for three days and then returned separately to the mainland.[28]

———

FRANCE SURRENDERED ON JUNE 21, 1940, but by October Britain had defeated the Luftwaffe in the Battle of Britain. Stalin thus had reason to hope that the violent, internecine struggle of the European capitalists would drag on for some time. Hitler, however, was secretly looking again toward the east. Japan proclaimed its New Order for Greater East Asia and a Greater East Asia Co-prosperity Sphere. In September Japan, Germany, and Italy concluded their Tripartite Treaty of Alliance, aimed not at Communist Russia but at capitalist-democratic America. Stalin authorized the beginning of negotiations with Tokyo on a Soviet-Japanese nonaggression or neutrality accord. Soviet aid to Nationalist China began to diminish.

As the European war gathered momentum, in China tensions between the Nationalists and the Communists escalated sharply. Chiang ordered all of the CCP's New Fourth Army to move north of the Yangtze by the end of 1940. In January 1941 Nationalist forces attacked one element of the Communist army that was moving south. The New Fourth Army Incident, as the battle was known, reaffirmed the determination of both parties, even at this desperate stage of the struggle against Japan, to give priority to the postwar showdown between them. The "united front" was henceforth an armed truce at best.[29]

The Incident also further diminished Soviet interest in helping the Nationalist government. At this point, however, President Roosevelt sent

China 100 P-40 fighters and American air force "volunteers" to fly them. The Flying Tigers, commanded by Claire Chennault, started to inflict serious damage on the Japanese. America's increasing material and financial support for the two nations resisting fascist juggernauts—Great Britain and China—was now changing the dynamics of the global struggle. Stalin was pleased to be on the outside of the polarization of world politics. On April 13, 1941, with Stalin beaming by their side, Molotov and Foreign Minister Matsuoka signed a five-year Soviet-Japanese Neutrality Pact. In a joint statement attached to the Pact, the Soviet Union pledged to respect the territorial integrity and inviolability of Manchukuo, and Japan promised to treat similarly the Mongolian People's Republic. Japan was now free to transfer elite army units from Manchuria to join the expected war against the Western democracies in southeast Asia and the Pacific.[30]

In the face of Soviet courtship of Japan, Ching-kuo became more outspokenly anti-Communist. He wrote two anti-Communist articles in the *Youth Daily:* "Dr. Sun Yat-sen's Criticism of Marxism," and "The CCP Is the Violator of the Chinese Race."[31] He made no more speeches defending the Soviet Union.

In Moscow the warm spring of 1941 seemed to presage a peaceful year for the Russian people. But on June 22 the awesome German *Blitzkrieg* into Russia began. Despite Hitler's appeal to Tokyo to join in the dismemberment of the Soviet Union, Japan—again taken completely by surprise—stuck to its new course of expansion to the south. On July 21 Imperial troops occupied southern Indochina, and Washington imposed a total trade embargo on Japan. Determined on their southern conquests and feeling that war with the United States was inevitable, the militarists in Tokyo decided to strike Pearl Harbor, decimate the American fleet, and seize all of southeast Asia.

Like Winston Churchill and Joseph Stalin, Chiang Kai-shek and Mao Zedong were immensely pleased by the dramatic entry of America into the war. Roosevelt appointed General Joseph W. Stilwell as his military liaison with Chiang Kai-shek, commander of American forces in the China-Burma-India theater, and administrator of American Lend Lease to China. Stilwell also was to serve as Joint Chief of Staff to the Generalissimo—together with Ho Ying-ch'in—making him Chiang's supposed subordinate as well as an American theater commander. The Flying Tigers eventually became part of the U.S. Fourteenth Air Force, and Chennault returned to active duty as a general. Stalin now saw no need to help Nationalist China or coddle Chiang Kai-shek. In 1942 the Soviet press once again began to heap criticism on the Generalissimo and the Chinese government. In remote Kannan, Ching-kuo told his friends that with the Americans in the war, the internal conflict in China, and thus their own work, would become increasingly important.[32]

IN JANUARY 1942 Chiang Kai-shek sent his remaining German-trained units, the Fifth and Sixth Armies, into Burma to help the British defend their colony, most especially the Burma road.[33] A few weeks after the fall of Rangoon in late February, the Generalissimo flew into Burma to inspect his troops at Lashio. Traveling with him, but unannounced, was Chiang Ching-kuo. "Vinegar Joe" arrived in Lashio from Calcutta on the same day on his way to assume his command in Chungking. The Gimo and Stilwell met briefly. The American reported he received a "cordial welcome," which was about the last pleasant remark he ever made about Chiang Kai-shek.[34]

Ching-kuo, who went unnoticed by Stilwell, stayed behind for a week and visited almost every company in the Chinese Sixth Army. He rose every morning before the soldiers and waited for them when they turned out for their morning workout and drill. He visited their kitchens and latrines and encouraged officers to volunteer to write letters home for the soldiers, virtually all of whom were illiterate. In his talks with the officers, Ching-kuo stressed that troop morale was the key to victory. It was essential that the common soldier know the reason he was fighting, and that there be unity between officers and men. After returning to Kanchow, Ching-kuo wrote to each of the officers he met.[35]

The Generalissimo gave Stilwell overall command of the Chinese forces in Burma. The Chinese generals, however, frequently did not implement Stilwell's orders, or the Gimo himself overrode them, sometimes without telling the American. While Stilwell had had some experience of China and knew the language, he was not the ideal personality to deal with Chiang or almost any Chinese leader in the situation that existed. The American officer's taciturn, hard-boiled, opinionated, and blunt approach made him in many circumstances a good combat leader but an ineffective diplomat. His frustration with Chiang's unwillingness to reorganize his armies, go on the offensive, or fire corrupt and inept generals was understandable. But from the Gimo's perspective, each of these actions threatened a major, unsettling change in the factional balance of power in Nationalist China. Stilwell heard good things about Ching-kuo, but the two never met. This was unfortunate, as Ching-kuo agreed with most of Stilwell's proposed reforms.[36]

AFTER CHING-KUO HAD BEEN in Kannan for three years, his father wrote him a glowing appreciation. "The people adore you and Kannan has been well developed. I am very delighted."[37] The Gimo now began thinking that down the road Ching-kuo, in light of his Russian language skills and administrative talent, could become governor of Sinkiang.[38] By 1942, although supplies from Russia were no longer coming through Sinkiang, political developments in this key province had turned favorable for the KMT. A vast, mostly Moslem land of majestic mountains, arid plains, and deserts, Sinkiang was also known as the Northwest. In 1934, Sheng Shih-ts'ai, a Nationalist general who had served Chiang Kai-shek during the Northern Expedition, had consolidated his control of the region with the assistance of Soviet troops. Sheng's regional government became a virtual Soviet puppet, and Russian advisers had effectively run the territory.[39] But in early 1942, when the Soviet Union appeared to be on the verge of defeat by the German army, Sheng began to reassess his ties to the USSR. Thus as the Moscow-Chungking friendship cooled, relations between Sheng and Chiang began to improve.

In late April, shortly after the two Chiangs returned from Burma, the Gimo asked his son to make a trip to the Northwest and suggested he take Wei-kuo along. The objective was to allow Ching-kuo an opportunity to see the situation in Sinkiang at first hand and to make policy recommendations.

It was a mission fraught with dangers, including extensive travel near the front-lines. At their last meeting before leaving, Chiang gave his son a poison capsule to take if the Japanese were about to capture him.[40]

Ching-kuo flew from Chungking to Ch'engtu, where he caught a train to Paochi. From there he motored to Hsian and met up with Wei-kuo, who was an officer in an armored unit stationed outside the city.[41]

Together the two brothers rode the train to Tungkuan, not far from the Japanese lines. They traveled by truck to Luoyang in a two-lane, 14-foot-deep ditch that an army of laborers had built by hand to protect military traffic from Japanese fire.[42] Tens of thousands of Chinese peasants working on massive defense projects in and around Luoyang moved Ching-kuo to proletarian poetry. "The voices of the workers," he wrote, "have converged into a labor of marching music."[43]

The two Chiangs picked up a convoy of twenty trucks loaded with cloth and other gifts for the minority leaders they intended to meet. Declining a military escort, Ching-kuo and Wei-kuo traveled to the end of the Great Wall at Chiayukuan, where a crumbling fort looked out at the rock-strewn desert. The stark and beautiful countryside made a strong impression on Ching-kuo: "Northwest, your name is great . . . you . . . the old hometown of the Chinese race, the tomb of our ancestors, the place of their treasures, the long buried roots of our culture . . . you and your . . . unyielding people are the forces we need for waging war against the Japanese and building our nation. . . . Ambitious youth, . . . go to the Northwest, return to your old hometown."[44]

As long as there is economic development, he reported to the Gimo, "the political issues in Sinkiang can definitely be solved."[45] But he also believed it was necessary to intensify efforts to counter both the Soviets and the CCP in the region.[46] Shortly after Ching-kuo's visit, Sheng Shih-ts'ai speeded up his reconciliation with Chiang Kai-shek. He rejoined the KMT in early 1943, and the last of the Russian troops withdrew from the area. That same year, claiming he had unearthed a Soviet-CCP plot, Sheng executed all the CCP members he could lay his hands on, including Mao Zedong's brother, Mao Ts'e-min, the Communist representative in Urumchi.[47]

TWO MONTHS BEFORE THE NEWS of Pearl Harbor had reached Kan-chow, Ching-kuo's secretary, Ya-juo, told him that she was pregnant. Within a few weeks the two lovers said good-bye. Ya-juo, accompanied by her friend Kui Hui, boarded a rickety bus for the long ride to Kuilin. She chose this enchanting town of erotic peaks to have her baby because she had a brother who was a magistrate in a nearby county. The two women moved into a house on Lishih Road, checked in with the doctor, kept out of sight, and waited for the happy but anxious day to arrive. Ching-kuo gave them enough money for their upkeep. Ya-juo had already given birth to two children, and she soon realized she was larger than during her previous pregnancies. The doctor said he suspected twins.[48]

On May 21, 1942, Ya-juo delivered two sons. Until Ching-kuo could arrive, she gave them temporary birth names "Li" and "Shih" from the name of the road on which she was then living. A few days after the birth, Ching-kuo came to see his new sons and proudly held them in his arms. He stayed for only two days and then left for Chungking to tell his father about his affair with Ya-juo and the birth of the twins.[49] The Generalissimo accepted the event and, exercising the right of grandfathers, proposed names for the two boys—Hsiao-yen and Hsiao-tz'u. The twins would thus share the generational name of all Chiang Kai-shek's grandchildren—Hsiao, meaning "filial piety."[50] The Gimo, however, proposed that the boys take their mother's family name. Ya-juo understood the implications of this suggestion—she and her sons would not be part of the Chiang family.[51]

Ya-juo, a liberated woman and activist, was not willing to live a life of seclusion. She began to make her name in the city.[52] Among the many Americans in Kuilin (which had more than a dozen American organizations), she found one willing to give her English lessons. Kui Hui reports that about six months later, sometime in November, when she and Ya-juo were out shopping, they thought someone was following them. A couple of days later a burglar broke into their house. Hearing of this incident, the Director of Civil Affairs of Kwangsi province, Ch'iu Ch'ang-wei, sent soldiers to protect the house. Ya-juo visited Ch'iu at his residence to express appreciation. When she returned home, she had diarrhea and complained of severe stomach cramps.[53]

Kui Hui rushed her friend to the hospital and stayed the night with her. In great pain, Ya-juo asked Kui Hui to care for the babies if she should die. Ching-kuo, she said, had promised that the boys would someday be taken into the Chiang family. She also wanted Kui Hui to have the mirrored compact that Ching-kuo had given her. The next morning Ya-juo seemed better, although she still had severe stomach pains. A doctor came to examine her and gave her an injection. In a few minutes Ya-juo cried out that she could not see. The medical staff hastened back into the room and sent Kui Hui for ice. When she returned, they informed her that Ya-juo was dead. As is customary in southern China, the burial was the next day. When Wang Sheng informed him of the news, Ching-kuo cried and for several days wore dark glasses to hide his swollen eyes.[54]

Kui Hui took the twins to Ya-juo's mother, Chang Ching-hua, and told her that she suspected foul play. From her account the Chang family came to believe that Ya-juo had been murdered and that a dark plot lay behind it. They feared for the lives of the twins and registered the boys as having been born in different years to confuse any effort to track them down.[55] Rumors and speculation about Ya-juo's death continue to this day. Ch'i Kao-ju, the editor of *Right Spirit Daily* in Kanchow, asserted in his biography of Ching-kuo that shortly before the death of Ya-juo, he overheard the shady Huang Chung-mei, the Moscow alumnus and spy, say that Chang Ya-juo was causing problems in Kuilin by calling herself Mrs. Chiang Ching-kuo. "Just kill her," Huang allegedly said to an associate: "I will take responsibility." Ch'i also remembers Huang complaining that he had done everything for Ching-kuo, but that the young Chiang "does not understand me." Ch'i speculates that Huang on his own authority may have murdered Ya-juo. This theory has been picked up by other Chinese biographers. Other than the statements recollected by Ch'i decades later and Kui Hui's suspicions, however, there is no other basis for believing Ya-juo was killed on the orders of the Communists, the Generalissimo, or Ching-kuo himself.

Faina remained unaware of her husband's relationship with Ya-juo and the birth of the twins. She did not inquire into her husband's work, and he laid down strict rules on her contacts, excluding, for example, wives of rich businessmen and others who might want to exploit the relationship. She and Ching-kuo appeared to be a modern and close couple. Faina regularly greeted her husband at the airport with a hug and a kiss—to the wonder and embarrassment of Chinese spectators.[56] At this time, Ching-kuo and his wife often if not usually spoke Russian together. Ching-kuo also still liked to read Russian literature like that of the nineteenth-century Ukrainian poet Shevchenko.[57] Later he and Faina would abandon most of their cultural ties to Russia in order to diminish speculation that they were pro-Soviet.

—

THROUGHOUT 1942 and 1943 Ching-kuo continued to oversee the implementation of his three-year plan. Visitors were struck by how well off the once very poor region of Kannan appeared compared to other parts of China. The *New York Times* corespondent, Brooks Atkinson, reported that Ching-kuo's program of reform had transformed the area. Before the war Kanchow only had three factories, now it had forty-four, including an alcohol plant, a flour mill, a match factory, and spinning mills. Through double cropping and new agricultural methods, Kannan—long a food deficit area—produced sufficient food for ten months consumption and expected complete self-sufficiency by 1944. Kanchow was in Atkinson's view the most modern and the cleanest city in China.[58]

In 1943 thousands of children without parents lived in shacks and makeshift tents in refugee camps along the Kung River. Ching-kuo ordered the construction of a school (called New Village School) about one hour's drive out of Kanchow on the banks of the Kung. After its completion, some 1,300 primary and high school orphans moved into New Village. In a radical departure for China, Ching-kuo prohibited all forms of corporal punishment at the school. He had the students form committees to manage their own affairs, elect their own mayor, and appoint their own police force.[59]

During the summer of 1943 Chiang often stayed at the school. He would rise at dawn with the students and lead them in calisthenics and then on a mad dash into the cold river. The sign on his office simply said, "Mister Chiang Ching-kuo." Today the visitor finds on the reception room walls an array of fading photos, including one of Ching-kuo and Faina and one that probably was not there in Ching-kuo's days, a picture of the pretty Chang Ya-juo. Upstairs, there is a small office with a rickety desk. Here Ching-kuo met at least two Americans, the journalist Harrison Forman, and Richard Service from the American consulate in Kuilin.[60]

—

CHENNAULT AND STILWELL had been arguing over strategy since 1942. Chennault wanted priority for the air war, while Stilwell insisted that building a well-trained ground force had to be the first goal. Chiang Kai-shek and Roosevelt sided with Chennault, and in 1943 the Air Force General began construction of a ring of airfields on the outer edge of the territory controlled by the National government. Chennault's plan was to use these air bases for sorties of B-29 bombers, which could reach the Japanese home islands and Japanese bases as far away as Thailand. As part of this strategy, the United States 14th Air Force wanted to establish an airfield near Kanchow for emergency landing by reconnaissance P-38 flights returning from Japan.

Robert Service, Vice Consul and Attaché of Embassy stationed at Kuilin, took the long, bumpy ride to Kanchow in a weapons-carrier to make arrangements for the construction. Service met Ching-kuo in his office at the New Village School. The American diplomat recalled that Ching-kuo was "very friendly, cooperative, and helpful." He was different from most Chinese officials Service had met during his many years in China in that he seemed "genuinely interested in the welfare of the public." Ching-kuo invited the American to dinner at his home, the only time that Service had received such an invitation from a ranking government official.

Service remembered that Ching-kuo's attractive Russian wife spoke Ningpo-accented Chinese but did not say much. Everyone "had quite a merry time with much finger game playing, which Ching-kuo usually won." Ching-kuo was full of jokes. After dinner he performed several impressive physical feats. For example, he lay his head on the back of a chair and his toes on the back of another while his rear rested on a third chair in the middle. Faina pulled the middle chair away, leaving him suspended. The American ascribed these macho displays to Ching-kuo's acquired Russian temperament.

According to Service, Ching-kuo's administration of his eleven counties was thought by Americans to be "near utopian as far as China was concerned." Ching-kuo had eliminated prostitution and gambling, put criminals to work, and trained them so they could find jobs after release. Even "Vinegar Joe" Stilwell noted in his diary that he had heard Ching-kuo "was doing a fairly good job."[61]

During the construction of the airfield Ching-kuo was on the site almost every day. He made friends with the American army engineers and had them to his house for meals. After the field was finished, he drove down to Kuilin and had dinner with Service at the residence of American Consul General Arthur Ringwalt. At the dinner table Ching-kuo was again thoroughly at ease, amiable, and open. While young Chiang was unassuming and relaxed, Service recalls, he "already basked in a certain aura of importance." Most of the American foreign service officers in China at the time thought the Generalissimo was botching both the war effort and the governing of China, but his thirty-three-year-old son struck them as just what China so desperately needed—an energetic, competent, and honest leader.[62]

Service remembered one other episode involving Ching-kuo. In mid-1944 General Kan Chieh-hou told Service about a secret organization of provincial military leaders unhappy with the conduct of the war. Service sent a classified dispatch to the embassy in Chungking reporting his conversation with Kan. In a serious professional lapse, the American ambassador showed the cable to Foreign Minister T. V. Soong. Soong was able to identify the source of the report, although it did not directly name Kan. Tai Li's men immediately arrested Kan for giving the Americans sensitive information, and a military court sentenced him to death. Service brought the case to the attention of Ching-kuo, who intervened and saved Kan's life. Tai-li was not pleased.[63]

THE GIMO CONTINUED to find time to write letters of pedantic instruction to Ching-kuo. In one epistle in August 1943, for example, Chiang warned that in learning, "haste makes waste." He suggested Ching-kuo study math and English "for no more than six hours a week each."[64] In addition to guiding Ching-kuo on academic studies, classical Chinese works, and Sun Yat-sen's writings, the Generalissimo also encouraged him to study the Bible and other Christian works. In a 1956 tribute to his father, Ching-kuo stressed the importance of Christian faith in the Gimo's life.[65] Apparently, the father did effective missionary work: the dutiful son began reading the Bible sometime shortly after his arrival in

Kanchow in 1939. On Easter Day 1943 in Chungking, Pastor Pi Fan-yu baptized Ching-kuo and his family.

Ching-kuo became a Methodist, just as he became a Confucian and an admirer of Mencius, because this was his father's wish. Like his father, he took his oaths seriously. Henceforth he would always carry with him two books—his diary and his Bible. On his father's recommendation, Ching-kuo also read a collection of Christian testaments—one for each day of the year—called *Streams in the Desert*.[66] Chiang Kai-shek had noted down his thoughts beside each of the daily inspirational messages or stories, and he suggested Ching-kuo add these to his own copy of the book.[67] The dominant theme of *Streams in the Desert* is a message of stoic perseverance and unwavering faith in the face of failure, disaster, and tragedy. A contribution by one H. C. Trumbull is typical: "Every person and every nation must take lessons in God's school of adversity. We can say, 'Blessed is night, for it reveals to us the stars.' In the same way we can say, 'Blessed is sorrow, for it reveals God's comfort.' "[68] The Generalissimo's copy of *Streams in the Desert* is in his coffin with him in Tzuhu, Taiwan, waiting for the journey home. Whether out of filial piety or sincere admiration, this book also became one of Ching-kuo's favorites.

In the early 1950s American military officers would see Ching-kuo reading a dog-eared Bible in the field.[69] Aides who traveled with him and went into his room at night for final instructions usually saw an open Bible lying on the bed or desk.[70] Ching-kuo read the Good Book from cover to cover several times. On each complete reading, he put a check mark on the front page. When he died, there were seventeen checks.[71]

But according to Chou Lien-hua, the Chiang family pastor in Taiwan, on the subject of religion as in other matters Ching-kuo was not closed-minded or dogmatic. He was instead a "seeker." He studied the Bible on his own, but he did not discuss religion with Chou or other pastors and only occasionally attended services. He prayed at Christian churches other than Methodist but also in Buddhist temples, including at his favorite Hole-in-the-Snow Monastery.[72]

CHING-KUO CONTINUED to be frustrated with the failure of the Youth Corps to become a dynamic force capable of mobilizing Chinese youth.

As in the administration of Kannan, the key to success with the corps, he believed, was to develop a large contingent of honest and dedicated young cadre. In 1943 Ching-kuo attended the First National Conference of the Youth Corps in Chungking, where he proposed that the corps expand its training classes into a large Youth Cadre School in Chungking that would produce thousands of youth leaders. With the elder Chiang's blessings, the conference endorsed the idea, and in December the Gimo appointed Ching-kuo as dean of education with responsibility for establishing the new school and its curriculum from scratch.

Ching-kuo retained his positions in Kannan and flew frequently between his posts. Japanese fighters twice pursued his plane. Soon he was spending most of his time in Chungking. Wang Sheng and some of Ching-kuo's other subordinates in Kanchow followed him to the war capital to become students at the new school.[73] Then on January 17, 1944, the Japanese ordered the Ichigo offensive, aimed at the new U.S. airfields. Within a few days the Imperial Army was on the outskirts of Kanchow, and Ching-kuo flew back there to deal with the crisis. When it was apparent that the town was about to fall, he evacuated most of those closely identified with him and the government, sending Faina, the children, and Ah Wang to Chungking. On February 3, as fighting could be heard in the hills, Ching-kuo flew out on a DC-3 from the airfield he had built for the Americans. On February 5, when the Japanese seized the town, it was largely deserted.[74]

MAKING ALLOWANCES for propaganda and legend, Ching-kuo's accomplishments in Kannan were real enough and in the circumstances of the day even spectacular. Among the most notable of his successes was the imposition of law and order without losing his local popularity. The secret was a reputation for personal incorruptibility, a genuine rapport with common people, and thus an ability to convince them that he was working on their behalf. For example, he met his conscription quotas, but in contrast with most parts of China, the process of drafting young men out of the villages of Kannan did not create fear and hatred of the authorities. At least such resentment was not remembered or recorded in Kannan.

But aside from the unique will of the leader and the dedicated officials under him, it would have been difficult, even impossible, to create new Kannans across the country for other reasons. Ching-kuo, for example, generated additional funds by retaining all the grain tax collected locally instead of transmitting it to the provincial government—a policy most local government officials could not duplicate.[75] Likewise, he was probably more able than his counterparts to compel banks to make low-interest loans.[76] In addition, Ching-kuo received assistance from the provincial and central governments that other regional commissioners of similar territories did not enjoy. According to a Chinese journalist who worked in Kannan at the time, special help included additional internal security personnel (Peace Preservation Corps and self-defense teams) and extra military and civilian police. Furthermore, young Chiang had direct command of these internal security forces, unlike other regional administrators. In addition, Kannan had more civilian government employees than similar regions.[77] According to one source, his office had 100 staff members compared to an average of 20 in other regions.[78] Special appropriations from the central government and perhaps from Madame Chiang's own purse may have paid for a number of projects in Kanchow, such as the large new stadium.[79]

THE KANNAN EXPERIENCE provided Ching-kuo with a solid base on which to build his future career. He had earned a reputation as a competent, energetic, creative, and incorruptible leader with experience in administration and local development, including education, youth work, and internal security. He also had begun to collect a group of subordinates he could trust as well as a circle of enemies. During his time in Kiangsi province, Ching-kuo came to understand the basic problems that afflicted the Kuomintang—corruption and factionalism. He was also well aware of the generally poor and often shocking treatment of conscripts, the padded personnel rolls of military units, and other widespread forms of corruption. His trips to Chungking helped him to grasp the fundamental conundrum of the Nationalist military—its division into jealous cliques, independent kingdoms, and under-strength divisions and armies. He had also come to distrust the CCP even more than in the past. In his speeches and sloganeering, he artfully mixed in with his egalitarian and anti-establishment terminology suitable allusions to the great neo-Confucianists so admired by his father. Nevertheless, the most conservative elements in the KMT returned his dislike and continued to float rumors alleging that Ching-kuo was a secret Soviet tool.

Chiang Kai-shek, a man without true friends, now had two he could confide in—his wife and his son. Father and son had begun exchanging their diaries for each other to read—an indication of the closeness their relationship had attained. At this time Ching-kuo had no difficulties with his stepmother. As for Wei-kuo, he did not have a serious political role, and thus his relationship with Madame Chiang was purely a family one. It is commonly believed that Soong Mei-ling preferred Wei-kuo because he was handsome, suave, and spoke good English. Ching-kuo, however, was also a model of filial piety. On Chinese New Year he would go to Chungking to visit his parents to pay his respects. Dressed in a traditional black robe, he would enter the room, kneel, and perform the "kowtow."[80] In contrast to this ritual behavior, Ching-kuo's life and work in Kiangsi underscored his steadfast refusal to take himself too seriously—a character trait absent at the top levels in both Chungking and Yenan.

7

Dean and General

THE YOUTH CADRE SCHOOL, housed in several old buildings ten miles outside of Chungking, opened on May 5, 1944. The Generalissimo predicted that it would serve the revolution "just like Whampoa," and the school began using the slogan, "the second Whampoa." This analogy excited apprehension in some quarters, as it suggested a new political contingent based on the Youth Corps and Ching-kuo.[1]

Ching-kuo selected 280 students for the first class through an examination process. They were recent college graduates or cadre who had significant experience in youth work. There was also an independent unit of 60 to 70 women.[2] Most of the students came from middle- or upper-class urban families. They were educated, patriotic, idealistic young people, and in their eyes Ching-kuo embodied the fresh and dedicated leader they had so eagerly sought. Ch'en Chih-ching, for example, in 1944, had just graduated from university. Like many college students, he was fervently patriotic and anti-Communist but saw the Kuomintang as "hopeless and corrupt." He and his friends heard about Ching-kuo, the radical reformist son of the Gimo who practiced what he preached. When Ch'en went to the Youth Cadre School to take the entrance exam, he saw over the doorway the slogan: "No Admission to Those Who Want to Be Officials or to Be Rich." The man in work clothes who received him at the door was Ching-kuo.[3]

Ching-kuo enjoyed the academic role. From this time on, including after he became president of the Republic of China, his closest associates from the old days would in private call him "dean" or "principal" (Hsiao Chang). The dean lived in a small house on the school grounds. He ate with the students and engaged in daily labor with them. During one of his impromptu inspections of the barracks, Ching-kuo found in one room a biography of Stalin and works by Marx and Engels. He thumbed through the books and then walked away.[4] After morning muster and exercise, despite the cold, the dean would tear off his shirt and lead the students in a charge up a nearby hill, shouting, "True men follow me!" The slope soon received the name True Men Hill.[5] Often he would go with a group of teachers and students to Chinese opera in Chungking. One night, despite a heavy rain, Ching-kuo insisted they jog the ten miles back to the school and sing the whole way.[6]

As he had done in his schools in Kannan, Ching-kuo introduced student government into the new training center. Military discipline prevailed, but he forbade the students to salute him. Rules were enforced strictly and without favoritism.[7] Above all he preached selfless service. A group of students suggested that after completing the course they should receive masters degrees. At the next assembly, Ching-kuo said he was surprised that soon after they enrolled they were so concerned about degrees. "All right," declared the dean, "I will make each of you a Doctor of Revolution." The students burst into laughter and did not raise the degree issue again.[8]

Despite the retreat from Kannan, the first half of the year was a time of great optimism at the Youth Cadre School. The prestige of the Generalissimo and Madame Chiang were at an all-time high. Pictures of the Gimo in his wicker chair beside Roosevelt and Churchill at Cairo circulated widely. The Allies belatedly but finally abolished the imperial legacy of extraterritoriality under which citizens of Western nations living in China were exempt from Chinese law. Also inspiring were the victories in Burma by the American-trained New First Army and New Sixth Army, the former under the Virginia Military Institute (VMI) alumnus, Sun Li-jen. Stilwell, unable to avoid insults even in his praise, declared these successes "the first sustained offensive in Chinese history against a first-class enemy."[9] Meanwhile, the United States Navy at the Battle of the Coral Sea decimated much of the remaining Japanese fleet, and U.S.

Marines, while suffering heavy loses, steadily advanced across the islands of the Pacific.

The war in China, however, was not going so well. Neither Chennault's pilots nor the Chinese army were able to stop the Japanese Ichigo offensive. Chinese military commands failed to cooperate, headquarters held back supplies to less favored generals, and huge casualties piled up as the Gimo ordered whole divisions to defend virtually surrounded cities. The Ichigo campaign created a profound military and political crisis for the Nationalist government and also provoked a change in American policy. Stilwell called for Chennault's ouster, but Roosevelt pulled out Vinegar Joe instead and replaced him with the more diplomatic Major-General Albert C. Wedemeyer. Wedemeyer, the new China-Burma-India Commander, got along well with Chiang Kai-shek, but in his confidential messages his views were not much different from those of Stilwell.[10]

CHINESE TROOPS AT SHANGHAI, Wuhan, Changsha, and other battles had shown themselves to be courageous fighters. They had skilled military leaders such as Ch'en Ch'eng, Pai Ch'ung-hsi, Li Tsung-jen, and Sun Li-jen, but divided leadership and terrible conditions for the enlisted men, most of them simple peasants, destroyed their fighting spirit. As outnumbered Japanese units again sliced through Chinese defenses, Ching-kuo grew increasingly frustrated. One day he took his father to a camp near Chungking. In the barracks the Gimo saw soldiers who had died in their bedrolls of sickness or starvation. Chiang Kai-shek flew into a rage and with his cane beat the officer in charge, then removed him from command. In August 1944 municipal workers carted off the bodies of 138 soldiers from the streets of Chungking. Ching-kuo also reported this to his father, but this time the Gimo did not go to see for himself.[11]

According to a military officer who served for many years as executive officer of Ching-kuo's office, Ching-kuo never confronted his father head-on but would instead plant an idea and encourage the Generalissimo to believe it was his own.[12] What China desperately required, Ching-kuo frequently told his father, was a new sort of military force composed of literate and patriotic youth led by officers of high quality and dedication. The Youth Corps, which was "in but not of" the Kuomintang, would be an obvious source of recruitment for such an elite army.

At this point, the Americans were committed to training and arming 39 Chinese divisions. Accepting his son's proposals, Chiang Kai-shek decided that nine of these divisions, or about 100,000 personnel, would constitute the new, educated youth army. On October 10 the Generalissimo called on educated youth throughout the country to join this elite military organization. While hoping for many volunteers, particularly for the officer corps, Chiang also established a national committee to handle conscription of educated young men into the ranks.[13]

In China, drafting middle school and college students and graduates was a novel step. Seven years into the war, the Chinese government had not conscripted college students or graduates with the exception of some doctors, engineers, and English majors, the last to serve as interpreters. There were only 40,000 college graduates in all of China at the beginning of the war, and it was believed that these and other educated youth coming on stream were needed to keep the economy and the government functioning.[14] Less explainable was the fact that high school students and graduates also usually escaped military service. The Gimo's decree would change this situation, at least for some educated youth.

In November the Generalissimo named Minister of War Ch'en Ch'eng to command the officially named Educated Youth Expeditionary Army. Ching-kuo became head of the unit's corps of political officers, which the Gimo made subordinate to the Training Directorate of the Military Council, not to its Political Department.[15] This unusual step gave Ching-kuo and the Youth Army unique independence from the regular army's established political system. Ching-kuo was determined to have a tough and truly effective corps of commissars.[16]

By the end of the year the Youth Army had signed up or drafted 140,000 students. Ching-kuo's officers were culling from these numbers enough personnel to form the nine divisions—the 201st through the 209th—and a Women's War Auxiliary Corps of 3,000. Ching-kuo created a professional corps of line commanders through the appointment of veteran officers formally selected by the Generalissimo. At the same time, Ching-kuo himself personally appointed all the political commissars, drawing largely on persons outside the military.[17] With about six months training, the first class in the Youth Cadre School received early graduation, and more than one hundred signed up as political officers in the Youth Army.[18]

By February 1945, 40,000 recruits were in training, with the remainder awaiting the availability of facilities. According to Youth Army veterans, when Ching-kuo visited the training camps, he continued his practice of rising before reveille, greeting the trainees as they arrived for muster, and then inspecting kitchens and latrines.[19] In an address to the first class of officer trainees, the Generalissimo called them a "revolutionary vanguard" whose fighting spirit would allow "one to defeat ten of the enemy."[20] The Youth Army was to be the Gimo's *tour de force*.[21]

Chiang Kai-shek also assigned his son to yet another job—director of the Youth Corps's separate political department.[22] As the CC brothers had feared, it was evident that the Youth Corps (which now numbered about 500,000) as well as the Youth Army and youth in general were Chiang Ching-kuo's turf. It was only a matter of time before ex-Blue Shirt K'ang Ts'e would be out of his key Youth Corps job and sent to the front, where he would be killed in action.

CHING-KUO, the man with the easy smile, cultivated the habit of never laughing when he was in his office. His father, always concerned with appearances, had urged him to adopt a more serious mien. But Ching-kuo continued the egalitarian habits of a lifetime, including rising from his chair when anyone came into his office. Relaxing after work with food and drink, he would put an arm around his subordinates, tell jokes, and of course play the finger game. Despite his heavy after-hours drinking, his undiscovered diabetes still only occasionally caused him problems.[23] Ching-kuo was physically at his peak, still rather lean, certainly dashing, confident, ebullient, and powerful.

With all his responsibilities, Ching-kuo had less time to spend at home with Faina and the children. A way of life that had evolved steadily since his marriage in 1935 now became set in concrete. According to long-time aides, Ching-kuo separated his work, his family life, and his social life. He loved his family and played with the children when he had the chance but spent little time at home. As always, he attracted women who were good-looking and smart, whether married or single. One friend, a daughter of an Air Force general, became pregnant and left for the United States.[24]

IN DECEMBER the Japanese suddenly halted the Ichigo offensive. With the war in the Pacific going badly, Japan did not want or need any more Chinese territory. Military planning was under way for a Chinese offensive and an American landing in South China. But with the Ichigo campaign crisis over, the Gimo again gave even higher priority than before to preparing for the coming contest with the Communists. He appointed Ch'en Ch'eng to the concurrent post of Commander-in-Chief of Active Service in the Rear (occupied) Areas. Building up the Youth Corps in order to counter the CCP's recruitment of students also became a high priority.

Many of those who were close to Ching-kuo during the mid-1940s believe that at this time the Gimo had settled on Ch'en as his likely successor and Ching-kuo as the second choice. For his part, Ching-kuo knew that some people now referred to him as "the Prince" and that his father was at least entertaining the thought that someday his son might become the leader of China. Ch'en Ch'eng and Ching-kuo tried to make their relationship work and generally got on well together. Ch'en was one of the few KMT generals whom Ching-kuo respected. But competition and tension inevitably developed. Ching-kuo told an associate, "If Ch'en is right, I will obey him, but how can I obey him when he is wrong?"[25]

The global war news now was virtually all good. The U.S. Marines captured Iwo Jima, and B-29s roamed the skies of Japan at will. In early February General Sun Li-jen and his New First Army retook Lashio and reopened the Burma Road. The land blockade of China finally ended.

NEAR THE END OF 1944, the newly appointed American Ambassador to China, Patrick Hurley, stopped off in Moscow on his way to Chungking. Stalin and Molotov told him the Soviet Union had lost all interest in the

Chinese Communists and the USSR desired better relations with Nationalist China. Shortly after Hurley's arrival in Chungking the Soviet chargé d'affaires approached Ching-kuo and suggested that a meeting be arranged between Stalin and Chiang Kai-shek. Nothing came of this, however, probably because Stalin decided to wait until after the upcoming Yalta meeting.[26]

At this time, the United States military believed that only a land campaign could defeat the Japanese on the mainland of Asia, and that the Chinese army was not up to the task. The Ichigo offensive and other events, including the Gimo's threat at one point to withdraw from the war if he did not receive more support, had caused Roosevelt to lose faith in Nationalist China. The constant criticism of the KMT by American foreign service officers, journalists, and others in China—not to speak of Stilwell's tirades—and the good news that always seemed to come from the Communist camp in Yenan played a part in Washington's perception of the China tangle. For all these reasons, at the Yalta summit in February 1945, Roosevelt was prepared to have the Chiang regime and the Republic of China unknowingly pay a major political price for a Russian pledge to attack the Japanese in Manchuria. The American leader agreed to return Port Arthur and the Eastern Chinese Railway, both in Manchuria (that is, in China), to Soviet control. Dealing with another piece of Chinese territory, Roosevelt accepted a resolution of Outer Mongolia's status by a plebiscite that the Soviets themselves were to administer. He further agreed not to inform America's ally in Chungking of these provisions affecting their country until the German defeat and the redeployment of 25 Soviet divisions to the Far East.

The Russian leader told the ailing American president that the Chinese Communists were "radish Communists," red on the outside but white inside, and he promised that before sending his troops into Manchuria, he would conclude a pact of friendship and alliance with the Chinese government and once again render military assistance to Chungking. In reality, Stalin at this point believed that a CCP victory in China could bring about the same sort of geopolitical transformation in the Far East that the Soviet Red Army was leaving in its wake in Eastern and Central Europe.[27] Mao's forces were steadily growing. For some time, the American embassy in Chungking had been predicting in its dispatches that a civil war in China was inevitable. Because of the corruption and ineptness of the KMT army, most American diplomats and journalists believed that the Communists very likely would win. The Soviet embassy's analysis and that of Stalin's representatives in Yenan no doubt were similar to that of the Americans. The Russians knew that once the Soviet Union occupied Manchuria, the postwar outlook for the Chinese Communists would become even more promising.

At Yalta and then Teheran, the Allied powers agreed on a postwar atlas in which there would be a divided Korea and a divided Germany. From Stalin's perspective a divided China, half Communist, half Nationalist, would have many advantages. But if in fact all of China should fall to the Communists, so much the better. While Chiang was kept in the dark until June about the Yalta agreements on the Far East, Stalin early on probably informed Mao, and joint military planning got under way for the insertion of Chinese Communist troops behind the planned Red Army invasion. It turned out to be much sooner than anyone expected.

AT THE URGING OF THE AMERICANS, the KMT and the CCP had been holding on-again-off-again talks on a coalition government since the end of 1944. During several meetings in Chungking, Zhou insisted on the establishment of a coalition regime before the CCP would dissolve its military organization. Chiang naturally wanted it the other way around. In March Chiang proposed convening a National Assembly to end one-party rule and draft a new constitution. In an effort to reinforce its "radish Communist" image, the CCP National Congress in April removed references in its constitution to the Soviet Union and the world Communist revolution. Instead, the new CCP charter sanctified Mao's "thought" as the Party's guiding light.

Also in April, the KMT held its Sixth Party Congress in Chungking. Unlike at the CCP Congress in Yenan, significant open criticism of the ruling establishment came up at the KMT meeting. The criticism, which came from members of the Youth Corps, was not directed at the Generalissimo but at widespread malfeasance and ineptness in the Party, the government, and the military.[28] Without question, Chiang Ching-kuo, now a member of the Central Committee, had, with his father's approval, sanctioned these verbal attacks on the KMT establishment. The Gimo presumably thought that such criticism would counter charges that the KMT was not democratic and perhaps also pressure the Party to clean up.[29] Reflecting Ching-kuo's desires, the Congress legally divested the Youth Corps of its loose KMT affiliation and converted it into a government organization responsible for training youth.[30]

On May 8, 1945, Germany unconditionally surrendered. Close to the end of the month Stalin told Harry Hopkins, President Truman's envoy, that the Russians would be able to begin operations in Manchuria on August 8 and that the USSR would negotiate a treaty with Chiang Kai-shek before the invasion. As he had said in 1927 and 1937, the Soviet leader again asserted that Chiang was the only man qualified to lead China. He also promised that Chiang's government would be permitted to organize local governments in areas of Manchuria under Soviet occupation. In June the Americans informed the Generalissimo of the Yalta agreement and the Soviet plans to attack the Japanese in Manchuria.

The Gimo had to make the best of the situation. If he was to prevail in the postwar internal struggle, he would need American assistance and a hands-off policy from Moscow, or at least restraint. Knowing for sure the Soviets would occupy Manchuria made it even more imperative that Chiang exhaust every possibility of reaching a new accommodation with Stalin.

SINKIANG WAS ANOTHER AREA where it would be essential to win Soviet restraint. Chiang Kai-shek and Ching-kuo believed that if they gave way on the independence of Outer Mongolia, Stalin might cooperate with the KMT in both Manchuria and Sinkiang. Since their withdrawal from the Northwest in 1943, the Soviets had continued to meddle in the region's affairs. Meanwhile, the policies of Sheng Shih-ts'ai had alienated the majority, non-Chinese peoples of the region. In late 1944, after the Gimo forced Sheng's departure, Uzbek leader Farkhad established an independent East Turkestan Republic seventy miles from Urumchi.[31]

To make matters worse, the new KMT governor and the military commander in Sinkiang were at odds. The Generalissimo sent Ching-kuo to sort things out. He arrived in Urumchi on April 13, 1945, and conferred with provincial officials and the new Soviet Ambassador to China, A. A. Petrov, who was there on his way to assume his duties in Chungking. According to the American Consul in Urumchi, Robert S. Ward, Ching-kuo's appearance seemed to indicate that "for the first time there was a sincere effort on the part of the Chinese to seek Soviet good will."[32] Ching-kuo's visit sparked hopeful speculation in Urumchi that he would become the new governor.[33] In June a "special delegate" from Chungking suggested to Ward that the U.S. government recommend to the Generalissimo the appointment of Ching-kuo as governor.[34]

Ching-kuo had unusual qualifications for the Sinkiang job, which necessarily involved dealing with the Soviets. Furthermore, unlike many Chinese officials, he would happily have gone to live and work there. But although the Gimo at one point had probably planned that the governorship in Sinkiang would be his son's next posting, by the spring of 1945 he had changed his mind. In view of the coming Soviet occupation of Manchuria and with the end of the war in sight, he wanted Ching-kuo to work on national affairs and to be nearby so that the two could continue their increasingly close relationship. This second trip to Sinkiang, however, did help prepare Ching-kuo for his next assignment—a return to Moscow after an eight-year absence.[35]

IN JUNE T. V. SOONG, the brother of Madame Chiang, assumed his new office as Premier (President of the Executive Yuan), while retaining his position as Foreign Minister. Chiang instructed T. V. to lead a delegation to Moscow at once to discuss the promised treaty, and he proposed that Soong take along Ching-kuo as an adviser. Soong of course agreed, although he resented young Chiang's role as his father's principal expert on the Soviet Union. In fact, while Soong was away for two months in San Francisco, the Generalissimo and Ching-kuo worked out a broad outline of the strategy to be followed in the talks with Stalin. The thrust of this policy was that China would make concessions in Mongolia in return for Soviet recognition of China's sovereignty in Manchuria, and a firm Soviet agreement to halt aid to the CCP and to rebel groups in Sinkiang. Initially, the Chinese delegation was not to indicate any flexibility on the question of Outer Mongolia, but newspapers in Chungking, obviously reflecting guidance, indicated that there was some room for compromise.[36]

Using an American airplane and crew, Soong and his entourage took off from Chungking on June 26. Ching-kuo, a lieutenant general in the Youth Army, on this delegation carried the rank of colonel. Molotov warmly greeted the party at the military airdrome—where he had so cordially welcomed Hitler's Foreign Minister Ribbentrop in 1939 and the Japanese envoy Matsuoka in 1941. Soong had five meetings with Stalin, at least two of which Chiang Ching-kuo attended.[37] Soong, a Harvard graduate, spoke in English, and a Soviet interpreter translated into Russian. Stalin was utterly charming, and the exchanges were very cordial.

Although Ching-kuo adopted a low posture in the delegation, he played a key role in the talks. To T. V. Soong's dismay, young Chiang had a private session with Stalin. It is safe to assume that Ching-kuo conveyed a personal message from his father and that Stalin was once again effusive in his praise of Chiang Kai-shek and in his promises of close Soviet cooperation with the Nationalist government. Stalin also asked how Faina and their Russian-born son were faring and gave Ching-kuo the present of a rifle for Alan.[38] Ching-kuo noted in Stalin's outer office a portrait of Peter the Great in the spot where he remembered seeing, years earlier, a large painting of Lenin standing on a tank. To his mind this change reflected the supremacy of nationalism over ideology in Stalin's outlook—on balance, he thought, a promising development.[39]

When the Chinese delegation returned to Chungking in mid-July, Ching-kuo was in an optimistic mood. Stalin had assured the Chinese that three weeks after the capitulation of Japan Soviet troops would begin to withdraw from Manchuria, and could complete the pullout within three months. On July 20, despite opposition within the KMT to any concessions on the status of Outer Mongolia, the Gimo approved final instructions to give way on this issue provided Stalin was prepared to promise noninterference in China's internal affairs.[40] Before returning to Moscow with the proposal, Soong told Hurley that it would politically destroy the man responsible for putting it forth.[41] He did not want to be the official who gave away Outer Mongolia. Finally, Soong agreed to lead the delegation to Moscow but depart before the signing of the pact.

Ching-kuo was not on the second delegation; the Gimo apparently decided to keep him at home in order to reduce his son's exposure to the expected backlash from the right wing. In addition, on August 6 (the day before the delegation's departure), China heard the news of the nuclear destruction of Hiroshima. Washington had not given the Chinese advance notice of the bomb, but Chiang Kai-shek was of course delighted. By enhancing Stalin's respect for the power of the United States, the atomic blasts could help China in the final round of negotiations and, equally important, encourage Russia's implementation of the expected treaty.

The Sino-Soviet Treaty of Friendship and Alliance, signed on August 14, 1945, pledged mutual support in the event of a repetition of Japanese aggression, mutual respect for sovereignty and for the principles of territorial integrity, and noninterference in each other's internal affairs. In an exchange of notes, China agreed to recognize the independence of Outer Mongolia if a (Soviet-run) plebiscite confirmed this was the wish of the people. For its part, Moscow undertook to render moral support and material aid entirely to the national government of China and declared (with reference to the recent developments in Sinkiang) that "it had no intention of interfering in the internal affairs of China."

The day after the Chinese delegation had arrived in Moscow, the Soviet Union declared war on Japan, and 700,000 Red Army veterans of the Western Front swept into Manchuria. In the treaty, Moscow reiterated its commitment to begin troop withdrawal from Manchuria three weeks after the Japanese surrender and to complete the process within three months. A Chinese government representative and staff would be appointed for the liberated territory of Manchuria, and as soon as any part of the territory ceased to be a zone of immediate military operations, the National government would assume full authority.[42] The American embassy in Moscow warned that Russia's moderation on Manchuria was "superficial" and that Stalin would continue to seek maximum influence in the region through the use of "those trained to accept their discipline and share their ideology"—that is, the CCP.[43] But the Allies, including China, had no real alternative but to assume Soviet good will. Russia had made a critical contribution to the Nazi defeat, suffering enormous losses in the process. The postwar order would have to be based initially on the assumption of Soviet cooperation.[44] On August 14 the new Foreign Minister, Wang Shih-chieh, put his signature on the treaty. The next day, Emperor Hirohito, speaking in "the Voice of the Crane," made his famous broadcast of surrender.

FOR TWENTY FIVE YEARS—eight of them in blood drenched battle—the contest had raged for the direction of civilization in the new age of revolutionary energy, knowledge, and power. Almost at the half-way point in the twentieth century, the two streams of the Enlightenment—the Jacobin and the democratic (the latter with authoritarian allies like China)—triumphed over the antediluvian counterstream of fascism. The next half century would be the second stage of this global civil war—a struggle between the radical/utopian idealists and the liberal/democratic camp, each side with its Third World adherents. As with the first epic conflict, the violent aspect of this struggle initially erupted in China, and again specifically in Manchuria. On one side stood a clear example of leftist totalitarianism—the Chinese Communist Party. On the other stood the Kuomintang, a conglomerate of ideologies and political forces, which only on the eve of the struggle with the Communists declared itself ready for representative democracy but which did not have the time or the will to convincingly implement this ideal.

8

Manchurian Candidate

JAPAN'S ONCE VAUNTED KWANGTUNG ARMY and its Manchukuo allies put up little resistance. Close behind the Soviet troops, 100,000 men of the Eighth Route Army under Lin Piao poured into Manchuria.[1] Except in the largest cities, the CCP everywhere quickly took charge of local administration, swept up the puppet troops, and appropriated the Japanese weapons captured by the Soviets. Believing that the Chinese National government would not have the strength to reestablish its authority over North China if it also attempted to occupy Manchuria, General Wedemeyer recommended that Chiang Kai-shek call for a temporary five-power guardianship over the region by the United States, Great Britain, France, China, and the Soviet Union.[2] Chiang rejected this advice.

The dynamics of the KMT-Communist struggle as well as the continuing intra-Kuomintang battles made Chiang's decision virtually inevitable. Manchuria was a vast territory of fifty million people, bordering on the Soviet Union and containing China's most important industrial and mining assets. The war had begun with Japan's aggression in Manchuria, and failure to assert the government's authority over it would have been a striking sign of weakness. It would have also cost Chiang Kai-shek the support of the large contingent of Manchurian troops fighting under the

Nationalist flag. But the issue of national unity was the most critical factor. Since 1911, unity had been the primary goal of all Chinese nationalists, whether KMT, Communist, or democratic. To have accepted Wedemeyer's advice would have meant Chiang Kai-shek's acquiescence in a *de facto* divided China. This he feared from a historical point of view, but also because such a move could have dislodged him from the leadership.[3]

Moreover, the Generalissimo believed he could prevail against the Communists in Manchuria. Encouraged by Chiang Ching-kuo, his principal adviser on Soviet affairs, the Gimo thought it was possible to induce Soviet cooperation by a combination of concessions and show of strength. Father and son calculated that there were compelling reasons for Stalin to live up to his commitments. The USSR was now one of only two superpowers. Its prestige was at a dizzying height. But Russia badly needed a breathing period, time to restore order, reconstruct a severely battered country, and develop its own nuclear arsenal to break the American monopoly. Thus a cooperative policy in a critical area like Manchuria seemed to be in its interest. In China itself, the Soviet leader's primary short-term goal was removal of the American military presence, which also required a reasonably benign Soviet posture.

Both Chiangs concluded that diplomacy with Moscow might succeed, but they also believed that there had to be a compelling military component to their strategy. Strengthening their hand, American planes flew 110,000 Nationalist troops into Peking, Tientsin, and other cities in North China. But none went into Manchuria because the Russians would not permit them to land. Concurrently, the Americans increased their pressure on the KMT and the CCP to find a political settlement. Ambassador Hurley flew to Yenan and escorted Mao and Zhou Enlai back to Chungking for a prolonged series of talks that would last from August 28 to October 11. Mao and Chiang Kai-shek had not met since 1926, when their parties were in the midst of the first united front. Now the dynamics were different. The Soviet Union occupied Manchuria, and CCP forces, not warlords, were entrenched in the countryside of North China and above the Great Wall.

Ching-kuo sat in on the Chungking talks and for the first and last time shook hands with Mao.[4] The mood was positive as both sides strove to appear genuinely committed to an agreement that would avoid civil war. At several receptions Mao led the gathering in shouting, "President Chiang Kai-shek, ten thousand years!"[5] Military skirmishes between the National Army and Communist forces, however, were already taking place on a regular basis in North China.

—

ON SEPTEMBER 4, 1945, Chiang Ching-kuo was appointed Special Foreign Ministry Commissioner for Manchuria. The Gimo also named Hsiung Shih-hui to be the senior Nationalist government official in Manchuria during the transition. Thus Hsiung, leader of the intellectual faction called the Political Science Clique, again would be Ching-kuo's superior. On October 1 the Soviets informed the ROC that Russian army withdrawal from the region would start at end of October. On the 12th, Ching-kuo and Hsiung flew to Ch'angch'un. Also on the team was Chang Kia-ngao, a respected economist and banker, whose responsibility was dealing with the Russians on economic affairs. Almost two months had gone by since the Russian attack into Manchuria, and Chinese Communist troops were now camped in the vicinity of Mukden and Ch'angch'un.[6] Nevertheless Ching-kuo was optimistic about the forthcoming talks with the Red Army Commander-in-Chief in Manchuria, General Rodion Y. Malinovsky. In his conversations with Chang Kia-ngao, Ching-kuo stressed the "great importance" of the Sino-Soviet relationship to China's future.[7]

The two teams met on October 13. The rugged, burly, and outspoken Malinovsky was a Soviet war hero, one of the commanders under Marshal Zhukov who had turned the tide at Stalingrad. Afterwards, Malinovsky led the Red Army in its streak across Manchuria.[8] The Russian general was agreeable, even friendly. Before the Chinese could ask, he pledged that the Red Army would disarm nongovernment forces in Manchuria. Ching-kuo then sought Malinovsky's permission to land Nationalist troops in Dairen and Port Arthur, both occupied by the Soviets under the Yalta agreement. The Russian refused, saying Dairen was a commercial port and Port Arthur a free port and thus military landings were inappropriate. The general suggested the government army land at the port of Hulutao. American ships with Chinese troops on board promptly sailed to Hulutao, but found unfriendly Chinese Communists already occupying the harbor. The American task force finally landed the troops south of the Great Wall, not in Manchuria at all.

When it came to implementation of other Soviet commitments, Ching-kuo ran into more stone walls. If he tried to make an appointment with Malinovsky or his staff, the general's office would often say it did not know where the officers were. Days went by without a response.[9] Ching-kuo noted in his diary, "Since our nation is not strong, I have to learn to swallow insults."[10] Chang Kia-ngao's efforts to talk in detail about economic matters did not fare much better. The Soviets demanded that virtually all industrial and mining enterprises in the region come under joint Sino-Soviet control.

The Nationalist military commander for the Northeast, General Tu Yu-ming, arrived in Ch'angch'un on October 29. Tu, a Whampoa graduate, had fought in Burma under Stilwell, who once described him as "Okay (and) . . . good on tactics," but later changed his mind. Chungking appointed Ching-kuo to the concurrent post of Director of the Political (now called, in deference to the Americans, the Information) Department of Tu's military forces in Manchuria.[11] That month, 500 Nationalist officials and bureaucrats flew into Ch'angch'un with the intention of fanning out through the region to assume control of local governments. But weeks went by and the Russians did not give permission for the officials to leave the city. As an explanation, Malinovsky's political commissar cited alleged anti-Soviet demonstrations throughout the region, which he blamed on the National government. Ching-kuo replied that Japanese or "traitors" had provoked any such activities.[12] At the same time, however, Ch'en Li-fu was arranging a series of anti-Soviet student demonstrations in various cities in China. At Ching-kuo's request, the Gimo rebuked Ch'en for these activities.[13]

Malinovsky finally gave permission for the Nationalist administrative personnel to take over various local governments, but he turned down Ching-kuo's request to borrow cars and aircraft for transport. In effect, the bureaucrats were still stuck in Ch'angch'un.[14] Malinovsky also informed Ching-kuo that Nationalist troops could only land by air four days prior to the Soviet withdrawal, the date of which was now becoming less certain. The Soviet commander again charged that thousands of secret KMT personnel were sabotaging Soviet facilities. When Ching-kuo raised the issue of surrendered Japanese arms, the general responded that all such weapons had been taken to the Soviet Union.[15]

On November 9 the Russian commander told Ching-kuo that his government had ordered him to turn over all post and telecommunications facilities and surplus weapons to the Chinese government. Instead, three days later, 2,000 of Lin Piao's soldiers moved into Ch'angch'un itself.[16] Ching-kuo, however, continued to urge patience. In this regard, he had increasing differences with Hsiung Shih-hui. Ching-kuo thought his superior was an "old bureaucrat" whose anti-Soviet attitude was "superficial" and lacked a "strategic perspective." For example, despite Soviet rejection of the idea, Hsiung wanted to send civilian personnel out to recruit and organize local troops. Ching-kuo believed this would be a disastrous move.[17]

Ching-kuo continued to tell his colleagues that they had to try everything possible to accommodate the Soviets in order to keep the Chinese Communists from consolidating their hold over the countryside.[18] But on November 7 Communist forces besieged Ching-kuo and several hundred Nationalist officials in the South Manchurian Railway Building in Ch'angch'un. A few days later, Malinovsky informed General Tu that the Soviet evacuation of Manchuria would be effected in three phases. After December 25, he said, Chinese National forces would be free to land anywhere in the region, except the two ports controlled by Russia.

About the same time, President Truman informed Chiang Kai-shek that he wished to send General George C. Marshall to mediate the dispute between the Nationalists and the Communists. Ch'en Li-fu warned the Gimo that Marshall's appearance would cause problems with the Soviets—and if, as was likely, Marshall failed in his mission, he would blame the Nationalists. It would be better, Ch'en suggested, to talk with the Soviets about the KMT-CCP problem. Ching-kuo agreed with this approach.[19]

Following this approach, the Gimo wrote to Stalin (probably in early November) suggesting a meeting to resolve the crisis. On November 13, Ching-kuo received a handwritten note from his father informing him that the government had decided to withdraw its Northeast headquarters.

"Let's see what the Soviet reaction is after a day or two," Chiang suggested. "If there is still hope of retrieving the situation, we can then indicate that *we really do not wish to establish our military power in the Northeast;* neither do we wish to provoke anyone. To create local political organizations we can use popular elections. In economics we can cooperate with the Soviets." (Italics added.)[20]

The most intriguing point in the Gimo's letter to Ching-kuo was the implication that under certain circumstances, Nationalist China would not seek to establish its military power throughout Manchuria and would in fact agree to extensive economic cooperation with Russia in the region. This language, very likely inspired by Ching-kuo, seemed to suggest a number of possibilities, including withdrawal of both government and Chinese Communist forces from parts or all of Manchuria, leaving Soviet troops in place in those areas. Meanwhile Chinese-Soviet economic cooperation throughout the region would blossom and local elections could be held.

At the same time, Chungking informed the Soviet embassy that because of the threatening activities of the Chinese Communists troops in Ch'angch'un, the Chinese government had no recourse but to withdraw from the city. The USSR, it warned, would be responsible for the consequences. Except for a handful of officers, including Ching-kuo and Chang Kia-ngao, the civilian government team in Manchuria departed for Peking on November 17, and the KMT military headquarters removed to Shanhaikuan on the coast.

The Soviet attitude in the talks suddenly changed. On November 21 Malinovsky told Ching-kuo that he was sorry the National government had withdrawn and that he did not know that Chinese Communists troops had surrounded their headquarters. The Russians then began to negotiate the economic issues in a seemingly serious manner. Chang Kia-ngao and Ching-kuo believed that the Nationalist withdrawal from Ch'angch'un and the threat of U.S. pressure had prompted the Soviets to move ahead with the negotiations.[21] By late November General Tu's troops, including Sun Li-jen's New First Army, were advancing northward along the coast, and this was thought also to have influenced the Russians. Around the beginning of December, Stalin, in response to the Gimo's message to him, suggested that a Nanking representative come to Moscow to discuss the Manchurian impasse.

Chang Kia-ngao and Ching-kuo argued that the government should not be too concerned about the potential economic loss in Manchuria. At Ching-kuo's urging, the Nationalists did not even make a public case against the extravagant Soviet pillaging of equipment and factories in the region.[22] Most of the facilities being carted off, Ching-kuo pointed out, were built by the Japanese. Realities, he believed, required "leaning toward the Soviets."[23] On November 24 the Russians presented Chang with a proposal for Sino-Soviet cooperation in 80 percent of Manchuria's heavy industry. Chang and Ching-kuo both favored giving the Russians what they wanted and working out an agreement along these lines.

A few days later the three senior Chinese officials in Manchuria went to Chungking for a meeting with the Generalissimo, Premier Soong, and Foreign Minister Wang. Soong argued that before discussing future economic cooperation with the Soviet Union, the political difficulties between China and the USSR had to be resolved—meaning Soviet withdrawal from Manchuria and the effective assumption of full administrative and economic control by the National government. Wang also opposed serious economic concessions at this point. Chiang Kai-shek appeared to back T. V. Soong and Wang. The Gimo authorized Chang Kia-ngao to tell the Russians that detailed discussions about economic cooperation would take place after withdrawal, but the two sides could begin to draw up a joint plan for economic reconstruction in Manchuria.[24]

The suggestion seemed to have a positive result. At a meeting on December 5 with Ching-kuo, Malinovsky agreed to several important points. He guaranteed the safe arrival at the Ch'angch'un airport of one division of government troops and did not object to the transport by rail of two divisions to Mukden. He also said the Soviets were making increased efforts to have armed forces not recognized by the government surrender their weapons. In addition, he agreed that the mayors appointed by the government could assume their duties. At the same meeting, the Russian indicated that to assure an orderly transition the withdrawal should be delayed until February 1, 1946.

It was in fact Mao who had requested the delay, but unaware of that, Ching-kuo and his colleagues believed that a postponement would be to the advantage of the Nationalists, and they convinced the Gimo of this.[25] Four days later, Ching-kuo informed Malinovsky that the Chinese government accepted the delayed deadline. A few weeks later the Gimo even approved payment of hard currency to the Soviet side to compensate it for "expenses incurred . . . as a result of postponing the date for withdrawing their troops." CCP and Soviet officials spread the word that the Nationalist government had requested the delay.[26]

Ching-kuo and Chang Kia-ngao were "delighted" with the new Russian attitude.[27] The Generalissimo told General Marshal on December 21 that the Russians had "stopped helping the Chinese Communists." As a result, he said, the Communists had suffered heavy losses in their actions against government troops and in order to gain time were now saying they wanted a political settlement.[28] Chiang Kai-shek and Ching-kuo, however, still believed that it was critical to demonstrate that the Nationalist government was willing and able to take over the region militarily if necessary.

Government forces were in fact moving quickly up the coast and along the major rail lines into the Northeast. By the end of December the Nationalists had captured most of the Manchurian ports, except Soviet-occupied Dairen and Port Arthur. Secretly, Malinovsky permitted the Communists to build a munitions complex in Dairen and to draft thousands of military recruits from the city and its suburbs.[29] Sun Li-jen's New First Army was well into central Manchuria, heading toward China's key industrial city of Mukden.[30]

Sun Li-jen by this time enjoyed a wide reputation as "100 percent a soldier," one of the few Chinese generals who did not play politics. At the end of the war with Japan, Eisenhower had confirmed Sun's status as America's favorite Chinese general by inviting him to tour the battlefields of Europe.[31] Sun's blunt and outspoken manner, however, strained his relations with his commander, Tu Yu-ming.[32] According to a former aide, if Sun had been an American, his nickname would have been Vinegar Joe.[33]

While Nationalist forces occupied lines of communications and the cities, Lin Piao was strengthening his control of the Manchurian countryside. With four months of forced conscription and incorporation of Manchukuo puppet forces, he increased the number of his PLA regulars and assembled a People's Self-Defense Army of around 150,000. He also brought in about 25,000 soldiers from the old Northeast Army of Chang Hsueh-liang. The CCP installed the Young Marshal's brother as titular commander of these forces and "governor" of Liaoning province.[34] By contrast, the Gimo assigned non-Manchurians to virtually all the key posts in the region.

Ching-kuo believed that the Nationalists were doing a poor job compared to the Communists in appealing to regional loyalties.[35] He was among those who, in the fall of 1945, suggested to the Gimo that he rehabilitate the Young Marshal and put him in charge of forming a new, locally recruited Northeast Army.[36] The Generalissimo rejected the idea, and Chang remained under house arrest. Soon he, his guards, and his companion, Miss Chao, moved to a new abode in the mountains outside Kanchow—the site of the Buddhist caves where Ching-kuo's family had spent the summers. At this tranquil site, the one Nationalist general who had at least some popular following in Manchuria sat out the critical period of the struggle for the Northeast.

The Gimo now asked Ching-kuo to go to Moscow and talk personally to Stalin about Manchuria. Before leaving, Ching-kuo approached Andrei Ledovski at the Soviet embassy. The Russian told Ching-kuo he enjoyed a good reputation in the Soviet Union and should simply speak to the point with Stalin and not try to flatter him.[37] Ching-kuo revealed to Ledovski an important concession that the Chinese side was prepared to make as part of an overall settlement—American capital investments would not be permitted in Manchuria, and the Soviet Union would not be denied any economic rights in China that were enjoyed by the United States.[38] Traveling alone, Ching-kuo left for the Soviet Union on Christmas Day, 1945. The trip was kept secret within the Chinese government, but Chiang Kai-shek informed General Marshall.

Ching-kuo's discussions with Stalin on December 30 and then again on January 3 took place in the context of the continued advance of Sun Li-jen's army and General Marshall's first diplomatic success. The KMT and the CCP accepted Marshall's proposals for a nationwide cease-fire to begin on January 10. The two Chinese parties also agreed to convene the multiparty Political Consultative Committee (PCC) that Chiang and Mao had accepted in principle in October. These developments should have improved the chances that Ching-kuo and Stalin could reach agreement on the future of Manchuria, provided the Russian leader was prepared to settle for something less than Communist control of the entire region.

In his briefing memorandum to Stalin, however, Foreign Minister Molotov offered a skeptical assessment of the young ex-Bolshevik:

> Now, about Chiang Ching-kuo. Just as Chiang Kai-shek is trying to maneuver between the USA and the USSR, Ching-kuo as a former Bolshevik Party member would also like to maneuver between us and his father, pretending he is a true friend of the USSR. Ching-kuo might even resort to criticism of his father. Chiang Kai-shek, however, would never send his son unless he was 100% sure that he would pursue his father's political goals. People close to Chiang Kai-shek don't like his son not only because in the past he belonged to the left, but also because he is the political heir. In practice, Ching-kuo is very mediocre and cannot even be compared to such a manipulator and politician as T. V. Soong. Conclusion: it is highly unlikely that Chiang Ching-kuo is authorized to sign any agreements with us. The objective of his trip to Moscow is to talk and maybe prepare the visit of Chiang Kai-shek himself.[39]

Molotov reported that Ching-kuo would seek Stalin's "moral and political assistance" against the "coming danger from the left" (the CCP) and in support of the Nationalist government's efforts to make the Communist troops cease fighting for control of Manchuria and northern China. The minister noted that Ching-kuo would float some concessions regarding the future role of America in China. He recounted Ching-kuo's indication that, as part of a comprehensive agreement, the Nationalist government would keep American capital out of Manchuria, and elsewhere in China the United States would receive no privileges denied to the Soviet Union. The young envoy, Molotov suggested, would question any further delay in the withdrawal of Soviet troops from Manchuria.[40]

Molotov recommended that, in response, Stalin demand the immediate pullout of all Americans from China, Nanking's recognition of the Mongolian Peoples Republic, and 50/50 joint ventures to run all former Japanese enterprises in Manchuria. He suggested Stalin stall on the troop withdrawal issue, explaining that Soviet outposts might be required for two to three years to protect rail lines and Soviet citizens.[41]

In their talks Ching-kuo did ask Stalin to negotiate between the KMT and the CCP and suggested that KMT-CPSU relations could be restored to the level of close cooperation like that which had existed in 1923–24.[42] Ching-kuo hinted at neutralization for China between the USSR and the

United States and a loosening of ties with Washington.[43] All American troops, he promised, would leave China as soon as they accomplished their mission of disarming and repatriating the Japanese. Presumably, he repeated the conditional pledge to which Molotov had referred of excluding American economic activity from Manchuria.[44] Further, he may have floated the policy line suggested by the Generalissimo in his November 13 letter to Ching-kuo, that the KMT government might not seek to establish its military power throughout Manchuria.

In response, Stalin declared that the KMT and the CCP should co-exist or else the KMT would grow ever more corrupt; the U.S. "open-door" policy was an instrument of imperialist invasion; and Nationalist China appeared to be friendly toward the Soviet Union but was actually hostile. If this continued, the Russian leader warned, the relationship could not last. The United States, he charged, wanted to use China as a tool, but when necessary would sacrifice China's interest. He said he did not want to interfere in China's internal affairs; the USSR was willing to have close relations with its neighbor, but the continued presence of American troops in China worsened the situation. The Soviet Union could help China establish heavy industry in Manchuria and develop the economy of Sinkiang, but Russia's most important condition was that China should not allow a single American soldier to remain in the country.[45]

Concluding on a conciliatory note, Stalin told Ching-kuo that if the American military withdrew from China, he would tell the CCP to come to an understanding with the Generalissimo and to support the KMT government. Ching-kuo responded that he thought he could get his father's approval for this condition in return for some convincing Soviet action. Stalin suggested that he and the Generalissimo meet somewhere on the border to discuss the issues.[46]

In between his meetings with the Soviet dictator, Ching-kuo took time to walk along the frozen Moscow River where he, Deng Xiaoping, and their girlfriends, Feng Fu-neng and Chang Hsi-ch'iung, used to stroll. He turned up Volkhonka Street to the old building at number 16. There, 20 years earlier, he and his friends had begun their grand and romantic adventure, determined to transform China and the world. Looking up the steps, he might have seen in the doorway the ghost of that wild revolutionary Karl Radek. There were many such ghosts wandering Moscow.

—

ON JANUARY 14 Ching-kuo returned to Chungking. Faina met him at the airport, but instead of going home he went immediately to report to the Gimo. Chiang Kai-shek was not impressed with Stalin's proposal that the Nationalists first kick the Americans out of China and then seek a Soviet deal in Manchuria. Despite his troubles with the Americans, Chiang at this stage was not about to swap still generous American assistance for vague promises from Stalin.

—

THE FAILURE OF CHING-KUO'S POLICY of accommodating Russia in hopes of winning its cooperation stirred strong criticism within the KMT. T. V. Soong adopted an attitude of "great indifference" to the issue, and Foreign Minister Wang, that of "extreme discretion."[47] After his return to Ch'angch'un, Ching-kuo found that his old Nanch'ang mentor, the intelligence officer Wen Ch'ang, had been posted there as head of Tai Li's operations in the region. In 1995 the aged Wen denied that he had been under instructions to keep a close watch on Ching-kuo in Manchuria.[48] But the younger Chiang's Trotskyite past, Russian experience, and pro-Soviet reputation made him particularly suspect to KMT elements that saw Communist conspiracies everywhere. The Gimo's enemies in the Party could now blame the failed policy toward Russia on his decision to give his son primary responsibility in this area. As a result, Ching-kuo's role in Manchuria sharply diminished. In late January Chang Kia-ngao reported that suspicion and mistrust between the Chinese and the Soviets were growing on a daily basis.[49]

On February 22 the CC brothers organized another series of large-scale anti-Soviet protests in Peking and other cities. Students destroyed the office of the CCP newspaper in Chungking and the *New China (Hsinhua) Daily* and broke into the Soviet embassy. The secretary of the Youth Corps in Ching-kuo's Youth Cadre School in Chungking, Ts'ai Hsing-san, planned for students at the school to participate in the demonstrations. As soon as Ching-kuo heard of the plans, however, he instructed Ts'ai to cancel them. Such protests, Ching-kuo said, would not have significant impact on the Soviet Union or the Chinese Communists but only cause trouble for the government.[50] As Ching-kuo predicted, Russian officers in Manchuria again cited the demonstrations as proof that the KMT was behind alleged anti-Soviet activities in Manchuria. These activities, they said, threatened public order and hence prevented compliance with the requests of the Nationalists.

In early March the Chinese government asked for the immediate withdrawal of all Russian forces from Manchuria. At this point. General Marshall and other U.S. officials believed that Chiang's government was bent on a policy of complete military occupation of Manchuria and the elimination of all Communist forces encountered.[51] It was also evident that the CCP sought the opposite goals. After the beginning of the cease-fire on January 10, Chinese Communist forces continued heavy deployment into Manchuria.[52] By mid-March Lin Piao's troops probably far outnumbered the 137,000 government forces in the region. On March 27 the Soviets informed the Chinese Foreign Ministry that they would be out of Manchuria by the end of April.

Meanwhile, the ROC's Political Consultative Council adopted a resolution demanding an investigation of the policies of Hsiung Shih-hui and Chiang Ching-kuo on the Manchurian issue. The attacks on Hsiung included accusations that he had also appropriated some ancient treasures in the Northeast and shipped them back in 150 pieces of luggage. The resolution called for Hsiung's removal and an end to the "localization" of negotiations, that is, Ching-kuo's assignment.[53] Some delegates directly criticized Ching-kuo's trip to Moscow.[54]

The Generalissimo said publicly that his government was trying to reach a reasonable settlement in the Northeast and that the Chinese people must not be misled by "groundless speculation."[55] He ordered that responsibility for negotiations with the Soviets over Manchurian issues be "returned to the central government," that is, back from Ch'angch'un to the Foreign Ministry. This was a victory for T. V. Soong and a rebuke to Ching-kuo. At the same time, however, the Gimo again reprimanded Ch'en Li-fu for organizing the recent student demonstrations.[56]

ON APRIL 15, the day after the Soviets withdrew from Ch'angch'un, Chinese Communist forces, which were already in the city, completed their occupation. In the words of the White Paper, "This was a flagrant violation of the cessation of hostilities order . . . It made the victorious Chinese Communist generals in Manchuria overconfident and less amenable to compromise, but (it also) . . . greatly strengthened the hand of the ultra-reactionary groups in the government."[57]

The Communists also took over the cities of northern Manchuria, including Harbin, a city of 800,000 situated only 350 miles from the Russian border. But overall, the military situation looked promising from the restored Nationalist capital of Nanking. Sun Li-jen's New First Army continued to advance steadily north from Mukden.[58] In the spring, the New Sixth Army defeated the Communists east of Mukden and joined up with Sun's force. The two American-trained armies recovered Ch'angch'un on May 23. In early June they pushed across the Sungari River. Another cease-fire order on June 6—agreed to as a result of pressure from General Marshall—saved Lin Piao's headquarters and permitted the central Manchurian front to stabilize along the Sungari for the remainder of 1946. Later, Chiang Kai-shek said this was his "most grievous mistake."[59]

More general world trends began to feed militancy in Moscow as well as in Nanking and Yenan. The Cold War was in its early stages. On March 5 Churchill proclaimed the descent across Europe of the Iron Curtain. Feeling more confident, the Gimo demanded Communist withdrawal from specified provinces and cities in North China as part of any peace agreement. Not surprisingly, Mao refused.

CHANG KIA-NGAO BLAMED the diplomatic failure in Manchuria not only on Soviet intentions but on "radicals in the Nationalist Party who stirred up a crazy, anti-Communist, anti-Soviet movement, which eventually resulted in the breakdown of Sino-Soviet negotiations."[60] But Chang also concluded that given Soviet power and the situation in Manchuria, a military victory there for the National government was highly unlikely. Therefore, he concluded, Nanking should simply have taken the best deal it could from the Russians and accepted for the time being *de facto* partition of China at the Great Wall.[61]

Ching-kuo, on the other hand, believed that if his government demonstrated it had a military option on the one hand, and made major concessions to Moscow on the other, some acceptable solution was possible, such as the "temporary" partition of Manchuria. Although Ching-kuo adopted a low posture on Soviet affairs, he remained deeply involved behind the scenes. He was in fact still his father's principal adviser on Russia, and he still advocated keeping the door open for better relations. Ching-kuo also kept in touch with the Soviet embassy and in April or May paid a call on the Soviet military attaché, General Roschin. Speaking tentatively, Ching-kuo revived the possibility of a summit between Chiang Kai-shek and Stalin. According to Roschin, Stalin accepted the idea, proposed a meeting in Moscow, and put a Soviet airplane at the Gimo's disposal, but nothing happened.[62]

A minor but interesting example of Ching-kuo's persistent hope that there could be a rapprochement with Moscow was a message he sent to General Wedemeyer's office on April 18, 1946. In it Ching-kuo insisted that the American air force give up a hostel in Nanking so that it could be turned over to the Soviets to use as part of their embassy.[63]

WITHIN A YEAR the military tide would begin to turn, and Manchuria would prove to be the trap that Wedemeyer, Chang Kia-ngao, and others feared. Chiang Kai-shek, however, felt compelled to stake everything on the outcome in Manchuria, and from a political and even a military perspective this was probably the right decision. To have done otherwise would have created a divided China and probably a more bloody civil war than the quite terrible one that did occur. It might also have been a conflict that could have drawn in the United States.

Criticized for his failed mission in Manchuria, Ching-kuo's political standing diminished. For the next two years his visibility was relatively low. This would have the unintended effect of minimizing his responsibility for the shattering economic, political, and military failures that were to come.

9

Defeat

IN THE EARLY STAGES of the civil war, the strength of the Nationalist armed forces fell from 3 million in August 1945 to 2.6 million in 1946.[1] Trimming down to a leaner, more effective force had been a key recommendation of the Americans. Ching-kuo moved to the Ministry of Defense in Nanking and took charge of the office responsible for demobilization of the Youth Army. Unlike most other discharged soldiers, who were lucky to receive a small packet of mustering-out pay and be sent on their way, Youth Army veterans enjoyed various types of support and a high-level patron who looked after their interests.[2]

Ching-kuo instituted a sort of GI Bill for his soldiers.[3] Youth Army veterans returning to civilian life received many favors—an advantage in the competition for teaching positions, for example—so they constituted a strong core of Ching-kuo supporters.[4] Ching-kuo and his father also envisaged the demobilized Youth Army veterans as forming elite units of the National Army Reserve.[5]

To retain all of his veterans as an organizational force, Ching-kuo established branches of a civilian Youth Army Soldiers' Federation in Peking, Shanghai, and several other cities. His main hope was that his young veterans would be able to counter the political activities of pro-Communist youth.[6] Meanwhile, Ching-kuo's trusted associate, Hu Kui, became the executive secretary in charge of day-to-day operations of the Youth Corps.[7]

—

IN NANKING CHING-KUO LIVED ON CHUNGSHAN ROAD, the tree-lined thoroughfare of government buildings, in a military hostel (in the late 1990s it was still functioning as the Chungshan Guest House). Ching-kuo's former personal secretary, Ts'u Sung-Ch'iu, shared a room with him. For a Nationalist lieutenant general this was a modest living arrangement. A fifteen-minute walk away was the presidential office and the Ministry of Defense. Over the next two years, Ching-kuo would begin his day with a morning jog. After a shower, he would call on his father, who was more likely to want to discuss Mencius than Manchuria. He spent long hours at his own offices in the ministry and on inspection trips to Youth Corps and Youth Army headquarters and offices around the country.

According to his colleagues, Ching-kuo chose to have his family live separate from him in Hangchow because of his long work hours and frequent trips out of Nanking. He also wanted to shield his children as much as possible from the attention and catering that the Gimo's grandchildren would inevitably receive. But Ching-kuo went home on a regular basis, and sometimes Faina and the children—a second boy, Alex, had been born in 1945—came to Nanking and stayed with the Generalissimo and his wife, both of whom were very fond of their handsome, Eurasian grandchildren—or step-grandchildren in her case.

One aide recalled taking twelve-year-old Alan to a swimming pool, but he found the lad so willful and disobedient that he spanked him.[8] On at least one occasion, Chang Ya-juo's brother quietly brought the twins to see Ching-kuo in Nanking. But sometime after this Ching-kuo made a pledge, perhaps to his father but more likely just to himself, that he would never see the boys again. Although he continued to provide support through Wang Sheng and later established an affectionate relationship from a distance, quite remarkably and rather strangely he lived up to this pledge for the rest of his life.[9]

In the Chekiang capital Faina once again found herself in a city where she knew no one. She had lived in China ten years but was still a foreigner. Her Ningpo dialect, however, was much better understood in Hangchow than in Kanchow or Chungking, and she made friends with several wives of local Chinese officials. She took up Chinese painting and also mahjong, a pastime Ching-kuo disliked.[10]

An officer who worked with Ching-kuo reported that because Ching-kuo was an "honest and clean" official, his wife had to manage her household with a limited budget, and Madame Chiang, without telling Ching-kuo, frequently provided small gifts of money to help out.[11] Despite the long separations and very likely Ching-kuo's occasional affairs with other women, he and Faina remained close as man and wife in appearance and apparently in reality. At this time Feng Fu-neng, his Moscow sweetheart, was married and living in Nanking, but there is no indication that she and Ching-kuo ever met again.[12]

Shortly after the war with Japan ended, Ching-kuo and his father made a short visit to Hsikou and arranged for workers to restore the war-damaged Feng Hao Fang and the rest of the Chiang properties. In December Ching-kuo went back to Hsikou with his family to attend his mother's reburial. In contrast to the stunning mountain view from the tomb of Ching-kuo's grandmother, his mother's resting place was an eight-foot high mound of earth behind a small temple on the outskirts of town. Following the traditional procedure, Ching-kuo sought a distinguished person to write the epitaph. His old mentor, Wu Chih-hui, obliged. Wu's inscription, "My late mother, Grand Madame Mao," discreetly avoided any reference to a relationship with Chiang Kai-shek.[13] According to those who were present, Ching-kuo wept profusely at the ceremony.[14]

CHING-KUO WENT FREQUENTLY to Shanghai to deal with growing student agitation. His most important asset in trying to counter Communist activity on the campuses of Shanghai were the several thousand Youth Army veterans in the city, especially the 500 or so who were now university students. Although he could have used the mass organizations at his disposal in an intimidating manner, he refused to do so. The head of the Youth Army Federation in Shanghai at the time, Ch'en Chih-ching, recalled how on one occasion Ching-kuo responded to a student strike at

Fudan University. Chiang mobilized a mass meeting of Youth Army veterans who were also students to demand a return to classes. The veterans rallied as instructed, but a large group of leftist students formed a wall at the entrance to the University and barred their entry. Instead of ordering the pro-KMT students to break through the human barrier, Ching-kuo commanded them to move to Hungku Park where he would address them. In his speech Ching-kuo stressed that it was the Communists who were using force to prevent students from meeting on their own campus. This showed that "in the future, we have much more work to do at the universities."

In Manchuria the war continued. Ching-kuo approached Roschin again in August and October, denied that the Nationalist government was following a pro-American policy, and once more raised the possibility of a summit with Stalin.[15] In August President Truman warned the Generalissimo that American aid would not continue unless there was genuine progress toward a peace settlement. New truces in the civil war fell apart, however, and Nationalist troops occupied two key towns in North China long held by Communist forces now called the PLA (Peoples Liberation Army). Lin Piao's troops crossed the frozen Sungari and attacked Sun Li-jen's soldiers in their winter camps, then retreated north again. In December 1946 Truman reaffirmed the American policy of noninterference in China's civil war. The U.S. Marines in North China withdrew, and Marshall departed China to become the new American secretary of state. Prior to leaving he issued a statement blaming "reactionaries" on the KMT side and "radicals" in the CCP for the failure of his peace mission.

IN THE COURSE OF THE NEXT MONTH, tragic events in Taiwan highlighted the fundamental weakness of the KMT—the large number of senior officials for whom high office meant primarily the opportunity, indeed the obligation, to enrich themselves and their families and associates. Japan had seized Taiwan in the Sino-Japanese War of 1895. In September 1945, Nationalist forces assisted by small American teams had landed on the island and taken over its administration. Taiwan had prospered economically under the Japanese, was agriculturally self-sufficient, and enjoyed a moderate industrial base. Although its ports and transport facilities had suffered heavy damage in the war, the island's economy was in better shape than that of any other province in China. Nevertheless the islanders—98 percent ethnic Chinese—had always resented Japan's harsh colonial rule, and at first they welcomed the Nationalists as liberators.

The Gimo had appointed as governor of Taiwan sixty-two-year-old General Ch'en Yi, an associate since 1911. A large retinue of mainlanders accompanied Ch'en to the island and took over political, administrative, and security posts. They also assumed control of state-run economic enterprises and immediately began a process of personal enrichment. General Wedemeyer, who tried to help the Chinese government in every way he could, reported that the Nationalist troops had "conducted themselves as conquerors."[16]

On February 28 protests in Taipei over the arrest of a woman selling cigarettes escalated into a major rebellion. Ch'en Yi blamed the uprising on pro-Japanese members of the Taiwan elite and radical elements who opposed having the island revert to China. Chiang Kai-shek sent a high-level delegation to Taiwan to confer with local leaders and restructure the provincial government. The Taiwanese community, represented by a hastily organized Taipei Resolution Committee, also adopted a moderate tone, retracting its earlier demands for abolishment of the Taiwan Garrison Command and the disarming of Nationalist troops. Dissidents in the streets, however, were out of control, and some extremists attacked government, police, and military offices.[17]

On March 9 Nationalist troops executed hundreds of listed individuals and mowed down thousand on the streets. These were traditional "pacification" tactics intended to "kill the chicken to scare the monkey." (In 1995 the Kuomintang apologized for its handling of the February affair and admitted to the staggering figure of 18,000 to 28,000 deaths.) On March 17 Defense Minister Pai Ch'ung-hsi led a delegation of military and political leaders, including Ching-kuo, to Taipei to investigate the situation.[18] After a three-week stay, Pai issued a statement that defended the governor's handling of the matter. On April 17 the American ambassador gave President Chiang a completely different view of the uprising. Within a few days Chiang replaced Ch'en Yi with a civilian governor, but found another appointment for him.

—

IN THE EARLY PART OF 1947, although Lin Piao launched several successful small scale offensives across the Sungari, the Gimo's forces generally appeared to retain the initiative in Manchuria. In March of 1947, in what was their high water mark in the war, the Nationalists captured Mao's capital of Yenan.

The Kuomintang, meanwhile, continued with its internal squabbles. A struggle over control of the Central Political Institute highlighted the growing rivalry between the CC Clique and Ching-kuo. The Gimo appointed Ching-kuo to replace Ch'en Kuo-fu as Dean of the Institute, but Ching-kuo declined the position after the Ch'ens "had stirred up the students to demonstrate against his appointment."[19] On the real field of battle, Lin Piao mustered 400,000 troops and struck across the Sungari River in June. Rolling back Sun Li-jen's outnumbered First Army, the Communists drove deep into Nationalist territory, seized large quantities of military equipment and supplies, and then advanced toward Mukden. Tu Yu-ming counterattacked, using to good effect his control of the air, and Lin Piao retreated back to the Sungari. Both sides suffered serious losses in this campaign, but it was clear the Communists were growing stronger.

Ching-kuo became pessimistic about the prospects in Manchuria. He did not criticize Tu by name but privately complained that government troops sent to Manchuria "did not have the support of the people, nor did they maintain good relations with the local armed forces." In the end, Ching-kuo said, Tu's troops were "a burden" to the government, "not an asset."[20]

On July 4, 1947, the State Council adopted a resolution for a general mobilization to suppress "the Communist rebellion." The Gimo shook up the Manchurian command, removing Tu Yu-ming as regional commander.[21] In September, Mao issued his directive ordering the PLA to go on the strategic offensive. With alarming speed, the promising military situation suddenly grew bleak. Ching-kuo and his colleagues, like the "old China hands" in the State Department, blamed the setbacks on continued corruption and ineptness at the senior levels of the KMT, the government, and the army. The disaster on Taiwan, which Ching-kuo had seen firsthand, underscored this reality.

Associates of Ching-kuo once more talked among themselves about the desirability of making the Youth Corps a competing political party to challenge the corrupt KMT. Ching-kuo wrote a booklet entitled "Our Suggestions for the Corps" that seemed to hint at this possibility. In early September the Youth Corps held its second National Congress at the mountain resort of Lushan. Prior to the meetings, Ching-kuo stalwarts met in his room at the conference site to discuss the concept of a competing party.

Ch'en Li-fu, members of the Whampoa clique, and other KMT seniors heard of the discussions, however, and stormed the Gimo's office to denounce the very idea.[22] While Chiang Kai-shek was himself frustrated with the Party's performance and that of his ministers and generals, he was opposed to the notion of a competing party. In view of his father's position Ching-kuo backed off the proposal, though some of his followers persisted in pushing for establishment of a new Youth Corps Party. Ching-kuo's cadre raised the possibility at the conference. Chiang Kai-shek came to the podium and put his foot down in no uncertain terms: "You are so muddle-headed! . . . I am already chairman of the Kuomintang. Can I lead another party at the same time?"[23]

Yet the Generalissimo went on to lament that the KMT as well as the Youth Corps were "mere empty shells without any real strength."[24] Going in the opposite direction of a competing party, the Gimo ordered the merging of the Youth Corps back into the KMT and elimination of its separate executive committee. Thus ended the corps's brief, formal status as a supposedly independent organization. The CC brothers and other factions were pleased. As compensation, Ching-kuo became a member of the Party's highest ruling body and in addition assumed the position of vice-chairman, under the Gimo's nominal chairmanship, of a new Central Training Committee in Party headquarters.[25]

Desperate for some organizational salvation to counter the Communists, Ching-kuo conceived the idea of special units of Youth Army veterans to be called—in the stilted language of Chinese organizational names—Insurrection Suppression and National Reconstruction Brigades. These brigades were to do political work in combat areas, winning hearts and minds and preventing the loss of popular support that seemed to follow in the train of the National Army. The Gimo approved the plan, and Ching-kuo proceeded to organize a number of the units—again, mostly with volunteers who were Youth Army veterans.[26] Ching-kuo officially became commander of the new brigades, but the effort was too little, too late, and the brigades had virtually no impact.

The Communists resumed their offensive in Manchuria, repeatedly severing the rail lines connecting the principal cities. Nationalist garrisons more and more relied on Clair Chennault's new private company, Civil Air Transport (CAT), to fly in supplies. The Gimo knew that militarily and politically he had lost the initiative. Increasingly, he made disparaging comments about his senior army officers. The spirit of most commanders, he said on one occasion, was broken and "their morality was base." Once he even expressed admiration for the discipline and honesty of the Communist officers.[27]

In December, as pessimism was suddenly spreading in Nanking, Vice Minister of Foreign Affairs George Yeh told Ambassador Stuart that the Soviets had lately been sounding more conciliatory. The principal channel of this "flirtation," according to Yeh, was a group of high-ranking officers in the Ministry of Defense who had received training in the Soviet Union and who spoke Russian—most prominently, Chiang Ching-kuo.[28] According to Yeh, Ching-kuo and his colleagues were advocating a political settlement with the Communists as "the only solution" and seeking a "closer understanding" with the Soviet Union to achieve this goal. General Roschin, the Soviet military attaché, was reportedly encouraging Ching-kuo and his group.[29]

After the military setbacks in the second half of 1947, Ching-kuo did in fact again advocate exploration of the possibilities with Moscow. The Gimo saw that such an initiative might at least serve as a pressure tactic against the Americans. This thinking was evident in early December, when Vice President Sun Fo publicly warned that if the United States did not provide major assistance to the Nationalist government, it would fall into the Soviet orbit.[30] About the same time, the young Chiang told Roschin that his father was now ready to consider the points made by

Stalin during the January 1946 meetings with Ching-kuo, and that the Gimo would be willing to visit Moscow.[31]

General Chang Chih-chung told Stuart that at a lunch he had on December 19 with the Gimo and Ching-kuo, Chiang Kai-shek had authorized him to feel out the possibilities with Moscow of renewing negotiations with the CCP. Chiang also indicated that Ching-kuo had already made a preliminary approach on this subject to the Soviet embassy.[32] In his reporting cable to Washington, Stuart speculated that the Gimo was perhaps trying to stir American interest by letting it out that he was exploring the possibilities with Moscow. Stuart concluded that because the Communists were "winning on all sides," it seemed "inconceivable" that they would accept peace talks.[33]

The Soviet leader probably chuckled when he read the cables from his embassy in Nanking reporting the overtures from the Chiangs. At this stage Stalin, who apparently never authorized a response, would have replied to these feelers only if Mao had agreed.[34] Stalin had waited twenty years for this. Now the time had come for the final twisting of the lemon.

No sooner had the new Nationalist commander, the respected Ch'en Ch'eng, proclaimed the military crisis in Manchuria to be over, than Lin Piao captured key towns in Liaoning and opened up a sea link with Shantung. Although the Nationalists now possessed almost half a million men in the region, they controlled only one percent of the area. Lin Piao settled down to refit his troops with newly captured American weapons. Ch'en Ch'eng, pleading illness, departed his headquarters in Ch'angch'un.[35]

The head of the U.S. Military Advisory Group in China, Major General David Barr, urged Chiang to withdraw his forces from the Northeast before they were destroyed. If the Gimo had in fact saved his nearly half million men and enormous arsenals in Manchuria, the outcome of the final showdown battle of Huaihai, below the Great Wall, might have been different. Chiang, however, still believed that such a retreat would signal the loss of the "mandate of heaven," and that it was far better for his forces to fight to the last man.

By early 1948 Stalin knew that Mao Zedong would be able to take all of Manchuria sometime within the year. Direct American intervention on the mainland now seemed highly unlikely. For the Soviet leader the outlook in Manchuria confirmed the prospect of another revolutionary upsurge around the world. A Communist China now seemed inevitable, and this momentous event would be a major factor in the changing "correlation of world forces."[36]

Indeed, sometime during the year, Soviet scientists informed Stalin that they would explode their first atomic bomb in 1949. In a show of force the Red Army blockaded West Berlin in June, and the Allies responded with a massive airlift. Czech Communists ousted the democratic government in Prague; the Malayan Communist Party began its guerrilla war against the British; and Ho Chi-minh and the Vietnam Peoples Army trained and waited in the mountains for the arrival of their Chinese Communist allies on Vietnam's northern border.

One major setback for Moscow was Marshal Tito's break with Stalin. Some in the West hoped that eventually Mao would become a Chinese Tito. Stalin did not fully trust Mao, but in 1948 he recognized that if his global strategy was to succeed, he could not treat the Chinese as he had other Communist leaders. He understood that China would be "his partner and rarely if ever his pawn."[37]

ONE HOT AUGUST DAY Lin Piao made the final inspection of his 700,000 troops. They were ready, even eager for the assault on the Nationalist Army ensconced in Ch'angch'un, Mukden, and a few other urban strongholds in Manchuria. The Peoples Liberation Army was well armed and morale was high. In contrast to Nationalist units, which consisted mainly of boys from the south, three of Lin Piao's best divisions were composed of ethnic Korean residents of Manchuria.[38]

After installing a Communist regime in Pyongyang in 1945, Soviet advisers had quickly built up a large and well-equipped North Korean army. Between 1946 and 1948 Kim Il-sung was able to send the PLA more than 2,000 railway cars of war material and even some of his own Soviet-trained troops as "volunteers." North Korea's key role as a strategic rear base and safe haven for the PLA was another key factor in the struggle for the Northeast.[39] This historic contribution to the CCP's cause would ensure that Mao in 1950 would send his own "volunteers" to save Kim.

ON THE WAR MAP most of China above the Yellow River was now splashed crimson, except for major cities and corridors along the rail lines connecting them. To many Chinese, however, the main enemy was inflation, not the Communists. The cost of the war had created huge budget deficits, and speculators, profiting from the chaos, fanned the resulting flames of inflation. Wholesale prices in Shanghai increased five-fold from September 1945 to February 1946, and thirtyfold again one year later. The government tried everything, including pegging wages to the cost of living, freezing prices and wages, and rationing industrial materials as well as consumer goods, but nothing worked. A standard sack of rice sold for 6.7 million yuan in June 1948, and 63 million yuan in August.[40]

On August 18 a government edict required all citizens to turn in any gold and silver bullion they held, plus all of their old currency, the *fabi* yuan, in exchange for a new currency called the gold yuan. The rate of exchange was 3 million *fabi* to 1 gold yuan. At the same time, Nanking forbade wage and price increases and banned strikes and demonstrations. There was widespread hope, if not belief, that this time the government meant what it said and would strictly enforce its decree. The government's three special control areas centered on Shanghai, Canton, and Tientsin.[41] The test was Shanghai, whose control region included Nanking and the provinces of Kiangsu, Chekiang, and Anhui. If the reforms could work in Shanghai, they could work anywhere.

On August 21 the Gimo appointed O. K. Yu as Supervisor of Economic Control in Shanghai and granted him police powers. Yu was from a wealthy business family in Shanghai and had done graduate work in the United States at the University of Michigan.[42] O. K.'s appointment, however, was a ceremonial one. His deputy was Chiang Ching-kuo. Few had any doubt that young Chiang would be in charge. Chiang Kai-shek noted in his diary: "Although I know that this appointment may cause Ching-kuo resentment and may sacrifice his career as well, I need to send him anyhow. Ching-kuo is the only person who can undertake this job."[43]

CHING-KUO ARRIVED IN SHANGHAI on August 20 and set to work. The English-language press referred to him as "the general-in-charge of economic war in Shanghai."[44] As a first step, he sent instructions to Wang Sheng to bring the Sixth Suppression and Reconstruction Brigade to Shanghai. When the brigade arrived, Ching-kuo expanded its size with Youth Army veterans in the city. He dispatched additional brigades to the three provinces under his authority. Not trusting the municipal bureaucracies, Ching-kuo also appointed squads from the brigade to the various security organizations in the city, including the Shanghai police, the garrison command, the economic police, and the railway police.[45]

Notices soon appeared that informants who denounced noncompliers would receive 30 percent of the value of confiscated gold, silver, foreign currency, or hoarded material.[46] Citizens could also write down tips and drop them in streetcorner suggestion boxes. Reports from the public began flowing into Ching-kuo's office in the Central Bank Building on Chiuchiang Road.[47] Meanwhile, unorganized groups of young men and women rushed to supplement the work of the police and Wang Sheng's brigade. Both official and unofficial posses spread out across the metropolis, making random searches for hoarded goods in markets, godowns (warehouses), and factories, checking reported inventories with actual quantities on hand.

Ching-kuo and his associates reviewed the reports of skullduggery and, when appropriate, ordered raids on suspected establishments.[48] Miscreants received speedy trials and fines or jail sentences. Corrupt officials faced the most severe punishment. A special criminal tribunal sentenced a secretary in the Finance Ministry and two Garrison Command officers to death.[49]

David Kung, a member of both the Kung and Soong families, owned an import-export business in the city (the Yangtze Company), and his business practices had earned him the nickname of Nanking Tiger. He was close to Tu Yue-sheng, the Green Gang leader, who himself had several nicknames: Big Ears Tu and Fruit Yue-sheng was also sometimes called Economic Tiger.[50]

In addition to heading the underworld, Tu held important posts in the Bank of China, the Communications Bank, and the Shanghai Stock Exchange. He had long maintained close contacts with T. V. Soong and H. H. Kung and was allegedly a sworn brother of Chiang Kai-shek's. When Chiang Ching-kuo arrived in Shanghai, Tu invited him to dinner, but young Chiang sent regrets. Tu was not used to such rebuffs.[51]

Another "tiger" was Wan Mou-lin, a trusted follower and "nephew" of Tu's who had made large profits dealing in rice during the Japanese occupation. Wan enjoyed the cognomen Rice Tiger.[52] Early on, one of Ching-kuo's brigade-police teams arrested Rice Tiger for illegally storing rice, forcing the price up, and misappropriating government grain loans. In an even bolder move, Ching-kuo took in Tu's son, Tu Wei-p'ing, for speculation, hoarding, and illegal stock transactions. On the same day (September 3) he arrested the managers of the Sung Sing Cotton Mill, the Yung Tai Ho Cigarette Company, and the Wing On Cotton Mill (in which T. V. Soong had an interest) as well as the chairmen of the Cotton Cloth Dealers Guild, the Paper Dealers' Guild, the Edible Oil Dealers Guild, and the Rice Dealers' Guild. The brigade members developed a chant, "We beat tigers, we do not swat flies!" and were soon known as Tiger-Beating Teams.

Ching-kuo instructed the guild leaders to order their respective members "to dump their stocks at the market prices quoted on August 19." Wing On, for example, was charged with holding its production of cloth in godowns after the price controls went into effect. Except for young Tu and one or two others, the businessmen were permitted to post bail and return home.[53] The next day there were more arrests of leading businessmen.[54] On September 7 the Shanghai Bankers Association agreed that all commercial banks in the city would turn over their foreign currency and gold bullion holdings to the central government.[55] With intelligence reports in hand, Ching-kuo went to Nanking and insisted on the arrest of the Finance Ministry's Currency Department head, Tai Ming-lin. Tai reportedly implicated a number of other high officials and financiers in illegal smuggling of foreign currency and gold from Shanghai banks to Hong Kong.[56]

Even the international community in Shanghai was impressed. The English-language *North China Daily News* observed on September 11 that "The experience of the past three weeks, which has shown the masses that it is possible to import a degree of reality into existing circumstances, has aroused a very considerable amount of hope."

By then the new reforms had been in effect for almost one month, and prices had stabilized remarkably.[57] The wholesale index had risen only 6 percent in this period.[58] Over three thousand profiteers had been arrested. But Ching-kuo concluded that inflation was not the core problem. The only way the KMT could reverse its decline was to cease being the party of the establishment and to become again a party of social revolution. On September 12 he addressed a mass meeting of 5,000 Youth Army veterans in the Shanghai Gymnasium. He led the crowd in singing a song called "Two Tigers" and in shouting "down with profiteers and speculators," "make revolution," "root out corrupt forces!" The hall shook with enthusiasm.

Ching-kuo made it clear that his real goal was not merely to hold down prices but to end the unequal distribution of wealth throughout the country. While making only one reference to "Communist bandits," he focused on the depredations of the rich:

> We had to fight our foreign enemy . . . the imperialists . . . now we have enemies at home . . . local tyrants and evil gentry in the rural areas and speculators and profiteers in urban areas.[59] . . . the new economic policies promulgated by the government are not simple laws and decrees but are designed for a social revolutionary campaign and mark the beginning of the implementation of the Principle of the People's Livelihood. Stabilizing prices is only a technical work; our objective is to put an end to the unequal distribution of wealth. To be more specific, we should prevent the rich from getting richer while the poor are becoming poorer.[60]

He dismissed criticism that because of his controls some factories might close: "Those who can afford to buy perfume and eat plenty of pork are very few. It does not matter if pork and perfumes disappear from the markets. As long as the people do not starve, it does not matter if all the department stores and big restaurants are closed."[61]

In his diary Ching-kuo expressed his distaste for the rich even more vividly: "Their wealth and their foreign-style homes are built on the skeletons of the people."[62] He assured the business community that the government would continue to protect private property and encourage private enterprise, but he also denounced "so-called economists who claim that if we want to solve economic problems, we should proceed from the economic point of view." Such people are wrong, he asserted: "the economic structure is based on social and political forces."[63]

At this stage in his life Ching-kuo still read Marxist books: one Sunday morning a staff member found him in the garden of his house at

2 Yi Ts'un Road reading Lenin's *Collected Works* in Russian.[64] Ching-kuo also drafted slogans for posters that appeared around the city. One of these was "Down with wealthy family capital!" This was widely interpreted to be an allusion to the Four Families (the Soongs, Chiangs, Kungs, and Ch'ens), so Ching-kuo changed the wording to "Down with bureaucratic capital," another leftist term.[65]

The key slogan, and Ching-kuo's favorite, was "make revolution, fight on two fronts!" "Make revolution," he explained, meant carrying out the behest of Sun Yat-sen, supporting Chiang Kai-shek, and accomplishing the national revolution under the Three Peoples Principles. "Fight on two fronts" meant opposing the Communist Party but at the same time fighting corrupt, reactionary forces within the Kuomintang and local gangsters.[66]

Ching-kuo gave a simple, low-key statement of the challenge facing the Chinese people: "China is a fine nation with abundant resources and manpower. If all these can be well utilized under able leadership, not only can China become a strong nation but she may also lead the world."[67] The moment of truth was fast approaching. The success or failure of their campaign, he told his friends, would "determine the destiny of the nation . . . and of our group as well."[68]

To the north, catastrophic defeat for the Nationalist government, unimaginable only a year earlier, now loomed on the horizon. The Liaoshen campaign to defeat the Nationalists in the Northeast was gathering dramatic momentum. Mao issued a death list of the "enemies of the people," which of course included Chiang Ching-kuo, Chiang Kai-shek, and all the Soongs and Kungs, except Ching-ling. The number of Communist agents, organizers, and agitators in the city was legion: indeed, they infested Ching-kuo's own office. Yet Ching-kuo did not stress the threat of Communist subversion. In his public remarks he continued to avoid political invective against the Communists, aside from occasional routine references to them as "bandits." He had no desire to repeat his father's 1927 purge of the Communists in Shanghai. More importantly, he recognized that any such pogrom would backfire.[69]

ALTHOUGH CHING-KUO WORKED LONG HOURS, seven days a week, at night he usually relaxed at lively dinners with his friends. Sometimes an affable Moscow classmate, Wang Hsin-heng (head of the city's Military Investigation Bureau), arranged parties that included Shanghai movie stars and "social butterflies." Faina and the children came for visits to the Western-style house at No. 2 Yi Ts'un, but lived mostly in Hangchow. According to a close associate, however, Ching-kuo did not, during this short Shanghai period, become involved in an extra-marital affair.[70]

Ching-kuo obtained his father's approval for his basic policies in Shanghai and kept O. K. Yu and Mayor K. C. Wu informed. But essentially he ran the city's economic, financial, commercial, and related police functions without seeking anyone's approval. K. C., a Princeton graduate close to Madame Chiang, felt that he had lost face and he submitted his resignation to Chiang Kai-shek. The Gimo rejected it.[71] Another Shanghai Wu, however, was happy with Ching-kuo's performance and encouraged him to stick to his guns: this was Ching-kuo's old mentor, Wu Chih-hui. One day a businessman who was under investigation came to the Economic Control Office with a letter written by Wu Chih-hui to Ching-kuo. The letter asked Ching-kuo not to punish the letter bearer for the economic crimes with which he was charged. A half hour later another letter arrived from Wu explaining that the businessman, an acquaintance, had threatened suicide if Wu did not write Ching-kuo. Wu urged his former student to disregard the first letter and handle the case according to the law.[72]

In the last half of September, for a brief, happy moment Ching-kuo thought he could succeed in replicating in Shanghai and then in Central China the complex of popular reforms he had instituted in Kannan. According to a *Central News Agency* report, the workers of Shanghai fervently believed that "so long as the 'great friend of the little man' is here beside them, they can rest assured that they will never go through exploitation at the hands of 'big-time speculators.'"[73] The same news agency reported, however, that "big business and influential families" were brewing intrigues to unseat Ching-kuo.

ROBERT SERVICE, then in the American Consulate General in Hong Kong, reported to Washington that Tu Yue-sheng, the Green Gang leader, was extremely angry at the arrest of his son. To demonstrate to Ching-kuo that his scion was being singled out, Tu provided evidence of economic crimes in Shanghai linked to "the four families" as well as to certain North China military leaders.[74] A few days later Service reported that T. V. Soong had sent his wife to Shanghai to persuade Ching-kuo to adopt a lenient attitude on the Wing On case.[75]

Ching-kuo talked to his father about Tu's son, and on September 24 the Gimo dispatched a telegram to Tu that was published in a Shanghai newspaper, the *Shen Pao*: "I would be grateful if you would assist Ching-kuo in his economic control in Shanghai."[76] This seemed to be a public declaration by the Gimo that he would not intervene to free Tu's son. The scenario is obscure, but apparently, after receiving the telegram, Tu came to see Ching-kuo, complained that he and his son were being singled out, and gave Ching-kuo a list of firms that were illegally storing goods (including the Yangtze Company of David Kung).[77]

A few days later Ching-kuo's friend, Chia Yi-pin, pounded on his boss' desk: "If Kung Ling-kan [David Kung] did not violate the law, then who did?" Ching-kuo did not reply, but afterward told Chia, "I cannot seek fidelity at the expense of filial piety or the other way around."[78] Chia went back to his hotel and wrote Ching-kuo a 14-page letter describing his disappointment. "I had originally thought the Kuomintang was hopeless, but I still placed hope in you. . . . But this matter has enlightened me. It is said that you 'swat only the flies and do not beat the tigers.'"[79]

Chia left Shanghai. Before the end of the year he made contact with the CCP and began to cooperate secretly with the Communists.[80] Shortly after that, with the information provided by Tu Yue-sheng, Ching-kuo charged the Yangtze Company with economic crimes and arrested some of David Kung's employees. According to one version, Ching-kuo put Kung under house arrest and as a matter of courtesy informed Soong Mei-ling. She traveled immediately to Shanghai and met together with Ching-kuo and her nephew. "You are brothers," she said to the two step-cousins. "You have no reason to fight each other." Kung hinted that if Ching-kuo did not drop the charges, he would expose things embarrassing to the Chiang family and the government.[81] In the end David Kung made a large settlement, reportedly turning over US $6 million to the government, and then left for Hong Kong and later New York. Tu Yue-sheng also departed for Hong Kong, shortly after which his son made a substantial payment to the government and was allowed to close his company and join his father. The Wing On company dumped its large stock of cotton at 25 percent less than it had cost. The principal family owners of Wing On, the Kwoks, also migrated to Hong Kong.[82] Shanghai was at last rid of the Kungs and the Tus. But by this time Ching-kuo's economic controls were coming apart, and the impression was widespread that he had been forced to capitulate on the Yangtze case.[83]

PRICE CONTROLS ARE DIFFICULT to sustain in a capitalist society even under the best of circumstances. Unless the root problem of inflation—usually, a large public-sector budget deficit—is addressed, such controls will surely fail. The currency reforms in Nationalist China collapsed in six weeks, including in the only area where they were seriously enforced—Shanghai. The fundamental problem was the failure to implement the program uniformly throughout the country.[84] Since prices rose rapidly outside of Shanghai, merchants and individuals flocked to the city to buy up all the goods they could lay their hands on. Although there was a bumper harvest that fall in neighboring Kiangsu and Chekiang provinces, there were serious food shortages in Shanghai. Raw materials were likewise not available as manufacturers stopped producing.

In the first week of the reform, the Central Bank issued 30 million gold yuan to the public in exchange for gold, silver, and foreign currencies, but as optimism faded, those who had held back were proved wise and those, mostly middle class citizens, who had obeyed the law were financially ruined.[85] The harsh inequities of the program also became more apparent. Those with foreign currency or bullion assets abroad valued at more than $3,000 were only required to declare them, not to turn them in. This exception included holdings in Hong Kong and was a great boon to millionaires like the Soongs, Kungs, Kwoks, and Tus. Those with less than $3,000 in foreign-held assets—a fortune to the average Chinese—did not even have to declare them. *Time and Culture* magazine

(Shih yu wen) lamented that the whole process was simply another way of "effecting a nominal change to preserve an old order."[86] Nothing at all was done to meet Ching-kuo's call for measures to reduce the great disparities of wealth. By the end of October medicines, toilet paper, cotton, coffins, and other items had disappeared entirely from the market.[87] Teachers, professionals, and small business people who had never entertained the idea of supporting the Communist Party began to think that anything would be better than the KMT.[88]

In the midst of this crisis came the terrible war news. Chinan, capital of the key province of Shantung, fell with little resistance on September 24. The few Nationalist-held cities in Manchuria were teetering. The new commanding general in Manchuria, Wei Li-huang, proposed to break out and evacuate his armies by sea to North China. The Gimo ordered him to fight on. In seven weeks Chiang Kai-shek lost 400,000 men; 140,000 escaped on ships.[89]

At the end of October, as Ching-kuo brooded over the fate of China, he received an urgent order from his father to report to Nanking.[90] There, at a special meeting, the Executive Yuan unfroze prices throughout Nationalist China. The decree stipulated that after consultations with merchants, prices would be re-frozen based on production costs.[91] This assertion at least brought a laugh. The next day Ching-kuo's office released a statement from him apologizing to the people of Shanghai and telling them what they already knew—he had failed to accomplish his mission. He accepted responsibility for having increased rather than diminished their suffering, but the statement was more defiant of the decree than repentant. "I will never shift to others any responsibility which should be borne by me . . . I firmly believe that the direction I have pointed out as regards 'whither Shanghai' [his September 12 speech] is absolutely correct. I sincerely wish the citizens of Shanghai to use their own strength to prevent unscrupulous merchants, bureaucrats, politicians, and racketeers from controlling Shanghai. I firmly believe a bright future lies ahead for Shanghai."[92] Immediately, prices rocketed skyward. By November 6 the cost of goods in Shanghai had increased more than ten times their levels in August.[93] Working round the clock, printing presses churned out the now worthless gold yuan.

In November 1948 Harry Truman scored an astounding upset over Thomas Dewey in the American presidential elections, ending any hope of an immediate turnaround in American policy toward China. A few days later, the last Nationalist soldiers withdrew from Manchuria. In three years Mao Zedong had conquered the vast Northeast region of China and occupied most of the North China plain. Now he and his comrades launched the next stage—driving the Nationalists back to the Yangtze.

CHING-KUO PLEADED WITH HIS FATHER to carry out a sweeping over-haul of his government, including the military. Instead, the Gimo turned down the resignation of Prime Minister Weng Wen-hao, a move that sources close to Ching-kuo interpreted as meaning the President did not intend to carry out a major personnel reshuffle.[94] Chiang Kai-shek now accepted the inevitability of defeat on the mainland. Already he was planning the retreat to Taiwan, although he would go through elaborate measures to keep Mao guessing as to where his last stand would be. Loyalty would be more important than ever in the coming days. This was not the moment, the Gimo believed, to purge his old supporters like the CC and Whampoa cliques and the Soong in-laws. But he re-established the Political Department in the armed forces, which under American pressure had been changed to an Information Department, and put Ching-kuo informally in charge. Ching-kuo immediately began re-assigning commissars down to the battalion level.

On November 5 Ching-kuo returned to Shanghai and gathered his closest comrades for a meeting. "Now, we have failed," he said. "I do not know where we should go and what we should do. We may find out later. In the future you should maintain discipline and take care of yourselves. I am not sure whether we will be able to work together again."[95] As he bade his friends farewell, he wept.

Most of his team then dispersed. Ching-kuo told Wang Sheng to take the Tiger-Beating brigade south. The remaining brigades and various other paramilitary units were gathered into a new Youth Regiment for National Salvation under Hu Kui. Youth Army veterans from this regiment and elsewhere would provide a large number of the new political commissars assigned to National army units slated for evacuation to Taiwan.[96]

THE PEOPLES LIBERATION ARMY pushed on to Hsuchow, less than two hundred miles up the rail line from Nanking. Chu Te, now commander in chief of all the Communist armies, committed 600,000 men to what was called the Battle of Huaihai, one of the most massive military engagements in history, extending over the provinces of Shantung, Anhui, and Kiangsu.[97]

The battle raged for sixty days. As senior commissar, Deng Xiaoping was the responsible PLA officer in this critical campaign.[98] Chiang Wei-kuo commanded a tank regiment. Near the end of the year, most of the surviving Nationalist forces in the Hsuchow area surrendered; some, however, retreated to Nanking, including the bulk of Chiang Wei-kuo's American M3-A1 tanks. The tanks did not stop to defend Nanking but went by rail and barge to Shanghai to prepare for evacuation to Taiwan.[99] The American Military Mission in Nanking concluded that "the military position of the National Government had declined beyond possible recoupment."[100]

Before the end of the year, some senior KMT leaders and military officers were pushing for peace talks with the Communists. Vice President Li Tsung-jen was the leader of the peace faction; likewise his old Kwangsi compatriot, Pai Chung-hsi, and a good number of other KMT officials, eager to gain time if nothing else, were also urging a ceasefire and a renewal of negotiations. After the Battle of Huaihai, however, Mao was willing to talk only about the unconditional surrender of the KMT.

10

End Game

AS 1949, THE YEAR OF THE OX, began, the Generalissimo refused to accept that he no longer possessed the mandate of heaven. He found solace in *Streams in the Desert* and guidance in Sun Ts'u's *The Art of War,* especially the sections on deception. His life-long stoicism did not fail him nor did his tenaciousness and sense of destiny. Now facing the victory of the Communists, he believed—as he had done after his military defeat by the Japanese—that if he could retreat and survive, world events would eventually turn to his advantage. But he needed as many months as possible to carry out the withdrawal to Taiwan, just as Mao needed time to refit his army for a mass crossing of the Yangtze. Chiang coolly plotted to save what he could, although this would come at great cost. Retreat to the island across the Strait was now a matter of timing and tactics. He would carefully shape his political moves to detach himself from the coming loss of the mainland, gain time, and complicate Mao's military decisions.

Ching-kuo's innate optimism and ebullience also returned. With Madame Chiang away in America promoting the desperate cause of "Free China," the son became the only real *confidant* of the Generalissimo. In December the Kuomintang Central Committee had named Ching-kuo chairman of its Taiwan Provincial Committee, but it was soon apparent that Ching-kuo was not rushing off to Taipei.[1] This anomaly was another way to complicate the CCP's calculations about the Gimo's ultimate destination. Ching-kuo was now by his father's side throughout the day and stayed with him at night in the large home Soong Mei-ling had built in the Purple and Gold Mountains outside the Nanking city walls.

When it came to evacuation priorities, two key items were China's great assembly of art treasures and its gold and foreign currency reserves. Before the Japanese attack in 1937, the Palace Museum in Peking had crated up most of its vast collection and sent it off, first to Nanking and then to Chungking. After the war, the curators carted their treasures, many of which were thousands of years old, back to Nanking. A number of pieces were lost or stolen, including the bones of the Peking Man, but the collection was so immense that the losses hardly mattered.

In early January of 1949 the Gimo gave Ching-kuo responsibility for seeing that the collection arrived safely on Taiwan. A few days later Ching-kuo was at the navy pier supervising sailors loading more than 100 huge museum crates aboard two frigates. At night the ships quietly slipped anchor and sailed full speed down the Yangtze. Without stopping in Shanghai, they steamed with their invaluable cargo directly to the port of Keelung in northern Taiwan.[2]

Ching-kuo next went secretly to Shanghai to begin the initial transfer of the Central Bank's gold bullion, silver coins, and foreign currency. Following his father's instructions, he sent the first shipment of these assets to Amoy in Fukien province. This was another of the Gimo's stratagems to keep Mao guessing as to whether or not he would try to hold on to part of the mainland.

By the first of the year, navy and commercial ships packed with refugees were steaming back and forth between mainland and Taiwan ports—the latter being Keelung in the north and Kaohsiung in the south. One steamer sank and more than a thousand people were lost. The Gimo ordered Chang Hsueh-liang and his companion, Miss Chao, moved to Taiwan. A house was found for them and their guards in the small town of Hsinchu, 50 miles south of Taipei.[3]

For many Taiwan was not the final destination. Those who had money in America or elsewhere abroad planned to retire to a safer refuge and one near their assets. Ching-kuo thought briefly of sending his wife and children to Hong Kong or to England. But he had no funds to support them, and he refused to accept money from the Soongs.[4] More importantly, he knew that such a move would have been another blow to his father's rapidly fading cause. Ching-kuo sent a message to Faina in Hangchow and told her to be prepared to leave on short notice. He also sent instructions to Chang Ching-hua, the grandmother of Ya-juo's twin boys. The Chang family, including the grandmother, the twins, the uncle and his wife and six or seven children, made it to Fuchow, where political officers put them on a navy ship headed for Taiwan.[5]

On January 15, following a brief siege, the city of Tientsin surrendered to the PLA. Chia Yi-pin, who was now secretly reporting to the CCP, called on Ching-kuo at the Lichih Guest House in Nanking and found him out back burning his papers. Chia asked why he was throwing a stack of invitation cards into the fire. "We will not be inviting people to dinner," he replied.[6]

ON JANUARY 19 Chiang Kai-shek presided over his last meeting on the mainland of the Executive Yuan. With Li Tsung-jen taking the lead, the majority of those present called for a cease-fire and peace negotiations. On January 21 the Generalissimo announced he was stepping down, although to Li's consternation he did not use the word "retirement."[7] Notably, he retained his position as Director General of the KMT.[8] That same day, the Generalissimo and his son, accompanied by a smaller than usual entourage, flew out of Nanking in a private plane named "Mei-ling," property of Madame Chiang. Chiang Wei-kuo was in Shanghai loading his tanks onto freighters, and to his chagrin his brother forgot to inform him of his father's imminent withdrawal from office and departure from Nanking. He read about it in the newspapers.[9]

On its way from Nanking the Gimo's party stopped over in Hangchow, where Governor Ch'en Yi, whose misrule had led to the Taiwan uprising and its bloody suppression in 1947, gave them a state banquet. Ching-kuo was not smiling. Ch'en Yi's days were numbered.[10]

WITH FAINA AND THE CHILDREN ABOARD, the Gimo's plane put down once more on a grass airfield near Elephant Mountain. A convoy of army trucks and cars took the "inactive" president, Ching-kuo and his family, the rest of the party, and the guard detachment to Hsikou. As usual, the villagers turned out and cheered as the vehicles drove under the arch and down Wuling Street. This time, however, except for the children, the people of Chiang's hometown looked decidedly nervous. Father and son and the latter's family spent the night at Feng Hao Fang. Faina bedded the children down in a cold upstairs room and pretended that this was another vacation trip to Hsikou, not another flight for their lives.[11]

At breakfast the first morning his father informed Ching-kuo, "We will be here three months." The forecast was accurate to the day.[12] Chiang also told Ching-kuo to instruct the air force immediately to build an airfield at Tinghai on the island of Chousan, not far from Ningpo and less than 100 miles from Shanghai. The Gimo was thinking of his army's impending staged retreat from that great metropolis. The first cable of the day reported that General Fu Ts'o-yi had surrendered Peking and 200,000 troops without a fight to Mao Zedong.[13] That same morning, by the ruins of the old Summer Palace outside the ancient capital, Mao sipped a cup of green tea and read reports of Chiang Kai-shek's arrival in Hsikou. Very likely the Chairman smiled, rubbed his chin, and tried to anticipate his old enemy's last moves.

CHING-KUO FLEW BACK TO SHANGHAI to oversee the final removal of the Central Bank's gold and other assets—this time to Taiwan. Chiang cautioned his son to continue to keep the operation secret, as Li Tsung-jen would want to use the gold reserves as a bargaining chip with the Communists. On February 10 Ching-kuo, employing his Youth Army veterans as drivers and guards and working late at night, loaded the last of the bullion on a navy ship tied up at a secure military wharf. Before dawn the ship weighed anchor and sailed for Keelung.[14] The total value of the transferred Treasury assets in 1949 U.S. dollars was $300–350 million—at least $10 billion in 1998 dollars.[15] But when Ching-kuo reported on his mission, the Generalissimo was not yet satisfied. He remembered an enormous box of diamonds and other jewelry that the government had confiscated from individuals during the war and which was now stored in the vault of the Central Bank. He sent Ching-kuo back to retrieve the jewels. Meanwhile, Acting President Li Tsung-jen heard that Ching-kuo had made off with the entire Treasury and flew into a rage. He ordered the Central Bank not to turn over the jewels and dispatched the official with the keys to the vault to Hong Kong. Ching-kuo felt that the value of the gems did not warrant creating further trouble with Li and returned to Hsikou without them. The Gimo was angry. "When we need to pay the troops on Taiwan," he told Ching-kuo, "every dollar will help.[16]

Another step in preparation for the move to Taiwan was the arrest of Chekiang Governor Ch'en Yi. Li Tsung-jen, who had no foreknowledge of this action, charged that Ching-kuo had instigated it. The surprised Ch'en was sent off in chains to Taiwan and soon executed, allegedly for plotting with the Communists.[17] Ching-kuo's real motive, however, was to try to palliate Taiwanese resentment of the 1947 massacres.[18]

ABOUT THE TIME the Generalissimo and Ching-kuo were arriving in Hsikou, Anastas Mikoyan, a senior member of the Soviet Politburo, made a secret visit to the CCP headquarters near Peking. Chinese Communist officials would later claim that Mikoyan, speaking on Stalin's behalf, urged Mao not to seek total victory as this could provoke U.S. intervention on the side of the Nationalists and suggested that the PLA stop at the Yangtze River.[19] Mikoyan's report to Stalin on the meeting is now available and refutes this claim. In fact, Mikoyan urged Mao not to delay taking Shanghai and other big cities and establishing the new Communist government. In an exchange of letters, Mao and Stalin agreed that peace terms offered to the KMT should be calculated to fail and that the revolutionary war should be pushed through to the end.[20]

On the question of foreign policy, Mao reaffirmed his readiness to align the new China with Moscow in the struggle against imperialism.[21] Mikoyan, in turn, discussed Soviet economic and military assistance to the future Communist China.[22] Soon after, Mao announced to the world that in the event of a third world war, the Chinese Communists would side with the Soviet Union.[23]

———

AT HSIKOU, the Generalissimo stayed much of the time on Hole-in-the-Snow Mountain at the small cabin he had constructed 28 years ago, not far from his mother's tomb. Sometimes he went on long walks in his black robe. Similarly outfitted as a "gentry man," Ching-kuo usually accompanied his father. On several occasions father and son together climbed the path to the monastery. When asked what the Gimo was doing in those days, surviving staff members say, "He was thinking."[24] Soon, however, Chiang began to receive a stream of visitors, including loyal military commanders and anxious government and Party officials seeking instructions. A plane from Shanghai would arrive every day at 5:00 AM. Major Konsin Shah, the Gimo's young pilot and *aide de camp*, was the official greeter as well as general *factotum*, and during this period managed only three or four hours sleep a day.[25]

Ching-kuo asked several of his associates, including Chia Yi-pin, Hu Kui, and Ch'en Chih-ching, to come to Hsikou, where he saw each one privately. Ch'en said he would take his chances and stay on. Ching-kuo gave him a few silver dollars for traveling money if he changed his mind.[26] Chia Yi-pin, the secret turncoat, feared that Ching-kuo had become suspicious of him, but if so, he had changed his mind, asking Chia to lead the Reserve Officers (Probationary Cadre) Team, consisting of about 10,000 men to be trained as company and platoon leaders, to Fukien, in preparation for evacuation to Taiwan.[27]

———

U.S. POLICY AT THIS TIME was to accept the inevitability of a Communist China and hope for the eventual emergence of Chinese Titoism. Taiwan, however, continued to present sticky political and moral dilemmas. In late 1948 the U.S. Joint Chiefs of Staff (JCS) informed the National Security Council (NSC) that Communist domination of Taiwan would have "seriously unfavorable" strategic implications for the security of the United States. The White House and the Department of State also wanted to prevent Taiwan from becoming part of the soon-to-be-Communist China. But they were convinced that the KMT regime that had failed so miserably on the mainland could not possibly defend the island, even with large-scale U.S. material assistance.

At the same time, the JCS said that any overt military commitment by the U.S. forces to defend Taiwan would be unwise, "so long as the present disparity between our military strength and our global obligations existed."[28] Equally important, American allies would have strongly opposed direct U.S. military action to deny Taiwan to Communist China. Thus, throughout 1949 and until June 1950, the Americans took various political and economic measures to try to head off Communist control of the island but did not have much hope that such maneuvers could succeed.[29]

In pursuit of this objective, in early 1949 the State Department began to assess various possibilities: replacing the Generalissimo with a more effective and democratic leadership within the KMT; encouraging a Taiwanese independence movement; or establishing a U.N. trusteeship over Taiwan. Secretary of State Dean Acheson at one point believed that if the KMT, even without the Gimo, was deemed incapable of governing the island in a manner that would deny it to the Communists, the United States should examine the possibility of developing "a spontaneous independence movement in Formosa which could then lead to an agreement in the UN on the future of Formosa and thus international sanction for US intervention." The American diplomat assigned to investigate these possibilities, Livingston T. Merchant, concluded that Governor Ch'en Ch'eng, whom the Americans still viewed favorably, would probably not be able to produce a more effective and popular government than the current one. On Merchant's recommendation, American officials suggested to Acting President Li Tsung-jen in Nanking that he replace Ch'en Ch'eng as governor with General Sun Li-jen.[30]

Sun was then in Taiwan, commanding the remnants of Ching-kuo's three Youth Army divisions on the island and the army training center near Kaohsiung. The general was recruiting local Taiwanese youth to supplement his forces, but he had little ammunition and no heavy machine guns or artillery. In early March Sun Li-jen received an invitation from General MacArthur to visit him in Tokyo. Sun obtained the Gimo's approval and flew off to Japan. MacArthur, who had talked with Merchant, told Sun the Nationalist government was doomed. If Sun took over responsibility for Taiwan's security, the American general said, the United States would support him. Sun replied that he was loyal to the Generalissimo. When he returned to Taiwan he reported MacArthur's remarks to Ch'en Ch'eng, who hurried off to Hsikou to brief the Gimo.[31]

A few weeks later Sun also crossed the Strait to reassure the Generalissimo. The Gimo told him, "Go back to Taiwan and keep up the good work training the Army."[32] Meanwhile, Acting President Li told Ambassador Stuart that he was powerless to appoint Sun as governor; only the "retired" Chiang Kai-shek could do that.[33] The Americans did not follow up. The episode confirmed to the Gimo what was already obvious—Washington wanted desperately to elbow him aside. The event of course also reassured him regarding the loyalty of Sun Li-jen, but at the same time it heightened his and Ching-kuo's watchfulness over this favorite of the Americans. Having approached Sun once, the Americans might do so again.

Sun, in fact, continued to convey pessimistic assessments to the Americans. In May he told U.S. officials in Taipei that he had been promised the position as commander-in-chief of ground forces in Taiwan, but that this assignment would not include the troops retreating to Taiwan from Shanghai. Sun said he thought Taiwan would fall as a result of internal fighting and lack of organization, rather than from the actions of an external foe.[34]

The Americans were even more despairing than Sun about Taiwan's future, but they now concluded that any effort to unseat the Gimo and his military team was unlikely to succeed. The KMT's leaders' grip on the armed forces on Taiwan, thanks in good part to Ching-kuo's reinvigorated commissars, was too tight. The idea of a U.N. trusteeship also dissipated. Chiang would certainly not agree, the Soviets would block any such move, and the British and other U.S. allies would refuse to support it. Taiwan's independence was even less plausible. In mid-March the CIA concluded that a victorious Taiwanese rebellion in the near future was "quite impossible."[35]

Over the next 15 months, as domestic political pressures regarding events in China increased, key officials in the Truman administration continued to cast about for a way to save Taiwan without U.S. military intervention. Meanwhile the U.S. government continued to deliver economic and military aid to Taiwan and supported the Joint Commission on Rural Reconstruction (JCRR), a successful Chinese-American intergovernmental body for planning and coordinating rural development on Taiwan.

IN EARLY APRIL 1949 General Chang Chih-chung headed a Nationalist delegation to Peking to discuss peace terms. Seeing the writing on the wall, he defected, along with several other Nationalist delegates, including Shao Li-tz'u, the Gimo's secretary and apparent long-time underground Communist who had introduced the young Ching-kuo to Communist leaders in Peking in 1925.[36] Chang Chih-chung had been one of the Gimo's most trusted supporters, a senior political officer known for his integrity and thus admired by Ching-kuo. His defection was a serious blow to the already severely depressed Nationalist morale.[37] Shao's betrayal also stunned Ching-kuo and heightened his fear of Communist infiltration among his own associates, a threat he had previously taken lightly. This reaction intensified when Ching-kuo learned that Chia Yi-pin, with whom he had talked only a few weeks before, had gone over to the Communists with his 10,000 officer trainees.[38]

Li Tsung-jen was convinced that the Gimo, determined to abandon the mainland, would not be happy if Li's government was somehow able to hold the line at the Yangtze. Such a turnaround could cause America to change its attitude and provide substantial support to Li. Chiang Kai-shek, however, had crippled any chance the government might have had on the military front by transferring the navy and air force to Taiwan and sending many of the remaining central army troops to Shanghai.[39]

The Gimo and Ching-kuo were watching a Peking opera performance at the Wuling School in Hsikou when the message arrived that the Communist General Ch'en Yi (not related to the late KMT governor) had led the PLA across the Yangtze along a two-hundred-mile front and captured Nanking.[40] Li and his government escaped and moved to Canton. On the same day that Nanking fell, Republican Senator William F. Knowland submitted a concurrent resolution in Congress calling for an investigation of America's foreign policy in the Far East. A few days earlier, Senator Styles Bridges accused Secretary Acheson of "sabotage of the valiant attempt of the Chinese Nationalists to keep at least part of China free."[41]

BACK IN HSIKOU the Gimo gave the order to move out, equivocating whether his destination was Fukien or Taiwan. On April 24 Ching-kuo said goodbye to Faina and the four children, who then traveled by car to the airfield near Ningpo. The infant, Eddy, was running a fever. The family, together with the loyal Ah Wang, boarded a military plane and for the fourth time took flight from their enemies. They landed at Taichung, then a small city in the middle of Taiwan. The next morning Ching-kuo and his father paid a last visit to his grandmother's tomb. Ching-kuo went alone to his mother's grave and then climbed one of the hills immediately behind the town. For the last time he looked out at his enchanting ancestral land.[42]

The Generalissimo and a small party including Ching-kuo, Major Shah, several secretaries, a doctor, and a reduced security detachment drove out of Hsikou. Among the few items Ching-kuo took in his baggage was a cast of the inscription on his mother's tombstone and a book from the Wuling School on the history of the Chiang family.[43] The convoy sped under the Wuling gate and down the dirt road. The Generalissimo did not look back. Nor did he and Ching-kuo wave to the confused townspeople who raised their hands in a tentative farewell.[44] By this time the town had lost a good bit of its population. Most Chiang families of any standing were already on their way to Taiwan. The local police and a large number of the Gimo's guards, most of whom came from Fenghua county, were left behind.

As the party prepared to board a frigate at the small dock at Elephant Mountain, the Gimo spied Major Shah. "What are you doing here?" he demanded. Shah explained that he was loading the ship. "Go back to the village," the Gimo ordered, "and arrange for a ship from Shanghai to take all the police, the guards, and their families to Amoy." The odds are that Chiang Kai-shek did not think of the low-level followers he had abandoned in Hsikou, but that Ching-kuo reminded him. After boarding the ship, the Gimo announced for the first time that he was going not to Taiwan or Amoy but to Shanghai. This surprised Ching-kuo and the others as the situation in the city was exceedingly dangerous.[45]

Shah returned to Hsikou and by radio arranged for an LST to pick up the security people and their families, numbering about 400 in all. Shah then caught a military plane to Shanghai and went to see the Gimo at the headquarters he had set up in a hostel on Rue Pere Robert. Shah reported that the evacuation from Hsikou had been organized, but he asked if it would not be better to send the evacuees directly to Taiwan rather than to Amoy. Chiang paced about his office and then declared, "Ch'en Ch'eng has political troubles." Shah saluted and returned to Hsikou. He understood that dispatching the security personnel to Amoy was part of the Generalissimo's effort to confuse Communist intelligence about his intentions and to give Ch'en Ch'eng time to strengthen Taiwan's defenses and consolidate KMT control.[46]

Another game of deception was played out in Shanghai. Chiang made several speeches proclaiming that Shanghai would be another Stalingrad and predicting total victory within three years. General T'ang En-po's troops and an army of coolies chopped down hundreds of trees, including those on the golf course, dug a vast moat around Shanghai, and erected a ten-foot palisade made of sharpened bamboo. The U.S. consul general reported that troops were "fortifying roof tops and sandbagging main buildings and junction spots . . . with apparent expectation of heavy street fighting."[47] The American diplomats did not observe, however, that planes and ships were evacuating most of T'ang's soldiers to Taiwan and to Tinghai on Chousan island. Although Chiang had often ordered garrisons in doomed cities to hold out to the end, he had no intention of doing so in Shanghai. But he did not want his whole army at this point rushing off to Taiwan.

On May 5 Li Tsung-jen sent a private letter to President Truman blaming Chiang Kai-shek for the Communist triumph in China and asking for American support of his (Li's) government. Washington demurred.[48]

Ching-kuo described Li's letter as "a fawning gesture to foreigners."[49] Meanwhile, in Shanghai, workers who, if they were lucky, had received their pay in products and goods, crowded the streets trying to barter what they had for what they needed. Hundreds of thousands jammed the docks along the Huangpu and at the airport terminal to the west of town. In view of this chaotic situation, there was concern over wholesale Communist infiltration into Taiwan. Ching-kuo's political officers were busy trying to prevent this. Before boarding a plane or ship for Taiwan, each refugee needed a paper showing approval from the Political Department for evacuation.[50]

On May 6 the Gimo and Ching-kuo boarded a frigate, which early the next morning steamed down the winding, sluggish Huangpu River.[51] The Communist 3rd Army had taken the ancient town of Suchow on the Grand Canal and was only fifty miles away, but Chiang Kai-shek seemed in no hurry. CCP spies following the ship's movements were puzzled. The vessel did not head for Taiwan but stopped at the Chousan Archipelago. The Gimo calmly conducted an inspection of the 125,000 troops who had come to the islands from Shanghai.[52]

On May 15 the Gimo instructed Ching-kuo to fly back to Shanghai to take charge during the city's last days. When he arrived, Ching-kuo could hear the explosion of artillery shells in the distance. The Bund was jammed with refugees from surrounding towns. Freighters clogged with passengers crammed on deck were still steaming down the river. Ching-kuo met with the rear guard commanders and gave them their final instructions—there was to be no effort to wreck Shanghai before the pullout.[53] The arrest and public execution of black marketeers and suspected and real Communist agents continued to the end, but apparently in the dozens or hundreds, not thousands.[54]

The next day Ching-kuo flew to the Pescadores (P'enghu Islands) off Taiwan's west coast, then to Fuchow to consult with the governor of Fukien about the construction of defense forts—another false trail for CCP agents to report.[55] Returning to Taipei, Ching-kuo discussed with Ch'en Ch'eng the handling of the exodus on the receiving end. The task of providing food and shelter to hundreds of thousands of men, women, children, and soldiers clogging the two major ports seemed insurmountable. About 5,000 new refugees were arriving each day.[56] Ching-kuo also reviewed with Ch'en and General P'eng Meng-chi the status of defense and internal security preparations.[57]

P'eng was an entrenched figure on the island, having been the military chief in Kaohsiung in 1945, and in charge of the island's Peace Preservation Corps since just after the 1947 uprising. P'eng's 60,000 to 80,000 men were paid and fed and were thus relatively disciplined. Some officials in the State Department, however, considered him "one of the most thoroughgoing scoundrels in the Chinese Army."[58] This was the beginning of the period Taiwanese refer to as The White Terror. Ch'en Ch'eng had declared martial law, and P'eng's Peace Preservation Corps and other competing security organizations were busy sweeping up suspects, both Communists and presumed Taiwanese nationalists. Many former members of the Student Reading Society at National Taiwan University were arrested and killed.

While he was in Taipei, Ching-kuo also rented a house for his family at 18 Ch'angan East Road. The house and land were owned jointly by the Hua Nan Bank and the First Commercial Bank. The banks readily offered to sell the property to him at a bargain price, but he refused. When he died forty years later, neither Ching-kuo nor his wife had ever owned a piece of real estate.[59]

On May 22, in Taipei, Major Shah read the morning reports from Shanghai saying that the fall of the city was imminent. He rushed to the radio room and sent an urgent message to Chiang Wei-kuo, who was still in Shanghai supervising the final embarkation of his tanks. Wei-kuo saw to it that Shah's mother and his own wife made it out on one of the last boats. Ching-kuo told Shah he wanted to return to Shanghai, although it was now tightly encircled. On May 25, they took off in a C-47 and headed across the Strait. Twenty minutes from Shanghai airport, the tower informed them that PLA troops were on the perimeter of the field. Shah veered south and made radio contact with the Gimo's frigate, which was somewhere near Chousan Island. As instructed, Shah landed at Tinghai. PLA troops entered Shanghai that day.[60]

It was a "soft ending" for the city. American consulate general officials had predicted that Ching-kuo would tackle "the job of demolishing Shanghai with special relish," destroying "the utilities, dockyards and other infrastructure of the city."[61] In fact, he ordered that it be left essentially undamaged. After the withdrawal, Nationalist planes, according to a subsequent American report, did not randomly bomb Shanghai but concentrated on oil storage facilities and airfields on the outskirts. An evaluation by the same consulate general of the economic situation in Shanghai one month after Ching-kuo ordered the final retreat indicated that utilities were functioning, there was approximately 40 days of fuel oil in stock, and essential food needs were being met. The docks had not been destroyed; factories had not been razed; and Shanghai mills even had about a six-week supply of raw cotton on hand.[62]

Shanghai's Vice Mayor Wu Shao-shu did not flee the city as Tang En-po's rear guard pulled out. He stayed in his office and handed over to the Communists the files and membership lists of KMT organizations in the city, including Ching-kuo's Youth Corps and Youth Army Federation.[63] Wu became a counselor in the Ministry of Communications of the Peoples Republic, indicating that his was not a late defection.

WHILE CHING-KUO WAS PURSUING his hectic schedule, the Generalissimo continued to linger on for some days at Chousan Island, where T'ang En-po's troops were furiously digging in. The Gimo visited a temple dedicated to Kuanyin, the patron goddess of Taiwan, and two famous monasteries in the region. He spent a good part of the time in meditation. This detached, unhurried, and contemplative behavior in the face of disaster was part of the Gimo's charisma. His success in keeping up this image of calm resoluteness explains in part why so many in the army and the government carried on with their duties when utter defeat seemed inevitable. Thousands of loyal soldiers and officers were still dying in the struggle to delay the advance of the PLA to the coasts opposite Chousan. As Major Shah recalls, "we had blind faith in him."[64]

As the presidential frigate steamed quietly into Kaohsiung harbor, General Sun Li-jen was there to greet the Generalissimo and his party. On June 25 the Gimo and Ching-kuo flew to Taipei to take part in a key conference on reorganization of the military. Ching-kuo insisted on some immediate reforms in the armed forces, such as centralization of all financial matters, including pay. Commanders would no longer control the pay rolls for their own troops. A more basic overhaul of the military establishment, however, would have to wait. Meanwhile the Generalissimo moved into a house outside Taipei near the top of Grass (later Yang Ming) Mountain, which belonged to the state-owned Taiwan Sugar Company. The house had a stunning view but one drawback—the American consulate general owned a small weekend house that overlooked the garden. Soon after the Gimo took up residence, Chinese security men erected a tall bamboo wall that blocked the view of the Americans. The Americans complained but to no avail.[65]

ON THE INTERNATIONAL POLITICAL FRONT, Mao provided further grist for those who warned that Communist China posed a powerful threat to the American position in Asia and that Taiwan should be saved as a major ally in the coming struggle. Following up his strong pledges of solidarity to Mikoyan and his April 4 pronouncement on a third world war, Mao again made explicit and official the intention of Communist China to ally itself with the Soviet Union in his paper of June 30, "On People's Democratic Dictatorship." The Chinese people, he wrote, "must lean either to the side of imperialism or to that of socialism. There can be no exception. There can be no sitting on the fence. There is no third road."[66]

The day after Mao's pronouncement, one of his principal lieutenants, Liu Shao-ch'i, left Peking for a secret meeting in Moscow. The visit was an ideological and political milestone. In his talks with Liu, Stalin propounded a major new development of his world view—a division of labor between the new Socialist China and the Soviet Union that explicitly affirmed an equal partnership. As Stalin put it to Liu, the center of world revolution had gravitated from Europe to Asia, and the Chinese Communist Party's destiny was to lead the anti-imperialist revolution in Asia.[67]

Stalin believed that a third world war was inevitable, a war that would deliver the death blow to imperialism and capitalism. The Soviet Union needed as much time as possible to build its strength, while diverting the United States and weakening its alliance system. To this end, the Soviet leader encouraged an aggressive Chinese Communist posture in Asia that would operate under the Soviet umbrella without directly involving the Soviet Union. A key operational goal of this global strategy would be Communist China's continued isolation from the West and hostility toward America.

Dazzling victories had left both Mao and Stalin in an elevated state of confidence. But with the Cold War stalemate in Europe and a nuclear standoff just down the road, the focus of the struggle against America and its allies would now shift to Asia. In this arena the Soviet Union's alliance with China would be key. Nevertheless, Stalin rejected Liu's request for direct Soviet air and naval support in the liberation of Taiwan. The imperialists, he warned, would use such aid as pretext to start a world war, for which the socialist camp was not ready. Instead, he offered extensive military equipment and advisory assistance, including the building of a modern air force. Large numbers of Soviet military advisers soon began to arrive in China, and Soviet MIGs flew into airfields near Shanghai.[68]

WHILE LIU SHAO-CH'I AND STALIN were discussing the new Chinese-Soviet partnership and Kim Il-sung was preparing his invasion of South Korea, Chiang Kai-shek was trying to rally international support from anti-Communist governments in the region. The Gimo and Ching-kuo flew to Baguio in the Philippines to meet President Elpidio Quirino and on July 11, 1949, issued a communiqué that called for an anti-Communist alliance in East Asia. Chiang also confidentially raised with Quirino the possibility of transferring a portion of the KMT's gold reserves on Taiwan to the Philippines—just in case.[69] The two Chiangs then flew to Canton for a meeting with Acting President Li Tsung-jen. Chiang Kai-shek told a meeting of the Central Executive Committee of the KMT that he shouldered a great deal of responsibility for the defeats they had suffered, but that Canton must be held and he himself was "ready to perish with the city." But he rejected pleas that the Nationalist Air Force return to the mainland to help hold Canton.[70]

On these trips Ching-kuo still served as personal assistant to his father. When the Gimo was in Canton, Li Tsung-jen gave a Cantonese dinner for his honored guest. Li saw "Ching-kuo running hither and thither" during the meal. The young Chiang, according to Li, was inspecting the ingredients and the preparation of each course. "Obviously," Li concluded, "he suspected that I wanted to poison his father."[71]

On August 7 father and son headed for South Korea to see President Syngman Rhee, who had endorsed the idea of an anti-Communist alliance. Shortly afterward, President Quirino visited Washington and subsequently both he and President Rhee dropped the proposal. It was also in August that the State Department issued its White Paper on China, which put the blame for the defeat of the KMT on popular discontent and ineptness and rampant corruption in the regime.

General Hu Ts'ung-nan was still ensconced in distant Szechwan with almost 300,000 men. On August 24 the Gimo and Ching-kuo flew to Chungking for a visit with Hu that lasted almost a month. Such a long stay in such critical days lent credence to the Gimo's talk of a final redoubt in Szechwan and neighboring areas.[72] Meanwhile, Pai Ch'ung-hsi fell back from Hunan to Kwangtung and Kwangsi.

BY NOVEMBER a total of almost two million military and civilian personnel, including families, had moved to Taiwan. Despite this 20 percent surge in population and the Americans' predictions of disaster, Ch'en Ch'eng and the JCRR increased agricultural production, and there were no food shortages and no major health crisis. Ch'en told American officials that he had set a limit on the numbers of refugees that would be accepted, implying that many more would have come if given the opportunity. He also oversaw implementation of the first stage of a gradual but far-reaching land reform program designed by the JCRR. In its 23 years on the mainland, the KMT had been unable to implement in any meaningful way Sun Yat-sen's promise of "land to the tiller." Entrenched economic and social interests had repeatedly scuttled the Party's efforts at land reform. But on Taiwan the KMT could reform someone else's land—that of the Taiwan gentry, many of whom were seen as pro-Japanese anyway. It could also sell to poor farmers the vast lands the state had expropriated from Japanese owners, which accounted for 21 percent of all cultivable land.[73]

The reform program began with mandated sharp rent reductions in August 1949. Its immediate success had major political as well as economic and social consequences. As Ch'en Ch'eng over the next seven years introduced the other aspects of land reform, Taiwanese farmers would become an important base of support for the Kuomintang. The former landlords, who in exchange for their land would receive bonds and stock in state-owned industries inherited from the Japanese, evolved into a new capitalist class with a large vested interest in political stability.

Ching-kuo had no formal role in these economic decisions, but according to some who did, he often sat in on key meetings on questions like land reform and reported back to his father.[74] Later in the year Ching-kuo met with a number of the biggest Taiwanese landlords and urged them to cooperate in the land reform program. One of these, Koo Ch'en-fu, recalls that Ching-kuo reminded him of the patriotism of Koo's family and asked him to help persuade other landlords to support the reform.[75] There is no doubt that Ching-kuo encouraged the Generalissimo to move ahead quickly and decisively with Ch'en Ch'eng's program, which was more far-reaching than the reforms young Chiang had been able to accomplish in Kannan.

In September Chiang Kai-shek named Sun Li-jen Taiwan Defense Commander, a move aimed in part at pleasing the Americans. Sun's command of ten divisions included five that were originally trained and armed by the Americans: the three Youth Army Divisions and the 52nd Army's two divisions.[76] Sun, however, told the Americans that Ch'en Ch'eng, as regional military commander, refused to give him adequate supplies or support. He therefore thought the odds of the invasion from the mainland succeeding were "good." The Communists, he predicted, could land 200,000 men within 24 hours from an armada of 1,000 junks, whereas only 60,000 of his 300,000 troops were combat soldiers.[77]

———

ON OCTOBER 1, 1949, Mao Zedong and his Politburo stood on the walls of the Forbidden City and proclaimed the beginning of the Peoples Republic of China. Among those in the first row were second-rank CCP leaders like Deng Xiaoping and Yang Shang-kun, both Moscow alumni; a contingent of non-Communists, including Soong Ch'ing-ling; and several former Chiang Kai-shek loyalists, most prominently generals Fu Ts'o-yi and Chang Chih-chung. In the third rank of VIPs were some of Ching-kuo's friends from Moscow days and later: people like Shao Li-tz'u with his wife and son, Ch'u Wu, and Chia Yi-pin.

A few days later the indomitable Pai Ch'ung-hsi pulled out of Canton and retreated with his worn-out forces to Kwangsi, where he and many of his soldiers had started on the road a quarter century before. In a speech in Taipei on October 10 ("Double Ten Day," the anniversary of the 1911 Revolution), Generalissimo Chiang denounced Soviet imperialism and promised to fight on until he defeated the Communists. Five days later, Canton fell. Some Nationalist units escaped to Hainan island, and the capital moved to Chungking, not Taipei.

At last some encouraging events occurred. In late October, after taking Amoy, the PLA landed several thousand troops on Quemoy, but the Nationalist defenders killed or captured most of the invaders. A smaller PLA attack on Chousan Island likewise failed. Then on November 3 the American consul general in Taipei delivered an important *demarche* personally to the Generalissimo—the first official American approach to him since 1948. The purpose of the statement, which reflected the latest fretting in Washington about the imminent loss of Taiwan, was to shock Chiang into his senses, to highlight the "mis-government of Formosa" and current unrest among the native Taiwanese, and to let him know that U.S. troops would not be coming to his rescue. American attitude toward Formosa, the *demarche* declared, would "depend largely on the action of the present (KMT) Chinese administration in establishing an efficient administration which would seek to bring to the people a higher level of political and economic well-being."[78]

After the meeting Chiang immediately called Ching-kuo, Ch'en Ch'eng, K. C. Wu and a few others to discuss it. The meeting lasted "late into the night." Far from feeling chastened, Chiang was ecstatic. The message had been delivered to him personally. Now, he said, the United States once again was "willing to deal with him." In addition, the United States seemed to be saying that if the Gimo would carry out sufficient reforms, America could fundamentally change its attitude concerning assistance to the island. Chiang called in the American consul general on

November 10 and read his reply, the tone of which was "not that of some-one who had been put on notice but of a partner with Washington in a great crusade to save Taiwan." Of course, he assured the American diplomat, all the changes Washington desired would be achieved.[79] Ch'en Ch'eng indicated to the Americans that the Chinese government was willing to attempt almost anything the United States would suggest.[80]

Greatly encouraged by the American approach, the Gimo wanted to demonstrate that he had still not abandoned the mainland. On November 14 he and Ching-kuo, with Major Shah in the cockpit, once more flew to Chungking.[81] The situation in Szechwan was clearly hopeless. Next door in Yunnan, the warlord Governor Lu Han, who had promised Ching-kuo and Chiang Kai-shek in August that he would fight to the end, was negotiating his surrender with CCP agents in Hong Kong. After the Gimo's arrival in Chungking, Pai Ch'ung-hsi escaped from Kwangsi with his army into Vietnam. A cable from acting-President Li Tsung-jen informed the Gimo that he (Li) was going to the United States for medical treatment. At one point during the Chungking stay Chiang sent Ching-kuo to a Nationalist redoubt in the mountains of nearby Sikang. "Tell them to die a significant death, and never give up," he commanded.[82]

After returning from this mission, Ching-kuo urged his father to leave Chungking before it was too late. But the old man refused, saying he was waiting to instruct the general in command of the rear guard, who was away in the field, on how to conduct the retreat. Several days later the general came to be briefed.[83] The next day the Generalissimo and Ching-kuo visited the Military Council in Chungking and found it deserted. The provincial officials had fled. Because of a surging mass of refugees, the Gimo's car could not get back to his residence at Old Eagle Rock. The Chiangs walked the rest of the way by foot.[84] That night they could hear gunfire. Major Shah roused the party before dawn, and they drove to the air base.

The Gimo ordered the air base commander, General Tu Chang-ch'eng, to blow up the squadron of P-47s on the airfield if they could not be flown out. At first light the small Chiang party took off for Ch'engtu. The next day General Tu arrived in Ch'engtu and reported that bad weather and the PLA had unexpectedly rolled in at the same time, and the fighter planes had unfortunately been left behind.[85] In a few days Deng Xiaoping entered Chungking, the city he had not seen since he left for France 29 years before. He became mayor of the city and political commissar of the region's Military Command.

In Ch'engtu Ching-kuo and his father paid their respects at the grave of Wei-kuo's biological father, Tai Chi-tao, who had committed suicide. On December 8, 1949, the Nationalist government formally and finally moved to Taipei (as did the American embassy). On December 16, as Deng Xiaoping's forces were on the outskirts of Ch'engtu, the Gimo's party took off in a DC-4 heavily loaded with fuel. Major Shah was serving as navigator. The cloud cover precluded ground orientation, and there were no radio stations operating to provide headings. Shah directed the plane by dead reckoning, including a guess as to the wind. As the plane droned on over the vast territory now controlled by the Communists, it grew dark. At 9:00 PM, just as there was a break in the clouds, Shah looked down and recognized the dim outline of Ping Tan Island off the coast of Fukien. He went back to the passenger compartment and told the Gimo that they would be landing in Taiwan in twenty-four minutes. Shah's seat-of-the-pants navigation had saved the day. Chiang, however, simply nodded and as usual gave no word of thanks.[86]

BACK IN TAIPEI, a debate broke out within the KMT. Ch'en Li-fu and other Party veterans urged Chiang to resume the office of president. Chiang Ching-kuo strongly argued that he should not take this course. He said that if his father took back the presidency, this would allow Acting President Li Tsung-jen to blame the Generalissimo for any failure to win support in the United States. Chiang accepted his son's advice.[87] He also made another important decision, appointing K. C. Wu, the former mayor of Shanghai, as governor of Taiwan. Wu privately pressed the Americans for a commitment of aid to strengthen his position—and, he said, that of the Generalissimo—against the KMT hard-liners who opposed reform. Sun Li-jen also joined in what was probably an orchestrated appeal for help to the Americans by officials they trusted. The American consul general, after another conversation with Sun, reported that the general was making progress and "the entire situation as far as defense of the island is concerned may be said to be more encouraging now than two months ago."[88] Likewise inflation was brought under control, 2,000 Taiwanese were placed in the lower and middle grades of the Provincial Civil Service, and K. C. Wu promulgated regulations for local elections.

—

NOW IT WAS TIME TO TAKE A BREAK. Chiang and his son traveled to Sun Moon Lake, a scenic spot in the central mountains of Taiwan. Shortly after their arrival, a cable reported the fall of the last Nationalist redoubt on the mainland. The Generalissimo sat silent for an hour, then he rose and said to his son, "Let us go to the mountain and have a walk." Waving back the bodyguards, they strolled to the edge of the woods, and again the Gimo sat down for a long period of meditation. Afterward, a local fisherman rowed them out into the lake. The Gimo cast out a net. As he dragged it back into the boat, he saw that he had landed a huge fish. The fisherman, perhaps moved to hyperbole by the occasion, exclaimed that in twenty years he had never caught such a fish. "It is a good omen," said Chiang.[89]

—

THERE WERE OTHER PORTENTS. The Soviet atom bomb test seemed more terrifying to most Americans than the dangers posed by the recent world war. Mao's words and actions appeared to confirm that a massive and forbidding Red China in alliance with the USSR was bent on threatening America and its allies. The new "correlation of world forces" was apparent when on December 16, after a frigid ten-day trip in Chiang Kai-shek's former armored train, Mao Zedong, arrived in Moscow to meet the great leader of both the powerful Sino-Soviet bloc and the world Communist movement.

In the United States, Madame Chiang's efforts on behalf of her husband were supported by the ever more aggressive China Lobby—an informal amalgam of politicians, businessmen, interest groups, conservative media, individuals, retired military officers, and others who were strong advocates of Chiang Kai-shek's position. Acting along the same lines, MacArthur was firing off cables from Tokyo to the Joint Chiefs of Staff stressing the critical importance of preventing the early fall of Taiwan. Defense Secretary Louis Johnson was doing all he could to reverse the policy on Taiwan, including keeping Madame informed. Near the end of the year, the U.S. Military Joint Chiefs changed their position to recommend that the United States provide small amounts of military material assistance to Taiwan, but they reiterated their opposition to sending American troops to the island.[90] Secretary of State Acheson rejected the recommendation on military aid on the grounds that it would provide Moscow with magnificent diplomatic and propaganda opportunities.[91] Despite some improvements in Taiwan's defense readiness, CIA and State Department assessments remained unchanged—the Chinese Communists would seize Taiwan by the end of 1950.[92]

The hamlet of Hsikou (c. 1934). *KMT Central Committee Archives.*

Ching-kuo with his grand-
mother, Wang Ts'ai-yu. *KMT
Central Committee Archives.*

Ching-kuo with his father (c. 1925). *KMT Central Committee Archives.*

Chiang Kai-shek with the war lords Yen Hsi-shan (left) and Chang Hsueh-liang (right) (c. 1935). *KMT Central Committee Archives.*

Ching-kuo (to the right, in dark undershirt) with fellow workers from the Uralmash complex (c. 1934). *Courtesy John Chang.*

Ching-kuo with Faina shortly after their return to China (c. 1937). *KMT Central Committee Archives.*

Ching-kuo with Faina, who is pregnant, and his mother, Mao Fu-mei, holding Alan (c. 1937). *KMT Central Committee Archives.*

Ching-kuo (center), Wang Sheng (fourth from right) and Kannan region inspection cadre (c. 1940). *KMT Central Committee Archives.*

Chang Ya-jou, mother of
Chiang Ching-kuo's twin
sons, ca. 1941. *Courtesy
John Chang.*

Ching-kuo reviewing
troops of the Educated
Youth Army (1945).
*KMT Central
Committee Archives.*

Chiang Wei-kuo, adopted son of
Chiang Kai-shek (1942). *KMT
Central Committee Archives.*

Ching-kuo in Nanking just prior to his Shanghai appointment (1948).
KMT Central Committee Archives.

KMT Reform Committee. Ch'en Ch'eng (front row, center), Ching-kuo (front row, far right) (1950). *KMT Central Committee Archives.*

Ching-kuo (right) with the Generalissimo and Madame Chiang Soong Mei-ling (c. 1955). *Kwang Hwa Mass Communications.*

Deputy Defense Minister Chiang Ching-kuo (left), Ambassador Wellington Koo, and Secretary of State John Foster Dulles (1953). *KMT Central Committee Archives.*

Ching-kuo and Faina with their children: (right to left) Alex, Amy, Alan, Alan's wife, Nancy Zi, and Eddy (c. 1960). *KMT Central Committee Archives.*

As Taiwan Defense Minister, Ching-kuo visits President John F. Kennedy (1963).
KMT Central Committee Archives.

Ching-kuo as President, talk-
ing to the nation, Oct. 1980.
*Kwang Hwa Mass
Communications.*

Ching-kuo with Vice-President Lee Teng-hui (c. 1984). *Kwang Hwa Mass
Communications.*

PART TWO

The Island

11

An Unintended Consequence

SOON AFTER REMOVING TO TAIWAN, Ching-kuo established a Political Action Committee in Kaohsiung to try to coordinate the myriad intelligence and secret police operations that crowded on to the island in 1949.[1] In addition to Ching-kuo, the senior members of the committee were P'eng Meng-ch'i, Air Force Commander Chou Chih-jou, and the commander of the Military Police. During most of the year Ching-kuo was preoccupied with his father's peripatetic travels and exercised only loose overall responsibility, while three staff members ran the committee: Ching-kuo's alter ego Wang Sheng, a former Moscow student, Cheng Chieh-min, and Mao Jen-feng, successor to the late military intelligence chief Tai Li. Mao had close ties to Madame Chiang.[2]

Some Taiwanese estimate that during 1949 the secret police arrested 10,000 Taiwanese for interrogation, while military courts sentenced many to long detentions and execution squads put more than a thousand to death.[3] The *New York Times* correspondent on the scene referred to the "indiscriminate ferocity" of the campaign. The U.S. mission in Taipei reported critically on the violence, and on occasion the State Department authorized a diplomatic remonstrance on the subject to the ROC.[4]

In the first half of 1950 Ching-kuo took a more active leadership role in internal security. Pressure on the native Taiwanese markedly relaxed.

The Gimo and his son were now focusing every possible resource on preparing for the mass invasion expected in early summer. The secret police thus began to concentrate almost entirely on uncovering CCP agents who had come over during the chaotic influx of the previous year. In the first half of 1950 the security network broke 300 alleged Communist spy cases, involving more than 3,000 people.[5]

CIA reports indicated that Mao's intelligence units were in fact concentrating heavily on infiltrating the Nationalist military, with the navy and air force as principal targets.[6] Among senior officers who allegedly proved to be CCP sleepers and went to their death were the deputy chief of the General Staff and his wife, the chief of Military Conscription, the vice minister of National Defense, the chief of Army Supply Services, and the CO of the 70th Division.[7] In one month—May 1950—reputedly 400 Communists gave themselves up.[8] These arrests were largely the work of Ching-kuo's political officers, although other bureaus played a significant part. The security forces executed about 15 percent of enemy agents who were apprehended.[9]

For the other prisoners Ching-kuo set up a re-education school. Named New Life Institute (Hsin sheng chiao tai suo), it was reminiscent of the New Man rehabilitation school he established in Kannan. The inmates had no fixed terms; rather, their release depended on "how rapidly they reformed their thinking."[10] Ching-kuo frequently visited the school, located on Green Island off the east coast, to check on living conditions and treatment of the "students."[11]

A number of U.S.-educated officials were unhappy with the high number of security arrests. K. C. Wu privately complained to the Americans about the overzealous activities of internal security and the commissars, and he said they were the ones that needed purging.[12] Sun Li-jen told the embassy that the problem was that all of the KMT secret police from the mainland now jammed onto the island had to justify their existence.[13]

Madame Chiang, who had been gone more than a year, returned on January 13. The American right wing was in full cry, vehemently denouncing the administration's abandonment of the KMT government. The Pentagon again recommended sending supplies and equipment to the beleaguered island, but President Truman publicly reaffirmed the policy of disengagement from the Chinese civil war. He declared unequivocally that the United States would not provide military aid or advice to Nationalist forces on Formosa. Soon after this declaration, Dean Acheson publicly described an American defense perimeter in East Asia that left out South Korea and Taiwan.[14]

At their meeting in Moscow, Mao and Stalin read these statements with great interest. Almost fifty years after that first Sino-Soviet summit, the Chinese in Peking keep telling interested Westerners that Mao's first visit to Moscow was a flop, marked primarily by the Chairman's reputed complaint, "I have nothing to do but eat and shit."[15] There were testy moments, to be sure, but the most recent studies of Soviet and Chinese documents underscore the deep geopolitical and ideological interests that bound the two leaders together. Stalin saw his alliance with Mao's China as the centerpiece of his global strategy, one whose "importance would be on the same level as the wartime cooperation between the Big Three." Mao believed that his own fundamental goals and those of China required that he demonstrate "his allegiance to Stalin and his willingness to comply with Soviet demands . . . while exploiting every opportunity to demonstrate his independence and his adeptness."[16] In Stalin's eyes, Mao's task was "to promote revolutionary struggle in Vietnam and southeast Asia, threaten to attack Taiwan and assist Kim Il-sung in his takeover of South Korea . . . [thus] causing the United States to split its forces and face combat on two global fronts."[17]

There is no official record of any discussion between Stalin and Mao regarding Kim Il Sung's planned invasion, but Khrushchev recalls that Mao approved the idea and expressed the opinion that the United States would not interfere.[18] In the post-Mao era some Chinese writers have reported that the Chairman had cautiously urged the Koreans to take American intervention into account, but thought Kim was determined to attack the South regardless.[19] Hence Mao, very likely recalling the assistance he had received from North Korea in the fight for Manchuria, suggested to Stalin that they "should help 'Little Kim.'"[20] In response to Kim's request, Mao, while still in Moscow, ordered the transfer to the North Korean Army of an additional 14,000 PLA soldiers of Korean nationality.[21]

Militarily, the capture of South Korea seemed a far less formidable and risky undertaking than the invasion of Taiwan. The South Korean army of 100,000 had equipment for only about 65,000, no tanks, and almost no airplanes.[22] Mao might logically have concluded that if Kim acted first, the fall of South Korea would devastate what remained of morale on Taiwan and very possibly preclude the necessity of a PLA invasion of the island. To facilitate both invasions, greatly increased shipments of Soviet arms began pouring down the Manchurian rail lines into China and over the Trans-Siberian into North Korea. Over the next few years the USSR would provide China almost two thousand front-line aircraft, including the most modern MIG 15s, as well as pilots, instructors, parts, and ordinance.[23]

ON TAIWAN THE KMT ORGANIZATION was trying to retrench amid intrigues and uncertainty. Ch'en Li-fu, who with his brother had long dominated the KMT, learned that Ching-kuo intended to arrest him. Li-fu thought that both Ch'en Ch'eng and Ching-kuo had persuaded the Gimo to turn against him. He decided to resign and soon ended up in New Jersey, where he and a friend bought a chicken farm with $4,000 of Ch'en's own money and a loan from H. H. Kung.[24] Plenty of the old guard remained, however. The Legislative Yuan and the National Assembly together harbored more than two thousand of them. In addition, a new old guard was already in place—middle-aged party, military, and security officers, including military commissars, whose outlook on life and governance was similar to that of the myopic generation that had dominated the KMT since 1928.

In March 1950, when Chiang resumed the presidency, he appointed low-key and honest Ch'en Ch'eng as Premier and promoted a number of American-trained officials to senior rank, such as K. C. Wu and George Yeh (a graduate of Amherst and Cambridge who became the new Foreign Minister).[25] Madame Chiang was a strong supporter of all the American graduates. Another favorite was the general manager of the Central Trust of China, K. Y. Yin, graduate of the American-run St. John's University in Shanghai, who had in this chaotic period achieved what seemed a miracle, a stable currency—the New Taiwan Dollar (NT$).

Chiang Kai-shek formally appointed Ching-kuo director of the renamed General Political Department of the Ministry of Defense. The new director planned a fundamental restructuring of the political officer corps back along Soviet lines, including a new surveillance system within the military, strengthened counterintelligence, and reinstallation of KMT activities throughout the military.[26] Meanwhile in the spring there was a new wave of arrests of suspected Communists within the armed forces and also of generals closely associated with Li Tsung-jen.[27]

Among senior commanders General Sun Li-jen was the one most disgruntled with the growing activism and independence of the political officers, and he continued to complain to his American contacts. In a March 20 memorandum, the CIA cited reports that Sun was planning a coup. If the CIA had picked up these reports, so had Ching-kuo. Surveillance of the VMI graduate and his closest associates increased, even as his star rose.[28]

One day in February Konsin Shah, now a colonel, visited Sun's training command in Kaohsiung. Shah returned to Taipei and at a breakfast meeting with the Gimo and Ching-kuo said that the training command was remarkable, far better than anything he had ever witnessed on the mainland. The Generalissimo finished his meal and said, "First, we go to Sun Li-jen's Training Command and take a look."

Sun had an hour's notice of the arrival of the leader's party, including Ching-kuo and Madame Chiang. The only honor guard at the airport was a bugler. As the Chiangs observed the day's training activities, Ching-kuo was impressed, and Madame even more so. Later that same day the Gimo was on the dais at the parade grounds at the Navy High Command. Numerous admirals were gathered around, but Chiang gestured to Sun Li-jen. "Here, General Sun, stand here on my right." Everyone knew Sun would be the next army commander.[29] The presidential appointment came within the month. One of Sun's achievements was the recruitment and training of a fresh force of 35,000 volunteers, mostly Taiwanese.

Chou Chih-jou, a solid Chiang loyalist, was appointed Chief of Staff and became Sun's boss[30] But aside from Chou, the other five top posts under Chiang Kai-shek, including the new Army Commander and overall Island Defense Commander (Sun Li-jen), were held by individuals respected by Americans and the American government. Four of the five held American degrees and spoke fluent English, and three were in their early forties. This was an attractive team and one difficult for the United States to abandon.

———

THE GIMO'S VARIOUS STRATAGEMS since his temporary "retirement" had won a year to prepare Taiwan for the expected invasion. On a territory the size of Florida the KMT possessed an army grown to about 670,000 soldiers, of whom 377,000 were now combat-ready. It had 250–300 light tanks under the command of Wei-kuo and 270 first-line combat aircraft.[31] At this time the Gimo abandoned Hainan and Chousan islands, although Ching-kuo argued for trying to hold the latter. Chiang planned to concentrate his resources on Taiwan, except for two small but important island outposts.

The two key footholds were Quemoy, off the port of Amoy, and Matsu, off the port of Fuchow, also in Fukien province. If the Nationalists could hold these piles of granite, they would stand as symbols that the Generalissimo's writ extended beyond Taiwan and the Pescadores. They could also be strategically important in detecting and trying to thwart a PLA invasion across the Strait. Ching-kuo visited both islands frequently and reported that they were indeed formidable redoubts. While pulling out of the Chousans, Chiang ordered larger commitments of military resources to Quemoy and Matsu. He also ordered holding a group of smaller islands, the Tachens, as a base for commando raids against the mainland.

But as summer approached, the fate of all these tiny outposts seemed beside the point. In May the CIA reiterated that the Chinese Communists would probably seize Taiwan before the end of the year.[32] The agency estimated that 370,000 troops of the PLA's Third Field Army were in position along the coast and at least 450,000 troops of Lin Piao's Fourth Field Army could support the invasion. The PLA had assembled some 5,000 junks and towed craft for the assault.[33] As a safeguard, Ching-kuo made contingency asylum arrangements in the Philippines for his father.[34] Expecting the onslaught before the typhoon season, Sun Li-jen's men worked day and night digging gun emplacements and tank traps along Taiwan's western shores.

———

KIM IL-SUNG VISITED MOSCOW from March 30 to April 25, 1950. He told Stalin that his invasion and occupation of South Korea would be completed in three days. Stalin approved the attack in principle but said the situation in the West dominated Soviet attention; he urged Kim to consult with Mao because "he had a good understanding of oriental matters." Stalin also told Kim that if the United States should intervene, the Soviet Union could not join the fray. Korea was no longer in the Soviet sphere. In the new partnership, it was a Chinese responsibility. Kim then went to see Mao. The Chinese leader expressed some reservations but in the end again gave his blessing.[35]

MEANWHILE, General MacArthur and Defense Secretary Louis Johnson continued to maneuver behind the scenes to reverse Truman's Taiwan policy.[36] Complicating matters, Senator Joseph McCarthy shifted the focus of his charges to the China field. In February he revealed his phantom list of Communist agents in the State Department. Smelling political blood, many Republican congressmen rallied behind the senator.[37] But most Republicans as well as Democrats and the American public in general still drew back from the thought of actually getting into a war with Communist China over Taiwan. The White House continued to write off the island as a lost cause.

Nevertheless, as disaster for Taiwan loomed, infighting within the U.S. government on the issue escalated. More Washington officials, including Assistant Secretary for Far Eastern Affairs Dean Rusk, became enamored of George Kennan's idea of replacing Chiang Kai-shek with a more liberal Chinese leader and seeking a U.N. trusteeship of some sort. The most frequently cited successor to the Gimo in this scenario was Dr. Hu Shih, the best-known Chinese intellectual of the time and a former Chinese ambassador to the United States from 1938 to 1942. But the key flaw in this strategy was that Chiang Kai-shek would not go quietly. The thoughts of those pushing for his replacement inevitably centered once again on General Sun Li-jen.

A year earlier Sun had turned down MacArthur's suggestion that he assume political leadership on Taiwan. But even if Sun now agreed, it seemed unlikely to those who knew much about Taiwan (and they did not include MacArthur) that he could in fact carry off a coup. To do so he would first have to wipe out 100 or so senior Nationalist officers stoutly loyal to the Gimo, including Chiang Ching-kuo. Ching-kuo's surveillance system was too good for anyone to think of such an elaborate plot. In addition, three of Sun's best divisions in the south were Youth Army divisions, whose loyalty to Ching-kuo was probably as strong as it was to Sun. Ch'en Ch'eng had transferred Sun's other crack divisions, those of the 52nd Army, to the Pescadores, where they could play no role in any coup scenario. In another anti-coup move, Ch'en positioned troops under a separate command between Kaohsiung and Taipei.[38]

As the prospect of a Communist invasion looked closer, Sun seemed to have changed his mind. In April 1950 the American military attaché in Taiwan reported that a high-level official, assumed to be Sun, told him that under Chiang Kai-shek the prospects were hopeless and "drastic measures" were needed. Dean Rusk saw the cable as did Paul Nitze, who had replaced George Kennan as director of Policy Planning. Nitze had his own fanciful scheme for promoting a coup on the mainland as well as on Taiwan.[39] On May 30, he, Rusk, and other senior officials drew up a plan to inform Chiang Kai-shek that the only recourse to avoid a bloody Communist takeover of Taiwan was for Chiang to request U.N. trusteeship, leave the island, and turn control over to General Sun.[40]

John Foster Dulles, whom Rusk had brought in as an adviser, was to inform the Gimo that the condition for American military protection of Taiwan was his resignation. A strong conservative, Dulles in private essentially favored the independent Taiwan option. It was "scandalous," he wrote "to adopt the theory that Formosa is part of China and that, therefore, the Formosans must be subjected to the cruel fate of being the final battleground between the Red regime and the Nationalist Army."[41] Neither Rusk nor Dulles understood the strength of both Chiang's and Mao's resistance to the idea of permanently dividing China.[42]

In a 1990 interview Rusk confirmed that in early June 1950 he received a secret, hand-delivered note from Sun Li-jen in which the general himself proposed to lead a *coup d'état* against the Gimo.[43] Sun asked for the support or acquiescence of the United States. Alarmed that the Gimo would kill Sun if the message got back to Taipei, Rusk burned the note and reported the incident directly to Secretary Acheson. Acheson promised to take the matter up with President Truman.

—

IN HIS ASSESSMENT of the situation in Taiwan, the American chargé in Taipei stressed in his cables that the Gimo, who was aware of the frustrated brainstorming going on in Washington, would never voluntarily turn over power to General Sun.[44] American military intelligence reported ever larger numbers of Communist troops massing on the coast opposite Taiwan. For the first time, PLA MIG fighters were in the air.[45] The State Department urged Americans on the island to leave. Unbeknownst to all the elaborate intelligence agencies, however, Mao Zedong had ordered the invasion of Taiwan postponed until the summer of 1951. According to one account, the Central Military Commission in Peking decided that PLA troop deployments to the coast were taking longer than expected and the attack force could not be ready before the typhoon season.[46] But the most important consideration was probably knowledge of Kim Il-sung's plans. Mao did not know the exact date of the coming North Korean attack, but he knew it was coming soon. The Chairman may have ordered postponement of the assault on Taiwan in hopes that the fall of South Korea would make invasion of the island unnecessary.

On June 23 Rusk talked with Hu Shih, who resided in New York. Assuredly, the conversation was about the possibility of his replacing Chiang if the latter would retire for good. Hu apparently refused. Now, the only option for getting rid of Chiang was the hazardous and dubious one of backing a *coup d'état* by Sun. But on the same day Rusk talked with Hu, Acheson held a news conference and announced that American policy was unchanged—the United States would not intervene in Taiwan. Acheson's public remarks reflected President Truman's rejection of the Rusk/Nitze/Dulles plans, Sun's secret coup proposal, and MacArthur's recently renewed demands of military material assistance to Taiwan.[47]

Truman understood that a failed coup attempt in Taiwan would bring chaos to the island, further depress the already low morale of Nationalist troops, and possibly excite Mao into launching his invasion. Critics would blame the administration, claiming that Truman and Acheson's plotting against the Gimo had been directly responsible for the island's fall to the Communists. Why Sun himself in June thought he could carry out a successful coup is puzzling.[48]

While Ching-kuo knew that Sun needed careful watching, it is uncertain whether his agents learned of the June note to Rusk. Possibly they did. But if so, at the end of June Ching-kuo and his father decided not to arrest Sun but to let him continue in his key positions. There was no need to dismay the Americans by arresting their favorite Chinese general. The world had changed. America was back on their side.

ON JUNE 25, 1950, Ching-kuo's aide awakened him early in the morning with a report from the Nationalist embassy in Seoul. At 4:00 AM North Korean artillery had begun smashing the Ongjin area across the 38th parallel. Perhaps this was another border incident. Ching-kuo dressed and drove to his office in the Presidential Building in downtown Taipei. About 6:00 AM North Korean infantry and armor, half of which had been trained in China, crossed the border and made amphibious landings on the east coast.[49] It was time to wake the Generalissimo. As predicted in the Gimo's favorite book, a stream had appeared in the desert, a stream that would soon be a mighty torrent.

President Truman met the next morning at Blair House with Acheson, Rusk, and the Joint Chiefs. The Americans did not, as Kim Il-sung had assumed and Mao had hoped, treat the incident as an internal Korean matter. Instead, they saw a weak state, established under American auspices, suddenly falling victim of armed aggression supported by the Communist giants. The recent Sino-Soviet treaty was on everyone's mind. The North Korean action seemed part of a general Communist offensive in Asia.

Truman ordered military action to assist the South Koreans and instructed the 7th Fleet to dispatch naval forces into the Taiwan Strait. In addition to the tremendous political pressure that liberals and moderates had been under on the issue of Taiwan, they had personally felt guilty about abandoning the island. Moreover, to gain the support of the Republicans and the public at large for the defense of South Korea, it was necessary to reverse position on Taiwan and try to diminish the bitter division over Asian policy. The next day the President commanded the 7th Fleet to repel any attack on Taiwan, called on the government in Taipei to cease all air and sea operations against the mainland, and declared that "the determination of the future status of Formosa must await the restoration of security in the Pacific, a peaceful settlement with Japan or consideration by the United Nations."

The Gimo, with Madame and Ching-kuo, convened a series of policy meetings in Taipei beginning early on Sunday morning. The group approved a statement by Foreign Minister Yeh that the Republic of China was suspending its naval and air operations against the mainland as the United States had requested, but it also reasserted that Taiwan was a part of China. Truman's declaration did "not in any way affect China's authority over Formosa."[50] George Yeh also proposed that the Gimo offer to send Nationalist troops to fight in Korea. The Generalissimo and others were initially opposed to the idea, but eventually approved it on Yeh's assurance that the Americans would reject it, which they did.[51]

IF KIM HAD DELAYED HIS ATTACK on the South, and instead Mao had launched his invasion of Taiwan on June 25, the United States very likely would not have intervened to save the island. But North Korea went first, and the Korean War gave new life to the Gimo's expected short tenure on Taiwan.[52] The quick and forceful American response in Korea and in the Taiwan Strait shocked Mao. Nevertheless, he saw the crisis as an opportunity to whip up a frenetic wave of anti-American revolutionary fervor throughout Asia. The conflict also precluded the high risks involved in the PLA's planned invasion of Taiwan.[53]

Truman and Acheson wanted to limit the American commitment to Chiang Kai-shek in the hope of avoiding Chinese Communist intervention in Korea or a clash in the Taiwan Strait.[54] MacArthur, however, insisted from the start on all-out support for the Nationalists and the use of Taiwan as a strategic asset for the protection and projection of U.S.

power. On July 1 MacArthur, without the State Department's approval, flew to Taipei to see the Generalissimo. MacArthur promised that Taiwan would get all the military equipment and supplies it needed, and his staff immediately set up a liaison office in Taipei.[55] The American Military Advisory Group (MAAG) and major shipments of military material and weapons would not appear until the next year, but the presence of the 7th Fleet in the Strait had removed any real danger to Taiwan.[56]

In early September the outgoing American chargé complained that the Generalissimo and his top officials dealt with MacArthur's staff in Taipei and openly ignored the accredited U.S. representative, namely himself.[57] Ching-kuo sent some of his closest associates, including Tsu Sung-chi'u, as liaison officers to MacArthur's headquarters in Tokyo, where they received daily intelligence briefings on the war and on developments on mainland China.[58] The chargé departed Taipei, and Karl Rankin, a career diplomat who had always been strongly pro-Nationalist, took over the embassy. Thereafter embassy reporting would contain no more complaints about MacArthur or police measures on the island. The bamboo wall in front of Rankin's residence on Yangming Mountain came down.

Although official American policy on the island's future remained equivocal, the Gimo and Ching-kuo felt their position was strong enough to complete the party reform they had been planning since 1949. Less than a month after the beginning of the Korean War, Chiang abolished the Central Executive Committee of 286 members and in its place appointed a Central Reform Committee with only 16 members, including Ching-kuo and Ch'en Ch'eng. The new committee not only would make organizational changes in the KMT but would serve for the time being as executive body of the party.[59]

Part of the reform process was a purging of the party rolls. Younger and more educated officials, many with ties to Ching-kuo, took over the headquarters. One of his important changes was to require a college degree as a prerequisite for new KMT officials.[60] Now, there were no longer competing and powerful cliques within the party to which members and cadre could lend support in return for patronage. Nomination for membership in the Central Committee henceforth would require approval by Director General Chiang Kai-shek. The result was a much tighter control over organization and operation than had ever been the case on the mainland. As the outgoing chargé explained in his final cable to Washington, the principal effect of the party reform was to endow the Gimo's elder son with "great power in police, party, military, and political affairs."[61]

The new KMT political program formally promulgated on September 1, 1950, paid scant attention to political rights. Ching-kuo, his father, and the entire KMT leadership knew that totally free and democratic elections would result in a Taiwanese, non-KMT, and probably pro-independence government. One-party local elections in which independents could run were the only concession to a more democratic system. This was considered the minimum necessary to engage the Taiwanese in the new order and placate the Americans.

The program also reflected continuing socialist influence—at least its state centrism—in the economic thinking of the old KMT generation as well as of Ching-kuo and his contemporaries. The party dedicated itself to encouraging family farming and private enterprise and was preparing to turn over many factories to private hands. But it also transferred from the provincial government to the central government major industrial sectors inherited from the Japanese, including steel, mining, petroleum, electric power, ship building, sugar, and fertilizer. The provincial government retained ownership and management of alcohol, tobacco, and forestry.[62]

DESPITE THE DELUGE OF HOSTILE WORDS flowing out of Peking, there had been no military conflict or even a skirmish between Chinese and American forces. In August and early September of 1950 the North Koreans continued to roll back the shattered South Korean army and the first contingents of American troops who had arrived on the peninsula. At this point, MacArthur made the last brilliant military move of his career. On September 15, U.N. (mostly American) forces landed at Inchon, just below Seoul. Cut off from its supplies, the overextended North Korean Army collapsed.[63] As the invaders fell back in disarray, Stalin cabled Mao asking if China was in a position to send troops to help the North Koreans.[64] Zhou Enlai rushed to Moscow, where Stalin proposed the first concrete implementation of the division of labor in the new Sino-Soviet global partnership: China would provide the manpower to assist Pyongyang, while the Soviet Union would furnish ammunition, planes, artillery, tanks, and other equipment.[65]

The Soviet leader believed that at all costs a nuclear world war had to be avoided, given the great American superiority in this area.[66] But, he calculated, massive Soviet material aid to Chinese "volunteers" in Korea and even limited employment of Soviet jets (with PLA or North Korean markings) was a gamble worth taking. By distracting the United States, a prolonged Korean conflict could significantly advance Soviet interests in Europe. A clear American defeat would, of course, have even more far-reaching implications. At the same time, Stalin minimized the possibility of direct clashes between American and Soviet personnel by withdrawing all Soviet advisers from North Korea.[67] When Zhou Enlai left his office, Stalin could have puffed on his pipe with satisfaction. United States-China hostility and consequently Chinese reliance on the USSR appeared assured for a long time to come.

Also as a result of the war in Korea seen from another perspective, Taipei would gain enormous leverage over the United States and a long-term effective shield against its powerful enemy. But again, Mao was not dismayed by the escalating U.S. intervention. Since a horrendous war between China and "U.S. imperialism" was inevitable, it was best to confront it in Korea.[68] The Chairman and the CCP leadership had in fact made the decision to enter the war even before the Inchon landing.[69] The Americans could not believe that Mao would really pay the great price and take the enormous risks that a mass assault into Korea would entail. On November 24 General MacArthur told his troops that they would be home by Christmas. Three days later, 300,000 Chinese "volunteers" led by General P'eng Te-huai attacked advance units of the American army and marines.

A deep sense of crisis seized the United States. Over the next two and a half years, tens of thousands of Americans would die fighting the Chinese Communists. Military assistance for an anti-Communist, Chinese ally on Taiwan would be a high priority for the United States. The CIA would receive virtually unlimited funding for its collaborative efforts with Ching-kuo's intelligence and special operations units. For two decades the United States would recognize the authoritarian regime on an island off the coast of Fukien as the legitimate Chinese government. This government would, next to Japan and South Korea, be the major US ally in the Far East.

12

Secret Wars

AS THE CONFLICT IN KOREA ESCALATED, Taiwan became the principal U.S. base for collecting intelligence and waging clandestine war against mainland China. Taiwan was not so much "an unsinkable aircraft carrier" as it was an "unsinkable station" for the CIA. As one former agency officer recalled, over the course of twenty years since the Korean War the agency provided to the Nationalists "a cornucopia of money, arms, equipment, and training." A succession of CIA station chiefs in Taipei thought and acted as if they were the premier U.S. decision-makers on the island. It became common practice for the station chief not to inform his nominal boss, the American ambassador, of major activities the agency was undertaking.[1]

In the first two years of the Korean War the Office of Policy Coordination (OPC), which was the successor of the famous World War II Office of Strategic Services (OSS), ran all U.S. covert operations out of Taiwan. In August 1949, with OPC support, Chennault arranged for the sale of his bankrupt airline, CAT, for $950,000 to the CIA. This gave the OPC and later the CIA its own commercial flying company—which at the same time remained the flag carrier for the Republic of China—to use for covert air operations against China and North Korea, and later against enemies in Indochina and Indonesia.[2] CAT and subsequently other front corporations, notably Air America and Air Asia, held by a OPC/CIA proprietary holding company called Pacific Corporation, operated out of Taiwan for the next two decades.[3] During the Korean War the operation flew 15,000 support missions and overflights of enemy territory. The agency even owned a B-17 bomber, which made flights as long as twenty hours over China and ranged as far as Tibet.[4]

The OPC/CIA station in Taipei ballooned to over 600 American employees. It operated behind a thin facade known by most taxi drivers in the city—a phantom company called Western Enterprises on Prestige Road. The first station chief in the new era was an ex-policeman named Charlie Johnston, "a full-steam-ahead sort of guy." During World War II Johnston had been in OSS and worked for a time in joint operations with Tai Li's military intelligence. Johnston's main objective was to support the 1.6 million guerrillas the Gimo and Ching-kuo claimed were still active on the mainland. The U.S. MAAG and military intelligence units also soon became heavily involved in the paramilitary business, sometimes coordinating with OPC/CIA and sometimes not.[5]

SOONG MEI-LING REMAINED her husband's primary adviser on diplomatic and political matters involving the United States. She now extended her portfolio to senior-level liaison with OPC/CIA on intelligence and covert action, reporting directly to the Gimo on these subjects.[6] But it was Ching-kuo who supervised and actually ran all of Taiwan's clandestine intelligence and paramilitary operations, including those done in cooperation with the Americans.[7] The Special Warfare Center, which he controlled, commanded the units that carried out covert activities. The center included two Special Forces groups with a total of 7,000 men and the Anti-Communist National Salvation Corps (ACNSC) of 5,500. The Americans described them as "highly qualified troops . . . with high *esprit de corps* but not always amenable to strict military discipline."[8] There was also an "orphans unit" of some 600 boys being trained for guerrilla war, sons of KMT officers killed in combat on the mainland. The U.S. MAAG supported two additional Special Forces groups totaling 6,000 personnel, also under Ching-kuo's Special Warfare Center.[9]

According to several Chinese officers close to Ching-kuo, and confirmed by CIA officials in Taiwan at the time, there were occasional policy differences between Madame Chiang and her stepson over intelligence and covert activities. But it was not in their style to show open conflict of any sort. Normally, they met separately with the Gimo to discuss issues on which they disagreed.[10]

WITH THE RAPID CLOSING of the "bamboo curtain," the CIA had virtually no reliable intelligence assets on mainland China. Consequently, the agency was eager to support Ching-kuo's clandestine collection activities, including communications intercepts and air reconnaissance as well as agent intelligence inside China. These collection activities soon employed thousands of people on Taiwan, Americans as well as Chinese.

Ching-kuo's sources on the mainland were agents left behind by Tai Li's bureau and other organizations in the Nationalist clandestine establishment. Taipei maintained contact with some of its agents by shortwave radio, but the Communists quickly tracked down and destroyed these sources. Many were "turned" into double agents and began sending back information under the control of CCP and PLA intelligence organizations.[11]

Most American officials soon came to put a low value on the intelligence produced by Ching-kuo's agents and infiltrators working on the mainland. All but one of more than a dozen CIA and military officers interviewed for this study who were familiar with the KMT's agent-based intelligence described it as basically useless and sometimes manufactured either by the Communists or the Nationalists themselves. Numerous State Department officers of the time were unanimous in their low opinion of it.[12]

Intercepts of mainland communications or "sigint" intelligence, aided by the CIA and the National Security Agency (NSA) became the most reliable source of information. Soon after the Korean War began, the NSA opened an elaborate radio monitoring facility near Taipei. The Nationalist counterpart agencies, which Ching-kuo controlled, provided most of the several thousand personnel to record and analyze military and governmental radio transmissions on the mainland. In other operations, Nationalist pilots made overflights of China and recorded transmissions by PLA radar. This sort of "sigint" provided excellent order of battle information to American and Nationalist military commanders.[13]

———

IN EARLY 1950 the gutsy Nationalist General Hu Ts'ung-nan attempted to regroup the remnants of his destroyed 3rd Army as a guerrilla force on the Sino-Burmese border. Within a few months this effort collapsed, and Hu fled back to Taiwan. Several thousand of his troops under General Li Mi, however, escaped into the mountains of Burma. In the fall of 1950 these KMT remnants faced an uncertain future, but assistance was on the way. Before the end of the year Ching-kuo's special forces devised a plan for the invasion of southern China using Li Mi's ragtag soldiers. The American covert specialists in OPC supported the plan, but the director of the CIA, Walter Bedell Smith, opposed it as doomed to failure. President Truman, however, overruled him. American conservatives at this time were demanding that the White House allow MacArthur to launch air strikes at military targets inside China and that Chiang Kai-shek be "unleashed" to fight the Communists. The White House could not afford to spurn such apparently low-cost opportunities to hit the enemy in his "soft underbelly."

The invasion plan out of Burma was premised on the Nationalist claim that several hundred thousand KMT guerrillas supposedly hiding out in south China needed only a little encouragement to go on the offensive. Without a doubt, Ching-kuo knew that these remnants could not conceivably become an effective force. But he and his father were happy to go along with an adventure that would intensify China-U.S. hostility, tie the Americans more closely to the Nationalist government, and bring funding, equipment, and jobs into Ching-kuo's special operations apparatus. With the secret cooperation of the Thai government, CAT planes began to fly arms, equipment, and trainers as well as American OPC advisers to Li Mi's bases.[14]

In April of 1951 General MacArthur went public with his call for an all-out war against China, including acceptance of Chiang Kai-shek's offer of troops to fight in Korea, and proposing U.S. support for the opening of a second front in China by the Nationalists. Few Americans understood that the Gimo had no desire to launch an invasion of the mainland even with U.S. air and sea support. Truman removed the hero of the war in the Pacific from his command and appointed General Matthew Ridgway as his successor. Under bitter and intensifying criticism for his policy of limited war in Korea, the President was now more inclined than ever to let the covert operations advocates have their way in regard to the KMT irregulars.

In June Li Mi and 2,000 men crossed the border and trekked 60 miles into Yunnan. At that point PLA militia attacked in force, killing a large number of the KMT soldiers and several Americans. Li Mi and his men fled back to Burma. Another attack further south met a similar fate. Despite these failures, loud protests from the Burmese government, and *New York Times* disclosures of the secret flights from Taiwan, the CIA-supported buildup of Ching-kuo's irregulars continued.[15] In late 1951 Li Mi flew to Taipei for a three-month stay and met with Ching-kuo to plan his next move. Returning to Burma with 700 regular Nationalist soldiers, Li Mi launched his last major assault in August 1952. Once again the PLA inflicted heavy loses on the intruders, who then scurried back into Burma, leaving many casualties behind.

Walter Bedell Smith was outraged at the debacle and abolished the OPC, merging it with the CIA's Office of Special Operations. For their part, the KMT officers and men in Burma settled down to a new life. They took local wives and occasionally made "intelligence-gathering" raids into China. But they spent most of their time in the lucrative opium trade, acting as middlemen, transporters, and security. Soon they controlled 90 percent of the drug traffic.[16]

BEFORE 1949 Ching-kuo was known to many foreigners and Chinese as incorruptible, energetic, determined, amiable, pragmatic, unassuming, and above all as an official who actually seemed to care for the welfare of the ordinary man. His enemies called him idealistic, naive, and left-leaning, but almost everyone (even, in private, the Communists) agreed his heart was in the right place. But on Taiwan, after 1950, he would come to be identified as the enforcer of the White Terror. The Taiwanese (such as Henry Kao, for instance, the non-KMT mayor of Taipei in the 1950s) who recognized Chiang Ching-kuo's honesty and concern for the common people, nevertheless believed he was personally responsible for the brutal suppression of the early 1950s.[17]

ONCE THE U.S. NAVY steamed into the Strait, Ching-kuo and the Gimo had much less reason than before to be concerned about either Communist infiltration or Taiwanese resistance. CCP agents already under cover on the island were disheartened, and more such agents began to turn themselves in. In December 1950 the Peace Preservation Headquarters announced that another 500 "underground Communist workers" had surrendered.[18] Later, Ching-kuo would state that by the end of the year the CPP no longer posed a menace on the island.[19]

But after June 1950 the security priority shifted back to Taiwanese suspected of anti-KMT and pro-independence sympathies. The CIA reported a noticeable increase in "repressive activities" and a resultant "popular [Taiwanese] revulsion against the regime."[20] The American chargé before Rankin called it a "reign of terror," although "more silken than in other countries and in other times." Even mild criticism of the regime, according to the chargé, could result in arrest and disappearance.[21] A senior operations officer in the CIA enterprise in Taipei reported hearing executions in the stadium. "Ching-kuo got all the Communists," he said, "but also a lot of others."[22]

Yet very few Taiwanese were likely at this time to engage in plotting violent or even nonviolent opposition to the KMT regime. After the crackdown of 1949 and with the memory of 1947 still very much alive, Taiwanese seemed profoundly subdued. In 1996 Wang Sheng stated that the Taiwan Independence Movement in the early 1950s "was a problem, but a relatively small one . . . not too serious."[23]

Judging by CIA data and statements from K. C. Wu, Ching-kuo, and the Peace Preservation Headquarters, it appears the number of individuals convicted of subversion was around 600 in 1951 and 1952 and around 750 in 1954. Many more were probably detained and released.[24] The numbers began to decline in 1955. In the mid-fifties there were about 14,000 political prisoners on Green Island.[25] The official figure for all arrests in Taiwan under martial law from 1949 to 1987, when the decree ended, is 29,407.[26] If Wang Sheng's estimate is correct and about 15 percent of those arrested were executed, this would give a total death toll in the 36-year period of very roughly 4,500. This is consistent with the 1997 estimate by a Taiwanese writer and TV documentarist.[27] Even a death toll half this figure would make for a comparable figure proportional to the population of the United States today of between 50,000 and 70,000 executions.

IN AUGUST 1950 Ching-kuo again reorganized the intelligence and secret police networks, pulling its various wings even more under his control. This restructuring provided him an unrivaled opportunity to know a great deal about all civil as well as military officers on Taiwan.[28] In 1954 he made the National Security Bureau (NSB) the central intelligence coordinating body. He held the nominal title of deputy head of the NSB but in reality acted as chief.[29] His simultaneous position as deputy chief of the 6th Division of KMT headquarters, which dealt with security and intelligence matters, gave him another line of direct authority over all organizations in this field.[30]

Ching-kuo inserted his own people—Youth Army and Youth Corps veterans—into the key intelligence bureaus as well as into the Taiwan Garrison Command (the former Peace Preservation Corps). Among other functions, this office controlled censorship, officially through post-publication sanctions. Among other new measures, Ching-kuo implemented a system in which every major business had to have a retired security or military officer in a high position in its personnel office.[31] One of Ching-kuo's immediately successful reforms was to sever the historic connections between the security services and various gangs and secret societies. A number of individual intelligence agents and military officers retained their personal ties to such groups, but for the next 30 years this unsavory link did not exist on the official level.[32]

Ching-kuo was an empathetic and not a brutal man. He and his friends, however, rationalized the "white terror" as necessary to preserve the integrity of the regime and thus Chinese unity. From their political point of view, they faced a serious potential threat of subversion—not just to their rule but to Chinese nationalism. By taking extreme measures to assure the survival of their regime and their political principle—Chinese unity—Ching-kuo and his men of course also served their personal and power interests. In the 1990s Ching-kuo's surviving associates from those early days on Taiwan argued that if they had not suppressed latent resistance, agitation for Taiwanese control would have emerged and escalated, and in the ensuing turmoil the Nationalist-mainlander military and the hard right in the KMT would have taken over and carried out a much worse reign of terror.

Whatever the rationalization, the political killings in this period were not only grossly inhuman but unnecessary. History is not without other examples of individuals who wielded great authority and were essentially people of good will rationalizing a terrible abuse of their power. One story reflects Ching-kuo's own humanness and lack of political vindictiveness on a personal level, even while he was overseeing a brutal suppression campaign. An officer in the 52nd Army, who had known Ching-kuo since 1942, came to tell him that his wife and children had not been able to escape the mainland, and he wished to join them. Ching-kuo offered to find the officer another wife. But the man replied that he loved his family and would like to go home. Ching-kuo suggested they change the subject. In a few days, however, the officer was surprised to receive orders assigning him to a KMT front organization in Hong Kong. From there he easily returned to Nanking, where, having survived a harrowing series of purge campaigns, he and his family still lived in 1996.[33]

IN 1951 CHING-KUO SET UP a new Political Staff College (originally called the Political Warfare Cadre School) in the small town of Peitou, a few miles down the river from Taipei.[34] Wang Sheng became Dean of Students, senior political instructor, and eventually director of the new college. Wang would prove to be the foremost ideologist of the KMT.[35]

Chiang Kai-shek's dictum that the struggle against the Communists was 30 percent military and 70 percent political was the foundation of the school's curriculum. The basic course lasted four years and was considered the equivalent of a university or military academy degree. The curriculum included military science and classes in history and foreign languages. The ideological education stressed the KMT's commitment to modernization and the public welfare, and also to the preservation of traditional Chinese culture.[36] The philosophy justified authoritarian rule but had no relationship to fascist beliefs, nor was it otherwise totalitarian, racist, or malevolently nationalistic. The KMT police state did not seek to eliminate autonomy in social, cultural, and economic life, although it monitored all these sectors. Its professed ideals of humanism and eventual democracy, while extravagantly dishonored in terms of political rights, would shape the values of the upcoming generation.

The school's graduates became the new political officers in the armed forces. They had no voice in combat operations, but were responsible for detecting disloyalty or subversion among officers and men alike, as well as rooting out corrupt and abusive practices. They compiled a political report on every officer in their respective units. Special sections ran psychological warfare operations designed to win over enemy troops and populations; for example, sending balloons over the mainland with propaganda tracts or dropping pamphlets from aircraft.[37] In 1953 the GPWD reported it had dropped 300 million leaflets on the mainland.[38] When the winds shifted, the Communists sent similarly laden balloons the other way.

Political officers were also responsible for troop welfare—pay, food, living accommodations, and dependent care. Within a few years, the GPWD transformed living conditions for Nationalist troops and their dependents. Among the new facilities were housing units, hospitals, and primary schools. The department provided compensation to survivors of those killed on active duty and rehabilitation and job placement for wounded or disabled servicemen. This was a revolution in the treatment of the common soldier in the Chinese Nationalist army. In one of its more popular operations, the GPWD ran 37 "tea houses" or brothels employing almost a thousand "hostesses."[39] Quemoy and Matsu each featured a "tea house," whose ladies were flown over for six-month engagements.

By 1957 there were 17,139 political officers serving in the three military services, or about one for each 35 personnel in the armed forces.[40] Ching-kuo had shaken the hand of each of these political officers and personally signed off on their promotions. Approximately 86 percent had undergone training at the Political Staff College. Thus emerged a new corps of young, educated, and enthusiastic commissars dedicated to the ideals of the Party, to Chiang Kai-shek, and to Chiang Ching-kuo.[41] These officers would also honor a traditional tie to their headmaster, Wang Sheng.

Along with reinstating political officers in the ROC armed forces, Ching-kuo restored Party control of the military, reintroducing Party cells at the company level and up. By 1954, 210,000 of the 600,000 members of the armed forces belonged to the KMT. Virtually all regular officers were Party members and thus participated in the KMT committees of their respective units. Party control restored the authority of the political officers, who could now take up differences with their line commanders in these committees or appeal unresolvable problems through Party lines of authority.[42]

Many senior line officers grumbled over this state of affairs. Wei-kuo, for example, once complained loudly to Wang Sheng about the activities of the political officers. These words got back to Ching-kuo and "deepened the misunderstanding" that was developing between the brothers.[43] On the arrival of the American MAAG in 1951, its commander, Major General William C. Chase, made no bones about his disapproval of the concept of political officers in the military. In his first report to the Generalissimo Chase declared, "There is throughout the Armed Forces a highly objectionable system of Political Commissars, that acts to penalize initiative and undermine the authority of commanders at all echelons."[44] At a June 1953 meeting, the Chairman of the Joint Chiefs, Admiral Arthur W. Radford, told President Chiang that "excessive political indoctrination and control had a stultifying effect on younger officers, created widespread insecurity, and weakened the chain of command."[45]

The Gimo had no intention this time of fundamentally altering the political officer corps to suit the United States. Ching-kuo, however, impressed the Americans by his willingness to discuss the role of the GPWD and to hear their point of view. He downplayed the aspect of Party control of the military and stressed the political officers' role in welfare and morale, as if they mostly organized sports days and handed out doughnuts. At Ching-kuo's invitation, the American military assigned an adviser to the GPWD in order to provide the MAAG an insight into what went on in this unfamiliar branch of service. As another concession to the Americans, Ching-kuo also officially reduced the percent of training hours the military spent on political subjects from 25 percent to 10 percent.[46] These gestures placated the U.S. government, which was not prepared to make fundamental changes in Ching-kuo's political officer system a condition for the extensive U.S. military aid that was flowing into the island.[47]

Nevertheless, the opposition of the Americans to the commissars in the early years of the MAAG encouraged Sun Li-jen to disapprove more outspokenly. He told U.S. officers that the dual system in the Nationalist military presented "an almost insuperable barrier to the achievement of good military discipline, high morale, and effective combat potential."[48] Friction over the role of political officers reflected the latent but growing rivalry between Ching-kuo and Sun for leadership in a future, post-Chiang Kai-shek era.[49] Some senior officers, including Chou Chih-jou, also were resentful of the forty-year-old Ching-kuo's high rank (general 2nd class) and power.[50] In an effort to reduce these feelings, Ching-kuo downplayed his military rank and seldom wore his uniform, a practice he had followed on the mainland.

TAIWAN'S GOVERNOR K. C. WU also became increasingly frustrated with the activities of Ching-kuo and his security people. One of the first signs of trouble, Wu relates, was when he ordered the release, because of a lack of evidence, of a mainlander businessman charged with Communist connections. Ching-kuo and P'eng Meng-chi came to Wu's office and told him the Gimo wanted the manager shot and his company confiscated. Wu wrote a protest to the Generalissimo, who in this case made a concession, saying that the businessman would receive only seven years in prison. In January 1952 Wu went to the Gimo to complain about "outrages of the secret police and the mockery of the military courts." "If you love your son," he claims he told the Gimo, "do not have him as head of the secret police. He will become the target of the people's hatred."

Ching-kuo pressed the Gimo to ease Wu out of the governorship, although he was a favorite of Madame Chiang.[51] Wu later asserted that he wanted to resign, but the Generalissimo refused and then indirectly threatened him. Shortly after that an automobile accident convinced Wu there had been an attempt on his life, and with the assistance of Madame Chiang he and his wife left hurriedly for the United States.[52]

In March the next year, in his American exile, Wu publicly broke with Chiang Kai-shek, sending open letters to him and the National Assembly cataloguing the iniquities of Chiang Ching-kuo. Wu charged the Generalissimo had delegated most of his powers to his son and that "hardly a day passed without some bitter struggle with the secret police. . . . They made numberless illegal arrests. They tortured and they blackmailed." Wu also claimed that the secret police constantly thwarted his efforts to hold free elections at the local level. Before the December 1952 local elections, the secret police, he alleged, rounded up 398 Taiwanese on charges they were "rascals." The Taiwan public heard little of Wu's charges. Instead, accusations were floated in Taipei charging that he had absconded with half a million dollars. The affair did Ching-kuo's image little good on the island and had a strong impact in the United States, where it reinforced his growing reputation for ruthlessness.[53]

IN JANUARY 1953 Dwight Eisenhower became President, John Foster Dulles Secretary of State, and his brother Allen Director of the CIA. Eisenhower's first priority was to conclude an armistice in Korea. In his first State of the Union address, Ike announced the removal of Truman's prohibition on Nationalist China's military operations against the mainland.[54] After he was "unleashed," however, Chiang did not make a serious proposal to the Americans for a grand counterattack, although he constantly talked about the idea and put forward a stream of unrealistic schemes.

Peking's refusal to allow repatriation to Taiwan of those Chinese Communist POWs in Korea who so wished—about 70 percent of the 21,000 captured "volunteers"—had stalled the armistice talks for more than a year. Two factors caused Mao's reluctant July 1953 decision to back down on the POW issue. The first was the death of Stalin on March 5.

The second was Eisenhower's message to Peking that if the fighting did not end in Korea, he would authorize the use of nuclear weapons and expand the war into China.[55] There is no record of the Gimo or Ching-kuo either in public or private at this time opposing the use of nuclear bombs on Chinese troops and on China itself if the People's Republic continued to block an armistice agreement in Korea. In fact, Ike passed his warning to Peking through two private channels—Prime Minister Nehru of India *and* Chiang Kai-shek.[56]

The Gimo was no doubt delighted to be asked to convey the warning. Without question, it was Ching-kuo who saw that the American message was delivered, probably via Hong Kong, to the Gimo's old colleague from Whampoa days, Zhou Enlai. Ike's nuclear ultimatum alarmed the new leadership in Moscow even more than it did Mao. The Soviet Union was bound in a military alliance with the Peoples Republic. An American nuclear attack on China could have calamitous consequences. The USSR made clear to the Chinese that it was time to declare victory in Korea and end the fighting.[57] Although Peking could claim it had fought the United States and its allies to a standstill, the inconclusive end of the war, forced as it was by an American nuclear threat and tainted with the major loss of face on the POW issue, was a serious reversal for Mao. The Americans were not after all paper tigers; the world revolution in Asia had not been advanced; the prospect of getting Chiang Kai-shek off his island redoubt was the reverse of what it had been three years before; and Peking was now heavily dependent on Soviet military support, including its nuclear umbrella.

The POWs were held at a vast prison camp on the South Korean island of Cheju. The Americans in charge, the Chinese Nationalists, and the South Koreans used various tactics, including intimidation and favorable treatment, to encourage defections. The historian Rosemary Foot makes a telling indictment of the situation, but since most of the POWs were former Nationalist soldiers thrown into the war by the PLA as cannon fodder, it seems likely the great majority did freely opt for Taiwan. Competition between pro-Communist and pro-Nationalist factions in the prison barracks led to several riots and incidents, including the brief capture of the American camp commander by pro-Communist POWs.[58]

Ching-kuo furnished 23 linguists and 55 "instructors" to work with the POWs. After Mao agreed that prisoners appearing before an international repatriation commission could choose to go to Taiwan, Ching-kuo sent more political officers to train the pro-Nationalist inmates on how to give "correct answers" during their interviews.[59] A short time later, at a mass rally in Taipei, Ching-kuo wiped tears from his eyes as he welcomed the former POWs to their new life on Taiwan. Most were older veterans of the Nationalist army, but for some their adventures were not over. Incorporated into Ching-kuo's special commando units, they would be sent on small-scale raids against the mainland, where they were killed or captured. The majority of the rugged but worn down soldiers, however, would simply add to the problems posed by the mass of aging Nationalist veterans. The ex-POWs would eventually form an ultra-right political organization called the Anti-Communist Heroes.[60]

IN THE UNITED STATES Senator McCarthy and his campaign against alleged spies in the government were coming under increasing criticism. One telling charge against the senator was that he had used forged documents provided by Nationalist intelligence organizations—in other words, Ching-kuo's specialists in misinformation.[61] At the same time, *The Reporter* magazine, Congressman Wayne Morse, and other American liberals were highlighting the allegedly nefarious nature of the China Lobby. Ching-kuo and his father agreed that it was time for him to establish a better image in America. A trusted aide of Ching-kuo's traveled to the United States to find out how a visit would be received. State and Defense strongly endorsed it, hoping the trip would enlarge Ching-kuo's "intellectual horizon—on which Soviet Russia looms so large." CIA analysts advised that he was "a proponent of the authoritarian school."[62]

On September 12, 1953, Ching-kuo and one companion, his interpreter and secretary, Samson Shen, departed for the United States. Five hundred government officials and high-ranking generals were at Taipei airport to see him off.[63] American diplomats observed that Ching-kuo was viewed with "a certain measure of dread."[64] In San Francisco, Los Angeles, Sacramento, Chicago, Detroit, Buffalo, and New York the Chinese community entertained the general with large receptions and buffets. People noted that he usually went to the kitchen after such affairs to talk with the cooks. He himself had to ask to visit public schools and factories. On September 28 Ching-kuo called on President Eisenhower at the White House.[65]

After the opening pleasantries, the President raised the question of Burma. With the end of the Korean War, the continued involvement of America's ally with an exile army of drug traffickers inside this neutral country was an increasing international scandal. Ching-kuo told Eisenhower that about 2,000 of the KMT forces would soon be evacuated to Taiwan.[66]

On October 1 Ching-kuo called on Allen Dulles at CIA headquarters. The Chinese complained that he was in the dark about certain aspects of the supposedly cooperative work undertaken by the CIA on Taiwan. He proposed that all information on China gathered by the two sides should be fully exchanged, mutual conclusions drawn, and follow-up efforts coordinated.[67] Dulles accepted these ideas in principle, and the two men agreed that their respective agencies on Taiwan would take up specific proposals to improve the relationship. Dulles did not raise the issue of the KMT irregulars in Burma, an omission that Ching-kuo would surely have noted.[68]

The same day Ching-kuo called on the other Dulles brother. Following a friendly exchange, the Secretary of State said he had "heard from some of our representatives that the General was a little rough in his methods." Samson Shen, the interpreter, did not translate this remark and there was a brief silence. Dulles reiterated that he had "heard that the General was a little rough in his handling of security matters." America, he went on, had dealt with problems of subversion without infringing on basic human rights. He hoped the general would "consider the adaptability of these methods to the circumstances in his own country." Shen translated these remarks and Ching-kuo "murmured an inaudible acknowledgment."[69]

AS THE AMERICANS HOPED, Ching-kuo did return to Taiwan with admiration not just for America's strength but for its open society. Little as well as big things impressed him. He did not see a guard at the Hoover Dam and told Samson Shen that this said a lot about the United States.[70] He also found Americans more disciplined and harder-working than he had thought—not as frivolous as Hollywood films made them out to be. But, he believed, Taiwan's conditions were quite different from those of the United States, and such an open democratic society was a distant goal for his country.[71]

Criticisms of his methods did not greatly disturb him. Limited knowledge of actual conditions on Taiwan and reliance on the views of Western-educated Chinese, he believed, had distorted the views of many Americans on what was happening on the island. Chinese critics in America of the KMT regime had few "grass roots" among the Chinese people and could not speak for them.[72] Security arrests in Taiwan in the year after his return were in fact more frequent than they had been in 1951 and 1952, although after 1954 there were "practically no executions."[73] It was also clear to Ching-kuo that despite Secretary Dulles' remarks, U.S. military and CIA assistance to his government would not only continue but would increase, whatever the degree of "roughness" in his methods. Upon returning to Taiwan, he took over from Madame Chiang her high-level liaison with both the CIA and the MAAG. CIA station chiefs were told that they should give much higher priority than before to developing close relations with Ching-kuo.[74]

Despite the favorable impression that Ching-kuo had made in the United States, some individuals, including John Foster Dulles, remained deeply suspicious. Two years after the visit Dulles referred to the young Chiang as "the possible leader of an anti-American defection (sic)."[75] The unfavorable intelligence on Ching-kuo through the 1950s came from the DDI or analysis side of the CIA, as distinct from the field operatives under the DDO. The analysts based their concerns on the private comments of "many Nationalist leaders" who were not admirers of the young Chiang.[76]

IN DECEMBER 1953 the U.N. General Assembly passed a resolution condemning the Taipei government for its activities inside Burma. Finally, an agreement was reached between Taipei, Rangoon, and Bangkok for

evacuation of the irregulars. CAT transported to Taiwan 5,583 KMT soldiers and 1,040 dependents. Many of the departing soldiers, however,
were either old men or local hill people, rather than Chinese nationals.
Most of the officers and men of the KMT units stayed behind and continued their opium business.[77] Even if he had wished to do so, Ching-kuo
probably could not have compelled all the irregulars to leave, but it is
likely that he instructed Li Mi to retain many of his combat-effective soldiers in Burma and Thailand. Ching-kuo knew the CIA also continued
contact with the KMT forces left in the region, and while neither he nor
the Americans approved of the opium business, both knew how their
"irregular" allies maintained themselves.

13

Family, Friends, Enemies

IN 1955 CHIANG KAI-SHEK was sixty-eight years old, his image more than ever that of the sage leader. Confident of American protection and with Ching-kuo in charge, he could relax in the august, detached style of leadership he preferred. His routine became even more set than in the past. He rose at dawn, and after meditation, exercise, and morning prayers with his wife, he would eat a bowl of wet rice and pickled vegetables and drink a glass of cold water. Then he would go over the folders that Ching-kuo had sent up.[1] His other daily rituals—time for solitary meditation, three walks a day, reading the classics and neo-Confucianist texts, the Bible, and *Streams in the Desert*, and conscientious writing in his diary— underscored his limited involvement in day-to-day affairs. An army general who worked for Ching-kuo in the 1950s said that even in these early years on Taiwan the Gimo lived in an "ivory tower," isolated from much that was going on. Chiang Kai-shek made all "the big decisions" but more and more relied on his son, to be his right hand and also his eyes and ears.

Ching-kuo had also settled into a routine. Rising at dawn, he would exercise and then shower. At 6:30 aides would bring him a stack of folders, yellow for routine matters and red for urgent. After going over these, he would have a quick meal similar to that of his father, which he insisted on getting from the kitchen himself.[2] He would select the folders to take to the Generalissimo and made notes and recommendations on each paper.[3]

In 1954 the MAAG political adviser posted to the GPWD, Lt. Colonel Charles H. Barber, had seen a good deal of Ching-kuo over the previous two and a half years. In personnel actions, Barber reported, Ching-kuo was ruthless, taking decisions without regard to friendship or who got hurt. On the other hand, Ching-kuo's affability and lack of presumption and self-importance were extremely disarming to his critics. "Many people who meet him socially for the first time find their previous conceptions of his appearance and character greatly altered."[4]

Robert Martin, a *US News And World Report* correspondent who had known Ching-kuo on the mainland, came to Taipei and had several meetings and two private dinners with him. Martin was impressed that this man, who possessed so much "naked and brutal power" and whom "the politicians" and some generals hated, dared to travel around and go to restaurants without bodyguards, was "totally unpretentious, frugal, modest, and informal," and displayed none of "the obsequiousness which usually is found among top Nationalist officials." Martin was struck by Chiang Ching-kuo's "questing mind; a total disdain for what we call democratic rights balanced by a dedication and singleness of purpose that is rarely found out here; an internal and spiritual drive that gets him out of bed at 6:30 AM and keeps him working at top speed until mid-night; [and] an ability to relax and enjoy himself simply because he is a fairly earthy man."

———

BUT ONE NEVER FORGETS, Martin added, that "he is a man with terrible power."[5] Visitors to the Ching-kuo household in the early or mid-fifties were surprised to find a modestly furnished abode ducked away on East Ch'angan Road. There was an air of both austerity and informality in the home. Except for a row of telephones, there was no sign this was the residence of the second most powerful man on the island. When entertaining a foreign guest at his residence, Ching-kuo would often wear his long Chinese gown and himself ladle out the hot Chinese dishes. The American scholar and writer, Allen Whiting, recalled Ching-kuo's tanned round face crinkling into an infectious grin as he chatted about his amusing problems in studying English or recounted the escapades of his boys romping around in their "Hopalong Cassidy" outfits. Ching-kuo loved movies and Marilyn Monroe. After dinner the Chiangs would occasionally pile into their Jeep and take off to the local movie house to watch an American film. They would stand in line with the shoving crowd and then try to find seats together in the stuffy and sometimes smelly theater.[6]

When he was home, however, Ching-kuo often was busy with official business, and despite his playfulness with his children, in their eyes he was an august figure. He expected a lot from his sons, and they were afraid of not living up to his expectations. Eddy recalled that when he was a young boy he held his father in "fear and dread." The older boys, Alan and Alex, were bright and, according to family friends, "spoiled brats," whom Ching-kuo would thrash whenever Faina reported serious misbehavior. Ching-kuo wanted at least one of his sons to attend the Military Academy. Alan followed his father's wishes and in 1955 entered the academy as a cadet. In his third year, however, Alan said he could not take the constant pressure in the cadet corps of being the Gimo's grandson and wanted to withdraw. Ching-kuo prevailed on his American military contacts to have the Virginia Military Institute, Sun Li-jen's old school, accept Alan. But despite a crash course, the young man's English was not up to university-level in the United States, and after eight weeks he withdrew from the Institute.[7]

IN DEALING WITH THE AMERICANS Ching-kuo relied on the advice of Jimmy Wei, publisher of the English-language *China News*. Wei was Ching-kuo's sometime interpreter, personal "chum," and drinking companion. Some American officials described him as "foil" and "court jester."[8] Ching-kuo also kept his old friends—his Moscow classmate, Wang Hsin-heng, was godfather to Ching-kuo's second son, Alex, and a close friend. But when the Taiwan Cement Company chose Wang as its chairman, Ching-kuo told an aide that he could not have a close companion in such a powerful business position and henceforth treated Wang as an acquaintance.[9] In a separate category was the "Young" Marshal,

Chang Hsueh-liang. Ching-kuo persuaded his father to move Chang's house arrest from Hsinchu to Peitou and to permit the Marshal to visit public places though not private homes.[10] Once every month or so, Ching-kuo would take Chang out for a late-night dinner, sometimes, it was rumored, with beautiful and accomplished women.[11]

The "friends of Ching-kuo" club convened with their wives at the house on Ch'angan East Road or at the Yangming Mountain house, calling the latter "The Drunken House" after a famous restaurant in Ch'engtu. When each new dish arrived, the whole table would toast, draining their glasses of rice wine. Of course the finger game was the most dangerous event, with the defeated draining not a small tumbler but a vessel of wine. Ladies as well as gentlemen slipped under the table. But the Dean (as he was still known to his pre-1949 friends—even after he became president) never seemed besotted. Occasionally, the guests left with different shoes or coats than the ones with which they arrived. Wives were not among the items confused at such times, but the occasions may have led to some of the affairs Ching-kuo is alleged to have had with the spouses of subordinates.[12] In public he was never seen accompanying a woman other than Faina, but he did apparently carry on several liaisons in the 1950s and 1960s.

As Ching-kuo's power increased, he tried to maintain his contact with ordinary people by taking Sunday walks in the countryside. From 1950 until he became president in 1978, he visited 320 towns and villages, dropping in on families unannounced and eating a simple lunch with the locals in dirt-floored cafes.[13] Sometimes he took dried noodles along to supply his own food. Even in Taipei in the 1950s he occasionally drove himself around town unescorted. One day, when driving a Jeep back to the city, he picked up a hitchhiker. He asked the man where he was going and then went out of his way to let the rider off at his destination. The man thanked him and rewarded him with a NT $10 tip. Ching-kuo accepted the note and when he arrived home gave it to Faina. "Look," he said, "I actually earned some money today."[14]

IN THE THEN SLEEPY TOWN OF HSINCHU, an hour's drive from Taipei, Ching-kuo's illegitimate twin sons, Hsiao-yen and Hsiao-t'zu, also were growing up. They lived with their Grandmother Chang and Uncle Han-lou and his large family in a small house on Central Street. Their school friends were almost all native Taiwanese, thus, in addition to Mandarin, the twins grew up speaking fluent Taiwanese or Minnan. In 1955 the boys were thirteen years old, but their grandmother had not told them who their real father was. They believed he had been trapped somewhere on the mainland. Wang Sheng made occasional visits to check on the family's welfare. Han-lou remained convinced that his sister had been murdered and would not allow the family to go to the government hospital in Hsinchu for treatment. Wang Sheng repeatedly assured him that his anxieties were groundless, but Han-lou would not believe him.[15]

In the late 1950s, when the twins were in high school, they selected their own English names—John for Hsiao-yen and Winston for Hsiao-tz'u. It was at this time that their grandmother, with Ching-kuo's approval, told them who their father was. The boys were shocked to learn they were the sons of Chiang Ching-kuo and the grandsons of Chiang Kai-shek. They felt immense pride, but this was tempered by the grandmother's strict injunction that they must not reveal this secret to anyone. They also realized that they would not be publicly acknowledged by their powerful father or famous grandfather. John Chang believed that over the years Mei-ling may indirectly have provided some of their financial support.[16]

BY 1954 THERE WERE SEVERAL THOUSAND U.S.-trained and equipped paramilitary personnel on Quemoy, Matsu, and the Tachen group of islands further to the north.[17] The CIA continued to keep the American embassy uninformed about raids and other covert activities from these places. Ambassador Rankin complained in one cable that in order to learn what the CIA and the MAAG were up to, he had to rely on Nationalist sources and "odd bits of gossip." At the same time, the CIA and the MAAG were involved in a running battle over which one would have responsibility for paramilitary operations against the mainland. Other American organizations, such as the U.S. Army's notoriously inept 500th Military Intelligence Unit, also got into the act, providing training and equipment to Ching-kuo's outfits without even informing the MAAG or the CIA, much less the ambassador. Rankin gently noted in his cable that these Ching-kuo/CIA/U.S. military covert operations, the scope of which he could only guess, bore on questions of war or peace in the area and thus required "far more attention from the policy angle than [they] appear to have had to date."[18]

The CIA and the MAAG did not let the embassy know of these covert operations in part because they knew the diplomats would describe them as provocative and pointless, especially since the fighting had stopped in Korea. Rankin observed that the clandestine activities were like "tickling the Communist tiger with a feather duster." Such tickling, he said, might provoke Peking into military action against the offshore islands.[19] In 1954 Rankin twice expressed his concern about it to Foreign Minister George Yeh. On each occasion Yeh neatly dismissed the complaint, saying he understood the American military representatives on the island were of quite a different opinion.[20]

After the Korean armistice, the Generalissimo continued to insist that only the destruction of the Communist regime in Peking would bring peace to Asia. He told American visitors that he had the necessary 600,000 troops to establish a secure beachhead on the coast, after which there would be large-scale defections away from the Communists, and Mao would soon have to flee to Moscow. This operation, Chiang admitted, would require a 3- to 6-year effort by the United States to upgrade the arms and equipment of the Nationalist forces, including a massive build up of the air force and navy.[21]

The Gimo knew the limited capability of his armed forces. He also understood that a failed all-out attack against the mainland would decimate the effective core of the Nationalist Army and possibly lead to the collapse of the KMT regime. As always, he had no intention of actually launching a massive invasion or even a large-scale raid directly from Taiwan unless he could be assured of victory. Such a condition could only be met if the Communist regime, including the PLA, was in an obvious state of collapse, or if the Americans were prepared to carry the main burden.

While pinprick raids against the mainland served the purposes of the Taipei government, the Nationalists carried out even these operations with caution. American CIA and military officers who served with Ching-kuo's special operations troops on the offshore islands during the Korean War remarked on the refusal of their Nationalist allies to launch serious raids against the mainland. The Nationalists were afraid, one officer recalled, that if they really hurt "the Chicoms," the latter would do what was necessary to chase them off these small islands. Covert operations launched from the Tachens amounted essentially to encouraging the pirates traditional to the area. The results, according to the Americans, amounted to only a nuisance to the Communists.[22]

John Foster Dulles, who had privately indicated his support for Taiwan independence in 1950, had no expectation of rolling back the Chinese Communists. His real strategic objective was containment of China and the defense of Taiwan. As Nancy Tucker has documented, from the beginning of Chiang's "unleashing" Dulles sought control over the Gimo's actions. In December 1953, in an exchange of letters between Dulles and Foreign Minster Yeh, the ROC once again gave a formal undertaking that its forces would not attack the mainland without prior consultation and agreement with the United States.[23]

SECRETARY DULLES WAS DETERMINED to avoid American involvement in another land war in Asia. In January he declared that the policy of "massive retaliation," meaning reliance on nuclear weapons rather than on American ground forces as in Korea, was already in effect in the Far East. The containment policy and the threat of massive retaliation, however, soon encountered a serious dilemma in Indochina. By 1954 the American military aid program in Vietnam had reached $1 billion, paying 74 percent of the cost of the French war effort. But after the armistice in Korea, Chinese cannon, mortars, bazookas, ammunition, and other supplies began flowing to the Viet Minh from the north, more than offsetting the American aid to the French.[24] At one point Eisenhower toyed with the idea of sending Chiang Kai-shek's troops to reinforce the French, but he abandoned the notion when told that any such move would risk large-scale counterintervention by the Chinese Communists. In addition, the French themselves rejected the option, noting that Nationalists troops would be "highly unwelcome" in Vietnam.[25]

In March General Giap began the siege of the French garrison of 16,000 at Dien Bien Phu. The American Joint Chiefs devised a plan to use "three small tactical atomic bombs to destroy the Viet Minh positions and relieve the garrison." But Eisenhower and Dulles both felt that only overt Chinese Communist aggression would be sufficient provocation for such a drastic step.[26] The problem was that the North Vietnamese were winning without direct Chinese involvement. In an operation that Ching-kuo oversaw, CAT planes based in Taiwan helped to supply Dien Bien Phu in its last days. The French garrison surrendered in May, and 14,000 survivors marched off as prisoners of war.[27] The American nuclear threat, however, did persuade Moscow and Peking to compel Ho Chi-minh to settle for the time being for half of Vietnam.[28]

THE INDOCHINA compromise settlement was part of a new Sino-Soviet international policy of peaceful coexistence that had been under way for a year. Mao had gone along with Moscow's post-Stalin leaders on this global strategy, but he wished to make clear to them and everyone else that peaceful coexistence did not mean that China would accept the permanent "occupation" of Taiwan by the United States. Probably for this reason Mao promptly initiated a crisis over Quemoy and Matsu. Nationalist and Communist aircraft clashed over the islands, and the two sides began to exchange heavy artillery barrages.

The Americans saw the Chinese Communist pressure as a sign that invasion of Quemoy and Matsu was imminent. To the world and to the United Nations it appeared that another war was about to break out in the Far East. Mao, however, almost certainly had no intention of launching a major attack at this time on either Quemoy or Matsu. It is also doubtful, as many then assumed, that Mao hoped his sword-rattling would discourage the ongoing American effort to form an anti-PRC security alliance in Asia or the American-Taiwan security pact that Chiang Kai-shek was demanding.[29] Mao essentially wanted to show his domestic audience and the world at large, including Taipei, Moscow, and Washington, that the Chinese civil war and the quest for Chinese unity were not over.

The Quemoy crisis of 1954 in fact gave impetus to the idea of a U.S.-ROC Mutual Security Treaty. Hoping to maintain flexibility with China for the future, John Foster Dulles had not favored such a pact. As the perceived threat to Quemoy and Matsu built up, Dulles wanted to take the crisis to the Security Council, but Chiang Kai-shek would only agree if Washington committed itself in a treaty to defend Taiwan. Reluctantly, in October 1954, Dulles and Eisenhower agreed to such a treaty provided Chiang was "willing to assume a defensive posture" in the Strait. Ike wanted to make it clear that "we are not going to defend our partner [the ROC] while our partner attacks [mainland China]."[30] Dulles refused explicitly to extend the treaty to cover the offshore islands. But far more important for Chiang—and for Mao—was that the treaty of alliance between the United States and the ROC strongly reinforced the principle of "one-China."

IN THE SUMMER OF 1954 most American military advisers in Taiwan, and probably most Chinese as well, expected Sun Li-jen to be the next Chief of Staff of the Nationalist armed forces. Privately, Sun had continued to express unhappiness with the commissar system and with the Gimo's decision to stake so much on Quemoy and Matsu. On one occasion Sun told Wellington Koo, back briefly in Taipei, that the Gimo's decision to plan for an all-out defense of Quemoy sacrificed military strategy to political considerations. Koo warned the General "to be a little more careful because not everybody . . . would understand or appreciate his views or manner."[31]

Clandestine reports of Sun's *lèse majesté* would have convinced the Gimo and his son that "Vinegar Joe's" admirer and think-alike was positioning himself for a move after the Gimo's death, if not before. In August 1954 Chiang Kai-shek suddenly removed Sun from all his command posts and appointed him his personal Chief of Staff, an entirely ceremonial position. In May 1955 the military police arrested Colonel Kuo Ting-liang, a former aide of General Sun's, on the charge that he was involved in a conspiracy to incite rebellion in the armed forces. Shortly after, the military police told Sun he was under house arrest.

The Chiangs understood that charges of sedition against the highly respected general would generate disbelief among Americans, but they were surprised by the strength of the U.S. reaction.[32] After hearing

Ambassador Koo explain his government's case against General Sun, Admiral Radford was flabbergasted. He said Sun was the most able general in the Chinese army and "could not be and never was pro-Communist." "Something must be quite bad in the Chinese Army," Radford said, "if [as charged] 100 officers scattered [in different units] had volunteered to join in the conspiracy against the Generalissimo." Growing more outraged as he talked, Radford said he agreed with Sun Li-jen that the GPWD was a bad system: "Promotions [in the Nationalist military] depend not on the recommendations of commanders but their political commissars . . . consequently morale [is] bad . . . [and] the commanders [have] no control over their men." Such an army, the Admiral concluded, cannot fight effectively. The report of this conversation must have shaken the Gimo and his son.[33]

The Chiangs decided to compromise. A commission of inquiry headed by Ch'en Ch'eng found that Sun had maneuvered to create a clique, that he had instructed Colonel Kuo to "intensify" this activity, and that he knew of Kuo's planned conspiracy. But, the commission found, Sun did not know Kuo was a Communist, and there was no proof Sun was "the prime mover in the conspiracy." The panel recommended leniency. The Generalissimo thereupon decreed that there would be no further disciplinary action against the general, but requested that the Ministry of Defense "Keep observation on him from time to time so that any sign of his reform may not go unnoticed." For the next 33 years, Sun was effectively under house arrest.

Aside from Sun Li-jen, the most outspoken critic of the GPWD was Chiang Wei-kuo. After Wei-kuo returned from the United States in early 1955, Chiang Kai-shek intended to appoint him deputy director of the Defense Ministry's 2nd Bureau (or G-2), which dealt with military intelligence. The 2nd Bureau was primarily responsible for tactical and strategic intelligence, such as enemy order of battle, as distinct from the IBMND, which focused on espionage and counterintelligence. Still, it was intelligence and thus a sensitive post. Ching-kuo suggested to his father that since Wei-kuo spoke good English, he was needed more in the 3rd Bureau (G-3), which dealt with operations. The Gimo changed the appointment to the 3rd Bureau.[34]

THE MILITARY CRISIS around the off-shore islands continued into 1955. Dulles offered a concession: if the Nationalists would withdraw from the Tachens, the administration would arrange for a congressional resolution authorizing the president to assist the Nationalists in defending not only Taiwan and the Pescadores but "related positions." The Gimo agreed, and Ching-kuo went to the islands to oversee the evacuation, accompanying many of the villagers as they placed ribbons across the doors of their houses signifying they would return. He was on the last landing boat that left the Tachens.[35]

At the same time, Chiang Kai-shek continued to expand the Nationalist military presence on Quemoy and Matsu.[36] The two garrisons of 100,000 men were digging more tunnels and stockpiling massive supplies of food and ammunition. The reinforcement raised the psychological and political costs of the potential loss of the two islands and thus escalated the stakes for the United States as well. Then in April Mao turned off the heat. Both he and Chiang had achieved what they wanted. An additional factor was that the Bandung Conference of nonaligned nations, which was to highlight peaceful coexistence, was about to begin in Indonesia.

Although it had just maneuvered the Formosa Resolution through Congress, the U.S. administration now quietly sought to get Chiang off Quemoy and Matsu. During an April meeting with the Generalissimo, Admiral Radford and Assistant Secretary Robertson said that despite the Formosa Resolution, President Eisenhower had decided not to sanction the use of U.S. forces to defend Quemoy and Matsu. But if the Nationalists withdrew from the island outposts, they added, U.S. naval forces would interdict the sea lanes along the China coast from Swatow in the south to Wenchow in Chekiang province north of Taiwan. In other words, to pry the Gimo off of Quemoy and Matsu, the United States was willing to engage in a renewed *de facto* state of war against Communist China in the Strait. Chiang, however, refused to consider this far-reaching and astounding proposal. The link to the mainland that the off-shore islands symbolized was more important to him. The Gimo understood that the proposed American naval action would, along with Nationalist withdrawal from its last two offshore outposts, freeze the status of Taiwan as an isolated and separate entity.[37]

IN 1955, DESPITE DIFFERENCES over the off-shore islands, Washington and Taipei seemed to be close allies. So did the two Communist giants, regardless of some ideological differences. Molotov declared that the socialist camp was led by both the Soviet Union and China.[38] The two powers were cooperating closely on the peaceful coexistence strategy. At the Asian-African Conference in Bandung, Zhou Enlai said China wanted to have friendly relations with all countries and proposed that Peking and Washington enter into negotiations to eliminate tensions in the Taiwan area. As a result of China's new posture, a number of countries broke relations with Taipei and recognized the People's Republic as the government of China. Most disturbing for Taipei was that Washington and Peking began ambassadorial-level talks in Geneva in August 1955. The Americans explained to the Gimo and Ching-kuo that the purpose of this exchange was to press Peking to renounce the use of force in the Strait. But that was just what the Nationalists feared. If such a pledge was ever given, it would undermine the *raison d'etre* of their autocratic rule.[39]

In fact, a few months into the talks the Chinese suggested a joint United States-China statement that the two countries would settle disputes between them by peaceful means without resorting to the use or threat of force. Making a key clarification, the Chinese representative, Wang Ping-nan, "made clear [that] disputes between the two countries referred to in the proposed statement would include the dispute between the United States and China in the Taiwan area."[40] In other words, in 1955 Mao Zedong was prepared to sign a joint Sino-American renunciation-of-force agreement in which the official record would cite the PRC representative as acknowledging that the pledge applied to matters relating to Taiwan. Acceptance of Peking's proposal would have significantly advanced Dulles' goals of promoting long-term peace in the Taiwan Strait, leaving open the status of Taiwan and gaining flexibility for future relations with China. Elated, the American negotiator, Ambassador U. Alexis Johnson, sent a flash cable strongly urging acceptance of the Chinese proposal.[41]

At the time, CIA analysts were predicting that even without a breakthrough in Sino-American relations, Taiwan's international position would steadily deteriorate, while China's diplomatic, military, and economic strength would grow.[42] But Dulles and Eisenhower feared that any agreement between China and the United States ending tension in the Strait, no matter how well it served America's declared goals, would provoke a furious reaction from the Gimo and the Republican right wing and set off a stampede of nations switching diplomatic recognition from Taipei to Peking. Strategically, the proposal was a good deal. Politically, however, it was messy. The administration rejected the Chinese offer and instead reverted to the usual demand that Peking formally and specifically "renounce the use of force in general and with particular reference to the Taiwan area."[43] Peking's December 1955 proposal suggests that despite Mao's philosophical differences with Khrushchev over whether peaceful coexistence was a tactical or strategic policy, he was at that moment prepared to follow Moscow in pursuing a fundamental rapprochement with America. Washington's rejection of his proposed compromise on the issue of Taiwan would play a role in Mao's radicalization over the next few years and his ultimate break with Moscow. The United States would not get such an offer again.

14

Managing the Great Patron

IN 1957 THERE WERE 10,000 Americans in Taiwan, the great majority
CIA and military personnel and their families.[1] One spring evening, in a
small house outside of Taipei, the wife of Master Sergeant Robert
Reynolds of the U.S. Army screamed for her husband. Someone had
peeped at her through a bathroom window while she was in the shower.
Reynolds grabbed his pistol, rushed outside, and shot a Chinese man
who was in their garden. In keeping with bilateral agreements, an American military court in Taipei tried Reynolds for manslaughter. On May 23
the court found the sergeant innocent, and an Air Force plane quickly
flew him and his wife to the Philippines.

There was an immediate uproar in the Taipei press. On May 24 the
victim's wife and hundreds of young demonstrators gathered to protest
outside the American embassy. The crowd grew in size and anger and
pelted the embassy with stones. The American chargé called Foreign
Minister George Yeh and demanded protection, whereupon Yeh con-
tacted the Garrison Command and asked them to break up the demonstration. The local commander told him that such an order had to come
from the President.[2]

Meanwhile, Lee Huan alerted Ching-kuo, who sped to the Youth
Corps headquarters to monitor the situation.[3] The demonstrators be-

came increasingly violent, and as they climbed the walls, Marines inside the compound fired tear gas. George Yeh called Ching-kuo urging immediate action. The Garrison Command officer in charge of the nearby riot squad requested permission to restore order. Ching-kuo instructed him not to use force. Instead, he ordered plainclothesmen to infiltrate the mob to try to contain the violence.

The demonstrators swarmed through the tear gas into the compound. When the Marines withdrew, the rioters ransacked the embassy and hurled the ambassador's safe out of a second story window. CIA personnel took photos that showed the police standing by, doing nothing. Some containers burst open and undercover Chinese security men (the CIA presumed) grabbed armloads of papers and scurried away. The crowd then descended on the American library and destroyed it as well. Ching-kuo and Lee Huan stayed up through the night "to handle the incident."[4]

There followed much hand wringing, protests, and apologies. The final American assessment came in the shape of an August 27 National Intelligence Estimate prepared by the CIA but co-signed by the intelligence organizations of State and Defense. The committee-written document tried to have it both ways: "Although some officials probably knew that a demonstration was planned and some advantage was taken of the situation, the pillage of the Embassy probably was not premeditated. There was a long delay in controlling the mob after the demonstrations turned to violence, reflecting seriously on the ability of the government to take prompt action in the event of an emergency situation."[5]

THE CIRCUMSTANCES OF THE RIOT rankled Eisenhower, but Washington had such a strong commitment to the Nationalist government in both the domestic and international contexts that it was eager to forget the whole matter. The mild American reaction confirmed to Ching-kuo and his father how much leverage Taipei had over the powerful United States.

The troubles had begun when Youth Corps members, outraged by the Reynolds case, sought approval to demonstrate before the embassy.

This request had gone to Ching-kuo himself. Remembering his own student days and personally miffed over the court martial verdict, he approved the petition with the injunction that it be kept peaceful. The demonstration got out of hand, however, as outsiders swelled the crowd.[6]

Twenty years later, during another crisis, Ching-kuo would tell a subordinate that so long as he had authority, government troops would not fire on the people in the streets of Taiwan.[7] Since he took responsibility for security in late 1949, he had overseen wide-scale arrests, detentions, and in the early years, several thousand executions, but there was no case in which the Nationalist military or police during this time fired on a public demonstration. Ching-kuo believed the Americans could afford a new embassy, recalled a senior aide of the 1980s who was then a Youth Corps member. "Better that than have the police in Ching-kuo's name shoot down citizens in the streets."[8]

The riots, however, further fed suspicions of Ching-kuo in American circles. In 1958 several ranking Republican senators and congressmen vigorously protested to the State Department and in person to President Eisenhower against a planned visit by Chiang Ching-kuo. A spokesman for the group said Ching-kuo was "entirely pro-Communist" and his Youth Corps had helped to instigate the attack on the embassy.[9] Senator Everett Dirksen privately observed that State Department Assistant Secretary Walter Robertson was a "great anticommunist, but his one blind spot was Chiang Ching-kuo."[10]

HAVING RECEIVED COMPENSATION and apologies from their host, the Americans repaired their embassy, bought new safes, and prepared to welcome a new ambassador—career diplomat Everett Drumright. Like Rankin, Drumright worked on the basis of the official policy assumption that the power, security, and prestige of the government of the Republic of China was of vital importance to the United States. On almost all matters he was—even more than his predecessor—sympathetic to the views of Chiang Kai-shek and Chiang Ching-kuo. Drumright dealt with George Yeh and on special occasions with the Gimo himself, but he had little to do with Ching-kuo, contact with whom was the jealously guarded prerogative of the CIA.

In the early spring of 1958 the new CIA station chief, Ray S. Cline, arrived in Taipei. The station's flimsy cover name had been changed from Western Enterprises to the Naval Auxiliary Communications Center (NACA). Cline was a scholarly, amiable, and earnest man. Over the next four years he and Ching-kuo would establish a professional and personal relationship of a quality probably unsurpassed in the CIA's dealings with foreign intelligence chiefs. The Chiang and Cline families also became close. Ching-kuo's children called the CIA chief "Uncle Ray," and Ching-kuo took English lessons several times a week from Ray's wife, Marjorie. Mrs. Cline also helped him with the preface of an English version of the recollections of his Soviet years, written in Hsikou in 1937.

The Chiangs took to attending CIA staff parties at the agency club in Taipei. They would wear the prescribed costume—for example, cowboy shirts—and join in the slow dancing. One evening Ching-kuo obliged and donned a waiter's jacket, put a napkin over his arm, and joined a barbershop quartet in song. According to Cline, everyone realized Ching-kuo "was a regular guy."[11] On occasion, the two middle-aged spy chiefs, who even looked alike, would go on a "bash" by themselves.[12]

At Cline's recommendation, the United States supplied several U-2 spy planes to the Nationalists and trained pilots for the high-flying craft. Under Ching-kuo's supervision, the ROC Air Force maintained and flew the U-2, but the CIA tightly controlled all flight operations. The U-2 flights became the most successful and important joint intelligence collection activity on Taiwan. During this period the Gimo kept requesting ever more advanced military technology. In January 1958 he made eight especially bold requests. Forty years later, the State Department has not yet released documents related to these proposals. Inadvertently, however, a memorandum that was declassified in 1998 described Washington's rejection of the most dramatic of Chiang's solicitations—an appeal for nuclear weapons and guided missiles.[13]

IN EARLY 1958 a group of Indonesian officials and military officers launched a rebellion against President Sukarno in central Sumatra and east Sulawesi. In March, during a meeting with Secretary Dulles, President Chiang said that if left-leaning Sukarno put down the rebellion, it would greatly enhance the position of the Communists in Indonesia. Dulles agreed.[14] Cline and Ching-kuo followed up with a plan to provide tactical air support as well as arms and other supplies to the anti-Sukarno rebel forces. If Sukarno could not be toppled, then the second goal of the joint project was to break up the Indonesian Republic, on the assumption that Sukarno intended to take his country into the Communist camp.

The operation soon turned into a fiasco. The Indonesian army shot down one of the CIA planes and captured the American pilot, Alan Pope. The incident played into the hands of the Indonesian Communist Party (PKI), which was able to say, with some justification, that America, the advocate of the rule of law in international relations, was secretly supporting the violent breakup of a member of the United Nations.[15] Following the covert American intervention on the side of the dissidents, the Soviet Union rushed a supply of MIG-16s to Sukarno.

When Washington dropped the rebels and shifted to a policy of strengthening the Indonesian army as a bulwark against the Communists, an odd situation emerged. Ching-kuo's CIA-supported B-26 bombers continued to fly missions in support of the rebellion, while the United States began shipping to the Jakarta government arms that would help them put down the uprising.[16] Washington had reconsidered. Maybe Sukarno was salvageable. In September Dulles remarked privately that "Sukarno is not a fanatic like Chiang Kai-shek . . . but rather a schemer and a smooth, adroit politician."[17] The Secretary of State grossly underestimated the Generalissimo, who was much more adroit at playing the Americans than was the Indonesian leader.

Despite occasional excitement like the Sulawesi misadventure, Ching-kuo's Special Operations staff was restless. The MAAG had trained 3,000 Nationalist soldiers as Special Forces troops, but after the evacuation of the Tachens in 1955, the CIA and the MAAG had "retired from practically all" involvement in penetration raids against China. Finally noting that the Communists "were highly successful in nipping all such efforts in the bud," Washington issued official directives to American agencies in Taiwan to stop their allies from engaging in such activities.[18]

But with Drumright and Cline on board, Ching-kuo and the Gimo began to push for an escalation of these operations. Shortly after Cline's arrival, Ching-kuo discussed with him a proposal for the United States to arm and train 30,000 paratroopers, who would be ready to jump into the mainland when a major rebellion broke out. Drumright strongly endorsed the idea. The State Department replied that the subject might be carefully discussed with the Gimo but reminded Drumright of the total failure of all previous such efforts.[19] In another gesture certain to be turned down, Chiang and his son proposed a rapid-deployment force of Nationalist troops that could act as a fire brigade "to protect free world interests in Asia." The American Joint Chiefs noted that most countries in Asia would not welcome such a force, and its use would bring Communist China into every incident in which it was committed.[20]

IN FEBRUARY 1956 Khrushchev informed the CPSU 20th Party Congress that peaceful coexistence was a "fundamental principle" and not a tactical ploy. This was an important declaration that caught the attention of his audience, but the reaction was nothing compared to the shock wave that ran through the chamber (Deng Xiaoping was there too) during his subsequent dramatic denunciation of the crimes of Joseph Stalin.[21] Mao's first response to these revelations was to launch his own liberalization effort—The Hundred Flowers campaign to encourage political discussion and criticism. But then in June 1957, faced with a wave of intellectual disapprobation and the lesson of the Hungarian Revolution, he abruptly chopped off the Hundred Flowers and launched a harsh crackdown on those who had spoken out. He put his favorite Party man, Deng Xiaoping, in charge of the suppression campaign, which branded 300,000 intellectuals as "rightists," sent tens of thousands to reeducation camps, and resulted in many executions.[22]

In August the USSR tested its first intercontinental missile, and six weeks later Sputnik roared into orbit, the first man-made satellite. The world, including Mao, was impressed. One month following Sputnik, the Soviets and Chinese signed a secret agreement in which the USSR undertook to provide scientific and technical assistance to enable China to manufacture its own nuclear weapons.[23] These events excited Mao into renewed visions of earth-shaking, revolutionary upheavals. In a speech at the November 7 celebrations in Moscow of the 40th Anniversary of the Bolshevik Revolution, he reiterated a militant view of the course of world politics.[24] Immediately upon returning from Russia, the Chairman started to plan a Great Leap Forward in Chinese agricultural and industrial production. Seeing Olympian gains for his beloved Party, Deng again enthusiastically supported Mao's ideas.

—

IN MAY 1958 the Great Leap Forward officially began. This radical program would have a profound effect on the internal politics of the CCP, on Mao himself, on Sino-Soviet relations, and on the shaping of China's radicalism of the 1960s. It also provided a catalyst for the Quemoy crisis of 1958. The Leap was intended to be Mao's Sputnik in the realm of politics—a revolutionary transformation of human society.

Khrushchev arrived secretly in Peking in July of that year, bearing what he thought was a generous proposal to strengthen the partnership by forming a joint Sino-Soviet fleet in the Pacific.[25] But by the time of Khrushchev's arrival Mao was receiving glowing reports from the countryside on the initial introduction of his grandiose rural reforms. In no mood to cooperate, Mao replied to the fleet proposal with conditions that the Russian leader was hardly likely to accept. Khrushchev then cautioned the Chinese leader to be prudent in dealing with the Taiwan issue.[26] Such advice rankled the Chairman, confirming his suspicion that the Soviets were prepared to acquiesce if not connive with the United States in a two-Chinas situation. [27]

—

ON AUGUST 23 Communist shore batteries fired 50,000 shells at Quemoy within two hours. Over the next five days a torrent of explosives rained down on the island. Mao explained privately to his doctor that the dramatic shelling was "pure show." He did not want to take Quemoy or Matsu because they were China's sovereign link to Taiwan. Besides, he said, "The islands are two batons that keep Khrushchev and Eisenhower dancing, scurrying this way and that."[28] This was Mao's version of the

Dulles policy of brinkmanship; he intended to threaten but not to invade Quemoy and its sister island.

At a NSC meeting in August, Ike protested that the United States was "being shoved into something that we do not think is correct [defending the offshore islands] because of someone else's [Chiang Kai-shek's] intransigence."[29] But he could not or did not rebut the argument of the Joint Chiefs and John Foster Dulles that because Chiang, in the face of Washington's stern opposition, had put 100,000 troops on Quemoy, the island was *ipso facto* strategically important—enough so that America would now go to war and use nuclear weapons if necessary to defend it.[30] On September 4 Dulles declared publicly that U.S. forces would be used for the protection of Quemoy. Although Moscow, like Washington, did not approve of its ally's actions regarding Quemoy either, the Russians felt compelled to warn that "an attack on the Chinese Peoples Republic, which is a great friend, ally, and neighbor of our country, is an attack on the Soviet Union."[31]

The Pentagon's experts agreed that if the Communists persisted in their shelling, only nuclear weapons could break the blockade. Dulles and the Joint Chiefs confidently discussed the types of nuclear weapons that would be used if necessary.[32] The United States rushed to Quemoy eight-inch howitzers capable of firing nuclear shells. A massive American air and sea armada moved westward to defend a little island U.S. leaders believed should not be defended.[33] The fact that Ching-kuo's forces had continued to use Quemoy as a base for pinprick raids against the mainland further weakened the rationale for American action. At one meeting, even Secretary Dulles blurted out that the United States "shouldn't really expect the Communists to refrain from attacking the islands if they were being used as bases for hostile activities against the mainland."[34]

During the Quemoy crisis Chiang Kai-shek and Ch'en Ch'eng met frequently with Drumright, and Ching-kuo saw Cline virtually every day. The Nationalist leaders expressed dismay at the Communist threat, warned against the dangerous futility of negotiations with Peking, reiterated the dire consequences should Quemoy be abandoned, pressed for strong U.S. action to break the blockade, and sought more advanced American weapons.[35] In his reports to Washington Cline echoed Ching-kuo's view that "it was essential" to counter the threat to Quemoy.[36]

Ching-kuo flew to the island several times during the period of most intense bombardment and once brought back to Cline the breech plate of an armor-piercing shell that had crashed through a bunker.[37]

—

THE CHIANGS had to convince the Americans that the KMT regime was a strong and stable ally, while at the same time insisting that the government's hold on Taiwan was so tenuous that if it abandoned the tiny, faraway islet of Quemoy, it would collapse. Quemoy, of course, remained important to the Generalissimo for the same reason it did to Mao. If the Nationalists pulled back from the offshore redoubts, two Chinas and ultimately an independent Taiwan would—even more than four and eight years earlier—seem to be the logical outcome. Mao orchestrated the crisis, but the Chiangs also skillfully played the game. As a direct consequence of the Quemoy incident, America rushed to Taiwan $350 million worth of advanced artillery, aircraft, tanks, amphibious ships, and other war materiel over and above the large amounts of military aid originally programmed.[38] Among the new weapons were the latest air-to-air Sidewinder missiles, which gave the ROC Air Force a decided edge over Communist MIGs. Yet Chiang Kai-shek would pay a price for providing a new but unwanted "brink" for the administration in Washington.

Eisenhower insisted that the United States, while gearing up for war over Quemoy, show a willingness "to conciliate and negotiate" on the issue, and he succeeded in having the United States-China ambassadorial talks resume in Warsaw. The first in this new round of exchanges took place on September 15. Suddenly, on October 6, on Mao's instruction, Peking announced a cease-fire in the shelling. About the same time, Eisenhower and Dulles received a full assessment of America's nuclear options regarding Quemoy and quickly reined in at the edge of the precipice.

On October 21 Dulles flew to Taipei to hand to the Generalissimo a stunning list of things he would have to do if he wished to prevent his government from being "liquidated." These included actions that would make clear that the Taipei government intended to conduct itself "as though there were an armistice" with the mainland regime; reflect a willingness "to conclude an armistice" with Peking; and underscore that the Nationalist government would not attempt forcibly to return to the mainland. Taiwan, Dulles insisted, must promise to avoid commando raids and like provocations; accept any solution of the offshore island problem that would assure the civilian population would not be turned over to the Communists or uprooted; and review "the character and perhaps the size of the Nationalist military establishment in order to achieve greater mobility and perhaps . . . less burden on the people of Taiwan."[39]

The Generalissimo was shocked. In a private meeting with the Gimo—with George Yeh, recently appointed Nationalist ambassador to Washington, present as interpreter—Secretary Dulles warned that the Nationalist government was perceived abroad as "militaristic . . . apt to precipitate a world war" and with only "a limited life expectancy." "It is doubtful," Dulles cautioned, "whether even the US can long protect the GRC [Government of the Republic of China] under present circumstances."[40]

A few hours after this tense meeting, Huang Shao-ku, the new Foreign Minister, urgently summoned Drumright. "The suggestions" advanced by the Secretary, Huang protested, "appeared to be of such a nature as almost to shake the foundation of the Republic of China." They were tantamount to demanding that his government publicly accept the "two Chinas idea."[41]

That evening, during a second meeting with the Secretary, Chiang ignored the far-reaching "suggestions" Dulles had made that morning and launched into a fervent exposition of the need to enhance the defense of Quemoy and counter the Communist shelling, which was wearing down the Nationalist defenders. Dulles replied that conventional weapons could not take out the PLA gun emplacements near Amoy harbor. "This would be like using a pea gun to attack a stone wall." Only nuclear weapons, he declared, could do the job. Did Chiang want "the United States to use nuclear weapons" against Communist China? Taken by surprise, the Gimo replied that "the use of tactical atomic weapons might be advisable."

The Secretary, who had learned some things since his meeting with the Joint Chiefs in early September, proceeded to describe the unsettling facts. To destroy the artillery emplacements threatening Quemoy would require nuclear weapons with the power of the Hiroshima or Nagasaki bombs, but the explosion of such weapons in the air would still have no effect on the Communist gun positions; surface or sub-surface nuclear explosions, on the other hand, would kill twenty million Chinese, including everyone on Quemoy. Finally, "The use of nuclear weapons would involve Taiwan, and if [Soviet] nuclear weapons were used to attack Taiwan, there would be nothing left of Taiwan."[42]

By previously accepting U.S. Air Force jets armed with nuclear weapons under American control on Taiwan, Chiang Kai-shek had, well before the 1958 crisis, acquiesced in the possibility that the United States would use the devices against China. At least one American intelligence document, the details of which have still not been declassified, reported in September 1958 Nationalist efforts "to involve the United States in a nuclear war with China."[43] But all along the Chiangs were, as the U.S. Taiwan Defense Commander later said, "abysmally ignorant" of nuclear warfare. In any event, the Gimo was hardly in a position to argue the case with Dulles, and he replied meekly that he "would not want to use nuclear weapons [in the Quemoy crisis] if their use would start a world war or involve the United States in large-scale hostilities."[44] It is inexplicable that all of this had not been thought through earlier. In September Dulles and the American Joint Chiefs were themselves contemplating with confident equanimity the use of small nuclear air bursts to wipe out the offending Communist guns.

After all, the United States had successfully employed nuclear threats to end the Korean War and to obtain a temporary settlement in Vietnam. These victories had led the administration initially to contemplate and threaten the use of such weapons in the unpromising tactical situation and potentially calamitous political and moral context of Quemoy. President Eisenhower's continued skepticism, the negative views of United States allies, and increasing criticism in the American media and Congress resulted in a painful reassessment of what was at stake.

Before flying away from Taipei, Dulles acceded to a joint communiqué with the Gimo, which was a greatly watered-down version of his list of "suggestions." In the document Taipei said that "the principal means" for restoration of freedom to the Chinese people on the mainland would be implementation of Sun Yat-sen's Three Principles, and that "the foundation of this mission resides in the hearts and minds of the Chinese people." The two sides recognized that "under the present conditions the defense of the Quemoys, together with the Matsus, is closely related to the defense of Taiwan."[45] Privately, the Nationalists agreed to withdraw 15,000 men from Quemoy.

———

DESPITE THE TONED-DOWN PUBLIC STATEMENT, Dulles had made it clear to the Chiangs that even a conservative Republican administration in Washington would not easily be drawn into a war with China, and that Americans in general favored a *de facto* if not *de jure* "two Chinas" solution. If Peking seriously wanted to take Quemoy, the United States could not prevent it with conventional weapons and would not employ nuclear weapons. As soon as Dulles' plane was in the air, the Gimo and his son discussed the disturbing exchange and decided on a dramatic move— they would approach Peking and seek to calm the waters.

The source of information on this reported approach was one of China's most senior leaders, Ch'iao Shih, until 1998 Chairman of the National Peoples Congress and before that long-time head of China's intelligence and security apparatus. In December 1994 Ch'iao told a distinguished Chinese American (Dr. Wang Chi, at the time head of the Chinese section of the Library of Congress) that during the period of heavy Communist shelling of Quemoy, Chiang Kai-shek sent a message to Zhou Enlai saying that if the PLA did not stop the firing, he (Chiang) would have to do what the Americans wanted—withdraw from Quemoy and Matsu—and this over time would threaten the indivisibility of China.[46] The message simply underscored what Mao and Chiang both already accepted: Quemoy had become key to the unity of China.

Ching-kuo presumably approached the CCP's intelligence apparatus in Hong Kong and delivered the message. China soon announced a new policy of shelling Quemoy only every other day. Supplies for the island garrison could land on the off-days. The crisis was over. The Nationalists and the Communists would continue to be enemies, seeking where possible to weaken the other, but at the topmost level there was an understanding—the two sides had a common interest in and commitment to

Chinese unity, while their respective superpower allies simply wanted peace in the Strait.

In December Washington finally rejected the Nationalist request of the previous January for nuclear weapons.[47] The Gimo then approved establishment of the first clandestine nuclear weapons research laboratory in Taiwan. According to Ching-kuo, it was he who broached the idea.[48]

———

THE KMT HAD ARRIVED on Taiwan with an army of almost half a million unattached males plus more than 100,000 officers and senior NCOs with families. By 1959 at least half of these men were in their thirties and forties and many in their fifties.[49] Given the high percentage of officers among those who fled the mainland, by then they and noncommissioned officers far outnumbered enlisted men—329,000 to 286,000.[50] Some special infantry units (so-called "officer combat regiments") were made up entirely of surplus officers.[51]

Since mainlander soldiers had highly uncertain prospects of ever returning to their homes or of having a family of their own on Taiwan, the theme of the counterattack was critical for keeping up their morale and retaining political loyalty. It was also essential that once out of the armed forces they did not become a social or economic problem and further alienate the local Taiwanese.

In the late 1950s Ching-kuo took on this huge, vexing problem by becoming chairman of the Vocational Assistance Commission for Retired Servicemen (VACRS). The Americans recognized its relevance for stability on Taiwan and coughed up large sums to fund its operations.[52] VACRS provided grants or loans to help the veterans start small businesses such as food stalls and pedicabs (three-wheel bicycle taxies). Private companies on Taiwan found themselves under heavy pressure to cooperate in the program. VACRS also started up an engineering company, which employed about 6,000 ex-soldiers in construction projects such as building the East-West Highway across the mountains of central Taiwan. In addition, the organization undertook to provide medical and home care for those who could not work. Finally, Ching-kuo approved the idea of issuing to each veteran a land deed that granted a small farm plot, location unspecified, to be redeemed after the recovery of the mainland. VACRS issued more than 700,000 such "deeds."[53]

The Veterans Hospital outside of Taipei (Chung min ts'ung yi yuan) not only grew into an enormous facility but also eventually became famous for the quality of its medical care and its outstanding doctors. The Chiang family used this facility as its primary hospital.[54] As with his other responsibilities, Ching-kuo's leadership of VACRS was characterized by attention to detail and frequent on-site inspections. He personally asked the president of Taiwan University to recommend a group of scholars who could devise suitable aptitude tests for the veterans so VACRS could try to find an appropriate job for every demobilized soldier.[55] He frequently visited the construction site on the East-West Highway, eating with the worker-veterans and inspecting their sleeping quarters, latrines, and recreational facilities. One former VACRS official recalls accompanying Ching-kuo on a visit to a leper hospital for veterans. To the dismay of his guards, Ching-kuo insisted on shaking hands with all the patients he met. A doctor said that some of these patients had not shaken hands with anyone for twenty years.[56]

IN 1957 THE GENERALISSIMO had created a new position in the Kuomintang of deputy director general and had appointed Ch'en Ch'eng to the position. By this move, he hoped to end speculation about a Ch'en Ch'eng-Chiang Ching-kuo rivalry. Ch'en was now the formal successor to the Generalissimo in both the Party and the government. In the minds of most observers Ching-kuo was still the second most powerful man on Taiwan, but he was content to progress slowly in his climb up the official ladder. He remained especially deferential to Ch'en, his nominal superior and—going back to Youth Corps and Youth Army days in the 1940s—his long-time boss and mentor. In the early 1950s, when Ching-kuo's security people insisted he stop jogging through the streets of Taipei, he thought of taking up golf, but Ch'en Ch'eng told him, "everyone else is playing golf. The two of us should not." Ching-kuo's major exercise thereafter was his long walks in the countryside and on Yangming Mountain.[57]

Still, political jockeying inevitably continued. The most serious episode of infighting between Ch'en Ch'eng and Ching-kuo took place in early 1959, after Ch'en met with a group of generals who had long-standing ties to him. One of the topics that came up was arrangements for President Chiang's succession, on the assumption that the Gimo would adhere to the constitution and not seek yet another term in 1960. Ching-kuo's intelligence people had bugged the meeting, and the senior officers involved soon found themselves retiring or assigned to noncommand positions.[58] One of these officers was the Chief of Staff, General "Tiger" Wang Shu-ming. Ching-kuo had cultivated close relations with Tiger, but Wang had older and stronger connections to Ch'en Ch'eng.[59] P'eng Meng-chi, who owed his position to Ching-kuo, became the new Chief of Staff.

The reassignment of Chiang Wei-kuo about this time may also have been related to the removal of Tiger Wang and other senior line officers connected to Ch'en Ch'eng. The strain in Ching-kuo's relations with his brother had grown over the years, although they maintained a surface cordiality. Wei-kuo's first wife, Shih Ching-yi, had died in childbirth, and in 1957 Wei-kuo was planning a wedding in Tokyo to a good-looking woman of Chinese-German parentage, Ellen Chiu. Upon hearing the news Ching-kuo asked if the location of the wedding could be changed. This was the only time, Wei-kuo recounts, that he lost his temper in front of his brother. Nevertheless he switched the site of the ceremony in Tokyo to the Chinese embassy.[60]

In 1958 Wei-kuo became Director of the Planning Bureau (G-5) in the Defense Ministry. Later that year he resumed leadership of the Armored Force Command, but this assignment lasted less than a year. Shortly after Tiger Wang's dismissal Wei-kuo was sent off to America to attend the U.S. Army Air Defense School. He never had any responsibility for air defense and never commanded troops again.[61]

OVER THE YEARS since the KMT moved to the island, local factions had sprung up in the countryside to compete for KMT nominations for local office and for the related patronage and power that went with these positions. In Taipei and a few other cities a number of Taiwanese independents had begun to criticize the government—within vague but generally understood limits, to be sure. Toleration of the independents made the elections seem more democratic to the home audience as well as to the Americans. Ching-kuo's internal security organizations, however, kept a close watch on the oppositionists, giving them warnings if they seemed to be going too far, and co-opting others. Independent politicians who went over the line could be harassed in various administrative ways, or, if they persisted, detained without charge or public knowledge.

According to Henry Kao, the KMT organization did not take him seriously when he first ran for Taipei mayor in 1954, so it allowed a free election and an honest count of the vote. To the Party's surprise, Kao won a clear majority. KMT headquarters and the Garrison Command wanted to nullify the elections. The American embassy, however, had already reported Kao as the winner. He learned that the Gimo had looked at his record and, almost certainly on Ching-kuo's recommendation, decided to approve the results.[62] In private, including to his friends at the American embassy, the mayor described the KMT-mainlander regime as an unjust dictatorship, but mostly he got on with the job of trying to improve the large, crowded, and polluted capital. Three years later, Kao ran for reelection, but he was not permitted to assign poll watchers and lost to the KMT candidate. In 1960 the election authorities again rejected his request for poll watchers, and he did not run.[63]

———

AFTER THE TRAUMATIC VISIT of John Foster Dulles in late October 1958, Ching-kuo's Special Warfare Center curtailed its mainland raids and infiltration efforts. To keep the large numbers of personnel involved occupied, Ching-kuo began resupplying the KMT irregulars in Burma with arms and equipment and even reintroducing Nationalist armed forces into the area for training purposes.[64] Ching-kuo's office also developed a "Four Point program for mainland operations" that stressed expanded collection of intelligence and psychological operations while waiting for signs of "serious resistance."[65]

In March 1959 such resistance did erupt, at "the top of the world" in Tibet. According to the common version of events, following popular agitation in Lhasa, rumors spread that Communist officials in the capital were planning to arrest the Dalai Lama and carry him off to Peking. Tibetans flocked to the city to protect their religious leader. Disorders spread. Khamba tribesmen attacked PLA outposts, and the Dalai Lama and a large caravan of priests and other followers fled Lhasa into the mountains and eventually into India.

At a March 26 meeting of the NSC, Allen Dulles reported that the Gimo was "extremely anxious to do something to encourage" continuation of the rebellion in Tibet.[66] Ching-kuo and Cline submitted recommendations on how Taipei and Washington could provide assistance to the rebels. The CIA, however, already had a "Tibetan connection." Declassified archival materials contain numerous references to an extensive CIA covert operation to supply and encourage anti-Communist Tibetans before as well as after the uprising.[67] The CIA Tibetan program, code-named "ST Circus" and which included training of Tibetans in the United States, actually was initiated in 1956, "based on U.S. government commitments made to the Dalai Lama in 1951 and 1956." Covert supply of weapons to the Tibetan resistance began in September 1958.[68] These operations were carried out with Ching-kuo's cooperation but not direct involvement inside Tibet. In a 1996 interview, one ranking Nationalist officer confirmed that clandestine CIA flights to Tibet from Taiwan took place before 1959. These operations encouraged the uprising and fostered the agitation and rumors that led to the Dalai Lama's decision to flee Lhasa.

Following the outbreak of the rebellion Drumright, for once, advised against a joint operation with Ching-kuo, pointing out that the Tibetans did not like the Chinese regardless of their political affiliation.[69] There was apprehension in Washington that Chinese Nationalist involvement could undermine sympathy in India and elsewhere for the Tibetans.[70] The White House nevertheless approved a Tibetan covert action program that included "exploratory discussions" with the Taipei government.[71] At this point the CIA apparently went ahead with its own plan and increased arms drops to the Tibetan guerrillas. According to one former CIA officer, the covert supply flights following the uprising were based in India.[72]

On May 3 the Gimo expressed strong displeasure that the United States had failed to cooperate with his government to exploit the uprising and said his forces would proceed, implying paratrooper landings in Tibet.[73] But the Tibetan resistance had already collapsed. As early as April 23 Dulles reported that the anti-Communist guerrillas had been badly beaten and were trying to flee to India.[74] Nevertheless the CIA's program of support continued and soon did become a joint operation with Ching-kuo's covert units.[75] A year later, the American NSC extended the program, although Eisenhower suggested that the only result would be more brutal reprisals by the Chinese Communists against the Tibetan people.[76]

IN ADDITION TO CONTINUING the joint action in Tibet, the Nationalists now made another push for American cooperation in paramilitary actions elsewhere in China. By this time the world knew the Great Leap Forward had been a disaster. Liu Shao-ch'i replaced Mao as President of the Peoples Republic, increasing speculation that the Chairman was in a weakened position. In February 1960 Ching-kuo informed Ray Cline that in response to spreading dissatisfaction on the mainland, the Gimo planned to airdrop paramilitary teams of 200 to 300 special forces into Szechwan and other areas. Ching-kuo said they would carry out this operation in the spring, unilaterally if necessary. Cline reported to Washington that he was trying to "moderate" these ambitious plans.[77]

During Eisenhower's state visit to Taipei in June 1960, the Generalissimo said it was time to establish guerrilla bases in a number of areas in the border regions. Resistance, he promised, would spread and lead to the downfall of the Communist regime. All that was needed from the United States was a few airplanes and telecommunications equipment. Ike promised to study the proposal.[78] Back in Washington, the Pentagon's judgment again was that the project would "meet with almost certain defeat with undesirable consequences for both [Taiwan] and the United States." Nevertheless, to placate the Generalissimo, Eisenhower approved joint planning "for the purpose of encouraging an anti-Communist movement on the mainland." The details of this project have not been declassified, but it appears that little action took place beyond more planning and training. [79]

Although the rebellion in Tibet was a tragic failure, it did contribute to tensions in Sino-Indian relations, which in turn contributed to a worsening of Moscow-Peking ties. On July 16 Moscow informed Peking of its decision not only to cancel the 1957 secret nuclear accord but to bring home all Soviet military and civilian technicians from China. By then Deng Xiaoping had drawn the painful but now obvious lesson from the debacle of the Great Leap. Along with other senior leaders, he was carefully promoting pragmatic policies to try to repair the damage.

15

China Leaps Backward

THROUGHOUT THE 1950s and into the 1960s, mainlanders—comprising only about 15 percent of Taiwan's population—occupied almost every senior position in the central government, the military, KMT headquarters, and the large state-owned economic sector. On the local level mainlander dominance was almost as pervasive. In 1963, for example, there were no Taiwanese among the 24 police regional bureau directors, and only five among the heads of the 120 sub-bureaus.[1]

Native provincials saw no feasible alternative to the KMT. Harsh security controls effectively discouraged even mild expressions of opposition. The Garrison Command could find few targets that needed suppression or even a serious "warning." Yet five thousand or so Taiwanese remained in detention as political prisoners, serving as living lessons to potential activists.[2]

It was not coercion alone, however, that maintained law and order. The KMT enjoyed support in varying degrees among most Taiwanese farmers and businessmen, who continued to be the beneficiaries not only of the government's economic policies but also of the political stability it enforced. Eighty percent of private entrepreneurs were native Taiwanese. In 1949 about two thirds of Taiwanese farmers were tenants. By the early 1960s, the same percentage were owner-farmers. The dramatically enhanced social status and self-esteem of the new landowners gave them a sense of pride and responsibility. One result was their active participation in local KMT-controlled elections as voters and candidates.[3] It was widely assumed, however, that the support of the KMT by farmers and business persons would rapidly diminish if a vigorous and free opposition was ever permitted.

Some non-KMT political leaders, such as former Taipei Mayor Henry Kao, had hoped the United States would back their efforts as independents willing to play the limited game of local politics and elections. In the mid-1960s Kao and others were bitter because they felt that their willingness to collaborate had not been reciprocated by mainlanders or appreciated by the Americans.[4] Nevertheless they continued to work within the limited system of participation that the Chiangs permitted. There was no direct pressure on Taipei from Washington to expand these limits, but attitudes on the subject were gradually changing both in America and in Taiwan.

A few Taiwanese did begin to rise through the ranks in the government and the party. Ching-kuo selected one, Hsu Ch'ing-chung, as deputy secretary general of the KMT Central Committee. Hsu in turn promoted the career of his young Taiwanese protégé, a fellow agriculturist named Lee Teng-hui. Lee became a member of an informal group of officials and academics called "the agricultural economics school" (*nung ching p'ai*). In the 1960s the leading figure in this school was the secretary general of the Joint Commission on Rural Reconstruction, Y. S. Tsiang, a Chekiang man and Ph.D. holder (University of Minnesota) in agriculture.

After his return from America, Tsiang had risen rapidly in the JCRR. In the early 1950s Chiang Kai-shek told his senior associates to be on the lookout for promising young men and to bring them to Ching-kuo's attention. One day, after a surprise introductory meeting with the Generalissimo, Tsiang received a telephone call from Ching-kuo suggesting they get together; soon after that Ching-kuo paid him a visit.[5] Tsiang became JCRR commissioner in 1961. Over the years he grew increasingly close to Ching-kuo personally as well as professionally. One reason, it was widely rumored, was because Tsiang also enjoyed the occasional night out and the company of women.

As Tsiang moved up, he also promoted Lee Teng-hui's career. Unknown to Tsiang or anyone else on the island, as a young graduate student in agricultural economics at National Taiwan University (NTU) Lee had secretly joined a Communist party front group. According to some reports, he became a member or a candidate member of the CCP. But he soon came to the conclusion that communism conflicted too deeply with his Christian beliefs, and sometime before the February 28, 1947, uprising he formally applied to his party cell to withdraw. During the troubles all those who knew of his affiliation were killed or fled to the mainland, and Lee escaped detection.[6] In 1965 Lee won a Rockefeller scholarship to Cornell University. Subsequently, Tsiang brought Lee's Ph.D. dissertation, entitled "Intersectional Capital Flows in the Economic Development of Taiwan," to Ching-kuo's attention. Despite the less-than-compelling title, the work apparently impressed Ching-kuo, and after Lee returned to Taipei in 1969, he was appointed chief of JCRR's rural economic division.[7] In 1970, at the urging of Y. S. Tsiang and Hsu Ch'ing-chung, Lee finally joined the Kuomintang. Like Ching-kuo, Lee was one of the few people who had been a member or candidate member of the CCP before joining (or in Ching-kuo's case, rejoining) the KMT.[8]

TOGETHER WITH THE AGENCY FOR INTERNATIONAL DEVELOPMENT (AID, the new name for ICA), the Chinese team of economic technocrats worked out a package of nineteen fundamental reforms to speed up development and push the island to the point where it would no longer require U.S. assistance. Many veteran Kuomintangers still glorified public enterprises and resented the intrusion of private capital, including Japanese and American investments, and strongly opposed the reforms.[9] Despite his inclination to favor government enterprises, Ching-kuo stayed on the sidelines of this debate. Ch'en Ch'eng and the leading planners, however, pushed the program vigorously, and Chiang Kai-shek soon endorsed it.

ACCORDING TO THE CIA, beginning in the late 1950s Peking attempted several times to communicate with the leaders in Taipei through secret channels. K'ang Sheng, the commissar who had accompanied Ching-kuo across Siberia in 1937, had made a political comeback in the CCP, and he as well as Deng Xiaoping may have been among those sending messages. The CCP offered a post of honor to Chiang Kai-shek in a unified China, an autonomous Taiwan, and an amnesty for "war criminals."[10] Although it appeared that these offers had elicited no response, Ching-kuo never-theless did not choose to share the approaches with his friend Ray Cline. The Americans had their own bilateral contact with Peking, and Ching-kuo wanted to maintain his covert channels for possible contingencies such as the Quemoy crisis in 1958.

Despite contacts, assessments of developments on mainland China produced by intelligence units under Ching-kuo continued to be heavily politicized. Ching-kuo's analysts had no feel, for example, for the fast-evolving dynamics of Sino-Soviet relations. In 1961 they were still main-taining that the Peking-Moscow dispute was a diabolic trick to throw the free world off its guard. Ching-kuo, however, was himself skeptical of the propagandistic intelligence his analysts produced. To provide a more bal-anced perspective he established a special office in the Defense Ministry staffed by civilian scholars. Later he turned this unit into an independent think-tank called the Institute of International Affairs, which was increasingly dominated by American-educated academics.

From the United States' point of view, the successful areas of clan-destine intelligence cooperation with Ching-kuo continued to be in the technical fields of communications (or signal) intercepts and air recon-naissance, both of which were closely controlled by the Americans. The U-2 spy planes flown by Nationalist pilots since 1958 were now providing unique information regarding China's rapidly developing nuclear weapon and missile programs. In September 1962 Peking shot down the first of three Nationalist U-2s that were lost over the years. Senior Nationalist flyers were unhappy with the CIA's operational control of the U-2s, but the division of labor continued. As this was one of the two suc-cessful clandestine operations conducted out of Taiwan, the Agency was not about to relinquish its authority over the spy planes.[11]

NOT ONLY TAIWANESE VOICES called for more democracy. Throughout the 1950s a mainlander named Lei Chen had acted as a troublesome gadfly to the KMT regime. His *Free China* magazine called for a non-party military, more local autonomy, adoption of a cabinet system, and other reforms. Conservative supporters of the Gimo began to suspect that Ch'en Ch'eng was secretly encouraging Lei Chen and other intellectuals in order to bolster his succession.[12] Ching-kuo and his father tolerated Lei Chen's criticism in the interest of demonstrating openness and because of the magazine's connection to the scholar Hu Shih, the prestigious intellectual still living in the United States. It was also difficult to suppress Lei since he took a firm anti-Communist and one-China line, arguing that the mainland could only be recovered through peaceful means—Taiwan's transformation into a prosperous democratic model. Intellectually, this argument may have appealed to Ching-kuo, as it was the one that he himself would eventually adopt.

Lei skirted the edge of the permissible, however, when he turned from intellectual and theoretical expositions to organizational work. In 1960 he began planning formation of a new China Democratic party. Creation of a competing political party was a direct challenge to the regime, but within the KMT there were now differences on how to react. Ch'en Ch'eng, and perhaps more importantly those around him hoping to build a future base of political support among the Taiwanese, advocated tolerance. The vice president startled political observers when he said publicly that a serious opposition party could exist so long as it was not "a party of warlords, hoodlums, and rascals." This was interpreted as a green light for Lei Chen.[13]

In contrast, Ching-kuo took a tough position against Lei's initiative, no doubt believing, as did some American observers, that "if an effective political opposition should ever be able to organize, it would inevitably devolve into a Taiwanese organ and portray the KMT as a mainlander dominated party . . . [and] in honest elections, the KMT would almost certainly be doomed."[14] The 1960 overthrow of South Korean strongman Syngman Rhee by pro-democracy students, following a rigged election, caused the Gimo and his son to be especially leery of letting any opposition raise its head on Taiwan. But trends in American policy also deeply concerned them. The implications of John Foster Dulles' startling lecture to the Gimo in late October 1958 grew more obvious every year—

the Americans, Republicans and Democrats alike, would incline to a two-Chinas policy, prompted by both American interests and ideals. At the same time, the Cold War was changing into a battle for the "hearts and minds" of the Third World, and America had begun to hold itself and its allies to a higher standard on human rights. In the fall of 1960 the Democratic nominee, John F. Kennedy, was making an issue of America's moral leadership. Ching-kuo and his father believed that if an opposition party on Taiwan got its nose in the tent, the Americans would push it all the way in. Their idea was to keep the animal locked up, but still leave the impression that it might some day be allowed entry.

Shortly after Ch'en Ch'eng's conciliatory remarks about an opposition party, internal security officials received Ching-kuo's permission to suppress the China Democratic Party. Bribes and threats persuaded one of the new party's leaders to leave the country, two were beaten by unknown persons, and several had their business licenses revoked.[15] In September security police arrested Lei Chen and an associate. Ch'en Ch'eng learned of the arrests in the newspaper.[16]

LEI RECEIVED A TEN-YEAR SENTENCE from a military court for alleged involvement in a Communist plot to overthrow the Gimo.[17] The Eisenhower administration initially was in high dudgeon over the Lei case. The State Department cabled Drumright expressing concern that Lei's arrest was "politically motivated," and commented that "any GRC policy of freezing the political status quo would conflict directly with long-established U.S. policy objective of working toward responsible representative government capable of attracting growing support [from the] people [of] Taiwan." The message even suggested that "a presentation of the U.S. attitude on the events leading to Syngman Rhee's downfall . . . might indirectly demonstrate U.S. concern that the GRC not make the same fatal mistakes."[18]

Drumright wasted no time in setting Washington straight. Chiang Ching-kuo, the ambassador reported back, had indeed pressed for the arrest of Lei because of the latter's persistent efforts to organize a political opposition. Washington can rest assured, Drumright said, that the

Gimo and his son will take whatever steps they think "necessary to retain political control, including the use of force." The ambassador explained that it would be useless for the United States to try to change things, because Chiang "is prepared to reject any U.S. intervention if it comes." It was not in America's interest, Drumright declared, to promote any more democratic change on Taiwan than the Generalissimo and Ching-kuo believed wise, noting the stark fact that free elections would doom the KMT. And, in a more debatable conclusion, he warned that the resulting instability would be "disastrous to U.S. interests," because the "Taiwanese are mainly unprincipled opportunists."[19] Washington made no further move to chastise the Gimo or Ching-kuo over the Lei case.

BY THE TIME JOHN KENNEDY was sworn in as president, more news was pouring out of China about the disastrous consequences of the Great Leap Forward. The average amount of grain per person had fallen from 205 kilos in 1957 to 154 kilos in 1961. Although it would not be known for several years that 20 million or more had died prematurely, it was apparent that malnutrition was on a grand scale.[20] Distended bellies were a common sight throughout rural areas, including in the Chiangs' home village of Hsikou. Soon thousands of desperate refugees from Kwangtung were pouring into Hong Kong.[21]

For the first time since 1949 a major invasion of the mainland began to look remotely possible. But, as in the past, the Gimo was not about to stake everything on a maximum effort until there was near collapse and civil war inside China. In 1961 and 1962 conditions on the mainland did not come close to meeting these requirements. But given China's economic disaster, the outpouring of refugees, the growing Sino-Indian dispute, and the now undeniable Peking-Moscow troubles, Chiang had to make a show of impatience to go on the attack. His leadership, the rule of the KMT, and the strong pro-Nationalist lobbies in the United States and among overseas Chinese all required it. Besides, excited demands by the Gimo for military action against the mainland usually resulted in efforts by the Americans to placate their ally with additional military equipment.

Thus in early 1961 the Gimo instructed Ching-kuo to begin secret planning for a surprise attack on the mainland.[22] Chief of Staff P'eng Meng-chi drew up two alternative scenarios: invading through Burma and attacking directly across the Taiwan Strait. The Gimo favored the Burma option.[23] Over the previous two years, Ching-kuo, on his father's instructions, had already flown several thousand elite Special Forces soldiers into northern Burma. These troops had joined the 5,500 irregulars and their dependents who had remained in Burma after the 1953–54 "evacuation." The combined forces began new probing raids across the border into China.[24] In early January 1961 Ching-kuo sent General Lai Ming-t'ang, his chief of G-2, to survey the prospects in Burma.[25]

Both Rangoon and Peking were fed up with the activities of the KMT irregulars and their reinforcements and concluded a secret agreement for combined operations against the KMT base at Mong Pa Liao, the main landing field for CAT planes flying in from Taiwan via Thailand. Burmese and PLA troops attacked and overwhelmed the base, and the KMT soldiers retreated into Laos. At the captured base Burmese officers discovered American arms of recent manufacture and five tons of U.S.-made ammunition.[26] Angered that Taipei had violated its categorical assurances in 1953 and 1954 that it would cut all ties with the irregulars, Dean Rusk instructed Drumright to berate the Generalissimo in unusually severe language for acting "recklessly" and to demand the complete withdrawal of all Nationalist forces from the area. Drumright did not directly confront the Gimo with this message but passed it to Ching-kuo through Ray Cline.[27] In a memo prepared for the White House, the State Department noted that the United States was not in a position to apply serious pressure on the Gimo on this—or other—issues because of "the important role that Taiwan plays in our strategic efforts to contain Chinese Communist expansionist pressures," including the "variety of intelligence operations conducted on and from Taiwan that are dependent on the cooperation of the Government of the Republic of China."[28]

Nevertheless, Washington's strong reaction and the military defeat in Burma resulted in yet another agreement by the Chiangs to withdraw their forces. In April Taiwan announced that it had repatriated 4,200 personnel, but it disavowed any responsibility for the 6,000 irregulars and dependents remaining in Laos and in the mountains of northern Burma.

Within months the CIA reportedly began hiring the disowned KMT remnants as mercenaries for its expanding secret operations in northwestern Laos.[29]

———

THE SAME MONTH that Ching-kuo's units came back from Burma, the disastrous CIA defeat at the Bay of Pigs in Cuba underscored the folly of assuming that a small-scale invasion by an exile force could set off a popular uprising against a powerful Communist regime. Chiang and his son knew that the Kennedy White House, even more than the Eisenhower administration, would reject the notion of a serious attack on the mainland. Yet in June 1961 the CIA station in Taipei reported that Chiang Kai-shek was again planning an assault across the Strait. Ching-kuo had briefed Ray Cline, informing him that mobilization would begin on August 1 and D-Day would be in January or February of 1962. Ching-kuo told Cline that Chiang Kai-shek had informed the heads of the three military services that they could not expect prior United States support for the planned assault, but "once the Nationalist troops had established a bridgehead anywhere on the mainland, the Americans would surely provide all necessary aid."

In his report to Washington Cline apparently did not express any skepticism that Chiang Kai-shek would be so foolhardy as to risk everything on such an assumption. Should the Nationalist assault fail and as a result resistance to a Chinese Communist counterattack on Taiwan crumble, the plan specified that President Chiang and a small number of other government leaders "would be evacuated from Taiwan to a safe haven."[30] The latter point was apparently intended to bring home to the Americans the potential loss of Taiwan if the counterattack failed.[31] When Cline was back in Washington on consultations in July, he warned McGeorge Bundy, the President's Special Assistant for National Security Affairs, that the Nationalists were so uneasy about the direction of U.S. policy that they might actually carry out a suicidal landing. Cline urged that to placate the Gimo the United States should join him in making "certain reconnaissance probes on the mainland."[32] As a result of Cline's persistent efforts, President Kennedy approved a plan developed by Ching-kuo's Special Warfare staff to drop six 20-man Nationalist teams into South China.[33] Some months later two such teams bravely parachuted onto the mainland, and their members were quickly killed or captured.

Cline, nevertheless, had impressed McGeorge Bundy, and during October, with Bundy's authorization and without informing Drumright or Ambassador Yeh in Washington, he negotiated an agreement with Ching-kuo on handling the issue of Outer Mongolia's entry into the United Nations. Taipei had sworn to veto any such move, although this would have lost it critical political support in the United Nations. In their talks with Cline Ching-kuo and his father agreed that Taipei would not veto Mongolia's entry after all, and for this "concession" wrung a pledge from Kennedy to veto Peking's entry into the United Nations if such a veto was "necessary and effective." Again, by threatening a counterproductive move, the Gimo had gained an important American commitment.[34]

In January 1962, amidst a continuing flood of news about troubles on the mainland, Chiang and his son again met privately with Cline, once more excluding Ambassador Drumright. Chiang told the station chief that he wished to know whether President Kennedy felt it timely to exchange views on "the circumstances under which GRC (Nationalist) intervention on the mainland might be feasible and necessary or at least desirable from the Free World strategic viewpoint." Chiang said he would certainly consult with the United States prior to any action, but "he hoped to have U.S. sympathy and support even though international factors might make it necessary for America to remain tacit about its sympathy." Now enthusiastically embracing the reality of a Sino-Soviet split, Chiang declared that the Russians would not intervene.[35] In February McGeorge Bundy visited Taipei, and the Gimo again pressed for at least "tacit agreement" to an assault on the mainland, and perhaps secret logistical support. Bundy was noncommittal. Like Cline, Drumright, who had sat in on this meeting, urged Washington not to reply to the Gimo's entreaties with a flat negative. Otherwise, he warned, Chiang might be provoked and take the leap into the flames.[36]

Although Cline had won the trust of McGeorge Bundy, Kennedy's Assistant Secretary for Far Eastern Affairs, Averill Harriman, developed a "jaundiced view" of Ambassador Drumright as "captive" of the KMT.

Having completed a four-year tour, the ambassador left Taipei; shortly thereafter Harriman flew to Taipei and met with the Gimo.[37] Chiang told Harriman the time was ripe for an assault on the mainland, and if he did not act he "might loose control." Harriman replied he had no fear the Generalissimo would lose control and stressed patience and the need for better intelligence about conditions in China.[38] A few weeks after Harriman departed, Chiang asked Cline to send yet another message to Kennedy saying that if the Nationalist government failed to heed growing pressures for early action against the mainland, there would be a risk of losing "leadership and control of Taiwan." Ching-kuo also personally cautioned Cline that should the Generalissimo step down, there could be a military coup and "anti-Americanism" might erupt.[39]

Ching-kuo argued that the previous teams had been too small. Airdrops of teams numbering at least 200 men each were needed if there was to be any chance of success. He also requested five electronically configured C-123 planes to carry out these covert missions. Cline, returning to Washington, gave credence to the Gimo's threat that if the ROC's requests were rejected he could be forced to resign. Instability and unrest on the island would follow, and the various joint-intelligence programs aimed at Peking would be at risk.[40] At an NSC meeting, which included the president, Cline strongly promoted Ching-kuo's latest proposal. Secretary Rusk said it was "nonsense," but Harriman favored again placating the Gimo with some gesture. Kennedy agreed that joint training and planning for the 200-man airdrops could begin, but said no such drops should be made until both governments agreed that conditions were right. He also offered to provide two of the five special C-123 aircraft Ching-kuo had requested and training for their crews.[41] The most interesting decision at the meeting, however, was McGeorge Bundy's instruction to Cline—made "very strongly"—that the CIA officer was to tell Ching-kuo that when the new U.S. ambassador to Taiwan arrived, he would take over the special political role heretofore played by the CIA.[42]

THE NEW ENVOY was to be retired Admiral Alan G. Kirk, commander of the U.S. naval armada at the Normandy landings in June 1944. As a distinguished military man and a contemporary of Chiang Kai-shek's, Kirk could speak with authority about the feasibility of amphibious operations against a well-equipped and dug-in military force. But Kirk did not arrive until July. Meanwhile Ching-kuo stepped up secret military training in the mountains and sent additional deployments to Quemoy and Matsu. Cline returned to Taipei and he, Ching-kuo, and the U.S. military set up an operational planning group called the 420 Committee to review GRC plans for airdrops of up to 200 men each. In the meantime, they agreed to cooperate with Ching-kuo's Special Warfare Center in dropping nine more 20-man teams to try to contact underground resistance elements. The Gimo then requested 16 B-57 bombers and 20–25 landing craft.[43]

The CIA was greatly pleased with Ray Cline's work on Taiwan, and he returned to Washington to become the deputy director for Intelligence. The Chiangs were delighted, as Cline was now in an even more powerful position to influence policy. Indeed, he wasted no time in using his new position as the senior CIA official in charge of all intelligence analysis to push the Chiang view of the mainland situation and what to do about it. In a May 17 meeting Cline told President Kennedy that controls were "crumbling" on the mainland and it would be very difficult for the Gimo to postpone military action beyond October. Cline urged the president to provide the B-57s, which were "necessary to neutralize [Communist China's] IL-28s," and the LSDs for Taiwan's amphibious forces.[44] A few days after this meeting Ching-kuo gave the CIA station an outline plan for landing commandos to initiate and support resistance movements in Fukien and Kwangtung, followed by assault landings at four points abreast of Taiwan. The indefatigable Cline won over CIA Director McCone, who urged Rusk and then Kennedy to authorize the U.S. military to begin stockpiling air and amphibious equipment to support a possible Nationalist invasion of the mainland.[45]

Mao apparently had his own interpretation as to why Kennedy planned to send the "D-Day" admiral to Taipei as ambassador: to place his expertise at the service of the Nationalists for a possible attack. Hence the PLA significantly strengthened its forces along the east coast. At this point Kennedy and his advisers thought the Kabuki play had gone far enough.[46] On June 23, at the Warsaw meeting with the Chinese, the U.S. representative said his country would dissociate itself by word and deed from any Nationalist attack against the mainland, and if such an attack did happen, the United States would seek to restore peace. Kennedy followed up with a more vague public statement to this effect.[47]

—

KIRK FINALLY ARRIVED IN TAIPEI and met with the Gimo. The ambassador advised that without large-scale US air, naval, and logistical support the Gimo's plan would surely fail.[48] He said the United States could not support an ROC invasion across the Strait and would not condone it. Any such action would seriously disrupt stability in the region. He also told Chiang that President Kennedy had decided conditions did not warrant making the B-57 bombers and the landing craft available at that time.[49] After this September meeting, the Gimo declined to receive Ambassador Kirk again.[50]

In October the Cuban missile crisis made contemplation of the use of nuclear weapons even more traumatic for Americans, and gave momentum to U.S.-Soviet efforts to prevent accidental war and control the spread of nuclear weapons. This effort in turn fed the fires of the Sino-Soviet dispute. In the midst of the ten-day Cuban missile standoff, the Chinese Communists launched a major offensive against India in the Himalayas. After bloodying India's nose, the Chinese withdrew back to their original lines. Mao apparently undertook this action to teach a lesson not only to India but also to the Russians on how to deal with a provocative enemy. In response, the CIA began carrying out active contingency planning for another round of covert operations "to free Tibet of ChiCom occupation," almost certainly in collaboration with Ching-kuo's Special Warfare units and possibly again with the cooperation of the Indian government.[51] Meanwhile, in the previously agreed-to joint operation with the CIA, nine more 20-man teams parachuted into the mainland. Again PRC security units killed or captured the infiltrators. Peking accused the United States of fostering the whole operation.[52]

When Kirk resigned because of a heart problem, his replacement, another retired admiral, Gerald Wright, carried the same negative message about the counterattack.[53] Despite the rebuffs, the Gimo continued in public to promise liberation of the mainland and in private to badger the Americans with new proposals. In March 1963 Chiang wrote

Kennedy once again, warning that unrest on the mainland was growing rapidly and his government could no longer ignore the popular demand for prompt action. By this time, however, senior Nationalist officials, including the Defense Minister, were telling American diplomats in private not to take the Gimo seriously.[54] In a May 1963 assessment that differed considerably from Cline's reports a year earlier, the new CIA station chief in Taipei concluded that "The GRC probably does not anticipate that either the current situation in Communist China or the current international situation favors a successful GRC attack. The GRC, even in the planning of small scale operations against the mainland, has demonstrated caution and absence of integrated planning."[55]

IN JUNE 1963 the Chinese Communists released a long twenty-five point indictment of the Soviet ideological line. Khrushchev suggested the two parties hold secret talks in Moscow. Deng led the Chinese delegation, but after two weeks the meetings ended inconclusively.[56] Three months later Ching-kuo held talks in Washington with *his* government's superpower ally. He carried a letter from the Gimo proposing yet another attack plan, this one called "Secret Dragon," involving a number of Nationalist airdrops of 100 to 300 men and seaborne attacks of 300–500 men. As usual, the intended goal was to set off revolutionary uprisings on the mainland.

During his September 10 meeting with McGeorge Bundy. Ching-kuo downplayed this proposal and said that the way to weaken and overthrow the Communist regime should be "more political than military," and he asserted that the Nationalist government was not planning a large-scale attack on the mainland. He did, however, urge that the United States and the Nationalist governments work together on ways to destroy Chinese Communist missile sites and atomic installations.[57] During his talk with President Kennedy the next day, Ching-kuo dutifully explained that Secret Dragon would be the first step in seizing one or more provinces in South China, not a large-scale invasion. He requested five C-130s (four of the promised five C-123s had been delivered). In response to a question from Kennedy, Ching-kuo said that 300 to 500 special troops could successfully be dropped at the Chinese Communist nuclear installations. Kennedy again stressed the need for better information on what was happening inside China.[58]

POSSIBLE ATTACKS on the PRC nuclear facilities were the focus of Ching-kuo's meeting with CIA Director John McCone on September 14. The talks concluded that the two sides would study ways of improving "capabilities to hurt the Chinese Communist regime" such as possible sabotage operations and attacks on strategic targets, including nuclear installations on the mainland. But the memo again stressed that execution of any such operations would require mutual agreement and should "avoid action that would run the risk of precipitating a world conflict or which by its failure would be detrimental to their joint interests."[59]

Ching-kuo's initiative regarding China's nuclear facilities coincided, probably deliberately, with proposals that had recently been floated by the CIA. According to Ray Cline, on the basis of U-2-derived intelligence the CIA projected that Peking would explode its first nuclear bomb within a year, and suggested to President Kennedy several alternative ways of dealing with the threat. These included an approach to Khrushchev for a joint strike against the Chinese nuclear facilities and covert teams from Taiwan to blow up the critical installations.[60] Kennedy had already been toying with the idea of some sort of collaboration with the Soviet Union aimed at "limiting or preventing Chinese nuclear development."[61] In the following months, however, the administration concluded that China's small-scale nuclear capability would have only marginal strategic and political impact, and the idea of a Nationalist paramilitary raid on the facilities deep inside China was shelved.[62]

After Ching-kuo's second visit to Washington, hardly any American leaders worried about his true ideological sympathies. The Chiangs, however, began to worry more about the reliability of the Americans. Shortly after Ching-kuo's return to Taipei, a military junta in Saigon deposed South Vietnamese dictator Ngo Dinh Diem and executed Diem and his brother Ngo Dinh Nhu, head of the secret police. Ching-kuo had met with Nhu in Taiwan in 1960, and at the request of the Vietnamese he had sent Wang Sheng to Saigon to advise on setting up a political officer service in the South Vietnamese Army.[63] Immediately after the 1963 coup, it was widely reported that the U.S. government had backed the plotters led by General Duong Van Minh. The coup confirmed the Chiangs' determination to maintain, and where possible strengthen, the political surveillance system in the Nationalist military. Three weeks later news reached Taipei of the assassination of President Kennedy. Ching-kuo was the first Nationalist official to call at the American embassy to express his condolences.

———

DURING THAT EVENTFUL FALL Ch'en Ch'eng become ill with what turned out to be liver cancer. In November 1963 the Ninth KMT Congress elevated to the Central Committee several top police and military officers in intelligence and security, including the directors of the IBMND, the GPWD, and the Garrison Command.[64] Ch'en was "extremely upset" over these changes.[65] In December the Gimo accepted Ch'en's resignation as concurrent premier and, surprisingly, chose as the new executive head of government the accomplished technocrat, Finance Minister C. K. Yen. Yen was widely regarded as competent, intelligent, and honest, but politically "soft" and unlikely ever to challenge Ching-kuo's authority. Particularly close to Madame Chiang, he was acceptable to all the leading figures in the KMT. Even Taiwanese liked him because of his focus on development.

In 1964 Taiwan's business boom seemed impressive. The third Four-Year Economic Development Plan that terminated in that year raised GNP by 35 percent, per capita income by 19 percent, and industrial production by an impressive 72 percent.[66] Politically, however, it was not a good year. President Charles de Gaulle recognized the Peking regime and closed down the French embassy in Taipei. Guided by Liu Shao-ch'i and Deng Xiaoping, China seemed to be recovering from its economic debacle of 1959–1962.

Also in 1964 Chiang Wei-kuo virtually disappeared as a possible political factor because his successor as commander of the First Armored Division, General Chao Chih-hua, made a farcical coup attempt. Chao had been Wei-kuo's deputy during the Battle of Hsupang in late 1948, had been captured, and later escaped. Ching-kuo's political officers would normally have been highly suspicious of such officers, but

Wei-kuo had strongly vouched for Chao. Chao remained a trusted officer for the next fourteen years. Then on January 21, 1964, he assembled the troops, officers, and tanks of his division and over loudspeakers announced that they would move on Taipei and seize the government because the Generalissimo was not acting vigorously enough against the Chinese Communists.

The assembled ranks of several thousand were stunned. A senior political officer shouted his support and rushed to the platform. Instead of saluting Chao, however, the commissar seized the commander and pinned him to the floor. That was the end of the two-minute coup. Chiang Kai-shek was angry with Wei-kuo over his long endorsement of Chao, and the incident put an even darker cloud over the career of the younger son.[67]

FAR REMOVED FROM THE MILITARY, a prominent Taiwanese intellectual, P'eng Ming-min, edged toward confrontation with the regime. The professor had been meeting privately with a few like-minded students and others to discuss the political situation. Ching-kuo's agents closely monitored these meetings, and in early 1964 the Garrison Command arrested P'eng and two young comrades for printing a manifesto calling for an independent Taiwan. The subsequent trial attracted a good deal of attention abroad, especially in Canada and the United States. Ching-kuo decided that P'eng would receive a light, eight-year sentence. But only seven months later, after signing a note worded by Ching-kuo's security officers saying he repented his action, P'eng obtained presidential clemency and went home.[68]

Ching-kuo also continued to allow some leeway to Taiwanese politicians like Henry Kao. In the 1964 elections for Taipei mayor, with Ching-kuo's approval, the election authorities granted Henry his poll watchers—500 to cover 360 polling stations. Although the KMT put a lot of resources into the mayoral campaign and covertly backed a third "independent" candidate to drain off votes, Kao won a narrow victory as did other independents in the mayoral races in Tainan and Keelung.[69]

16

The Minister

IN JANUARY 1965 Premier Yen appointed Chiang Ching-kuo Minister of Defense—a title that did not go to his head. One day an American congressman paid a call on the new Minister, accompanied by Embassy Second Secretary Herbert Levin. The congressman expressed the hope that the Nationalists would be able to retake the mainland in the next few years. The problem, the congressman said, was that if the Communists had control over a young person for ten years, that person would remain "forever a hard-core Communist." Ching-kuo, who had spent twelve years as a young Communist acolyte, nodded. He then turned and gave Levin "a big Western wink."[1]

That spring Ch'en Ch'eng died, at 67 years of age. Well before his death, however, Ching-kuo had been the country's real CEO—except for the key areas of economic and financial affairs. The Generalissimo was now 78 years old and increasingly detached from events of the day. Because of his failing eyesight, he did little reading and his staff kept unpleasant news from him.[2] After Ch'en's death, Ching-kuo allowed C. K. Yen to continue to manage the economy pretty much as he and his pragmatic, market-oriented associates wished. But virtually everyone in Taiwan recognized that Ching-kuo's informal authority now extended to these fields as well.[3]

CHING-KUO WAS ALSO THE KEY behind-the-scenes negotiator with the United States on sensitive international matters, such as France's recognition of Peking the previous year.[4] Despite Washington's stated intention to end high-level policy discussions with Taipei in intelligence channels, the Chiangs were still able to call on Ray Cline to act as a principal interlocutor. Cline and Director McCone, however, continued in vain to promote the Gimo's proposals to use Nationalist troops to fight in Vietnam and to destroy the Communist nuclear installations on the mainland.[5]

In the spring of 1965 the war in Indochina sharply escalated, the Sino-Soviet rift widened from an ideological breach into national hostility, the pro-Peking Indonesian Communist Party virtually ceased to exist following its failed coup in Jakarta, and Peking's foreign policy across the board became increasingly radical. Ching-kuo sent a message to the CIA that his father wanted to talk with Ray Cline again. There was a prolonged discussion in Washington about the wisdom of rushing to send the Gimo's personally chosen American envoy whenever he sent out the call. Cline finally received permission to fly once more to Taipei. On arrival he had a short meeting with the two Chiangs in the presence of the American chargé; then Ching-kuo took his friend to Sun-Moon Lake for a five-hour private session with the Generalissimo. The time to attack the mainland was "now or never," the Gimo insisted.[6] Cline rushed back to Washington to plead the Gimo's case anew, but "no one in Washington paid the slightest attention." The Americans could not tell whether Chiang was still posturing for the historical record and his domestic right-wing audience or becoming addled.[7]

Ching-kuo himself discounted his father's increasingly ritualistic calls for a military attack. Only a few weeks after Cline's visit Ching-kuo met with the new CIA station chief (the Station's cover name was now the U.S. Army Technological Group) and spelled out in a candid way his own position on the recovery of the mainland and on United States-Republic of China relations:

> While the Nationalist Government must nourish the hope of returning to the mainland in order to sustain morale on the island of Taiwan, the key men of [my] generation realize that it may be a long time before a

non-Communist regime can be re-established in mainland China—perhaps not in their lifetimes. Nevertheless, [we] wish to do everything of which [we] are capable to insure that no opportunity is lost to defeat Chinese Communist ambitions and gain any position of strength which will weaken and undermine the Peiping [Peking] regime . . . [thus] the young generation of [Nationalist] leaders . . . feel their primary aim . . . and strategy should be to maintain an intimate and cooperative understanding with the United States and to support U.S. policy in East Asia.[8]

Shortly afterwards, Ching-kuo participated in some high-level meetings in Washington and dutifully passed on his father's latest proposals for military action. In his talks with Defense Secretary McNamara, Ching-kuo said his father had asked him to leave behind a "concept paper" proposing to seize China's five southwest provinces, a plan dubbed Great Torch Five. Ching-kuo stressed, however, that Great Torch Five was not an operational proposal and that more joint studies were required. His emphasis was on the need for the United States and Nationalist China to act as a real partnership or alliance, not only on the question of Communist China but on policy and strategy throughout Asia. He told McNamara that a return to the mainland depended "on winning over the people and the Communist armed forces," and that the question was how to make use of Chinese Nationalist strength without touching off a wider war.[9]

Speaking to Secretary Rusk and others, Ching-kuo gave what seemed to the Americans an objective analysis of Peking's intentions, saying he doubted the Chinese Communists would intervene directly either in Vietnam or South Asia. In his talk with President Johnson, Ching-kuo noted that he had raised some military proposals, but his key goal was not military action against the mainland, but "penetrating and sustained" consultations in order to "integrate" U.S. and Nationalist policies regarding not only China but all of Asia.[10] According to Ching-kuo, internal dynamics would primarily shape developments on the mainland, and Taiwan's role in the long-term transformation of Communist China would be as an economic, cultural, social, and political model—pretty much what Lei Chen had preached.[11] American officials welcomed Ching-kuo's presentations. They believed he had designed the visit to show greater flexibility and accommodation to U.S.

views. In return they promised better consultations and, yes, more joint studies.[12]

—

CHING-KUO DID REPEAT the Generalissimo's old offer to make Nationalist forces "available" to support free-world interests in Asia. Ray Cline followed up the visit by again pushing for an NSC decision to use Chinese Nationalist forces in Indochina, but the State Department and the White House once more rejected the proposal as a dangerous move that America's allies would strongly oppose.[13] Clandestine personnel, however, was another matter. By the time of Ching-kuo's 1965 trip to Washington, several hundred military and paramilitary personnel from his Special Warfare Center were already in Vietnam, where they constituted the third largest foreign contingent.[14] The most important among them were members of a paramilitary unit called the Sea Swallows, led by a Catholic priest, Father Nguyen Loc Hoa.[15] Taipei also assisted South Vietnam in other ways. Most important were the CAT and Air America facilities in Taiwan, which supported CIA air activities throughout Indochina. Following Wang Sheng's initial trip to Saigon in 1960, the Vietnamese Armed Forces established their own General Political Warfare Department modeled on Ching-kuo's system.[16]

The new South Vietnamese military junta, headed by General Nguyen Van Thieu and Air Force General Nguyen Cao Ky, had actually come to power in mid-1965 with behind-the-scenes assistance from Ching-kuo. His intelligence operatives in Saigon had channeled funding from a wealthy ethnic Chinese businessman to General Thieu, and also facilitated connections between Thieu and the CIA.[17]

—

BUT CHING-KUO WAS NOT BANKING EVERYTHING on Taiwan's ties to America. In June 1965 the Gimo approved his proposal that the secret nuclear bomb study project move out of the research stage into development. Some "high ranking Nationalist officials and presidential advisers" told the President that a Manhattan Project for Taiwan would be economically unsound, technically unfeasible, and politically un-wise.[18] But Ching-kuo took on overall responsibility for the project and appointed General T'ang Chung-po as the director. A super-secret divi-sion of the Chungshan Institute of Science, the military's R&D body, car-ried out the laboratory work, while General T'ang worked out a strategy for acquiring the necessary reactors, reprocessors, enriched uranium, and delivery technology. Among the people General Tang recruited for his team was a young, science-inclined officer just out of the military academy, Chang Hsien-yi. The CIA, however, had been quicker this time and had already recruited Chang as a spy.

AFTER HE BECAME MINISTER OF DEFENSE IN 1965, Ching-kuo moved his family into a navy guest house called Seven Seas. The house, some-what larger than the abode on Ch'angan East Road, was in a compound near the Grand Hotel.[19] By then, Ching-kuo was 56 years of age. He had finally taken his doctor's advice and cut down on his drinking; some say he quit entirely. In the late 1950s he had taken up Chinese painting as a hobby, but because his legs had begun to hurt—a diabetic symptom—he could no longer stand for long periods and in the mid-1960s gave up this pastime. The parties with his inner core of friends continued until he became Vice Premier in 1969. The gatherings, as in the past, were all chitchat and jokes and, of course, the finger game. But now Ching-kuo delegated a "tai piao" or representative to stand in for him in the drinking contests. If Americans were invited, the Chinese still tried to get them drunk. Once, in the 1960s, a newly arrived station chief was sent home "drunk as a dog."[20]

According to some sources, Ching-kuo stopped his occasional affairs with women in the 1960s. Others maintain the womanizing persisted, although more modestly, into the 1970s. One story that comes from friends of the woman involved regards his friendship with the most famous Peking Opera singer in Taiwan, the beautiful Ku Cheng-ch'iu. Ching-kuo pursued her, but she repeatedly rejected him because she had been long involved with a married man, Jen Hsien-ch'un, with whom she had two children. Jen got into trouble when a cousin for whom he had provided a "guarantee" for entry into Taiwan was arrested as a spy in 1956. When Jen was sentenced to a short prison term, rumor had it that Ching-kuo had sought to get him out of the way. But, although Ku was outraged at the arrest of her lover and the father of her children, she apparently did not blame Ching-kuo. She did meet with her powerful admirer and pleaded with him to pardon Jen. According to the story, Ching-kuo did not take advantage of Ms. Ku's situation and regretfully declined to release Jen.[21]

Neither the rumored nor the real affairs interfered with Ching-kuo's family life. Faina followed the rules her husband laid down, but on some things she went her own way. In the late 1950s, because Amy objected, she gave up mahjong, but still smoked cigarettes. She took up golf and bowling and also did volunteer work in supporting local schools. In the 1950s her small circle of friends had included several "White Russian" wives of both Chinese and Americans, including CAT pilots, but in the 1960s, as Ching-kuo moved to higher positions, she stopped seeing them. Her English was good. At a dinner party, a visiting U.S. Congressman naively asked Faina, "Which are you, White Russian or Red Russian? " Without hesitation, she replied, "I suppose you could say, I was born one and raised the other."[22]

Ching-kuo once told an aide, "to manage a country is easy, to manage a family is difficult." While he was always pressed for time, he took his family responsibilities seriously. One young man named Mao Kao-wen, distantly related to Ching-kuo through the latter's mother, Mao Fu-mei, was about to depart for graduate study in America and called on his esteemed cousin to say farewell. Ching-kuo questioned the boy for an hour about his plans, taking notes on the replies; years later, the relative recalled thinking, "here was a serious man."[23]

AFTER HIS SHORT STAY at a small Kansas school, Alan Chiang entered Armstrong College in California. He met and married a beautiful and smart young woman named Nancy Zi. Like Alan, Nancy was a Eurasian. In 1907, her grandfather, Hsu Hsi-lin, had assassinated a Ch'ing dynasty official, and as punishment had suffered the cutting out of his still living heart. Her mother was Maria Bordan, a German national. Alan and Nancy were married in a Catholic Church in Laguna Beach, after which they went to school for a year in Washington, D.C. In 1961 she presented Ching-kuo with his first grandchild, a blond, blue-eyed daughter named Yomei (Yu-mei). Madame Chiang bestowed on the child one of her English baptismal names, Marguerite, the other being Faina Maria, but she would always be called Yomei.[24]

In addition to ruling out private business as a vocation for his sons, Ching-kuo set down other strict rules to avoid the impression that his family was profiting from their position. He told Nancy that she could not buy the sports car she wanted even with her own money, nor could she go on a trip to Australia with her parents.

Alan was a bright, charming young man with a sense of humor. He created scrolls of calligraphy that he presented to his friends, signed "drunken soldier." He did not, however, have his father's tolerance for spirits. When Alan was in his late twenties, doctors at Veterans Hospital informed him that he had diabetes, but he continued to drink.

One day, as Y. S. Sun, president of Taiwan Power Company (a state enterprise), was escorting the Gimo through a new power station, Chiang drew him aside and said he would be grateful if Sun could find a job for his grandson and try to help the young man make something of himself. Sun started Alan off as an apprentice, and after a year the young Chiang was promoted to a small Taipei office as manager.[25] One result of this connection for Alan was that Ching-kuo became close to Y. S. Sun, a fellow engineer who had trained at the Tennessee Valley Authority. Ching-kuo soon brought Y. S. into the government, where he became part of the second generation of intellectual technocrats.

Of all his children, Ching-kuo was closest to his daughter, Amy. Until his death he kept a picture of her and Yomei on his desk. Servants in the household described her as a very kind girl but strong willed.[26] When she went to the United States to university, Ching-kuo asked the Minister of Defense, Yu Ta-wei, to have his stateside son, Yu Yang-ho, look after her. Amy soon fell in love with Yu, a forty-year-old, thrice-divorced business-man, and planned to marry him. Ching-kuo was furious. He objected to the proposed union because of the 18-year age difference and Yang-ho's three failed marriages. Ching-kuo also felt it was as inappropriate for his daughter to marry a businessman as it would be for one of his sons to become one. Madame wrote Ching-kuo a letter in English—her written Chinese was never very good—and asked him to accept Amy's decision. When Amy returned to Taipei for a visit, Ching-kuo took her on a weekend trip to Sun-Moon Lake, where they spent many hours paddling around and talking. Amy promised not to marry before finishing university, and father and daughter were reconciled.[27]

Shortly after her return to the States, however, Amy and Yang-ho married in Reno, Nevada. When he heard the news, Ching-kuo was eating lunch. In a rage, he pushed over the dining table. Faina wept and beat her head against the bedpost.[28] Eventually they accepted their daughter's decision. The same year that Nancy Chiang delivered Yomei, Amy bore Ching-kuo's first grandson, Theodore (Yu Tsu-sheng). Soon grandfather Ching-kuo was rolling and tumbling on the floor with Theodore and Yomei. But he never really accepted Amy's husband. As a result, the couple visited Taipei less and less.

For the second son, Alex, the first half of the decade was a period of teen-age hell-raising. Like his older brother, he created much anguish for his father and mother. He was, however, more disciplined in his studies, and the only child of Ching-kuo's who saw himself as a future political leader. The youngest son, Hsiao-yung, or Eddy, caused his parents relatively little worry.[29] To Ching-kuo's great pride, Eddy entered the Military Academy preparatory school.

At Christmas and Thanksgiving—the latter American holiday being a favorite of Madame's—the clan would gather at the presidential residence for a festive dinner. By the late 1960s the group was rather large: the Gimo and his wife, Ching-kuo and Faina, their four children (if Amy was in town), the spouses of two, two Ching-kuo grandchildren, Wei-kuo, his second wife, Ellen Chiu, their son Gregory, a young woman named Dorothy Wu, a granddaughter of the Gimo's long-departed sister, and several descendants of his late half-brother. Except for the deceased Ya-jou's twin boys and their offspring, all the Gimo's grandchildren and subsequent descendants would be Eurasian. Before dinner, the extended family attended services at the chapel presided over by Pastor Chou. Also present at the services were Young Marshal Chang Hsueh-liang and Miss Chao, whom he finally married.

Ching-kuo continued to abide by his decision never to see his illegitimate twin sons, John and Winston. Of the extended family, only the Gimo and Madame, Ching-kuo, and possibly Wei-kuo knew of their existence. In 1960 the boys entered private Suchow (or Dongwu) University on the outskirts of Taipei. Winston was set on an academic career in legal studies but took his first degree in Chinese Literature. John focused on public service, specifically foreign service. While in college, the two boys held part time jobs to support themselves, and Wang Sheng occasionally provided "small amounts of money" to help out. Still, they often had to request a delay in the payment of their tuition. They mentioned to no one, not even their closest friends, that they were the sons of Chiang Ching-kuo. After his junior year, John, who had become active in the Youth Corps, attended a political cadre summer camp for college students. Alex Chiang was there too but did not know that he had a half-brother, much less one in the same room.[30]

Women in the Generalissimo's past also lingered out of sight. Yao Yeh-ch'eng, "Mama Yao," lived out her old age in nearby T'aoyuan. Wei-kuo visited regularly and provided her living expenses. Ching-kuo's "Shanghai Mother" (Ch'en Chieh-ju) re-entered the picture in 1961, when, with the help of Zhou Enlai, she received permission to move from the mainland to Hong Kong, into a house that Ching-kuo had purchased for her.[31] In March 1965 she accepted $170,000 from an agent of Ching-kuo's for the manuscript of her memoirs and a promise not to publish them.[32]

SINCE HIS RELEASE IN 1964, P'eng Ming-min had been unemployed. In early 1966, to his surprise, an official came to his house to inform him that Defense Minister Ching-kuo would like "to hear his advice." When P'eng entered the minister's office, Chiang stood up to greet the former political prisoner, and asked about his family and whether there was anything he could do to help him. Responding to the warmth in Ching-kuo's questions, P'eng said he would like to return to the university. Ching-kuo indicated he would look into it. Shortly after, P'eng was invited to join Ching-kuo's "think tank," the Institute of International Affairs. The professor turned down the offer. Over the next few years P'eng continued under surveillance but persisted in occasional meetings with like-minded intellectuals. Meanwhile, intelligence agents sent by Ching-kuo repeatedly made clear to P'eng that "liberals in the Party [the KMT]" still hoped to persuade him to work for change from within.[33]

While Ching-kuo could not entice the professor into cooperation, he did succeed in winning over a major figure in the Taiwan independence movement. In May 1965, Liao Wen-yi (Dr. Thomas Liao), who for years had headed the Taiwan Independence Party based in Tokyo, publicly forsook the movement and flew back to Taiwan. The authorities thereupon returned properties confiscated from Liao and his family—no doubt a key component of his deal with Ching-kuo.[34]

In 1966 the National Assembly elected the Gimo to a fourth term as president, but also—reluctantly—approved a constitutional amendment pushed by Ching-kuo that allowed special balloting to fill a number of new seats to reflect population growth on Taiwan. Only 26 of the Legislative Yuan seats, or about 5 percent of the total, would be at stake in the elections, which were not to be held for three years. Nevertheless, under Ching-kuo's direction, the KMT was taking its first tiny but symbolically significant step toward empowerment of the majority.

Meanwhile, the KMT organizational department, firmly under Ching-kuo's control, continued successfully to run local elections that included anti-KMT candidates. Ching-kuo's strategy was to have honest polling and vote-counting in order to attract credible independents to compete, and then to rely on tight restrictions on campaigning, including what could and could not be said, as well as on the KMT's huge financial advantage and control of the media, to assure victory in the great majority of contests. As the new election for Taipei mayor approached, however, Wang Sheng and others warned Ching-kuo that it was too dangerous to allow anti-KMT politicians (like Henry Kao) to run the capital city. Ching-kuo agreed and arranged for his father to declare Taipei a special municipality, which meant that the central government would appoint the mayor. But on Ching-kuo's recommendation, the Gimo, to the surprise of many, appointed Kao to the position. Kao grumbled but accepted the arrangement. On meeting the mayor after his appointment, Ching-kuo told him he should concentrate more on improving the daily livelihood of the poor and less on widening streets, planting trees, and "putting up bunting."[35]

———

THE RATE OF DISCHARGE of older mainlanders from the military services increased, but the continued lopsided proportion of commissioned and noncommissioned officers indicated that Ching-kuo did not want to move too fast, lest he affect the stability of the military establishment. Generals and admirals were still virtually all mainlanders, but Ching-kuo realized this would have to change.

The new Defense Minister arranged a retreat at Sun-Moon lake for his most senior officers. After dinner one night, Ching-kuo, returning from a walk, stopped at the edge of a group talking on the patio about the security risks of promoting native Taiwanese into the higher ranks. He interrupted the conversation: "Gentlemen, this is a serious subject. If we don't treat the people here as Chinese, we will have a big problem."[36] Ching-kuo soon retired 500 generals and 2,000 colonels—all mainlanders—while the number of Taiwanese in the military academies steadily grew, and the first Taiwanese field-grade officers pinned on their new emblems of rank.[37]

Mainland soldiers and aging veterans constituted the largest group of poor on the island, and their situation was a constant source of concern for Ching-kuo. One day he went to see Reverend Chou Lien-hua, the pastor at the President's chapel, to discuss the morale of the old veterans. Ching-kuo said that their nostalgia for home and family seemed to be growing. Some active-duty soldiers as well as retired servicemen from the mainland often went to the seashore facing China to burn incense. "This is a problem in the realm of the metaphysical," Chiang said, and he asked Chou if he would consider visiting units of the armed forces and "preaching to them."

Chou thought about this request for a few days and eventually visited several military units and spoke to large groups of officers and men about personal values and the meaning of religious belief. Later Ching-kuo told the reverend that the army men did not understand much of his preaching and the air force men also had some problems. But, he said, the political officers, being likewise concerned with matters of the heart, understood him very well.[38]

―

AS PLANNED, the U.S. AID program officially ended in June 1965. Taiwan's growth rate that year was 9 percent. Per capita income was $174 (in 1965 dollars). By the standards of the late 1990s, this seems a very low figure. But it represented rapid growth over the previous 15 years—the highest rate in the world after that of Japan.[39] Total U.S. economic aid to the island since 1950 topped out at about $1.4 billion. This was the largest amount of aid the United States had expended per capita in any country. Economic assistance continued after 1965 in the form of loans, surplus food sales, and technical assistance. In addition, just as Japan's economy had surged in the early 1950s because of U.S. military procurement related to the Korean War, so Taiwan was beginning to benefit substantially from the Indochina conflict. In 1965 U.S. military procurements on the island for use in the Indochina theater were running about $130 million a year.[40]

For those living in Taiwan at that time, the rising levels of consumption, education, and health were vividly apparent. The political ramifications were also obvious. The booming private sectors—commerce, manufacturing, and agriculture—were principally "Taiwanese sectors."

17

The Golden Cudgel

BY 1966 IT WAS APPARENT that Washington intended to make a major commitment of fortune and blood to stop what it perceived as Chinese-Communist expansion in Indochina. The American intervention in turn further convinced Mao that his world view in 1950 was correct: "imperialist America" had to be confronted and the revolutionary momentum pushed forward wherever possible. Events in Algeria, the Congo, Latin America, and Indonesia seemed to confirm the polarization of world politics. They also hastened Mao's determination to carry out a revolutionary transformation of his own party and Chinese society. Thus began the Great Proletarian Cultural Revolution, Mao's effort to cleanse Chinese society of the ossification, routinization, and pursuit of self-interest that he believed had brought about the death of true socialism in the USSR. Mao thus purged Deng Xiaoping because he was the epitome of the Party man—the very quality that over the years had made "Little Cannon" the Chairman's most useful and trustworthy supporter. Deng and his third wife, Cho Lin, mother of his five children, went off to prison.[1]

The resulting disorder and infighting on the mainland looked like another prayer answered to readers of *Streams in the Desert*. To exploit the trashing of Chinese traditional culture by the Red Guards, the Gimo mandated a Movement for China's Cultural Renaissance. Ching-kuo publicly declared that the Nationalists would answer an appeal for assistance from the mainland within six hours. He ordered his Special Warfare Center to conduct yet more studies on possible operations across the Strait.[2]

Despite such posturing in Taipei, Ching-kuo's China-watchers did not think the Communist system was on the verge of collapse, primarily because of the continuing cohesion of the PLA. Wang Sheng, officially deputy director of the GPWD and in practice its chief, met bi-weekly with the American Political Counselor David Dean to exchange views on the strange happenings in China. Wang's analysis was surprisingly objective.[3]

The Chinese Communist threat to world peace that the Americans and the Chinese Nationalists had so often invoked now began to look real to many countries, including even the Soviet Union. Mao declared Soviet "social imperialism" to be as evil as "American imperialism." He and Lin Piao called for "peoples wars" across the globe and supported Maoist guerrillas in India, Burma, Thailand, Malaysia, and the Philippines. Radicals in the camp of Mao's wife, Chiang Ch'ing, seized control of foreign policy. Red Guards burned down the British embassy in Peking and harassed Soviet diplomats and their families. The deification of Mao—"the red, red sun in the hearts of all the people of the world"—reached the level of that accorded to Stalin and Hitler.

The triumph of extremism in China and Taipei's important contributions to the U.S. effort in Indochina temporarily strengthened Ching-kuo's hopes for a new, stronger, no-nonsense United States-Taiwan partnership. By 1967 the number of American military and CIA personnel and their families in Taiwan had grown to 20,000.[4] Several American Phantom jets with tactical nuclear bombs were still based at an airfield near Taichung for possible use against China, should the Vietnam War drastically escalate with direct Chinese intervention as had happened in Korea.

But there was also a disturbing and ironic countertrend. Washington and the West in general showed increasing signs of wishing to come to terms with Mao Zedong—however extreme his revolutionary gyrations—since he was no longer an ally of the Soviet Union. Dean Acheson had predicted such a break would come and would open the door to normalization of relations between America and China. In dealing with China, the Senate Foreign Relations Committee introduced the concept of "containment without isolation" and suggested that America's goal should be the inclusion of China in the world community.[5] There were other omens of a geopolitical shift. In June 1967 the PRC exploded a test hydrogen bomb, and although the Johnson administration poured hundreds of thousands of troops into Vietnam, they could not suppress the Vietcong insurgents.

While Indochina-related activities on Taiwan remained at a high level, Taiwan's most important ally in the American government, the CIA, began to cut back on its largess to Ching-kuo's operations aimed at China. The agency reduced the size of the station and canceled several joint mainland-targeted programs.[6] The CIA even sold off its airline, the legendary CAT, and suspended the special low-level air reconnaissance mission ("Gosbeak"), which for several years had probed and mapped Chinese Communist air defenses. After the station chief informed Ching-kuo that the specially fitted aircraft for this mission were to be withdrawn, the normally cool leader lost his temper. The station chief explained that new U.S. satellites made the program unnecessary, but Ching-kuo assumed that the United States was primarily seeking to end a provocation of the Peoples Republic.[7] To demonstrate his unhappiness, he refused to see or talk to the station chief for some months and closed the Joint Operations Office.[8]

Selected CIA-ROC intelligence operations, including the U-2 flights and signals intercepts, continued. One new combined undertaking began—an over-the-horizon radar site designed to monitor China's missile firings. But the trend was apparent: the American and Taiwan clandestine services "began to watch each other as much as they cooperated." The CIA station observed "a certain malaise" in the senior ranks of the Taipei regime about their position in the world.[9]

As signs of creeping U.S. disengagement increased, the Gimo still occasionally badgered visiting Americans to support an assault on the mainland.[10] At one point, however, Ching-kuo persuaded his father to tell the Americans that while the return to the mainland would still be 30 percent military, it was now evident that political means would come first, "after which, at a later time, some military action may be necessary 'to clean up the mess.'"[11] Ching-kuo approved a new program for "strengthening operations behind enemy lines" that specifically rejected an invasion, because the international situation was unfavorable and because an attack would reunify the Communists. The plan called for political and psychological warfare and centered on the expectation that Taiwan's economic, cultural, and other successes would eventually influence political events on the mainland. This was a far-fetched scenario at the time, but it would materialize in the 1980s.[12]

BY 1968 CHING-KUO KNEW that his vision of a close strategic partnership with America would not be realized. After the Tet offensive in South Vietnam and the murders of Robert Kennedy and Martin Luther King, a grave malaise settled over America, with strong anti-war and anti-military fevers. On November 1 Johnson halted the bombing of North Vietnam. Four days later Richard M. Nixon was elected president. Nixon had long been a great friend of the KMT, but only a year earlier he had declared that the world simply could not afford to leave China outside the family of nations.[13] The Nationalist position in the United Nations also continued to slip.

During the summer of 1968 the deterioration of Sino-Soviet relations led to an interesting KGB gambit toward Chiang Ching-kuo. Mao had perceived the United States-USSR Nuclear Nonproliferation Treaty and Moscow's invasion of Czechoslovakia as omens of future Soviet military pressure against China. Zhou Enlai called the invasion of Czechoslovakia "the most barefaced and typical specimen of fascist power politics."[14] More Soviet Red Army divisions rumbled up to the Sino-Soviet border. Among them were rocket units carrying nuclear-tipped surface-to-surface missiles.

Two months after the Soviet invasion of Czechoslovakia, a Russian national named Victor Louis (also known as Vitaly Yevgeniyevich), Moscow correspondent for the *London Evening Star*, approached the press officer of the Nationalist embassy in Tokyo. Louis said he wished to visit Taiwan.[15] The Taiwanese intelligence service immediately and no doubt correctly assumed Louis to be a KGB agent; Ching-kuo wondered what Moscow was up to, but the request was too intriguing to ignore. He approved the visit and asked his friend Jimmy Wei, who was then director general of the Government Information Office, to be the principal contact. He did not inform the Americans at this time of the forthcoming visit—the first contact of any sort between the Nationalist Government and the Soviet regime since 1949.

Louis arrived and had several meetings with Wei. He said that because of the hostility of the Peking government toward the USSR, Moscow was interested in a rapprochement with Chiang Kai-shek and suggested that, as a beginning, the two governments set up trade offices in each other's capital. Louis then made a startling declaration: now was the best chance for the Nationalists to recover the mainland and the key was Russian neutrality. Moscow, he said, would regard a Nationalist attack on the mainland as an internal war, provided Taipei could convince the USSR that it would not permit U.S. bases in China once it returned to power there.

Indeed, Louis soon went beyond the promise of neutrality in the Chinese civil war and suggested that since Mao was a threat to both governments, they should explore ways to cooperate to bring about his fall. Under instructions from Ching-kuo, Wei told Louis that abrogation of the USSR-PRC Treaty of 1950 "would help Taipei reorient its mind." In the meantime the Nationalists were willing to discuss areas of cooperation, including supply of Soviet ammunition, military hardware, and intelligence. Wei suggested that if the Nationalists launched an attack on the mainland, the USSR could contribute by creating another crisis on the Soviet-Sinkiang border. On the question of U.S. bases in China, Ching-kuo instructed Wei to say that the Nationalist government would pursue "an independent foreign policy."

Ching-kuo was highly skeptical. He suspected that Louis's approach was another piece of Soviet psychological warfare against Peking. Still, the way things were going, it was now more than conceivable that the Sino-Soviet crisis could actually lead to large-scale military conflict. The ironic idea that the Soviet Union could actually support the Nationalist cause against the CCP naturally appealed to Ching-kuo. At several points in his life he had believed this was possible. He authorized Wei to say that after Mao's overthrow, northeast and northwest China could be designated special areas for cooperation between China and the USSR—the same enticements that he had vainly offered Stalin in January 1946. Under instruction, Wei emphasized to Louis that questions of great importance between the two governments would have to be decided by "the highest authority."

Ching-kuo himself agreed to see Louis in the latter's position as a foreign correspondent. On October 29, speaking Russian with the visitor, Ching-kuo talked mostly about conditions in the Soviet Union.[16] But he did tell Louis that once the Nationalists recovered the mainland, they could "consider their relations with the United States," implying that *reconsideration* was possible. Although Ching-kuo put little stock in the Soviet approach, he was prepared to make such a statement because it was clear that a long-term, strategic partnership between Taiwan and the United States was not going to materialize.

He instructed Wei that he and Louis should continue their discussions in Europe. The day after Louis left Taipei, Ching-kuo called on American Chargé David Dean, and casually mentioned that he recently met "a fellow from the *London Evening Star,* who spoke Russian very well." The CIA station was chagrined that Ching-kuo had not told them first of the Victor Louis visit.[17]

After arriving in Hong Kong, Louis told the *Washington Post* correspondent of his visit to Taipei, thus leaking it to the world and stirring up a flurry of speculation—which was no doubt the intent. Peking fumed that "the Soviet revisionists have degenerated so low as to utilize the stinking political mummy of the Chiang Kai-shek bandit gang." Taipei media responded by describing incidents along the Sino-Soviet border as a "Chinese Communist invasion of the Soviet Union." The KMT's 10th Party Congress in 1969 declared that Mao was creating the frontier crisis with the USSR to divert attention from his grave internal problems. In Taiwan derogatory references to the Soviet Union ceased, and political groups and organizations with names carrying anti-Soviet implications received orders to change their names. Taipei media and official speeches began to employ the term "anti-Mao" in place of "anti-Communist." On November 26 Peking proposed to Washington another Warsaw meeting to take place the following February.

Over the next three years Wei made six trips abroad to meet with Louis. In the mid-1990s Ching-kuo associates said that Wei had been politically naive and overplayed the importance of the exchanges. But in

1969 Soviet and Chinese forces actually began killing each other along the Sinkiang and Manchurian borders. Ching-kuo thought the exchange was well worth maintaining. Moscow further increased its forces on the border and probed for U.S. reaction should the Soviet Union attack China's nuclear installations at Lob Nor in Sinkiang province. The Soviets circulated a secret memo to their East European allies which also envisaged a preemptive attack.[18] As with Victor Louis's approach to Ching-kuo, this gambit was no doubt intended to get back to Peking.

In the midst of the threat of war between the Communist giants, President Nixon expounded his Guam Doctrine. This edict asserted that the United States would assist its allies and friends in East Asia to resist Communist insurgency, but these countries would have to carry the principal burden of protecting their own security; in other words, do not expect U.S. troops. Soon after, Nixon and his National Security Adviser, Henry Kissinger, appeared to be taking a number of "small steps" to relax tensions with China. In reality, the two men saw the opportunity of rapprochement with Peking as a grand geopolitical maneuver that would alter the global balance of forces and also contribute to a peaceful and politically acceptable end to the Vietnam War. The administration lifted the ban on travel to China for seven categories of U.S. citizens. In the fall, during a speech at the United Nations, Nixon said the United States wished to have a dialogue with Peking as it had with the Soviet government. In December Washington permitted U.S. companies to trade with China in "nonstrategic" goods. And, most symbolic of all, the Seventh Fleet ceased to patrol the Taiwan Strait.

For many of the hard liners in the KMT, the possibility of growing isolation for the Taipei regime meant that the Party had to tighten its grip. They believed that if the government gave in even minimally to the demands for more civil rights, KMT mainlanders would soon be surrendering power and along with it their privileges and fundamental political commitment to China's reunification. But for Ching-kuo and his reformers, the troubling world developments as well as changing conditions within Taiwan strengthened the argument for a gradual, controlled broadening of political participation.[19]

To promote this process of change, Ching-kuo arranged the appointment of Lee Huan as chairman of the KMT provincial committee and placed another contemporary technocrat, Chang Pao-shu (a fisheries expert), as Secretary General of the KMT Central Committee. Ching-kuo, Lee Huan, and Chang Pao-shu adopted a fundamentally new long-term goal—the KMT would seek to become a popular and democratic political organization even though that meant it would eventually be dominated by native Taiwanese. The long and drawn-out process would involve co-opting many more Taiwanese into the KMT leadership while cautiously nurturing and controlling the growth of a moderate opposition.[20]

Under Lee Huan's supervision the KMT initiated a rapid turnover of county- and municipal-level Party executives, almost all of whom previously had been mainlanders. Within a year, one third were native Taiwanese. More Taiwanese received posts at KMT headquarters. In honestly conducted island-wide elections for county and city officials, 61 of 71 Provincial Assembly seats went to the Kuomintang, and KMT candidates won 14 of 15 contests for county magistrate. Independents, however, won the races for mayor in Kaohsiung, Taichung, and Hsinchu. Opposition Taiwanese (including KMT-appointed Henry Kao in Taipei) now controlled three of the four largest cities on the island, suggesting that the "nonparty" forces enjoyed the support of the most urban and better educated Taiwanese. In private the new, independent, nonparty mayors were bitterly critical of the KMT-dominated system, but once in office they devoted themselves to administration and development as well as to patronage.[21] However much they hated the KMT, they still played by its rules.

IN THE MID AND LATE SIXTIES Ching-kuo began to recruit a new generation of future leaders—products of the Taiwan school system with advanced, mostly American degrees. Whereas officials like Y. S. Tsiang and Y. S. Sun constituted Taiwan's second generation of technocrats who were on the threshold of their ascendancy, the third generation of mostly American-trained scholar-officials would run not only the economy but increasingly political strategy as well. These young mainlanders were 4 to 12 years old when they left their homes and arrived as refugee children on the island. They had received high school and undergraduate diplomas on Taiwan and grew up with Taiwanese neighbors and friends, thus gaining a relatively liberal outlook. Among them were Ching-kuo's twin sons, John and Winston, and a Yale-educated Ph.D. named Fred Chien. At the end of the 1960s Chien, at the age of 34, was director of the North American Desk in the Ministry of Foreign Affairs, having served as English secretary to both Ch'en Ch'eng and Ching-kuo. Another prominent member of this cohort was a mainland-born but island-raised Taiwanese with a Chicago Ph.D. named Lien Chan.

In June of 1969 Ching-kuo finally assumed a formal leadership role in the overall administration of the government. The Gimo named him deputy premier. The following month he took over the concurrent posts of chairman of both the Council for International Economic Cooperation (CIEC, the economic policy-making body) and the Financial, Economic and Monetary Conference (FEMC, the coordinating agency). Ching-kuo carefully briefed himself on the issues that came before the CIEC and FEMC, and, reflecting his style of leadership, called a series of meetings with Chinese businessmen and foreign investors to hear their suggestions on how to keep the economy moving. The businessmen urged a reduction of red tape, noting, for example, the one hundred separate "chops" (bureaucratic stamps) needed just to import an automobile. Ching-kuo promised to simplify government procedures. He also launched an offensive against corruption, giving young prosecutors in the Ministry of Justice permission to go after ranking government and Party officials suspected of graft. The most prominent episode involved the so-called Great Banana Case, which resulted in the dismissal of a governor of the Central Bank linked to Madame Chiang and her family.

Clearly, there was no point in making major changes in an economy that was working so well. The rate of growth in 1969 was 10 percent. The economy had expanded almost ten times since 1952.[22] Every child on Taiwan now received nine years of compulsory education. The increasingly affluent rural population and the educated and rapidly growing middle class eagerly purchased the cornucopia of consumer goods that were flooding the market.[23]

Ching-kuo did, however, oppose the technocrats on the issue of family planning. Since the mid-1960s, K. T. Li and other senior economic reformers had pushed for an active government program to reduce the fertility rate in what was the second most densely populated country in the world. At a Central Committee meeting on November 1967, Li had argued that population pressures not only threatened full employment and rising per capita income but also could become a cause of social unrest. The subject provoked "heated debate," Ching-kuo being one of the principal dissenters. Possibly speaking from his Marxist background, he argued that the more working people a country possessed, the stronger it would be. The arch-conservatives and the military shared his view on this point and also strongly opposed family planning, which Sun Yat-sen had denounced as "race suicide." In contrast, C. K. Yen and the entire team of technocrats supported the program. Although Chiang Kai-shek had previously endorsed Sun Yat-sen's views on the matter, he approved the plans for extensive manufacture and distribution in Taiwan of "the loop," or intrauterine device. Partially as a result, population growth on the island steadily dropped.[24]

Ching-kuo's position on family planning may have been a gesture to conservatives. Around this time he took another step to protect his right flank. For some time he had been urging "big brother" Ch'en Li-fu to return to Taiwan to live out his retirement. In April Ch'en accepted the invitation, gave up his chicken farm in New Jersey, and flew back to Taipei.[25] Although he had left the island in 1950 fearing Ching-kuo was about to arrest him, the two now reconciled and Ch'en encouraged the remnants of his old CC Clique in the Legislative Yuan and the National Assembly to support the Generalissimo's son.[26]

In December, during the long-promised supplementary elections for the national representative bodies, Ching-kuo permitted unprecedented attacks on the regime. The restrictions on campaigning, the large sums of money spent by the KMT, and the KMT's control of the media were for the first time subjects of open criticism in the more independent press. Nonparty candidates like "Big Gun" Kuo Kuo-chi and Huang Hsin-chieh protested discrimination against native Taiwanese and the allocation of the lion's share of government revenue to the military. They even demanded direct election of the governor of Taiwan and the end of martial law. Huang went so far as to say that return to the mainland was hopeless and the country would suffer if President Chiang remained in office for long.[27] Both "Big Gun" and Huang Hsin-chieh won, which meant that for the first time the Legislative Yuan would have two real opposition members.[28]

IN JULY, shortly after naming Ching-kuo vice premier, the President and Madame Chiang were riding in their limousine with two escorting security cars up the steep curving road to the house on Yangming Mountain, now used as a retreat. A jeep sped down the hill and swerved across the center line. The first security car slammed on its brakes, and the Gimo's limousine plowed into its rear. The Generalissimo flew across the seat into the driver. Although badly shaken up, Chiang escaped without apparent serious injury, but after the accident, his health and mental faculties further declined.[29]

The President soon began to experience a problem with frequent urination. The Americans sent a U.S. Army urologist, who recommended a prostate operation. The Gimo demurred but his wife urged him to agree. She still had faith in the Americans. According to a Chinese physician who was present, the American doctor's hands shook during the operation. The procedure appeared to be successful, but while there were no direct complications, Chiang never really recovered, and his already limited involvement in state and Party matters further declined.[30] The Gimo still received major visitors and gave occasional public speeches, but, in all but name, Ching-kuo was the leader of the Republic of China.

ANOTHER, less expected health crisis struck the family. Ching-kuo's eldest son, who had risen to become manager of the T'aoyuan office of Taipower and had also set up the electric utility on Quemoy, was slated to become general manager of a chemical factory. He continued, however, to have problems with his drinking, and when intoxicated verbally abused his wife.[31] According to one story, in the late 1960s Alan was involved in a fracas in a bar in Taichung and a bouncer tossed him out. Alan called the Taichung garrison commander and ordered him to close the bar, which the officer did. When Ching-kuo heard of this, he called the commander to Taipei and, in his usual style, told him, "you have been working too hard. You should take a rest." The officer resigned.[32]

Alan was also now having a diabetic attack almost monthly. On October 15, 1970, just before he was scheduled to move to the chemical factory, he drank heavily and that night went into a coma. Ching-kuo, who knew that he had passed on diabetes to his son, visited him every day in the hospital. Holding his son's hand, he would whisper, "Alan, Dad is here to see you, please wake up."[33] Eventually he did wake up, but remained in the hospital for almost five years, much of the time in a small house on the hospital grounds, where Nancy and Yomei also lived.

Ching-kuo's second son, Alex, had turned 25 that year. Like Alan, he was now a famous party-goer, loved women—and also had diabetes, though he was more disciplined about his drinking than his older brother had been. He had attended the Munich Political Science Institute in Germany, where he met and married an attractive young woman named Wang Chang-shih. Eddy, the son who most wanted to please his father, graduated from the Military Preparatory School and entered the Military Academy; Ching-kuo was immensely proud. The Chiang tradition of military service would, it seemed, continue. Unfortunately, Eddy injured his foot and eventually withdrew from the Academy, entering NTU, where he majored in political science.

The twin brothers graduated from Suchow University in 1968. John entered the Foreign Service and in 1970, during his service as a diplomat in a small town in Belgium, married Helen Huang (Huang Mei-lun). Helen was a strikingly beautiful fellow graduate of Suchow. Just minutes before the ceremony, he told his bride that he was the son of Chiang Ching-kuo and the grandson of Chiang Kai-shek. Helen was stunned but proud. The next year she gave birth to their first daughter. John informed Wang Sheng, who sent back a Chinese name proposed by Ching-kuo—Huilan. After graduation from Suchow, Winston went into the army for two years, returned to Suchow, and obtained a bachelor's degree in law.

EARLIER IN 1970 Vice President Spiro Agnew flew to Taipei for a one-day visit. He went directly to Sun-Moon Lake, where he met twice with the Gimo and had a "working breakfast" of almost two hours with Ching-kuo.

Ching-kuo presented him with a memo outlining the PRC threat to Taiwan and the Pescadores.[34] Agnew promised that the United States would keep its commitment to defend these two territories but was evasive about Quemoy and Matsu. His comments concerning American political intentions toward Peking were meant to be reassuring—Agnew after all had no idea that Nixon and Kissinger were exploring real détente with Communist China—but his words were hardly categorical.[35]

Taiwan remained an important support base for the now slowing but still enormous U.S. military effort in Indochina, and joint U.S.-Nationalist military exercises continued. Washington still viewed the island as a critical intelligence collection base targeting China—critical, that is, so long as America perceived China as a grave military threat. But the concept of a strategic relationship as well as the political bond between Taipei and Washington were slipping virtually every month. Following the suspension of Seventh Fleet patrols in the Strait, the U.S. Air Force began to remove its nuclear-armed B-52s from Okinawa, which the United States had agreed to return to Japan. Ching-kuo ordered $30 million worth of runway extensions and other improvements to several Taiwan air bases and offered to station the B-52s at these fields. Washington, however, never seriously considered the possibility.

These moves coincided with a marked decline in the influence of the China Lobby in America. To be sure, powerful friends of the Republic of China still existed; friendly congressmen, for example, were able to arrange the transfer of three submarines to Taiwan. But key organizations such as the Committee of One Million Against Admission of Communist China to the United Nations were losing support.[36] The Vietnam War and the upheavals it was causing in society were making many Americans ready for rapprochement with Peking, whether they knew it or not.

In the spring of 1970 Ching-kuo made an official visit to Washington to find out what concessions Nixon intended to offer Peking.[37] The Americans rolled out the red carpet for the visitor from Taiwan. Vice Premier Ching-kuo, a second-level cabinet official, received his bed and board at Blair House, usually reserved for chiefs of governments or heads of state. His hosts assumed they were entertaining the successor to the Generalissimo. But foremost in Nixon and Kissinger's minds were

their ongoing, secret exchanges with Peking, and the possible effect a breakthrough with China would have on Taiwan. Only weeks before Ching-kuo's arrival, the State Department had sent Kissinger studies on a possible renunciation of force agreement with Peking and the consequences of improved China-United States relations.[38] If relations with Mao's China went as Nixon and Kissinger hoped, their goal regarding Taiwan would be to moderate the reaction there and keep the island stable and prospering. A restrained reaction in Taiwan would help to mitigate the expected outrage among conservative Republicans.

The President spent 75 minutes with Ching-kuo in the Oval Office—a very lengthy meeting for a vice premier. During their conversation Nixon employed the technique that Ching-kuo practiced on his own visitors—asking questions but saying little. James Shen, the Nationalist Vice Minister of Foreign Affairs who accompanied Ching-kuo and acted as his interpreter, said Nixon "listened to Ching-kuo very closely but did not make any promises" regarding U.S. relations with Peking.[39] Nixon explained that the talks with the Chinese were exploratory in nature and would not affect America's friendship with the Republic of China. "The United States," he said, "would never forsake its allies and friends . . . to use a colloquial expression, 'I will never sell you down the river.'"

That night, during his toast at a black-tie dinner in Ching-kuo's honor, Nixon reiterated his government's determination to stand firm with the ROC in international affairs. Ching-kuo, however, understood that this commitment would not necessarily be inconsistent with a sharp improvement in U.S. relations with the Peoples Republic. He knew that the issue of Taiwan was *the* key to a Peking/Washington breakthrough. Zhou Enlai in fact had recently sent Nixon a private message through the Romanians reiterating his public line: "there is only one outstanding issue between us—the U.S. occupation of Taiwan."[40]

In another show of respect for Ching-kuo, on April 22 Henry Kissinger walked across Pennsylvania Avenue to Blair House to meet with him. The two men talked alone in English for half an hour. According to John Holdridge (Kissinger's Chinese affairs assistant), this was a very unusual arrangement—most especially for a visiting vice premier.[41] Kissinger asked Ching-kuo for his reaction should the Sino-American talks shift from Warsaw to Washington or Peking. The question itself

suggested the seriousness of these discussions. The White House had postponed the next Warsaw meeting with the Chinese to May 20, so that it would not come too close on the heels of Ching-kuo's visit. Later James Shen asked Ching-kuo whether Kissinger had delivered any other important message. Ching-kuo only smiled.[42]

Ching-kuo also met with Secretary of State William Rogers, Secretary of Defense Melvin Laird, and other top American officials, all of whom assured him of the unstinting support of the United States for the ROC. Ching-kuo was not as experienced as his father in dealing with the Americans, but he was not a novice. Nixon was the fourth U.S. president with whom he had met. More importantly, Ching-kuo was more perceptive and objective than was the Generalissimo in assessing world trends. If not before his trip then certainly after, he understood more than most American observers that for the first time America and Communist China simultaneously saw a compelling interest in establishing good relations.

———

TWO DAYS AFTER MEETING with Kissinger Ching-kuo was in New York, where he was scheduled to address the East Asian-American Council of Commerce and Industry. The Vice Premier's party and accompanying American Secret Service guards and police arrived at the opulent Plaza Hotel shortly after noontime. Ching-kuo could see about 25 students from the Taiwan Independence Alliance waiting near the Hotel entrance, holding signs and shouting protests. The Vice Premier alighted from his limo and walked up the stairs; just as he was pushing through the large revolving door, two men with guns drawn jumped out from behind marble pillars flanking the entry. As one of the would-be assassins fired, a New York City detective pushed the gun away. A bullet whizzed by Ching-kuo's head and passed through one of the glass wings of the door. The detective and Wen Ha-hsiung, a military aide, wrestled the assailant to the ground. Other security personnel seized the accomplice.[43]

Ching-kuo stopped briefly and looked at the fracas. He then went on into the lobby and took the elevator to the floor where the function was being held. In a few minutes the police caught up with him to report that

everything was under control and to show him the gun. Ching-kuo said he would be happy to talk with the young men who tried to kill him. The police suggested that would not be practical. Ching-kuo proceeded to speak to the assembled guests without mentioning that he had almost been murdered a few minutes before.[44] Upon returning to his hotel he called Faina to tell her not to worry. On the schedule for that night was a large reception by the Chinese-American community. Ching-kuo's aides and security people advised him not to go; the New York police recommended he leave town. "No more discussion," Ching-kuo said. "Everything will proceed as scheduled."[45]

The young man who almost killed Ching-kuo was Huang Wen-hsiung, a Taiwanese graduate student in industrial engineering at Cornell University. Ching-kuo's security organs immediately began an investigation of all of Huang's contacts at the university. They discovered that the prominent Taiwanese agriculturist, Lee Teng-hui, and his wife had been actively involved in Taiwanese social life at Cornell, although not with the independence movement. Nevertheless the Lees did know Huang. The security agencies put a red flag by the professor's name. But Interior Minister Hsu Ch'ing-chung and Y. S. Tsiang, recently promoted to secretary general of the cabinet (the Executive Yuan) by Ching-kuo, assured their leader that Lee had no connection to Huang or to the Taiwan Independence movement.[46]

Huang's accomplice was his brother-in-law, Ch'eng Tzu-ts'ai. Pleading guilty at their arraignment, they both jumped bail and escaped to Sweden. Ch'eng was later extradited back to the United States and served five years in a federal prison. Huang remained in hiding. When Ching-kuo returned to Taipei, 10,000 people turned out to greet him.

———

SHORTLY AFTER HIS WASHINGTON TRIP Ching-kuo visited Saigon, to see what the Nixon Doctrine meant for Indochina. This was at the time of the large-scale American military incursions into Cambodia against the North Vietnamese sanctuaries there. Nixon was determined to combine American withdrawal from Vietnam with occasional, bold, aggressive action. In Peking, Defense chief Lin Piao seized upon the attacks to denounce Zhou's policy of exploring détente with America. In a notably belated reaction, three weeks after the start of the Cambodian incursion, Peking finally canceled the Warsaw meeting scheduled for May 20.[47] It was clear to Ching-kuo that his hosts in Saigon faced at best a dubious future. While the Chinese leader was in South Vietnam, Nixon announced the pullout of another 150,000 American troops. Here was a stark lesson in the need for self-reliance and a broad base of popular support.

ON JUNE 19, 1970, Secretary of State Rogers sent a memo to President Nixon warning that support for Taipei in the United Nations was eroding fast. He warned the President of the possible need to shift to a "dual representation" formula. The always latent support—among Republicans, Democrats, and independents alike—for a "two Chinas" solution to the Taiwan issue was quickly resurfacing. To many this seemed the logical way to let China into the world community while supporting the rights and interests of the people of Taiwan. Kissinger and Nixon understood, however, that should the United States succeed in formalizing the concept of "two Chinas," this would not open the door to détente but would instead lock America into another long-term confrontation with the Peoples Republic.[48]

Ching-kuo was now certain that Nixon was determined to open up a new era of relations with Peking during his first term. Although he believed that Nixon would, as he had promised, maintain a U.S. military umbrella over Taiwan and the Pescadores, he feared that American détente with Communist China would sweep away for good the strategic relationship between the United States and the Nationalist government. It would also shred the *raison d'être* of one-party rule on Taiwan—the KMT claim to be the government of all China—and seriously weaken the moral authority Taipei had gained at home and abroad as the guardian of traditional Chinese culture.[49]

Upon returning from Saigon Ching-kuo made a number of changes to strengthen his control, replacing, for example, all of the Chiefs of Staff. He had himself selected the incumbents, and he found prestigious jobs for each, but an even younger set of military chiefs further increased the level of loyalty. In Premier C. K. Yen's name Ching-kuo also re-shuffled a number of cabinet positions.[50] At the same time, Taiwan's Atomic Energy Council established a new Nuclear Energy Research Center, purportedly to work solely on the peaceful uses of nuclear power.[51] A clandestine wing, however, pursued the work on nuclear weapons. The CIA spy, Chang Hsien-yi, steadily rose in rank and responsibility in this unit and kept his CIA handlers up to date.

SOVIET MILITARY THREATS, like a bucket of cold water, had had a sobering effect on Mao—there were now 40 nuclear-armed Red Army divisions on his borders. The results of the grand Cultural Revolution—chaos, economic stagnation, *de facto* military rule, and runaway factional intrigue—also had cooled the fevered brow of the aging Chairman, as had the rank failure of the international line of polarization. But the growing sentiment for a "two Chinas" solution in the United Nations, together with the sharp change in Washington's attitude toward Peking, were equal or even greater factors in his calculations and those of Zhou Enlai.

In the autumn of 1970 a veritable drumbeat of signals reached Peking from the White House. Washington proposed a hotline between the two capitals, and for the first time in public Nixon employed the official name, "the Chinese Peoples Republic." Mao decided that these signals required a positive response, even though this would entail a more wrenching ideological shift for him than for the American president. At an August-September Central Committee meeting of the CCP, Mao told the delegates that China's most dangerous enemy was now the Soviet Union and informed his compatriots of the ongoing talks with the United States on restoring relations between the two countries.

In October Canada broke with Taipei and recognized the Peking government. There were public hints from Washington that the following year Taipei would have to accept a "two Chinas" arrangement if it hoped to retain its seat in the United Nations. The same month, Victor Louis and Wei met again in Vienna. Louis stressed that a pro-China faction in the Kremlin was gathering strength, and he requested intelligence from Taipei to support the thesis that even after Mao, Communist China would remain hostile toward the USSR. There was in fact a marked improvement in Peking-Moscow relations just after the CCP meeting in the fall and the Vienna session between Wei and Louis. The two Communist governments returned their respective ambassadors to the other's capital and exchanged surprisingly warm messages on their revolutionary anniversaries (October 1 and November 7). Louis told Wei that the CPSU Party Congress the following March would be crucial for the future direction of Soviet policy on China. He said the Soviet side wanted Taipei to affirm that Moscow and Taipei agreed in principle on military cooperation.[52]

Wei returned to Taiwan in November and reported to Ching-kuo. At the end of the meeting Wei handed over an envelope that Louis had asked him to deliver. It was, said Wei, a letter from Faina's sister, whom she had not seen in 33 years. Ching-kuo opened the letter and read the Cyrillic text. "Yes," he said, "this is from her sister." He then crumpled the notepaper in his hand and dropped it in the "burn bag" for classified documents. "Do not mention this to anyone," he ordered. This reaction seemed cruel, but apparently Mrs. Chiang had begun to suffer from "melancholia," and it is possible that Ching-kuo feared the letter would only depress her more.[53] He may also have thought that the Soviets would try to exploit the relationship between the sisters, and that word of it would revive the old fears on Taiwan that Ching-kuo was pro-Russian and even a secret Communist.[54]

As the first year of the decade ended, most people in Taiwan cared little about world affairs. They were happily going about their business, and good business it was. United States-Taiwan trade had surpassed the $2.5 billion mark. The export processing zone at Kaohsiung was booming, with 120 firms operating manufacturing and assembly plants there. Island-wide industrial production increased 17 percent during the year.

18

The Premier

IN MARCH 1971 Peking invited an American table-tennis team to visit China. The next month President Nixon announced that the United States would issue visitor visas to individuals and groups from China, and lifted the ban on the import of Chinese commercial goods. In an effort to counter the Mao-Zhou line, Lin Piao and his faction backed Hanoi in its Tet-like offensive against a large-scale South Vietnamese incursion into Laos, while Zhou advocated a gradual (and more cautious) response. Taking an even more dangerous initiative, Lin apparently attempted to promote a partial Sino-Soviet rapprochement or at least an even-handed treatment of China's two adversaries. As if in reply, Moscow now offered more concessions to the CCP and proposed a nonaggression agreement.[1] As Kissinger was packing his bags for Peking, the *People's Daily*, in what later appeared to be a reference to Lin Piao, warned of "enemy agents" in the Party and "hidden traitors" who have "illicit relations with foreign countries."[2]

On July 9 "Dr. K" arrived secretly in Peking via Pakistan. The conditions that Zhou Enlai set out for a settlement with the United States all involved Taiwan. He demanded the United States acknowledge that Taiwan was a part of China, withdraw its military forces from Taiwan by a fixed deadline, and abrogate the 1954 Mutual Defense Treaty. Kissinger accepted the first condition, said troop reductions could begin once the

Vietnam War was ended, and hedged on the third demand. He also offered to support China's admission to the United Nations but said the United States would support Taipei in keeping its seat in the General Assembly. Full normalization of relations on the basis of one China, he said, would come in the second Nixon administration.

Kissinger completed his mission and secretly departed Peking. Half an hour before Nixon went on the air to reveal his and his envoy's *tour de force* in diplomacy, Ambassador Walter MacConaughy telephoned the Nationalist Foreign Ministry to alert them to the event. MacConaughy and the Secretary of State had been informed less than an hour before. KMT diplomats had known something was cooking, but still they were disturbed that the American president would not give Taipei even an hour's notice. Fred Chien immediately typed up a memo for President Chiang, Ching-kuo, and Premier Yen. Meanwhile, Foreign Minister Chou Shu-k'ai telephoned the news to other senior officials. Ching-kuo immediately called Chien and asked him to come to his office to give a personal report.

Chien hurried across the street to the presidential office. The Vice Premier asked Chien for his analysis of Kissinger and his strategic thinking.[3] After the discussion, he ordered issuance of a mild public statement in the name of Premier Yen, which said the news had come as a "great surprise," denounced the Communists in the usual terms, and proclaimed that the Republic of China would not yield "to any violence or might."[4] The next day both KMT and independent newspapers avowed that the United States could no longer be trusted, and the National Assembly charged Nixon with "betrayal." But the overall reaction was surpassingly calm.

As Kissinger left China, both he and Zhou had exuded a mood of triumph. But inside China the reaction to the visit, although kept hidden for many months, was dramatic in the extreme. According to later charges by the Chinese government, Lin Piao plotted to kill Mao and take power, but loyal officers discovered the plot, and Lin fled with his wife, son, and several fellow conspirators in a military jet transport. The plane flew into Mongolian air space heading for the Soviet Union, abruptly changed course, and crashed in the Gobi Desert. There were no survivors. Lin apparently believed that Mao's embrace of America spelled his own political demise, but that it could also provide the political and moral justifications for a military coup to oust the Chairman.

———

THE INTERNATIONAL CONSEQUENCES of the "Kissinger surprise" were stunning. Nations that had long been supporters of Nationalist China as well as those leaning toward a "two Chinas" solution in the United Nations rushed to embrace Peking. In August Nixon authorized Secretary Rogers to proceed with the proposal for dual representation in the United Nations. The Gimo muttered that he would rather be "a broken jade on the ground than a whole tile on the roof." But Taipei eventually agreed to go along, in effect accepting the loss of its Security Council seat as the price of remaining in the United Nations. Because of the Gimo's rapidly declining health, this dramatic decision was essentially Chiang Ching-kuo's.[5]

On October 25, 1971, however, the U.N. General Assembly voted to seat the representatives of the Peoples Republic and "to expel the representatives of Chiang Kai-shek." Nixon and Kissinger had made a convincing show of trying to corral votes for Taipei, thus hoping to temper the dismay of the avid pro-Chiang right wing of the Republican Party and moderate the reaction in Taiwan. State Department officers, including Secretary Rogers, believed they had made an all-out effort to save Taiwan's Assembly seat. But the extensive American lobbying looked less than fervent when the world learned that on the day of the vote in the General Assembly, Kissinger was back in Peking making arrangements for the President's visit the coming year.

While Taiwan's ejection from the United Nations was a humiliating blow to the pride of the old KMT, public as well as official reaction was again calm.[6] In fact, the defeat had a stabilizing effect on Taiwan, sharply underscoring the point that mainlanders and Taiwanese now shared a common destiny. The strong diplomatic effort that Washington had made in New York on Taipei's behalf also made a difference. There was little fear in Taiwan that the United States intended to remove its security umbrella. Moreover, Mao's turn to the Americans virtually ended the likelihood of Chinese military pressure against Taiwan.

Earlier in the year the GIO and the KMT's 4th Division had approved publication of a new journal, *The Intellectual* (*Tahsueh*, literally, "University"), under the editorship of NTU Professor Yang Kuo-shu. Behind *The Intellectual* was a coalition of Taiwanese and mainlander liberals—mostly teachers, professors, and writers, but also a few "rising young businessmen." The journal soon proved to be more political than academic, with articles that called for a "revitalization of the national power structure" and specifically demanded complete re-election of the central government representative organs.[7]

The Intellectual also sharply criticized the government for not taking action to prevent the inclusion of the Tiaoyut'ai (or Sinkaku) islets in the American reversion of Okinawa to Japan. These uninhabited rocks northeast of Taiwan had suddenly gained importance because of reports of oil-bearing strata in the region. The establishment press and some members of the Legislative and Control Yuans joined the chorus of criticism. Tiaoyut'ai committees sprang up at almost every college, ushering in an unprecedented period of intellectual ferment on the campuses.

Under Ching-kuo's orders, the security bureaus and the Garrison Command closely watched this movement but did not take direct action to discourage it. The Tiaoyut'ai issue appealed to loyal KMT youth, especially mainlander activists in the Youth Corps who thirsted for some uplifting goal that would allow them to make common cause with their Taiwanese peers. Ma Ying-jeou, then a student at NTU, recalls that he and his friends who took part in the Tiaoyut'ai movement were under heavy surveillance. In one incident Ma joined a group of mainlander and Taiwanese students who went to the airport to throw eggs at the Japanese ambassador.[8]

To give a clear warning to the young intellectuals to temper their expectations, Ching-kuo in March ordered the arrest of a prominent mainlander dissident, Li Ao, along with Professor P'eng's two former associates and jail mates, Hsieh Ts'ung-min and Wei Ting-ch'iao. Detention of these "usual suspects" suggested the paucity of real subversive threats. According to Hsieh, he was interrogated and tortured by each of the three principal security bureaus. Eventually he succumbed and falsely accused Li Ao of engaging in anti-government plotting.[9]

The dissidents, however, were unfazed. On October 15 students and teachers associated with *The Intellectual* issued a joint Declaration on

National Affairs that called for a rule of law and a pluralistic and open society. The signers denounced the "elite privileged group" as "bloated, aging, and . . . isolated from the masses." At NTU there were unprecedented discussion meetings on free speech. Instead of clamping down or raising new warning flags, Ching-kuo sent an invitation to the leading participants in *The Intellectual* to hold a panel discussion. In it he listened to the group's opinions and declared that "youth should speak out more [and] should be more concerned with national affairs."[10] He also granted amnesty to a small group of political prisoners.[11]

ON AUGUST 29 the Tainan Giants baseball team from the southern part of the island won the Little League World Series in the United States. This was the second championship for Taiwan within three years. An estimated ten million watched the game on TV—two thirds of the men, women, and children on the island. Half of Taipei, mainlander and Taiwanese, turned out to greet the Giants on their return. The event reflected remarkable changes in life style and attitudes, such as widespread ownership of television sets, a modern mania for Western spectator sports, and a common pride in Taiwan's accomplishments.[12]

Social and economic changes of fundamental importance continued. There were now more than 6,000 civic organizations on the island with 22,000 branches, ranging from Rotary clubs to Buddhist organizations to collectors of Chinese snuff bottles. Eighty percent of schoolchildren were going on to middle school, while the number of college students had increased fivefold.[13] The new generation in general was less prone automatically to respect authority. While some college students gathered for earnest political discussions, long-haired young men and short-skirted women began to appear on the streets looking for a good time. The police took to dragging offending males into their stations for forced haircuts, but the rebellion continued.

BEFORE PRESIDENT NIXON left Washington on his dramatic 1972 visit to Peking, Ching-kuo assured the American ambassador in Taipei that his government would make no "unusual movements or actions" in the Strait that might create an incident.[14] A few days later Ching-kuo watched the live TV broadcast of Nixon's arrival, his greeting by Zhou Enlai, and other scenes of the dramatic occasion. There was no televising of the initial meeting between Nixon and Mao Zedong, and the television audience missed Mao's first words: "Our common old friend, Generalissimo Chiang Kai-shek, doesn't approve of this."[15] The evening of February 27 Ching-kuo read wire service reports of the now famous Shanghai Communiqué. The key part was the short section dealing with Taiwan:

> The United States acknowledges that all Chinese on either side of the Taiwan Strait maintain there is but one China and that Taiwan is a part of China. The United States Government does not challenge that position. It reaffirms its interest in a peaceful settlement of the Taiwan question by the Chinese themselves. With this prospect in mind, it reaffirms the ultimate objective of the withdrawal of all US forces and military installations from Taiwan. In the meantime, it will progressively reduce its forces and military installations on Taiwan as tension in the area diminishes.[16]

ALTHOUGH THE AMERICAN DECLARATION was not a categorical assertion that Taiwan was a territorial part of China, it was politically and psychologically the equivalent. After Nixon flew home from Shanghai, Assistant Secretary of State for East Asian Affairs Marshall Green and Kissinger's assistant John Holdridge flew to Taipei to brief the leadership in Taiwan. While the Americans had a long and cordial meeting with Ching-kuo, the Generalissimo was "not available." Ching-kuo was surprisingly calm. He did not berate the Americans but stressed that as long as the Mutual Security Treaty and American military assistance continued, he was not "too disturbed."[17] According to a later statement of his, the Americans had assured him that while the United States intended to seek normalization of relations with Peking, this did not mean establishment of diplomatic relations.[18] The U.S. envoys, however, assert that they simply informed Ching-kuo that the U.S.-ROC political relationship would continue.[19]

Following the Shanghai Communiqué, speculation arose whether Taiwan would now try to play the Soviet card. When asked about this possibility in an interview with Hearst reporters, Taipei Foreign Minister Chou Shu-k'ai said that the Republic of China would not rule out "shaking hands with the devil." Chou suggested Warsaw-type talks between Taipei and Moscow. Wild rumors spread: according to one story, Ching-kuo intended to lease the Pescadores to Moscow for use as a naval base.[20] The publisher Yu Chi-chung made a report on the pros and cons of exploring an alliance with the USSR—the cons heavily outweighed the pros. Ching-kuo ordered the release of a statement ruling out "a Soviet card," and three months later relieved Foreign Minister Chou of his portfolio.[21] Ching-kuo also replaced his chum, Jimmy Wei, as head of the Government Information Office with the 38-year-old Fred Chien. Chien stopped the contacts with Victor Louis and other clandestine activities by the GIO of which Wei had been so fond.[22]

THIRTY-SEVEN YEARS after Ching-kuo began his apprenticeship, he decided it was time formally to take charge. His father agreed, and C. K. Yen conveniently decided to step down from the premiership. On May 26, 1972, the Legislative Yuan, with a vote of 381 out of 394, confirmed Chiang Ching-kuo as premier. In his first public statements he renewed the promise of an eventual return to the mainland, but stressed administrative reform in Taiwan and a crackdown on corruption. He asked the people to excuse him for "talking less" so that he could get more done. His economic team headed by K. T. Li in finance and Y. S. Sun in economic affairs continued, but he made several major Taiwanese appointments, including Hsu Ch'ing-chung as Vice Premier, Chang Feng-hsu as Interior Minister, and independent Taipei Mayor Henry Kao as Minister of Communications. Before the announcement Ching-kuo summoned the pesky Kao to his office to request that he join his cabinet. Kao demurred, but Ching-kuo said he was planning ten big construction projects, six of which would be in communications. "I need you," he said. Kao did not quite believe him, but there was "nothing [he] could do." So he accepted.[23]

And twenty-seven years after the KMT took over the island from the Japanese, Ching-kuo appointed the first Taiwanese as governor of the island. Hsieh Tung-min was among the so-called "half-mountain" Taiwanese, patriotic Chinese islanders who left home during Japanese rule, joined the KMT on the mainland, and worked in government or Party jobs until Taiwan was returned to China in 1945. The nickname implied that only "half" of their hearts belonged with their fellow Taiwanese.

Ching-kuo's formal elevation was timely. In July the Generalissimo suffered cardiac arrest. Reports leaked to the press claimed it was nothing serious, only a minor case of pneumonia. But in reality the President would be an invalid for the rest of his life. He no longer met distinguished visitors and remained at his residence in Shihlin, mostly in bed or in a wheelchair. Ching-kuo visited his father first thing in the morning and in the evening. He reported good news to him but no longer went through the formality of seeking his approval for major decisions.[24] Madame Chiang, who had long accepted that Ching-kuo would succeed his father, now limited her overt political activity to organizations like the Women's Anti-aggression League.[25]

CHING-KUO'S CABINET MEETINGS were unusually short—about forty minutes. "He hated formalities and blah blah blah." He displayed his impatience by twiddling his thumbs or folding his hands in front of his face. In a final gesture that usually brought long-winded presentations to an end, he would vigorously rub his jaw.[26] He handled KMT Standing Committee sessions the same way. This august body of 21 members included five arch-conservatives whose response to Taiwan's growing isolation was to cling ever tighter to Party orthodoxy. Ching-kuo never argued with them.[27]

At his first cabinet meeting he stressed coordination, integrity, and image, pronouncing the Ten Rules Of Reform or "the ten taboos." Officials of any rank were not permitted to go to "girlie restaurants," "black coffee shops," or karaoke bars, indulge in extravagant weddings or funerals, or engage in several other types of listed diversion. Police began visiting the proscribed establishments and checking ID cards; several officials lost their job for throwing lavish weddings.[28] More serious was Ching-kuo's crackdown on bribe-taking and abuse of office. The Investigation Bureau arrested more than 50 government officers, including several in the Garrison Command, on charges of involvement in a smuggling ring. The prosecutors also charged the director general of the Government Personnel Bureau, Wang Cheng-yi, with taking a large bribe from a building contractor. Wang was a cousin of Ching-kuo's and a former confidential secretary to the Gimo.[29] Ching-kuo personally approved the arrest and the life sentence Wang received, as well as the death sentence given a vice director of the Tax Bureau.[30]

Ching-kuo told his cabinet that the Chinese people had suffered thousands of years of arrogant treatment from officials.[31] One way to simplify the bureaucracy was through openness. He decided to make public the national budget, except for Defense and Foreign Affairs. For the first time in the history of the Nationalist government, in fact in all of Chinese history, citizens could see where at least some of their taxes were going.[32] In June *The Intellectual* declared that Premier Chiang's first year of administration "had been the year of greatest accomplishments since the government's removal to Taiwan."[33]

THE PREMIER CONTINUED TO HANDLE the Taiwanese opposition with a mixture of toughness and finesse. As the December 1972 elections approached, one hundred "nonparty" politicians met in a hotel in Taipei to press for changes in the electoral laws. This was the first formal meeting of nonparty figures since 1960. Along with "Little Gun" Kuo Yu-hsin and Huang Hsin-chieh, a new opposition star, K'ang Ning-hsiang, dominated the gathering. This former gas station attendant and now Taipei City Councilman would play a key role in the transition to democracy. As the elections approached, K'ang was leading the demand for the right of candidates to assign poll watchers to each election ward and to make speeches outside the officially approved fora.[34] Twice he was warned about contravening the national policy of "mobilizing for the suppression of the Communist rebellion." Throughout the campaign Ching-kuo received reports detailing the provocative rallies of the nonparty candidates and recommending selective detentions, including the arrest of K'ang. Wang Sheng warned that K'ang was a Communist agent. Ching-kuo ignored these warnings.[35]

After the polling Ching-kuo was highly pleased with the results. More than 70 percent of eligible voters had gone to the polls and cast their votes for the Kuomintang in embarrassingly large numbers—97 percent of Party candidates won, including all the mayor and magistrate races. Nonparty representation ended up somewhat higher than that figure would suggest, because a number of positions were left open for independent candidates.[36]

Although K'ang Ning-hsiang was later considered a relatively conservative oppositionist, in the early days he ranked among the more radical of the "in-system politicians." His interpolations in the Legislative Yuan, including those directed at the head of government, were sharp but not polemical. Ching-kuo asked his subordinates why KMT members in the legislature did not ask such questions.[37] Eventually he invited K'ang to tea, and the two discussed the issues that were on the legislative agenda.[38]

Except for the ultra conservatives who continued to grumble, most senior KMT officials accepted Ching-kuo's decision to allow a vociferous opposition to emerge in the Yuan. The Taiwanese nonparty activists were a tiny group and seemed to pose no threat for the foreseeable future. Some hardliners, including several in the security bureaus and the military, thought it was a relatively harmless way to let the opposition blow off steam and also to appeal to Americans as a sign of growing freedom. Indeed, some American academics wrote that the outlook for democracy in Taiwan appeared "encouraging."[39]

But pressure on the intellectuals came from a different source. Shortly after the release of several detained scholars, the president of NTU dismissed 14 of the most activist professors in the Philosophy Department and successfully curtailed political meetings like those that had been held on the campus since 1971.[40] In December 1973 the editor of *The Intellectual,* Yang Kuo-shu, was pressured into stepping down after an article called for the KMT to allow an opposition party. Differences between the mainlanders and the Taiwanese backers of the magazine came to the surface. At Ching-kuo's initiative, some of the young intellectuals associated with the journal (mostly mainlanders) were invited into the government and the Party with promises that they could bring about the reforms they desired by working within the system. A good number accepted the offer.[41] The dissident movement outside the officially sanctioned political system experienced a "low tide."[42] On the campuses, reform-minded mainlander professors continued to act as loyal opposition, calling in measured terms for greater democracy and an end to martial law.[43]

The Nixon shock had served to diminish prospects for independence and had thus temporarily taken the wind out of the sails of the Taiwanese opposition. It had also shaken the prospect of continuing the mainlander-controlled regime indefinitely. In August 1973, Ching-kuo told Ambassador MacConaughy that a "more open society" on Taiwan was necessary to strengthen unity, which in turn was essential to face Peking's increasingly energetic unification campaign. The changes he envisioned, he said, would contrast Taiwan favorably with the PRC. People could then draw their own conclusions.[44]

EXPORTS OF LABOR-INTENSIVE MANUFACTURED GOODS—toys, apparel, shoes, and many others—had provided the basis of Taiwan's rapid economic growth since 1962. In the 1970s, under Ching-kuo's leadership and that of his technocrats, industry shifted increasingly to the manufacture of high-technology products. In 1970 the Ministry of Economic Affairs merged several applied industrial research organs into the Industrial Technology Research Institute (ITRI) to promote this national goal. For the first time, significant numbers of Taiwan residents with American graduate degrees in engineering and science were coming home.

But the state sector continued to account for a large portion of Taiwan's economy. Premier Chiang's first major economic initiative involved enormous government expenditures. He called for Ten Major Development Projects, including an East Coast rail line, a North-South expressway, new harbors, a major new airport, and railway electrification. The Big Ten also included the construction of capital-intensive industries producing petrochemicals, iron and steel, aluminum and copper. These joint state-private ventures appealed to the instincts of the former Marxist engineer.

The initial estimated total cost of the Ten Projects was $5 billion. The actual cost would end up as more than double the estimates. Some observers said the country could not afford such undertakings during an economic crisis. Ching-kuo replied, "if we don't do it today, tomorrow we will regret it." Generals worried that the result would be increased pressure to reduce spending on the military. Domestic savings, however, provided 60 percent of the required funds, and the government's high credit worthiness enabled it to borrow the rest from abroad. Defense spending actually increased.[45] First-generation technocrats like K. T. Li were caught up in the Premier's enthusiasm and supported most of the Big Projects. Driving to a meeting on the subject of the North-South Freeway project, a vice minister asked K. T. where the money was going to come from. Li replied, "Never mind, we'll start the project and get the money somehow."[46]

Ching-kuo launched his ambitious construction program in the midst of the world energy crisis and a global economic downturn. With total exports equal to 53 percent of its gross domestic product, Taiwan was particularly vulnerable to international currents. In 1974 the island experienced a large trade deficit, and GNP grew only 1.1 percent. The cabinet increased taxes and sharply raised interest and electricity rates as well as the domestic price of gasoline and oil. Not content simply to wait for the free market response to these measures, Ching-kuo gave instructions for the government to supply soybeans and wheat at low prices and impose a price ceiling on several commodities.[47]

Despite the spiraling costs and the world recession, the Premier ordered the Ten Big Projects to proceed on schedule. The additional expenditures stimulated the economy and played a significant role in Taiwan's ability to ride out the oil crisis without a recession. In fact, in 1974 per capita income rose to U.S. $465. The projects also created an integrated industrial complex and infrastructure that would support the coming surge in high-tech business.[48] Ching-kuo also carried out reforms in agriculture: he abolished the compulsory rice-fertilizer exchange system, lowered rural taxes, set guaranteed rice prices, and revised regulations on the selling of farmland to encourage larger and thus mechanized holdings.[49] In addition, he sought to diversify Taiwan's export markets to reduce the heavy dependence on the United States and Japan, and he sped up the process of nuclear electrification.

MAO ZEDONG, in ill health for some time, now had difficulty speaking. "The slightest physical activity took his breath away." He was increasingly erratic and crotchety, but his mind remained reasonably clear. Unlike his old enemy, the Gimo, who was his elder by six years, Mao was still in charge. Medical tests discovered Zhou Enlai's cancer, but Mao would not give permission for surgery, fearing that if Zhou died, the camp of radicals around Mao's wife's would be unchecked. Suddenly, in one of his erratic swings in the internal power struggle, Mao decided, at Zhou's recommendation, to reinstate Deng Xiaoping.[50]

In March 1973 the "Little Cannon" rejoined the Central Committee, and Zhou turned over most of foreign affairs to his old friend. Deng immediately announced that Peking was ready to hold direct reunification negotiations with Taipei. At this stage, he said, "priority consideration . . . [will be] given to the peaceful method. . . . [of unification]."[51] Old Nationalists on the mainland who had made their peace with the Communists sent public and private entreaties to the Chiangs. But Ching-kuo brusquely rejected all such approaches. "Any contact with the Chinese Communists," he told the *New York Times,* "would be suicidal and we shall never be that stupid."[52]

Ching-kuo believed that any suspicion in Taiwan that he was seeking a secret settlement with the mainland or even considering a relaxation of the ban on personal contact would at that time create a strong, possibly violent reaction, not only among Taiwanese but also among investors. Such suspicions would undermine two of his three fundamental responses to Taiwan's isolation—rapid economic growth and gradual, stable advance on the political front toward a consensus government.

THE COROLLARY OF CHING-KUO'S REJECTION of secret talks with Peking was to forge the strongest possible relations with the United States regardless of further improvements in Sino-American ties. Kissinger's latitude for maneuver with regard to China was much more curtailed than it had been before the Watergate scandal and Nixon's 1974 resignation. The new Ford administration informed Ching-kuo that while it would continue the process of normalizing relations with the

PRC, "the existing form of the relationship meets our needs."[53] But even so it was clear that Washington's next step—switching diplomatic recognition from Taipei to Peking—was only a matter of time. Thus Ching-kuo was determined to do everything possible to encourage sympathy for Taiwan in America and to counter the burgeoning influence of the Peoples Republic in the American Chinese community and among Chinese students in the States.

Part of this effort was open and aboveboard. The Foreign Ministry and the Government Information Office received funding for various outreach programs. Numerous American congressmen, journalists, and others visited the island as guests. Taipei poured more money into groups like the Free Chinese Association, Chinese-language newspapers and journals, and American lobbying and PR firms. Ching-kuo also expanded purchases of American military equipment, which strengthened the powerful U.S. defense industry's interest in Taiwan. Much more important, however, was the new explosion of trade in civilian goods.

Between 1971 and 1978 exports and imports between Taiwan and the United States soared from $1.3 billion to $7.4 billion, with a heavy balance in the island's favor.[54] Ching-kuo dispatched a number of "Buy American" missions on shopping tours of the States. The U.S. government cooperated in the quantum leap in economic ties by encouraging and guaranteeing private investment. Billions of dollars for the Big Ten projects came from American sources.[55] But at the same time American business saw even greater opportunities in China and did not wish to jeopardize them.

CHING-KUO'S CAMPAIGN to win the hearts and minds of America also had a covert side. A meeting of Nationalist intelligence officials reportedly even suggested a clandestine program of physical violence, including letter bombs to American academics who were deemed pro-Peking. There is no evidence that Ching-kuo ever seriously considered such proposals or an alleged earlier scheme to assassinate Zhou Enlai.[56] Nevertheless he did sign off on assigning more than 30 additional intelligence officers to the Nationalist embassy in Washington and increasing the number of consulates around the United States.[57] In 1975 Ching-kuo approved an NSB plan secretly to buy twenty state-of-the art U.S. torpedoes from a presumed organized crime source in the States. The source was an undercover FBI agent. Just as the FBI was about to make arrests in the case, the White House ordered the affair handled with a serious but private demarche to Ching-kuo. Ambassador Leonard Unger delivered a strongly worded protest to Ching-kuo, who recalled the Nationalist officials in America involved in the case.[58]

The Premier was embarrassed by the torpedo debacle. But like previous intelligence failures he had lived through, including the many joint operations with the CIA, this one too carried little cost for the Nationalists. Consequently, he did not institute any major reforms in clandestine operations. Indeed, his new intelligence chief in the ROC embassy in Washington, Admiral Wang Hsi-ling, turned out to be more of a "cowboy" than his predecessor. Wang had been naval attaché to the Generalissimo for five years and was personally known to Ching-kuo. His orders apparently did not enjoin him to tone down the clandestine operations in the United States but simply to be more careful. Once in Washington, he upgraded efforts to recruit Chinese-Americans to provide confidential documents and information from U.S. government offices, including the FBI. He also sought to use Chinese-Americans who visited China to collect intelligence on the mainland. Finally, he increased the budget for financing anti-PRC demonstrations and infiltrating Chinese and Taiwanese student organizations in America.[59] Wang reputedly was "a long-time primary asset of the CIA," meaning he was reporting without authorization to the CIA on his own government—or the CIA thought he was.[60] Very likely it was the latter case, and the reason he was chosen for the Washington job.

CHING-KUO ORDERED speeding up the secret project to develop nuclear weapons. By 1973, using uranium obtained from South Africa and a 40 megawatt reactor purchased from Canada, the Taiwan scientists were making progress. Washington successfully cut off Nationalist negotiations for reprocessing equipment and services from French and British companies, but not before Taiwan had obtained a number of vital components.[61] In September 1974 the CIA declared that Taipei would be in a position to fabricate a nuclear weapon in "five years or so."[62] Ching-kuo's secret enterprise was now the major collection target of CIA case officers on the island.[63] The agency's mole in the Nuclear Research Center, Chang Hsien-yi (promoted to colonel), met his CIA handlers regularly in the *hutongs* of Taipei to pass on his reports.[64]

—

IN 1975 ALAN CHIANG WAS MOVED with the family to a residence on Yangming Mountain. Alan was able to walk around with an aide and a nurse in attendance and to form sentences, but, according to one friend, he often had little idea of what he was saying. Unable to communicate meaningfully with her father, Yomei grew ever closer to her grandfather. Even as a ten-year-old she would sit in Ching-kuo's office and have hour-long chats with him.[65]

The youngest son, Eddy, was still living at home. After dropping out of the Military Academy he completed his political science degree at NTU, but at this point still had no interest in a political career. Because his father forbade his children to work in the private sector, Eddy took a job at a KMT-owned company, the Chunghsing Electronic and Machinery Company, and following the example of his brothers, married a beautiful woman, Fang Chih-yi, in 1973. The young couple lived at Seven Seas for several years, until they began to have children. In 1974, during a trip to the States, Madame Chiang was discovered to have breast cancer. Without informing her sick husband, she first elected radiation treatment and then agreed to a mastectomy.[66]

Middle son Alex and his wife, Wang Ch'ang-shih, produced two grandchildren in succession—in 1971 a girl, Yolang (Yu-lang), and the next year a son, Yosung (Yu-sung). Madame Chiang awarded the girl the name Alexandra and called the boy Jonathan. Alex was unfaithful, and he and his wife had numerous shouting matches, sometimes in the family home, greatly distressing Ching-kuo. Relations between father and son became tense. At times the Premier, trembling with rage, would berate his son over reports of his scandalous activities.[67] At one point his wild behavior was such that his father had him locked inside Seven Seas with instructions to the guards not to let him out.[68] Eventually Alex's wife divorced him and returned to Europe, but, "as was the Chinese custom," she was required to leave Ching-kuo's grandchildren behind.[69]

Alex obtained an MA degree from the Graduate School of Sino-American Relations at the Chinese Cultural College in Taipei and worked as a counselor at VACRS. In 1976 he seemed to get some control of his drinking and went into broadcasting, a field controlled by the government and the Party. He rose quickly to become director of the KMT-owned Central (Radio) Broadcasting System. Sharing with his father a fascination with clandestine operations against enemies of the state, he developed friendships with ranking officials in intelligence and internal security. [70]

In the mid-1970s Ching-kuo's twin sons John and Winston were in their early thirties and well established in their respective careers. Ching-kuo told Wang Sheng that after his and Faina's death he wanted the twins "brought into the Chiang family."[71] John was now serving at the Nationalist embassy in Washington and also attended Georgetown University, where he received an MA in international relations. While living in Washington, he and Helen had another daughter. From afar grandfather Ching-kuo suggested the name, Huiyun. In 1978 John returned to Taipei and worked as a section chief and then deputy director in the Department of North American Affairs. His brother Winston studied for six years in the United States. Working as a waiter and security guard to pay his way, Winston eventually obtained an MA in political science from Southern Methodist University and a law degree and law doctorate from Tulane. He then returned to Taipei and became a law professor at his and his brother's alma mater. Winston married Irene Chao (Chao Shen-de); they had a daughter and a son.

19

Old Orders Passing

IN JANUARY 1975, at age seventy, Deng Xiaoping returned to the CCP Politburo and again took charge of the day-to-day affairs of the Party. He set the course of government to follow a rational, comprehensive program of industrial, scientific, and economic development and brought back officials disgraced during the Cultural Revolution. He soon ordered the release of a large number of Nationalist prisoners, including nearly 300 senior officers who had been jailed for 25 years. Peking announced that ten of the former KMT generals would be leaving for Taiwan via Hong Kong.

Ching-kuo, however, instructed that only the personnel captured in raids on the mainland since 1950 would be considered for settlement in Taiwan. The rest, mostly men who had remained loyal to the Generalissimo through war and imprisonment, were left to eke out a miserable existence in China or Hong Kong. One committed suicide in his hotel room in the colony.[1] Chiang Kai-shek probably never heard of the appeal of the long-imprisoned, old KMT officers. Throughout the year he had grown markedly weaker. Ching-kuo told his step-brother Wei-kuo not to enter their father's room as too many people would make the air unclean.[2] One day near the end the Gimo's physician, Dr. Hsiung, found the door to the bedroom ajar and saw Ching-kuo standing by the bed with his back to his father and talking, while looking out the window. The doctor thought this was strangely disrespectful behavior. He told a nurse to go into the room and find out what the Premier was saying. She reported that Ching-kuo was reciting Mencius.[3]

April 5, 1975, was the last day of the Tomb Sweeping (Ch'ing Ming) Festival. On that night, according to tradition, the ghosts of the ancestors are pacing about, preparing to go back into their chambers. Dr. Hsiung was in the garden of the presidential palace late that evening admiring the immense scattering of stars in the clear night sky. Shortly after Hsiung returned indoors and retired for the night, the doctor on duty called him in a state of high alarm. The President's heart had stopped. Hsiung threw on a robe and rushed downstairs into Chiang's bedroom. He injected a stimulant into the President's heart and it resumed beating. Madame Chiang Soong Mei-ling arrived and was at the bedside when her husband's heart stopped again. The doctor administered another injection and was preparing a third when she sighed. "Just stop," she said. It was a few minutes before midnight.[4] Just then a huge storm with thunder and lightning swept over the island from Taipei to Kaohsiung. Even Harvard-educated officials in the city thought this was more than a coincidence.[5]

In obituaries around the world most observers dismissed Chiang Kai-shek as the man who had lost China by tolerating corruption and ineptitude on a Great Wall scale. At home, however, official mourning was extraordinary. Movie houses and other places of entertainment closed for a month. No one dared play golf or billiards. For four days television stations broadcast only black and white films on his life or activities connected with the funeral. In accordance with custom, the two Chiang brothers wrapped the corpse of their father in a white cloth for burial. Later, Wei-kuo was resentful that Ching-kuo in his journal did not mention his younger brother's role at the funeral—not even his name.[6]

It was clear that—in death as in life—the Generalissimo's heart was not in Taiwan. In keeping with his will, his bones were placed not in the magnificent structure to be erected in his memory in the capital city, but thirty miles outside of town in a modest, black marble sarcophagus in an unadorned room in the small mountain retreat of Tzuhu. There his spirit still waits for the "recovery of the mainland" and for someone to take him home to China.

Within twelve hours of Chiang's death, C. K. Yen took the oath of office as President. Ching-kuo submitted a *pro forma* resignation as Premier. The KMT's Standing Committee unanimously rejected the gesture and instead elected him Chairman of the KMT Central Committee. Although Ching-kuo was mostly out of touch for thirty days of mourning, there was no rumor of a possible challenge to his leadership.

Five days after the death of the Gimo Saigon fell to the North Vietnamese. While in mourning for his father, Ching-kuo had a long talk with Ambassador Leonard Unger about the implications of the American defeat. He told Unger that though the fall of Saigon would bring a temporary satisfaction to the Communist camp, it would in the long run intensify conflict between Peking and Moscow. At the time few observers anywhere perceived this scenario. In 1970 Ching-kuo had seen developments in South Vietnam as a lesson pointing out the critical need for a supportive population: the total collapse of the Saigon regime dramatically drove home the point.[7]

Shortly after his father's death Ching-kuo commuted the sentences of 3,600 inmates, including about 200 political prisoners. This was his most important gesture of reconciliation with the opposition to date, and probably one that he would have undertaken only after the passing of his less forgiving father.[8] Ching-kuo next transferred authority over approval of new publications from the Garrison Command to the Government Information Office (GIO), which Fred Chien headed. The KMT's 4th Division and the Garrison Command still retained the authority to close down offending journals.

In August Chien okayed an application submitted by K'ang Ning-hsiang, Huang Hsin-chieh, and other opposition leaders to publish a new journal, *The Taiwan Political Review. The Review*, run primarily by Taiwanese, immediately raised the level of political criticism, not only attacking the KMT and calling for the reelection of all the national bodies, but also openly demanding a more even distribution of power between mainlanders and Taiwanese—a heretofore taboo subject.[9] But the fifth issue went too far, publishing an article by a Chinese professor in Australia who declared that the people of Taiwan had either to overthrow the KMT dictatorship or struggle for early unification with the motherland. Ching-kuo agreed with the Garrison Command that this was "incitement to sedition," and let stand their decision to close the magazine.[10] In May two well-known nonparty politicians received long prison terms for "intent to overthrow the government by illegal means." Military courts, understanding that they had the nod from on high, also handed down stiff sentences for sedition to 30 family members and friends of a non-KMT legislator.[11]

THE U.S. COLLAPSE IN INDOCHINA spurred Ching-kuo's interest in Taipei's secret weapons project, including a missile delivery system. In early 1975 fifteen engineers from the Chung Shan Institute went to the Massachusetts Institute of Technology (MIT) to take advanced training in inertia navigation, ostensibly in connection with the manufacture of commercial navigation equipment. In response to press reports, Ching-kuo in a report to the Legislative Yuan revealed that research on nuclear weapons had started as far back as 1958, and that the government had been ready since 1974 to manufacture them. But, he declared, while he himself had suggested moving ahead with production, the Generalissimo had vetoed the proposal, asserting that his government would never use nuclear weapons "to hurt our own countrymen."[12]

In fact work continued on both the weapons and a delivery system. The Taiwan engineers had almost completed their program at MIT in inertia navigation, when other students charged that Taipei intended to use the training to construct a weapons delivery system. This presented the pretext for the State Department, guided by the CIA spy's information, to request that MIT cancel the program. The Taiwan engineers went home—but with most of the know-how they had come to Cambridge to obtain. In June 1976 inspectors of the International Atomic Energy Agency, also instructed by intelligence from Colonel Chang, found that ten barrels of used fuel containing 500 grams of plutonium were missing. In August the *Washington Post,* backed by official U.S. sources, wrote that Taiwan had been secretly reprocessing for some time and had been producing plutonium for a nuclear weapon.[13]

Washington demanded that Ching-kuo dismantle the reprocessing facility and ship back related equipment to the United States.[14] After talks with Ambassador Unger, Ching-kuo accepted these demands and cleared off on a diplomatic note to the Americans that affirmed that his government "had no intention whatsoever to develop nuclear weapons or a nuclear explosive device or to engage in any activities related to reprocessing purposes."[15] On January 23, 1977, Ching-kuo also issued a statement supporting President Jimmy Carter's call for a total ban on nuclear testing.[16] He noted that Taipei had signed the Nuclear Non-Proliferation Treaty (NPT) in 1970, thereby committing itself not to develop nuclear devices. Privately, Ching-kuo ordered the reprocessing program put on hold for the time being but for research work to continue.[17]

—

ZHOU ENLAI DIED ON JANUARY 8, 1976. By this time CCP radicals had succeeded in turning Mao once again against Deng Xiaoping. Newspapers controlled by Mao's wife, Chiang Ch'ing, openly attacked Deng and the deceased Zhou. On Tomb Sweeping Day, which fell on April 4, crowds flocked to the Square of Heavenly Peace with floral wreaths to honor Zhou. The next day the demonstration turned violent, and toward evening protesters burned a police station. Five battalions of security forces and ten thousand militiamen surged into the Square, beating and arresting the demonstrators.

Chiang Ch'ing convinced her husband that Deng was behind the "counterrevolutionary" action in the Square and that the entire revolution was at risk. On the orders of the enfeebled Chairman, the Politburo purged Deng once again of all his Party and government posts. A provincial CCP secretary named Hua Kuo-feng, who had risen to prominence during the Cultural Revolution, became successor to both Mao and Zhou. This time Deng went off to comfortable seclusion in Canton.[18]

A few minutes after midnight on September 9, Chiang Ch'ing stormed into an earthquake-proof bedroom in Building 202 in the Forbidden City. The Chairman's vital signs had drastically weakened. "Will someone tell me what is happening?" she demanded of the doctors and the Politburo members crowding around the hospital bed. Mao's named successor, Hua Kuo-feng, politely responded. "Comrade Chiang Ch'ing, the Chairman is talking with Dr. Li right now."

"It's all right, Chairman," the doctor whispered to the patient. "We will be able to help you." But at this moment, the Chairman's eyes closed and the electrocardiograph went flat. The doctor looked up at Chiang Ch'ing, his eyes full of dread. "What were you people doing?" she shouted. "You will be held responsible!"[19] But she was more afraid than any of them.

After Ching-kuo learned that Mao had died, he told Ambassador Unger that there was a good possibility that Deng Xiaoping would return to a position of power in Peking. He saw continuing attacks on Deng in the Chinese media as evidence that some persons in authority feared his old classmate's strong potential for a comeback. At this point Deng was still officially under house arrest, and his return to power—much less his ascendancy—was hardly a common expectation. Ching-kuo also understood that Deng's return and a purge of the radicals would further improve the chances of a full normalization of United States-China relations. He did not share this deduction with the ambassador. Four weeks later, in Peking, a cabal of senior Politburo members arrested Chiang Ch'ing and her "gang," elected Hua Kuo-feng as Party Chairman, and summoned Deng back to the capital. The post-Mao era had begun.[20]

ONE OF THE PEOPLE with whom Ching-kuo consulted on mainland as well as U.S. affairs was Deputy Director of the Institute of International Relations Wei Yung, a mainlander scholar who had studied and taught political science and international relations in the United States for 15 years. Advisers like Wei contributed to Ching-kuo's balanced and reasoned analysis of world events.[21]

Another American Ph.D. who joined the group of young scholar officials around Ching-kuo was James Soong. Born in Hunan, at age 21 he left Taiwan for eight years of study in the United States. He received an MA from Berkeley and a Ph.D. from Georgetown. When Fred Chien took over the Information Office, he recommended Soong to replace him as Ching-kuo's confidential secretary. In 1974 Soong began a close, almost familial relationship with Ching-kuo that would last until the President's death.

In November 1976 the KMT held its first Congress since the death of the Generalissimo. Of the 48 new Central Committee members 16 were Taiwanese, including Lee Teng-hui and Taipei Mayor Lin Yang-kang. The new Standing Committee of 22 members included five Taiwanese, up from three in 1972.

—

WITH MAO GONE, the Gang of Four put away, and Deng back in Peking, China's international stature loomed larger every day. Taiwan's global standing, by contrast, was in a downward spiral. Fifty countries had broken diplomatic relations with Taiwan since the Kissinger surprise of July 1971. In 1977 the Nationalist government seemed on the verge of the ultimate desertion. On April 20 the new Assistant Secretary for East Asia and Pacific Affairs, Richard Holbrooke, told Ching-kuo that President Carter intended to move toward normalization with Peking but would consult the Taipei government "on all matters affecting it."[22] In August Holbrooke returned to Taipei to brief Ching-kuo on Secretary of State Cyrus Vance's trip to Peking. Holbrooke said that the United States would not accept any normalization of relations with the PRC that "would undermine the security and well-being of the people of Taiwan," but he confirmed that the conditions being discussed implied the end of the Mutual Security Treaty. Indeed, Vance had informed Deng that the United States was prepared to end the treaty, remove all American troops from Taiwan, and terminate diplomatic relations with the ROC.[23]

Ching-kuo told Holbrooke that there was indeed only one China and that the ROC embodied and represented this national concept. He admitted this might seem farfetched, but it was the only solution to the Taiwan-mainland problem. At the end of the meeting, Ching-kuo evinced no ill humor. Instead, he sent his greetings to President Carter and said he was glad the United States had a "new and great President."[24]

As suggested by the mood of the meeting, Ching-kuo was satisfied that he could deal with the new challenge and again turn it to Taiwan's advantage. Still, it was necessary to do what he could to slow down the pace of events. Five months after the Gimo's death, Madame Chiang, with 17 attendants and much baggage, flew to New York for medical treatment.[25] Now she was busy on the phone rallying the support of key Americans. Ching-kuo authorized a press campaign that resulted in 250,000 individual letters from Taiwan residents to President Carter urging America not to desert its old ally. Under various auspices, hundreds of American opinion makers came to the island to observe its prosperity and stability. Full page ads expounding Taiwan's position appeared in the *New York Times* and other American papers. These extensive people-to-people and other public relations efforts had some effect. Polls showed the majority of Americans favored diplomatic relations with Peking but not at the expense of breaking ties with Taipei. Still, newspapers on Taiwan closely chronicled the increasing U.S. tilt toward Peking. The state tobacco monopoly in Taiwan began printing on all cigarette packages a favorite injunction of the Chiangs: "Stay calm in the face of adversity."[26]

Admiral Wang Hsi-ling stepped up his covert efforts to mobilize Chinese students and the ethnic Chinese community in America to influence public and congressional opinion. Friendly sources passed on inside information regarding American policy vis-a-vis China and Taiwan.[27] Fred Chien once revealed inadvertently to an American official that he had seen a top secret U.S. document.[28] The FBI took notice of the admiral's activities. The bureau's counterespionage office had in fact infiltrated Wang's network of clandestine agents—mostly Chinese-Americans—and had a good handle on what Taiwan intelligence was up to.[29] In June 1977, in a confidential decision, federal officials formally placed Taiwan on the "criteria list" of nations whose "intelligence activities are hostile to or of particular concern to the national security of the United States so that counterintelligence activity is required." This meant the FBI, NSA, and CIA would begin intensive surveillance of the activities of Nationalist officials in America.

Sometime in the fall of 1977 Admiral Wang had lunch with a mainland-born, Taiwan-educated journalist named Henry Liu. The GPWD had originally trained Liu as a journalist and agent and he was also receiving funds from the IBMND for reports on his trips to the mainland. But when in China, Liu reported to Chinese intelligence on developments in Taiwan. Then when he returned to the States, he provided the FBI information on both his Taiwan and Chinese contacts. Admiral Wang told Liu that his writings had for years embarrassed his homeland. Appealing to Liu's patriotism, he urged him to soften his criticism of the Chiang family. Liu, who was an agreeable sort, said he would tone down his writings. He immediately regretted having made this commitment, however, and proceeded to pen articles lambasting Ching-kuo, calling him "the last emperor of China."[30] The admiral, having reported his earlier luncheon success in bringing Liu around, was incensed.[31]

THE CARTER ADMINISTRATION's promotion of human rights also had an impact on Taiwan. Anticipating Carter's emphasis on this subject, Ching-kuo had initiated Taiwan's "human rights year" on December 25, 1976. Such rights, he proclaimed, were guaranteed in Taiwan, but the Communist threat and the consequent need to protect order made some restraints on freedom necessary.[32] In private interviews with Americans Ching-kuo had used this argument since the early 1950s. But its public assertion put the regime intellectually and morally on the defensive in trying to justify every exception it made to the principles of individual freedom.

The record of his government on human rights, Ching-kuo asserted, had been misinterpreted. Only 254 persons were in jail charged with sedition, and only one had been executed. He invited well-intentioned states to send observers to see for themselves.[33] Taiwanese opposition figures abroad charged that there were 8,000 political prisoners on the island. A U.S. Senate subcommittee held hearings on the subject, and later it became evident that Ching-kuo's figures were close to the mark. Some observers noted the meticulous collection of evidence, circumspection in making arrests, and relatively light sentences involved in the handling of sedition cases in Taiwan.[34] The State Department's first Human Rights Report concluded that "the average Chinese [in Taiwan] goes about his business without anxiety over repressive government."[35]

The combined local, provincial, and Legislative Yuan elections in November presented an insightful example of evolving politics in the controlled and very limited democracy of Taiwan. Lee Huan was still director of the organizational section of the KMT (as well as Youth Corps director), and as such was in charge of the selection of candidates and

KMT campaigning. The KMT expected Lee to produce another sweeping victory. The Standing Committee decided to hold local and national elections at the same time, over the opposition of Lee Huan, who argued that the KMT could better concentrate its resources in separate elections.[36] Also against Lee's advice, the Standing Committee decided to renominate KMT incumbent magistrates regardless of their performance and popularity.[37]

Before polling day Lee reported to Ching-kuo that because of these decisions, the KMT would probably lose a number of important seats. Ching-kuo told him that the Party should use its advantages, but no irregularities should be permitted. "All we need," he said, "is 51 percent."[38] On election day various rumors spread alleging irregular practices. Around 2:00 PM, at the Chungli polling station, an election official was seen helping an illiterate couple mark their ballots. Poll watchers for the independent candidate, Hsu Hsin-liang, loudly protested. A crowd gathered and threatened the election officials. The police escorted the officials to the Chungli police station across the street from the polling place. The crowd in front of the station kept growing. Hsu's campaign workers appealed to the protesters, promising the matter would be pursued in the courts. Some shouted, "What good is the law . . . they own the courts!" About 4:00 PM, the demonstrators smashed windows in the police station and burned several police vehicles.[39]

The police radioed their predicament to Taipei headquarters, which immediately called the Premier's office. Ching-kuo hastily gathered a small group of officials in his office. Some recommended sending in troops to restore order. Riot police were on the scene and a Garrison Command unit was not far away. "No," Ching-kuo declared, "we will not make use of the Army." Told that under no circumstances should his men fire on the crowd, the chief of the Chungli police station ordered the use of tear gas only when the rioters stormed the second floor. The noxious fumes had little effect, and the riot troops clambered out through an upstairs exit. The fire spread to the police dormitory and nearby residences as the crowd dispersed, some rushing to save their own homes.[40]

The KMT won "only" 76 percent of the 1,318 contests in that election, but lost several magistrate and mayoral races. Senior KMT members told Ching-kuo that Lee Huan was responsible for the losses.

Ching-kuo sent for Lee and said, "Many people are criticizing you. I know the failure was due to the Party's decisions. But you had better resign."[41] As acting chairman of the Provincial Party Headquarters, Ching-kuo brought in another Youth Army veteran, the scholarly P'an Ch'en-ch'iu.

IN ADDITION TO GUIDING foreign and domestic affairs, Ching-kuo increasingly put his own stamp on economic policy. He established a new, more interventionist Council for Economic Planning and Development (CEPD) under loyalist Yu Kuo-hua. Modeled on Japan's Ministry of Industry and Trade, the CEPD recentralized economic decision-making, taking responsibility for macro-planning, setting priorities, coordination, and sector evaluation. The CEPD's central goal was to nurture Taiwan's capacity "to develop new products, to raise value added and vertically to integrate its electronics industry."[42]

Half the island's population was now living in urban areas, and many rural residents were actually employed in local industry or working temporarily in the cities.[43] On his walks Ching-kuo saw striking examples of the growing affluence of the former peasant society. Not all of it pleased him. Advertisements that touted "luxury flats," "luxury cars," and "luxury vacations" irritated him. He hated the word "luxury." Per capita income reached US$900. Equally or more important was its increasingly balanced distribution, more equitable than in any other capitalist country in the world. By 1976 the share of the bottom 40 percent had risen from 11 to 22 percent, and that of the richest fifth had dropped from 61 to 39 percent.[44]

20

The Divorce

IN 1978 C. K. YEN AGAIN conveniently decided to step down—this time from the presidency—and he recommended Ching-kuo as his successor. From Quemoy to Taipei to Tainan, dragon dances and firecrackers marked the news that the KMT had nominated Chiang Ching-kuo as the Party's candidate for president in the National Assembly elections. "Big character posters" appeared on campuses across the island hailing the news.[1] Ching-kuo chose the seventy-one-year-old Taiwanese governor, the "half mountain" Hsieh Tung-min, as his vice presidential running mate, and electrical engineer Y. S. Sun as the new premier.

On March 21, 1978, the more than 1,200 members of the National Assembly elected the KMT ticket almost unanimously. Two months later Ching-kuo officially assumed the presidency in a grand celebration. The aging Peking opera singer, Ku Cheng-ch'iu, one of the few women Ching-kuo had pursued unsuccessfully, came out of her long retirement to give a performance.[2] Some noted that the new president's daughter, Amy, and her family had not come from America for the inauguration.[3] The next day Ching-kuo's office issued an advisory to the press that he was not to be called "leader" (ling hsiu). The word also went out that on no occasion should the royal exclamation "long live" (wan shui, literally, "ten thousand years") be applied to the new president as it had been to all previous Chinese rulers, including the Gimo and Mao Zedong. This was, Ching-kuo said, the era of democracy, and he considered himself a common Party member and a common citizen.[4]

Everyone noted that President Carter sent a low-level delegation to the inauguration and, in another example of gauche timing, Zbigniew Brzezinski arrived in Peking for talks that very day. Ching-kuo asked Fred Chien to draft up a memo of the policy challenges and options the Nationalist government would face if the United States broke relations. Each scenario should include a set of countermeasures the government would pursue in the event that contingency occurred.[5]

His intention was to deal cautiously and realistically with Taiwan's unique international situation. Taipei showed increasing flexibility on representational issues. In April the Taiwan Olympic Committee executed a major policy aboutface, declaring it would not oppose Peking's admission into the Olympics so long as Taipei's membership remained intact. During a May 29 meeting with Ambassador Unger, President Chiang reiterated his government's "total objection" to the normalization of relations between the United States and the PRC, but expressed the hope that if Washington nevertheless proceeded, it would at the same time assure Taiwan that its relations with the United States would continue essentially as in the past. This was an almost blasé acceptance of the inevitable. In his reporting cable Unger concluded that however bitter the pill of normalization, including a break in America's diplomatic and military ties with Taiwan, Ching-kuo would want to continue as close a relationship with the United States as Washington would permit.[6]

MEANWHILE, IN CHINA, Deng Xiaoping was riding a counter-Cultural Revolution tide. He announced new pragmatic policies on education, and intellectuals and reformers began to pen articles on such themes as "seek truth from facts" and "practice is the sole criterion of truth." Students wrote "big character posters" about the horrors of the Cultural Revolution and the urgent need for democratic reform and posted them in parks and campuses. Deng was also busy managing international affairs, including the increasing tensions with Vietnam, which Ching-kuo had foreseen. Because of these tensions, Sino-Soviet relations once again became strained, and the Soviets reinforced their troops on the borders. With the leftists on the defensive, Deng revived the process of negotiations with America, maneuvering for the May visit to Peking by National Security Advisor Brzezinski, who strongly favored moving ahead on normalization with the PRC.

—

NOW THAT HE WAS PRESIDENT, the 68-year old Ching-kuo had a medical team to look after him. In the first checkup the head of the team, Dr. Chiang Bi-ling, found the head of state in reasonably good health. For many years he had been receiving daily shots of insulin, but for the moment his diabetes was considered under control. His heart was "okay." He was not athletic, but almost every week he still walked in the countryside, in the mountains, or at various project sites.[7] Soon after his first presidential examination, however, he began to complain that his feet and legs were not feeling right.[8]

Ching-kuo nevertheless continued to pay little attention to his diet. He told his good friend Hsiung Yuan (the Gimo's doctor) that "it was necessary to listen to one's doctor, but not too much."[9] Often the family ate leftovers because he decreed that they could not be thrown away. President Chiang and his family remained at the rather modest Seven Seas. When he became president, professional cooks expert in both Western and Chinese food took over the kitchen.[10] The presidential food bill, however, was a fraction of what it had been under the senior Chiangs.[11]

The government bought a bulletproof Cadillac for the new head of state, but Ching-kuo continued to use his old Buick and turned the new limo over to Vice President Hsieh. The result amused onlookers at official gatherings. The VP would arrive in his fancy new limousine, then the President would drive up in his aging Buick. Ching-kuo moved into the big office suite his father had occupied in the presidential building. But despite his creaking legs, he continued always to stand up whenever his staff or anyone else entered the room.[12]

—

DURING 1978 Taiwan security organs demonstrated that they would still act not just against serious sedition, but also against those who had wandered across the shifting line of permissible political activity. Police charged eight people with involvement in the Chungli riots and confiscated 10,000 copies of a book on the 1977 elections and the disturbance. In September one of the few outspoken independent newspapers, the Chinese-language *Taiwan Daily News*, under pressure from the authorities, was sold to the government.[13]

Nevertheless the political mood on the island was upbeat. The opposition steadily widened the boundaries of debate. Interest in the elections to the national parliamentary bodies scheduled for late December steadily built up. In the Provincial Assembly some members strongly criticized the police, and in October a leading newspaper actually raised the issue of ending martial law. In an interpolation in the Legislative Yuan, K'ang Ning-hsiang called on the President to take specific steps toward political democracy. In his response Ching-kuo stressed that to achieve the ideal of democracy it was necessary to deal with reality, and this required a "step by step" approach.[14] He followed up by instructing the military commands not to influence the voting of soldiers or their dependents in the upcoming polling. At the same time, he ordered the security services to stop harassing the oppositionists.[15]

As the year-end elections neared, nonparty candidates for the 38 open seats in the Legislative Yuan and the 56 National Assembly seats formed an ad hoc group to coordinate their campaigns. The group, led by K'ang Ning-hsiang, issued a twelve-point platform including a call for the end of martial law, an amnesty for all political prisoners, and direct elections of officials.[16] Such a platform was unprecedented. For the first time the established press, mostly owned by loyal KMT members, began carrying photos, names, and even the platforms of the nonparty candidates. In early December many papers covered a gathering of some 500 opposition candidates and supporters. The Garrison Command unsuccessfully tried to persuade the press to tone down its coverage. Ts'u Sung-Ch'iu, in charge of the Party's Cultural Affairs office, publicly stated that the new openness of the press was a "good sign."[17] TV and radio stations, all government or KMT-owned, continued virtually to ignore the opposition, but still, the campaign and the election itself promised to be a significant step forward.

International developments, however, soon threw the political process off track. On November 3 Moscow and Hanoi signed a new Treaty of Friendship and Cooperation that appeared to be a response to Vietnam's increasing tensions with Pol Pot's Cambodia and China. During the year pro-Soviet military officers seized power in Afghanistan and South Yemen. Mengistu Haile Mariam, who had taken over in Ethiopia the year before, was also clearly in the Soviet camp, as were the new Communist governments in Angola and Mozambique. In the Western hemisphere pro-Castro forces had seized power in Nicaragua and Grenada, while Communist guerrillas seemed to be on the verge of winning in El Salvador. The Soviet Union's influence was on the rise. China and the United States perceived an urgent need to advance their strategic relationship. In the fall of 1978 China signed its own peace and friendship treaty with Japan, and Deng signaled flexibility on the Taiwan issue in the context of United States-China normalization. With an acrimonious political fight over the Panama Canal Treaty behind it, the Carter administration was ready to move ahead on recognition of Peking. Serious, confidential Sino-American negotiations began on formal diplomatic relations.

IN ADDITION TO ITS CLANDESTINE SOURCES, the Nationalist embassy had many friends in the executive branch as well as in Congress, but Taipei knew nothing about these secret negotiations. Secrecy was as important to Carter and his team as it had been to Nixon and Kissinger. Ching-kuo knew that Jimmy Carter wanted dearly to make his deal with Peking before his term was up, but he thought this step was still a good ways down the road. U.S. officials had promised Chiang that the administration would at least consult with him before taking the final plunge. On December 13, secret negotiations in Peking on the normalization communiqué nearly collapsed over the sole remaining question—the future of U.S. arms sales to Taiwan. Deng protested to American Ambassador Leonard Woodcock that if America continued to sell weapons to Taiwan after normalization with the Peoples Republic, "Chiang Ching-kuo's tail will be 10,000 meters high," and why would Chiang then want to negotiate with Deng on reunification? At the last moment, Deng agreed to finesse the issue. The United States would accept a moratorium of one year on such sales but no further restrictions, while the Chinese side would record its strong opposition to any transfers of this sort by the United States.[18] When Carter received word of the breakthrough, he decided on an announcement two days later and instructed the State Department to inform Chiang Ching-kuo two hours before the broadcast. Later the time interval was changed to twelve hours.[19]

It was 10:00 P.M. in Taipei on December 16, when a "flash" cable arrived at the U.S. embassy instructing the ambassador to go immediately to the U.S. Taiwan Defense Command headquarters, the only U.S. facility with a secure phone line to Washington, for an important call. Breaking with his common practice, Unger had neglected to leave word with the Marine Guard where he could be reached. Political Counselor Mark Pratt finally found him, in his tux and red bow tie, at an American University Club Christmas ball. Unger and Pratt sped to the TDC facility, and shortly before midnight the ambassador was on the secure phone with Harvey Feldman, Director of Taiwan Affairs at the State Department. Feldman told Unger to inform Ching-kuo immediately that President Carter would announce an agreement with Peking on the establishment as of January 1 of diplomatic relations and the simultaneous breaking of U.S. diplomatic ties with the Republic of China. The timing of this news was a surprise to Unger: in Washington in October he and Feldman had agreed that Ching-kuo would need two weeks to prepare for the break.

IT WAS ALMOST 3:00 A.M. in Taipei before Unger reached Ching-kuo's aide and GIO deputy director James Soong by phone and told him he needed to see the President on an urgent matter. Soong checked with the President's appointment assistant and then called Unger to confirm a meeting at 9:00 A.M. Soong then called on Fred Chien at home, waking him up. Fred knew nothing that would explain such an urgent request. Soong had no sooner returned home than Unger telephoned him again. The ambassador was distraught that the advance notice would only be two hours and asked to see the President as soon as possible. "Has that thing happened?" Soong asked. Unger replied simply, "I have to see the President."[20]

Soong returned to the residence, woke up the President, and said that Ambassador Unger wanted to see him immediately. Unger and Pratt arrived at Seven Seas and with Soong and Chien present gave the official U.S. statement to the President. Ching-kuo was calm. The United States, he told Unger, would regret this decision. The Republic of China had always been a friend and loyal ally, and would remain so. The Communists could never be either one or the other. Unger asked that the Nationalist government not leak any word of his message until 8:00 A.M. Ching-kuo made no commitment. "I am President of the Republic," he said. "I am responsible for the security of my people and I will do what I think necessary."[21]

When Unger and Pratt left, Ching-kuo told Soong to call an urgent meeting of selected officials. Soong and Chien began telephoning the cabinet and other senior officers on Ching-kuo's list. At 7:00 A.M. the leaders convened at Seven Seas. Foreign Minister Shen Ch'ang-huan offered to resign, but Ching-kuo rejected the gesture. The meeting continued through breakfast. The President and his colleagues then decamped to Party headquarters for an official meeting of the Standing Committee. The GRC had a statement on radio and television as soon as Carter made his announcement. Soong and others believed this quick response helped to calm the nation. The Standing Committee also decided to postpone the elections which were due in seven days. At 10:00 A.M. Ching-kuo watched Carter's announcement on his satellite TV:

> As of January 1, 1979, the USA recognizes the Peoples Republic of China as the sole legal government of China. . . . On that same date . . . the USA will notify Taiwan that it is terminating diplomatic relations and that the Mutual Defense Treaty between the USA and the Republic of China is being terminated in accordance with the provisions of the treaty. . . . In the future, the American people and the people of Taiwan will maintain commercial, cultural and other relations without official government representation and without diplomatic relations.

CARTER TRIED TO ADD a note of reassurance for America's old ally, stating "that normalization of relations between our country and the Peoples Republic will not jeopardize the well-being of the people of Taiwan." But such a pledge seemed to carry little weight. Taiwan's diplomatic status was now completely in limbo. That evening Ching-kuo made a televised address to the nation in which he asked the people to be strong and confident. The United States, he said, had dishonored its treaty commitments and caused a "tremendously adverse impact on the entire free world." The Republic of China would neither negotiate with the Communist regime nor give up its sacred task of recovering the mainland. Privately, Ching-kuo told his associates that there was no point in worrying. They simply had to stay firm and work doubly hard. Always practical, he focused on the need to step up foreign investment.[22]

Despite his own calm reaction, Ching-kuo apparently agreed to a controlled display of anger at the Americans. For two nights following Carter's announcement, crowds of young protesters threw stones and eggs at the American embassy in Taipei. At one point U.S. Marines fired tear gas to repel rioters storming the building. American diplomats assumed the Youth Corps had organized the protest. Meanwhile, Carter and Deng appeared vindicated in their anti-Soviet geopolitical calculations when, on Christmas day, Vietnamese troops invaded Cambodia and within two weeks occupied Phnom Penh. The Chinese representative in the Security Council, Ch'en Chu, denounced Moscow for using Vietnam as its "Asian Cuba" in a drive for worldwide hegemony.

On December 27 Deputy Secretary of State Warren Christopher arrived in Taipei for two days of talks about the future framework of unofficial relations between the United States and Taiwan. Fred Chien coolly greeted Christopher at the airport. Unger and Pratt were there as well. As the motorcade drove past the gate, a throng of protesters began throwing paint, eggs, and rocks at the vehicles carrying the Americans. As the cars stopped, the crowd grew more violent, shattering windows. One demonstrator reached through and punched Christopher in the face, breaking his glasses. Before hunkering down on the floor, Pratt and his besieged colleagues noted plainclothes security men trying to prevent the most extreme attacks, even throwing themselves across the car windows.

After half an hour the assault suddenly ended, and the motorcade moved on its way. Nerves were badly frayed, but no one was seriously hurt. It appeared that the authorities had carefully staged the riot—

someone had placed portable toilets along the road—so there would be a great show of violent activity but no real injuries. The next morning, a crowd of 20,000 gathered in front of the Foreign Ministry shouting anti-American slogans and stomping on peanuts as a sign of disregard for President Carter. The demonstration forced postponement of the first day of talks. American diplomats believed Wang Sheng was the organizer of these events, employing Youth Corps and GPWD agents.[23]

On December 29 Ching-kuo and Christopher finally met. Ching-kuo said that future ties between Taiwan and the United States must rest on five underlying principles—"reality, continuity, security, legality, and governmentality." By the later, he meant, that a government-to-government level mechanism would have to be set up to carry on relations between the two countries.[24] Christopher replied that this would not be possible. The meeting ended on a cold note.

———

ON THE FIRST DAY OF 1979 the United States and China officially opened a new era of diplomatic relations. A few days before that Ambassador Unger paid a farewell call on Ching-kuo. The President was gracious and friendly.[25] In Washington the State Department gave a formal one-year notification to the Nationalist government of its intention to withdraw from the Mutual Defense Treaty. The Carter administration also revealed its last-minute concession to Deng—the agreement to a moratorium on arms sales to Taiwan for a year. The Carter break initially frayed nerves on the island more than the 1971–72 events. On the black market the new Taiwan dollar plunged in value, and the Taipei stock market tumbled by almost 10 percent. The island's malaise intensified as Deng and the mighty Peoples Republic enjoyed an enormous public relations boost around the world. In China the *Zeitgeist* of change, encouraged by the Dengists, was rapidly growing among intellectuals and urban youth. "Big character posters" had now grown into a dramatic political phenomenon. Thousands of students were pasting up proclamations, manifestos, and poems calling for a more just society. An area just west of the Forbidden City became the most famous site for such displays and it soon achieved a name known around the world—Democracy

Wall. Deng declared that these expositions were "an appropriate exercise of individual rights."[26]

On January 29, just after *Time* magazine picked Deng as its Man of the Year, the most powerful leader in the Chinese Communist Party arrived in the United States. His six-day whirlwind tour, including a rodeo in Texas where he wore a cowboy hat, captivated the American people. Two weeks after Deng's return to Peking, the PLA invaded Vietnam "to teach Hanoi a lesson" and force it to withdraw its front-line troops from Cambodia. One major consequence of this undeclared Sino-Vietnamese war, and perhaps one intended by Deng, was to turn the attention of the Chinese military further away from the liberation of Taiwan and to focus it on countering the Soviet bloc, of which Vietnam now seemed distinctly a part. On March 5 the PLA withdrew from Vietnam, but a prolonged series of artillery barrages and skirmishes ensued. It would be the bloodiest war ever between Communist countries.

Despite the enthusiastic welcome Deng received in America, a coalition of conservative and liberal senators (including Ted Kennedy, who was preparing to challenge Carter for the presidential nomination in 1980) was determined to shore up the continuing U.S. commitment to Taiwan. The senators were irate that the administration had not consulted with them on the termination of the defense treaty. Senator Goldwater proposed privately that Taipei wage a full-scale lobbying effort to preserve both the treaty and government-to-government relations. The Republicans were eager for an all-out confrontation with the administration. Some congressmen dashed to the island to show their support.[27]

Madame Chiang again emerged, ready to lead the fight. As always, she believed that she was by far the best person to deal with the Americans. She and her Kung relatives had been on the phones since December 16, encouraging key American friends to thwart the President's plans. When early in the year Vice Foreign Minister H. K. Yang arrived in Washington, Madame Chiang sent for him. "It would be better if you did not handle the negotiations with the Americans," she told Yang. Instead, she wanted her nephew, David Kung, one of Ching-kuo's least favorite relatives, to carry on the dialogue. Yang replied that President Chiang had instructed him to negotiate with the United States on the matter, and it was his duty to do so.[28]

Ching-kuo did what he could to exploit the backlash in the Congress. He authorized Premier Sun publicly to urge American lawmakers to protect the interests of Taiwan, approved another vigorous public relations program in the United States, and sent Yang instructions to insist on some level of nondiplomatic official relationship, if only in the form of liaison or consular offices. But he also intended to avoid a showdown with President Carter. He rejected Senator Robert Dole's invitation, on behalf of the Coalition for Peace Through Strength, to come to America immediately to confront the administration. Madame Chiang was aghast at this restraint, and American pro-Nationalists were dismayed. The American Heritage Foundation, which had been demanding nullification of the entire Carter-Deng agreement, protested that the Foundation ought not to have to be "more Catholic than the Pope." Ching-kuo's flexible pragmatism in the face of strong criticism among conservatives at home and in the States reflected his confidence in the ability of Taiwan, seemingly abandoned by the world, to carry on. He also realized it would be a mistake to destroy relations with the Democratic Party. Taiwan would still need broad sympathy in the United States.[29]

Carter was determined not to go back on his commitments to Deng, and in their negotiations with Yang, American diplomats insisted on the formality of a "nonofficial" relationship, although it would in most respects amount to *de facto* official ties. Yang stalled. Eventually, the State Department threatened to close the Nationalist consulates in the United States and to cease all American government operations on Taiwan if agreement was not reached before March 1. Ching-kuo authorized Yang to accept nonofficial ties—a U.S. office called the American Institute in Taiwan (AIT) and a Taiwan office in Washington called the Coordination Council for North American Affairs (CCNAA).[30] Madame Chiang could not directly criticize Ching-kuo, but she accused his envoy of having given away everything. To show his support, Ching-kuo met Yang at the airport when he returned from Washington.

CHING-KUO'S DUAL APPROACH—negotiation with the administration and appeals to Taiwan's friends in Congress—paid off. The administration submitted to Congress its Taiwan Enabling Act, which was intended to give legal sanction to the agreed on "nonofficial" relationship with Taiwan. The draft bill provided for the continuity of 60-plus treaties and agreements between the United States and the ROC, including the sale of enriched nuclear fuel for Taiwan's nuclear power reactors. A bipartisan group of congressmen, however, set to work to strengthen the bill in Taiwan's favor, most dramatically on the issue of security. Whereas Carter's Enabling Act draft had said nothing about Taiwan's security, the legislation that emerged, renamed the Taiwan Relations Act (TRA), affirmed commitments that were very similar to those of the soon to be defunct Mutual Defense Treaty: U.S. establishment of diplomatic relations with Peking rested on the expectation that the future of Taiwan would be determined by peaceful means; any attempt to determine that future by other than peaceful means, including boycott or embargo, would be regarded by the United States as a threat to the peace and security of the Western Pacific and a matter of grave concern to the United States; the United States would continue providing defensive arms to Taiwan without regard to the views of the Peoples Republic; and the United States would resist any form of coercion exerted against the security or social or economic system of Taiwan.[31]

The changes wrought in the TRA represented a political triumph for Taiwan and personally for Chiang Ching-kuo. Extending U.S. concern over Taiwan's security interests to embargoes and boycotts seemed to go even beyond the existing defense treaty. At the last moment Taipei also obtained a U.S. concession to allow it to maintain eight "unofficial" offices in the United States rather than four as Washington had originally insisted. In addition, while the Americans termed the new relationship strictly nonofficial, they acquiesced in Taipei's public statement that described the future work of AIT and CCNA as having the "qualities of officiality."

At home Ching-kuo orchestrated an extensive campaign to restore the nation's confidence. In speeches and slogans, on the radio and TV, officials, media persons, writers, and other private citizens harped on the themes of unity and self-reliance. Ching-kuo announced a 12 percent increase in defense spending. Citizens rushed to contribute to a Self-Strengthening National Salvation Fund to purchase jet fighters. Through the Garrison Command, the government bought Taiwan dollars on the black market, driving the rate back up. Moderate nonparty politicians, led by K'ang Ning-hsiang, also initially joined the national unity parade.[32] The result of all these efforts was a rapid return of optimism. The island's economic statistics resumed their exuberant climb. American, Japanese, and other foreign investment was soon running above the level of the previous year. Some observers speculated that the normalization of United States-China relations had actually improved the investment climate, clearing the air and putting the long-dreaded but inevitable action in the past.[33]

ON DECEMBER 16 the PLA ceased its every-other-day shelling of Quemoy and Matsu, which had been going on since 1958, and the Nationalists in turn silenced their guns. The KMT now faced a more energetic and focused Communist peace offensive.[34] On New Year's Day, the National Peoples Congress in Peking issued a conciliatory "Message to Compatriots on Taiwan . . ." The letter proposed to open up trade, travel, and communications links with Taiwan. Liao Cheng-chih, head of the Taiwan Affairs Office in Peking, wrote an open letter to Ching-kuo, his "little brother," proposing that the KMT and the CCP enter into a third united front with the patriotic goal of reuniting the country. Liao had been a schoolmate and friend of Ching-kuo a half century earlier, when both were left-wing students in Shanghai. As part of the new campaign, Liao's Taiwan Affairs Office opened branches in every province in China, down to the county and city level. These local Taiwan committees embraced more than 100,000 cadre, many of whom were former KMT members and Nationalist officials or relatives. The committee members wrote thousands of letters to friends and kin in Taiwan, Southeast Asia, and around the world, urging reconciliation between the island and the motherland.

CHING-KUO'S REACTION to the united front campaign was much more subtle than Deng understood. Deng believed that despite the failure to achieve an end to American arms sales to Taiwan, events had fundamentally changed the political dynamics of Taiwan-mainland relations, opening up the possibility of Taipei's coming to terms with its long-time political adversary. Chiang Ching-kuo understood, however, that the process that Peking was now fervently encouraging—of social, cultural, and economic contact and engagement across the Strait—could in the long term have much more positive than negative consequences for Taiwan. If travel and trade evolved carefully, such interaction would elevate the image and influence of Taiwan throughout China and encourage the remarkable but still embryonic democratic movement bubbling up on the mainland. Thus the stage was set for the remarkable rapprochement between Taiwan and the mainland in the 1980s.[35]

But, in Ching-kuo's view, 1979 was not the time to take concrete steps in this direction. The break in relations with America had put the KMT again on the defensive. Internal unity and stability once more were the over-riding priorities. Consequently, Ching-kuo and his government vigorously denounced the appeals from Peking and proclaimed the policy of "three no's"—no compromise, no contact, and no negotiations with the Communists. But soon there were signs that Ching-kuo intended gradually to modify the "no's" by acquiescing in private actions by the people and businesses of Taiwan.[36]

AT A STANDING COMMITTEE MEETING on January 29, Ching-kuo proposed a small senior group to recommend strategy and tactics in countering the CCP's political offensive. Ching-kuo said defense was not enough. "We also have to learn how to launch our own political offensive." After the meeting, he asked to see Wang Sheng and told him that he should head a new secret office for this purpose. Taiwan, he said, had not been "creative or aggressive" enough in countering Peking, and it had to launch "its own united front offensive against the mainland."[37] Over the long term the goal was to produce a countercurrent within China—sympathy for a united China based on the Taiwan, not the Communist, model.[38] This was a serious matter, Ching-kuo told his old friend. "If I give you the responsibility, I know you will carry it out to the end." Wang believed that he could achieve the goals the President had laid out, but feared that in the process "my reputation could be wrecked." Nevertheless he accepted the appointment, and it was agreed he would report through Y. S. Tsiang, then Foreign Minister.[39]

The measures that the secret office—code named Liu hsiao-k'ang (LSK)—devised were simply an expansion of previous information efforts to undercut Peking's propaganda and promote Taiwan's image. These included, for example, warning Taiwanese going abroad against falling for united front appeals they might encounter from friends or relatives. One less than bold proposal was for a "filial piety month" to highlight Taiwan's traditional values as opposed to Communist ones.[40]

These activities hardly needed the full attention of Wang Sheng, arguably the second most powerful man on the island. The "offensive actions" that Wang feared could "destroy his reputation" were in the familiar field of covert warfare. The most secret of the planned clandestine actions involved physical intimidation of individuals inside and outside Taiwan who were suspected of being used by Peking to serve its cause. For this purpose, for the first time on Taiwan the intelligence organizations would establish links with ultra-rightist groups and at least one mainlander criminal gang operating on the island. The result would be the opposite of what Ching-kuo intended—serious damage to Taiwan's image and moral authority. There is no direct evidence linking the LSK office to this activity, but almost certainly it was among the sensitive "offensive actions" Ching-kuo referred to in his talk with Wang. The new office was to coordinate all of Taipei's strategic and operational decisions that might affect the political struggle with Peking. The IBMND's forthcoming link-up with a criminal gang was a major decision of this sort.

The LSK office, with a small staff of twenty, moved into the Liming Cultural Company Building in Taipei and began work. Wang devoted most of his time to this office but continued as director of the GPWD and as informal adviser to Ching-kuo on all internal security matters. The LSK essentially came up with ideas, which Y. S. Tsiang and Premier Sun endorsed and then passed on to Ching-kuo for final approval.[41]

21

Riot and Trials

IF TAIWAN WAS TO BE the example for China, it had to continue making progress toward a full-fledged democracy. To this end Ching-kuo approved personnel changes in 14 key posts in KMT central and provincial headquarters. The new appointments were mostly young, moderate, and often academic reformers, both mainlanders and Taiwanese. The chairman of the KMT Provincial Committee, Sung Shih-hsuan (Ching-kuo's cousin), appointed many young Taiwanese with college degrees to head the Party's local branches. By 1984, half of city and county Party chairmen were youthful Taiwanese.[1]

March 10, 1979, was, by Chinese reckoning, the President's 70th birthday, by custom an important occasion, which called for a gala celebration. But Ching-kuo refused to accept the banquet his friends and family proposed. Instead, he took a boat to Matsu island and had breakfast with the soldiers posted there and for dinner ate a bowl of noodles with the officers.[2] In April he officiated at the grand opening of the $70-million national shrine to his father. The enormous multi-arched marble gate at the entry to the 25-hectare site carried four carved characters translated as "Great Golden Mean, Great Righteousness." Ching-kuo was confident Taiwan had weathered the shock of losing its U.S. diplomatic recognition and, as he expected, actually emerged stronger. The key was to show strength and resolve, but also to demonstrate that he intended to lead the island in the direction of liberalization and the rule of law. But he also found that political relaxation inevitably led to even stronger liberal (Taiwanese) pressures and conservative (old-line KMT mainlander) counterpressures.[3]

The latter were in some ways more disturbing than the former. In 1979 the split within the Kuomintang became more open than any time since its arrival on Taiwan. At the end of May a group of senior conservative parliamentarians demanded an end to the "thought pollution" allegedly flooding the island, and warned that the opposition was opening the way for the "communization" of Taiwan.[4] From its point of view, the right wing had reason to be concerned that Ching-kuo and the reformers were heading down a slippery slope in attempting "controlled liberalization." How (and for how long) could a reform-dominated leadership that espoused constitutional democracy justify continued restrictions on the opposition, denying them even the right to have an opposition party and an organization? For their part, the conservatives were also right in believing that the nonparty opposition and their increasingly vocal supporters in the United States would not be satisfied with half a loaf of reform. To paraphrase Alexis de Tocqueville, authoritarian governments are in greatest danger when they begin to reform themselves. Nonetheless the political struggle between the regime and the Taiwanese opposition still reflected a Confucian approach to a dangerous, conflictive situation, with both sides—the authoritarian but reformist leadership and the moderate oppositionists—avoiding all-out confrontation.

AN UNUSUAL BIRTHDAY PARTY was illustrative. Back in January of 1979 Hsu Hsin-liang, the opposition magistrate of Taoyuan county whose supporters had rioted at Chungli, and other prominent dissidents had marched in Taoyuan and in Kaohsiung city without a permit. The next day, perhaps hoping to attract favorable attention from Ching-kuo, Provincial Governor Lin Yang-kang rushed to investigate Hsu's behavior and threatened to depose him.[5] To demonstrate support, opposition leaders organized a birthday celebration on May 26 for Hsu in his home town of Chungli, where the gutted police station had been repaired. The

Garrison Command sent a letter to each of the host politicians, including K'ang Ning-hsiang, warning that "should any unfortunate incidents that affect social order occur, all the consequences will be the responsibility of you and the other hosts." Ching-kuo received a briefing on this upcoming event and gave instructions that so long as it was orderly the police should not interfere.[6]

On the day of the birthday party, Chungli had a festive air. Thousands of people, including a few American observers, wandered around the square examining banned or unauthorized books and reading colorful posters pasted on a Democracy Wall. Numerous plainclothes and uniformed policemen kept watch but took no action. At 5:00 PM, between 300 and 500 nonparty supporters ate box lunches and imbibed nonalcoholic drinks at a restaurant. Then, two hours later, some 20,000 people gathered in the town square to hear speeches that ranged in tone "from calm and thoughtful to rapid and inflammatory." Hsu Hsin-liang concluded the affair with a joking explanation of the impeachment process against him then under way. The birthday party, he said, was "the largest unapproved peaceful political gathering in Taiwan's history."[7]

WANG SHENG AND OTHER HARDLINERS were disturbed at the permissiveness shown by the authorities during the Chungli birthday party. The tug-of-war intensified between the coalition of reformers (principally in the GIO and Party headquarters) and the diehards (mainly in the security organs, the Central Committee, the Legislative Yuan, and the National Assembly). Even in the Standing Committee the tone became "very political." While not directly attacking Ching-kuo, the archconservative minority became more belligerent and hawkish, denouncing the "traitorous" happenings that were undermining venerable KMT principles. Ching-kuo, as usual, rubbed his hands and listened, but said nothing. Outside the meetings he let it be known that he was "personally pushing a policy of dialogue."[8]

When K'ang Ning-hsiang applied to publish a new journal called *The Eighties (Pa shih nien tai)*, the GIO, now headed by another of the young Ching-kuo protégés, James Soong, approved the application, as did Ts'u Sung-ch'iu's Fourth Division at Party headquarters. Antonio Chiang, editor of *The Eighties,* sought to make the new journal a forum for the moderate opposition. Chiang publicly declared that he wanted to avoid "language that incited and to walk the fine line of acceptable criticism."[9] In August the GIO approved yet another political magazine with an opposition publisher, the dissident Legislative Yuan member, Huang Hsin-chieh. Unlike *The Eighties,* the latest journal, called *Formosa (Mei li tao)* immediately pursued a confrontational, edge-of-the-law strategy. It was at this point that a distinct division appeared between the moderate or mainstream, nonparty oppositionists like K'ang Ning-hsiang and Antonio Chiang, both associated with *The Eighties,* and a new, more radical faction that would be known as the *Formosa* Group.[10]

Mimeographed newsheets, a feature of the democracy movement in Peking, also began to be seen on the streets in Taiwan. These free one-pagers, such as *The Tide* and *News,* focused on opposition activities and speeches critical of the government. As with the "underground" press in Peking, the newsletters also did not cross the official bounds of sedition—in Taiwan the line would be crossed by using language that was pro-Communist, pro-independence, or in favor of the violent overthrow of the government. But their sharply critical content showed how far the impermissible had retreated. All the while, Ching-kuo's reformers continued to meet informally with prominent nonparty individuals.

At the same time ultra-rightist magazines appeared on the newsstands, and radical anti-Communist groups of mainlanders became more outspoken. These included the Anti-Communist Heroes (the original members were the Korean War POWs whom Ching-kuo had brought to Taiwan in 1953), other fanatical nationalistic groups like the Iron Blood Patriots Society, and moribund triad societies from the mainland that were enjoying a resurrection. The right-wing organizations held a conference in July and heard calls for "eradication" of the "disloyal" nonparty opposition. Military newspapers gave the right-wing groups positive coverage. In the summer and fall, right-wing vandals thought to be from the Anti-Communist Heroes and the Iron Blood Patriots sacked a number of regional offices of the dissident journal *Formosa* as well as the home of Huang Hsin-chieh.[11]

The reformist momentum, however, persisted through the fall. With Ching-kuo's endorsement, KMT moderates, including James Soong and Ch'en Lu-an and Ts'u Sung-ch'iu at KMT headquarters, arranged for

National Development Seminars to include committees on politics and foreign affairs. Ching-kuo declared that these nonpartisan seminars aimed at scholars and overseas Chinese should "absolutely not evade (political) issues." The sharper and more sensitive the issue, "the more decisively and clearly the government must handle it." Every informed person on the island knew this was a reference to democratic reforms. The Chinese-language *China Times* and *United Daily News* began to publish articles supporting electoral and other reforms, although they opined that "now was not the time to form an opposition party."[12]

GAINING STRENGTH, the native Taiwanese *Formosa* group was growing more impatient, ebullient, and popular (estimates of the magazine's circulation ranged from 100,000–300,000). The new journal had in fact begun to act as a proto-party organization, articulating a party line, setting up local *Formosa* branches, and sponsoring street activities.[13] *Formosa* requested permission to hold an evening torchlight rally and parade on December 10 in Kaohsiung in celebration of World Human Rights Day. The Garrison Command rejected the application on the grounds that the expected crowd of 30,000 would threaten public order. K'ang Ning-hsiang opposed conducting an illegal rally, but Huang Hsin-chieh and his supporters decided to go ahead. It was evident that the year-long failure of the police to enforce the procedures and strictures regarding rallies and written material had convinced the *Formosa* oppositionists that Ching-kuo could not or would not use deadly force to stifle a mass expression of public dissent.[14]

When Wang Sheng and other security officials briefed the President on the imminent crisis. Ching-kuo reaffirmed his instructions that in any civil disturbance, if the police were being beaten, they must not retaliate.[15] The military police sent to the scene were to have no firearms. On the morning of December 10, Chairman Chiang opened the fourth plenum of the eleventh KMT Central Committee with an important speech. He told the 780 delegates that 1979 had been "the most difficult and dangerous year in the history" of the Party. He then spelled out his vision of creating an ideal, model society—the same sort of vision that he had had for Kannan forty years before.

But now he saw this model as one that would eventually transform the mainland. Noting the "economic deterioration and social chaos" across the Strait, Ching-kuo believed the Chinese people were asking, "why can't we have a national economy like that of Taiwan?" Communist control of the mainland, he declared, "must and will be changed in compliance with the aspirations of the people." He reiterated that the policy of "never negotiating and never compromising with the Chinese Communists" was written in stone. Democracy on Taiwan, however, was the central theme of his long discourse:

> We affirm that democratic and constitutional government is a broad thoroughfare along which national politics must move. We shall continue to march forward and never retreat. From now on, we shall address ourselves more actively to developing the basics of democracy, including further fulfillment of the functions of public opinion, strengthening of the rule of law and enhancing the concept of responsible politics. These three goals will be sought simultaneously.

He added the caveat that all his KMT Young Turks—both young and aging—accepted: "Although we attach importance to the safeguarding of human rights and freedom, we attach even greater importance to the security of the nation and society so as to establish a stable democracy in which freedom will not be transformed into permissiveness and democracy will not take a turn toward violence."[16]

AT 6:00 PM THAT AFTERNOON, crowds began gathering in front of the local *Formosa* office in Kaohsiung. Speakers in sound trucks bitterly attacked the government and vowed that the rally would proceed. About this time, the head of the Southern Taiwan Garrison Command met Huang Hsin-chieh at the railway station. The commander told Huang that a rally in front of the *Formosa* office had been approved, but not the parade. The commander said that the demonstrators were armed with torches, iron bars, and chemicals, and he won a promise from Huang that the organizers would keep the rally peaceful.

By 8:40 PM, speakers had whipped the crowd of several thousand into a high state of excitement. Shih Ming-te, the general manager of *Formosa,* climbed on top of a sound truck and led a group of young men down the street. Bystanders joined in and the crowd swelled. A few hundred meters away, "military police on strict orders not to fight back" stood in a line across the road. The marchers pushed their way through this thin line, while back at the rally site mobs assaulted nearby security forces and a police station. The riot continued on until midnight, when riot squads sprayed tear gas and dispersed the mob. A total of 183 policemen and 92 demonstrators were injured that night.[17]

Oppositionists confirmed to AIT officers that the security forces had not used force but tried to fend off attackers with their shields. But they also charged that certain security services had arranged for gang members to infiltrate the rally and provoke the violence, thus creating a pretext for a crackdown on the opposition.[18] In a 1995 interview, the secretary general of Ching-kuo's Presidential Office in 1979 was asked whether the IBMND was involved. "There is no evidence whether this is true or not,"[19] he replied. From the point of view of those responsible for internal security, serious domestic opposition of the sort the *Formosa* group was fomenting served the purposes of Peking's united front campaign and deserved to be suppressed by any means.

If the security services were involved, this may well have taken the form of informally encouraging criminal gangs or ultra-rightist groups like the Iron Blood Patriots to infiltrate the crowd and provoke the violence. The CIA and the State Department had no inside information, but key officers involved at the time with Taiwan affairs believed this was a likely scenario.[20] On the other hand, foreign observers and numerous photos and videos confirmed that opposition leaders stirred up the demonstrators to a frenzy, and that Shih Ming-te himself led the group that assaulted the military police down the street. K'ang Ning-hsiang believed there was "probably some provocation by security agents, but the opposition failed to exercise good crowd control and the crowd reacted to the provocateurs."[21] In any event, another potentially bloody confrontation had passed, a mob of thousands had attacked the Nationalist police, which obeyed Ching-kuo's orders not to use lethal force and itself took most of the serious injuries.

News of the riot shook the members of the KMT Central Committee as they gathered drinking jasmine tea on the second morning of their plenum. The stalwarts were, of course, outraged. Ching-kuo was dismayed. The riot had seemed to mock his talk on the very day of the disturbance of a peaceful and harmonious society. The violence also shocked the inner circle of reformers, including new and old Young Turks. John Kuan, who had been leading the dialogue with the opposition, including the *Formosa* group, lamented bitterly that mutual understanding was not possible because the words of the nonparty leaders belied their actions.[22] But thanks to the forbearance of the police and the mostly one-sided nature of the violence, the affair appeared initially to have been "a magnificent public relations coup" for the government.[23] Not only did KMT-affiliated groups denounce the rioters, but so also did the respected *Independence Evening News* and several nonparty elected officials.[24] Lee Teng-hui presented a gift of NT $2 million to the wounded law officers on behalf of the people of Taipei.[25]

A KMT BACKLASH was to be expected. The Central Committee elected Wang Sheng and senior military commanders to the Standing Committee. A number of scholar reformers lost their jobs. Yet at the same time several elder Chiang Kai-shek arch-conservatives were asked to retire, and Taiwanese again increased their representation in the Standing Committee from 5 to 9, constituting a full third of the body.

Ching-kuo convened an ad hoc group to review the options on the aftermath of the riot. After thinking it over for a few days, he approved the arrest of the senior officials of the *Formosa* group and banned that journal as well as the moderate *Eighties.* He decided on a major crackdown in part to maintain a consensual approach within the KMT, but also because he felt that to do otherwise would invite more violence and a loss of control of the reform process. On December 14 security police began rounding up over a hundred opposition leaders, including Huang Hsin-chieh. The magazine's director, Shih Ming-te, managed to escape and was hidden by the Reverend Kao Ch'un-ming, the head of the Presbyterian Church.

The events of December sparked increased speculation about the rise of Wang Sheng and a military faction. Earlier, the assassination of South Korean President Park Chung Hee by military-intelligence conspirators had stirred speculation about the possibility of a similar coup in Taiwan. In his closing address to the Central Committee, Ching-kuo went out of his way to underscore the regime's intention to abide by constitutional democracy. He promised to resume the suspended parliamentary elections and categorically rejected the possibility of "military rule."[26]

During 1979 the new "unofficial" relations between Taiwan and the United States had fallen into place. Career diplomat Charles T. (Chuck) Cross arrived in June to head AIT, while the first director of AIT's office in Washington (actually across the Potomac in Rosslyn, Virginia) was David Dean, who as political counselor in Taipei in the mid-1960s had, with his wife Mary, become friends of Ching-kuo and Faina. When Dean visited Taipei in September, Ching-kuo told him that he wanted to improve relations with the United States. Citing a Chinese saying, "to swallow the blood on one's teeth," he said the ROC could not let emotions and resentment rule.[27] To the Americans it seemed that, despite the Kaohsiung riot and its aftermath, the normalization trauma had cleared the air on Taiwan. Taipei appeared "more interested in moving ahead on a variety of practical matters to be able better to meet the challenges of the future."[28]

READING ABOUT THE RIOTS IN TAIWAN, Deng Xiaoping must have wondered what Ching-kuo was doing by allowing such violent protests to take place. A year earlier Deng had endorsed the Democracy Wall in Peking. Now he tried to define the limits of freedom of speech in the new post-Maoist China. In March 1979 he issued his Four Cardinal Principles of acceptable political behavior, essentially repeating the "four no's": no criticism of socialism, the dictatorship of the proletariat, the leadership of the CCP, and Marxism-Leninism/Mao Zedong thought. Over the next ten years Deng remained ambivalent about the notion that it was both possible and necessary to democratize the Party. In Peking as in Taipei, tension between the desire for a more open political system and the perceived need to preserve the rule of the Party dominated leadership dynamics.

In 1979 the CCP officially accepted that the purpose of socialist production was to meet the common needs of the people, a philosophical watershed that not only opened the way for a competitive consumer society but also washed away what remained of the justification for absolute political control. Chinese liberals could now argue that a more open political system had to accompany economic reforms if modernization—in the sense of a consumer society like that on Taiwan—was to be achieved. Like Ching-kuo's cohort, liberal Dengists assumed that a more free and vibrant political system could be achieved in a gradual manner that would not seriously threaten the Party's control. The liberals included new Politburo members, Hu Yao-pang and Chao Tzu-yang, both handpicked by Deng to lead China into the new era. Hu and Chao were not only "soft authoritarians," but intellectually they inclined to the more humanist and secularist point of view.

In the fall of 1979, however, the Democracy Wall proved too threatening and, no doubt with Deng's approval, the city of Peking imposed explicit rules about which posters could be put up and where, effectively ending the movement's spontaneous and democratic character. The sedition trial of the most prominent Democracy Wall pamphleteer, Wei Ching-sheng, took place in October and November.[29] But despite the termination of the Wall and the example made of Wei, who received a 15-year sentence, the relatively liberal view still seemed to be very much alive in the CCP's top ranks.

ON DECEMBER 25, 1979, Soviet forces invaded Afghanistan, occupied the major cities, executed the Communist president previously backed by Moscow, Hafizullah Amin, installed a new leader, and themselves took over the major "counterinsurgency" role in the country. This move plunged the Soviet chiefs into a quagmire which would eventually have a powerful impact on intellectual and political trends in the Soviet Union and thus on world politics, including in Taiwan and on mainland China. Referring to the U.S. experience in Vietnam, a senior Soviet diplomat told an American colleague in Peking, "now its our turn."[30] Another result was to further convince China that Moscow was engaged in a strategic pincer movement around the Peoples Republic. This in turn gave a further boost to the informal Sino-American strategic partnership and thereby strengthened the reformers in China. For the next ten years, international events and the ups and downs of the respective democracy movements in China, the Soviet Union, and Taiwan would interact.

—

IN HIS YOUNGER DAYS Ching-kuo had been serious at work but able to relax with friends, drinking, joking, and enjoying idle chatter. Now he was seventy, ailing and more restricted physically. A biopsy revealed a cancerous prostate. On January 16 he underwent a transurethral resection of the prostate at Veterans Hospital. On January 18, 1980, an official announcement informed the public of the operation—another first for a Chinese leader. The President soon resumed his duties but became more contemplative, as always keeping his deepest thoughts to himself.[31] One day Doctor Chiang Bi-ling accompanied him on a flight to Quemoy during which the President did not say a word. He was not reading; he was looking out the window, thinking.[32]

Ching-kuo quickly decided on his strategy in dealing with the Kaohsiung defendants: project the image of a strong leader dispensing stern justice to the guilty and light sentences to those led astray, while assuring the public that he remained committed to a gradual opening up of the political system.[33] On February 1 the Garrison Command released 50 of the detainees on bail and forty one on probation, while keeping 61 under arrest. Eventually, 32 defendants were handed over to civilian prosecutors to face trial for assaulting police officers and other common criminal offenses, and eight, including Huang Hsin-chieh and Shih Ming-te (who had finally been captured), received indictments charging them with the capital crime of sedition. The indictments declared that the defendants had completely confessed to their crimes, and that the prosecution would recommend mercy in view of their cooperation and repentance.[34]

The KMT scholar reformers and other moderates, including Ts'u Sung-ch'iu, pushed for an open trial at the military court. The AIT director in Taipei, Chuck Cross, also urged the government to let the world and the people of Taiwan see its case against the accused. He argued that the opposition was not that potent, and the KMT was doing itself no good by over-reacting.[35] The public, worried about violence and instability, continued generally to support the government over the affair, but there was growing sympathy for the accused.[36] More importantly, in America, the media and human rights organizations portrayed the opposition leaders as the victims, highlighting allegations that an official provocation lay behind the violent night in Kaohsiung. Finally, Ching-kuo decided that the military court proceeding would be open, and statements of the accused made in court could be reported in the local press.[37]

———

A LITTLE AFTER NOON ON FEBRUARY 28—the anniversary of the 1947 Taiwanese uprising—assailants broke into the home of one of the eight defendants in the treason trial, Provincial Assemblyman Lin Yi-hsiung, slashed to death his mother and his twin six-year-old daughters and badly wounded a third child. The murderers took no valuables. Ching-kuo responded to the ghastly crime by immediately releasing Lin on bail and ordering a large reward for information on the case. The police began an extensive investigation.[38]

Most Taiwanese believed that either an ultra-right group or a mainlander gang had carried out a "kill the chicken to scare the monkey" operation. They did not think Ching-kuo was aware of the plot but doubted that he would be able or willing to unmask the real killers.[39] Some U.S. officials suspected the Iron Blood Patriots were behind the crime. The Americans also heard rumors linking Ching-kuo's son Alex to the murders. According to one source, during a heavy drinking session Alex had told a group of Iron Blood Patriots it would be good "to teach them [Lin Yi-hsiung's trouble-making family] a lesson." The brutal and shocking murder, which the police never solved, further sullied the image of the KMT, particularly in the eyes of the American press and human rights activists in the United States.[40]

Ching-kuo accepted the official briefings he received, which suggested the perpetrator was someone with a personal or political grudge against Lin. But at the time his internal security forces, presumably with the authorization of the LSK Office, had been forging links with criminal gangs capable of vicious murder. In 1980, according to veterans of the Bamboo Gang, Taiwan intelligence organizations approached a former gang leader, Ch'en Ch'i-li, who was in retirement following a long prison term. Under Ching-kuo and Wang Sheng's supervision of domestic security and police work on Taiwan, Shanghai-type gangs and triad societies essentially had not previously existed on the island. Contacts with triad gangs in Hong Kong reportedly continued, but organized crime had no significant influence or role in Nationalist intelligence organizations.[41] David Kaplan asserts that between 1949 and the end of the 1970s, neither the Green Gang nor any other of the infamous Chinese triads had succeeded in establishing a foothold in criminal activity in Taiwan. "Not until the early 1980s, when the opposition began to pose a major challenge, did secret societies openly assert themselves, but these were largely as political lobbies, not criminal gangs."[42] The Iron Blood Patriots were such a group.

The Bamboo Gang was not a secret society but a typical Taiwan street gang formed in the 1960s whose members were mainlanders. In the 1980 meeting with the Bamboo Gang godfather Ch'en Ch'i-li, IBMND officials told him that the gang's patriotic energies were needed to help protect the nation. "The now-emboldened opposition had turned to native Taiwanese gangs for support," they said, "and was using them to strike at KMT political campaigns and candidates. The country needed the Bamboo Gang to fight back."[43] Some ranking intelligence officials reportedly opposed recruiting a criminal gang as a paramilitary arm,[44] and Wang Sheng categorically denies every having known of, much less been involved in, a decision to use a gang for covert operations. If there was such connection, he asserts, the IBMND was acting without authorization.[45]

But a unilateral decision by the IBMND or the NSB on this serious matter seems improbable. Very likely, Wang Sheng wearing his LSK hat or Ching-kuo himself authorized this policy. If Ching-kuo did so, presumably the decision was based on his assumption that the more democratic society he envisioned would impose increasing constraints on the official internal security apparatus. Thus he might have been convinced by Wang Sheng or others that an unofficial or "private sector" covert tool would at times be necessary to carry out illegal or distasteful measures to protect national security interests.[46] In any event, Ching-kuo's continued view of clandestine activities in general as a valuable weapon of internal as well as external policy provided the background for this fateful step.

THE TRIAL OF THE KAOHSIUNG DEFENDANTS, which began on March 18, was unprecedented. Observers from Amnesty International and other human rights groups attended, as did American and other "nonofficial" diplomats and foreign corespondents. At first the government attempted to limit the space allocated in local newspapers to the proceedings, but soon gave up. The independent press began devoting two or three pages to the drama, thereby presenting the political views of the opposition to 8 million readers. The defendants stated they had "confessed" only after days of endless questioning without sleep—a procedure the press called "fatigue bombing." Despite the open proceedings, the verdict was a foregone conclusion. On April 18 the court found all the defendants guilty of sedition. The tribunal had planned to sentence Shih Ming-te to death, but Ching-kuo sent word that no one was to be executed. As long as he was President, he would "allow no bloodshed on the island of Taiwan."[47]

The court then sentenced Shih Ming-te to life imprisonment, Huang Hsin-chieh to 14 years, and the other six defendants to 12 years each. While the sentences were mild given the supposed crimes, there was an outcry in America. The negative public reaction grew worse when in June a military tribunal handed down prison terms of up to six years to the head and nine other members of the Presbyterian Church who had admitted to sheltering Shih Ming-te before his arrest. What had started out as a political coup for the KMT and the government had turned into a victory for the democratic movement.

The trial of the churchmen was especially painful for Taipei Mayor Lee Teng-hui, a devout Presbyterian. At the time Lee was also devastated by the death of his son from cancer and considered giving up politics and becoming a preacher. He talked with friends and his minister about his intentions. Chou Lien-hua and other Christian clergymen told him that he would be only a mediocre preacher, but a great political leader. Lee decided to stay in politics.[48]

SHORTLY AFTER THE TRIAL, hawks in the Party, the Legislative Yuan, and the military-security complex complained to Ching-kuo that the decision to have an open trial had been a disaster for the KMT. Ching-kuo called in the Party's cultural and public relations director, Ts'u Sung-ch'iu (he had been one of those who had successfully pushed the idea of an open court), and expressed pleasure that in the whole Kaohsiung affair and its aftermath there had been no loss of life. It apparently did not occur to him to think of the family of Lin Yi-hsiung. Ts'u agreed it had turned out as well as could be expected.

"They say you are liberal," Ching-kuo remarked to his old friend of four decades, "they" being the right wing.

"Well, I majored in Western political science," Ts'u replied.

Ching-kuo smiled. "I understand."

Then, in an unusually critical if friendly comment, Ts'u said, "You are so good at listening, but you never give your opinion."

"That is the best way to get the true picture of things," Ching-kuo replied. "Besides, it saves energy."

Ching-kuo noted the increasing criticism of Ts'u within the Party. "Maybe you should change to another job,"[49] he suggested. Ts'u became director of China Television (CTV), and Lee Huan, who had been in that post since 1977, went off to assume the presidency of Chung Shan University in Kaohsiung.

The postponed elections, which the authorities rescheduled for December 6, reflected the continuation of Ching-kuo's policy of a gradual move toward representative democracy. A new law increased the number of seats up for election in the Legislative Yuan to 70, a 78 percent increase over the 1978 figure. As usually only about 100 of the 300 or so surviving mainland-elected members tottered in to attend each session, the increase meant that the Yuan was at least coming in sight of being a true representative body.

22

Island and Mainland

BY CRACKING DOWN on the radical opposition after the Kaohsiung riot, Ching-kuo made it clear that he would not tolerate street violence. Now he wanted to make a different point. He told his KMT electoral team that the coming election would be democratic and clean. The KMT, he said, "is pursuing reform not for the sake of winning an election, but is holding an election during the course of reform."[1]

The leaders of the radical wing of the opposition were mostly in jail and could not take part in the coming election. Their relatives and lawyers, however, became candidates. Meanwhile, opposition moderates continued the struggle in their own fashion. With *The Eighties* banned, the irrepressible K'ang Ning-hsiang applied for a permit to publish yet another magazine, *The Asian (Ya chou jen)*. GIO and the 4th Division at Party headquarters approved. The editor of the banned *The Eighties*, Antonio Chiang, became editor of the new journal, in which he hoped "to project the image of a loyal opposition such as exists in Western democracies . . . this will be difficult to pull off, since criticism is equated with rebellion in traditional Chinese culture, but if we fail, moderate Taiwanese opposition will die and be replaced by radicals willing to resort to violence."[2]

Antonio's words were music to the ears of the reformers, both the young scholars and the Ching-kuo veteran liberals. But the Garrison

Command soon found reason to ban *The Asian,* whereupon K'ang and Antonio received permission for yet another publication—*Warm Currents* (Nuan liu)—which the military watchers also proscribed in short order. Likewise, the brother of the jailed Huang Hsin-chieh rushed out his own anti-government, officially sanctioned journal, *Political Monitor,* only to have the Garrison Command immediately squelch it.[3]

The December (1980) election campaign went off without major incident. Nonparty or "outside party" candidates said "almost anything they wished," although they avoided the most provocative subjects, such as Taiwan independence and direct attacks on the Chiang family. In return, the government prevented right-wing groups and veterans' organizations from disrupting the rallies and campaigns of the nonparty candidates.[4] The result was a victory for Ching-kuo and his coalition of reformers.[5] Of the 70 seats up for election in the Legislative Yuan, the opposition won only seven, with K'ang Ning-hsiang among the winners.

Like a good politician anywhere in an election year, Ching-kuo had shaped his legislative agenda to win popular approval, particularly among workers and the middle class. Beginning in 1979, the government introduced and the Legislative Yuan passed a broad range of liberal economic and social laws. These included new welfare legislation, a revised company law, and special courts to handle labor-management disputes. The minimum wage rose from US $67 to US $84 per month, and workers were guaranteed a proportion of annual profits of their respective enterprises as well as 10 to 15 percent of new stock issues. Other bills set aside impressive funds for housing loans to workers; greatly expanded construction of new public housing; and increased welfare payments to poor families. Most interesting of all was a law unprecedented in Chinese history and thought—a State Compensation Act providing payment to individuals whose freedoms or rights were infringed upon by public officials and corporations acting on behalf of the government.[6]

THE 1980 ELECTION of Ronald Reagan had seemed a major victory for Taiwan since during his campaign the Republican candidate had promised to re-establish official relations with the Republic of China in

Taipei.[7] But Ching-kuo understood both the strategic realities that shaped Washington's China policy and the fickle nature of American public opinion. He would not expect sweeping change from Reagan, the seventh American president with whom he had dealt. In fact, he realized that should the new president move toward a resumption of official relations with Taipei, a major crisis could erupt in both Sino-American and mainland-Taiwan relations, with unpredictable results. Taipei would revert to total dependence on America, and those most pleased with this outcome would be the advocates of Taiwan independence.

Any move to restore official relations would also complicate continued American military sales to Taiwan, which had resumed at the beginning of the year. In 1980 the Carter administration had approved almost US $300 million in the sale of "defensive weapons" to Taipei, including shipboard air defense missiles and 1,000 TOW anti-tank missiles plus launchers. The focus of ROC procurement ambitions, however, was for an advanced U.S. jet fighter. If this objective was to be achieved, it had to be done quietly and in the context of reasonably positive United States–China relations, a point the "unofficial" American representative, Chuck Cross, kept emphasizing in his conversations with Nationalist officials.

Taipei had put off its decision on which advanced or "FX" aircraft it desired until after the U.S. election. Following Reagan's smashing victory, Vice Foreign Minister Fred Chien strongly counseled restraint in seeking concessions from the new government in Washington.[8] When the *Far Eastern Economic Review* asked Ching-kuo what he expected of the Reagan administration, he did not mention the campaign pledge to restore an official relationship; instead, he replied simply: "Our expectation is the faithful implementation of the Taiwan Relations Act."[9]

Indeed, two years after the break, the sense of isolation on the island was lifting. Ching-kuo's government continued its vigorous and increasingly flexible policy of strengthening ties with foreign governments and international bodies, accepting when necessary the fiction of nonofficial and nondiplomatic relations. These connections multiplied in number but also began to deepen and expand in character.

Business was good, and businessmen in Taipei were becoming vocally optimistic about the prospects for the China market's developing into a natural outlet for Taiwanese machine tools and consumer goods.

Some even foresaw Taiwanese components and materials flowing into the export processing zones that were appearing on the mainland. The Peking-guided Hong Kong publication, *Ta kung pao,* declared that China had abundant resources and a large market, making it a perfect fit with Taiwan's economy. The Chinese Foreign Trade Ministry announced that custom duties would not apply to Taiwan goods. Two-way trade through Hong Kong was still tiny, but growing.[10]

Meanwhile, with Ching-kuo's authorization, the Taipei government signaled for the first time that some people-to-people contact with the mainland was permissible, even desirable. The *United Daily News* quoted the chairman of Taiwan's Council for Agricultural Planning and Development to the effect that if the Chinese Communists wanted to "Taiwanize" their agriculture, the council would be willing to help "in order to improve the living standards of our fellow countrymen." In a separate article in the same paper, a Taiwan academic was cited as suggesting that contact abroad with persons from the mainland could be useful in opening their minds.[11] During the year, the government strikingly liberalized its approval of passport applications. Of the 150,000 residents of Taiwan who received passports the first ten months of the year, many went to Hong Kong and then on to visit their old homes on the mainland. Two of the "three no's" were rapidly eroding. This quiet evolution of policy reflected Ching-kuo's belief, as expressed to Wang Sheng, that "to be more anti-communist, we will have to become less anti-communist."[12]

IN 1980 INDIRECT TRADE between Taiwan and the mainland was around US $300 million. On the docks of Fuchow and Amoy in Fukien province, a foreign observer could often see warehoused stacks of cardboard boxes containing TVs and other appliances made in Taiwan. The Garrison Command continued to warn that such trading was illegal, but Taiwanese fishermen who transported these direct shipments to mainland ports paid little heed.[13] K'ang Ning-hsiang publicly charged that the "three no's" was an "ossified policy" that was "detrimental to the interests of the people of Taiwan." "Taiwan's ultimate survival," he declared, "depends on friendship [with China]."[14]

Although the International Monetary Fund had ousted Taiwan in 1980, the ROC did not worry. Its reserves were US $7 billion and its foreign debt only US $3.5 billion.[15] Spending for industrial research and development had increased by 58 percent. Trade with Southeast Asia, Western Europe, and even the Eastern bloc was booming. Foreign banks were scrambling to open branches in Taipei. For the first time, Taiwan capitalists were making substantial investments abroad. As a result of the second global oil crisis stemming from the Iran-United States confrontation, Taiwan's oil import bill jumped by 100 percent, but the government dealt with the problem effectively, raising gasoline prices and speeding up its nuclear power program.[16] It seemed that the boom had helped to blur both class lines and ethnic (mainlander-Taiwanese) differences. Families in all classes sought to climb up the social ladder through the same strategy—hard work, education, and saving.[17]

TAIPEI MAYOR LEE TENG-HUI regularly attended cabinet meetings. He had been a senior official now for almost ten years. He was not one of Ching-kuo's insiders, but he made a point of seeing the President two or three times a week to seek his political counsel on municipal problems. No doubt Lee learned a great deal; the visits also gave him the opportunity to impress the President with his earnestness. When several Taipei students died in a drowning accident that was laid to negligence of the city government, Ching-kuo called in the mayor to stress the need to demonstrate contrition and sympathy, and Lee hurried out to call on the families of the victims.[18]

Lee was American-trained, English-speaking, a scholar-official, tall, seemingly modest, a Christian, a good manager of people, and a good administrator.[19] In addition, he was personally friendly with a number of opposition leaders.[20] Y. S. Tsiang continued to push this Taiwanese protégé of his as the KMT's "best bet."[21] Y. S., Wang Sheng, and others were thinking more seriously than ever before about the succession. The 72-year-old President had constant pain in his legs. He could not sleep at night and was often under heavy sedation.

THOUGHTS ABOUT THE NEXT GENERATION of leaders brought to mind the young, American-trained members of Ching-kuo's circle. Another young scholar soon joined the group. In 1978 the KMT paper in Taipei, the *Central Daily News,* published a piece by a Chinese Harvard-trained lawyer named Ma Ying-jeou, who was working in a prestigious law firm in Boston. Ma had written on the inevitable collapse of Communism, and Ching-kuo was intrigued by the argument that Communist systems could and would collapse sooner rather than later through a natural dynamic. This was considered an eccentric opinion in the early 1980s, but Ching-kuo had already become a believer. Young Ma also published several articles in Taipei newspapers on how Taiwan could deal with the break in relations with the United States. In September 1981 Ching-kuo interviewed Ma, and three months later Ma took over as deputy director of the President's office.

In November 1981 local elections again went off well. There were no reports of violence or charges of ballot tampering or harassment of opposition candidates, and some nonparty leaders expressed satisfaction with the fairness of the polling (as distinct from the campaign). The KMT won 77 percent of the 189 seats in the various councils, but 19 of the nonparty's 31 "official" candidates won. The oppositionists also won 4 of the 19 magistrates' seats.[22] Following the elections Premier Sun made sweeping changes in his cabinet, with the newcomers being on average nine years younger than incumbents. Observers saw the new faces as advancement for KMT reformers. Taiwanese appointments were also notable. For the first time a Taiwanese, Ch'en Shou-shan, headed the Garrison Command—an appointment less revolutionary than it may seem, for Ch'en was a "half-mountain" Taiwanese and a protégé of Wang Sheng. Also close to the internal security czar was the new head of the NSB, Wang Ching-hsu, the former Garrison Commander.

IN 1981 DENG STEPPED UP HIS EFFORTS to woo Ching-kuo. Peking ceased commemorating the anniversary of the 1947 Taiwan uprising, and in July Hu Yao-pang, the new CCP chairman, invited Ching-kuo and other KMT officials to visit their ancestral homes. This was just the beginning: the full-court press began in September, when China made a nine-point proposal for reunification that included Taiwan's retention of its own armed forces, full autonomy, no interference in Taiwan's domestic affairs, and even joint leadership in running China proper. Peking's statements began stressing the common heritage of the KMT and the CCP. Orders went out to the CCP committee in Hsikou to repair the Feng Hau Fang complex and the graves of Ching-kuo's mother and grandmother.[23] The PRC offered to sell Taiwan oil, coal, and medicines at preferential prices.[24]

Deng Xiaoping also provided a legal framework for his "one country, two systems" formula on reunification. He directed revisions to the constitution of the Peoples' Republic that provided a unique status—Special Administrative Regions (SAR)—for Taiwan and Hong Kong. The SARs were guaranteed a "high degree of autonomy," including control over their existing economic, political, social, and judicial systems. Peking alone would represent China in international fora, but Taiwan and Hong Kong would have "considerable diplomatic powers to handle some external affairs."[25] To further improve the atmosphere, the PLA withdrew a substantial portion of its forces stationed in Fukien opposite Taiwan.

Rhetorically, Taipei's "three no's" continued in force. But articles now began appearing in the pro-KMT press concluding that for the foreseeable future a military attack on the island by China was highly unlikely, and that peaceful and gradual reunification was the correct path, starting with mail, tourism, and indirect trade.[26] The author of one such article was Kao Ying-mao, a native Taiwanese professor at Brown University. Kao was invited to meet with the President and explain his views. At the meeting that followed and several others over the next few years, Ching-kuo asked questions, and Kao, perforce, did all the talking. Nevertheless, it was clear the President agreed with Kao's analysis.[27]

SOON AFTER THE NEW REAGAN ADMINISTRATION took office, a number of senators, including Barry Goldwater and Jesse Helms, demanded approval of an advanced fighter plane sale to Taiwan. A split within the administration immediately ensued. Senior White House staff, including

National Security Adviser Richard Allen, was supportive of the opening to China but willing to take the chance of provoking Peking by enhancing the character of U.S. relations with Taiwan. Allen had drafted Reagan's campaign pledge to resume official relations with Taipei. But Secretary of State Alexander Haig, like his two immediate predecessors, gave much higher priority to consolidating the strategic relationship with Peking. Haig won the first battle, compelling the White House to withdraw an invitation to Taipei to send a ranking official for the inauguration. Publicly and privately, Peking warned that a sale to Taiwan of the FX or advanced fighter would end the budding strategic relationship between China and the United States.[28]

Later in 1981 the CIA and the Defense Department concluded that such a sale was not necessary for Taiwan's defense. Chuck Cross, who favored the sale of the FX, continued to urge his Nationalist interlocutors to be patient. A debate ensued in the KMT leadership on how strongly and publicly Taiwan should push for the FX. In the summer Reagan conveyed a personal message to Ching-kuo through a "non-American channel," assuring him that Taiwan would get "some sort of advanced aircraft" that Ching-kuo "would find acceptable." Haig was not aware of this message, which presumably originated with Richard Allen.[29] The "channel" was Lee Kuan-yew, who had a private meeting with the American president when he visited Washington in June, shortly before coming to Taipei for unannounced talks with Ching-kuo.[30] Lee had become the key behind-the-scenes interlocutor in the China-Taiwan-America triangle. Shortly after receipt of this message, the GIO (on July 15) released "a very authoritative and important policy statement" by Ching-kuo in which he said President Reagan was "a man of principle and a staunch foe of Communism"; thus Taiwan should be patient in its relations with America and "move little by little with maximum patience and perseverance."[31]

When President Reagan met Chinese Premier Chao Tzu-yang, at the North-South Summit in Cancun, Mexico, in October, Chao underscored Peking's strong opposition to arms sales to Taiwan and stressed that recognition of the principle of Peking's sovereignty over the island was the best way to assure Taiwan's security and the continuation of its status quo. Subsequently, Peking pressed Washington for a definite date when all U.S. arms sales to Taipei would cease. It stepped up warnings that China would downgrade relations with the United States if it sold an FX fighter to Taiwan.

For the next year Haig was able to dominate Washington's China policy. The Secretary convinced President Reagan that critical strategic interests required Washington to settle the arms sales issue left over from the Carter administration. In a memo to the President, Haig argued that because Carter had mishandled the arms sales issue with Peking, the critical strategic tie now hung in the balance. Washington announced that it would not approve the sale of an FX-type fighter to Taiwan but would approve local production in Taiwan of the less advanced F-5E fighter. The U.S. Ambassador in Peking, Arthur Hummel, began to negotiate with his Chinese counterparts a new understanding on the Taiwan arms sales question.

AS THE NEW DENG ERA WAS RAPIDLY UNFOLDING on the mainland, Ching-kuo's ideas about how reform on Taiwan would extend across the Strait were coming more into focus. At least since the early 1970s, Ching-kuo had believed that Taiwan would have to become a successful political as well as economic model if over the long term it was to remain viable. Now, with the unfolding of Deng's reforms on the mainland, it was also increasingly apparent to Ching-kuo that political progress on Taiwan would encourage the same dynamic on the mainland. He knew from experience that once the process of political reform had begun, it would be difficult to reverse. The key was to create a process that would not only retain stability on Taiwan but would also be valid for all of China.[32] James Soong, Ma Ying-jeou, and Ching-kuo's other young scholar-officials began to suggest publicly that the Taiwan model could actually win out peacefully on the mainland. "We are now the better alternative," Soong said in a 1981 speech. "When we talk about recovery [of the mainland], it may not be direct—it is the presentation of a different [alternative]."[33]

Ching-kuo alerted the Americans to his intentions. Early in the year, before the new AIT Director James R. Lilley left Washington to take up his post in Taipei, a prominent Chinese with close ties to Ching-kuo came to see Lilley. The envoy, clearly speaking for his President, said that Ching-kuo had a four-point program. Point one was democratization, including "comprehensive elections." Number two was "Taiwanization." The days of mainlander control were coming to an end, and across the board Taiwanese must take an increasingly prominent role. The third point was "key to accomplishment of the first two": more rapid increases in income and standards of living, objectives that in turn required more infrastructure and even greater stress on technology and exports. The fourth and most striking point in the program was "development of working relations with China."[34]

Taipei welcomed the assignment of Jim Lilley, a retired, distinguished CIA officer close to the Reagan administration and to Vice President Bush.[35] With one exception (David Dean), Ching-kuo did not trust State Department types and had better relations with American CIA and military officials. Chuck Cross never met with Ching-kuo except at receptions. Lilley, however, called on Ching-kuo at Seven Seas a number of times for long private exchanges. The President, always friendly but reserved, struck Lilley as "a visionary and a strong leader."[36]

In early 1982, while Ching-kuo was in Veterans Hospital recovering from a retina operation to deal with his growing vision problem, he approved including a team from mainland China in the women's softball world championship to be held on Taiwan. The Liu Hsiao-k'ang office had urged Ching-kuo to okay Peking's participation. Like Ching-kuo, Wang Sheng believed that gradually opening up contact with the mainland would have more advantages than disadvantages for Taiwan.[37] In the end, however, Peking surprisingly elected not to come, but the new director of North American Affairs in the Foreign Ministry told Lilley that although this time the connection was not made, there would be other opportunities in the future.[38] The Foreign Ministry official was Ching-kuo's son, John Chang, who had recently moved back to Taipei from Washington with his family.

IN MAY 1982 the priority of American strategic interests with Peking was apparent in separate letters that Reagan sent to Deng, Premier Chao, and Chairman Hu Yao-pang. In his letter to Hu, drafted by Haig's officers, Reagan reiterated the commitment of the United States to the principle of one China and added, "we will not permit the unofficial relations between the American people and the Chinese people on Taiwan to weaken our commitment to this principle." Of even more interest to Ching-kuo was Reagan's statement in his letter to Deng: "we fully recognize the significance of the nine-point proposal of September 30, 1981," which set out Peking's terms for unification. Reagan told Chao that "the United States expects that in the context of progress toward a peaceful solution [of the Taiwan-mainland issue], there would naturally be a decrease in the need for arms by Taiwan." Vice President Bush, who had headed the U.S. Liaison Office in Peking in the mid-1970s and inclined to the Haig view, followed up the letters with an official visit to Peking, conveying the same conciliatory message.[39]

Conservative senators led by Goldwater, Helms, and Thurmond, and most of Reagan's White House staff, strongly disagreed with Haig on China and a whole range of other international issues. Behind the scenes they were pushing Reagan to fire Haig.[40] Goldwater decided on a trip to Taiwan. Almost certainly he talked with Reagan before his departure, and we can safely assume that the senator, who arrived in Taipei on June 4, briefed Ching-kuo on Haig's negotiations with Peking and told him not to worry—Reagan would not approve an agreement with the PRC that violated the TRA and its commitment to Taiwan's security. We do know that Goldwater assured Ching-kuo that Reagan would live up to his promise of getting Taiwan "some sort of advanced aircraft."

Shortly after the Goldwater visit, Haig's diplomats and Peking negotiators reached agreement on a draft communiqué. The United States pledged to limit "the quantity and quality" of its arms sales to Taiwan and affirmed that such sales would gradually diminish, "leading over a period of time to a final resolution." In the unusual document, the Chinese dropped their demand for a "time certain" for the ending of U.S. arms sales to the island and tacitly permitted the Americans to link their commitment to reduce and ultimately end such sales to China's statement that its "fundamental policy" was "to strive for the peaceful solution to the Taiwan question." Goldwater and the pro-Taiwan conservatives in the White House were outraged when they learned of the contents of the draft communiqué. At a meeting of congressmen with Reagan on

June 23, Goldwater alleged that Haig had lied to the President, himself, and others about where the negotiations were headed.[41]

Two days later, without giving Secretary Haig a chance to defend himself, Reagan informed him that he would accept his resignation. On June 25, 1982, Haig resigned, charging that unspecified opponents had waged "guerrilla warfare" against his management of foreign policy.[42] On July 9 representatives of 28 conservative groups warned the President of an "extremely acrimonious backlash" if he agreed to any reduction of arms to Taiwan.[43] The pro-Taiwan group in the Reagan camp thus regained the upper hand it had lost after the 1980 elections. Reagan believed he could not back down from the agreed draft with the Chinese, but to offset its effect, on July 14 he signed off on "six assurances" to Chiang Ching-kuo. These pledged that the United States would live up to the TRA; it had not and would not set a date for ending arms sales; it would not pressure Taipei into talks with Peking; and would not act as a mediator. In addition, the White House announced its intention to sell more F-5E aircraft to Taiwan than the number approved in December.[44] Later the United States also agreed to make arrangements for Taiwan's early purchase of excess F-104s from West Germany.[45]

Reagan finally approved the communiqué with Peking as drafted under Haig with only slight changes. When Lilley informed Ching-kuo of the final version of the agreement, he was "remarkably balanced and sensible" in his response.[46] Reagan's personal commitments and assurances from Goldwater and others had convinced Ching-kuo that the communiqué would not make any substantial difference in U.S. arms sales to Taiwan.

After the communiqué became official on August 17, a clarifying U.S. government statement and President Reagan's remarks at a later news conference asserted that the reduction in arms sales was linked to Peking's commitment to a peaceful resolution of Taiwan's future. The linkage was in fact key, but it was an informal one. Forced by the Reagan statement to clarify its position, Peking issued its own statement asserting that there was no linkage implied or otherwise.[47] Ching-kuo's policy of patience and restraint had again paid off. In addition to the F-5Es and the F-104s, he knew that eventually Taiwan would also receive a new advanced fighter. In fact, the political ramifications of the communiqué would on balance be favorable to Taipei. For the first time since 1960 the leadership in the State Department and the NSC was highly sympathetic toward Taiwan, although it was still committed if possible to retaining the U.S. opening to Peking.

———

ALTHOUGH THE COMMUNIQUÉ was essentially negated, the public perception of it as another blow at Taiwan's security once again united the island and diminished the prospects for an independent Taiwan. K'ang Ning-hsiang even led a group of four opposition legislators to Washington to argue against limitations on military sales to Taiwan.[48] The media on the island encouraged public discussions on how to enhance unity and consensus in face of the latest inimical American move. Ching-kuo dispatched Fred Chien to take over the CCNAA office in Washington. In another reaction, Ching-kuo told his military chief of staff to speed up the weapons development program. Nuclear weapons were clearly high on the list.[49] AIT officials warned senior Nationalists against proceeding with research on or actual fabrication of a nuclear weapon and received categorical denials of any such activity.[50]

Meanwhile, Ching-kuo continued gradually to relax his government's posture regarding the mainland, including negotiations. One trial balloon was Premier Sun's public remark that the ROC position toward talks with Peking was similar to President Kennedy's declaration in 1961 that the United States would never fear to negotiate but would never negotiate out of fear. Reunification, Sun said, should be based "on the free will of the Chinese people as a whole. . . . If the political, economic, social and cultural gaps between the Chinese mainland and free China continue to narrow, the conditions for peaceful reunification can gradually mature."[51]

The next month Liao Ch'eng-chih sent another letter to Ching-kuo, his "schoolmate and friend," offering to visit Taiwan to discuss unification. The response was a firm "no." The Communist proposals for a dialogue, Ching-kuo said, were simply "pouring spoiled wine into old bottles." The Chinese people, he declared, were sick of communism, while Taiwan's success inspired them to desire "freedom, democracy and a prosperous way of life."[52]

———

DURING REAGAN'S FIRST YEAR IN OFFICE, another killing had embarrassed the Taipei government. In May 1981 Ch'en Wen-cheng, a permanent resident of the United States and a statistics professor at Carnegie Mellon University, returned to Taiwan to visit relatives. On July 1 the Garrison Command brought him in for questioning. The next morning his body was discovered on the campus of NTU with numerous broken bones and massive internal bleeding. There was an immediate uproar in the United States. According to Chuck Cross, "there was clear evidence of official involvement" in the murder.[53] The U.S. House of Representatives Subcommittee for East Asian and Pacific affairs held hearings on the matter.[54]

Ching-kuo apparently accepted the official explanation that the government had nothing to do with the professor's death. No aide recalls the President having raised any questions about the affair.[55] This murder, also never solved, was again the sort of "pro-active" offensive action that veterans of the spy wars could condone in the name of national security.

———

THE LIU HSIAO-K'ANG OFFICE under Wang Sheng had gradually assumed authority over various aspects of national policy-making. By 1983 Wang was in the habit of summoning the senior vice minister or number two official in a ministry or office and issuing orders, expecting them to be carried out. Liu Hsiao-k'ang seemed to be functioning as "a super cabinet or government within a government."[56] By Wang's own account, the office was involved in "virtually every policy question."[57] Some senior officials began to see a possibly sinister motive—preparation for a takeover after Ching-kuo's death. Next to Ching-kuo, the vast network of political officers and security/intelligence types owed their loyalty to Wang Sheng, providing him probably with the strongest potential power base for a takeover in the post-Chiang era.

Such an era seemed more than hypothetical. By early 1983 the President could barely walk—it was like "stepping on cotton," he told his doctors—but he refused to use a wheelchair. Severe headaches added to his suffering. On most days he went for one hour to his office downtown, but now he held almost all of his meetings at Seven Seas.[58]

Reflecting its new vigor and openness, the press speculated exten-
sively about the succession, something unheard of in Chiang Kai-shek's
days. Premier Sun was an obvious possibility. But he was 69 and not in
robust health. Foreign as well as local observers frequently cited Y. S.
Tsiang and Wang Sheng as those who would play key roles in a post-
Ching-kuo Taiwan.[59] A favorite theory was that Tsiang saw himself as
premier and Wang Sheng as KMT secretary general. A number of Standing Committee members and senior ministers, Shen Ch'ang-huan and
Chiang Kai-shek's old friend Chang Ch'un among them, took the
unusual step of talking to Ching-kuo privately about their concerns.
Wang Sheng, they thought, was a man who would be king.[60]

About this time Dean and Lilley thought it would be a good idea
to invite Wang to visit the States. The reason was the same that led to
the invitation to Ching-kuo 30 years earlier—the Americans hoped to
broaden the security czar's understanding of democracy. When Wang
informed Ching-kuo of the invitation, the President asked why the
Americans were doing this. Wang said he didn't know and asked if he
should refuse. Ching-kuo said no; Wang then made the trip a very public
one, calling on congressmen and high officials.[61] Shortly after Wang
returned to Taipei, Ching-kuo called him to Seven Seas. "The Liu Hsiao-
k'ang office," he told his old comrade, "seems to have become another
system of leadership. Two Standing Committee members have spoken to
me on this subject. I am concerned about the inner unity of the Party and
not allowing factions. If the Liu Hsiao-k'ang office continues I think it
will develop into a faction."[62] Wang claims he was at first happy when
Ching-kuo told him to close the secret office, thinking he could now
devote all his time to his beloved GPWD.[63]

Two weeks later, however, Ching-kuo called him back and said that
he was being transferred to an obscure post as director of the Department of Joint Operations and Training. Wang was stunned. In his own
mind he had bent over backward to avoid the creation of a faction. He
had 10,000 former students in Taiwan and around the world but, he
claimed, he had never tried to establish a network. Wang saluted and
walked out, ending a 45-year friendship.[64] For the new head of the
GPWD, Ching-kuo picked not a career commissar this time, but an army
line officer, General Hsu Li-nung.[65]

Subsequent remarks by Wang convinced Ching-kuo that he had done the right thing. In his farewell address to the Political Warfare College, Wang reportedly said, "killing one Wang Sheng is of no use, because there are thousands of Wang Shengs," clearly referring to all the political officers who had graduated from the school. In a letter to Chief of Staff Hao, Wang also referred to himself as "the most anti-Communist person." Wang later blamed his demotion on the President's ill health, "paranoia" ("his mind was going"), and the scheming of certain "influential people."[66] But the first demotion was not the end of it: Ching-kuo then sent Y. S. Sun to inform Wang that he had been assigned as ambassador to Paraguay, about as far away from Taiwan as one could get.

Before Wang departed for his new post, Ching-kuo called him in for a farewell chat. It was best, he said, that Wang "go abroad for a while as an ambassador," otherwise "he might become the focus of a faction." Wang claims he brusquely replied, "you ought to know me . . . Don't use your own fists to hit your head!"[67] Ching-kuo ignored the impertinence. "I was once a diplomatic envoy in Manchuria," he told Wang. "It was a good experience." He then added a Delphic remark—"To learn to swim, you must get into the pool."[68]

23

Successors, Brokers, Killers

IN 1983 CHING-KUO PICKED a new director of the IBMND—Wang Hsi-ling, the admiral who had been running intelligence operations from Washington. The Liu Hsiao-k'ang office was gone, but its mandate to recommend covert, pro-active measures apparently now lay with the NSB, headed by General Wang Ching-hsu, the former Garrison Commander known as "Big Wang." By this time the Bamboo Gang, with the support of the IBMND, had ballooned into a formidable crime syndicate with thousands of members.

The departure of Wang Sheng emboldened Taiwan's press. The Garrison Command continued to suspend periodicals, but the GIO and the KMT 4th Division as rapidly approved new ones. Yet under the loosened but still firmly controlled system, KMT rule seemed secure. The nonparty activists now fell into two sharply divided factions: the mainstream group led by K'ang Ning-hsiang, and the radical faction, now called the New Generation. The latter group's center were relatives and lawyers of the Kaohsiung defendants and younger militants. The rival oppositionists could not agree on candidates for the December elections, and thus in many constituencies the anti-government vote split. As a result, K'ang Ning-hsiang went down to a surprising defeat in his Taipei constituency. Only six candidates endorsed by the moderate Nonparty Nominating Committee won seats, compared to nine in the 1980 elections, but four of the seven relatives and lawyers standing in for the jailed dissidents were winners. Nevertheless the election was a major victory for Y. S. Tsiang, whom Ching-kuo had appointed secretary general of the Party.

Ching-kuo's nonconfrontational policy toward the United States also seemed to be paying off. In a notable interview with the German magazine *Der Spiegel* in May, he refused to be baited into criticism of the United States but insisted the two countries were "still trusted friends . . . and natural allies."[1] The private assurances he had received from President Reagan continued to satisfy him. In 1983 the Reagan administration approved a stunning US $530 million in missiles and other military sales to Taiwan. Peking's reaction was surprisingly mild, and Deng Xiaoping seemed optimistic about China's relations with America. In September Washington and Peking announced that Chao Tzu-yang would visit the United States in January, and Reagan would make an official trip to China in April. Meanwhile, the White House relaxed restrictions on technology transfers to the Peoples Republic.[2]

Ching-kuo did not view these developments as threatening. Senior Taiwan officials, notably Economic Minister Chao, began publicly to endorse the idea of trade with China.[3] Privately, Premier Sun proposed to Ching-kuo that it was time for Taipei officially to allow both open trade and tourism with the mainland. The President agreed such a step would be advantageous but took no direct action.[4] Without any official change of policy in Taipei, Taiwan-mainland dynamics were advancing in intriguing directions. Under Peking's no-tariff policy and Taipei's official blind eye, the island's indirect exports to the mainland were increasing as rapidly as illegal travel from Taiwan to China.[5] But for Ching-kuo, more important were the political and psychological watersheds in China that seemed to confirm profound possibilities. Deng had irrevocably abandoned communism as an economic system and as an all-encompassing, mobilizing ideology. Moreover, despite the political twists and turns since 1978, a powerful and popular democratic movement really seemed to be gaining momentum. Ching-kuo still thought it best to continue to let relations with China multiply spontaneously in the private sector and see how things developed.[6]

THE PRESIDENT'S DECLINING HEALTH as well as the Wang Sheng affair underscored the need to decide on his successor. During Ching-kuo's latest hospitalization, the secretary general of the presidential office formed an "eight person group" to exercise collective leadership in the event the President did not recover or could not perform his duties. This initiative displeased Ching-kuo.[7] His presidential term would be up in one year, in May 1984. The formal National Assembly election would be in March. Ching-kuo understood that the odds of his living until 1990 were at best uncertain.

Before the end of 1983 he decided that his successor would be a native Taiwanese.[8] The incumbent Vice President, Hsieh Tung-min, was old and had little credibility. Ching-kuo's favorable impression of Governor Lee Teng-hui, on the other hand, had continued to grow. As governor, Lee had done a good job, solving some practical problems his predecessor Lin Yang-kang had not. For example, the opposition of local people had blocked several flood prevention projects in northern Taiwan. Lee made personal trips to the area and met with the locals, in the end persuading them that the planned projects would be beneficial.[9]

Like President Chiang, Lee was originally a technocrat. He also projected the image of a man who was not grasping for power. In addition to Lee's talents as a politician, manager, and leader, in Ching-kuo's opinion he simply had the credentials and appearance of a president of the Republic of China. Ching-kuo was pleased when he thought of the distinguished impression Lee's towering and smiling figure would make on the world.[10]

Just as Ching-kuo was contemplating his final choice, he read one morning the transcript of Lee's denunciation of the idea of Taiwan independence during a debate in the Taiwan Assembly. China, Lee told the Assembly, had never rejected Taiwan and Taiwan could never forget China. Ching-kuo was highly pleased. On the spot, he told a senior aide to invite Lee to give a report to the Standing Committee meeting scheduled in a few days. The President asked for a short speech that would give "encouragement" to Lee. At the meeting, Governor Lee gave a brief, upbeat report on provincial affairs. After he sat down, Ching-kuo made one of his rare comments on these occasions: "Lee Teng-hui has performed very well" (fei ch'ang hao). Everyone in the room knew then that Lee would be the new Vice President and thus the successor to Ching-kuo, at least as state leader.[11]

In February 1984, although Wang Sheng had been at his diplomatic post in Paraguay only a few months, he received permission to return from Asuncion to Taipei to attend the KMT Central Committee meeting. Ching-kuo took note of the fact that a good number of retired GPWD officers went to the airport to greet the former chief commissar. If he had doubts before, Ching-kuo knew then that he had been correct in getting Wang out of Taiwan.[12]

The Central Committee, as usual, met at the Chungshan building on Yangming Mountain, but this was an especially important session. It was, of course, widely expected that the committee would draft Chiang Ching-kuo for a second term as president. The unknown was his own nominee as vice president—and likely successor as president. The secret was well kept inside the Standing Committee. The public and the media were surprised when Ching-kuo announced the winner—Lee Teng-hui, whom the Central Committee promptly approved.

It was some time after Lee's nomination as Vice President that the Security Bureau somehow learned of his youthful membership in or connection to the CCP in 1945–46 and informed the President of this startling bit of intelligence. Ching-kuo shrugged it off—"It can't be helped" (*mei yu panfa*).[13] Certainly, the President was thinking of his own much longer youthful allegiance to the Soviet Communist Party. But hard-line security and GPWD types had not been enthusiastic about Ching-kuo's selection of Lee, and they were decidedly unhappy when they learned the Taiwanese had a hidden Communist past, a serious offense under martial law.[14]

Some of Ching-kuo's own family did not consider the succession question settled. Ching-kuo's two sons Alex and Eddy, his foster brother Wei-kuo, and Madame Chiang now focused on the possibility of the party leadership, as distinct from the chief of state role, going to a loyal mainlander if not to a member of the family. The party position, they thought, would be where the real power would reside.[15] At this moment, Y. S. Sun, long thought a possible successor, suffered a stroke and was never able to return to political life. As his replacement, Ching-kuo chose the Chiang family loyalist and scholar official from Fenghua county, 70-year-old Harvard and London School alumnus, Yu Kuo-hua.

The February session of the Central Committee enlarged the Standing Committee from 27 to 31, raising the number of native Taiwanese to 12, or 39 percent of the total. But even more than in the past Ching-kuo relied on his trusted subordinates, both the older confidants and the younger third-generation scholar officials. He brought Lee Huan back from exile in Kaohsiung, appointing him Minister of Education. At this time Ching-kuo had a hospital-type bed set up in his bedroom at Seven Seas and began to conduct much of his business there with a small "bedside elite."[16]

FAINA WAS SUFFERING from insomnia and shortness of breath, but she was in better health than her visibly fading husband. Growing infirmity brought the couple closer. Their greatest pleasure was in their numerous grandchildren, who ranged in age from Yomei, now a budding artist in her twenties, to Eddy's two young sons: Edward (Yu-chang), born in 1979, and Demos (Yu-po), born in 1978. Alan remained a semi-invalid. Eddy preferred to stay out of the limelight and steered clear of the intelligence types who fascinated his brother Alex.[17]

After his wife returned to Europe, Alex hired a young and pretty Taiwanese woman, Ts'ai Hui-mei, to be the governess and English tutor of his children. Alex was now general manager of the (radio) Broadcasting Corporation of China (BCC) and also held the honorary post of baseball commissioner, which brought him favorable publicity in view of Taiwan's remarkable Little League victories. He continued to hobnob with movie stars and other celebrities in the new, affluent Taiwan jet set, including senior intelligence officers. By 1984 there was speculation in Taipei that the chain-smoking, hard-drinking, but also hard-working middle son could be the real successor to his father. The opposition claimed Ching-kuo was preparing to hand over power to Alex, who now had responsibility for overseeing his father's personal guard unit. But Ching-kuo, better than anyone, understood his son's failings and had no intention of permitting him to assume a key political position.[18]

Ching-kuo took pride in the steady accomplishments of his undeclared twin sons but continued to have no personal contact with them. As director of North American Affairs, John Chang, wrote memos for the use of the President on important policy issues, and dealt with key visitors from the United States and Canada. But, unlike other office directors in the Foreign Ministry, he did not accompany eminent visitors to see the President. About this time articles began to appear in Hong Kong and on the mainland identifying Ching-kuo's two undeclared sons. Eddy Chiang twice asked his father about these stories, but each time Ching-kuo denied there was anything to them. Eddy and his brother Alex, however, soon were convinced the rumors were true. Alex told one friend that he was sure the twins were fine men, but their presence in the city was a constant embarrassment to his mother. He then tried to thwart the careers of his twin half-brothers, objecting unsuccessfully to John's promotion to vice minister in the Foreign Ministry. Once, after the BCC interviewed Winston Chang on an educational issue, Alex called the producer and warned him never to have that person on the air again.[19]

WHEN CHING-KUO DECIDED the time had come for informal exchanges between Taipei and Peking, there was no shortage of would-be intermediaries. At one time Anna Chennault (the widow of Claire Chennault) and even Ray Cline (retired from the CIA) sought to play the part. Ching-kuo brushed them off, limiting this sensitive role to only one trusted individual—Premier Lee Kuan-yew of Singapore. Lee was the only world leader who was able to travel between the two competing Chinese capitals, although, ironically, Singapore—not wishing to alarm its ethnically sensitive Malay neighbors—had diplomatic relations with neither Peking nor Taipei. Lee had visited Peking for the first time in May 1976 and met briefly with the ailing Mao Zedong. In 1978, as the new era of reforms began in China, Deng Xiaoping himself went to have a look at the booming but politically quiescent Chinese city-state at the tip of the Malay Peninsula. In 1980 Lee made his second visit to China, and the next year Deng sent his then protégé, Chao Tzu-yang, to study Singapore's success at first hand.

Favorable reporting in Chinese media on Singapore's society and economy, as well as public and private remarks by senior officials in Peking in the early 1980s, underscored Deng's fascination with Lee Kuan-yew's prosperous and tidy country. Lee tried to educate Deng and other senior PRC officials about the situation on Taiwan, including the sympathy of most Taiwanese for the principle of independence and thus the need for China as well as Taiwan to proceed with flexibility and care on the reunification issue.[20] At some point during these years Lee began to make unpublicized visits to Taipei for talks with Ching-kuo.[21]

The positive chemistry that developed between Chiang Ching-kuo and Lee Kuan-yew surpassed that between Lee and Deng. Lee and Chiang were anti-Communist but pragmatic, and both took a long-term but cautiously optimistic approach to ending communism in China.[22] Deng, on the other hand, wanted to save communism by reforming it. During Lee's periodic visits to Taipei, he and Ching-kuo would spend many hours alone talking about China and the China-Taiwan issue. Ching-kuo believed Lee understood the dynamics of this question better than anyone. Ching-kuo's key associates agree that Lee was a major influence on the President's thinking about China. This was the only close, personal relationship with a foreign chief of government that Ching-kuo ever enjoyed. He sometimes went to the airport to meet Lee, which he never did for any other foreign visitor. He also instructed his secretary to include in his letters to Lee language reflecting his affection.[23]

At least once Deng sent his personal regards through Lee Kuan-yew to Ching-kuo, "my classmate in Moscow."[24] Deng also spelled out to the Singapore leader and other visitors how the Taiwan-mainland issue could be resolved in a way that protected the interests of all sides. Peking, Deng said, would never send officials or troops to the island, nor interfere in political or "personnel" (that is, leadership) matters, nor would it ever seek to revise the terms of a reunification agreement, which "could last a hundred years."[25]

According to Deng, Taiwan would also have "special rights to handle foreign affairs . . . issue special passports . . . grant visas . . . and sign some agreements with other countries." The relationship should be one whereby "you do not swallow me, I do not swallow you. You do not bother about me, and vice versa. Each of the two sides can go its own way." Deng again ruled out Peking's renunciation of the use of force before an agreement was concluded, but it was not necessarily ruled out as part of a final accord. Future disputes on implementation of the agreement would be handled through consultation. Apart from the principle of "one China," Deng stressed, "the mainland had no other absolute conditions. All other conditions and schemes are negotiable and adaptable."[26]

This was as flexible a starting position for talks as Taiwan would ever get from Peking. Ching-kuo, however, did not yet believe he had a mandate, and conditions had not changed sufficiently on the mainland to negotiate on reunification. Lee and Ching-kuo did agree that a growing engagement between the mainland and the prosperous and open societies of Taiwan and Singapore would lead China to evolve in a similar direction. As Ching-kuo told *Der Spiegel:* "the re-establishment of a free, democratic and unified China is neither a dream nor an illusion."[27]

By 1983 Ching-kuo believed that as a result of Deng's economic reforms and pragmatic foreign policy the Peoples Republic would grow stronger and stronger. If Taiwan and the mainland could get together, he told his colleagues, "China would have a great future." The key was to create the political framework that would make this possible. For a variety of compelling reasons, quite aside from the intellectual and moral choice, the framework would have to be democratic.[28]

ON SEPTEMBER 26, 1984, Deng Xiaoping achieved a striking victory in the long struggle for the unification of China—agreement on the Sino-British Joint Declaration on the Future of Hong Kong. As the first concrete manifestation of his "one country, two systems" formula, Deng and Prime Minister Margaret Thatcher agreed that Hong Kong would revert to Chinese administration in 1997, and that China would appoint the chief executive and be permitted to station PLA units in the territory. But for the next 50 years Hong Kong would continue to have its own economic, social, financial, and political systems. During their meeting Deng asked Thatcher to pass a message to President Reagan asking that the Americans "do something" to promote contact between Taiwan and the mainland.[29]

The Hong Kong Declaration strengthened Deng's already strong position in the CCP. Divisions still existed between reformers like Hu Yao-pang and Chao Tzu-yang on the one side, and on the other, arch-conservatives opposed to fundamental changes in economic and social policies, but Deng nevertheless continued to consolidate his role as paramount leader. In 1984 he reconfirmed his commitment to China's openness to the world and to economic reform by visiting the controversial special economic zones in Shenchen, Chuhai, and Amoy.[30] But he also remained determined not to let reform and relaxation get out of hand. As a party man above all, he was sensitive to charges that reforms were subverting party control. Hence he endorsed a campaign promoting the idea of a "socialist spiritual civilization," and in 1981 and 1983 approved a flood of polemics against "spiritual pollution" and "bourgeois liberalization." The former, we have seen, was a term conservatives on Taiwan also used to resist political liberalization.

IN MAY 1984 the informal Taiwan opposition formed another proto-party organization called the Nonparty Public Policy Association. The NPPA's frankly stated goal was establishment of a formal opposition. KMT reformers like James Soong hoped the opposition would be content for a while longer with the substance but not the form of a party structure. In a gesture of moderation, Ching-kuo in August approved parole for four of those sentenced in the Kaohsiung trials, including Lin Yi-hsiung, father of the murdered family. As two scholars described it, the KMT was responding to growing pressure and militancy from the opposition by a combination of selective repression, steady institutional liberalization, and accelerated efforts to co-opt more Taiwanese into the system.[31] Conservatives in the ruling mainlander elite were growing more bitter and fearful, however. In July Admiral Wang Hsi-ling met with the boss of the Bamboo Gang, Ch'en Ch'i-li. According to David Kaplan, Wang had a rather ambitious plan to make the Bamboo Gang a trained and integrated wing of covert action for use around the world, including Hong Kong and the United States. Although the LSK office was defunct, clandestine and illegal activities to counter anti-KMT individuals and groups continued in force.

Wang's first meeting with Ch'en was at the home of a well-known movie director, a reflection of the close ties between the movie industry, the intelligence apparatus, and organized crime. The guest of honor at the dinner was Chiang Wei-kuo. Wang followed up this initial meeting by inviting Ch'en to dinner on August 2, along with Major General Hu Yi-min, deputy director of the IBMND and an old Tai Li operator from mainland days, and a Colonel Ch'en Hu-men. Wang told Ch'en Ch'i-li that a traitor named Henry Liu had written a book slandering the President and smearing the image of the nation. Now this man was writing another book, *The Biography of K. C. Wu.* "Liu must be killed," said Wang. Ch'en readily accepted the assignment.[32]

Liu had promised Wang Hsi-ling to sanitize his book on Ching-kuo and had even taken money from the IBMND for this concession. Then, with only a few deletions, he had proceeded with publication. Now, in addition to a biography of K. C. Wu, he was also planning a book on the life of the purged General Sun Li-jen. Ching-kuo would star as villain in both books.[33] Admiral Wang was fed up with the author, who, he believed, had also become more loyal to Peking than Taipei.[34]

On September 14, after a farewell dinner by Wang Hsi-ling, Ch'en Ch'i-li boarded a plane for California to arrange the murder. A month later, three Bamboo Gang members shot and killed Henry Liu in his garage in Daly City, on the outskirts of San Francisco. But National Security Agency computers in Fort Mead, Maryland, recorded several incriminating international calls between Ch'en Ch'i-li in California and the IBMND.[35]

Ch'en Ch'i-li and the two actual assassins of Henry Liu, Wu Tun and Tung Kui-sen, returned to Taipei on October 21. IBMND officers greeted them at the Chiang Kai-shek International Airport and praised them for a job well done. Colonel Ch'en Hu-men told them that "the Big Boss" was grateful. Later, when Tung asked Ch'en Ch'i-li who was "the Big Boss," Ch'en allegedly replied that it was Chiang Hsiao-wu—Alex Chiang.

⎯

IN LATE OCTOBER and early November the Garrison Command took swift action against journals that were running stories implying official involvement in Henry Liu's murder. The government also began to sue media critics for libel. Unrelated to the Henry Liu story, civil courts convicted two editors of libel and sent them off to jail. Other opposition journals made a *cause célèbre* of these cases. Reflecting another gain by the hard-liners, the Interior Ministry ordered the NPPA to disband as an illegal organization.

But three weeks after the return of the assassins of Henry Liu, Taiwan police agencies launched the largest crackdown ever on criminal gangs on the island. Thousands of police and military personnel swept through the principal cities, arresting hundreds of suspected gang members, including many in the Bamboo Gang. The government had planned to begin Operation Clean Sweep *(Yi Ch'ing)* near the end of the year, but for some reason suddenly moved up the date. A police squad burst into Ch'en Ch'i-li's house and carted him off. Fearing for his life, Ch'en yelled out that he was an undercover agent of the IBMND. Ch'en was in the custody of the Justice Ministry's Security Bureau, a rival of the IBMND, and it was this bureau that interrogated him. The assassin Tung managed to escape abroad. The NSB, under the direction of General Wang Ching-hsu, coordinated this unprecedented crime sweep involving several security organs. This was the same "Big Wang" who had been Garrison commander in 1981 at the time of the murder of Professor Ch'en. Years later, Eddy Chiang suggested that Operation Clean Sweep was an effort to take the killers of Henry Liu out of circulation. He said the murder case probably involved "internal strife" between intelligence units, and that Admiral Wang Hsi-ling would not have undertaken such an action by himself.[36]

Ching-kuo's morning briefing on November 13 contained a report prepared by his presidential chief of staff on Operation Clean Sweep. The report noted that one gang leader arrested had claimed to be an agent of the IBMND, showing a document to prove this claim, and that he had also confessed that in this capacity he had carried out the murder of Henry Liu. Ching-kuo was shocked and angry. "It's unbelievable," he said. "Well, deal with it according to the law."[37] He instructed Big Wang to oversee the matter.[38] Big and Little Wang apparently at first believed they could successfully deny any connection of the IBMND to the murder. But when they learned that the Bamboo Gang leader had left tapes in the United States describing the plot in detail, they apparently told

Ching-kuo of the IBMND's involvement. They may or may not have revealed Big Wang's role. Ching-kuo ordered the Foreign Ministry to inform the U.S. State Department that the Nationalist government had arrested a suspect, an underworld figure, in the murder of Henry Liu. The ministry, however, was not to mention Ch'en's claim that he was working for the IBMND. The attempted cover-up would continue for two months, making the Americans, as Eddy Chiang said, "infuriated."[39]

In mid-December the FBI informed the State Department of evidence of IBMND involvement in the murder. Congressman Steven Solarz announced a hearing to determine whether this act of terrorism in America warranted the suspension of arms sales to Taiwan. State requested the extradition of Ch'en Ch'i-li and Wu Tun to stand trial in the United States. Ching-kuo declined but promised that Taipei would share information on the case with Washington.[40]

To underscore the importance of the issue, AIT Director Harry Thayer roused the secretary general of the President's Office out of bed to read to him a ten-point cable on the case.[41] Ironically, the senior Taiwan diplomat dealing with Thayer on the issue was John Chang, whose mother's death 42 years earlier was rumored to be the work of secret KMT agents. *The Eighties* launched its own investigation and published an article charging an official connection to the killing. The Garrison Command confiscated the entire issue. Soon confronted with irrefutable evidence the FBI had on the case, however, Ching-kuo finally approved admitting that Colonel Ch'en Hu-men had, without authorization, conspired in the murder. Washington said responsibility went higher than the Colonel. Taipei then offered up General Hu, Wang Hsi-ling's subordinate. No, said the FBI and the State Department, Wang Hsi-ling himself was involved.[42]

On January 13 the FBI obtained from a Bamboo Gang member in Houston a copy of Ch'en Ch'i-li's tape in which he named Wang Hsi-ling as personally directing the murder. Ching-kuo ordered the dismissal of Wang Hsi-ling and his two associates and their trial by military court for the murder of Henry Liu.[43] It was not until four days later, however, that GIO—which in November had threatened to sue publications that suggested an official connection to the killing—issued a statement saying that the government was "deeply shocked by the involvement of our intelligence officials," and that the authorities had suspended Wang Hsi-ling from his directorship of the IBMND.[44] Several more days passed, however, before the authorities actually detained the suspended IBMND chief, suggesting negotiations with him on conditions under which he would take the blame.

Ching-kuo told an aide that he felt "extraordinary pain" over what had happened. He kept protesting that he could not understand how Wang Hsi-ling could make such a foolish decision.[45] Until the debacle in Daly City, he lamented, Taipei had occupied the high road in relations with Washington. After the departure of Haig, the Republican administration had been highly sympathetic to the needs of Taiwan. Now the Liu murder put Taiwan on "shaky ground" and threatened all the recent and potential gains with the United States. Ching-kuo was worried about Reagan's personal support for Taiwan and about the impact on U.S. arms sales, which in 1984 had soared to US $700 million—and especially about the effect on Reagan's promise of the much desired advanced fighter plane.

The President told the next regular Wednesday Standing Committee meeting that gangsters had trapped government officials by socializing with them. He ordered all such contacts to cease. Ching-kuo appointed four seniors, Big Wang, Hao Pei-ts'un, Shen Ch'ang-huan, and Wang Shao-yu (general secretary of the Executive Yuan) to form a task force to deal with the immediate crisis and make long-term recommendations. Leaked stories began to appear in the Taipei press reporting that Ching-kuo was furious with evidence of official involvement and had ordered a clean sweep of the intelligence and internal security network and the arrest of anyone involved, whatever his rank.[46] Ching-kuo approved the American request that a Daly City detective and two FBI agents be permitted to come to Taipei to interview the accused gang members and administer polygraph tests. He knew the Americans were primarily interested in how high up culpability in this affair went in Taipei, including his own possible knowledge. He did not approve their request to interview Admiral Wang.[47]

The public relations problem in the States was nonetheless escalating. The *Washington Post* described the Taiwan government as "a favored friend acting like a thug."[48] The first day of hearings of the House

Subcommittee on Asian and Pacific Affairs—the same subcommittee that had investigated the death of Professor Ch'en—was a disaster for Taipei. The next day, February 8, Ching-kuo changed his mind and agreed that the Americans could also interview Wang Hsi-ling and administer a polygraph test. When Wang took the test, he denied both that he had specifically ordered the murder (he had only suggested that Ch'en Ch'i-li "teach Liu a lesson") and that superiors had approved the killing. According to Americans who were present, on all three answers Wang visibly "squirmed," and the needle indicated blatant deception.[49]

At this point President Chiang must have understood, if he did not know, why such a "discreet" and trusted intelligence officer had gotten involved in such a risky escapade that promised such inconsequential benefit. Extensive circumstantial evidence suggests that Big Wang gave Admiral Wang either the okay or the order to arrange the murder. Twelve years later, an old and close comrade of Ching-kuo said that Wang Hsi-ling was definitely covering up for someone.[50] Several ranking KMT officials of the time believe that the original idea came from Alex Chiang, whose "involvement with the intelligence apparatus" had been promoted over the years by Wang Sheng.[51] Rumors of Alex's involvement appeared in the press in Hong Kong and America and even in Taiwan. Because of the condition of his eyes, Ching-kuo now depended on his staff to read to him. Very likely one or more of his young aides or senior associates—or possibly his son Eddy—informed him in early 1985 of the rumors about Alex's involvement. Alex heatedly denied the stories and maintained he had never met Ch'en Ch'i-li and was in no way involved in the case.[52]

At the minimum, however, Ching-kuo came to believe that Alex's "love of intrigue," his life style, his unsavory friends, and his reckless comments had at the least led indirectly to the murder.[53] Almost certainly Ching-kuo himself knew nothing of the plan to kill Henry Liu, but nevertheless he also bore responsibility. His endorsement of pro-active or "offensive" measures (when he established the Liu Hsiao-k'ang office in 1979 with Wang Sheng in charge) led directly to the IBMND's decision in 1981 to make use of the Bamboo Gang as a covert tool. The prominent political murders in 1980 and 1981 were also very possibly or even probably related. Ching-kuo at the time did not demand a rigorous internal investigation of any of these incidents.

When Ching-kuo fired Wang Sheng in 1983, he did not use the occasion to rein in the covert forces that had been set loose to intimidate the opposition. At any point the President could have made absolutely clear that political assassination was excluded from the pro-active covert measures. Finally, Ching-kuo did not give effective guidance to his erratic son or his intelligence/internal security chiefs. This sector of the Nationalist government continued, as it always had, to live and work outside the normal precepts of human conduct.

ALONG WITH CHIANG CHING-KUO, the post-Haig Reagan appointees who ran China policy in Washington wanted to see the Henry Liu case wrapped up and forgotten as soon as possible. It was clear to officers at AIT that "in their heart of hearts" Reagan's new team "did not want to come down hard on Ching-kuo."[54] Under the leadership of Assistant Secretary Paul Wolfowitz, the East Asia and Pacific Bureau at State was pushing approval of the plan to allow General Dynamics (maker of the F-16) to enter into a joint venture with Taiwan for manufacture of a so-called Indigenous Defense Fighter (IDF). The IDF, to be largely assembled in Taiwan, was designed as a stripped-down version of the F-16, with a different engine and electronics and significantly reduced range that made it more purely defensive. It was Reagan's way of meeting his personal commitment to Ching-kuo to provide him with an "acceptable advanced fighter aircraft."

Some Foreign Service Officers in the State Department argued that the IDF was a violation of the August 1982 Sino-American communiqué, which stated that U.S. military sales to Taiwan would not increase in quantity or quality but would diminish over time. The matter was taken to Secretary of State George Shultz. The Liu case and the Solarz hearings seemed to put a cloud over the IDF proposal, but because of Reagan's secret commitment to Ching-kuo, in retrospect it is apparent that the decision was already made.[55]

But there was another White House interest in seeing the Liu case finished and buried. While the Solarz committee hearing was proceeding on Capitol Hill, Fred Chien received Colonel Oliver North in his Washington office, a meeting arranged by Gaston Siegur, NSC director of East

Asian Affairs. North brought along Nicaraguan rebel or "contra" leader Adolfo Caldero, who explained the plight of the anti-Sandinista guerrillas in Nicaragua, abandoned by the Congress. Caldero asked if "rich persons" in Taiwan might contribute US $1 million to the guerrillas.[56]

Ching-kuo had been depressed and angry over the employment of a criminal gang by a bureau of his government, probably at the instigation of his son, to carry out a cold-blooded murder inside the country that was the most important in the world for Taiwan. In these circumstances it was all the more startling to get Fred Chien's report of the White House's request to the Kuomintang for under-the-table money for a covert operation to be kept secret from the Congress. The unconstitutional and illegal covert program in Nicaragua was causing the deaths of hundreds in a small Central American country with which the United States and Taiwan still had diplomatic relations. Taipei in fact had an on-going aid program with the Sandinista government and had recently extended $9 million in low-interest loans to the leftist regime. Ching-kuo was delighted by North's request. To be safe, he ordered a further check with the White House to confirm that it was blessed at the highest level. The NSC replied that "President Reagan would appreciate a favorable response."[57]

Ching-kuo instructed the Security Bureau to meet the secret American request through the KMT-front organization called the World Anti-Communist League. The chairman of the league, retired U.S. Army Major General John Singlaub, soon visited Oliver North in his White House office. Wringing the situation to the utmost, Ching-kuo sent a further query—would the White House be "greatly pleased" by a KMT contribution to the contras? The response was a quick affirmative.[58]

On April 9 a civil court, after nine hours of testimony, found Ch'en Ch'i-li and Wu Tun guilty of killing Henry Liu and sentenced them to life imprisonment. Ten days later, a military court, following fourteen hours of testimony, convicted Wang Hsi-ling and his two subordinates. During his trial Wang said that "when the KMT was on the mainland and in the early days in Taiwan, it had carried out political killings, but only according to carefully drawn plans. For the last 10 to 20 years, using violence had been against government policy."[59] In neither trial did the prosecutors probe for possible involvement above the IBMND director. The

Admiral received a life term, but most observers expected correctly that he would be out within a few years. At the Solarz hearings, Deputy Assistant Secretary of State for East Asia and the Pacific William Brown stated that there was no evidence of "a consistent pattern of [KMT] harassment or intimidation [of its enemies in the United States]—nothing in terms of proof."[60] The hearings came to the same conclusion and thus resulted only in a token congressional resolution calling again for extradition of the perpetrators to the United States. As expected, Taipei again declined. The State Department then expelled all the IBMND agents from the United States whom the FBI could identify.

In June or July the Nationalist government, through the World Anti-Communist League, made the first of two clandestine deposits of US $1 million into Oliver North's secret Swiss account. As an example of the strict compartmentalization that Ching-kuo practiced, Premier Yu Kuo-hua and Party Secretary General Ma Shu-li never heard of these secret payments. In July Hao Pei-ts'un informed Ching-kuo that the White House had approved the IDF proposal. Ching-kuo smiled. "This is a great achievement for our military diplomacy," he said.[61]

Aside from the expulsion of the IBMND agents, Taiwan paid no price in its relations with the United States as a result of the murder of Henry Liu. Nevertheless, inside Taiwan, the Henry Liu case had a profound and lasting impact. Lee Teng-hui, Fred Chien, James Soong, and other American-trained scholar officials were aghast and ashamed, as were the aging liberals in the original Ching-kuo cohort. A government and a party that relied on criminal gangs to terrorize their enemies was not what they had in mind when they chose to make their careers with the KMT. The event badly tattered the political clout and moral authority of the KMT's arch-conservative wing and the internal security apparatus as a whole. From this point on, the idea of stamping out "cultural pollution," meaning public criticism of the government and its leaders, was dead.

The scandal at last shattered Ching-kuo's long-held belief in his clandestine services and their covert activities. For the first time he changed the fundamental goals and objectives of the intelligence establishment, ordering the merger of the IBMND and the Defense Ministry's Special Intelligence Bureau and appointing a field general, not a political or intelligence officer, to head the consolidated office. The new organ would henceforth collect only military intelligence.[62] Most significant of all, Ching-kuo forbade any covert activities in the United States. He instructed the NSB to focus on intelligence collection, analysis, and counter-intelligence, not covert action. After a decent interval, he removed Big Wang from the NSB.[63]

Ching-kuo knew it would be difficult to change the culture of the secret security forces. The line officer he had assigned to carry out the task, he remarked, was "jumping into a fire pit." In contrast to his earlier practice of recruiting promising youth for the intelligence services, he now made clear that he would no longer permit outstanding students and cadre to enter intelligence work. It is a "liability," he told Lee Huan, reflecting a sense of powerlessness over his Frankenstein creation.[64] The President also ordered severance of ties to the guerrilla forces in the Thai-Burma border area—ties that he had continued despite repeated promises to the Americans since 1953 to end them.[65] Finally, he decreed that arrests of important opposition figures in Taiwan and the closure of journals would have to have his personal approval before the fact. On the same day, he told General Hao that greater emphasis was required on promoting native Taiwanese generals.[66]

24

Building Consensus

IN FEBRUARY 1985 Ching-kuo asked Y. S. Tsiang to resign as Party secretary general. The departure of Y. S., who was closer to Ching-kuo than most of the loyalists from the 1930s and 1940s, was related indirectly to the collapse of the country's largest savings and loan institution, the Tenth Credit Cooperative. The case involved almost US $200 million in illegal loans, including some to government figures. Corruption had fatally crippled the Kuomintang on the mainland: now, just as the revelation of a renewed gang connection and an officially sanctioned murder had stunned the nation, a corruption case that rivaled anything in the days of H. H. Kung and T. V. Soong burst into public view.[1]

Ching-kuo called in the Finance and Economics ministers and they promptly resigned, a pattern never seen in the old mainland days. The more conservative banking and foreign exchange system that emerged from the scandal also reflected the President's usually suppressed preference for controls. Another explanation has been suggested for Y. S.'s fall from grace. According to one source close to Ching-kuo, the President had asked Y. S. to help look after Alex, and after the murder of Henry Liu, he felt that his friend had not done all he could have in this connection.[2]

The 74-year-old Ma Shu-li, Taiwan's unofficial ambassador to Japan, took over the post of secretary general. Ching-kuo told him that he was determined to implement a full range of democratic reforms over the next year or two.[3] To prepare the way, he asked Ma to convene ad hoc study groups for informal discussion of political change. C. K. Yen agreed to chair these small, unofficial meetings, which usually consisted of only four or five persons who "brain stormed" the positive and negative consequences of specific political reforms. The participants included Standing Committee members, ranking military and security officers, both young and old Ching-kuo Turks, aging conservatives from the Legislative Yuan and National Assembly, and finally, respected academics.[4]

Ching-kuo did not himself meet with these groups. Instead, he followed up by inviting one or two individuals at a time to his bedside.[5] When the chosen guests arrived, the President would push the button on his hospital bed and rise to a sitting position. "Excuse us, Doctor," he would say to Dr. Chiang, "we have some important matters to discuss."[6] The "discussions" were mostly one-sided, with Ching-kuo asking all the questions. Whatever the guests' views, invitations to the bedside flattered the recipients.

Although the Minister of Interior ordered the opposition Non-Party Public Association to disband, its leaders refused to do so. The KMT nevertheless continued the discussions, which gave a measure of legitimacy to the "nonparty" party.[7] After the Henry Liu murder trials ended, the Garrison Command renewed its campaign against the anti-KMT press. Between May and October it seized 976,000 copies of provocative journals.[8] But despite bannings, confiscation of issues, and libel suits, the rump opposition press in Taiwan and various media in Hong Kong continued to run daily stories on the Liu murder case, the financial scandals, and the endless rumors concerning Alex Chiang. Muckraking stories about the Chiangs, including Faina and the family finances, now became commonplace.[9] Copies of Henry Liu's biography of Ching-kuo were widely available in Taiwan, as was Sterling Seagrave's scathing, one-sided saga entitled *The Soong Dynasty*.[10]

WHILE PREOCCUPIED with his own domestic politics, Ching-kuo closely followed the tug of war in China between conservatives and liberals.[11] In June a mainland magazine began carrying a series of favorable recollections about Chiang Ching-kuo written by old comrades.[12] In November Lee Kuan-yew made his first announced trip to Taiwan. From Taipei he went to China for the third time, and on his way back to Singapore he seems to have made another of his unannounced stops in Taipei. During a December 5 meeting with David Dean, Ching-kuo casually commented that when Lee Kuan-yew was recently in town he had relayed Deng Xiaoping's personal regards.[13] Shortly after Lee's visit, Ma Shu-li was reading a report to the President on some mainland development. Ching-kuo waved his hand to interrupt. "Don't say 'bandit' *(kung fei)* anymore," he said, referring to the standard term in Taiwan for the long-time enemy. "Say 'Communist.' "[14]

On April 28 Economics Minister Li Ta-hai publicly reiterated what he said was the government's "long-standing policy" of *not* interfering with indirect trade with the mainland. He cited a think-tank report that concluded government control of such trade was neither necessary nor possible. The same government-funded think-tank announced a new quarterly journal providing information on markets in China. In addition to thousands of clandestine family visits, hundreds of Taiwan business persons were already "traveling illegally" to China via Hong Kong. One legislator publicly hailed the traffic as "a successful landing on the mainland."[15] The official estimate for the flow of goods in 1985—about 80 percent in the form of Taiwan exports—was US $700 million. A style of youth culture called "Hong Kong-Taiwan" (in Mandarin, "Gang-Tai"), in music, movies, karaoke bars, haircuts, and mod apparel, was spreading like wildfire among Chinese youth on the mainland, something previously unheard of in Communist China.[16] Even more striking were published reports that some Taiwan businessmen had already opened factories in China, primarily in Fukien, making items such as dresses, shoes, and sanitary napkins.[17] In 1985 direct investments in China from Hong Kong totaled almost $1 billion. For the first time, there was an estimated figure for such investments from Taiwan—US $500,000.[18]

AT 81, DENG XIAOPING WAS SIX YEARS OLDER than Ching-kuo. During his lifetime he had consumed as much alcohol as had his erstwhile friend and KMT counterpart and was still a heavy smoker. But he had a stronger constitution. In September of 1985 Deng retired from daily administration, although as unofficial "paramount leader" he continued as the supreme military and political authority.

In Taipei that summer, eye specialists determined that Ching-kuo's deteriorating retinas required another operation. Two local eye surgeons performed the procedure. After this operation, Ching-kuo's heath accelerated on its downhill course. Neuropathy in his lower legs increased.[19] Even with the assistance of young aides, he could hardly make it up the steps to the third floor meeting room in the old KMT headquarters building in downtown Taipei. Ma Shu-li proposed that the Party build an elevator, but Ching-kuo refused. Instead, the meetings moved to the Government Guest House. But after a while the President thought it was not appropriate to have Party meetings in a government building, and he agreed to installation of the elevator.[20]

His illness prompted Ching-kuo to increase efforts to prepare Vice President Lee Teng-hui for the presidency, and the two spent more time together, although Lee never entered the bedroom inner sanctum, which was for mainlanders only. Concerned that Lee had virtually no ties with the military, Ching-kuo told his Armed Forces Chief of Staff to talk to him more often. A month later he repeated the injunction, specifically asking General Hao to speak with Lee about the handling of the Henry Liu case.[21] Hao Pei-ts'un followed up, and he and Lee established a good relationship. The President arranged for Lee to take his place in addressing the graduates of the Political Warfare College and on a number of other prominent state occasions. To demonstrate Lee's ability to handle foreign affairs, Ching-kuo sent him on a three-week official tour of Central America, visiting the few countries in that hemisphere still in Taiwan's diplomatic ambit—Costa Rica, Panama, and Guatemala.[22] Ching-kuo also told Jim Lilley, the senior American official on the island, that he would like him to get to know Lee on a private basis, "without others hanging around." Lilley and Lee soon became good friends, once going with their wives on a three-day trip around the island.[23]

But questions remained about the succession. Some political analysts in Taiwan and abroad were saying that when Ching-kuo died, Lee Teng-hui would become a mere figurehead. Control of the Kuomintang would be key in the post-Ching-kuo era, and many still saw succession in this sector going to a Chiang family or military figure. "We don't see Lee as a tough guy who can beat back the tough guys from the mainland," was a typical comment.[24] A few observers even continued to view Alex Chiang as a possible successor: because of his family name, he "could add a note of stability when the time for change comes."[25] But increasingly speculation focused on the youngest son, Eddy.

Following the Henry Liu murder and Ching-kuo's new mistrust of the intelligence organs, Eddy became his father's confidant, briefing him every Tuesday and Friday on the latest political developments. Some opposition journalist began calling Eddy "the underground president."[26] To clarify matters, in an August interview with *Time* magazine, the President said that he had "never given any consideration" to the possibility of a succession to the presidency by a member of the Chiang family.[27] When Ching-kuo learned that both Alex and Eddy were intending to run for the KMT Central Committee, he told Ma Shu-li, as secretary general, to put a stop to it.[28] In a December 25 address to the National Assembly, he was even more categorical. Answering his own rhetorical question about whether there could be a family successor or military rule after his departure, he replied to both: "It can't be and it won't be."[29] Shortly thereafter, Ching-kuo sent Alex into virtual exile as Taiwan's deputy representative in Singapore, where Lee Kuan-yew promised to "look after him."

HALFWAY ACROSS THE GLOBE, in the capital city on the frozen Moscow River, another leadership succession came to completion. After the truncated reigns of Konstantin Chernenko and Yuri Andropov, Mikhail Gorbachev at 55 became the General Secretary of the Communist Party of the Soviet Union. Gorbachev and his like-minded friends thought that "everything pertaining to the economy, culture, democracy, and foreign policy—all spheres—had to be reappraised" and reformed. His astounding effort to put a human and democratic face on Soviet communism would eventually lead to the demise of the system itself. In the near term, his reforms added history-bending momentum to democratic movements in Eastern Europe, the Philippines, China, and Taiwan.[30]

In 1985 the KMT began to advance more openly the view that Ching-kuo and Lee Kuan-yew had been slowly evolving over the previous several years, which saw the possibility of profound change on the mainland. Shaw Yu-ming, a University of Chicago scholar who had returned to head the Institute of International Affairs, publicly argued not only that the CCP would have to adopt fundamental political reforms to survive, but that it was in fact capable of doing so.[31] "We believe that the opening of reform (on the mainland) will produce a kind of revolution of rising expectations which will seriously shake the political and ideological foundations of the communist government *as it is constituted today* [emphasis added], that for the sake of survival the Chinese people and their communist leaders will have to look for other models of state building and government administration."[32]

BY THE END OF 1985 more than a million foreign tourists and business persons were visiting the island each year. At the same time, tens of thousands of Taiwan citizens were traveling abroad, including the increasing numbers slipping off to the mainland. More and more Taiwan residents had money for such travel. In 1985, dividing the total national income by the entire population of 19 million produced a figure over US $3,000. The 1985 drop in world oil prices was a further boost to Taiwan's economy and the NT dollar. The cabinet decided to reduce gasoline prices for the public by NT $1. Ching-kuo said this was not enough and the cabinet increased the reduction to NT $3.[33]

The same year was also "a pretty good year for China's reformers." Deng trimmed his sails and tacked into a brisk ideological wind, holding his "Second Revolution" more or less steadily—if flexibly—on course.[34] By the new year, "spiritual pollution" and "bourgeois liberalism" were virtually dead issues. Hu Yao-pang asserted that a high degree of democracy was "one of the great objectives of socialism," and, in an intriguing echo of the imprisoned Wei Ching-sheng, declared that "without democracy there is no modernization." Even the director of the Marxism-Leninism Mao Zedong Thought Institute, Su Shao-chih, published excited articles calling for democratic reform and personal freedom. Gorbachev's idea that it was possible to humanize and democratize communism had found fertile soil in China among youth and intellectuals and even among some at the top of the old party of Mao Zedong.[35]

But at the pinnacle there was doubt. Deng at one point had seemed to believe that a controlled, Singapore-type democratization of the Party was necessary to prevent great abuses of power such as those of Stalin and Mao. But all along he had assumed that transplanting a small democratic heart into the Party would not threaten its monopoly of power, much less end its reign. Now, he was less certain. Through the first eight months of 1986 Deng continued to call for political reform, but he increasingly stressed reform of the structure rather than the system.

—

THROUGHOUT THESE YEARS, pro-government as well as opposition media people, politicians, and commentators in Taiwan had given extensive coverage to the unfolding *Zeitgeist* of human rights in China. Thus it became more and more difficult for KMT conservatives to oppose the emergence of a similar spirit on the island. A large nonpolitical sphere had always existed in Taiwan. But this traditional civil society was rather narrow in its differentiation, focusing on family, clan, religion, hobbies, and work. It did not contain groups willing to take on the government. But with expanding affluence, education, and urbanization, civil society on the island was rapidly expanding into more controversial areas. The Consumers' Foundation, established in 1980, mobilized public support on questions such as the price of rice and nuclear power. Local and national anti-pollution organizations soon appeared, including militant ones with international links, such as the Taiwan Greenpeace Organization. Likewise, by 1985 there was an active women's movement and an Aborigine Human Rights Movement. Moreover, the rapidly increasing number of labor disputes reflected the erosion of KMT and management-dominated unions.[36] The push for civil rights could not be stopped.

Ching-kuo's band of scholar-officials believed that they were riding this democratic wave of history, but that only he could navigate through the shoals and persuade the Kuomintang and the entrenched mainlanders on Taiwan to abandon their dictatorial power of their own accord. The Wang Sheng affair and the Henry Liu debacle had under-scored that the potential was still there for a reactionary takeover after Ching-kuo's death. Such a move, the reformers feared, would probably find support from some members of the Chiang family.

Chiang Wei-kuo was due to retire from the army. Ching-kuo sug-gested he become ambassador to Saudi Arabia or South Korea, but Wei-kuo declined.[37] Finally, Ching-kuo agreed to name him secretary general of Taiwan's National Security Council. This gave Wei-kuo political stand-ing and kept him in the country and involved in national affairs. The pos-sibility had apparently occurred to Wei-kuo and his friends that on the death of his ailing stepbrother, the KMT leadership might turn to him to head the Party. But the President himself believed nothing could be more disastrous for the country and the Party.

Ching-kuo wished he had more years to implement his plans, but he knew his time was quickly passing. On April 18, as a result of cardiac arrhythmia, his heartbeat became dangerously low—about 20 or 30 beats per minute. Dr. Chiang Bi-ling decided that his patient needed a pacemaker.[38] Before he went into the operating room, Ching-kuo noti-fied only five senior officials; his designated successor Lee Teng-hui was not among them. With the major series of reforms pending, the Presi-dent felt it was too delicate a time to let it be known, even to many of his closest companions, that he would be out of action for some time.[39] After the operation the President's heartbeat returned to normal, but he still complained of shortness of breath.[40] The Central News Agency reported the operation on August 26. At this point, the President finally began to use a wheelchair in public, but to visitors he still appeared "alert and always well briefed."[41]

He regularly asked James Soong for a run down on what the opposi-tion journals were saying.[42] One example illustrates his continuing high level of engagement and political knowledge. Before the city and county-level elections in February 1986, he predicted that the KMT candidates for magistrate in Changhua and Chiayi counties would lose badly, and recommended to Secretary General Ma Shu-li that the Party nominate no one in these races. But when the local Party organizations resisted, Ching-kuo accepted a compromise. The Changhua KMT committee did not name a candidate but Chiayi did; he went on to suffer a bad defeat.[43] Overall, however, the KMT again did well at the polls—a large turnout gave the ruling (and officially still the only legal) party more than two thirds of city and county council seats. The next month, the KMT Central Committee elected new members to the Standing Committee, bringing representation of the provincials up, just shy of fifty percent (14 out of 31).

HAVING WORKED AT BUILDING CONSENSUS within the Party for almost a year, Ching-kuo was ready to advance to the next stage, actual implementation of fundamental as distinct from incremental changes. At his behest, the Standing Committee established a new political reform committee of 24 people, divided into two task forces of 12 each. Each subgroup had three issues with which to deal. The three most important areas of reform again bore titles that did not refer directly to the key changes that were to be explored: "revision of national security laws" really meant ending martial law; "reinvigoration of the parliamentary bodies" meant ending the reign of the entrenched mainlander solons; and "research on the question of civil organizations" meant legalization of opposition parties.[44]

Abolition of martial law was the key reform. Once the government gave up its "emergency" powers, the ban on opposition parties and other limitations on democracy could no longer be rationalized. Some of the middle-aged Young Turks like Fred Chien had for several years been telling the President that martial law was unnecessary; its existence only gave ammunition to the government's critics. Taiwan, they argued, did not implement most aspects of martial law anyway. There was no curfew, and only four offenses were subject to military trial. In the past Ching-kuo had responded that "if we end martial law, the government will no longer be secure." But now it was time to end martial law. He sent word via his son Eddy to Fred Chien in Washington that Fred had been right.[45]

Still, the forces of inertia were powerful. Despite Ching-kuo's efforts and those of Ma Shu-li over the previous year, most Standing Committee members, not merely the extreme right-wing minority, saw their futures threatened by a truly democratic system. The aging Yuan and Assembly representatives, of course, were as adamantly opposed as ever.[46] The select consensus-building discussion groups chaired by C. K. Yen continued, until in the middle of one session Yen keeled over with a stroke. After that there were no more of these gatherings. Instead, Ching-kuo continued to massage the reactionaries during informal meetings at his residence and occasionally even ventured out to visit the wizened patriarchs who were even more infirm than he.

In these discussions Ching-kuo "acted as if his interlocutors were his superiors" and sought their advice. He could have issued an emergency edict and dismissed the Yuans and the National Assembly, but he felt he had to work within the legal and constitutional system he and his father had set up and under which they had ruled. It was critical, he believed, that the transition to a rule-of-law and democratic society be constitutional.[47] It would have been impolite and impolitic for any of Ching-kuo's interlocutors in their discussions to have openly opposed the idea of a real and final transition to democracy. This was especially true of the ranking military and security officials, all of whom were Ching-kuo appointees. Thus they contented themselves with pointing out the problems and dangers inherent in each of the proposed reforms. For example, Minister of Defense Admiral Sung Ch'ang-chih warned of possible destabilization if martial law was lifted. But he did not oppose it; he simply warned, "we must take care."[48]

25

Breakthrough

IN THE SUMMER OF 1986 Lee Kuan-yew returned to Taiwan for a three-day visit and met privately with Chiang Ching-kuo for long discussions on mainland developments. Ching-kuo updated Lee on his plans to transform the political system on Taiwan, and the two friends exchanged views on how these reforms would lend momentum to the growing ethos of democracy on the mainland. Ironically, Ching-kuo's program would make Taiwan more democratic than Singapore. In fact, in terms of freedom of speech and the press, it already was.

IN JUNE, DURING A PRIVATE MEETING in his bedroom, Ching-kuo impatiently reiterated his determination to introduce "step by step" a four-point plan for political reform, but it appears he intended to announce these reforms in 1987, after the December 1986 parliamentary elections.[1] Meanwhile, the native Taiwanese nonparty leaders, under increasing attack from militants for being too soft, decided it was time to push the process forward with a bold move. The dramatic advance of pro-democracy movements in both Peking and Moscow convinced them that the KMT would be extremely reluctant at this time to be seen cracking down on a democratic opposition at home. On September 28, as 135 members of the informal opposition met at the Grand Hotel, the non-party leaders surprised the assembled members by suddenly proposing a resolution to establish as of that day a new Democratic Progressive Party (DPP). The excited delegates passed the motion overwhelmingly. The platform of the new party demanded "self determination" for the people of Taiwan.

When an aide rushed into Ching-kuo's bedroom to inform him of the news, he nodded but did not react. Half an hour later he told the aide to call a meeting of the core group of senior officials. The luminaries of the Party, government, and military soon gathered expectantly in a small reception room in the residence. The President arrived in his wheelchair. "Times are changing," he said, " the environment is changing, the tide is also changing." He went on for some minutes in this philosophical vein. In the past, he said, the KMT had been "too proud and conceited"; now it "cannot act as before."[2] Although the Garrison Command had prepared an arrest list, Ching-kuo said there would be no detentions. "To arrest people cannot solve a problem. . . . The government should avoid conflict and remain calm."[3] He ordered the GIO to prepare an official announcement saying that the question of the formation of new political parties was being studied, and pending a decision, the current policy would continue in effect: that is, there would be no legal opposition parties. Therefore the government would not recognize the DPP at this time. The KMT Standing Committee, he added, should expedite its study of political reform and publish a timetable so that the public could understand the reformist direction the Party was taking.[4]

The Garrison Command had already called all the daily newspapers "suggesting" that they not publish the DPP announcement. Yu Chi-chung, the publisher of the Chinese-language *China Times* and a member of the Standing Committee, had told the caller that his paper would carry the report in the morning.[5] The next day, when the Standing Committee formally met to discuss the question, Ching-kuo repeated his declaration on the changing tide in human affairs. There was no further discussion. The government would not recognize the DPP until proper procedures were completed, but it would not in the meantime take any legal action against its members. No one at the meeting voiced criticism of the President's decision.[6] By contrast, a subsequent meeting of the honorary Central Advisory Committee, to which Ching-kuo had consigned many of the aging die-hards, including a number of former Blue Shirts, was a raucous affair. During the discussion of the DPP issue, some of the elders shouted "p'an kuo . . . p'an kuo" (treason, treason!).[7]

Radical mainlander groups like the Iron Blood Patriots held rallies denouncing the opposition's move and writing petitions in their own blood demanding the government arrest the leaders for sedition.[8] "Ching-kuo is too soft," elders complained to James Soong. "He should be like his father! Throw them [the oppositionists] in the sea!" When Soong reported these remarks to Ching-kuo, he said, "they're still complaining, are they? Well, be nice to them, but remain firm."[9] Since Ching-kuo was planning to legalize the opposition soon, he was not about to order another mass arrest that would provoke wide criticism and make it appear that Taiwan was going against the democratic current. "It is easy to use power," he told an aide, "but it is hard to know when not to use it."[10]

MAINLAND CONSERVATIVES were as upset by the liberal trend of domestic politics as were the hard-liners on Taiwan. CCP stalwarts viewed with dismay the beginnings of an unraveling of power in Russia. *Glasnost* had let loose a flood of open attacks on the Communist Party of the Soviet Union and revelations of the horrendous crimes of the past. Deng himself took alarm and began to view the democratic current as a potentially disastrous deluge that could inundate the mighty CCP. There were also elements of personal power and pride in Deng's reaction. Ruan Ming, then deputy director of the CCP's theoretical research department, believes that Deng's family and aides were afraid the democratization process would lead to his total loss of power and that this would strip them of influence and privilege.[11] For several years Deng had talked about his imminent retirement, but when in 1986 Hu Yao-pang began urging him actually to give up power, he became resentful and suspicious.[12] At the September CCP Plenum, Deng stressed the danger of losing control through political reform. Perhaps in indirect reaction to Ching-kuo and Lee Kuan-yew's strategy for encouraging change in

China, he warned that "speechifiers of Taiwan and Hong Kong . . . want us to practice bourgeois liberalism and accuse us of violating human rights." Among the masses, he cautioned, and especially the youth, there is a "trend in favor of liberalism."[13]

Despite Deng's warnings, the September plenum actually represented a high point for the reformers. The plenum called for cultural and artistic freedom and declared that China's opening to the world took place in ideological and cultural realms as much as in economic and technical ones. The informal and spontaneous democratic movement began to spread across the campuses and press rooms of China.[14] The Chinese public's admiration of Gorbachev shot up further when he announced the beginning of Soviet troop withdrawal from Afghanistan and indicated that some Red Army units in Mongolia might be withdrawn. Gorbachev even offered unilateral concessions on the Sino-Soviet frontier dispute. Moscow and Peking soon announced renewal of the border negotiations that had been broken off in 1978.[15]

The events in China and Russia had been very much on Ching-kuo's mind when he took no action against the "illegal" formation of the DPP in September, and they were again the following month, when he made an informal but major announcement. During a meeting on October 7 with *Washington Post* publisher Katherine Graham, Ching-kuo surprised his aides as well as his visitor by announcing that his government intended to "propose" an end to martial law. Ching-kuo, whom the subsequent *Post* report described as "relaxed, self-assured and mentally acute," also said the KMT was "vigorously" studying the question of legalizing new political parties and that he expected it would come to a conclusion very soon.[16] On October 15 the President told the Standing Committee that the KMT "must adopt new ideas and measures to meet the needs of an ever-changing situation."[17] The committee dutifully approved proposals to enact a new National Security Law to replace martial law, and to revise statutes governing civic organizations and elections to allow for the formation of new political parties.

Chiang was confident that a deep commitment to the "the system" by the military and security elites as well as by the legion of recalcitrants in the various national representative bodies would compel them to go along with a *fait accompli* on martial law.[18] But as the task force on the subject began drafting the National Security Act, ranking internal security officials suggested language that would have continued the government's broad authority to restrain freedom of speech whenever it chose. Ching-kuo dismissed the tactic. "That would simply be old wine in new bottles," he said.[19]

———

AT THE END OF OCTOBER Ching-kuo went to the airport to greet a visitor—his stepmother. For the first time in almost a decade, Madame Chiang Kai-shek, 85 years old, was returning to Taiwan. The announced reason was to attend the 100th anniversary (by Chinese calculation) of the birth of the Generalissimo, on October 31. The free-ranging press immediately speculated, however, that the conservatives had urged her to return to help slow down the avalanche of reform that seemed about to tumble down on top of them. One opposition journalist, Antonio Chiang, suggested that she intended to round up support for a family succession.[20]

After paying respects to her late husband's remains, Madame Chiang in fact did not fly back to the comforts of Long Island, but settled down for a prolonged stay at the old presidential residence in Shihlin. There she gave tea parties for selected government, military, and Party officials. To her, the political scene must have seemed dangerously out of control. She believed her son-in-law, in his final years, was slipping. On the eve of the December 6 elections, the major newspapers carried an article by Madame Chiang which reflected the fears of the conservatives. "There is instant coffee and there is instant tea," she wrote. "But only charlatanry can provide instant democracy. What the wildly ambitious want is to profit from anarchy, not law and order."[21]

Indeed, the campaign underway was as wild as any in the United States. Candidates unfurled banners reading "Oppose the Chiang Family" and "Oppose All Tyranny." Some cartoons of Ching-kuo portrayed him as a lackey of the United States; others as a pig. Some candidates openly referred to the President as "Piggy."[22] This was the end of the imperial presidency on Taiwan and a historic milestone in Chinese democracy—the great leader could be openly criticized and even mocked.

Protesters did not limit themselves to rhetoric. They burned the Kuomintang/national flag, and someone tossed a bomb into the courtyard of the KMT headquarters in Taipei. Martial law was still in effect, and the Garrison Command again urged the President to approve arrests of selected DPP leaders. Ching-kuo again refused. Instead, he ordered the release of 13 more political prisoners, leaving 110 oppositionists in jail.[23]

Shortly before polling day, Hsu Hsin-liang, the former T'aoyuan magistrate who had the famous 1978 birthday party in Chungli, tried to return to Taiwan. Charged with treason, Hsu had fled the country after the Kaohsiung riots. He now wanted to fly back to Taipei, hoping the authorities would arrest him, thereby creating sympathy for the opposition. The government, however, refused to allow the fugitive to return. When Hsu landed at Chiang Kai-shek International Airport without a valid entry visa, riot police protecting the approaches to the terminal hosed and tear-gassed a huge crowd of stone throwing DPP supporters. Hsu was immediately bundled onto a plane and flown out of the country. Both sides rushed out videos to prove the other had been responsible for the violence at the airport. The KMT controlled the TV and radio stations and won the argument.[24]

The Kuomintang obtained 70 percent of the popular vote and 59 of the 73 contested seats in the Legislative Yuan. The DPP could nonetheless point to the fact that only three months after its formation, the Party had established itself as the dominant force on the opposition side and had won 23 of the 44 seats it contested. Despite the DPP's bitter attacks on the undemocratic nature of the national elected bodies, its successful candidates promptly took their seats and abided by the house rules—most, although not all of the time. Ching-kuo was pleased with the results. In his New Year's message, he was upbeat and conciliatory, stressing a favorite image: "We must understand we are in the same boat, and we must help each other to achieve harmony in good faith and in a forgiving spirit. Rationalism dissolves extremism. We must muster the will and wisdom of all the people as the moving force for a complete reformation."[25]

Throughout the world news media reported the free, democratic elections in Taiwan. Chinese on the mainland also heard the news, via VOA and BBC broadcasts as well as directly from Taiwan. Three days after the Taiwan poll, students took to the streets of Hefei in Anhui Province, shouting slogans such as "We want democracy!" "No democracy, no modernization!" Demonstrations spread to Shenzhen on December 14, Shanghai on the 19th, and Canton on the 20th. Some banners asked why the CCP was not as successful as the KMT in promoting democracy and prosperity. CCP conservatives accused Taiwan's Radio Free China of encouraging the demonstrators.[26]

As he did periodically, Ching-kuo called in Shaw Yu-ming to discuss the events in China, in particular the reported pro-Taiwan aspects of the recent demonstrations. Shaw compared the young protesters in Shanghai to student activists in the Cultural Revolution in the 1960s. Ching-kuo disagreed. In the Cultural Revolution, he said, the participants were mostly juveniles. The current demonstrators were college students. This was a more serious expression of intellectual and political ferment.[27]

IN NOVEMBER, at a CCP Secretariat meeting, there had been an angry exchange between Deng and Hu.[28] Following the Taiwan elections and the subsequent student demonstrations on the mainland, Deng Xiaoping turned against the democratic cause. At a December 30 meeting he sounded like the most hard-shell KMT veteran: "We must adopt dictatorial measures that must not only be talked about but used when necessary . . . our method is to expose the conspiracy and avoid bloodshed and be willing to sustain some injuries. Nevertheless, those who are leaders of these chaotic incidents must be dealt with according to the law. If we don't take any measures and we retreat, we'll only be confronted with more troubles later."[29]

The student unrest, however, spread to Peking. Deng called a special Party meeting on January 7, 1987, during which he accused Hu Yao-pang of failure to deal resolutely with the young demonstrators. Hu lost his position as CCP chairman although he retained his seat in the Politburo. Chao Tzu-yang took over as Party leader. Deng, for the third time in the 1980s, ordered a campaign against "bourgeois liberalization."[30]

ON FEBRUARY 5, when the KMT announced another reshuffle of senior cadre, Western observers noted that Ching-kuo was stacking "the upper echelons of the Party with a new generation of pragmatists."[31] James Soong and Kao Ming-hui joined Ma Ying-jeou as deputy secretaries general (Kao was a Taiwanese with a Ph.D. from Southern Illinois University). Lien Chan, another Taiwanese, moved up to Vice Premier. The University of Chicago-educated China watcher, Shaw Yu-ming, took over as GIO director.

Yet Ching-kuo continued to show Confucian respect for the aging old guard. With his nod, the Party re-elected the incumbent president and vice president of the Legislative Yuan, 82 and 77 years of age respectively. But this was a tactical concession. Developments on the mainland and the shadow of his own death spurred on the President to work to complete the reform process in 1987.

He now spent most of his waking hours in bed or in his wheelchair. He still came to the weekly Standing Committee meetings, usually the first to arrive so that his aides could wheel him in unseen. The other members understood they were to leave before he did. His remarks lasted no more than 5 or 10 minutes, and his notes were in inch-high characters. He was nearly blind in the left eye and had very limited vision in the right. There was an oversized wall clock in his bedroom so he could tell the time. He told Dr. Chiang, "I feel like an old lamp down to its last drops of oil."[32] He continued his consultations lying in bed. But he also spent many hours alone in his room. Unable to read, he looked out his window and thought about what he must do in the little time left.[33] While he did not think his death was imminent, he knew he could not live more than a year or two at the most.[34]

Ching-kuo was pleased with Taiwan's relations with America and indeed its position in the world. In the spring he told David Dean that relations with the United States were "better than any time before," including the 1950s.[35] Because of the nonofficial nature of United States-Taiwan relations, the world now viewed the Nationalist government as an autonomous and increasingly important world actor. In the long run, presidents Nixon and Carter, he believed, had done Taiwan a favor. They had given the island an unprecedented status and prestige. Moreover, they had given the Taiwanese people, when offered a free choice, reason to support KMT governance and for the foreseeable future to reject the independence option.[36] In May Ching-kuo ordered the release of all but one of the remaining prisoners from the Kaohsiung trials of 1980. The exception was Shih Ming-te.

—

GETTING THE SECRET INTELLIGENCE AGENCIES under control was not easy. It had been more than two years since the President had ordered fundamental changes in the clandestine services, but it was necessary for him to repeat his instructions over and over again. In August 1985 he had instructed the Military Intelligence Bureau to cut all its ties with irregulars in the Golden Triangle and with gang members in Taiwan. In December that year, he again ordered the NSB and the military intelligence not to conduct "any intelligence collection in the United States." Three months later he issued new instructions to the NSB on its tasks and told the new director, Sung Hsin-lien, not to call joint meetings with KMT, government, and military officials. In September 1986 he had to instruct Hao Pei-ts'un once more to tell Sung Hsin-lien that his organization should not recruit spies in America. Such operations, the President said, "do not bring us any benefit but will only unnecessarily trouble U.S.-Taiwan relations."[37]

Right-wing parliamentarians responded to the increasing street demonstrations of the DPP by energizing existing organizations like the Iron Blood Patriots, and forming new groups of agitators. Two front organizations emerged early in the year embracing most of these groups. One called itself the Anti-Communist Patriotic Front (AFP) and the other the Republic of China Patriotic Society (PS). Some analysts charged that these fronts received financial support not only from conservatives in the KMT and the representative organs but also from the military and intelligence apparatus. Whenever the DPP held a rally, the rightists would hold a counter-rally. Sometimes violence broke out between the groups, as on June 12 in front of the Legislative Yuan.[38]

In the one year that had passed since Ching-kuo had appointed the Standing Committee task forces on reform, the government had still not formally implemented the promised changes legalizing opposition parties and ending martial law. In May 1987 Ching-kuo asked Minister of Education Lee Huan if he would become secretary general of the Party. Ma Shu-li was now 76 and worn out by the twelve-hour, seven-day-a-week job.[39] Following standard practice, Lee, who was himself 70 years of age, demurred. But the President insisted. During a long talk Ching-kuo told his old friend that he was impatient with the endless foot-dragging. He had three goals he wanted him to fulfill.[40]

First, the KMT required fundamental reorganization to compete in a fully open political system. "If we do not rejuvenate the KMT," he said, "people will give up on the Party . . . even its members will drift away." The second goal was "full political democracy." This meant lifting martial law, allowing people to form their own political parties, having a fully elected parliament, and, finally, lifting restrictions on the press.

The third objective was "reunification across the Strait." This was his most explicit and strongest comment indicating that he saw both the necessity and the opportunity for a nominal unification within a foresee-able time frame, even possibly within the short time remaining to him. "We have to take initiatives to put us on the road to reunification," he told Lee. "Taiwan and the mainland must eventually unify. If they do not, Tai-wan will find it harder and harder to exist independently."

American policy also took a nuanced turn on the question of reunifi-cation. Conservatives like Assistant Secretary Paul Wolfowitz wanted good relations with China but thought this was not so important as to warrant undermining the options for Taiwan, including eventually inde-pendence, although this was left unsaid. They were not prepared to encourage the island to explore openings with the mainland. After Wol-fowitz's departure, there was a swing back to underscoring the principle of one China as well as the requirement that it be pursued peacefully. Thus it followed that America would welcome any progress the two sides made in this direction. In Shanghai on March 5, Secretary of State George Shultz said that "one China and a peaceful resolution of the Tai-wan question [remained] the core" of American policy. The United States, Shultz declared, supported "a continuing evolutionary process towards a peaceful resolution of the Taiwan issue," and America would seek "to foster an environment in which such developments can continue to take place."[41] The State Department informed Fred Chien in advance of the Secretary's remarks in Shanghai. Chien "hit the roof," charging this amounted to pressure on Taiwan to negotiate with Peking. The next day Jim Lilley informed Ching-kuo at Seven Seas. Ching-kuo smiled. "Okay," he said, "that's fine."[42] Shultz's pronouncement was consistent with Ching-kuo's own determination to lend momentum to the cross-Straits process, thereby encouraging the democratic movement on the mainland.

About this time Deng Xiaoping met with a visiting professor from the University of Virginia, Shao-chuan Leng, who was C. K. Yen's son-in-law. Deng asked the professor to tell Lee Huan that he would send Yang Shang-k'un to meet with him at a time and place of Lee's choosing. Leng relayed the message, and Lee Huan immediately reported it to Ching-kuo. At first, Ching-kuo made no response. Two days later he told Lee, "The timing is not yet right."[43]

Under pressure from Lee, on June 23 the Legislative Yuan passed the new National Security Law, and on July 7 it unanimously approved the lifting of the Emergency Decree "in the Taiwan area." Shaw Yu-ming suggested that Ching-kuo copy the practice of American presidents and at a dramatic press conference sign the order ending martial law. He proposed using multiple pens and handing them out to the legislators. Ching-kuo declined.[44]

On July 14 the new law quietly went into effect. The cabinet transferred all criminal cases not involving military personnel to civilian courts. The new statute still prohibited advocacy of "independence," but this exception to free speech in reality had little effect except to provoke criticism. The few times it was enforced, the effort boomeranged. The DPP continued officially and vociferously to advocate "self-determination." The government declared January 1, 1988, as the date for submission of applications for registration of new political parties. Actually, four other political groups had already followed the DPP lead and established parties without official sanction. One of these was an ultra-right, mainlander organization, the Democratic Freedom Party.[45]

Lee and Ching-kuo agreed that the old Leninist structure that Sun Yat-sen, under Borodin's guidance, had adopted for the KMT in 1924 was long outdated. The original Kuomintang, like the CCP, had been a revolutionary and ideological party. In both cases a historic mission was used to justify a monopoly of truth and virtue, which was hardly compatible with a diversified and democratic society and an open and competitive political system. To win popular support on Taiwan, the KMT had simply to demonstrate in a convincing manner that it could meet the everyday needs of the people better than its rivals. Under the influence of Ching-kuo's American-trained scholar-officials and the original "young Turks" like Lee Huan, the Kuomintang had been reshaping itself along these lines since the late 1960s. By 1987 the KMT was well on the way to becoming a modern political party, and a predominantly native Taiwanese one. The new KMT members of the Legislative Yuan, mostly young reformists, had won their seats in competitive campaigns against the DPP. Ching-kuo made plain he also wanted a more dynamic and open leadership structure inside the Party, stunning the Standing Committee by telling them they were too compliant and should speak out more.[46]

ALMOST EVERY MONTH some world event added to the growing sense that the era of dictatorships was coming to an end, and a Cambrian-like explosion of democratic forms was taking place. Following the 1987 Washington summit between Reagan and Gorbachev, the Cold War began rapidly to recede. The Soviets affirmed their desire to withdraw from Afghanistan. In South Korea strikes, student demonstrations, and a concern to remain host of the 1988 Olympics led to a peaceful transfer of power from military dictatorship to democracy.[47] Ching-kuo's image from a year before of the changing tide in human affairs seemed manifest. Of all the changes on Taiwan itself that year, the most dramatic was the opening of legal travel to the mainland.[48] The corps of arch-conservatives whose long lives had been devoted to hating and fighting the Communists believed that permission for such travel would betray the entire struggle. Ching-kuo, however, ordered the immediate end of the almost 40-year-old ban.[49] Over the next two months tens of thousands of Taiwan residents rushed to apply for permits. The President welcomed the overwhelming response, which was in fact a major aspect of his strategy to encourage change on the mainland. "There is no need to worry," he told his companions. "The visits will let people on Taiwan understand the situation on the mainland and vice versa."[50] Many travelers ignored the official restriction to family visits. One Taipei paper sent two reporters to Peking and printed their stories datelined in the Chinese capital. Literally thousands of Taiwan businessmen joined the mad rush across the Strait.[51] Hundreds and soon thousands more small Taiwan-financed factories and workshops turning out labor-intensive products sprouted up in Amoy and other coastal cities.

In October Lee Huan publicly declared that the KMT policy was no longer to seek to replace the Communist Party on the mainland, but to push for "political reforms, freedom of the press, and economic liberalization."[52] The right wing was again livid—the top executive of the KMT was abandoning the Party's historic commitment to the destruction of the CCP. But Ching-kuo told the seniors who came to his bedroom to complain that the people of the mainland had the right to decide whether they wanted the CCP, the KMT, or some other party to run the government.[53]

———

THE MOST DIFFICULT of all Ching-kuo's reforms involved the overhaul of the national representative bodies. Lee Huan asked Ma Ying-jeou to work with the task force assigned this mission. Ma warned Lee that he would probably "step on some toes," and then proceeded to draft a plan for "voluntary" retirement of all the mainland-elected members of the national bodies, providing them with handsome stipends and various fancy titles, for example, "adviser to the President." At the same time, conservatives were telling Ching-kuo that if all the mainland-elected Yuan and Assembly members were forced to retire, it would be necessary to allot a suitable number of seats in the new Parliament and Assembly to represent the mainland provinces. In one of his meetings with Ying-jeou, the President said, "I want you to find out if our government made any declaration when [in 1949] we moved the seat of government from the mainland to Taiwan regarding our continued representation of all of China." Ma researched the question and reported back that the ROC government had made no declaration that its elected bodies would continue to represent provinces on the mainland. The President said that in light of this fact, there should be no seats designated for mainland representation.[54]

On the 16th of December, Lee Kuan-yew and his wife arrived in Taipei for a five-day visit. He and Ching-kuo spent several hours in private, discussing events on the mainland. Lee apparently was guardedly optimistic that China could make the transition into a Singapore-like polity—a controlled democracy, but a democracy nonetheless. Despite Deng's concerns and the ouster of Hu Yao-pang, the liberal tide in China still seemed to be rising. At the CCP's 13th Congress in October, Chao Tzu-yang, as General-Secretary of the CCP, had proclaimed the urgency of political reform.[55] Ching-kuo was fascinated with the impact of developments in Russia. Gorbachev had sharply criticized Stalin, and Boris Yeltsin had lost his Party posts and assumed the mantle as leader of a growing popular movement.[56] Both Ching-kuo and Lee Kuan-yew believed a historic stage in Chinese history was approaching. Lee told Ching-kuo that if Taiwan and the mainland did not resolve their political differences, eventually there would be a military solution.[57] Ching-kuo was not feeling well and did not offer a dinner to his distinguished friend. Instead, he asked Ma Shu-li and Yu Kuo-hua to do the honors. Lee sadly observed the deterioration of his friend's physical condition.

FOR THE FIRST TIME in more than ten years, Madame Chiang hosted the Christmas eve dinner at Shihlin for family members who were in town—Ching-kuo and Faina, Alan, Nancy and Yomei, Eddy and his family, and Wei-kuo and his wife and son. Dr. Hsiung Yuan was also there. The twins and their families were, of course, not included. At one point, Ching-kuo and Dr. Hsiung were alone. The President, who had repeatedly refused to go into the hospital when his doctors recommended it, whispered, "I am very uncomfortable. Please ask if some specialists can give me a check up." Hsiung said he would immediately arrange for a medical team to see him.[58] The next day, Christmas day, Hsiung called Ching-kuo's office to confirm a date for his admission. The staff told him that the President wanted to delay going into the hospital. Christmas was

Constitution Day, and Chiang Ching-kuo had one last public occasion to attend.

The President ignored the entreaties of Lee Huan and others and insisted on participating in the traditional commemorative session of the National Assembly. "You're afraid they will beat me up, right?" he said. "Well, let them. We're going to honor the custom."[59] As he drove to the meeting, 3,000 chanting demonstrators converged on the Assembly building. Riot police and barbed wire held them at bay. A few miles away, 3,000 KMT supporters held a counterdemonstration. Inside the building, the eleven DPP Assembly members unfolded banners reading, "Old Thieves, Out!" The other 900-odd members, including the targets of these imperatives, looked nervously around the chamber. Few of those present knew that Ching-kuo had hoped by then to have announced the staged retirement of the surviving mainland-elected members and an open election for all Yuan and Assembly seats.

Waiting in the wings, Ching-kuo motioned to his aides to wheel him on stage. After the ovation died down, the handful of DPP members continued shouting. Chiang did not seem troubled by the protests and proceeded with a brief greeting to the Assembly. He then remained in his wheelchair while the secretary general of the Assembly read out the five-minute address Chiang had prepared. The speech noted that it was necessary to "improve the composition of the parliamentary bodies," but that such a change could not violate the Constitution, which stipulated that the Nationalist government was the sole legitimate government of all China. After Ching-kuo departed and the meeting adjourned, the DDP members joined the demonstrators outside for a march through downtown.[60] The President smiled benignly during the trip home. Shortly after this event, James Soong showed Ching-kuo a magazine with a cover story alleging that the President intended to build a luxurious mausoleum for himself. Chiang chuckled. "I have not even built a house for myself," he said. "Why would I build a great tomb?"[61]

THE YEAR OF 1987 had been a good year, and not only for political reform. Ching-kuo's investment in and encouragement of high-tech industries were paying off handsomely. Taiwan was now the globe's tenth largest exporter of manufactured goods. Its foreign exchange holdings were approaching US $40 billion, the largest per capita in the world. During the year, Taiwanese capitalists invested almost US $2 billion abroad, mostly on the mainland. The official jobless rate was 2.5 percent. Taiwan factories were importing foreign workers. Most astounding, the average household income had soared to almost US $5,000.[62]

The island was no longer a pariah state, a dependent satellite of the United States, or a reviled dictatorship. It was a model of economic growth and of a peaceful, if chaotic, democratic transition.

26

A Chinese Democracy

ON JANUARY 1, 1988, under Ching-kuo's instructions, the government's restriction on the number of newspapers allowed (29) and their page limit (12) officially ended. Within a few days, the government registered about 200 new publications. A large number of tabloids soon appeared on the streets. At the same time, more than 60 political groups applied to register as parties. Eventually, 20 followed through and actually formed organizations (the DPP among them). Despite these liberalization measures, there was still pent-up anger at the regime and its leaders. Many of the new papers and political parties were bitterly anti-KMT. Political invective swept over the island. In the first four months of the year, over 700 street demonstrations, mostly anti-KMT, took place. Inside the Legislative Yuan, when the DPP furiously opposed passage of new laws regulating public demonstrations, fistfights broke out in the hall.[1]

On January 12 the task force on parliamentary reform finally passed the proposal drafted by Ma Ying-jeou, ending the era of mainlander control of Taiwan's political process. Ma planned to see Ching-kuo the next day to report the good news. That morning the President complained of being uncomfortable. Although his doctors could find no apparent cause for his discomfort, they administered intravenous fluids. Ching-kuo asked to see his disabled son, Alan. When Alan emerged from the room, he told his mother that his father looked very ill. At about 1:50 in the afternoon, while Ching-kuo was napping, he suddenly suffered a severe hemorrhage of the gastrointestinal tract. Blood obstructed his breathing, and he went into shock. Because his pacemaker maintained his heartbeat at 70 per minute, the organ could not pump fast enough to supply needed oxygen throughout the body, and before the doctors could begin to move him to the hospital, he died of hypovolemic shock. It was, Dr. Hsiung recalls, a nice, sunny afternoon.[2]

The GIO announced the death of the President four hours later. At 9:00 PM, Lee Teng-hui took the oath of office as the fourth president of the Republic of China.[3] For the first time in its history the Republic was without a strong man, but there was hardly a ripple on the political scene. The next morning the cabinet met for its regular session and spent two hours discussing how to clean up a polluted river. At the passing of the Generalissimo thirteen years earlier, the press and ranking officials had employed the contrived language of the imperial court to describe the "greatness" of the departed ruler. But following Ching-kuo's death, for the first time in four thousand years the traditionally extravagant and quasi-religious titles and praise were absent. Instead, media commentary and individual eulogies focused on Chiang Ching-kuo's empathy for the common person.[4]

Unlike his father, Ching-kuo deliberately did not leave a last will for the instruction of the nation. The ranking coterie, believing they had to correct this fault, instructed Ching-kuo's secretary, Wang Chia-hua, to draft a document expressing the President's hope that the people would "uphold the anti-Communist national policy and thoroughly carry out constitutional democracy . . ." The GIO released the document with the explanation that the deceased President had dictated and signed it on January 5, in the presence of several notables and his son Eddy.[5]

Likewise, after his death, to embarrass the opposition, Kuomintang officials let out the story that the disruption at the Assembly on December 25 had hastened the President's death. But his aides say this was not the case. He had warned them that democracy was chaotic and sometimes rather unpleasant, especially to its leaders.

Chiang Ching-kuo would not have been pleased with these charades. But he would have been delighted to have seen K'ang Ning-hsiang and several other DPP leaders coming to the shrine to pay their last respects. Despite the bad blood between the KMT and its adversaries, Ching-kuo had in the end left behind a key requirement for a stable democracy—a certain level of civility and restraint among the contenders. The DPP and the tiny Labor Party announced they would cancel all political demonstrations during the 30-day mourning period.[6] On January 16 the High Court handed down stiff sentences to two opposition figures accused of directly and publicly advocating Taiwan independence. The DPP was furious, but still postponed street demonstrations to protest the decision.

———

THE DAY AFTER THE PRESIDENT'S DEATH, Lee Huan called his three deputies, Ma Ying-jeou, Kao Ming-hui, and James Soong to a 10:00 AM meeting in his office. Lee said it was now necessary to choose an acting Party chairman to serve until the July Party Congress. Lee Huan declared that he believed Lee Teng-hui should be both Party and government leader. This was Chiang Ching-kuo's wish. His three colleagues concurred. Ma, Kao, and Soong divided up the list of Standing Committee members and set out to inform them of Lee Huan's recommendation. The next day they reported back to Lee Huan that all the mainlander members of the Standing Committee accepted that Lee Teng-hui should be the chairman. Some Taiwanese members had reservations, but Lee Huan talked separately to them and each agreed to move ahead with the appointment.

As senior Standing Committee member, Premier Yu Kuo-hua would be the one to nominate Lee as the new chairman. But on January 24 Yu received a letter from Madame, advising that it would be better not to choose an interim Party leader. For Mei-ling and the Chiang Kai-shek old guard, the notion that a native Taiwanese would become both president and leader of the Party seemed the death knell of the KMT's historic role.[7] Yu informed Lee Huan, who said that in his opinion the committee should move ahead with the appointment of Lee Teng-hui as acting Party leader. Afterwards, Lee Huan said, he would resign and write to Madame to tell her he was sorry that he could not do as she requested. Yu agreed with this approach.

Lee Huan then went to see Lee Teng-hui, showed him the letter, and explained the situation. The new President understood he should assume a low posture. Earlier, on January 22, dressed in a traditional dark blue gown and short black jacket, he had presided over the transfer of Ching-kuo's body from the Veterans Hospital to the Martyrs' Shrine. There he conducted a brief ceremony to put the soul at ease *(an ling)*. Subsequently, he and other members of the funeral committee took turns maintaining a 24-hour vigil by the body. Meanwhile, Chief of Staff Hao Pei-ts'un and Defense Minister Cheng Wei-yuan issued a statement to confirm that the armed forces would uphold the late president's will and support his successor, Lee Teng-hui.

Lee Huan called a meeting of the Standing Committee for the 27th. At 3:00 AM on the morning of the 26th, Eddy Chiang telephoned Yu Kuo-hua at home to underscore that Madame Chiang did not want the appointment to go ahead. Shortly before the committee meeting the next day, Yu told Lee Huan it would be impolite for him abruptly to turn down Madame's repeated request. When the other committee members arrived and were informed of the situation, most said that the nomination of Lee Teng-hui should proceed. Hao Pei-ts'un and a few others, however, agreed with Yu that the decision could be delayed to accommodate the lady.[8] James Soong suddenly announced to the gathering that Comrade Yu would make the nomination for new Party chairman. Yu hesitated. After an awkward silence, Soong spoke regretting the indecision and walked out of the room. Yu Chi-chung commented: "we must go forward, not backward." Yu Kuo-hua suddenly stood up and made the expected nomination. All the members voted "yes," whereupon Lee Huan telephoned the news to Lee Teng-hui.[9]

The next day the new President and leader of the Kuomintang went to see the Madame and promised to carry out the legacy of Chiang Kai-shek and Chiang Ching-kuo. He then proceeded to the Revolutionary Martyrs' Shrine to pay his respects once again to the man who had chosen him for a historic role. By this time 1.2 million people had filed by the casket. On the morning of January 30, Faina and her children, Alan, Amy, Alex, and Eddy, one by one looked for the last time on the face of the dead leader, father, and husband. Alan made the traditional three kowtows. Only the family and a selected few, including Lee Kuan-yew, accompanied the body to its "temporary resting place," a small house called Touliao near his father's remains at Tzuhu.[10] A million persons lined the route. At 9:00 AM all but a few of the 20 million people on the island ceased whatever they were doing. Trains and buses stopped. The bells of every temple and church on Taiwan rang out a last farewell.

DENG XIAOPING HAD BEEN WORRIED for some months about Ching-kuo's health and the possibility that the situation in Taiwan would become more complicated after the death of his old classmate. As soon as he heard about it, he immediately called an enlarged meeting of the Politburo. After listening to reports by the Taiwan Affairs Office and the Taiwan Working Group, Deng said that the reunification of China was a great issue of worldwide importance. Were Chiang Ching-kuo still alive, "the reunification of China would not be as difficult and complicated as it is now. The KMT and the CCP have cooperated twice in the past. I just don't believe that there cannot be a third co-operation between us. It is a pity indeed that [Ching-kuo] died too early."[11]

Deng went on to say that Ching-kuo had adhered to his father's principle of only "one China," but the CCP over the years had also lost opportunities to work things out peacefully with the KMT leaders. Only recently, he lamented, had Peking come up with the "correct road, namely, the principle of 'one country, two systems.'" He implied that it had carried the possibility of serious progress: "Although the KMT members seemed indifferent to this offer made by our Party, they have after all considered it seriously! There is a great divergence of views within the KMT!"[12]

A few months later, when Hu Yao-bang's replacement as Secretary General of the CCP, Chao Tzu-yang, was under severe criticism because of the failure of price reform, one of his supporters, journalist Tai Ch'ing, argued that China needed a benign autocratic leader like Chiang Ching-kuo:

> When Chiang died, mourners lined the street in the thousands. . . . All the fresh flowers on the island renowned for its abundance of flowers were sold out. Why? He arranged for an end to the rule of his own family and lifted the

bans on opposition parties and restrictions on the press. "All right, I am an autocrat, but I am the last. I am using my power to ensure the introduction of democracy." . . . Given our unique situation, only an enlightened autocrat [like Chiang Ching-kuo] can bring an end to autocracy in China.[13]

DENG XIAOPING WAS RIGHT. If Chiang Ching-kuo had lived a little longer, he probably would have "advanced the principle of reunification."[14] Over the coming years the government of Lee Teng-hui followed the course Chiang would very likely have pursued: a rapid expansion of cultural and economic engagement between the two territories, including trade, communications, investment, and travel. Most probably, Ching-kuo also anticipated the establishment of semi-official committees on each side to discuss cross-Straits matters. Beyond these practical engagements, however, Chiang apparently envisioned at least the possibility of an early comprehensive agreement that would consolidate a long-term peaceful relationship across the Strait, to make "permanent" Taiwan's adherence to the principle of "one China" but also strengthen in theory and practice Taiwan's autonomy and de facto sovereignty. One of Ching-kuo's young American-trained political scientists, Wei Yung, had publicly advocated "one country, two governments," a variation of Deng's "one country, two systems" concept. It is a good guess that Ching-kuo would have explored an agreement with Peking along these lines, including creation of a China Commonwealth or some other nonsovereign union and readmission of Taiwan to the U.N. General Assembly. Apparently, both Chiang and Deng believed that the two of them were in the best position to make the compromises that such an agreement would have required.

Given Ching-kuo's step-by-step effort to complete the democratization process on Taiwan, it is evident that he intended to limit his initiatives with the mainland to those that could win acceptance on the island. Thus movement toward an actual agreement that would have manifested the principle of reunification would have depended not only on major concessions from Peking, such as on U.N. membership, but also on China's further progress toward democracy. Ching-kuo was convinced that the process of economic, cultural, and democratic reform on the mainland, encouraged by the Taiwan and Russian examples, would put China on the same greased incline of liberalization that he and the Kuomintang had ridden. In what was probably his last interview, Ching-kuo suggested that the dynamic was working. The Communists, he said, "are changing to cope with our position, not vice versa." Completing democratization on Taiwan, he believed, would propel into motion the same dynamic on the mainland, perhaps within the coming year. He was not too far wrong.[15]

IN THE MID-1980s Ching-kuo and Deng were both looking to their place in history, wanting to be remembered not as old-style Sino-centric rulers but as modern patriots and pragmatic politicians. Both sought vindication of their respective and competing historic roles. The legacy that each wished to leave behind was broadly similar—prosperity, prestige, and peace for their people, but also preservation of the principle of China's great unity. For Ching-kuo, tranquillity and progress on the island required democracy, which also meant Taiwanization, which in turn carried a potential threat to the principle of unity. Consequently, he believed that deep and broad engagement across the Strait and a consequent liberalization of Chinese society on the mainland was the only way to make democratization of Taiwan compatible with the principle of Chinese unity. A free and open political system thus became central to all of Chiang Ching-kuo's objectives.

Ching-kuo could have moved sooner toward democracy, perhaps shortly after his father died or after becoming President in 1978. His close associates argue that such a move would have failed, provoking a military-rightist coup and possibly a civil war. If a truly fair and democratic vote had taken place at that time, they say, the KMT probably would have lost, and a victory by pro-independence Taiwanese could have provoked a war with China as well as civil conflict, dragging in America and changing the course of history.

During the 16 years between Ching-kuo's effective leadership in the late 1960s and his death, several hundred people paid with time in prison for political activity that would be normal in a democracy, and a few—such as Henry Liu and the family of Lin Yi-hsiung—paid with their lives. But over all one would have to conclude with Edwin Winkler that it was a period of "soft authoritarianism." Moreover, from at least the late 1960s on, Ching-kuo and his political cohort were committed to the ideal of a truly pluralistic democracy. Their reforms were not simply stratagems to let off steam.

In 1978 Ching-kuo probably thought he would have longer than ten years to complete the transition. But shocks in Taiwan's relations with America and the world provided both a powerful stimulus and a pretext for moving forward. Ching-kuo, in fact, was able to turn the island's international setbacks into an advantage, diminishing the prospects of the independence option in the minds of native Taiwanese and justifying the mainlanders' surrender of power. In the end he believed that Nixon and Carter had had a fundamentally positive impact. Events in China, the Soviet Union, and elsewhere in the mid-1980s convinced Ching-kuo that the almost inconceivable was possible—a Communist dictatorship could fall; China could get swept up in the dynamic of change. These factors as well as his own visibly sinking health provided the catalyst for his final push. When he died, there was much to be done to complete the democratic transition, and Lee Teng-hui, astutely managing the Taiwanese-mainlander conundrum, would fulfill these tasks. But for all practical purposes, by January 1988, democracy, imperfect and rowdy as it was, had made a soft touchdown in Taiwan.

IN THE MID-1980s, having successfully arranged the peaceful re-incorporation of Hong Kong and Macao under Chinese authority, Deng gave highest priority to convincing Taiwan to accept his "one country, two systems" approach to achieving Chinese unity. This goal gave Deng a strong incentive to support the liberal reformers in the CCP leadership, specifically Hu Yao-pang and Chao Tzu-yang. Deng knew that the more liberal and reformist China appeared to be, the more likely Ching-kuo would be willing and able to seek a comprehensive resolution. The death of Ching-kuo reduced Peking expectations of a possible breakthrough in relations with Taipei, and thus, to an unknowable but very likely significant extent, diminished Deng's interest in democratic reform and restraint.

All the same, the liberal reformers in Peking almost won. During the year after the death of Ching-kuo, inflation on the mainland that followed the freeing of retail prices left the reformers again in disarray. Nevertheless, among intellectuals and youth, the momentum in favor of more rather than less democracy accelerated. Peking University removed Mao's statutes from its campus. The National Peoples Congress witnessed a startling expression of independent views and even the casting of some negative votes. The Congress endorsed the right of the people to buy and sell their land-use rights, their recently acquired stakes in some enterprises, and their houses and apartments as well. A Chinese Sakharov appeared: the renowned physicist Fang Li-chih openly criticized the Peking leadership and suggested Taiwan was a model of development that the mainland should emulate.[16]

In August 1988 Chinese television broadcast the immensely popular six-part miniseries, "River Elegy," which called for radical cultural change. It was so liberal in its outlook that conservatives on Taiwan criticized it as an attack on Chinese history and culture.[17] A provocative writer from Taiwan, Po Yang, told Peking University students that "throughout Chinese history, the throne has never changed, only the ass that is on it." Democracy, he warned, is a way of life that can not be imposed but comes through the belief in equality among people that is disseminated through family, school, and community life.[18]

Reagan and Gorbachev ended the Cold War. The Soviets, as promised, withdrew from Afghanistan. There was a cease-fire in Nicaragua. The Iran-Iraq war ended. Hungary became a free nation and democratic movements elsewhere in Eastern Europe gathered momentum. Cuba, Angola, and South Africa agreed on peace and on independence for Namibia. Former enemies De Klerk and Mandela began to talk. When on April 8, 1989, Hu Yao-pang toppled over and died during a Politburo meeting, the outcome of the struggle between CCP liberals and conservatives was by no means certain.

The demonstrations in the Square of Heavenly Peace (Tienanmen) that began on April 22 in honor of Hu Yao-pang soon provoked a showdown between the contending forces. An estimated one million Peking residents poured out of their offices and factories to cheer the student protesters. Chao Tzu-yang persisted, like Chiang Ching-kuo, in his opposition to firing on citizens protesting in the streets. If the students had accepted Chao's promise of more reforms and returned to their classes, the crisis would very likely have ended as a major victory for democratic forces in China rather than a shattering defeat. Chiang Ching-kuo's hopes for a democratized China with which Taiwan could in truth unite might have been realized. But the perfect was once more the enemy of the good. The students refused to compromise. In early May Deng began to take charge. Elbowing Chao aside, he ordered the army to restore government control over Tienanmen Square and the city by all means necessary. In fact, he thought, shedding a little blood would be beneficial.

SOMETIME IN THE TWENTY-FIRST CENTURY China will have the largest economy in the world and will be a military superpower. If, like Taiwan today, China is then also democratic, it will not readily make war, at least not against other democracies. A democratic China will hardly be perfect, any more than America, but it will likely be a normal democratic power with all the pride, virtues, foibles, and mistakes inherent in such a status. This sort of outcome would contribute more than any other variable to stability and peace in the Pacific Rim, and indeed in the world. If democracy does triumph in China, history will in good part credit the impact of the Taiwan example of an open and free Chinese society and the man who more than any other brought this about—the Generalissimo's son.

Epilogue

- On January 11, 1988, the day before Ching-kuo died, the CIA spy, Colonel Chang Hsien-yi, and his wife and children were brought secretly to the United States and given new identities. Washington again demanded that Taiwan's nuclear weapons program cease and that related materials and equipment be destroyed. Lee Teng-hui's government shut down the project but presumably shelved copies of the blueprints.

- During that same year Lee Teng-hui freed the old VMI graduate, General Sun Li-jen, from his 33 years of house arrest. The general asked that his guards stay on, as he had become attached to them. He passed away in 1990.

- In 1990, freed of all restrictions, the "Young Marshal," Chang Hsueh-liang, and his wife flew off to Honolulu. Sotheby's sold his art collection for several million dollars, and he moved into an apartment in the Hilton Hawaiian Village. At the turn of the twentieth century, the ancient Manchurian who had kidnapped the Generalissimo and perhaps changed history was still in his room, looking down at the emerald surf rolling into Waikiki.

- Alan Chiang, at age 53, died of throat cancer in 1989 in Veterans Hospital in Taiwan.

- After serving only six years of a life sentence for the murder of Henry Liu, Admiral Wang Hsi-ling received a pardon in 1991 along with the Bamboo Gang leader Ch'en Ch'i-li. Ch'en became a prosperous businessman.

- Alex Chiang converted to Buddhism and settled down. He established a friendly relationship with his half-brothers. In 1991 he died suddenly in Taipei, apparently of heart failure and diabetes, 47 years of age.

- In 1992 Faina traveled to San Francisco to visit Amy and Eddy and their families. In 2000, having survived all three of her sons, she was living quietly at Seven Seas.

- In 1993 Winston Chang, then president of Suchow University, visited the grave of his mother in Kuilin, China. The cosmetic compact that Ching-kuo had given Ya-jou was returned to him. While on the mainland, he suffered a stroke and was flown back to Taiwan. He died in 1996, 54 years old.

- Huang Wen-hsiung, who tried to assassinate Ching-kuo at the Plaza Hotel in New York in 1970, returned to Taipei in 1996 at the age of 59. At a press conference, he said he did not regret having made the attempt on Ching-kuo's life.

- In 1996 the first direct presidential elections in Taiwan pitted the incumbent Lee Teng-hui against the returned independence leader, Peng Ming-min, the DPP candidate. Lee Teng-hui's visit to the United States and other gestures provoked Peking and won political points at home. The Peoples Republic, however, was more worried about P'eng. Shortly before the polling, China rattled missiles in the Straits; an American carrier steamed to the scene, and the crisis ended. But the Taiwanese voters got the message, and Lee, seen as by far the less likely to start a war with the mainland, won by an impressive majority.

- Eddy Chiang became an arch political foe of Lee Teng-hui. He and his family moved to Canada, then to San Francisco. Under treatment for cancer, he visited Hsikou and Peking in 1996, and in December of that year died at Veterans Hospital in Taiwan, only 48 years old.

- After nearly fifty years as the KMT's chief anti-Communist, Wang Sheng visited Shanghai in 1996 and met with CCP official Wang Tao-han, chairman of Peking's Association for Relations Across the Taiwan Strait.

- Alan and Nancy's daughter Yomei, Ching-kuo's favorite granddaughter, married a British insurance executive in London. In 1997 Yomei gave birth to Zoe Maria Chiang Maclellan, a great-granddaughter of the Generalissimo, who is one quarter Chinese, one eighth Russian, one eighth German, and one half English.

- Becoming a bitter "anti-mainstream" critic of Lee Teng-hui, Chiang Wei-kuo proposed to move the bodies of his father and brother to Hsikou for reburial. In his memoirs, published shortly before his death in 1997, he repeated the same unconvincing allegation that he had conveyed confidentially to me the previous year: that Ching-kuo (like himself) was not the biological son of Chiang Kai-shek.

- For eighty years Deng Xiaoping lived a Party man, and on February 19, 1997, he died a Party man. President Jiang Zemin led the mourners, who circled the bier in the pecking order decreed by their Party standing. Deng had requested a simple cremation and—following Zhou Enlai's example—a scattering of his ashes in the ocean.

- In 1998 more than 300 of the former Yuan and Assembly members elected on the mainland more than half a century before were still drawing their stipends. Thirteen were over 100 years of age.

- Lee Huan served one year as Premier under Lee Teng-hui. In 1999 he was 81 years old, and still a lively and optimistic man.

- Fred Chien eventually became Foreign Minister but reportedly disagreed with Lee Teng-hui's diplomacy toward America and the mainland. Chien was sent upstairs to become speaker of the National Assembly and then president of the Control Yuan.

- Lee Teng-hui sent a pot of orchids to Madame Chiang Soong Mei-ling on her 102nd birthday in New York.

- Hsu Hsin-liang, the ex-KMT politician involved in the Chungli riot of 1977, the "birthday party" and the Kaohsiung riot two years later, the airport fracas of 1986, and other adventures of the opposition, became leader of the DPP. In 1998, however, Lin Yi-hsiung, the Kaohsiung defendant whose infant daughters were murdered, replaced Hsu as party chairman.

- At the beginning of the new century, Ch'en Li-fu (born in 1900) was living in his modest house in Peit'ou, almost deaf but with an amazing memory of events from 73 years before, when he was a young aide to Chiang Kai-shek.

- Ching-kuo's surviving son, John Chang, rose steadily in the government of Lee Teng-hui, serving as Foreign Minister, Vice Premier, and Secretary General of the KMT. In 1999 he became Director General of the President's Office. But Taiwan's democracy reflected the American model in many ways, and early in the new year Chang resigned, after a tabloid's revelation during the election campaign of an extra-marital affair.

- James Soong became an unusually popular governor of Taiwan. According to Lee Teng-hui's critics, it was for this reason that Lee denied Soong the KMT nomination for president in the March 18, 2000 election. Soong then ran as an independent, coming in a close second to the DPP's candidate, Ch'en Sui-bian. Lee's choice as the KMT candidate, the scholarly but uncharismatic Lien Chan, came in a poor third. For the first time since the island's recovery from Japan in 1945, the KMT lost control of the government on Taiwan. Lee Teng-hui, who had planned to stay on as KMT chairman, was forced to resign.

- During the 2000 presidential campaign on Taiwan, Peking again issued serious warnings on the consequences of any move toward independence or even of continued delay toward reunification. Candidate Ch'en Sui-bian, previously a fervent advocate of independence, declared that neither formal independence nor a referendum on the subject were needed and that if elected, he would open direct trade and travel with the mainland and visit Peking for talks. Elected with 39 percent of the vote, Ch'en continued to make conciliatory statements and named the KMT Minister of Defense, a mainlander and former general, to be his Premier.

AS THE THIRD MILLENNIUM BEGAN:

- Per capita income on Taiwan was $14,200, and foreign exchange reserves of over $100 billion were the highest per capita in the world. Taiwan counted one business firm for every 18 people. Only 21 percent of the people of the island thought their children would be worse off than they, compared to 60 percent of parents in the United States.

- Controls on currency trading, capital flows, and banking instituted during Chiang Ching-kuo's administration had enabled Taiwan to escape virtually unscathed the economic downturn of the late 1990s in East Asia.

- Taiwan produced most of the computer scanners manufactured in the world, the majority of monitors and motherboards, and about half of all laptop PCs.

- As many as 32,000 Taiwan companies had invested US $15 billion in mainland enterprises and had concluded letters of intent for another US $34 billion. Taiwan residents were sending over $1 billion in annual family remittances to the mainland. Two-way trade, although officially still indirect, was $7 billion.

- Visits from the island to the mainland since 1987 totaled 13 million. (One taxi driver, a mainlander, told me he had made seven such trips.) Travelers the other way numbered 56,000.

- There were 2,500 different civic organizations in Taiwan, including 250,000 local committees or groups, with a total membership of more than 10 million individuals.

- Taiwan boasted professional soccer, baseball, and basketball leagues, including players with names like de los Santos, Hanibal, and Wishnevski.

- Including the reserves, 4 million men and women were serving in Taiwan's armed forces. The ROC air force possessed a wing of 100 "Ching-kuo" indigenous fighters, 40 out of an eventual 150 American F-16s, and 60 new French Mirage jets: the small island owned more advanced military jets than did mainland China.

⸺

BACK IN CHINA'S CHEKIANG PROVINCE, not far from the restored tomb of Chiang Ching-kuo's grandmother, the Hole-in-the-Snow Monastery was receiving several thousand Taiwan visitors every year. Taiwan funds were paying for restoration, general upkeep, and the monks' living expenses. One new hall paid for by Taiwan devotees is a massive artificial grotto with hundreds of miniature smiling kewpie-like Buddhas perched in crevices. Only a few are not beaming in happiness. A hawker in the doorway sells little plastic round-bottomed Buddhas. When rocked, the gold chubby figures laugh uproariously. According to the mayor of Hsikou, these represent the favorite Buddha of the people of Chiang Ching-kuo's old village—the Mila Buddha, the fat, optimistic God who is always smiling.

Appendix: Romanization Table

As Used in the Text	Wade-Giles	Pinyin
Names		
Ai Ch'i-ming	Ai Ch'i-ming	Ai Chiming
Chang Chih-chung	Chang Chih-chung	Zhang Zhizhong
Chang Ching-hua	Chang Ching-hua	Chang Jinghua
Chang Ching-yu	Chang Ching-yu	Zhang Jingyu
Chang Ch'un	Chang Ch'un	Zhang Chun
Chang Ch'un-hung	Chang Ch'un-hung	Zhang Chunhong
Chang Feng-hsu	Chang Feng-hsu	Zhang Fengxu
Chang Han-lou	Chang Han-lou	Zhang Hanlou
Chang Hsi-chiung	Chang Hsi-chiung	Zhang Xijiong
Chang Hsi-yuan	Chang Hsi-yuan	Zhang Xiyuan
Chang Hsien-yi	Chang Hsien-yi	Zhang Xianyi
Chang Hsueh-liang	Chang Hsueh-liang	Zhang Xueliang
Chang, John	Chang Hsiao-yen	Zhang Xiaoyan
Chang Kia-ngao	Chang Chia-ao	Zhang Jiaao
Chang Kuo-t'ao	Chang Kuo-t'ao	Zhang Guotao
Chang Pao-shu	Chang Pao-shu	Zhang Baoshu
Chang Tso-lin	Chang Tso-lin	Zhang Zuolin
Chang Ts'u-yi	Chang Ts'u-yi	Zhang Cuyi
Chang, Winston	Chang Hsiao-tzu	Zhang Shaozi
Chang Ya-juo	Chang Ya-juo	Zhang Ya-ruo
Chao Chih-hua	Chao Chih-hua	Zhao Zhihua

AS USED IN THE TEXT	WADE-GILES	PINYIN
Chao Tzu-yang	Chao Tzu-yang	Zhao Ziyang
Chao Yi-t'i	Chao Yi-t'i	Zhao Yiti
Ch'en Ch'eng	Ch'en Ch'eng	Chen Cheng
Ch'en Ch'i-li	Ch'en Ch'i-li	Chen Qili
Ch'en Chieh-ju	Ch'en Chieh-ju	Chen Jieru
Ch'en Chih-ching	Ch'en Chih-ching	Chen Zhijing
Chen Chiung-ming	Ch'en Chiung-ming	Chen Jiongming
Ch'en Chu	Ch'en Chu	Chen Zhu
Ch'en Hu-men	Ch'en Hu-men	Chen Humen
Ch'en Kuo-fu	Ch'en Kuo-fu	Chen Guofu
Ch'en Li-fu	Ch'en Li-fu	Chen Lifu
Ch'en Lu-an	Ch'en Lu-an	Chen Luan
Ch'en Shao-yu	Ch'en Shao-yu	Chen Shaoyu
Ch'en Shou-shan	Ch'en Shou-shan	Chen Shoushan
Ch'en Shui-bian	Ch'en Shui-pian	Che, Shuibian
Ch'en Tu-hsiu	Ch'en Tu-hsiu	Chen Duxiu
Ch'en Wen-ch'eng	Ch'en Wen-ch'eng	Chen Wencheng
Ch'en Yi	Ch'en Yi	Chen Yi
Ch'en Yu-shih	Ch'en Yu-shih	Chen Yushi
Cheng Chieh-min	Cheng Chieh-min	Zheng Jiemin
Ch'eng Tzu-ts'ai	Ch'eng Tzu-ts'ai	Cheng Zicai
Cheng Wei-yuan	Cheng Wei-yuan	Zheng, Weiyuan
Ch'i Kao-ju	Ch'i Kao-ju	Qi Gaoru
Chia Yi-pin	Chia Yi-pin	Jia Yibin
Chiang, Alan	Chiang Hsiao-wen	Jiang Xiaowen
Chiang, Alex	Chiang Hsiao-wu	Jiang Xiaowu
Chiang, Amy	Chiang Hsiao-chang	Jiang Xiaozhang
Chiang Bi-ling	Chiang Pi-ling	Jiang Biling
Chiang Ch'ing	Chiang Ch'ing	Jiang Ching
Chiang Ching-kuo	Chiang Ching-kuo	Jiang Jingguo
Chiang, Demos	Chiang Yu-po	Jiang Youbo
Chiang, Eddy	Chiang Hsiao-yung	Jiang Xiaoyong
Chiang, Edward	Chiang, Yu-chang	Jiang Yuzhang
Chiang, Faina	Chiang Fang-liang	Jiang, Fangliang
Chiang Hsi-hou	Chiang Hsi-hou	Jiang Xihou
Chiang Jui-ch'ing	Chiang Jui-ch'ing	Jiang Ruiqing
Chiang Jui-yuan	Chiang Jui-yuan	Jiang Ruiyuan
Chiang Kai-shek	Chiang Chieh-shi	Jiang Jieshi
Chiang Kuo-tung	Chiang Kuo-tung	Jiang Guodong
Chiang, Mei-ling	Chiang Mei-ling	Jiang Meiling
Chiang, Nancy	Chiang Nai-chin	Jiang Naijin

As Used in the Text	Wade-Giles	Pinyin
Chiang Pi-ling	Chiang Pi-ling	Jiang Biling
Chiang Su-an	Chiang Su-an	Jiang Suan
Chiang Wei-kuo	Chiang Wei-kuo	Jiang Weiguo
Chiang Yomei	Chiang Yu-mei	Jiang Youmei
Chiang Yu-piao	Chiang Yu-piao	Jiang Yubiao
Chiang Yu-sung	Chiang Yu-sung	Jiang Yousong
Ch'iao Shih	Ch'iao Shih	Qiao Shi
Chien, Fred	Ch'ien Fu	Qian Fu
Ch'in Wei-ying	Ch'in Wei-ying	Chin Weiying
Ch'iu Ch'ang-wei	Ch'iu Ch'ang-wei	Qiu Changwei
Chiu, Ellen	Chiu Ai-lun	Jiu Ailun
Cho Lin	Cho Lin	Zhuo Lin
Chou Chih-jou	Chou Chih-jou	Zhou Zhirou
Chou Lien-hua	Chou Lien-hua	Zhou Lianhua
Chou Pai-chieh	Chou Pai-chieh	Zhou Baijie
Chou Shu-kai	Chou Shu-kai	Zhou Shukai
Chou Tung	Chou Tung	Zhou Dong
Ch'u Ch'iu-pai	Ch'u Chiu-pai	Qu Qiubai
Chu P'ing	Chu P'ing	Zhu Ping
Chu Te	Chu Te	Zhu De
Ch'u Wu	Ch'u Wu	Chu Wu
Deng Xiaoping	Teng Hsiao-ping	Deng Xiaoping
Fang Chih-yi	Fang Chih-yi	Fang Zhiyi
Fang Li-chih	Fang Li-chih	Fang Lizhi
Feng Fu-fa	Feng Fu-fa	Feng Fufa
Feng Fu-neng	Feng Fu-neng	Feng Funeng
Feng Hung-chih	Feng Hung-chih	Feng Hongzhi
Feng Hung-kuo	Feng Hung-kuo	Feng Hongguo
Feng Yu-hsiang	Feng Yu-hsiang	Feng Yuxiang
Fu Ts'o-yi	Fu Ts'o-yi	Fu Zuoyi
Hao Pei-ts'un	Hao Po-ts'un	Hao Bocun
Ho Chung-han	Ho Chung-han	He Zhonghan
Ho Ying-ch'in	Ho Ying-ch'in	He Yingqin
Hsieh Ts'ung-min	Hsieh Ts'ung-min	Xie Congmin
Hsieh Tung-min	Hsieh Tung-min	Xie Dongmin
Hsiung Shih-hui	Hsiung Shih-hui	Xiong Shihui
Hsiung Yuan	Hsiung Yuan	Xiong Yuan
Hsu Chi-yuan	Hsu Chi-yuan	Xu Jiyuan
Hsu Chin-hu	Hsu Chin-hu	Xu Jinhu
Hsu Ch'ing-chung	Hsu Ch'ing-chung	Xu Qingzhong
Hsu Hsi-lin	Hsu Hsi-lin	Xu Xilin

As Used in the Text	Wade-Giles	Pinyin
Hsu Hsin-liang	Hsu Hsin-liang	Xu Xinliang
Hsu Li-nung	Hsu Li-nung	Xu Linong
Hsu, Nancy	Hsu Nai-chin	Xu Naijin
Hsu Tao-lin	Hsu Tao-lin	Xu Daolin
Hu Han-min	Hu Han-min	Hu Hanmin
Hu Kui	Hu Kui	Hu Gui
Hu Shih	Hu Shih	Hu Shi
Hu Ts'ung-nan	Hu Ts'ung-nan	Hu Zongnan
Hu Yao-pang	Hu Yao-pang	Hu Yaobang
Hu Yi-min	Hu Yi-min	Hu Yimin
Hua Kuo-feng	Hua Kuo-feng	Hua Guofeng
Huang Chi-ming	Huang Chi-ming	Huang Jiming
Huang Chung-mei	Huang Chung-mei	Huang Zhongmei
Huang, Helen	Huang Mei-lun	Huang Meilun
Huang Hsin-chieh	Huang Hsin-chieh	Huang Xinjie
Huang Shao-ku	Huang Shao-ku	Huang Shaogu
Huang Wen-hsiung	Huang Wen-hsiung	Huang Wenxiong
Jen Hsien-ch'un	Jen Hsien-ch'un	Ren Xianqun
Kan Chieh-hou	Kan Chieh-hou	Gan Jiehou
K'ang Ning-hsiang	K'ang Ning-hsiang	Kang Ningxiang
K'ang Sheng	K'ang Sheng	Kang Sheng
K'ang Tse	K'ang Tse	Kang Ze
Kao Ch'un-ming	Kao Ch'un-ming	Gao Chunming
Kao, Henry	Kao Yu-shu	Gao Yushu
Kao Li-wen	Kao Li-wen	Gao Liwen
Kao Ming-hui	Kao Ming-hui	Gao Minghui
Kao Ying-mao	Kao Ying-mao	Gao Yingmao
Koo, Wellington	Ku Wei-chun	Ku Weizhun
Kuan, John	Kuan Chung	Guan Zhong
Ku Cheng-ch'iu	Ku Cheng-ch'iu	Gu Zhengqiu
Ku Ch'ing-lien	Ku Ch'ing-lien	Gu Qinglian
Kui Hui	Kui Hui	Gui Hui
Kung, David	Kung Ling-kan	Kong Linggan
Kung, H. H	Kung Hsiang-hsi	Kong Xiangxi
Kuo Kuo-chi	Kuo Kuo-chi	Guo Guoji
Kuo T'ing-liang	Kuo T'ing-liang	Guo Tingliang
Kuo Yu-hsin	Kuo Yu-hsin	Guo Yuxin
Lai Ming-t'ang	Lai Ming-t'ang	Lai Mingtang
Lee Huan	Li Huan	Li Huan
Lee Kuan-yew	Li Kuan-yu	Li Guanyu
Lee Teng-hui	Li Teng-hui	Li Denghui

As Used in the Text	Wade-Giles	Pinyin
Lei Chen	Lei Chen	Lei Zhen
Leng Shao-chuan	Leng Shao-chuan	Leng Shaozhuan
Li Ao	Li Ao	Li Ao
Li, K. T.	Li Kuo-ting	Li Guoding
Li Li-san	Li Li-san	Li Lisan
Li Mi	Li Mi	Li Mi
Li Ta-chao	Li Ta-chao	Li Dazhao
Li Ta-hai	Li Ta-hai	Li Dahai
Li Tsung-jen	Li Tsung-jen	Li Congren
Li Wei-han	Li Wei-han	Li Wei-han
Liao Cheng-chih	Liao Cheng-chih	Liao Zhengzhi
Liao Chung-k'ai	Liao Chung-k'ai	Liao Zhongkai
Liao Wen-yi	Liao Wen-yi	Liao Wenyi
Lien Chan	Lien Chan	Lian Zhan
Lin Piao	Lin Piao	Lin Biao
Lin Yang-kang	Lin Yang-kang	Lin Yanggang
Lin Yi-hsiung	Lin Yi-hsiung	Lin Yixiong
Liu An-chi	Liu An-chi	Liu Anji
Liu Chien-ch'un	Liu Chien-ch'un	Liu Jianqun
Liu Po-ch'eng	Liu Po-ch'eng	Liu Bocheng
Liu Shao-ch'i	Liu Shao-ch'i	Liu Shaoqi
Lu Kuang-yi	Lu Kuang-yi	Lu Guangyi
Ma Shu-li	Ma Shu-li	Ma Shuli
Ma Ying-jeou	Ma Ying-chiu	Ma Yingjiu
Mao Fu-mei	Mao Fu-mei	Mao Fumei
Mao Jen-feng	Mao Jen-feng	Mao Renfeng
Mao Kao-wen	Mao Kao-wen	Mao Gaowen
Mao Mao-ch'ing	Mao Mao-ch'ing	Mao Maoqing
Mao Ts'e-min	Mao Ts'e-min	Mao Zemin
Mao Zedong	Mao Ts'e-tung	Mao Zedong
Pai Ch'ung-hsi	Pai Ch'ung-hsi	Bai Chongxi
Pai Ya-ts'an	Pai Ya-ts'an	Bai Yacan
P'an Ch'en-ch'iu	P'an Ch'en-ch'iu	Pan Chenqiu
P'an Han-nien	P'an Han-nien	Pan Hannian
P'eng Chen	P'eng Chen	Peng Zhen
P'eng Meng-chi	P'eng Meng-chi	Peng Mengji
P'eng Ming-min	P'eng Ming-min	Peng Mingmin
P'eng Te-huai	P'eng Te-huai	Peng Dehuai
Pi Fan-yu	Pi Fan-yu	Bi Fanyu
Po Yang	Po Yang	Bo Yang
P'u Tao-min	P'u Tao-min	Pu Daomin

As Used in the Text	Wade-Giles	Pinyin
Ruan Ming	Juan Ming	Ruan Ming
Shah, Konsin	Sha Kung-ch'uan	Sha Gongquan
Shao Chih-kang	Shao Chih-kang	Shao Zhigang
Shao Li-tzu	Shao Li-tzu	Shao Lizi
Shao Yu-lin	Shao Yu-lin	Shao Yulin
Shaw Yu-ming	Shao Yu-ming	Shao Yuming
Shen Ch'ang-huan	Shen Ch'ang-huan	Shen Changhuan
Shen, James	Shen Chien-hung	Shen Jianhong
Shen, Samson	Shen Ch'i	Shen Chi
Sheng Shih-ts'ai	Sheng Shih-ts'ai	Sheng Shicai
Shih Ming-te	Shih Ming-te	Shi Mingde
Soong Ch'ing-ling	Sung Ch'ing-ling	Song Qingling
Soong, James	Sung Chu-yu	Song Zhuyu
Soong Mei-ling	Sung Mei-ling	Song Meiling
Soong, T. V.	Sung Tzu-wen	Song Ziwen
Su Shao-chih	Su Shao-chih	Su Shaozhi
Sun Li-jen	Sun Li-jen	Sun Liren
Sun Yat-sen	Sun Yihsien	Sun Yixian
Sun, Y. S.	Sun Yun-hsuan	Sun Yunxuan
Sung Hsin-lien	Sung Hsin-lien	Song Xinlian
Sung Shih-hsuan	Sung Shih-hsuan	Song Shixuan
Sung Ts'ang-chih	Sung Ts'ang-chih	Song Cangzhi
Tai Chi-t'ao	Tai Chi-t'ao	Dai Jitao
Tai Ch'ing	Tai Ch'ing	Dai Qing
Tai Li	Tai Li	Dai Li
Tai Ming-lin	Tai Ming-lin	Dai Minglin
T'ang Chung-po	T'ang Chung-po	Tang Zhongbo
T'ang En-po	T'ang En-po	Tang Enbo
Teng Wen-yi	Teng Wen-yi	Deng Wenyi
Teng Yen-ta	Teng Yen-ta	Deng Yanda
Ts'ai Hsing-san	Ts'ai Hsing-san	Cai Xingsan
Ts'ai Hui-mei	Ts'ai Hui-mei	Cai Huimei
Ts'eng Kuo-fan	Ts'eng Kuo-fan	Zeng Guofan
Tsiang T'ing-fu	Chiang T'ing-fu	Jiang Tingfu
Tsiang Y. S.	Chiang Yen-shih	Jiang Yanshi
Ts'u Sung-ch'iu	Ch'u Sung-ch'iu	Chu Songqiu
Tu Wei-p'ing	Tu Wei-p'ing	Du Weiping
Tu Yu-ming	Tu Yu-ming	Du Yuming
Tu Yueh-sheng	Tu Yueh-sheng	Du Yuesheng
Tung Kui-sen	Tung Kui-sen	Dong Guisen

As Used in the Text	Wade-Giles	Pinyin
Wan Mou-lin	Wan Mou-lin	Wan Moulin
Wang Chang-shih	Wang Chang-shih	Wang Zhangshi
Wang Cheng-yi	Wang Cheng-yi	Wang Zhengyi
Wang Chia-hua	Wang Chia-hua	Wang Jiahua
Wang Ching-hsu	Wang Ching-hsu	Wang Jingxu
Wang Ching-wei	Wang Ching-wei	Wang Jingwei
Wang Hsi-ling	Wang Hsi-ling	Wang Xiling
Wang Hsin-heng	Wang Hsin-heng	Wang Xinheng
Wang Ming	Wang Ming	Wang Ming
Wang Ou-sheng	Wang Ou-sheng	Wang Ousheng
Wang Ping-nan	Wang Ping-nan	Wang Bingnan
Wang Shao-yu	Wang Shao-yu	Wang Shaoyu
Wang Sheng	Wang Sheng	Wang Sheng
Wang Shih-chieh	Wang Shih-chieh	Wang Shijie
Wang Shu-ming	Wang Shu-ming	Wang Shuming
Wang Tao-han	Wang Tao-han	Wang Daohan
Wang Ts'ai-yu	Wang Ts'ai-yu	Wang Caiyu
Wang Yang-ming	Wang Yang-ming	Wang Yangming
Wei Ching-sheng	Wei Ching-sheng	Wei Jingsheng
Wei, Jimmy	Wei Ching-meng	Wei Jingmeng
Wei Li-huang	Wei Li-huang	Wei Lihuang
Wei Ting-chiao	Wei Ting-chiao	Wei Dingjiao
Wei Yung	Wei Yung	Wei Yong
Wen Ch'ang	Wen Ch'ang	Wen Chang
Wen Ha-hsiung	Wen Ha-hsiung	Wen Haxiong
Weng Wen-hao	Weng Wen-hao	Weng Wenhao
Wu Chih-hui	Wu Chih-hui	Wu Zhihui
Wu, K. C.	Wu Kuo-chen	Wu Guozhen
Wu P'ei-fu	Wu P'ei-fu	Wu Peifu
Wu Tun	Wu Tun	Wu Dun
Yang, H. K.	Yang Hsi-kun	Yang Xikun
Yang Kuo-shu	Yang Kuo-shu	Yang Guoshu
Yang Shang-k'un	Yang Shang-k'un	Yang Shangkun
Yao Yeh-ch'eng	Yao Yeh-ch'eng	Yao Yecheng
Yeh, George	Yeh Kung-ch'ao	Ye Gongchao
Yen, C. K.	Yen Chia-kan	Yan Jiagan
Yen Hsi-shan	Yen His-shan	Yan Xishan
Yi Fu-en	Yi Fu-en	Yi Fuen
Yu Chi-chung	Yu Chi-chung	Yu Jizhong
Yu Chi-yu	Yu Chi-yu	Yu Jiyu

As Used in the Text	Wade-Giles	Pinyin
Yu Feng-chih	Yu Feng-chih	Yu Fengzhi
Yu Kuo-hua	Yu Kuo-hua	Yu Guohua
Yu, O. K.	Yu Hung-chuan	Yu Hongzhuan
Yu Ta-wei	Yu Ta-wei	Yu Dawei
Yu Tsu-sheng	Yu Tsu-sheng	Yu Zusheng
Yu Yang-ho	Yu Yang-ho	Yu Yanghe
Yu Yu-jen	Yu Yu-jen	Yu Youren
Zhou Enlai	Chou En-lai	Zhou Enlai

Provinces

Anhui	Anhui	Anhui
Chekiang	Chechiang	Zhejiang
Ch'inghai	Ch'inghai	Qinghai
Fukien	Fuchien	Fujian
Heilungkiang	Heilungchiang	Heilongjiang
Honan	Honan	Henan
Hopei	Hopei	Hebei
Jehe	Jeho	Rehe
Kansu	Kansu	Gansu
Kiangsi	Chianghsi	Jiangxi
Kiangsu	Chiangsu	Jiangsu
Kwangsi	Kuanghsi	Guangxi
Kwangtung	Kuangtung	Guangdong
Kweichow	Kueichou	Guizhou
Liaoning	Liaoning	Liaoning
Shansi	Shanhsi	Shanxi
Shantung	Shantung	Shandong
Shensi	Shânhsi	Shânxi
Sikang	Hsik'ang	Xikang
Sinkiang	Hsinchiang	Xinjiang
Suiyun	Suiyun	Suiyun
Szechuan	Szuch'uan	Sichuan
Tibet	Hsits'ang	Xizang
Yunnan	Yunnan	Yunnan

Cities

Amoy	Hsiamen	Xiamen
Canton	Kuangchou	Guangzhou
Ch'angch'un	Ch'angch'un	Changchun
Ch'angsha	Ch'angsha	Changsha

As Used in the Text	Wade-Giles	Pinyin
Ch'engtu	Ch'engtu	Chengdu
Chinan	Chinan	Jinan
Chungking	Ch'ungch'ing	Chongqing
Chungli	Chungli	Zhongli
Dairen	Talien	Dalian
Fenghua	Fenghua	Fenghua
Foochow	Fuchou	Fuzhou
Hangchow	Hangchou	Hangzhou
Harbin	Haerhpin	Haerbin
Hong Kong	Hsiangkang	Xianggang
Hsian	Hsian	Xian
Hsikou	Hsikou	Xikou
Hsinchu	Hsinchu	Xinjyu
Hsuchow	Hsuchou	Xuzhou
Kanchow	Kanchou	Ganzhou
Kaohsiung	Kaohsiung	Gaoxiong
Keelung	Chilung	Jilong
Kweilin	Kuilin	Guilin
Lanchow	Lanchou	Lanzhou
Lhasa	Lasa	Lasa
Luoyang	Loyang	Luoyang
Mukden	Shenyang	Shenyang
Nanch'ang	Nanch'ang	Nanchang
Nanking	Nanching	Nanjing
Ningpo	Ningpo	Ningbo
Peit'ou	Peit'ou	Beitou
Peking	Peiching	Beijing
Port Arthur	Luta	Luda
Shanghai	Shanghai	Shanghai
Shenchen	Shenchen	Shenzhen
Suchow	Suchou	Suzhou
Swatow	Shant'ou	Shantou
Taichung	Taichung	Taizhong
Taipei	T'aipei	Taibei
Tainan	T'ainan	Tainan
Tientsin	Tienchin	Tianjin
Urumchi	Wulumuch'i	Wulumuchi
Wenchow	Wenchou	Wenzhou
Wuhan	Wuhan	Wuhan
Yenan	Yenan	Yan'an

As Used in the Text	Wade-Giles	Pinyin
Islands		
Chousan	Chousan	Zhousan
Matsu	Mat'su	Macu
Pescadores	Penghu	Penghu
Quemoy	Chinmen	Jinmen
Tachens	Tachen	Dazhen
Rivers		
Huangpu	Huangp'u	Huangpu
Kan	Kan	Gan
Kung	Kung	Gong
Pearl	Chuchiang	Zhu Jiang
Yangtse	Ch'angchiang	Changjiang
Yellow	Huangchiang	Huangjiang
Yung	Yung	Yong

Notes

1. UPRIGHT STONE

1. Fenghua group interview, Sept. 27, 1995.

2. Sun Yi-shu, interviews, May 14, 1996 and May 30, 1996. Sun was personal secretary to Ching-kuo and to Chiang Kai-shek. His great-aunt was Chiang Kai-shek's sister, and his wife was a relative of Wang Ts'ai-yu. Wang Shun-ch'i reports that Wang Ts'ai-yu had been taught at home and knew some characters. Wang Shun-ch'i, interview, June 20, 1996.

3. Chiang Ching-kuo, *Chiang Ching-kuo hsien sheng chuan chi* (Chiang Ching-kuo, *Collected Works*). (Taipei: Government Information Office, 1989). Hereafter *CCKHSCC*. vol. 2, p. 204.

4. Fenghua group, interview, Sept. 27, 1995.

5. Ibid.

6. The account of the adoption of the half-brother and the division of the salt store and the bamboo grove is by Chiang Wei-kuo, from interview on June 5, 1996 (Taipei), and Wang Shun-ch'i, interview, Sept. 30, 1995.

7. Wang Shun-ch'i, interview, June 19, 1996.Wang Shun-ch'i, unpublished article, 1995; Sun Yi-shu, interview, May 14, 1996; a Chiang-Ching-kuo family member, notes to author, Feb. 10, 1999.

8. Ch'en Chieh-ju, *Chiang Kai-shek's Secret Past* (Boulder, Co.: Westview Press, 1993), pp. 54–55.

9. Howard L. Boorman, *Biographical Dictionary of Republican China* (New York: Columbia University Press, 1979), vol. 3, p. 200.

10. Ting I, "A Study of Chiang Kai-shek's Marital Life," *The Perspective Monthly*, Hong

Kong, Jan. 1973. Ting I is an earlier psuedonym for Henry Liu (Chiang Nan), the ill-fated CCK biographer.

11. *New York Times,* Feb. 12, 1936, p. 12.

12. Wang Shun-ch'i, answers to written questions by the author, 1996. In a 1996 interview and in papers published after his death in 1997, Chiang Wei-kuo said that Chiang Kai-shek was not Ching-kuo's natural father since Kai-shek did not see Fu-mei in 1909, much less sire a child with her. The reported trip to Shanghai, however, would seem to take care of the proximity problem. It is not likely Chiang would have accepted as his own another man's child by Fu-mei.

13. Wang Shun-ch'i, answers, 1996.

14. The information that Chiang Ching-kuo was registered as the son of Jui-ch'ing comes from Chiang Wei-kuo interview, June 5, 1996, and from Wang Shun-ch'i, who reported having seen the civil record of the birth (interview, June 19, 1996); Sun Yi-shu also confirms the story (interview, May 14, 1996). This was not an uncommon practice of the time.

15. Edward L. Dreyer, *China at War, 1901–1949* (New York: Longman, 1995), pp. 32–39.

16. Hollington Tong, *Chiang Kai-shek, Soldier and Statesman* (Taipei: China Publishing Company, 1953), p. 33. Wang Shun-ch'i, answers, 1996. Brian Crozier, *The Man Who Lost China* (New York: Charles Scribner's Sons, 1976), pp. 40–41.

17. Ch'en Chieh-ju, *Chiang,* pp. 83–85.

18. Han Shan-p'i, *Chiang Ching-kuo Chuan Chi* (Biography of Chiang Ching-kuo) (Taipei: 1988), pp. 23–36. Also Crozier, *The Man Who Lost China,* p. 44. Ch'en Chieh-ju, *Chiang,* p. 33, reports that Chiang told her that Yao was a "sing-song girl" he had met in 1916 while hiding out from assassins. Chiang's adopted son, Wei-kuo, whom Yao later raised as her own son, claimed she was a KMT activist. Chiang Wei-kuo, interview, June 5, 1996, Taipei.

19. Boorman, *Biographical Dictionary,* vol. 1, p. 320.

20. Brian G. Martin, *The Shanghai Green Gang, Politics and Organized Crime, 1919–1939* (Berkeley: University of California Press, 1996) pp. 79–80.

21. Fenghua group, interview, Sept. 27, 1995, and Wang Shun-ch'i, unpublished, 1995.

22. Fenghua group, interview, Sept. 27, 1995, and Wang Shun-ch'i, answers, 1996.

23. Wang Shun-ch'i, unpublished, 1995, citing Chiang Yuan-tung, a cousin and classmate of Ching-kuo.

24. Ibid.

25. Ibid.

26. Pinchon Loh, *The Early Chiang Kai-shek, A Study of His Persona* (New York: Columbia Unversity Press, 1971), p. 52, pp. 132–133.

27. Chiang Kai-shek letter to Ching-kuo, Feb. 9, 1920, quoted in Mao Ssu-Ch'eng, *Min-kuo shih wu nien i-ch'ien chih Chiang Chieh-shih Hsien-sheng* (Mr. Chiang Kai-shek, 1887–1926) (Hong Kong: Longmen, 1965), pp. 105–106.

28. Fenghua group, interview, Sept. 27, 1995. Boorman, *Biographical Dictionary,* vol. 1, p. 306, states that in December 1917 Chiang entrusted Ching-kuo's education to Ku

and to Wang Ou-sheng, implying that Ching-kuo withdrew from the Wushan School at that time.

29. Chiang Kai-shek, *Nanking Diaries,* entries for Feb. 7 and Mar. 4, 1920. Nanking #2 National Archives, Nanking.

30. Loh, *Early Chiang,* p. 60.

31. *Nanking Diaries,* entries for Nov. 30, 1920, and April 3, 1921. Also see Wang Shun-ch'i, unpublished, 1995.

32. Chiang Wei-kuo, *Chien shan tu hsing: Chiang wei kuo de jen sheng chih lu* (Walking Alone in the Midst of a Thousand Mountains: Chiang Wei-kuo's Life Journey) (Taipei: 1996), p. 20.

33. Chiang Wei-kuo, *Chien shan,* p. 36.

34. Chiang Wei-kuo, interview, June 7, 1996.

2. A TEACHABLE SON

1. Pinchon Loh, *The Early Chiang Kai-shek, A Study of His Persona* (New York: Columbia Unversity Press, 1971), p. 62.

2. Chiang Kai-shek, *Nanking Diaries,* #2 National Archives, Nanking, entry for Mar. 6, 1921. Letter dated Jan. 28, 1922.

3. Letter dated Mar. 3, 1922. Mao Ssu-Ch'eng, *Min-kuo shih wu nien i-ch'ien chih Chiang Chieh-shih Hsien-sheng* (Mr. Chiang Kai-shek, 1887–1926)(Hong Kong: Longmen, 1965), p. 144.

4. Chiang Ching-kuo, *Chiang Ching-kuo hsien sheng chuan chi* (Chiang Ching-kuo, *Collected Works*) (Taipei: Government Information Office, 1989), vol. 2, p. 252; henceforth *CCKHSCC.*

5. 1994 Russian Tele-Radio (RTR) TV documentary, *Cheloviek meniayet kozhu, ili Zhizn i nieobichainiye prevrashchieniya gospodina Dzian Dzingo* (The Man Changes the Skin, or the Life and Extraordinary Metamorphoses of Mr. Ching-kuo). Producer Samariy Zelikin. The reference to Fu-mei's pleas to remain in the house is found in Ching-kuo's letter to his mother in 1935, which he later asserted he was forced to write. *New York Times,* Feb. 12, 1936, p. 12.

6. Brian Crozier, *The Man Who Lost China* (New York: Charles Scribner's Sons, 1976), p. 114, citing Ting (Henry Liu).

7. Ch'en Chieh-ju, *Chiang Kai-shek's Secret Past* (Boulder, Co.: Westview Press, 1993), pp. 1–26.

8. Ch'en, *Chiang,* pp. 27–42.

9. Ibid. Fenghua group, interview, Sept. 27, 1995.

10. Ibid.

11. Ch'en, *Chiang,* pp. 27–42.

12. *CCKHSCC,* vol. 2, pp. 262, 264 (letter of Oct. 31, 1923).

13. Ibid., p. 249.

14. Ibid.

15. Ibid., pp. 250–251.

16. Ibid., pp. 247, 260.

17. Ibid., p. 260 (letter of August 4, 1922); pp. 264–265.(letter of Nov. 27, 1923)

18. Wei-kuo was named as the addressee at Chiang Wei-kuo interview, June 5, 1996.

19. Chiang Kai-shek, *Soviet Russia in China, A Summing Up at Seventy* (New York: Farrar, Straus, 1957), pp. 8–19.

20. Conrad Brandt, *Stalin's Failure in China* (Cambridge, Mass.: Harvard University Press, 1966), p. 71.

21. Ch'en Li-fu and Sidney H. Chang, *The Storm Clouds Clear Over China* (Stanford: Hoover Institution Press, 1994), pp. 9, 64.

22. Boorman, Howard L., *Biographical Dictionary of Republican China* (New York: Columbia University Press, 1979), vol. 1, p. 207.

23. Wang Shun-ch'i, unpublished article, 1995. The letter is in the Nanking Archives.

24. Ibid.

25. Hsiung, S. I., *The Life of Chiang Kai-shek* (Shanghai: World Book Company, 1948), p. 199.

26. *Shen Pao* (newspaper), Shanghai, May 31, 1925, p. 13.

27. *New York Times*, May 31, 1925, p. 3. *Shen Pao,* Shanghai, May, 31, 1925.

28. Chiang Ching-kuo (CCK), "My Days in Soviet Russia," in Ray S. Cline, *Chiang Ching-kuo Remembered* (Washington, D.C.: United States Global Strategic Council, 1989), p. 153.

29. Ch'en Ch'eng Ch'ing, archivist of KMT period, Shanghai Municipal Archives, interview, June 17, 1996, Shanghai. Han Shan-p'i, *Chiang Ching kuo ping chuan* (The Life of Chiang Ching-kuo) (Hong Kong: Tianyuan Chu ban she, 1988), p. 40.

30. *New York Times,* June 5, 1925.

31. Ibid., June 12, 1925.

32. Jonathan D. Spence, *The Search for Modern China* (New York: W. W. Norton, 1990), p. 340.

33. Edgar Snow, *Red Star Over China* (New York: Grove Press, 1944), p. 160.

34. Cline, *CCK Remembered,* p. 154.

35. Han, *Chiang Ching kuo,* pp. 42–45.

36. Cline, *CCK Remembered,* p. 148.

37. Alexander Pantsov, "From Students to Dissidents: The Chinese Trotskyites in Soviet Russia (Part I)," in *Issues & Studies,* 30/3 (March 1994), Institute of International Relations, Taipei, pp. 113–114.

38. Yen Ling-feng, a CCP-selected student at UTC 1926–1928, interview, August 30, 1995, Taipei.

39. *CCKHSCC,* vol. 2, p. 532.

40. Ch'en, *Chiang,* pp. 169–170.

41. Ibid, p. 171.

42. Ch'en Li-fu, interview, Taipei, May 29, 1996.

43. *Nanking Diaries*, Oct. 1, 1925.

3. DREAMS OF THE RED CHAMBER

1. Chiang Ching-kuo (CCK), 1957, in Ray S. Cline, *Chiang Ching-kuo Remembered* (Washington, D.C.: United States Global Strategic Council, 1989), pp. 154–155.

2. Deng Maomao, *Deng Xiaoping, My Father* (New York: Basic Books, 1995), pp. 108–109.

3. Howard L. Boorman, *Biographical Dictionary of Republican China* (New York: Columbia University Press, 1979), vol. 1, p. 231, notes that in late 1925 Ch'en was selected as a CCP nominee to attend UTC and arrived in Moscow in late November. The odds are that he made the trip with Ching-kuo.

4. Cline, *CCK Remembered*, p. 155.

5. Yueh Sheng, *Sun Yat-sen University in Moscow and the Chinese Revolution,* International Studies East Asian Series Research Publication #7, Center for East Asian Studies, University of Kansas (New York: Paragon Book Gallery, 1971), p. 29.

6. Yueh Sheng, *Sun Yat-sen University*, p. 32.

7. Alexander Pantsov, "From Students to Dissidents: The Chinese Trotskyites in Soviet Russia, Part 1," in *Issues & Studies,* 30/3 (March 1994), Institute of International Relations, Taipei, p. 57. John McCook Roots, *Chou, An Informal Biography of China's Legendary Chou En-lai* (New York: Doubleday, 1978), pp. 36–37. As a *New York Times* correspondent, Roots visited the university in 1926.

8. Alexander Georgievich Larin, a Russian historian and China specialist, interview in 1994 Russian Tele-Radio (RTR) TV documentary, *Cheloviek meniayet kozhu, ili Zhizn i nieobichainiye prevrashchieniya gospodina Dzian Dzingo* (The Man Changes the Skin, or the Life and Extraordinary Metamorphoses of Mr. Ching-kuo). Producer Samariy Zelikin. Henceforth, 1994 RTR documentary.

9. Yueh Sheng, *Sun Yat-sen University*, p. 88. Franz Uli, *Deng Xiaoping* (New York: Harcourt, Brace & Jovanovich, 1988), pp. 67–68.

10. For clips from Russian newsreels of the time see 1994 RTR documentary.

11. Pantsov, "Students," part 3, p. 113.

12. *Chiang shih fu tzu* (The Chiangs, Father and Son), a collection of articles and recollections by Ching-kuo's friends, colleagues, and subordinates, ed. by the Literature and Historical Materials Committee of the Political Consultative Conference of Chekiang Province (Fenghua City: Tian ching chu ban she, 1994), p. 170.

13. Pantsov, "Students," part 3, p. 121.

14. Trotsky, Leon, *Problems of the Chinese Revolution* (New York: Pioneer Publishers, 1932), p. 436.

15. Roots, *Chou*, p. 36.

16. *Chin jih ta lu* (The Mainland Today), 99, Oct. 15, 1959, Taipei, pp. 33-34. Cited by Yueh Sheng, *Sun Yat-sen University*, pp. 35–36.

17. Cline, *CCK Remembered*, p. 159.

18. Pantsov, "Students," part 3, p. 59.

19. Yen Ling-feng, interview, August 30, 1995, Taipei.

20. Uli, *Deng*, p. 67.

21. Ibid., pp. 67–68.

22. Yu Min-ling, "E kuo tang an chung te liu su hsueh sheng Chiang Ching kuo" (Chiang Ching-kuo's Student Years in the Soviet Union as Reflected in Russian Archives), Modern History Research Institute (Taipei: Academia Sinica, June 1998), p. 111. Yu found the letter at the Russian Center for Preservation and the Study of Documents of Contemporary History, sect. 530, index #4, file #49.

23. Yan Nung and Peng Che-yu in *Chiang shih fu tzu*, pp. 165–176. An article based on interviews with Ching-kuo's Moscow classmate Hsu Chun-hu and others. See also Li Hsin-chih and Wang Yue-ts'ung, *Wei ta teh shih hsien, kuang hui teh szu hsiang: Deng Xiaoping ke ming huo tung ta shih chi* (Great Achievement, Brilliant Thought: Chronology of Deng Xiaoping's Revolutionary Activities) (Peking: 1990). Cited by David Shambaugh, "Deng Xiaoping: The Politician" in Shambaugh, ed., *Deng Xiaoping, Portrait of a Chinese Statesman* (Oxford: Clarendon Press, 1995), p. 55.

24. Deng Maomao, *Deng*, pp. 108–109.

25. Ch'en Li-fu and Sidney H. Chang, *The Storm Clouds Clear Over China* (Stanford: Hoover Institution Press), 1994), p. 25.

26. Ch'en Li-fu, interview, May 29, 1996. Ch'en, *Storm Clouds*, pp. 28–29.

27. Yu Min-ling, "E kuo tang," p. 121.

28. Robert C. North and Xenia J. Eudin, *M. N. Roy's Mission to China* (Berkeley: University of California Press, 1963), p. 27.

29. Conrad Brandt, *Stalin's Failure in China* (Cambridge, Mass.: Harvard University Press, 1958), p. 73.

30. Politburo report March 25, 1996, "Problems of Our Policy with Respect to China and Japan," in Les Evans and Russel Block, *Leon Trotsky on China* (New York: Monad Press, 1996), pp. 103–108.

31. Ch'en, *Storm Clouds*, pp. 58–59.

32. Yen Ling-feng, interview, August 30, 1995.

33. Cline, *CCK Remembered*, pp. 160–161. The magazine was probably *Kuo chi P'ing lun* (International Review); see Pantsov, "Students," part 1, p. 118.

34. Yueh Sheng, *Sun Yat-sen University*, p. 160

35. Yu Min-ling, "E kuo tang," pp. 112–115.

36. Yueh Sheng, *Sun Yat-sen University*, p. 89.

37. The list can be seen in 1994 RTR documentary. Fu-neng is also identified as Ching-kuo's wife in a May 1927 document in which Pavel Mif argues for the detention in China of the Feng children. Pantsov, "Students," part 3, p. 79. Marriage practices described in Yu Min-ling, fax to author, June 26, 1998.

38. Cline, *CCK Remembered*, p. 158. Possibly an interpreter was used on these occasions.

39. Brandt, *Stalin's Failure*, p. 89.

40. Stuart Schram, *Mao Tse-tung* (New York: Simon and Schuster, 1967), p. 92.

41. Brandt, *Stalin's Failure,* pp. 88, 94, 95.

42. Brian Crozier, *The Man Who Lost China* (New York: Charles Scribner's Sons, 1976), pp. 94–95. Ch'en, *Storm Clouds,* p. 49.

43. Ibid. pp. 95–97.

44. Ibid.

45. Records at Sun Yat-sen University, Pantsov, "Students," part 1, p. 112.

46. Brandt, *Stalin's Failure,* p. 161.

47. Warren Lerner, *Karl Radek, The Last Internationalist* (Stanford: Stanford University Press, 1970), p. 145.

48. Cline, *CCK Remembered,* pp. 158–159.

49. Ch'en, *Storm Clouds,* p. 62.

50. Alexander Larin, interview in 1994 RTR documentary.

51. Yueh Sheng, *Sun Yat-sen University,* p. 122.

52. Trotsky, *Problems,* p. 384.

53. Yueh Sheng, *Sun Yat-sen University,* p. 122. *Izvestia* published an account of the speech in an article describing the reaction of the Sun Yat-sen students to the Shanghai coup.

54. *Time,* April 25, 1927, p. 44.

55. Quoted in 1994 RTR documentary.

56. Robert C. North, *Moscow and the Chinese Communists,* 2d ed. (Stanford: Stanford University Press, 1963), pp. 65–66.

57. North and Eudin, *M. N. Roy's Mission,* pp. 70–71.

58. Yueh Sheng, *Sun Yat-sen University,* p. 131. Pantsov, "Students," part 2, p. 64.

59. Ibid. Pantsov notes that Ching-kuo "was the first (among the Sun Yat-sen University students) to quit the (Trotsky) opposition." The date of Ching-kuo's decision is uncertain. Possibly it came at the end of April, only two weeks after the Shanghai coup. This would be consistent with Ching-kuo's statement that he graduated early in April. But it may have come later after the July collapse of the left KMT-CCP coalition in Wuhan.

60. North, *Moscow and the Chinese,* pp. 105–106.

61. *Pravda,* August 20, 1927.

62. Jonathan D. Spence, *The Search for Modern China* (New York: W. W. Norton, 1990), p. 371.

63. Pantsov, "Students," part 1, p. 118.

64. Percy Ch'en, *China Called Me* (Boston: Little, Brown, 1979), p. 182.

65. For the parade incident and the Fengs see Pantsov, "Students," part 2, p. 62; part 3, p. 79; and Yueh, Sheng, *Sun Yat-sen University,* p. 207.

4. SOCIALIST MAN

1. 1994 Russian Tele-Radio (RTR) TV documentary, *Cheloviek meniayet kozhu, ili zhizn i nieobichainiye prevrashchieniya gospodina Dzian Dzingo* (The Man Changes the Skin, or the Life and Extraordinary Metamorphoses of Mr. Ching-kuo). Producer Samariy Zelikin. Henceforth 1994 RTR documentary.

2. Ray S. Cline, *Chiang Ching-kuo Remembered* (Washington, D.C.: United States Global Strategic Council, 1989), p. 164.

3. Cline, *CCK Remembered*, p. 16. Chiang Ching-kuo 1934 autobiography attached to 1934 "Questionaire for the Communist Party Candidate, completed by Nikolai Elizarov (Chiang Ching-kuo)," photocopy in *Asia and Africa Today*, Moscow, August 1991, pp. 52–55. Henceforth CCK 1934 autobiography.

4. Brian Crozier, *The Man Who Lost China* (New York: Charles Scribner's Sons, 1976), pp. 115–118.

5. Cline, *CCK Remembered*, p. 165.

6. 1994 RTR documentary.

7. Yan Nung and Peng She-yu, "Chiang Ching-kuo tzai su lian," in *Chiang shi fu zi* (The Chiangs, Father and Son), ed. the Literature and Historical Materials Committee of the Political Consultative Conference of Chekiang Province (Fenghua City: Tien Jing, 1994), p. 172. The internal security organ was still called the OGPU. It became the NKVD (Ministry of State Security) in 1934 and KGB (Committee of State Security) in 1953.

8. Alexander Pantsov, "From Students to Dissidents: The Chinese Trotskyites in Soviet Russia," part 3, in *Issues & Studies*, 30/3 (March 1994), Institute of International Relations, Taipei, p. 79.

9. Wang Tsan-t'ing (an officer in the entourage of Feng Yu-hsiang), *K'en sui Feng Yu-hsiang erh shih yu nien* (Twenty Years Following Feng Yu-hsiang) (Jinan: Shangdong Renmin Chubanshe, 1983), p. 87.

10. Cline, *CCK Remembered*, p. 165.

11. Yan and P'eng, "tzai su lian," p. 172.

12. Yueh, Sheng, *Sun Yat-sen University in Moscow and the Chinese Revolution*, International Studies East Asian Series Research Publication #7, Center for East Asian Studies, University of Kansas (New York: Paragon Book Gallery, 1971), p. 211.

13. Yen Ling-feng, interview, August 25, 1995, Taipei.

14. Howard L. Boorman, *Biographical Dictionary of Republican China* (New York: Columbia University Press, 1979), vol. 1, p. 394.

15. Han Suyin, *Eldest Son: Zhou Enlai and the Making of Modern China, 1898–1976* (New York: Hill and Wang, 1994), p. 98.

16. Cline, *CCK Remembered*, p. 166.

17. Harrison E. Salisbury, *War Between Russia and China* (New York: Norton, 1969), pp. 37–39.

18. Warren Lerner, *Karl Radek, The Last Internationalist* (Stanford: Stanford University Press, 1970), pp. 149–152.

28. Wang Yueh-hsi, interview, Fenghua, Sept. 25, 1937.

29. A family member who has remained close to Faina Chiang. Also Chu P'ei-yang interview, Shanghai, Sept. 30, 1995. Ms. Chu was a second cousin of Ching-kuo.

30. *CCKHSCC*, vol. 1, pp. 245–249.

31. Ibid., p. 247.

32. StateDept Foreign Service dispatch, March 31, 1953, reporting the description by Hsu Tao-lin.

33. *CCKHSCC*, vol. 1, pp. 269–271. Yu Min-ling, "E kuo tang," pp. 128–130.

34. Ibid.

35. *CKHSCC*, vol. 2, p. 271.

36. Jonathan D. Spence, *The Search for Modern China* (New York: W. W. Norton, 1990), pp. 446–447.

37. Edward L. Dreyer, *China at War, 1901–1949* (White Plains, N.Y.: Longman Publishing Group, 1996), p. 218.

38. Ch'en, *Storm Clouds,* pp. 124–125.

39. *China Handbook, 1937–1945* (Shanghai: Commercial Press, 1946), p. 89. The aid was in the form of low interest loans paid for by shipments of Chinese raw materials.

40. *Chiang Ching-kuo tsai kan nan* (Chiang Ching-kuo in Kannan). Henceforth *CCKTKN.* A collection of articles by former associates of Ching-kuo given at a conference on "Chiang Ching-kuo in Kannan" held by the Kiangsi Provincial Committee and Kanchow Municipal Committee in Nanch'ang in 1989, pp. 1–14.

41. Spence, *Search,* p. 461.

42. Joseph J. Heinlein, *Political Warfare: The Chinese Nationalist Model,* Ph.D. thesis, The American University, Washington, D.C.. 1974, pp. 260–272.

43. Ts'ai Hsing-san and Ts'ao Yun-hsia, *Chiang Ching-kuo hsi shih hua* (History of the Chiang Ching-kuo Faction) (Hong Kong: 1988), pp. 29–32. Ts'ai served in Kannan with Ching-kuo in the late 1930s and early 1940s.

44. Ai Ch'i-ming, interview, Nanking, June 15, 1996. Ms Ai was head of the women's unit in the first class of the Youth Cadre School under Ching-kuo in 1944.

45. Ch'en, *Storm Clouds,* pp. 142–143.

46. Joseph Warren Stilwell, *The Stilwell Papers* (New York: Schocken Books, 1972), p. 196.

47. Howard L. Boorman, *Biographical Dictionary of Republican China* (New York: Columbia University Press, 1979), vol. 1, p. 362.

48. Ch'en, *Storm Clouds*, p. 143.

49. Ts'ai and Ts'ao, *Chiang Ching-kuo,* p. 33.

50. Luo Hsuan, *Chiang Ching-kuo Kiangsi chuan chi* (Biography of Chiang Ching-kuo) (Taipei: Hsiao yüan Publisher, 1989), p. 6. Luo served in Kannan with Ching-kuo.

51. Han, *Chiang Ching-kuo,* pp. 99–101.

52. Tai Yi-chin, "Ta lu shih ch'i Chiang Ching-kuo tsou wei te chin pu jen shih" (Progressive Colleagues of Chiang Ching-kuo in His Mainland Days), *Chuan chi ren hsueh* (Biographical Literature), 5/55, Taipei, May 30, 1992.

53. Wen Ch'ang, interview, Peking, Sept. 26, 1995.

54. Ibid.

55. Heinlein, *Political,* pp. 320–330.

56. Brian G. Martin, *The Shanghai Green Gang, Politics and Organized Crime, 1919–1939* (Berkeley: University of California Press, 1996).

57. Dreyer, *China,* p. 235.

58. Kan (referring to the river) was the ancient word for Kiangsi, and "nan" means "south."

59. Wang Sheng, answers to written questions, submitted undated, spring 1996.

60. Fang Shih-tsao, "Ta chi hsi tu tu po, ch'ang chi chi liu mang" (Policies and Actions Against Opium Smoking, Gambling, Prostitution and Banditry), in *CCKTKN,* pp. 121–129.

61. Chia Yi-pin, interview, Sept. 21, 1995. Ts'ai and Ts'ao, *Chiang Ching-kuo,* pp. 71–72, lists several others: Kao Su-ming, Hsu Chi-yuan, and P'eng Chien-hua.

62. Chiang Shu, interview, Shanghai, Sept. 30, 1995. Chiang worked in the Youth Corps in Kannan.

63. Forman, "Gissimo," p. 11. Chiang Nan, *Chiang Ching-kuo,* p. 101.

64. Forman, "Gissimo," p. 11.

65. Wang Sheng, answers to written questions, spring 1996.

66. Chiang Shu, interview, Shanghai, Sept. 30, 1995.

67. Ch'i Kao-ju, *Chiang Ching-kuo teh yi sheng,* pp. 31–31. Forman, "Gissimo," p. 11, 61. Wang Sheng, interview, Sept. 8, 1995.

68. Fang Shih-tsao, *CCKTKN,* pp. 121–129.

69. Luo, *Chiang Ching-kuo,* pp. 23–28.

70. Whiting, *"Mystery,"* 1955, p. 117. Also Fang Shih-tsao, *CCKTKN,* p. 126.

71. Fang Shih-tsao, *CCKTKN,* p. 127.

72. Wang Sheng, answers, spring 1996.

73. Fang Shih-tsao, *CCKTKN,* pp. 130–132.

74. Wang Sheng, answers, spring 1996.

75. Wang Sheng, interview, Sept. 11, 1995.

76. Hsu Hao-jan, "Hsin jen Hsueh Hsiao," in *CCKTKN,* pp. 299–310.

77. *CCKHSCC,* chronology, vol. 1, p. 76.

78. Forman, "Gissimo," p. 62.

79. Ibid.

80. Ibid.

81. Dreyer, *China,* p. 241.

6. THE KANNAN MODEL

1. Fenghua group, interview, Sept. 27, 1995.

2. Ibid.

3. Ibid.

4. Ibid. Also Wang Sheng, answers to written questions, spring 1996.

5. Luo Hsuan, *Chiang Ching-kuo Chiang-hsi chuan chi* (Chiang Ching-kuo's Kiangsi Biography) (Taipei: Hsiao yüan Publishing House, 1989), pp. 43–45; and Wang Sheng, interview, Taipei, Sept. 8, 1995.

6. One contributor to a collection of articles by former associates of Ching-kuo, Ch'en Ta, claimed that Ching-kuo deified his father and required others to do the same. See Huang Wen-yao, *Chiang Ching-kuo tsai kan nan* (Chiang Ching-kuo in Kannan), pp. 159–174, henceforth *CCKTKN,* given at a conference on "Chiang Ching-kuo in Kannan" held by the Kiangsi Provincial Committee and Kanchow Municipal Committee in Nanch'ang in 1989.

7. Huang Wen-yao, *CCKTKN,* p. 99.

8. Wang Sheng, answers, spring 1996.

9. John Chang (one of Ya-jou's twin sons), interview, Taipei, May 15, 1996.

10. Wang Sheng, answers, spring 1996.

11. Chang Su, "Chiang Ching-kuo yu Chang Ya-jou" (Chiang Ching-kuo and Chang Ya-jou), in *CCKTKN,* pp. 349–352.

12. Ibid., pp. 356–358.

13. Wang Li-hsing, "Chiang Hsiao-yung de sheng yang" (Last Words of Chiang Hsiao-yung), *Yuan chin Tsa chih,* Sept. 15, 1996, p. 111. This article is an interview with Eddy Chiang (Chiang Hsiao-yung), Ching-kuo's and Faina's youngest son.

14. Luo, *Chiang Ching-kuo,* pp. 37–38.

15. Chiang Ching-kuo, *Chiang Ching-kuo hsien sheng chuan chi,* (Chiang Ching-kuo, Collected Works) (Taipei, 1989), henceforth *CCKHSCC,* vol. 2, pp. 273–272.

16. *CCKTKN,* pp. 456–460.

17. Luo, *Chiang Ching-kuo,* pp. 104–105.

18. Ibid., p. 114.

19. *CCKTKN,* pp. 460–485.

20. Wang Sheng, interview, Sept. 8, 1995.

21. Ibid.

22. Various interviews in Kanchow, and Harrison Forman, "Gissimo, Junior," *Collier's,* July 31, 1943, p. 61.

23. Howard L. Boorman, *Biographical Dictionary of Republican China* (New York: Columbia University Press, 1979), vol. 1, p. 363.

24. Chiang Wei-kuo, interview, Taipei, June 5, 1996.

25. Chiang Wei-kuo, *Ch'ien shan tu hsing: Chiang wei kuo de jen sheng chih lu* (Walking Alone in the Midst of a Thousand Mountains: Chiang Wei-kuo's Life Journey) (Taipei: Tienhsia, 1996), p. 78. Interview, June 7, 1996. Boorman, *Biographical Dictionary,* vol. 1, p. 363.

26. Chiang Wei-kuo, interview, June 5, 1996.

27. Chiang Wei-kuo, *Ch'ien shan,* pp. 47–60, 83–84.

28. Chiang Wei-kuo, interview, June 5, 1996.

29. Robert C. North, *Moscow and the Chinese Communists,* 2d ed. (Stanford: Stanford University Press, 1963), p. 191.

30. Tien-Fong Ch'eng, *A History of Sino-Russian Relations* (Westport, Conn.: Greenwood Press, 1957), p. 220.

31. *Chiang Ching-kuo te nien biao tsai Kannan,* in *CCKTKN,* pp. 450–459.

32. Wang Sheng, answers, spring 1996.

33. Wang Ch'u-ying (an officer in the Sixth Army), interview, Nanking, June 15, 1996.

34. Joseph Warren Stilwell, *The Stilwell Papers* (New York: Schocken Books, 1972), pp. 68–69.

35. Wang Ch'u-ying, interview, June 15, 1996

36. Stilwell, *Papers,* pp. 148–149. Also, Stilwell, referring to Madame Chiang, noted: "Great influence on Chiang Kai-shek mostly along the right lines too. A great help on several occasions," p. 95.

37. *CCKHSCC,* vol. 2, p. 274.

38. Chiang Nan, *Chiang Ching-kuo chuan* (The Biography of Chiang Ching-kuo) (Los Angeles: Mei-kuo lun tan pao, 1984), p. 114.

39. Boorman, *Biographical Dictionary,* vol. 3, p. 123.

40. Eddy Chiang, interview, Taipei, May 19, 1996. Eddy's grandfather told him that he gave suicide pills to Ching-kuo whenever he went on a dangerous mission.

41. Boorman, *Biographical Dictionary,* vol. 2, p. 177.

42. Chiang Wei-kuo, interview, June 6, 1996.

43. *CCKHSCC,* vol. 1, pp. 187–229.

44. Ibid., p. 228.

45. Ibid.

46. Wen Ch'ang, interview, Sept. 26, 1995.

47. Boorman, *Biographical Dictionary,* vol. 3, p. 123.

48. John Chang, interview, Taipei, Sept. 15, 1995.

49. Ibid.

50. Chang Su, "Chang Ya-jou," pp. 360–362.

51. Ibid.

52. John Chang, interview, Sept. 15, 1995.

53. Chang Su, "Chang Ya-jou," p. 363–364.

54. John Chang, interview, Sept. 15, 1995. Wang Sheng, interview, Sept. 11, 1995.

55. John Chang, interview, Sept. 9, 1995.

56. Forman, "Gissimo," p. 62.

57. Forman observed Ching-kuo reading the Ukrainian poet Shevchenko during an airplane trip. Ibid.

58. Brooks Atkinson, *New York Times,* Nov. 5, 1943, p. 5.

59. Fang Shih-tsao and local guide, interview at site of the New Village School, June 13, 1996. Also see the recollections of Hou Tung-ho, in *CCKTKN*, pp. 243–253.

60. Ibid.

61. Stilwell, *Papers,* p. 149.

62. Robert Service, telephone interview, April 11, 1996.

63. Ibid.

64. *CCKHSCC,* Vol 2, p. 276.

65. Ibid., pp. 178–184.

66. Mrs. Chas. E. Cowman, *Streams in the Desert* (Los Angeles: Oriental Missionary Society, 1931), p. 23.

67. *CCKHSCC,* vol. 2, p. 184.

68. Cowman, *Streams,* p. 23.

69. Whiting, Allen S., "Mystery Man of Formosa," *Saturday Evening Post,* March 12, 1955, p. 26.

70. Lodge Lo, Ching-kuo aide from 1958–1964, interview, Taipei, Sept. 13, 1995.

71. Eddy Chiang interview, May 19,1996.

72. Chou Lien-hua, interview, Taipei, May 17, 1996.

73. Ch'i P'eng-fei, *Chiang Chieh-shih Chia Shih* (History of the Chiang-Kai-shek Family) (Peking: Hualing Publishing, 1994), p. 200.

74. Interviews in Kanchow, June 12, 1996, with Fang Shih-tsao and others.

75. Ch'en Ta, *CCKTKN,* pp. 159–174.

76. Ch'i Kao-ju, *Chiang Ching-kuo teh yi sheng* (The Life of Chiang Ching-kuo) (Taipei: Biographical Literary Press, 1991), p. 104.

77. Ts'ao Yun-hsia, "Wu you he shi duo" (The Five Haves and Ten Manys), in *CCKTKN,* pp. 330–344.

78. Ch'en Ta, *CCKTKN,* pp. 154–179.

79. Robert Service, interview, April 11, 1996. Researchers in Kanchow say there is no evidence of this, but it seems plausible.

80. This story was told by a Chinese-American with close connections to Madame Chiang; interview, Dec. 1995.

7. DEAN AND GENERAL

1. Ai Ch'i-ming, interview, Nanking, June 15, 1996. (Ms. Ai was in charge of the woman's unit at the school.)

2. Ibid.

3. Ch'en Chih-ching, interview, Shanghai, Sept. 30, 1995.

4. Wang Chih-ping, "Hui yi Chiang Ching-kuo" (In Remembrance of Ching-kuo), in *Chiang shi fu zi* (The Chiangs, Father and Son) (Fenghua: Tien Ching, 1994), pp. 249–258.

5. Ch'en Chih-ching, interview, Sept. 30, 1995.

6. Ts'ai Hsing-san and Ts'ao Yun-hsia, *Chiang Ching-kuo hsi shih hua* (History of Chiang Ching Kuo Faction) (Hong Kong: Tian Di Books, 1988), pp. 107–108. Ts'ai was a secretary in the Youth Corps (TPPYC) and before that worked for Ching-kuo in Kannan.

7. *Chiang Ching-kuo tsai kan nan* (Chiang Ching-kuo in Kannan), henceforth *CCKTKN*, a collection of articles by former associates of Ching-kuo given at a conference on "Chiang Ching-kuo in Kannan" held by the Kiangsi Provincial Committee and Kanchow Municipal Committee in Nanch'ang in 1989, pp. 407–424.

8. Lee Huan and Lin Yin-ting, *Chui sui pan shih chi: Li Huan yu Ching-kuo hsien sheng* (Lee Huan: Following Chiang Ching-kuo for Half a Century) (Taipei: Commonwealth Press, 1998), p. 30.

9. Howard L. Boorman, *Biographical Dictionary of Republican China* (New York: Columbia University Press, 1979), vol. 3, p. 166.

10. Edward L. Dreyer, *China at War, 1901–1949* (White Plains, N.Y.: Longman Publishing Group, 1996), p. 300.

11. Barbara Tuchman, *Sand Against the Wind: the Stilwell Experience in China* (London: Macmillan, 1971), p. 484.

12. Wen Ha-hsiung, interview, Taipei, May 17, 1996.

13. Ts'ai and Ts'ao, *Chiang Ching-kuo*, pp. 115–116. Wang Ch'u-ying, interview, June 15, 1996. Wang was a political officer in the Youth Army.

14. Ch'en Li-fu and Sidney H. Chang, *The Storm Clouds Clear Over China* (Stanford: Hoover Institution Press, 1994), p. 170. Ch'en was Minister of Education from Jan. 1938 until Dec. 1944.

15. Joseph J. Heinlein, *Political Warfare: The Chinese Nationalist Model,* Ph.D. thesis, The American University, Washington, D.C., 1974, pp. 479–480.

16. Ibid., pp. 415–425.

17. Ts'ai and Ts'ao, *Chiang*, pp. 115–116.

18. Ibid., pp. 133–134.

19. Wang Ch'u-ying, interview, June 15, 1996.

20. Heinlein, *Political Warfare,* p. 439–440.

21. Ibid., p. 450.

22. Han Shan-p'i, *Chiang Ching kuo ping chuan* (The Life of Chiang Ching-kuo) (Hong Kong: Tianyuan Press, 1988), pp. 173–180.

23. Lodge Lo, interview, Taipei, Sept. 14, 1995.

24. The source is a Chinese-American close to Madame Chiang: in 1996 the woman in question was still living in Washington, D.C. but declined to be interviewed.

25. Chia Yi-pin, interview, Peking, Sept. 21, 1995.

26. Herbert Feis, *The China Tangle* (Princeton: 1953), pp. 19–20. Ch'en, *Storm Clouds,* p. 178, asserts that the Gimo did not accept Stalin's invitation because he feared he would be kidnapped.

27. Jonathan Spence, *The Search for Modern China* (New York: W. W. Norton, 1990),

p. 482. In April 1945 the CCP claimed 1.2 million members, 900,000 troops under arms, and a population of 95 million under its control.

28. Spence, *Search*, p. 482.

29. Ai Ch'i-ming, interview, June 15, 1996.

30. Heinlein, *Political Warfare*, p. 482.

31. Ch'eng Tien-fong, *A History of Sino-Russian Relations* (Westport, Conn.: Greenwood Press, 1957), pp. 280–281.

32. Cable from the U.S. Consulate in Urumchi, April 18, 1945, in *Foreign Relations of the United States* (Washington, D.C.: Government Printing Office, 1945), vol. 7, p. 1000. Henceforth *FRUS*.

33. Ibid., pp. 1000–01.

34. Cable from the U.S. Consulate in Urumchi, June 22, 1945, in ibid., pp. 1001–02.

35. Boorman, *Biographical Dictionary*, vol. 4, p. 424.

36. Ch'eng, *Sino-Russian*, p. 270.

37. Aitch'en K. Wu, *China and the Soviet Union* (London: Methuen, 1950), pp. 287–288.

38. Ts'ai and Ts'ao, *Chiang*, p. 38.

39. *CCKHSCC*, vol. 2, p. 232.

40. Boorman, *Biographical Dictionary*, vol. 3, pp. 152–153.

41. Ch'eng, *Sino-Russian*, p. 271.

42. Ibid., pp. 271–273.

43. *United States Relations with China, with Special Reference to the Period 1944–1949* (The White Paper) (Washington, D.C.: Government Printing Office, 1949), p. 123.

44. Six million Soviet military personnel died in the war and 2.2 million in the Chinese armed forces. R. R. Palmer and Joel Colton, *A History of the Modern World* (New York: Knopf, 1995), p. 860.

8. MANCHURIAN CANDIDATE

1. Tang Tsou, *America's Failure in China, 1941–1950* (Chicago: University of Chicago Press, 1963), p. 305. Steven I. Levine, *Anvil of Victory: The Communist Revolution In Manchuria, 1945–1948* (New York: Columbia University Press, 1987), p. 103.

2. Albert C. Wedemeyer, *Wedemeyer Reports* (New York: Holt, 1958), p. 346.

3. Wellington Koo stresses this point in explaining the Gimo's decision, in *Reminiscences of Wellington Koo*, Oral History, Butler Library, Columbia University, pp. H-361–362.

4. Han Suyin, *Eldest Son: Chou En-lai and the Making of Modern China, 1898–1976* (New York: Hill and Wang, 1994), p. 189.

5. Ibid., p. 261.

6. Ibid., p. 275.

7. Chang Kia-ngao, *Last Chance in Manchuria* (Stanford: Stanford University Press, 1989), p. 45.

8. Nikita Khrushchev, trans. Edward Crankshaw, *Khrushchev Remembers* (Boston: Little, Brown, 1970), pp. 548–549.

9. Chiang Ching-kuo, *Chiang Ching-kuo hsien sheng chuan chi*, (Chiang Ching-kuo, Collected Works) (Taipei: GIO, 1989), hereafter *CCKHSCC*, vol. 2, p. 305.

10. Ibid., pp. 304–305.

11. Ibid.

12. Chang, *Manchuria*, p. 93.

13. Ibid., p. 45.

14. *CCKHSCC*, vol. 2, pp. 311–312.

15. Ibid., pp. 323.

16. Ibid., pp. 311–312.

17. Ibid., pp. 319–320.

18. Chang Lingau, "Chiang Ching-kuo tsai tung pei" (Chiang Ching-kuo in the Northeast), pp. 211–213, 234, in *Chiang shih fu tzu* (The Chiangs, Father and Son), ed. the Literature and Historical Materials Committee of the Political Consultative Conference of Chekiang Province (Fenghua City: Tien Jing, 1994).

19. Ch'en Li-fu and Sidney H. Chang, *The Storm Clouds Clear Over China* (Stanford: Hoover Institution Press, 1994), pp. 184–185.

20. Chang, *Manchuria*, p. 118.

21. Ibid., p. 33.

22. Ibid., pp. 32–33.

23. Ibid., p. 234.

24. Ibid., pp. 34–35, 137.

25. Sergei N. Goncharov, John W. Lewis, Xue Litai, *Uncertain Partners: Stalin, Mao and the Korean War* (Stanford: Stanford University Press, 1993), p. 11.

26. Chang, *Manchuria*, p. 159.

27. Ibid., p. 161.

28. Marshall Mission Files, lot 54-D270, *Foreign Relations of the United States*, 1945, vol. 2, p. 797. Henceforth *FRUS*.

29. CCKHSCC, vol. 2, pp. 311–313.

30. Edward L. Dreyer, *China at War, 1901–1945* (White Plains, N.Y.: Longman Publishing Group, 1996), p. 324.

31. Howard L. Boorman, *Biographical Dictionary of Republican China* (New York: Columbia University Press, 1979), vol. 3, p. 166.

32. Wen Ch'ang, interview, Sept. 25, 1997. Wen Ha-hsiung, interview, Taipei, May 17, 1996.

33. Wen Ha-hsiung, interview, May 17, 1996.

34. Jonathan D. Spence, *The Search for Modern China* (New York: W. W. Norton, 1990), p. 494.

35. Wang Chu-ying, interview, Nanking, June 15, 1996.

36. Boorman, *Biographical Dictionary,* vol. 1, p. 69.

37. Papers provided by Andrei Ledovski to the author, Sept. 1997.

38. Memorandum #453-L, Molotov to Stalin, Dec. 29, 1945, "Reference to the Visit of Mr. Chiang Ching-kuo," pp. 1–2, Archives of the People's Commissar of Foreign Affairs. Provided to the author by Andrei Ledovsky, an officer in the Soviet embassy in China in 1945–46 and later Soviet ambassador to China. Molotov indicated in his memo that Chiang-Kai-shek had made these commitments prior to Ching-kuo's trip, subject to overall agreement.

39. Memorandum #453-L, Molotov to Stalin, Dec. 29, 1945, pp. 4–5.

40. Ibid.

41. Ibid.

42. Papers provided by Andrei Ledovski, Sept. 1997.

43. Allen Whiting reports that an informed Nationalist official told him this in the 1950s. Allen Whiting, *Sinkiang, Pawn or Pivot* (East Lansing: Michigan State University Press, 1958), p. 141.

44. Papers provided by Andrei Ledovski, Sept. 1997.

45. Chang, *Manchuria,* pp. 207–208.

46. AmEmb Nanking, cable Jan. 4, 1949, *FRUS 1949,* vol. 8, p. 8. Ch'u Wu, a fellow ex-Trotskyite, described this Ching-kuo-Stalin exchange. Ch'u Wu's report is not necessarily accurate but rings true, with the added condition put forward by Ching-kuo that the Soviets show their good faith.

47. Chang, *Manchuria,* p. 208.

48. Wen Ch'ang, interview, Sept. 26, 1995.

49. Chang, *Manchuria,* p. 244.

50. Ts'ai Hsing-san, *Chiang Ching-kuo yu Su Lien* (Chiang Ching-kuo and the Soviet Union) (Hong Kong: Tian di Books, 1976), pp. 48–49.

51. *United States Relations with China, with Special Reference to the Period 1944–1949* (The White Paper) (Washington, D.C.: Government Printing Office, 1949), p. 146.

52. Ibid., p. 147.

53. *Shen Pao* (newspaper), Shanghai, April 1, 1946.

54. *Chung yang jih pao (Central Daily News),* Nanking, April 1, 1946, p. 2. Chang, *Manchuria,* pp. 280, 283. *New York Times,* April 1, 1946. *Shen Pao,* Shanghai, April 1, 1946.

55. *Chung yang jih pao,* Nanking, April 1, 1946, p. 2.

56. Chang, *Manchuria,* p. 258–259.

57. The White Paper, p. 149.

58. Dreyer, *China at War,* p. 324.

59. Ibid.

60. Chang, *Manchuria,* p. 343.

61. Ibid., p. 297.

62. AmEmb Nanking, cable Jan. 4, 1949, *FRUS 1949*, vol. 8, pp. 8–9. Andrei Ledovski says Ching-kuo's meeting with Roschin was on April 24. Ledovski, e-mail notes to the author, Sept. 1997.

63. April 22, 1946, top secret cable to ComGen China (Wedemeyer) from Nanking HQ (General Gillem), NatArch, College Park Maryland, RG 334 entry 90 (Army MAG China), box 3, item 9.

9. DEFEAT

1. E. R. Hooton, *The Greatest Tumult: The Chinese Civil War, 1936–1949* (London: Brassey's, 1991), pp. 65–68.

2. Wang Shao-yu, interview, Taipei, May 11, 1996. Wang worked for Ching-kuo in the Reserve Officers Bureau in Nanking in 1946–47.

3. Chia Yi-pin, interview, Peking, Sept. 21, 1995. Chia was head of the education office in the demobilization office in 1946.

4. Chiang Nan (pen name of Henry Liu), *Chiang Ching-kuo chuan* (Biography of Chiang Ching-kuo) (Los Angeles: Mei-kuo lun t'an pao, 1984), p. 130.

5. Chiang Nan, *Chiang*, p. 130.

6. Ch'en Chih-ching, interview, Shanghai, Sept. 25, 1995. Ch'en was head of the Shanghai branch of the Youth Army Soldiers' Federation from 1946 to 1949.

7. Ai Ch'i-ming, interview, Nanking, June 15, 1996. Ai was with Ching-kuo in the Cadre School, the Youth Army, and the Demobilization Bureau.

8. Konsin Shah, interview, Taipei, May 29, 1996.

9. John Chang, interview, Taipei, May 23, 1996.

10. Ts'ai Hsing-san and Ts'ao Yun-hsia, *Chiang Ching-kuo hsi shih hua* (History of Chiang Ching Kuo Faction) (Hong Kong: Tien Ti Books, 1979), p. 14.

11. Chia Yi-pin, interview, Sept. 21, 1995.

12. Feng Fu-fa, "Wo teh fu ch'in Feng Yu-hsiang" (My Father General Feng Yu-hsiang), in *Wen shih tsu liao hsuan pian* (Selected Historical Writings and Documents) (Peking: 1982), vol. 15, p. 19. Feng Fu-neng was then living in Nanking, where her father, Feng Yu-hsiang, was Vice Chairman of the National Military Commission. Her sister, Feng Fu-fa, reports that Fu-neng "married while on a trip," but does not provide details.

13. *Chiang shih fu tzu* (The Chiangs, Father and Son), ed. the Literature and Historical Materials Committee of the Political Consultative Conference of Chekiang Province (Fenghua City: Tien Jing, 1994), pp. 289–290.

14. Ai Ch'i-ming, June 15, 1996, Ai attended the ceremony.

15. Papers provided by Andrei Ledovski to the author, Sept. 1997.

16. *United States Relations with China, with Special Reference to the Period 1944–1949* (The White Paper) (Washington, D.C.: U.S. Government Printing Office, 1949), p. 309.

17. This and the following paragraphs on the uprising are drawn from the balanced

account by Lai Tse-han, Ramon H. Meyers, and Wei Wou, *A Tragic Beginning: The Taiwan Uprising of February 28, 1947* (Stanford: Stanford University Press, 1991).

18. AmEmb cable, March 18, 1947, *Foreign Relations of the United States* (Washington, D.C.: Government Printing Office, 1947), vol. 7, p. 442. Henceforth *FRUS*.

19. Ts'ai and Ts'ao, *Chiang Ching-kuo*, pp. 161–167. In 1996 Ch'en Li-fu said the incident was all a misunderstanding. Ch'en Li-fu, interview, May 29, 1996. Also see Ch'en Li-fu and Sidney H. Chang, *The Storm Clouds Clear Over China* (Stanford: Hoover Institution Press, 1994), pp. 196–198.

20. Wang Chu-ying, interview, Nanking, June 15, 1996. Wang was an officer in the 52nd Army that fought in Liaoning province.

21. Howard L. Boorman, *Biographical Dictionary of Republican China* (New York: Columbia University Press, 1979), vol. 3, p. 167; Donald Klein and Anne Clark, *Biographical Dictionary of Chinese Communism: 1921–1965* (Cambridge, Mass.: Harvard University Press, 1971), p. 132.

22. Chiang Nan, *Chiang*, pp. 156–157. Han Shan-p'i, *Chiang Ching kuo ping chuan* (The Life of Chiang Ching-kuo) (Hong Kong: Tian yuan Press, 1988), pp. 234–242.

23. Chiang Shu, interview, Shanghai, Sept. 30, 1995. Chiang Shu attended the Lushan conference.

24. Lloyd E. Eastman, "Who Lost China? Chiang-Kai-shek Testifies," *China Quarterly*, 88 (Dec. 1981), p. 661, citing *Collection of the Thoughts and Speeches of President Chiang* (Taipei: 1966).

25. Ch'en Chih-ching, interview, Sept. 30, 1997.

26. Ch'i P'eng-fei, *Chiang Chieh-shih chia shih* (History of the Chiang-Kai-shek Family) (Peking: Tuan Chieh Press, 1994), p. 203.

27. Eastman, "Who Lost China," pp. 660–661.

28. AmEmb Nanking, cable Dec. 19, 1947, *FRUS 1947*, vol. 7, p. 411.

29. Ibid.

30. StateDept, cable to AmEmb Nanking, *FRUS, 1947*, vol. 7, p. 410.

31. AmEmb Nanking, cable to StateDept Jan. 4, 1949, *FRUS 1949*, vol. 8, p. 9. The source of the information is Urumchi Mayor Ch'u Wu, Ching-kuo's friend and former ex-Trotskyite. His remarks have to be viewed skeptically, but they are consistent with the reports from George Yeh and Chang Chih-chung to Stuart.

32. AmEmb Nanking, cable Dec. 22, 1947, *FRUS 1947*, vol. 7, pp. 412–413.

33. Ibid.

34. In December 1949 Ch'u Wu claimed that the Soviets had given a favorable response to this December 1947 approach, but that Ching-kuo had then informed them that the situation had changed and the Generalissimo would not make the trip. It is possible that Madame Chiang and T. V. Soong heard of this approach to Moscow and turned the Gimo around. Roschin, however, was at the meeting when Ch'u said there had been a positive Soviet reply, and he did not deny it. AmEmb Nanking, cable to StateDept Jan. 4, 1949, *FRUS 1949*, vol. 8, p. 9. Goncharov reports that Stalin passed along to Mao a letter from Chiang Kai-shek in late summer of 1948, which might have referred to the December 1947 initiative. Sergei N. Goncharov, John W. Lewis,

Xue Litai, *Uncertain Partners: Stalin, Mao and the Korean War* (Stanford: Stanford University Press, 1993), p. 25.

35. Klein and Clark, *Biographical Dictionary,* p. 133.

36. Dimitri Volkogonov, *Stalin, Triumph and Tragedy,* ed. and trans. Harold Shukman (Rocklin, Calif.: Forum, 1996), pp. 537–539.

37. Goncharov, Lewis, Xue, *Uncertain Partners,* p. 25.

38. Klein and Clark, *Biographical Dictionary,* p. 133.

39. Chen Jian, *China's Road to the Korean War: The Making of the Sino-American Confrontation* (New York: Columbia University Press, 1994), pp. 107–109.

40. Jonathan Spence, *The Search for Modern China* (New York: W. W. Norton, 1990), pp. 501–502.

41. Suzanne Pepper, *Civil War in China: The Political Struggle, 1945–1949* (Berkeley: University of California Press, 1978), pp. 121–122.

42. Boorman, *Biographical Dictionary,* vol. 4, pp. 63–64.

43. Chiang-Kai-shek, *Nanking Diaries,* Nanking #2 National Archives, entry for August 23, 1948.

44. *North China Daily News* (henceforth NCDN), Shanghai, Sept. 1, 1948.

45. Ch'en Chih-ching, interview, Oct. 2, 1995.

46. Shanghai Municipal Archives, file Q6-7-90.

47. Ch'en Chih-ching, interview, Sept. 30, 1995.

48. Ibid.

49. Ch'i, *Chiang Chieh-shih,* p. 204.

50. Ch'i Kao-ju, *Chiang Ching-kuo teh yi sheng* (The Life of Chiang Ching-kuo) (Taipei: Chuan chi wen hsueh, 1991), pp. 204–205.

51. "Chiang Ching-kuo ta hu ch'uan tong de ku shi" (The Whole Story of Chiang Ching-kuo Beating the Tigers), *Li shih tzu liao (Historical Data)*, Shanghai, 6 (1988), pp. 137–146.

52. Ibid.

53. NCDN, Sept. 4, 1948.

54. NCND, Sept. 5, 1948.

55. NCND, Sept. 8, 1948.

56. NCND, Sept. 9, 1948.

57. Pepper, *Civil War,* p. 123.

58. Spence, *The Search,* p. 504.

59. Shanghai Municipal Archives, file Q6-7-90. Also NCND, Sept. 13, 1948.

60. Ibid.

61. Ibid.

62. Shanghai Municipal Archives, file Q6-7-90.

63. Ibid.

64. Ch'en Chih-ching, interview, Oct. 2, 1995.

65. Ibid.

66. Ibid.

67. Shanghai Municipal Archives, file Q6-7-90. Also NCND, Sept. 13, 1948.

68. Ch'en Chih-ching, interview, Oct. 2, 1995.

69. Ibid.

70. Ibid.

71. Ch'i, *Chiang Ching-kuo*, p. 206.

72. *CCKHSCC*, vol. 2, p. 524.

73. NCND, Sept. 10, 1948.

74. AmConGen Hong Kong, dispatch 40, Sept. 13, 1948, NatArch RG 59, General Records of the State Department 1945–1949, box 7275.

75. Ibid., dispatch no. 45, Sept. 25, 1948.

76. "ta hu ch'uan tung," *Li shih tzu liao*, pp. 137–146.

77. Ibid. Also Ch'en Chih-ching, interview, Oct. 2, 1995.

78. Chia Yi-pin, interview, Sept. 21, 1995.

79. Ibid.

80. Chia Yi-pin, e-mail Feb. 24, 1997.

81. Chia Yi-pin, interview, Sept. 21, 1995.

82. AmConGen Hong Kong, dispatch 45, Sept. 25, 1948, NatArch RG 59, StateDept file 1945–1949, box 7275.

83. An investigation concluded that the Yangtze Company had in fact "hoarded and smuggled goods and evaded taxes," and that Mayor K. C. Wu had tried to protect the company. Hsiung Tsai-wei and Chin Yueh-kuang, "Report on the Investigation of the Yangtze Company," Nov. 30, 1948, Shanghai Municipal Archives, Chiang Ching-kuo file Q-6-7-90.

84. Pepper, *Civil War*, p. 124.

85. The White Paper, pp. 400–401. *Chin yung erh pao*, Shanghai, August 28, 1948.

86. Pepper, *Civil War*, p. 122. *Shih yu wen*, Shanghai, August 27, 1948.

87. Ibid.

88. The White Paper, p. 401.

89. Steven I. Levine, *Anvil of Victory: The Communist Revolution In Manchuria, 1945–1948* (New York: Columbia University Press, 1987), pp. 134–136. The White Paper, p. 321.

90. Ch'en Chih-ching, interview, Oct. 2, 1995.

91. NCDN, Nov. 1, 1948.

92. AmConGen Shanghai, telegram 2284, Nov. 1, 1948, NatArch, StateDept. file 1945–1949, box 7275.

93. Pepper, *Civil War*, p. 126.

94. NCDN, Nov. 14, 1948.

95. Ch'en Chih-ching, interview, Oct. 2, 1995.

96. Ibid.

97. The battle raged from the Huai River to the sea (*hai*).

98. Richard Evans, *Deng Xiaoping and the Making of Modern China* (New York: Penguin Books, 1993), pp. 105–106.

99. Chiang Wei-kuo, interview, June 5, 1996.

100. The White Paper, p. 323.

10. END GAME

1. David M. Finkelstein, *Washington's Taiwan Dilemma, 1949–1950* (Fairfax, Va.: George Mason University Press, 1993), p. 110.

2. Konsin Shah, interview, Taipei, May 22, 1996.

3. A Chinese American who has known Chang Hsueh-liang for many years.

4. Konsin Shah, interview, May 22, 1996. Nancy Chiang, interview, Taipei, May 22, 1996.

5. John Chang, interview, Taipei, Sept. 15, 1995.

6. Chia Yi-pin, interview, Peking, Sept. 21, 1995

7. Hollinton Tong, *Chiang Kai-shek, Soldier and Statesman* (Taipei: China Publishing Company, 1953), pp. 439–440. Brian Crozier, *The Man Who Lost China* (New York: Charles Scribner's Sons, 1976), pp. 325–326.

8. Chiang Ching-kuo, *Chiang Ching-kuo hsien sheng chuan chi*, (Chiang Ching-kuo, Collected Works) (Taipei: GIO, 1989). Henceforth *CCKHSCC*, vol. 1, p. 385.

9. Chiang Wei-kuo, *Chien shan tu hsing: Chiang wei kuo de jen sheng chih lu* (Walking Alone in the Midst of a Thousand Mountains: Chiang Wei-kuo's Life Journey) (Taipei: Tienhsia Press, 1996), p. 113.

10. Konsin Shah, interview, May 22, 1996.

11. Ibid.

12. Tong, *Chiang*, p. 449.

13. *CCKHSCC*, vol. 2, pp. 216–217.

14. Ibid., pp. 380–399.

15. Tang Tsou, *America's Failure in China, 1941–1950* (Chicago: University of Chicago Press, 1963), p. 497. Li Tsung-jen and Te-kong Tong, *The Memoirs of Li Tsung-jen* (Boulder, Co.: Westview Press, 1974), pp. 506–507.

16. *CCKHSCC*, vol. 2, p. 221.

17. Howard L. Boorman, *Biographical Dictionary of Republican China* (New York: Columbia University Press, 1979), vol. 1, p. 254. *CCKHSCC*, vol. 1, p. 393.

18. Li and Tong, *Memoirs*, p. 511.

19. Nieh Rung-chen, *Hung hsing chih nei: Nie Rung-chen yuan shai hui yi lu* (Inside the Red Star: The Memoirs of Marshal Nieh Rung-chen) (Peking: New World Press, 1988), pp. 585–586.

20. "Memorandum of A. I. Mikoyan to the Presidium on his January and February visit

to China," doc. P2375, in Andrei Ledovsky, "Mikoyan's Secret Mission to China in January and February 1949," *Far Eastern Affairs*, 2, Moscow (1995), pp. 73–93.

21. Sergei N. Goncharov, John W. Lewis, Xue Litai, *Uncertain Partners, Stalin, Mao and the Korean War* (Stanford: Stanford University Press, 1993), pp. 40–44.

22. Alexander Larin, Moscow, e-mail to author, June 2, 1997.

23. Mao Zedong, *On People's Democratic Dictatorship* (Peking: Foreign Language Press, 1952), p. 10.

24. Konsin Shah, interview, May 22, 1996.

25. Ibid.

26. Ch'en Chih-ching, interview, October 2, 1995.

27. Chia Yi-pin, interview, Sept. 21, 1995.

28. NSC document 37/2, "The Current Position of the United States with Respect to Formosa," Feb. 3, 1949, *Foreign Relations of the United States* (Washington, D.C.: Government Printing Office, 1949), vol. 9, pp. 281–282; henceforth *FRUS*. For U.S. judgments and decisions during the year see State memo, Butterworth to Secretary Acheson, Dec. 16, 1949, NatArch RG 59, box 7386. On the vagaries of U.S. policy-making in 1949 and 1950 see the excellent work by Finkelstein, *Taiwan Dilemma*.

29. NSC document 37/2, Feb. 3, 1949, "The Current Position of the United States with Respect to Formosa," *FRUS, 1949,* vol. 9, pp. 281–282.

30. Finkelstein, *Taiwan Dilemma,* pp. 117–118.

31. *Lien ho pao*, Taipei, March 22, 1988. There are no American records available on the discussions between MacArthur and Sun. See Finkelstein, *Taiwan Dilemma*, p. 148.

32. Ibid.

33. Ibid.

34. AmConGen Taipei, cable May 18, 1949, NatArch RG 59, Box 7387.

35. Finkelstein, *Taiwan Dilemma*, p. 143.

36. Crozier, *The Man Who,* p. 332.

37. Boorman, *Biographical Dictionary*, vol. 1, p. 45.

38. Chia Yi-pin, interview, Sept. 21, 1995.

39. Li and Tong, *Memoirs*, p. 514.

40. Edward L. Dreyer, *China at War, 1901–1949* (White Plains, N.Y.: Longman Publishing Group, 1996), p. 347.

41. Tang Tsou, *America's Failure*, p. 501.

42. *Chiang Ching-kuo tzu shu* (Chiang Ching-kuo's Diaries) (Changsha: Hunan Peoples Press, 1988), p. 215.

43. Wang Shun-ch'i and Hu Yuan-fu, *Chiang Ching-kuo tsai ku hsiang yi shih* (Stories of Chiang Ching-kuo in His Hometown), ed. by the Literature and Historial Materials Committee of the Political Consultative Council (Fenghua City: Guji Press, 1994), pp. 291–292.

44. *Chiang Ching-kuo tzu shu*, p. 215. Konsin Shah, interview, May 22, 1996.

45. Konsin Shah, interview, May 22, 1996.

46. Ibid.

47. AmConGen Shanghai, cable 1656, May 16, 1949, *FRUS, 1949,* vol. 8, pp. 320–321.

48. Tong, *Chiang,* pp. 450–451.

49. *CCKHSCC,* vol. 1, p. 432.

50. Joseph J. Heinlein, *Political Warfare: The Chinese Nationalist Model,* Ph.D.. diss., The American University, Washington, D.C.. 1974, p. 492.

51. Ts'ai Hsing-san and Ts'ao Yun-hsia, *Chiang Ching-kuo hsi shih hua* (History of Chiang Ching Kuo Faction) (Hong Kong: Tien Ti Books, 1979), p. 260. Tong, *Chiang,* p. 453, gives the departure date as May 6.

52. Tong, *Chiang,* p. 451.

53. *Chiang Ching-kuo tzu shu,* p. 216.

54. Lionel Max Chassin, *The Communist Conquest of China* (London: Weidenfield and Nicholson, 1966), pp. 222–223. For an alarmist American view see AmConGen Shanghai, cable 1656, May 16, 1949, *FRUS, 1949,* vol. 8, p. 321.

55. *Chiang Ching-kuo tzu shu,* p. 216.

56. Konsin Shah, interview, May 22, 1996. Finkelstein, *Taiwan Dilemma,* p. 111.

57. Konsin Shah, interview, May 22, 1996.

58. StateDept memo, K.C. Krentz to Butterworth and Sprouse, June 8, 1949, NatArch RG 59, box 7386.

59. Konsin Shah, Taipei, interview, May 22, 29, 1996. Eddy Chiang, interview, Taipei, May 19, 1996.

60. Konsin Shah, interview, May 22, 29, 1996.

61. AmConGen Shanghai, cable 1635, May 14, 1949, NatArch RG 59, StateDept file 1945–1949, box 7279.

62. AmConGen Shanghai, cable 2496, June 26, 1949, *FRUS, 1949,* vol. 9.

63. Crozier, *The Man Who,* p. 338.

64. Konsin Shah, interview, May 22, 29, 1996.

65. Ibid.

66. Mao Zedong, *On People's Democratic Dictatorship* (Peking: Foreign Language Press, 1952), p. 10.

67. Goncharov, Lewis, and Xue, *Uncertain Partners,* p. 72.

68. Ibid., pp. 72–76.

69. Finkelstein, *Taiwan Dilemma,* p. 171.

70. Tong, *Chiang,* p. 454.

71. Li and Tong, *Memoirs,* p. 537. Boorman, *Biographical Dictionary,* vol. 4, p. 7.

72. Tong, *Chiang,* p. 460.

73. Ibid., p. 539.

74. K. T. Li, interview, Taipei, Sept. 4, 1995.

75. Koo Ch'en-fu, interview, Taipei, Sept. 11, 1995.

76. AmEmb Taipei, cable Sept. 14, 1949, NatArch RG 59, box 7386.

77. AmEmb Taipei, cable Sept. 15, 1949, NatArch RG 59, box 7387.

78. Finkelstein, *Taiwan Dilemma*, pp. 187–199.

79. Ibid. p. 194.

80. AmEmb Taipei, cable Nov. 5, 1949, NatArch RG 59, box 7387.

81. Wang Sheng, answers to written questions, spring 1996.

82. *CCKHSCC*, vol. 1, p. 226.

83. Ibid., p. 68.

84. Tong, *Chiang*, p. 475.

85. Konsin Shah, interview, May 22, 1996.

86. Ibid.

87. Crozier, *The Man Who*, p. 344.

88. AmEmb Taipei, cable Nov. 11, 1949, NatArch RG 59, box 7387. Memo Butterworth to Secretary of State from Bureau of Far Eastern Affairs, Dec. 15, 1949, NatArch RG 59, box 7386.

89. Tong, *Chiang*, p. 477. Tong claims the fish was five feet long!

90. Tsou, *America's Failure*, pp. 512–513. Finkelstein, *Taiwan Dilemma*, pp. 227–237.

91. Memcon, Dec. 29, 1949, Dean Acheson, Omar N. Bradley, et. al., NatArch RG 59, Box 7387.

92. Tsou, America's Failure, p. 529.

11. AN UNINTENDED CONSEQUENCE

1. Fred Chien, interview, Taipei, August 29, 1995.

2. Former CIA officers who served in Taiwan in the 1950s and 1960s, interviews, 1995–1998.

3. George Kerr, *Formosa Betrayed* (Boston: Houghton Mifflin, 1976), p. 368.

4. Kerr, *Formosa*, p. 395.

5. *Chiang Ching-kuo tsai kan nan* (Chiang Ching-kuo in Kannan), henceforth *CCKTKN*, a collection of articles by former associates of Ching-kuo given at a conference on "Chiang Ching-kuo in Kannan" held by the Kiangsi Provincial Committee and Kanchow Municipal Committee in Nanch'ang in 1989, p. 287. Hollinton Tong, *Chiang Kai-shek, Soldier and Statesman* (Taipei: China Publishing Company, 1953), p. 493. In a May 25, 1996, Taipei interview with the author, Wang Sheng said that in the 1949–1951 period more than 2,700 Communists agents were found.

6. CIA memo, May 11, 1950, file AOI, 878.OA12, FIO request.

7. Tong, *Chiang*, p. 493. Kerr, *Formosa*, p. 395. Wang Sheng, interview, Taipei, May 25, 1996.

8. Tong, *Chiang*, p. 493.

9. Wang Sheng, interviews, Sept. 8, 11, 1995, May 31, 1996. Wang Sheng, answers to written questions, spring 1996.

10. Wellington Koo, *Reminiscences of Wellington Koo*, Oral History, Butler Library, Columbia University, undated, p. H-338.

11. Wang Sheng, interviews, Sept. 8, 11, 1995, May 31, 1996. Wang Sheng, answers, spring 1996.

12. AmEmb Taipei, memcon, Jan. 16, 1950, *Foreign Relations of the United States* (Washington, D.C.: Government Printing Office, 1950), vol. 6, p. 280; henceforth *FRUS*.

13. AmEmb Taipei, cable April 27, 1950, *FRUS, 1950*, vol. 6, p. 335.

14. *State Department Bulletin*, Jan. 16, 1950, p. 79.

15. Harrison E. Salisbury, *War Between Russia and China* (New York: W. W. Norton, 1969), p. 97.

16. Sergei N. Goncharov, John W. Lewis, Xue Litai, *Uncertain Partners, Stalin, Mao and the Korean War* (Stanford: Stanford University Press, 1993), pp. 76–129.

17. Ibid.

18. Nikita Khrushchev, *Khrushchev Remembers*, trans. and ed. by Strobe Talbott (Boston: Little Brown, 1970), pp. 368–369. Also from the Russian text as cited by Goncharov, Lewis, Xue, *Uncertain Partners*, p. 325 n2.

19. Chen Jian, *China's Road to the Korean War: The Making of the Sino-American Confrontation* (New York: Columbia University Press, 1994), pp. 87–88.

20. Goncharov, Lewis, Xue, *Uncertain Partners*, pp. 130, 325 n1.

21. Ibid.

22. Gregory Henderson, *Korea: The Politics of the Vortex* (Cambridge, Mass.: Harvard University Press, 1968), p. 149.

23. CIA memo, May 11, 1950, file AOI, 878.OA12, FIO request.

24. Ch'en Li-fu and Sidney H. Chang, *The Storm Clouds Clear Over China* (Stanford: Hoover Institution Press, 1994),

pp. 218–221.

25. Howard L. Boorman, *Biographical Dictionary of Republican China* (New York: Columbia University Press, 1979), vol. 4, pp. 29–31.

26. Chiang Ching-kuo, *Chiang Ching-kuo hsien sheng chuan chi* (Chiang Ching-kuo, Collected Works) (Taipei: GIO, 1989), henceforth *CCKHSCC*, vol. 1, chronology, p. 154.

27. CIA memo, May 11, 1950, file AOI, 878.OA12, FIO request. Also Rosemary Foot, *A Substitute for Victory* (Ithaca: Cornell University Press, 1990), p. 296.

28. CIA memo for the President cited by David M. Finkelstein, *Washington's Taiwan Dilemma, 1949–1950* (Fairfax, Va.: George Mason University Press, 1993), p. 296.

29. Konsin Shah, interview, May 22, 1996.

30. *Republic of China Yearbook, 1951* (Taipei: Kuang hua Press, 1951), p. 492.

31. CIA, "Prospects," July 26, 1950, IM-312 D/FE, FIO request.

32. CIA memo, May 11, 1950.

33. CIA, "Prospects." July 26, 1950.

34. Bruce Cumings, *Origins of the Korean War* (Princeton: Princeton University Press, 1981), p. 531, citing American military intelligence documents.

35. Goncharov, Lewis, Xue, *Uncertain Partners*, p. 146. Chen, *China's Road*, pp. 120–125.

36. Nancy Bernkopf Tucker, "A House Divided: The United States, the State Department and China," in Warren I. Cohen and Akira Iriye, eds., *The Great Powers in East Asia, 1953–1960* (New York: Columbia University Press, 1990), pp. 330–331.

37. Tucker, "House Divided," p. 32.

38. Wang Ch'u-ying, interview, Nanking, June 15, 1996. Wang was an officer in the 52nd Army on Taiwan.

39. Cumings, *Origins*, p. 535.

40. Ibid., p. 537.

41. Dulles to Senator Arthur Vandenburg, letter of Jan. 1950, in Finkelstein, *Taiwan Dilemma*, p. 302.

42. StateDept memo, Rusk to Acheson, June 9, 1950, NatArch, StateDept RG 4254, Office of Chinese Affairs, box 17.

43. Tu Nien-chung, in *Chungkuo shih pao chou k'an (China Times Weekly)*, Taipei, Sept. 1–7, 1990, pp. 8–11. Tu interviewed Rusk in 1990 (month and day not given). After the interview, Rusk expressed dismay to learn that Sun was still alive in Taiwan and thus would be embarrassed by his revelations. Tu Nien-chung, conversations with the author, Taipei, May 1996.

44. AmEmb Taipei, cable June 7, 1950, NatArch, box StateDept.

45. *Hearings on the Military Situation in the Far East* (The MacArthur hearings), U.S. Senate Committee on the Armed Services and the Committee on Foreign Relations, 82nd Congress, 1st sess. (1951), p. 2621.

46. Goncharov, Lewis, Xue, *Uncertain* Partners, p. 152.

47. Leonard A. Kusnitz, *Public Opinion and Foreign Policy: America's China Policy, 1949–1979* (Westport, Conn.: Greenwood Press, 1984), p. 34. On MacArthur, see Finkelstein, *Taiwan Dilemma*, p. 315–317.

48. Tu Nien-chung, in *Chungkuo*, p. 11. Rusk said Sun had not proposed a "plan," but only an "idea."

49. *General MacArthur's Report to the United Nations Secretary General*, UN Publications, Sept. 18, 1950.

50. Tong, *Chiang*, p. 506.

51. Dean Rusk as told to Daniel S. Papp, *As I Saw It* (New York: W. W. Norton, 1990), pp. 175–176. According to Rusk, a "very high [Taipei] official" told him this story, almost certainly Yeh. Chiang's offer was conditional on the United States totally equipping the 33,000 troops with modern weapons and providing two years training.

52. A contributing factor may have been an epidemic that swept through the Chinese troops. Jonathan D. Spence, *The Search For Modern China* (New York: W. W. Norton, 1990), p. 526.

53. Chen, *China's Road*, pp. 130–133. Mao Zedong, *Wei ta te k'ang mei yuan chiao Yun tung* (The Great Movement to Resist the United States and to Help Korea) (Peking: Foreign Language Press, 1954).

54. Tucker, "House Divided," pp. 36–38.

55. Konsin Shah, interview, May 22, 1996. Shah attended the MacArthur meetings.

56. Ibid.

57. AmEmb Taipei, cable Sept. 6, 1950, *FRUS, 1950,* vol. 6, pp. 486–487.

58. Ts'u Sung-chi'u, interview, Taipei, June 6, 1996.

59. Ch'i Kao-ju, *Chiang Ching-kuo teh yi sheng* (The Life of Chiang Ching-kuo) (Taipei: Biographical Literary Press, 1991), pp. 220–221.

60. Steven J. Hood, *The Kuomintang and the Democratization of Taiwan* (Boulder, Co.: Westview Press, 1997), p. 35.

61. AmEmb Taipei, cable Sept. 6, 1950.

62. Hood, *Kuomintang,* p. 31.

63. Chen, *China's Road,* pp. 154–156.

64. Ibid., p. 161–162.

65. Khrushchev, *Khrushchev Remembers,* p. 370. Goncharov, Lewis, Xue, *Uncertain Partners,* p. 189.

66. George Kennan, *Memoirs, 1950–1963* (New York: Hutchinson, 1983), p. 94.

67. Khrushchev, *Khrushchev Remembers,* p. 370.

68. Chen, *China's Road,* p. 129. Donald Zagoria, *The Sino-Soviet Conflict, 1956–1961* (Princeton: Princeton University Press, 1962), pp. 164–165.

69. Chen, *China's Road,* pp. 180–181.

12. SECRET WARS

1. CIA and U.S. military intelligence officers who had served in Taiwan in the 1950s and 1960s, 1995–1998 interviews.

2. William Leary, *Perilous Mission: Civil Air Transport and CIA Covert Operations in Asia* (Montgomery: 1980).

3. Victor Marchetti and John D. Marks, *The CIA and the Cult of Intelligence* (New York: Knopf, 1980), p. 121.

4. Retired ROC Air Force officer familiar with these operations, interview, Taipei, May 1996.

5. CIA and U.S. military intelligence officers.

6. Ibid.

7. Ibid.

8. National Intelligence Estimate no. 43-6, June 20, 1961, "Prospects for the Government of the Republic of China," FIO request.

9. Ibid. Also, Wellington Koo, *Reminiscences of Wellington Koo,* Oral History, Butler Library, Columbia University, 1954, p. H-341.

10. CIA and U.S. military intelligence officers.

11. Ibid.

12. NIE no. 43-64 of March 11, 1964, stated that the Nationalist raiding parties "have so far produced little intelligence or much else of value." The one senior CIA officer interviewed who praised Nationalist intelligence in the 1950s and 1960s said it was "more sophisticated than that of Israel or France." Interview, Nov. 11, 1995.

13. Ray S. Cline, *Secrets, Spies and Scholars: Blueprint of the Essential CIA* (Washington, D.C.: Acropolis Books, 1976), p. 177.

14. Alfred W. McCoy, *The Politics of Heroin in Southeast Asia* (New York: Harper & Row, 1972), pp. 169–170.

15. *New York Times,* April 6, 1951, p. 12.

16. McCoy, *Heroin,* pp. 171–178.

17. Henry Kao, interview, Taipei, August 30, 1995.

18. *Republic of China Yearbook* (Taipei: Kuang Hua Press, 1951), p. 495.

19. Allen Whiting, "Mystery Man of Formosa," *Saturday Evening Post,* March 12, 1955, p. 117. Ching-kuo explained that continuing arrests and convictions after 1950 reflected ongoing infiltration of agents.

20. CIA, "Prospects for an Early Successful Chinese Communist Attack on Taiwan," July 26, 1950, IM-312 D/FE, FIO request.

21. AmEmb Taipei, cable Sept. 6, 1950, *FRUS, 1950,* vol. 6, p. 486.

22. Former CIA officer stationed in Taipei in 1950.

23. Wang Sheng, interview, May 25, 1996.

24. According to the CIA, in 1951 there were 264 cases of subversion resulting in convictions. Each case usually involved two or more persons. Thus the total number of persons convicted was probably around 600 (NIE, "Morale on Taiwan," April 16, 1955, *FRUS, 1955–57,* vol. 2, p. 484.) In 1952, according to K. C. Wu, there were 998 arrests, which, using the one-third conviction rate, would mean that the military court found about 330 individuals guilty. Given the figures available for other years in the period, however, Wu was probably referring to "cases" rather than "arrests." See Steven J. Hood, *The Kuomintang and the Democratization of Taiwan* (Boulder, Co.: Westview Press, 1997), p. 35. In 1954 the Peace Preservation Headquarters announced that 858 cases of subversion involving 1,745 persons "had been tabled" in the first three quarters of the year, resulting in the conviction of 597 of these individuals, or extrapolating for the whole year, a figure of around 750 (NIE, April 16, cited above). Ching-kuo told a visitor that in the first half of 1954, "we broke an average of 13 Communist conspiracies every month. (Whiting, "Mystery Man," p. 117.) These statements suggest that military courts convicted 350 to 400 people of espionage or treason that year.

25. Koo, *Reminiscences,* p. H-174, reports the figure given to Hu Shih by the Minister of Justice in 1953. In 1954 Koo was told the number was only 6,000, p. H-338.

26. Hsieh Ts'ung-min (Roger Hsieh), interview, Taipei, June 4, 1996: a KMT legislator told him that the figure was much higher—60,000 to 70,000.

27. The writer is Lan Bozhou, see *Far Eastern Economic Review,* June 5, 1997, p. 70; henceforth *FEER.* The Ministry of Justice informed opposition leaders in the 1990s that the files on executions had long since been burned. Hsieh Ts'ung-min, interview, June 4, 1996.

28. AmEmb Taipei, dispatch, March 15, 1954, NatArch, RG59 StateDept. file 1950-54, box 4218. Henceforth, NA-box 4218.

29. Ch'i P'eng-fei, *Chiang Chieh-shih Chia Shih* (History of the Chiang-Kai-shek Family) (Peking: Tuan chieh Press, 1994), p. 215.

30. Konsin Shah, interview, Taipei, May 22, 1996.

31. Henry Kao, interview, August 30, 1995.

32. CIA and U.S. military officers who served in Taiwan in the 1950s.

33. Interview with the Nationalist army officer, Nanking, June 14, 1996.

34. Wang Sheng, interview, May 25, 1996

35. Chiang Ching-kuo, *Chiang Ching-kuo hsien sheng chuan chi* (Chiang Ching-kuo, *Collected Works*) (Taipei: 1989), vol. 1, chronology, p. 154. Henceforth *CCKHSCC*. Ch'i, *Chiang*, p. 214.

36. Joseph J. Heinlein, *Political Warfare: The Chinese Nationalist Model*, Ph.D. thesis, The American University, Washington, D.C.. 1974, pp. 521–525.

37. Heinlein, *Political*, pp. 582–601.

38. *New York Times*, March 6, 1954, p. 3.

39. Heinlein, *Political*, pp. 584–585.

40. Ibid. p. 579. Fred W. Riggs, *Formosa under Chinese Nationalist Rule* (New York: Octagon Books, 1952), p. 17.

41. Heinlein, *Political*, pp. 580–581.

42. Ibid., pp. 601–616.

43. Chiang Wei-kuo, *Chien shan tu hsing: Chiang wei kuo de jen sheng chih lu* (Walking Alone in the Midst of a Thousand Mountains: Chiang Wei-kuo's Life Journey) (Taipei: Tien hsia Press, 1996), pp. 174–176.

44. AmEmb Taipei, cable Dec. 11, 1951, *FRUS, 1951*, vol. 7, p. 1865.

45. AmEmb Taipei, cable June 18, 1953, *FRUS, 1952–54*, vol. 14, p. 207.

46. Defense Department, memo Nash to Drumright, Feb. 23, 1954, *FRUS, 1952–54*, vol. 14, p. 365.

47. Charles H. Barber, "China's Political Officer System," *Military Review* (July 1953), p. 10. Major Barber was the officer assigned as MAAG advisor in the GPWD.

48. StateDept, memo Barnett to Rusk, Oct. 3, 1951, *FRUS, 1951*, vol. 7, p. 1820.

49. Wen Ha-hsiung, interview, Taipei, 1996.

50. Ch'i, *Chiang Chieh-shih*, p. 214.

51. Konsin Shah, interview, May 29, 1996.

52. K. C. Wu, "Formosa," *Look*, June 29, 1954, pp. 39–43.

53. "The K. C. Wu Story," *The Reporter*, April 27, 1954, pp. 18–20.

54. *FRUS, 1952–54*, vol. 14, p. 670.

55. Dwight D. Eisenhower, *Mandate for Change 1953–1956* (New York: W. W. Norton, 1963), p. 180.

56. White House memcon (President Johnson, former President Eisenhower), *FRUS, 1964–68*, vol. 2, p. 300.

57. *New York Times*, January 13, 1954, p. 3. Harold C. Hinton, "Sino-Soviet Relations, Background and Overview," in *China, the Soviet Union and the West*, ed. Douglas T. Stuart (Boulder, Co.: Westview Press, 1982).

58. Rosemary Foot, *A Substitute for Victory* (Ithaca: Cornell University Press, 1990), pp. 87–92, 97, 113–116, 192–193. 219–220.

59. Ibid., pp. 219–220.

60. David Dean, interview, Fairfax, Va., April 30, 1996. David E. Kaplan, *Fires of the Dragon* (New York: Atheneum, 1992), pp. 303–304.

61. Robert P. Newman, "Clandestine Chinese Nationalist Efforts to Punish Their American Detractors," *Diplomatic History, 7/3* (Summer 1983), pp. 205–222.

62. AmEmb Taipei, dispatch March 15, 1954, NatArch RG59, StateDept. file 1950-54, box 4218. StateDept office memo, Robertson to the Secretary, Sept. 21, 1953, NatArch document 033.9311/9-2153, FIO request.

63. *China News*, Taipei, Sept. 12, 1953.

64. AmEmb Taipei, dispatch March 15, 1954. NA-box 4218.

65. Koo, *Reminiscences*, pp. G-110–134.

66. Ibid., pp. G-133–134. Samson Shen, interview, Taipei, August 24, 1995.

67. Koo, *Reminiscences*, pp. G-79, H-353.

68. Ibid., p. G-131.

69. Memo for the files, MacConaughy, Nov. 13, 1953, *FRUS, 1952–54*, vol. 14, p. 253. Also Koo, *Reminiscences*, p. G-131–132

70. Samson Shen, interview, August 24, 1995.

71. AmEmb Taipei, dispatch, Oct. 13, 1954. NA-box 4218.

72. Ibid.

73. Wang Sheng, interview, May 25, 1996.

74. Former CIA officers who served in Taiwan in the 1950s.

75. StateDept memcon, March 14, 1955, Dulles/Menzies, *FRUS, 1955–57*, vol. 2, p. 369.

76. NIE, April 16, 1955. *FRUS, 1955–57*, vol. 2, p. 485. This interagency intelligence estimate, chaired by the CIA, stated that Ching-kuo "is strongly disliked by many Nationalist leaders and some of them have suggested that in a future emergency, he might defect or might even try to deliver Taiwan to the Communists."

77. Alfred W. McCoy, *The Politics of Heroin in Southeast Asia* (New York: Harper & Row, 1972), p. 173. Brian Crozier, *The Man Who Lost China* (New York: Charles Scribner's Sons, 1976), p. 370.

13. FAMILY, FRIENDS, ENEMIES

1. Brian Crozier, *The Man Who Lost China* (New York: Charles Scribner's Sons, 1976), p. 358.

2. Allen S. Whiting, "Mystery Man of Formosa," *Saturday Evening Post*, March 12, 1955, p. 26. Weng Yuan reports Ching-kuo ate poached eggs; see *Wo tsai Chiang*

Chieh-shih fu tzu shen p'ian ti jih tzu (My Days in the Chiang Kai-shek Household) (Taipei: Shu hua Press, 1983), pp. 266–269.

3. Whiting, "Mystery Man," 1955, p. 26.

4. AmEmb Taipei, dispatch March 15, 1954, NatArch, RG59 StateDept file 1950–54, box 4218. Henceforth, NA-box 4218.

5. AmConGen Hong Kong, dispatch 792, Nov. 10, 1955, NatArch, declassified NND 877406, 3/17/98, FIO request. Martin gave the consulate a copy of his background letter on Ching-kuo.

6. Whiting, "Mystery," p. 26.

7. Several Ching-kuo aides, interviews, 1995, 1996, 1998. Also Ch'i P'eng-fei, *Chiang Chieh-shih Chia Shih* (History of the Chiang-Kai-shek Family) (Peking: Tuan chieh Press, 1994), p. 359–360.

8. AmEmb Taipei, dispatch, October 13, 1954. NA-box 4218.

9. Fred Chien, interview, Taipei, August 29, 1995.

10. Chou Lien-hua, interview, Taipei, May 17, 1996.

11. Wang Chi, interview, Washington, Nov. 12, 1995.

12. The dinner parties are described by one of the intimate friends who attended the events. Stories that Ching-kuo had affairs with wives of some subordinates (one was reputedly the wife of a major general) come from several sources, among others Mark Pratt (interview, Dec. 2, 1995), and several ranking Chinese in Taipei who had been close to Ching-kuo professionally, but the rumors are not confirmed by any of his intimates.

13. Ma Ch'i-ch'uan, interview, Taipei, August 31, 1995.

14. A former senior aide to Chiang Ching-kuo, interview, August 30, 1995.

15. John Chang, interview, Taipei, Sept. 7, 1995.

16. Ibid.

17. *FRUS, 1952–54*, vol. 14, p. 639.

18. Ibid.

19. AmEmb Taipei, cable Feb. 20, 1954, *FRUS, 1952–54*, vol. 14, pp. 363–364.

20. Ibid., cable Sept. 13, 1954, *FRUS, 1952–54*, vol. 14, pp. 624–627.

21. Ibid., cable Nov. 30, 1953.

22. Former U.S. military officers who served in Taiwan in the 1950s, interviews, 1995–1998.

23. Nancy Bernkopf Tucker, "John Foster Dulles and the Taiwan Roots of the 'Two Chinas' policy," in Richard H. Immerman, ed., *John Foster Dulles and the Diplomacy of the Cold War* (Princeton: Princeton University Press, 1990), pp. 241–244. See also Nancy Bernkopf Tucker, *Taiwan, Hong Kong and the United States, 1945–1992* (New York: Twayne Publishers, 1994), pp. 36–38.

24. George K. Tanham, *Communist Revolutionary Warfare: The Vietminh in Indochina* (New York: Praeger, 1961), pp. 68–69.

25. George McT. Kahin, *Intervention: How America Became Involved in Vietnam* (New York: Doubleday, 1986), p. 41.

26. Richard M. Nixon, *The Memoirs of Richard Nixon* (New York, Warner Books, 1978), p. 150.

27. Victor Marchetti and John D. Marks, *The CIA and the Cult of Intelligence* (New York: Knopf, 1980), p. 120.

28. Chen Jian, "China and the First Indo-China War, 1950–54," *China Quarterly* (Dec. 1993), pp. 85–110.

29. He Di and Gordan H. Chang, "The Absence of War in the US/China Confrontation Over Quemoy and Matsu in 1954–1955: Contingency, Luck, Deterrence," *American Historical Review,* 98 (Dec. 1993). Bernkopf Tucker, *Taiwan*, pp. 38–42.

30. StateDept memo, Dulles to Robertson, Oct. 7 and 8, 1954, *FRUS, 1952–54*, vol. 14, pp. 708, 709.

31. Wellington Koo, *Reminiscences of Wellington Koo*, Oral History, Butler Library, Columbia University, undated, pp. K-287–288.

32. Ibid.

33. Ibid.

34. Chiang Wei-kuo, *Chien shan tu hsing: Chiang wei kuo de jen sheng chih lu* (Walking Alone in the Midst of a Thousand Mountains: Chiang Wei-kuo's Life Journey) (Taipei: Tienhsia, 1996), p. 151.

35. An American Marine officer stationed in the Tachens at the time, interview, 1996.

36. Koo, *Reminiscences,* pp. H-360–361.

37. StateDept memo, Parsons to Herter, August 10, 1960, *FRUS, 1958–60*, vol. 19, p. 706.

38. Harold C. Hinton, *China's Turbulent Quest* (New York: Macmillan, 1972), p. 62.

39. AmEmb Taipei, airgram A-902, May 8, 1963 (transmitting memcon between Foreign Minister Shen Ch'ang-huan and Joseph A. Yager), NatArch RG59, StateDept file, box 3669.

40. Cable from Johnson (Geneva), Dec. 1, 1955, *FRUS, 1955–57*, vol. 3, p. 194.

41. Ibid., Dec. 2, 1955, p. 200.

42. NIE 43-55, Nov. 1, 1955, *FRUS, 1955–57*, vol. 3, pp. 153–154. NIE 13-56, Jan. 5, 1956, ibid., pp. 230–232.

43. Cable from State Department to Johnson (Geneva), Dec. 6, 1955, ibid., pp. 206–207.

14. MANAGING THE GREAT PATRON

1. Operations Coordinating Board memo, "Report on Taiwan and the Government of the Republic of China (NSC 5723)," April 20, 1959, NatArch, Defense Dept. file 1959, box MNR2.

2. James P. Richards' memo, "Taiwan," Oct. 9, 1957, in *Foreign Relations of the United States* (Washington, D.C.: Government Printing Office, 1955–1957), vol. 3, pp. 625–627. Henceforth *FRUS*.

3. Lee Huan and Lin Yin-ting, *Chiu shui pan shih, Lee Huan yu Ching-kuo hsien sheng* (Lee Huan: Half a Century of Following Chiang Ching-kuo) (Taipei: Commonwealth Press, 1998), pp. 78–79.

4. "Report on Taiwan . . . (NSC 5723)." Lee and Lin, *Chiu shui,* pp. 78–79.

5. NIE 43-2-57, August 27, 1957, "The Prospects for the Government of the Republic of China," *FRUS, 1955–57,* vol. 3, p. 589.

6. Richards' memo, "Taiwan," pp. 625–627.

7. Lee Huan, interview, Taipei, May 18, 1996.

8. Ma Ying-jeou, interview, Taipei, March 10, 1998.

9. StateDept cable to AmEmb Taipei, March 22, 1958, NatArch, RG StateDept, 1956–59, central decimal file, box 3937.

10. Ralph Clough, interview, April 22, 1998. Dirksen made the remark to Clough.

11. Ray S. Cline, *Chiang Ching-kuo Remembered* (Washington, D.C.: United States Global Strategic Council, 1989), pp. 34–36.

12. Harvey Feldman, annotations to the author, Jan. 1999.

13. StateDept memo, Dec. 30, 1958, *FRUS, 1958–60,* vol. 19, pp. 509–510.

14. Memcon, Taipei, March 14, 1958, Dulles/Chiang-Kai-shek and others, *FRUS, 1958–60,* vol. 19, p. 9.

15. Victor Marchetti and John D. Marks, *The CIA and the Cult of Intelligence* (New York: Knopf, 1980), p. 122.

16. AmEmb Taipei, cable May 22, 1958, *FRUS, 1958–60,* vol. 17, pp. 145–146.

17. StateDept memcon, Dulles/Casey, Sept. 9, 1958, *FRUS, 1958–60,* vol. 17, p. 281.

18. Letter, Robertson to Drumright, April 29, 1958, *FRUS, 1958–60,* vol. 19, p. 19. AmEmb Taipei dispatch April 3, 1958, *FRUS, 1958–60,* vol. 19, p. 14.

19. Letter, Robertson to Drumright, April 29, 1958.

20. Nancy Bernkopf Tucker, *Taiwan, Hong Kong and the United States, 1945–1992* (New York: Twayne Publishers, 1994), p. 67.

21. Alan J. Day, ed., *China and the Soviet Union, 1949–1984* (London: Longman, 1985), pp. 5–7.

22. See Roderick MacFarquhar, ed., *The Hundred Flowers Campaign and The Chinese Intellectuals* (New York: Octagon Books, 1960).

23. *Cambridge Encyclopedia of China* (Cambridge: Cambridge University Press, 1991), p. 265.

24. Li Zhisui, *The Private Life Of Chairman Mao* (New York: Random House, 1991), p. 224.

25. Roy Medvedev, trans. Harold Shukman, *China and the Superpowers* (New York: Blackwell, 1986), p. 33.

26. Li, *Private Life,* p. 262.

27. Commander in Chief Pacific (Felt) to Chief of Naval Operations, cable Nov. 24, 1958, *FRUS, 1958–60,* vol. 19, p. 494.

28. Li, *Private Life,* pp. 270–271.

29. StateDept memo for the record, NSC meeting, August 14, 1958, *FRUS, 1958–60,* vol. 19, p. 53.

30. White House memo, "Meeting on Taiwan Straits," Aug. 25, 1958, *FRUS, 1958–60,* vol. 19, p. 73. See also p. 98 for Aug. 25 meeting and Eisenhower's complaint that Chiang Kai-shek, having "ignored our advice, comes whining to us."

31. Day, *China,* pp. 11–12.

32. White House memcon, "Taiwan Straits Situation," Dulles, Herter, Twining, and others, *FRUS, 1958–60,* vol. 19, pp. 115–122.

33. On Sept. 11 Ike said he "was quite prepared to see the abandonment of Quemoy," but the United States "was committed, indeed over-committed to backing up Chiang-Kai-shek." White House memcon, Eisenhower, Goodpaster, McElroy, Sept. 15, 1958, *FRUS, 1958–60,* vol. 19, p. 162.

34. StateDept memcon, Dulles, Robertson, Parsons, *FRUS, 1958–60,* vol. 19, p. 157. AmEmb Taipei, cable Sept. 10, 1958, detailed these activities. StateDept central files 793.00/0-1158, see *FRUS, 1958–60,* vol. 19 suppl.

35. AmEmb Taipei, cable Sept. 19, 1958, *FRUS, 1958–60,* vol. 19, p. 227.

36. Cline, *CCK Remembered,* p. 57.

37. Ibid., p. 62.

38. Operations Coordinating Board memo, "Report on Taiwan . . .(NSC 5723)," April 20, 1959.

39. Talking paper prepared for Dulles, Taipei, October 21, 1958, *FRUS, 1958–60,* vol. 19, p. 416.

40. Ibid., p. 415.

41. AmEmb Taipei, cable Oct. 21, 1958, in ibid., pp. 431–432.

42. StateDept memcon, Dulles/Chiang, in ibid.

43. Memo by Regional Planning Adviser, FEA Bureau, "Taiwan Straits Crisis: Where Do We Go from Here?" Sept. 18, 1958, in ibid., p. 222. The intelligence document has not been declassified, but the subject is clearly spelled out.

44. StateDept memcon, Dulles/Chiang, in ibid., pp. 431–432.

45. StateDept press release, Oct. 23, 1958, "Joint Communiqué," in ibid., p. 442.

46. Wang Chi, interview, Washington, Nov. 28, 1995.

47. StateDept memo, Dec. 30, 1958, *FRUS, 1958–60,* vol. 19, pp. 509–510.

48. This was revealed by Ching-kuo in a semi-annual report to the Legislative Yuan in 1975. *China Quarterly,* 64 (Dec. 1975), p. 808.

49. In 1959 the ROC armed forces numbered 630,000, of which the U.S. Military Assistance Program supported 600,000.

50. NIE 43-6, June 20, 1961. "Prospects for the Government of the ROC," FIO release. Sun Li-jen first recruited Taiwanese volunteers in 1949–50. In 1951, 12,000 to 14,000 were drafted, presumably commandeered by Sun. For several years after 1951, however, no Taiwanese were drafted. See NIE 295, Sept. 14, 1954, "Probable Developments in Taiwan through 1956," *FRUS, 1952–54,* vol. 14, p. 637.

51. Former U.S. military officers stationed on the islands.

52. Konsin Shah, interview, May 22, 1996.

53. Wang Lixing, *Hao Pei-ts'un Jih chi: Chiang Ts'ung Tong de tsui hou sui yueh* (President Chiang Ching-kuo's Late Years: Hao Pei-ts'un Diary) (Taipei: Tien Hsia Literary Press, 1995), p. 374.

54. Chiang Bi-ling, interview, Taipei, June 5, 1996.

55. Fred Chien, interview, Taipei, Aug. 29, 1995. The NTU president was Chien's father.

56. Wang Shao-yu, interview, Taipei, May 11, 1996.

57. Hao Pei-ts'un, interview, Taipei, August 25, 1995.

58. Sun Li-fan, *Ch'en Ch'eng wan nien* (Ch'en Ch'eng's Late Years) (Hofei: Anhuei Peoples Press, 1996), p. 151.

59. COMUSTDC/MAAG Taiwan Report of Taiwan-Kinmen Operations, Taipei, undated, *FRUS, 1958–60,* vol. 19, p. 503.

60. Chiang Wei-kuo, *Chien shan tu hsing: Chiang wei kuo de jen sheng chih lu* (Walking Alone in the Midst of a Thousand Mountains: Chiang Wei-kuo's Life Journey) (Taipei: Tien Hsia Literary Press, 1996), p. 174.

61. Howard L. Boorman, *Biographical Dictionary of Republican China* (New York: Columbia University Press, 1979), vol. 1, p. 364.

62. Henry Kao, interview, Taipei, August 30, 1995.

63. Ibid.

64. StateDept memo reviewing history of the KMT irregulars, Feb. 1961, *FRUS, 1961–63,* vol. 23, p. 90.

65. AmEmb Taipei, cable Feb. 11, 1958, *FRUS, 1958–60,* vol. 19, pp. 524–526.

66. NSC memo of discussion, S. Everett Gleason, March 26, 1959, in ibid., p. 751.

67. In an unusual commentary in the preface of *FRUS,* vol. 19, pp. x–xi, the historian of the State Department notes that because of the CIA position, the *FRUS* compilation on Tibet "falls short of the standards of thoroughness and accuracy mandated" by law. For example, the *FRUS* citation of a CIA Review of Tibetan Operations prepared just after the uprising omits eight pages of text that the CIA would not declassify. The context of the omissions indicates that they include details of CIA clandestine operations in Tibet before March 1959. See CIA memo to the White House, Dulles to Eisenhower, April 1, 1959, *FRUS, 1958–60,* vol. 19, pp. 752–753.

68. Memo for the 303 Committee, Jan. 26, 1968, *FRUS, 1964–68,* vol. 30, pp. 739–742. See also John Kenneth Knaus, *Orphans of the Cold War: America and the Tibetan Struggle for Survival* (New York: Public Affairs, 1999). Henry Kissinger finally stopped the Tibetan covert program in the early 1970s.

69. NSC memo for 5412/2 (covert action) Group, March 27, 1959, *FRUS, 1958–60,* vol. 19, pp. 556–557.

70. StateDept cable to AmEmb Taipei, April 2, 1959, in ibid., pp. 754–755.

71. Memo for President Eisenhower's files (Gordon Gray), April 6, 1959, in ibid., pp. 554–557.

72. This presumably is one reason the CIA is reluctant to declassify details—it would embarrass the Indian government.

73. AmEmb Taipei, cable May 3, 1959, *FRUS, 1958–60,* vol. 19, p. 562.

74. CIA briefing note prepared for the President, April 1, 1958, in ibid., p. 753.

75. CIA officer stationed in South Asia at the time, interview, 1996.

76. White House memo (Gray), Feb. 4, 1960, *FRUS 1958–60*, vol. 19, p. 808.

77. CIA memo, Bissell to Lansdale, Feb. 13, 1960, *FRUS, 1958–60*, vol. 19, pp. 660–662.

78. White House memcon, Eisenhower/Chiang, June 19, 1960, *FRUS, 1958–60*, vol. 19, pp. 684–687.

79. See ibid., p. 687, n2 for quotation from memo. Ike's agreement to some sort of plan is revealed in the Gimo's message of thanks to him of Dec. 14, 1960, in ibid., p. 748.

15. CHINA LEAPS BACKWARD

1. Tien Hung-mao, "Uncertain Future: Politics in Taiwan," in Robert B. Oxnam and Richard C. Bush, eds., *China Briefing: 1980* (Boulder, Co.: Westview Press, 1981), p. 69.

2. *New York Times,* Feb. 4, 1968.

3. AmEmb Taipei, airgram A-734, March 22, 1963, "Taiwanese Dissidence and the Prospects for Insurrection." NatArch RG 59, StateDept file, box 3669. Peter Colm and I drafted the report while I was a Foreign Service officer at the embassy.

4. Ibid..

5. Y. S. Tsiang, interview, Taipei, Aug. 29, 1995.

6. Ch'eng Hsiu-lien, "Lee Teng Hui Was CCP Underground Member," *Kuang Chiao Ching,* Hong Kong, 186 (March 16, 1988), pp. 22–24. Hsu Che, "Lee Teng-hui p'ing Chuan" (The Life of Lee Teng Hui) (Hong Kong: Focuswood Limited, 1988), pp. 16–17.

7. *Newsweek,* May 20, 1996.

8. Ts'ui Chih-ch'ing, *The Dictionary of Contemporary Chinese Figures* (Chengchou: Honan Peoples Press, 1994), p. 18. Hsu Che, *Lee Deng-hui,* pp. 19–23. Y. S. Tsiang, interview, Aug. 29, 1995.

9. K. T. Li, *Economic Transformation of Taiwan, ROC* (London: Shepheard-Walwyn, 1988), p. 111.

10. NIE no. 43-64, March 11, 1964, p. 5, FIO request.

11. Senior Nationalist air force officer at the time, interview, Taipei, 1996.

12. Sun Li-fan, *Ch'en Ch'eng wan nien* (Ch'en Ch'eng's Late Years), (Hofei: Anhuei Peoples Press, 1996), pp. 122–123.

13. *New York Times,* June 4, 1960.

14. This quote is not from Ching-kuo but from Ambassador Drumright's analysis of the situation, though Ching-kuo assuredly held the same view. AmEmb Taipei, cable Oct. 7, 1960, *Foreign Relations of the United States* (Washington, D.C.: Government Printing Office, 1958–60), vol. 19, pp. 725-726. Henceforth *FRUS.*

15. NIE no. 43-61, June 20, 1961, p. 7 (note), FIO request.

16. Sun Li-fan, *Ch'en Ch'eng,* pp. 123.

17. *Foreign Broadcast Information Service Daily Report* (henceforth *FBIS*), *Asia and Pacific*, Sept. 23, p. DDD 2; Sept. 27, p. DDD 13. John Israel, "Politics on Formosa," *China Quarterly*, 15 (July–Sept. 1963), p. 6.

18. StateDept, cable to AmEmb Taipei, Sept. 30, 1960, *FRUS, 1958–60*, vol. 19, p. 724, n.1.

19. AmEmb Taipei, cable Oct. 1, 1960, ibid., pp. 724–725.

20. Jonathan Spence, *The Search for Modern China* (New York: W. W. Norton, 1990), p. 583.

21. Wang Shun-ch'i described conditions in Hsikou, interview, Hsikou, June 19, 1996.

22. CIA field information report, Taipei, June 27, 1961, FIO request.

23. Fred Chien, then English secretary to Ch'en Ch'eng, interview, Taipei, August 29, 1995.

24. Enclosure to a State Department memo to the White House, Feb. 22, 1961, *FRUS, 1961–62*, vol. 23, p. 94.

25. Fred Chien, August 29, 1995.

26. Alfred W. McCoy, *The Politics of Heroin in Southeast Asia* (New York: Harper & Row, 1972), p. 176.

27. *FRUS, 1961–62*, vol. 22, doc. 5, p. 12; p. 18, n.6.

28. Enclosure to a State Department memo to the White House, Feb. 22, 1961, *FRUS, 1961–62*, vol. 23, p. 94.

29. McCoy, *Heroin*, pp. 176–177.

30. CIA field information report, Taipei, June 27, 1961, FIO request.

31. Ibid.

32. McGeorge Bundy to President Kennedy, memo July 7, 1961, *FRUS, 1961–62*, vol. 22, p. 89.

33. Roger Hilsman to Harriman, memo March 31, 1962, in ibid., p. 193, n.1.

34. See CIA channel messages and other documents, ibid., pp. 156–162.

35. CIA station Taipei, cable Jan. 25, 1962; no other identification; FIO request.

36. AmEmb Taipei, cable Feb. 28, 1962, *FRUS, 1961–62*, vol. 22, p. 186 and n.1.

37. Ralph Clough, interview, Washington, April 22, 1998.

38. LBJ Library, background paper, "Visit of Ching-kuo to Washington, US-GRC Consultations Concerning Possible Action Against the Mainland," Sept. 17, 1965, National Security File (China), memos, vol. 4, 7/65–10/65, pp. 1–2, henceforth: LBJ, Background Paper. Kennedy to Harriman, memo March 9, 1962, *FRUS, 1961–62*, vol. 22, pp. 192–193.

39. CIA report TDCS DB-3/649,714, March 23, 1962, FIO request.

40. Rice to Harriman, StateDept, memo March 28, 1962, *FRUS, 1961–62*, vol. 22, pp. 198–200.

41. LBJ, Background Paper, p. 2.

42. Hilsman, memo for the record of a "White House Meeting on GRC Plans," March 31, 1962, *FRUS, 1961–62*, vol. 22, pp. 204–205.

43. LBJ, Background Paper, p. 3. CIA report TDCSDB-3/650, 315, May 25, 1962, *FRUS, 1961–62,* vol. 22, p. 295 n.3.

44. Ray Cline, CIA memo for the record of White House meeting with President Kennedy, May 17, 1962, FIO request.

45. Richard Helms, memo for the record of meeting with President Kennedy, June 18, 1962, text and footnotes, *FRUS, 1961–62,* vol. 22, pp. 246–247.

46. NIE no. 43-64 of March 11, 1964, pp. 6, 15, FIO request.

47. AmEmb Warsaw, cable June 23, 1962, *FRUS, 1961–62,* vol. 22, pp. 273–275.

48. LBJ, Background Paper, p. 2. Ralph Clough, interview, Nov. 30, 1995. Clough drafted the cited paper for LBJ.

49. Kirk memcon on meeting with President Chiang, Sept. 6, 1962, *FRUS, 1961–62,* vol. 22, pp. 306–313.

50. Clough, interview, Nov. 30, 1995.

51. See references to McCone and Bundy memos on the subject, Nov. 10 and Nov. 16 respectively, *FRUS, 1961–62,* vol. 22, p. 321.

52. AmEmb Taipei, cable Jan. 10, 1963, ibid., p. 337–338 and note.

53. Clough, interview, Nov. 30, 1995.

54. AmEmb Taipei, airgram no. A-649, Feb. 22, 1963; airgram no. A-757, March 23, 1963. Those who discounted the Gimo's appeals included Defense Minster Yu Ta-wei and the secretary general of the President's office, Chiang's old comrade, Chang Ch'un.

55. CIA Taipei report no. TDCS DB-3/654,567, May 9, 1963, FIO request.

56. Alan J. Day, editor, *China and the Soviet Union, 1949–1984* (London: Longman, 1985), p. 39.

57. LBJ, Background Paper, p. 5. NSC draft minutes, September 10, 1962, Chiang-Bundy meeting, *FRUS, 1961–62,* vol. 22, pp. 283–284.

58. LBJ, Background Paper, p. 4.

59. CIA memo for the record, McCone-Chiang meeting, Sept. 14, 1963. See also LBJ, Background Paper, p. 5, and StateDept memo, undated, *FRUS, 1961–62,* vol. 22, p. 396.

60. Nancy Bernkopf Tucker, *Taiwan, Hong Kong and the United States, 1945–1992* (New York: Twayne Publishers, 1994), p. 65, from an interview with Cline.

61. Kennedy message to Harriman (then Under Secretary for Political Affairs), July 15, 1962, *FRUS, 1961–62,* vol. 22, p. 370.

62. Kromer to Bundy, NSC memo Nov. 5, 1962, ibid., pp. 404–405.

63. Thomas A, Marks, *Counterrevolution in China: Wang Sheng and the Kuomintang* (London: Frank Cass Publishers, 1998), p. 198.

64. AmEmb Taipei, airgram no. A-498, Dec. 4, 1963, NatArch, StateDept file RG 59, box 3867.

65. AmEmb Taipei, airgram no. A-534, Dec. 11, 1963, Nat Archives, StateDept file RG 59, box 3669.

66. *FEER,* Oct. 14, 1965, p. 55.

67. Wen Ha-hsiung, interview, Taipei, May 17, 1996.

68. P'eng Ming-min, *A Taste of Freedom: Memoirs of a Formosan Independence Leader* (New York: Holt, Rhinehart and Winston, 1972), pp. 131–181.

69. Henry Kao, interview, Taipei, August 30, 1995.

16. THE MINISTER

1. Herbert Levin, telcon, New York, October 9, 1997.

2. AmEmb Taipei, airgram, 1963, NatArch, StateDept file RG 59, box 3669.

3. CIA Taipei station, cable Sept. 17, 1965, FIO request.

4. AmEmbTaipei, cable Jan. 27, 1964, *Foreign Relations of the United States* (Washington, D.C.: Government Printing Office, 1964-68), vol. 30, pp. 13–15. Henceforth *FRUS*.

5. CIA memo, Cline to McCone, March 2, 1964, and NSC memo, Komer to President Johnson, March 3, 1964, StateDept cables to AmEmbassy Taipei, March 6 and 16, 1964, *FRUS, 1964–68*, vol 30, pp. 25–31. LBJ Library, Background Paper, "Visit of Ching-kuo to Washington, U.S.-GRC Consultations Concerning Possible Action Against the Mainland," Sept. 17, 1965, National Security File, country file China, memos vol. 4, 7/65–10/65, p. 6, henceforth LBJ Background Paper. Letter, Pres. Johnson to Pres. Chiang, Dec. 21, 1964, NSF, Special Head of State Correspondence, China, 1/1/65–3/1/66. See also *FRUS, 19663–64*, vol. 30, pp. 142–143. StateDept to AmEmbassy Taipei, cable Nov. 20, 1964, *FRUS*, vol. 30, p. 129.

6. NSC memo, Thomson to Bundy, August 5, 1965, *FRUS, 1964–68*, vol. 30, pp. 190–191.

7. CIA officer who served in Taiwan in the 1960s, interviews, 1995–1998.

8. CIA station Taipei, cable Sept. 22, 1965, FIO request.

9. Defense memcon, McNamara-Chiang, Sept. 22, 1965, *FRUS, 1964–68*, vol. 30, pp. 209–214. Defense memcon, McNamara-Chiang, Sept. 24, 1965, LBJ Library, NSF, China, 1/1/65–1/3/66. Defense memcon, McNamara-Chiang, Sept. 22, 1965, *FRUS, 1964–68*, vol. 30, pp. 209–214.

10. StateDept cable to AmEmb Taipei, Sept. 25, 1965, NSF, China, 1/1/65–1/3/66, LBJ Library. NSC memcon, Pres. Johnson-Ching-kuo, Sept. 23, 1965, *FRUS*, vol. 30, pp. 216–218.

11. State memcon, Rusk-Ching-kuo, Sept. 22, 1965, LBJ Library, NSF, China, 1/165–1/3/66. Also Lee Huan, interview, March 9, 1998.

12. AmEmb Taipei, cable Oct. 28, 1965, *FRUS, 1964–68*, vol. 30, pp. 221–223. JCS memo Nov. 16, 1965, ibid., pp. 224–226. AmEmb Taipei, cable Jan. 25, 1966, and StateDept cable to Taipei, Jan. 28, 1966, ibid., pp. 242–247.

13. George McT. Kahin, *Intervention: How America Became Involved in Vietnam* (New York: Doubleday, 1986), p. 207.

14. Ibid., p. 332.

15. Ibid., p. 333.

16. Thomas A. Marks, *Counterrevolution in China: Wang Sheng and the Kuomintang* (London: Frank Cass Publishers, 1998), pp. 200–209, 222. Joyce K. Kallgren, "Vietnam and Politics in Taiwan," *Asian Survey*, 6/1 (Jan. 1966), p. 28.

17. Gabriel Kolko, *Anatomy of a War: Vietnam, the United States, and the Modern Historical Experience* (New York: Pantheon Books, 1985), p. 211.

18. Min S. Yee, *The Boston Globe*, May 6, 1968.

19. The section on Ching-kuo's personal and family life is taken from interviews with aides, personal secretaries, Chinese and American friends of the Ching-kuo family, and family members. Secondary sources are cited.

20. A Chinese-American whose husband worked for the CIA at the time, telcon, Dec. 1995.

21. Hsu Ch'o-yun, telcon, Nov. 19, 1997. Ku's memoirs do not mention Ching-kuo's affection for her. Ku Cheng-ch'iu, *Hsiu lien shih Shui* (Taipei: Shih pao yun hua Press, 1997).

22. Former CIA officer, 1996.

23. Mao Kao-wen, interview, Taipei, May 24, 1996.

24. A family member in notes to the author, Feb. 10, 1999.

25. Y. S. Sun, interview, Taipei, August 30, 1995.

26. Weng Yuan, *Wo tsai Chiang Chieh-shih fu tzu shen p'ian ti jih tzu* (My Days in the Chiang Kai-shek Household) (Taipei: Shu hua Publisher, 1994), pp. 234–237.

27. A personal aide to Ching-kuo at the time. The aide remembered the letter because he had to type it out as Ching-kuo could not make out the English script.

28. Wang Mei-yu, *Chiang Fang-liang chuan chi* (Biography of Chiang Fang-liang) (Taipei: China Times Publishing Company, 1997), pp. 70–72. One family member states that Yang-ho was not wealthy then, and that he and Amy lived in a small one-bedroom apartment in San Francisco. This and Faina's reaction is from a family member's notes to the author, Feb. 10, 1999.

29. Weng, *Wo tsai Chiang*, pp. 243–246.

30. John Chang, interview with Shen Shiau-chi, Taipei, Nov. 20, 1997. Huang Meilun, *Chang Hsiao-yen li cheng shang you* (Chang Hsiao-yen: Always Striving for the Best) (Taipei: Chiu Ke Press, 1996), p. 69.

31. Ch'en Chieh-ju, *Chiang Kai-shek's Secret Past,* intro. by Lloyd E. Eastman (Boulder, Co.: Westview Press, 1993), pp. xxiii–xxiv.

32. Ibid., pp. xvii–xviii.

33. P'eng Ming-min, *A Taste of Freedom: Memoirs of a Formosan Independence Leader* (New York: Holt, Rhinehart & Winston, 1972), pp. 182–228.

34. *FEER,* June 17, 1965, p. 545.

35. Henry Kao, interview, August 30, 1995.

36. Lodge Loh, interview, Taipei, Sept. 13, 1995.

37. Mark Plummer, "Taiwan: 'The New Look' in Government," *Asian Survey*, 9/1 (1969), pp. 18–22.

38. Chou Lien-hua, interview, Taipei, May 17, 1996.

39. Melvin Gurtov, "Taiwan in 1966: Political Rigidity, Economic Growth," *Asian Survey,* 7/1 (1967), p. 43.

40. *FEER,* Sept. 9, 1955.

17. THE GOLDEN CUDGEL

1. Richard Evans, *Deng Xiaoping and the Making of Modern China* (New York: Penguin Books, 1993), p. 90.

2. CIA cable, Taipei to CIA headquarters, August 16, 1967, FIO request. Also Melvin Gurtov, "Taiwan in 1966: Political Rigidity, Economic Growth," *Asian Survey,* 7/1 (1967), p. 17.

3. David Dean, interview, Fairfax, Va., April 30, 1996.

4. Nancy Bernkopf Tucker, *Taiwan, Hong Kong, and the United States, 1945–1992* (New York: Twayne Publishers, 1994), p. 116.

5. Doak Barnett coined the term.

6. Senior CIA officers who served in Taiwan in the 1960s, interviews, 1995–1998.

7. Ralph Clough, interview, Washington, Nov. 30, 1995.

8. Senior CIA officer, interview, 1998. CIA memo for Secretary Rusk, undated, *Foreign Relations of the United States* (Washington, D.C.: Government Printing Office, 1964–68), vol. 30, pp. 476–477. Henceforth *FRUS.*

9. CIA memo for Rusk, undated, in ibid., pp. 476–477. Senior CIA officer, interview, 1998.

10. StateDept, cable to AmEmb Taipei, March 16, 1967, *FRUS, 1964–68,* vol. 30, pp. 539–540.

11. AmEmb Taipei, cable May 2, 1967, in ibid., pp. 256–257.

12. AmEmb Taipei, cable May 24, 1967, in ibid., pp. 571–572.

13. Richard Nixon, "Asia After Vietnam," *Foreign Affairs* (Oct. 1967).

14. Alan J. Day, ed., *China and the Soviet Union, 1949–1984* (London: Longman, 1985), p. 84.

15. This section is based on a series in the *China Times* (Taipei) in May 1995 on the Victor Louis episode. The series was in turn derived from Jimmy Wei's diaries. The section also draws from numerous interviews with Ching-kuo's subordinates and American officials in 1995 and 1996. Finally, see *Far Eastern Economic Review* (henceforth *FEER*), April 3, p. 7, and August 7, 1969, p. 318.

16. Fred Chien, interview, Taipei, Sept. 6, 1995.

17. David Dean, interview, April 30, 1996.

18. Harrison E. Salisbury, *War Between Russia and China* (New York: Norton, 1969), pp. 161–162.

19. Lee Huan, interview, Taipei, March, 9, 1998.

20. Ibid.

21. As the political officer in the American embassy covering Taiwanese political developments and attitudes, I met frequently with the independent politicians. To try to

discourage such contacts, the Ministry of Foreign Affairs on more than one occasion complained to the embassy that the meetings were provocative.

22. *FEER, Asia 1970 Yearbook,* pp. 283–284.

23. Thomas B. Gold, *State and Society in the Taiwan Miracle* (Armonk, N.Y.: M. E. Sharpe, 1986), p. 90.

24. K. T. Li, interview, Taipei, Sept. 7, 1995. "Family Planning in Taiwan," Ralph W. Huenemann, *Modern China,* 16/21 (April 1990), pp. 173–189.

25. Ch'en Li-fu, interview, Peitou, May 29, 1996.

26. Ibid.

27. Sheldon Appleton, "Taiwan Portents of Change," *Asian Survey,* 11/1 (Jan. 1971), p. 68.

28. *FEER,* Jan. 22, 1970, p. 44. Steven J. Hood, *The Kuomintang and the Democratization of Taiwan* (Boulder, Co.: Westview Press, 1997), pp. 47–48.

29. Hsiung Yuan, interview, Taipei, May 31, 1996. Weng Yuan, *Wo tsai Chiang Chieh-shih fu tzu shen p'ian ti jih tzu* (My Days in the Chiang-Kai-shek Household) (Taipei: Shu hua Press, 1983), pp. 128–131.

30. Hsiung Yuan, interview, May 31, 1996.

31. Weng, *Wo tsai Chiang,* p. 233.

32. Chi P'eng-fei, *Chiang Chieh-shih Chia Shih* (History of the Chiang-Kai-shek Family) (Peking: Tuan chieh Press, 1994), pp. 359–360.

33. Wang Mei-yu, *Chiang Fang-liang chuan chi* (Anecdotes of Chiang Fang-liang) (Taipei: China Times Publishing Company, 1997), p. 69. A family member in notes to the author, Feb. 10, 1999.

34. Records of the Assistant Secretary of Defense (International Security Affairs) for 1970, box 7, file China, Communist, 000.1-471.6.

35. *FEER,* May 22, 1970.

36. *FEER,* Feb. 5, 1970, p. 29.

37. James Shen, *The US and Free China: How the US Sold Out Its Ally* (Washington, D.C.: Acropolis Books, 1983), pp. 48–49.

38. Eliot to Kissinger, StateDept memo to the White House, "Renunciation of Force Agreement with PRC," March 24, 1971. NatArch, StateDept 71 27612.

39. Shen, *US and Free China,* p. 439.

40. Richard M. Nixon, *The Memoirs of Richard Nixon* (New York: Warner Books, 1978), p. 547.

41. John Holdridge, telcon, Washington, D.C., Oct. 10, 1997. Holdridge did not remember seeing a report on this meeting. Henry Kissinger, through an aide, informed me that he could not remember what had transpired.

42. Shen, *US and Free China,* p. 439.

43. Wen Ha-hsiung, interview, Taipei, May 17, 1996. Shen, *US and Free China,* p. 53.

44. Wen Ha-hsiung, interview, May 17, 1996.

45. Ibid.

46. Hsu Che, *Lee Teng-hui p'ing chuan* (The Life of Lee Teng-hui) (Hong Kong: Focuswood Limited, 1988), pp. 19–23, 65–66.

47. Nixon, *Memoirs*, p. 692.

48. Henry Kissinger, *The White House Years* (Boston: Little, Brown, 1979), pp. 771–774.

49. Ching-kuo's assessment of the rapidly changing geopolitics is derived from 1995, 1996, and 1998 interviews with several contemporary senior associates, including Y. S. Tsiang and Lee Huan and Ching-kuo's young protégés such as Fred Chien.

50. *FEER*, Dec. 26, 1970.

51. Ibid.

52. *China News,* May 30, 1995.

53. Weng, *Wo tsai Chiang*, pp. 216–226.

54. Lodge Loh, interview, Taipei, Sept. 13, 1995.

18. THE PREMIER

1. Jay Taylor, *Peking and the Revolutionary Movements of Southeast Asia* (New York: Praeger, 1976), pp. 165–169.

2. Taylor, *Peking*, p. 168. Eddy Chiang, interview, Taipei, May 19, 1996.

3. Fred Chien, interview, Taipei, May 16, 1996.

4. *FEER,* July 31, 1971, p. 7.

5. Harvey Feldman, notes to the author, Jan. 1999.

6. Sheldon Appleton, "Taiwan Portents of Change," *Asian Survey,* 11/1 (Jan. 1971), p. 35.

7. Chen Guying, "The Reform Movement among Intellectuals in Taiwan since 1970," *Bulletin of Concerned Asian Scholars* (July–Sept. 1982), p. 34.

8. Ma Ying-jeou, interview, Taipei, May 22, 1996.

9. Hsieh Ts'ung-min, interview, Taipei, June 4, 1996.

10. Chiang Nan, *Chiang Ching-kuo chuan* (The Life of Chiang Ching-kuo) (Los Angeles: Mei-kuo lun t'an pao, 1984), p. 458.

11. *FEER,* Dec. 25, 1971.

12. Appleton, "Taiwan Portents," p. 37.

13. *FEER, Asia 1972 Yearbook* (Hong Kong: 1973), pp. 310–312.

14. AmEmb Taipei, cable 3514, Nov. 22, 1974, NatArch, FIO request.

15. Richard M. Nixon, *The Memoirs of Richard Nixon* (New York: Warner Books, 1978), p. 1060.

16. William Bader and Jeffery T. Bergner, *The Taiwan Relations Act* (Menlo Park, Calif.: SRI International, 1989), p. 159.

17. John Holdridge, telephone interview, Washington, D.C., Oct. 10, 1997.

18. *FEER,* Jan. 12, 1979, p. 22.

19. Leo Moser, telephone interview, December 11, 1997. (Moser was director of the Office of Republic of China Affairs in the State Department.)

20. *FEER,* June 11, 1973.

21. Yu Chi-chung, interview, Taipei, May 24, 1996. (As noted earlier, Yu's company, The China Times Publishing Company, is the publisher of the Chinese edition of this book.)

22. Fred Chien, interview, May 16, 1996.

23. Henry Kao, interview, Taipei, August 30, 1995.

24. Interviews with numerous Ching-kuo subordinates of the time, 1995, 1996. Also Eddy Chiang interview, Taipei, May 19, 1996. Dr. Hsiung Yuan, interview, Taipei, May 30, 1996.

25. Konsin Shah, interview, Taipei, May 29, 1996.

26. Fred Chien, interviews, August 29, 1995, May 16, 1996.

27. Chang Tsu-yi, interview, Taipei, May 16, 1996.

28. Fred Chien, interviews, August 29, 1995, May 16, 1996. J. Bruce Jacobs, "Taiwan 1973: Consolidation of the Succession," *Asian Survey* 14/1 (1974), p. 22.

29. Chang Tsu-yi, interview, May 16, 1996.

30. Chiang Nan, *Chiang Ching-kuo,* p. 448.

31. Chang Tsu-yi, interview, May 16, 1996.

32. Ibid.

33. *Tahsueh,* Taipei, June 1973, pp. 8–10.

34. *FEER,* Nov. 11, 1972.

35. Fred Chien, interviews, August 29, 1995, May 16, 1996. Chang Tsu-yi, interview, May 16, 1996. Harvey Feldman, notes to the author, Jan. 1999.

36. *FEER,* Jan. 8, 22, 1973.

37. Chang Tsu-yi, interview, May 16, 1996.

38. K'ang Ning-hsiang, interview, Taipei, Sept. 1, 1995. Chang Tsu-yi, interview, May 16, 1996.

39. J. Bruce Jacobs, "Taiwan 1973," pp. 28–29.

40. Chen, "Reform Movement," p. 35.

41. Ibid., p. 36. These included John Kuan, Wei Yung, Li Chung-kui, and Ch'iu Hung-ta.

42. Ibid., p. 32.

43. Ibid., p. 36. Principal among these liberal but loyal professors were Yang Kuo-shu, Hu Fu, Li Yi-yuan, Li Hung-hsi, and Huang Yueh-ch'in.

44. AmEmb Taipei, cable 9414, August 7, 1973, NatArch, FIO request.

45. K. T. Li, *Economic Transformation of Taiwan, ROC* (London: Shepheard-Walwyn, 1988), p. 268.

46. Wang Shao-yu, interview, Taipei, May 11, 1996.

47. Peter P. Cheng, "Taiwan: Protective Adjustment Economy," *Asian Survey,* 15 /1 (Jan. 1975).

48. Thomas B. Gold, *State and Society in the Taiwan Miracle* (Armonk, NY: M. E. Sharpe, 1986), p. 98.

49. Ibid., p. 106.

50. Li Zhisui, *The Private Life Of Chairman Mao* (New York: Random House, 1994), pp. 573–574.

51. Ralph Clough, "Chiang Ching-kuo's Policies toward Mainland China and the Outside World," in Shao-chuan Leng, ed., *Chiang Ching-kuo's Leadership in the Development of the Republic of China on Taiwan* (Lanham, MD: University Press of America, 1993), p. 141.

52. *New York Times,* Jan. 2, 1974.

53. StateDept to AmEmb Taipei, cable 23368, April 27, 1974. AmEmb Taipei, cable 3505, Nov. 22, 1974, NatArch, FIO requests.

54. Clough, "Chiang Ching-kuo's Policies," p. 139.

55. William R. Kinter and John F. Copper, *A Matter of Two Chinas* (Philadelphia: Foreign Policy Institute, 1979), p. 27.

56. David E. Kaplan, *Fires of the Dragon* (New York: Atheneum, 1992), pp. 147, 177. The "US Senate Report" that Kaplan cites was in fact a controversial "personal report prepared for the subcommittee by its counsel, Michael Glennon," and some members of the Committee charged it was "partisan and unprofessional" (*FEER,* Sept. 4, 1981). Such an assassination proposal would not have been out of character for KMT (or, in the 1960s, American) intelligence organs, but there is no evidence it was seriously considered.

57. "Taiwan Agents in America and the Death of Professor Wen-chen Chen," Hearings before the House Subcommittee on Asian and Pacific Affairs and on Human Rights and International Organizations, July 30 and Oct. 6, 1981, pp. 11–16 and 37.

58. Kaplan, *Fires,* pp. 184–191.

59. Ibid., pp. 239–242.

60. Ibid., p. 242.

61. Steve Weisman and Herbert Krosney, *The Islamic Bomb: The Nuclear Threat to Israel and the Middle East* (New York: Times Books, 1981), pp. 152–153.

62. Ibid., p. 153.

63. Ibid.

64. *New York Times,* March 23, 1988; *Washington Post,* March 24, 1988.

65. A family member, notes to the author, Feb. 10, 1999. An American friend of Alan and Nancy's, interview, April, 1996.

66. *FEER,* Oct. 10, 1975, pp. 26–27.

67. Wang Mei-yu, *Chiang Fang-liang chuan chi* (Anecdotes of Chiang Fang-liang) (Taipei: China Times Publishing Company, 1997), p. 77.

68. Lee Huan and Lin Yin-ting, *Chiu shui pan shih, Lee Huan yu Ching-kuo hsien sheng* (Lee Huan: A Half Century of Following Chiang Ching-kuo) (Taipei: Commonwealth Press, 1998), pp. 167–268.

69. An American friend of Alex Chiang's, interview, Taipei, June, 1996.

70. Ts'ui Chih-ch'ing, *The Dictionary of Contemporary Chinese Figures* (Chengchou: Honan Peoples Press, 1994), p. 130. Wang Li-hsing, "Chiang Hsiao-yung de sheng

yang" (Last Words of Chiang Hsiao-yung), *Yuan chin Tsa chih,* Taipei, Sept. 15, 1996, p. 110.

71. Wang Sheng, interview, March 13, 1998.

19. OLD ORDERS PASSING

1. Interview with various aides to Ching-kuo, 1995, 1996, 1998. Ralph Clough, "Chiang Ching-kuo's Policies toward Mainland China and the Outside World," in Shao-chuan Leng, ed., *Chiang Ching-kuo's Leadership in the Development of the Republic of China on Taiwan* (Lanham, Md.: University Press of America, 1993), pp. 140–141.

2. Chiang Wei-kuo, *Ch'ien shan tu hsing: Chiang wei kuo de jen sheng chih lu* (Walking Alone in the Midst of a Thousand Mountains: Chiang Wei-kuo's Life Journey) (Taipei: Tienhsia, 1996), p. 217.

3. Hsiung Yuan, interview, May 30, 1996. Eddy Chiang, interview, Taipei, May 19, 1996.

4. Hsiung Yuan, interview, May 31, 1996.

5. *Far Eastern Economic Review (FEER),* April 18, 1975, p. 20.

6. Chiang Wei-kuo, *Ch'ien shan,* pp. 218–219.

7. AmEmb Taipei, cable 4969, April 26, 1975. NatArch, FIO request.

8. Peter P. Cheng, "Taiwan 1975: A Year of Transition," *Asian Survey,* 16/1 (Jan. 1976), pp. 61–62.

9. Chiang Nan, *Chiang Ching-kuo chuan* (The Biography of Chiang Ching-kuo) (Los Angeles: Mei-kuo lun t'an pao, 1984), p. 469.

10. Chen Guying, "The Reform Movement among Intellectuals in Taiwan since 1970," *Bulletin of Concerned Asian Scholars* (July–Sept., 1982) p. 38.

11. Ibid. The legislator was Huang Shun-hsing.

12. *China Quarterly,* 64 (Dec. 1975), p. 808.

13. *Washington Post,* August 29, 1976.

14. Ibid.

15. Clough, "Chiang Ching-kuo," pp. 118–119. "Hearings, Subcommittee on Arms Control . . . ," U.S. Senate, 94th Congress, 1st and 2nd sess. on Non-Proliferation Issues (Washington, D.C.: Government Printing Office, 1977).

16. *Washington Post,* Feb. 22, 1977.

17. Wang Li-hsing, *Hao Pei-ts'un Jih chi: Chiang Ts'ung T'ung de tsui hou sui yueh* (President Chiang Ching-kuo's Late Years: Hao Pei-ts'un Diary) (Taipei: 1995), pp. 83–84.

18. David S. G. Goodman and Gerald Segal, eds., *China in the Nineties: Crisis Management & Beyond* (New York: Oxford University Press, 1992), p. 85.

19. Li Zhisui, *The Private Life Of Chairman Mao* (New York: Random House, 1994), pp. 5–11.

20. AmEmb Taipei, cable 1046, Sept. 16, 1976.

21. Ts'ui Chih-ch'ing, *The Dictionary of Contemporary Chinese Figures* (Chengchou: Honan Peoples Press, 1994), p. 70. *Republic of China Yearbook* (Taipei: Kuang Hua Press, 1991–92), pp. 532–533.

22. AmEmb Taipei, cable 3283, April 22, 1977.

23. Harvey Feldman (appointed director of Republic of China Affairs at the State Department in Sept. 1978), notes to the author, Jan. 1999.

24. AmEmb Taipei, cable 5269, August 27, 1977.

25. *FEER,* Oct. 10, 1975, pp. 26–27.

26. *FEER,* June 17, 1977.

27. Citing two unnamed individuals involved in the case, David Kaplan reports that in 1977 the CIA discovered that Taipei's Intelligence Bureau was using the diplomatic pouch to smuggle heroin into the United States from Thailand, presumably to finance its operations. David E. Kaplan, *Fires of the Dragon* (New York: Atheneum, 1992), pp. 243–244. But Taipei had plenty of hard currency in the mid-1970s. And with such evidence as Kaplan alleges, the Carter administration would at the very least have required the recall of Admiral Wang, which did not happen.

28. Mark Pratt, written notes to the author, July 1998.

29. Mark Pratt, telcon, June 24, 1998.

30. Kaplan, *Fires,* pp. 258–259.

31. Ibid., pp. 175–176. Mark Pratt, letter to the author, July 8, 1998.

32. *Chung yang jih pao,* Taipei, Dec. 26, 1971.

33. Ibid.

34. Gerald McBeath, "Taiwan in 1977: Holding the Reins," *Asian Survey,* 18/1 (Jan. 1978), p. 19.

35. *FEER,* April 8, 1977, p. 18.

36. Lee Huan, interview, May 18, 1996.

37. Ibid.

38. Mark Pratt, interview, Dec. 14, 1996.

39. Ch'en, *"Reform Movement,"* p. 44

40. Lee Huan, May 18, 1996. Gerald McBeath, "Taiwan in 1976: Chiang in the Saddle," *Asian Survey,* 17/1 (Jan. 1977). *FEER,* Melinda Liu, December 2, 1977.

41. Lee Huan, May 18, 1996.

42. Thomas B. Gold, *State and Society in the Taiwan Miracle* (Armonk, NY: M. E. Sharpe, 1986), pp. 102–103.

43. Stuart E. Thompson, "Taiwan's Rural Economy," *China Quarterly,* 99 (Sept. 1984), p. 553.

44. Hung Mao Tien, "Taiwan in Transition: Prospects for Socio-Political Change," *China Quarterly,* 64 (Dec. 1975), pp. 614–644. McBeath, "Taiwan in 1977," p. 18.

20. THE DIVORCE

1. *Far Eastern Economic Review (FEER),* Melinda Liu, Jan. 20, 1978.

2. Hsu Ch'o-yun, telcon, Pittsburgh, Nov. 21, 1997.

3. Weng Yuan, *Wo tsai Chiang Chieh-shih fu tzu shen p'ian ti jih tzu* (My Days in the Chiang-Kai-shek Household) (Taipei: Shu hua Press, 1994), pp. 237–242.

4. Chiang Nan, *Chiang Ching-kuo chuan* (The Life of Chiang Ching-kuo) (Los Angeles: Mei-kuo lun t'an pao, 1984), p. 507.

5. Fred Chien, interview, Taipei, August 30, 1995.

6. AmEmb Taipei, cable 7581, FIO request. NatArch, doc. 78, Taipei 03352.

7. Chiang Bi-ling, interview, Taipei, June 5, 1996.

8. Ibid.

9. Hsiung Yuan, interview, Taipei, May 31, 1996.

10. Chiang Bi-ling, interview, June 5, 1996.

11. Weng, *Chiang*, pp. 266–269. The previous large food bill at the Shilin residence reflected the cost of entertaining the constant stream of visitors, relatives, and friends whom the Generalissimo and his wife entertained.

12. Chang Tsu-yi, interview, May 16, 1996.

13. *FEER*, Bill Kazer, Sept. 22, 1978.

14. Chiang Ching-kuo, *Chiang Ching-kuo hsien sheng chuan chi*, hereafter, *CCKHSCC* (Chiang Ching-kuo, Collected Works) (Taipei: GIO, 1989), vol. 14, pp. 257–260.

15. AIT Taipei, cable 03836, Oct. 23, 1979. FIO request.

16. *FEER*, Bill Kazer, Dec. 15, 1978, p. 30.

17. Ibid., Dec. 22, 1978.

18. Patrick Tyler, "The Abnormalization of U.S.-Chinese Relations," *Foreign Affairs* (Sept.-Oct. 1999), pp. 93–122.

19. Interviews: James Soong, Taipei, Sept.13, 1995; Fred Chien, Taipei, May 15, 1996; Leonard Unger, Maryland, Dec. 4, 1995; Wang Chia-hua, Taipei, August 24, 1995. Undated notes to the author from Mark Pratt, 1998. Annotations and oral comments from Harvey Feldman, Jan. 1999.

20. Ibid.

21. Ibid.

22. Y. S. Tsiang, interview, Taipei, August 29, 1995.

23. Mark Pratt, notes to the author, July 8, 1998.

24. For text of Ching-kuo statement, see Steven P. Gibert and William M. Carpenter, *America and Island China: A Documentary History* (Lanham, Md.: University Press of America, 1989), pp. 208–109.

25. Leonard Unger, interview, Maryland, Nov. 28, 1995.

26. Chen Guying, "The Reform Movement among Intellectuals in Taiwan since 1970," *Bulletin of Concerned Asian Scholars* (July-Sept. 1982), p. 45.

27. Harvey Feldman, Michael Y. M. Kao, and Ilpyong J. Kim, *Taiwan in a Time of Transition,* (New York: Paragon, 1988), pp. 147–149. Nancy B. Tucker, *Taiwan, Hong Kong and the United States, 1945–1992* (New York: Twayne Publishers, 1994), p. 136.

28. Yang Hsi-k'un, interview, Taipei, May 20, 1996.

29. Tucker, *Taiwan, Hong Kong*, p. 136. H. K. Yang, interview, Taipei, May 20, 1996.

30. Tucker, *Taiwan, Hong Kong,* pp. 136–137. The first head of the CCNAA office in Washington was Konsin Shah, the pilot/navigator who had been with Ching-kuo and his father during the hectic days of 1949.

31. Feldman, *Taiwan in a Time,* pp. 152–155.

32. Philip Patrick Newell, *Transition Toward Democracy in Taiwan: Political Change in the Chiang Ching-kuo Era, 1971–1986,* Ph.D. thesis, Georgetown University, Washington, Jan. 10, 1994, p. 472. J. Bruce Jacobs, "Taiwan 1979, Normalcy after Normalization," *Asian Survey* (Jan. 1980), p. 88.

33. *FEER,* July 20, 1979.

34. Ralph N. Clough, *Reaching Across the Taiwan Straits: People to People Diplomacy* (Boulder, Co.: Westview Press, 1993), p. 142.

35. Wang Sheng, interview, May 25, 1996. Ching-kuo's views of the new dynamic of Taiwan-mainland relations derive from multiple interviews in 1995–1998 with his closest associates from 1979 through 1987: Wang Sheng, Lee Huan, Fred Chien, Y. S. Tsiang, Ma Ying-jeou, Yu Chi-chung, Ts'u Sung-ch'iu, Ma Shu-li, Shaw Yi-ming, James Soong, and others.

36. Ni Luo, *Hsien yi yuan bu chih hsiung chung* (Wang Sheng: Steady in Chaos or Peace) (Taipei: Shih Chieh Literary Press, 1995), p. 355, quotes Wang Sheng on the negative effect of the "three no's" on the people of Taiwan.

37. Wang Sheng, interview, May 25, 1996, Ni, *Hsien yi yuan,* pp. 353–357. Thomas A. Marks, *Counterrevolution in China: Wang Sheng and the Kuomintang* (London: Frank Cass Publishers, 1998), p. 260.

38. Wang Sheng, interviews, May 25, 1996, March 13, 1998. Ni, *Hsien yi yuan,* pp. 396–404.

39. Ibid.

40. Ni, *Hsien yi yuan,* p. 385–396. The LSK name came from rulers of the Eastern Han dynasty. Wang Hsi-ling, *Hao Pei-ts'un jih chi: Chiang Ts'ung T'ung de tsui hou sui yueh* (President Chiang Ching-kuo's Late Years: Hao Pei-ts'un Diary) (Taipei: Tien hsia Literary Press, 1995), pp. 121–122.

41. Wang Sheng, interview, May 25, 1996. Marks, *Counterrevolution,* p. 262.

21. RIOT AND TRIALS

1. Tien Hung-mao, *The Great Transition: Political and Social Change in the Republic of China* (Stanford: Hoover Institution Press, 1989), p. 70.

2. Ma Chi-chuang, interview, Taipei, August 31, 1995.

3. For an excellent analysis of Ching-kuo's thinking and political dynamics at this time see AIT Taipei, cables 03880, Oct. 26, 1979, and 03836, Oct. 23, 1979. FIO request.

4. *Pa shih nien dai,* Taipei, 1/1 (1979), p. 62.

5. AIT Taipei, cable 03970, Oct. 31, 1979, FIO request. Also J. Bruce Jacobs, "Taiwan 1979, Normalcy after Normalization," *Asian Survey* (Jan. 1980), pp. 84–93; pp. 90–91. Philip Patrick Newell, *Transition Toward Democracy in Taiwan: Political Change in the Chiang Ching-kuo Era, 1971–1986,* Ph.D. thesis, Georgetown University, Washington, D.C., Jan. 10, 1994, p. 473.

6. Jacobs, "Taiwan 1979," p. 90. Chang Ts'u-yi, interview, Taipei, May 16, 1996. James Soong, interview, Taipei, Sept. 15, 1995.

7. Jacobs, "Taiwan 1979," 1980, p. 92. Jacobs was present at the birthday party.

8. AIT Taipei, cable 03836, Oct. 23, 1979, FIO request. Fred Chien, interview, Taipei, May 16, 1996.

9. Bill Kazer, *FEER*, July 6, 1979, p. 14.

10. Newell, *Transition*, pp. 477–478.

11. Ibid., pp. 477–478, 489–493.

12. Ibid., pp. 477–478.

13. Ibid.

14. John Kaplan, *The Court Martial of the Kaohsiung Defendants* (Berkeley: University of California Press, 1982), p. 16.

15. James Soong, interview, Sept. 13, 1995.

16. FBIS, *Daily Report Asia & Pacific*, vol. 4, Dec. 12, 1979, pp. B4–B19.

17. The story of the riot is drawn from Kaplan, *Court Martial*, pp. 16–20; Chen Guying, "The Reform Movement among Intellectuals in Taiwan since 1970," *Bulletin of Concerned Asian Scholars* (July-Sept. 1982), pp. 45–46; and the excellent account by Phil Kurata, *FEER*, Dec. 28, 1979.

18. Henry Kao, interview, Taipei, August 30, 1995. AIT Taipei, cable 04683, Dec. 11, 1979, FIO request.

19. Ma Chi-chuang, interview, August 31, 1995.

20. Former CIA officer, interview, Washington, 1996. Mark Pratt, interview, Washington, Dec. 1, 1996.

21. K'ang Ning-hsiang, interview, Taipei, Sept. 1, 1995.

22. Kurata, *FEER*, Dec. 28, 1979.

23. Ibid.

24. *Tzu li wan pao*, Dec. 12, 14, 26, 1979.

25. FBIS, *Daily Report Asia & Pacific*, vol. 4, Dec. 17, 1979, p. B1.

26. Ibid., p. B3. Hung-mao Tien, "Uncertain Future: Politics in Taiwan," in Robert B. Oxnam and Richard C. Bush, eds., *China Briefing: 1980* (Boulder, Co.: Westview Press, 1981).

27. David Dean, interview, Virginia, April 22, 1997.

28. AIT Taipei, cable 03896, Nov. 3, 1979, FIO request.

29. Joyce K. Kallgren, "China in 1979: On Turning Thirty," *Asian Survey,* 20/1 (Jan. 1980), pp. 3–11.

30. A remark made to the author by a senior officer in the Soviet embassy in Peking on Oct. 21, 1980.

31. FBIS, *Daily Report Asia & Pacific,* vol. 4, Jan. 18, 1980, p. B1.

32. Chiang Bi-ling, interview, Taipei, June 5, 1996.

33. AIT Taipei, cable 00271, Jan. 16, 1980, FIO request.

34. Kaplan, *Court Martial*, pp. 18–19.

35. Charles T. Cross, interviews, telcon, April 4, 1996, Dec. 1, 1997.

36. John F. Cooper, "Taiwan in 1980: Entering a New Decade," *Asian Survey,* 21/1 (Jan. 1981), p. 54.

37. Ts'u Sung-ch'iu, interview, Taipei, June 6, 1996.

38. Kurata, *FEER,* March 21, 1980, p. 38.

39. AIT cable 01157, March 10, 1980, FIO request.

40. David E. Kaplan, *Fires of the Dragon* (New York: Atheneum, 1992), p. 305. Kurata, *FEER,* March 21, 1980, p. 38.

41. See Kathleen Graf, *The Bamboo Gang and the Murder of Henry Liu,* M.A. thesis, Tufts University, 1987. Harvey Feldman notes to author, Jan. 1999.

42. Kaplan, *Fires,* p. 366. Kaplan, without citing his source, states also that thousands of triad members fled to Taiwan in 1949 and "were quietly reintegrated into the government. Military and intelligence officials found their promotions often depended on membership in the Green Gang or Hung societies. Chiang Ching-kuo, like his father, was said to be a longtime member of the Green Gang, and used the triads to consolidate his hold over the military." Of the 100 or so books and articles on Chiang Ching-kuo written in Hong Kong, China, Taiwan, and the United States, friendly, neutral, unfriendly, and hostile, not one confirms this story. On the contrary, Ching-kuo's loathing of the gangs is a recurrent theme. The many interviews conducted by the author reflect the same conclusion.

43. Kaplan, *Fires,* p. 368.

44. Ibid., p. 369.

45. Wang Sheng, interview, Taipei, March 13, 1998.

46. This was the theory of some American diplomats involved with Taiwan. Mary von Breisen, telcon, April 1, 1998.

47. Yu Chi-chung interview, Taipei, May 24, 1996.

48. Chou Lien-hua, interview, Taipei, May 17, 1996.

49. Ts'u Sung-ch'iu, interview, Taipei, June 6, 1996.

22. ISLAND AND MAINLAND

1. AIT cable 00846, Feb. 21, 1979, FIO request.

2. AIT cable 00723, Feb. 13, 1980, FIO request.

3. Phil Kurata, *FEER,* August 29, 1980

4. John Franklin Copper, "Taiwan in 1981: In a Holding Pattern," *Asian Survey,* 22/1 (Jan. 1982), p. 34.

5. For a full treatment see John F. Cooper, "Taiwan's Recent Election: Progress Toward a Democratic System," *Asian Survey* (Oct. 1981), pp. 1029–1039.

6. Ibid.

7. For the text of Reagan's statement see Steven P. Gibert and William M. Carpenter, *America and Island China: A Documentary History* (Lanham, MD: University Press of America, 1989), pp. 272–275.

8. Fred Chien, interview, Taipei, May 15, 1996.

9. *FEER*, May 22, 1981, p. 46.

10. Melinda Liu, *FEER*, July 20, 1979, p. 46.

11. Ibid., p. 24.

12. AIT cable 00430, Jan. 26, 1980, FIO request. For Ching-kuo quote to Wang Sheng see Ni Luo, *Hsien yi yuan bu chih hsiung chung* (Wang Sheng: Steady in Chaos or Peace) (Taipei: Shih Chieh Wen Wu Press, 1995), pp. 353–357.

13. The author saw such scenes in Fuchow and Xiamen in 1980 and 1981.

14. K'ang Ning-hsiang, interview, Taipei, September 1, 1995.

15. Cooper, "Taiwan in 1981," p. 55.

16. Ibid., p. 61.

17. Ibid., pp. 34, 59.

18. Lei Ming, *Lee Teng-hui Lin Yang-kang Tsui hou ta tui chueh* (Lee Teng-hui and Lin Yang-kang: The Last Fight) (Taipei: 1994), pp. 27–28.

19. Hsiung Yuan, interview, Taipei, May 31, 1996.

20. Hsieh Dongmin, interview, Taipei, June 4, 1996.

21. James R. Lilley, interview, Washington, August 15, 1996.

22. Andrew Tanzer, *FEER*, Nov. 20, 1981, p. 10.

23. Wang Shun-ch'i, interview, Hsikou, June 19, 1996.

24. Copper, "Taiwan in 1981," p. 50.

25. Deng Xiaoping, *Deng Xiaoping on One Country, Two Systems* (Peking: Foreign Language Press, 1984), pp. 67–72.

26. David Bonsai, *FEER*, Sept. 18, 1981, p. 10.

27. Kao Ying-mao, interview, Taipei, Sept. 4, 1995.

28. Copper, "Taiwan in 1981," p. 51.

29. Interview with a close aide to Alexander Haig at this time. Washington, May 28, 1998.

30. Charles T. Cross, unpublished memoirs, pp. 130–131. Fred Chien and James Soong described the content of the letter to Cross on July 18, 1981.

31. Cross, unpublished memoirs, pp. 130–131. Fred Chien and James Soong told Cross that Reagan's message to Ching-kuo had been the key factor in Ching-kuo's cautious and patient line on the FX.

32. Ching-kuo's views at this time come from multiple interviews with his closest associates, both the young and the older cohort. It is also consistent with the analysis of AIT in AIT cable 00846, February 21, 1980, FIO request.

33. *FEER*, May 22, 1981, p. 33.

34. James R. Lilley, interview, August 15, 1996.

35. Lilley, a Chinese speaker, served many years on Taiwan as a CIA officer and was the CIA's declared station chief in Peking when George Bush was chief of the U.S. Liaison Office there in the mid-1970s.

36. James R. Lilley, interview, August 15, 1996.

37. Thomas A. Marks, *Counterrevolution in China: Wang Sheng and the Kuomintang* (London: Frank Cass Publishers, 1998), p. 265.

38. James R. Lilley, interview, August 15, 1996. Ni Luo, *Hsien yi yuan*, pp. 381–384. Andrew Tanzer, *FEER*, July 16, 1982, p. 22

39. For texts, see Gibert and Carpenter, *America and Island China*, pp. 296–299.

40. Alexander M. Haig, Jr., *Caveat, Realism, Reagan and Foreign Policy* (New York: Macmillan, 1984), pp. 194–215.

41. Gibert and Carpenter, *America and Island China*, p. 39, from interviews of key actors by the authors. This account is also consistent with the background story heard by foreign service officers involved in the negotiations, including myself.

42. Haig, *Caveat*, pp. 194–215. Sherwood Goldberg, interview, May 27, 1998.

43. *Washington Post*, July 9, 1982, p. A13.

44. Richard Nations, *FEER*, June 4, 1982, p. 16. Gibert and Carpenter, *America and Island China*, p. 40.

45. James R. Lilley, interview, August 15, 1996.

46. Ibid.

47. Parris Chang, "Taiwan in 1982: Diplomatic Setback Abroad and Demands for Reforms at Home," *Asian Survey*, 23/1 (Jan. 1983), pp. 38–39.

48. Ibid., p. 40.

49. Wang Li-hsing, *Hao Pei-ts'un Jih chi: Chiang Ts'ung T'ung de tsui hou sui yueh* (Hao Pei-ts'un Diary: President Chiang Ching-kuo's Late Years) (Taipei: 1995). From Wang Li-hsing's interview with Hao, p. 58.

50. Various AIT officials involved in Taiwan affairs at the time. Interviews, Washigton, 1995–1997.

51. David Jenkins, *FEER*, Feb. 10, 1983, p. 31.

52. *FEER*, Dec. 17, 1982, pp. 32–33.

53. Charles T. Cross, interview, telcon, April 4, 1996.

54. Subcommittee on Asian and Pacific Affairs and on Human Rights and International Organizations of the Committee on Foreign Affairs, June 30 and October 6, 1981, *Taiwan Agents in America and the Death of Professor Ch'en* (Washington: 1982), pp. 7–8.

55. Former aides to Ching-kuo, interviews 1996, 1998.

56. Wen Ha-hsiung, interview, Taipei, May 17, 1996.

57. Marks, *Counterrevolution*, p. 263.

58. Chiang Bi-ling, interview, June 5, 1996. James R. Lilley, interview, August 15, 1996.

59. *FEER*, Dec. 17, 1982, pp. 34–35.

60. Ni Luo, *Hsien yi yuan*, pp. 413. David Dean, interview, April 22, 1996.

61. Ni Luo, *Hsien yi yuan*, p. 413.

62. Ibid., p. 414.

63. Marks, *Counterrevolution*, p. 274.

64. Wang Sheng, interview, May 25, 1996. Ni Luo, *Hsien yi yuan*, p. 413.

65. *FEER*, June 2, 1983, p. 15.

66. Marks, *Counterrevolution*, p. 9.

67. Ibid., p. 10.

68. Wang Sheng, interview, May 25, 1996.

23. SUCCESSORS, BROKERS, KILLERS

1. GIO, Taipei, *Documents series*, 1 (1983).

2. Richard Nations, *FEER*, July 28, 1983, p. 14.

3. James R. Lilley, interview, Washington, August 15, 1996.

4. Y. S. Sun interview, Taipei, August 28, 1995.

5. Robert Ash and Y. Y. Kueh, "Economic Integration within Greater China: Trade and Investment Flows," *China Quarterly*, 136 (Dec. 1993), p. 716.

6. Interviews, Taipei: Wang Sheng, March 13, 1998; Ma Shu Li, March 13, 1998; Lee Huan, March 9, 1998; Ma Ying-jeou, March 10, 1998.

7. Hsu Che, "Lee Teng-hui p'ing chuan" (The Life of Lee Teng-hui) (Taipei: Tien Yuan Press, 1988), pp. 111–112, 125–126.

8. Yu Chi-chung, interview, Taipei, May 15, 1996.

9. Chang Ts'u-yi, interview, Taipei, May 16, 1996.

10. Lei Ming, *Lee Teng-hui Lin Yang-kang Tsui ho ta tui chueh* (Lee Teng-hui and Lin Yang-kang: The Last Fight) (Taipei: Hanszu Press, 1994), pp. 106–107.

11. Chang Ts'u-yi, interview, May 16, 1996.

12. Wang Li-hsing, *Hao Pei-ts'un jih chi: Chiang Ts'ung T'ung de tsui hou sui yueh* (President Chiang Ching-kuo's Late Years: Hao Pei-ts'un Diary) (Taipei: Tien Hsia Literary Press, 1995), p. 129.

13. Interview of Eddy Chiang in Wang Li-hsing, "Chiang Hsiao-yung de sheng yang" (Last Words of Chiang Hsiao-yung), *Yuan chin tsa chih*, Sept. 15, 1996, pp. 112–113.

14. Various senior KMT officials, interviews, Taipei, 1995, 1996, 1998.

15. Ibid.

16. Lee Huan, interview, May 16, 1996.

17. *Republic of China Yearbook* (Taipei: Kuang Hua Press, 1989), p. 594.

18. Hsu Ch'o-yun, note to the author, April 1998. Lee Huan and Lin Yin-ting, *Chiu shui pan shih, Lee Huan yu Ching-kuo hsien sheng*, (Lee Huan: A Half Century of Following Chiang Ching-kuo) (Taipei: Commonwealth Press, 1998), p. 268. Wang Sheng, interview, March 13, 1998.

19. A family member, interviews August 1995, May 1996, March 1998.

20. Ma Shu-li, interview, March 13, 1998.

21. Lee's first publicly announced visit to Taiwan was in November 1985. In its November 5, 1985, report on this visit, the Central News Agency reported that Lee had made "many visits [to Taiwan] in recent years, but this was the first announced visit."

22. James R. Lilley, interview, August 15, 1996.

23. Ma Ying-jeou, interview, March 10, 1998.

24. Wang Li-hsing, *Hao Pei-ts'un*, p. 278. This is a quote from Ching-kuo from a meeting with David Dean cited in Hao's diary for December 1, 1985. Hao reported simply that Ching-kuo had mentioned Deng's message to Dean and made no further comment. Ching-kuo was almost certainly letting the Americans know of Deng's message in case they picked it up from the Singaporeans.

25. L. Y. Yang, *Ch'i shih nien tai*, Hong Kong, August 1, 1983. *BBC Summary of World Broadcasts, The Far East,* August 5, 1983. L. Y. Yang, a professor at Seton Hall University, described his long meeting with Deng, the specific date of which he does not mention.

26. Ibid.

27. GIO, Taipei, *Documents Series,* 1 (1983).

28. Yu Chi-chung, interview, March 9, 1998.

29. Martin L. Lasater, *U.S. Interests in the New Taiwan* (Boulder, Co.: Westview Press, 1993), p. 22.

30. Ruan Ming, *Deng Xiaoping, Chronicle of an Empire,* (Boulder, Co.: Westview Press, 1992), pp. 149–150.

31. Yangshan Chou and Andrew J. Nathan, "Democratizing Transition in Taiwan," *Asian Survey,* 27/3 (March 1987), p. 283.

32. David E. Kaplan, *Fires of the Dragon* (New York: Atheneum, 1992), pp. 375–408.

33. Ibid.

34. Mark Pratt, letter to the author, July 8, 1998.

35. Kaplan, *Fires,* pp. 391–392.

36. Eddy Chiang, interview in Wang, *Yuan chian,* p. 110.

37. Wan Tao-yuan, interview, Taipei, May 17, 1996.

38. Eddy Chiang, *Yuan chian,* p. 109. "When Father asked relevant officials about the case, they all lied . . . [or] they blamed one another. . . . some officials denied it [involvement of Intelligence organs] had taken place. . . ."

39. Ibid.

40. Wang, *Hao Pei-ts'un,* pp. 212–213.

41. Harry E. T. Thayer, interview, Washington, Dec. 6, 1995.

42. AIT officials concerned with Taiwan affairs, interviews, Washington, 1995–1999.

43. Wang, *Hao Pei-ts'un,* p. 213.

44. *New York Times,* Jan. 16, 1985.

45. Wang, *Hao Pei-ts'un,* pp. 209–214, 216.

46. *Tzu li wan pao,* Jan. 17, 1985.

47. Kaplan, *Fires,* p. 453.

48. Ibid., p. 456.

49. Mary von Breisen, telcon interview, March 30, 1998. Ms. Breisen, deputy director of the political section at AIT, attended all the meetings with the FBI, including the polygraph sessions.

50. Senior ROC official, interview, May 1996.

51. Eddy Chiang, interview in Wang, *Yuan chian,* p. 108. Eddy did not name Wang Sheng directly but referred to "people in the Liu Hsiao-k'ang office." Eddy charged that Wang had tried "to utilize the relationship between the two brothers [Alex and Eddy] so that they would check and balance or influence one another or whatever."

52. David Hess, interview, Taipei, May 26, 1996.

53. This was more or less the explanation given by Eddy Chiang in his 1996 interview in Wang, *Yuan chian,* p. 110, and very likely in part reflects conversations with his father on the subject. "The impression of [Alex's] involvement," Eddy said, "was eighty percent due to rumors and twenty percent due to the impression [he] left." In a June 7, 1996, interview with the author, Chiang Wei-kuo, when asked if Alex was involved in the Henry Liu murder, responded, "Yes, possibly."

54. Mary von Breisen. telcon interview, March 30, 1998.

55. I was then director of analysis for East Asia and the Pacific in the State Department and was involved in the debate. I took the view that the IDF would be a violation of the letter as well as the spirit of the 1982 communiqué.

56. Fred Chien, interview, Taipei, March 13, 1998.

57. A senior military and diplomatic officer whose connections to Ching-kuo went back to 1945, interview, Taipei, May 1996. Also confirmed by a senior Foreign Ministry diplomat of the period in a March 1998 discussion in Taipei. On the Taiwan aid program see *FEER,* Sept. 26, p. 38.

58. Ibid. *San Francisco Chronicle,* May 16, 1987. Kaplan, *Fires,* p. 458.

59. Carl Goldstein, *FEER,* April 18, 1995, p. 15; May 2, 1995, p. 20.

60. *Hearings and Markup, The Murder of Henry Liu,* Subcommittee on Asian and Pacific Affairs, House of Representatives, 99th Congress, February 7, March 21, April 3, 1985, Washington, p. 33.

61. *Iran Contra Puzzle, Congressional Quarterly* (Washington: 1987), p. A-12. Wang, *Hao Pei-ts'un,* pp. 254–255.

62. Wang, *Hao Pei-ts'un,* pp. 333–334. Wan Tao-han, interview, Taipei, May 17, 1996.

63. Wang, *Hao Pei-ts'un,* p. 273.

64. Lee and Lin, *Chiu shui pan shih,* p. 265.

65. Wang, *Hao Pei-ts'un,* pp. 233–236, 241–244, 260.

66. Ma Shu-li, interview, March 13, 1998.

24. BUILDING CONSENSUS

1. Wang Li-hsing, *Hao Pei-ts'un jih chi: Chiang Ts'ung T'ung de tsui hou sui yueh* (President Chiang Ching-kuo's Late Years: Hao Pei-ts'un Diary) (Taipei: Tien Hsia Literary Press, 1995), pp. 224–225. The Cathay Investment Trust owned by the same Ts'ai family was also involved in the crisis, sometimes referred to as the "Cathay scandal."

2. A former ranking Nationalist official who did not wish to be quoted, interview, Taipei, August, 1995.

3. Ma Shu-li, interview, Taipei, May 30, 1996.

4. Such as Kuo Wei-fan (Ph.D. University of Paris) and Huang Kun-hui (Ph.D. University of Colorado). Ma Shu-li, interview, Taipei, June 2, 1996.

5. Ma Shu-li, interview, Taipei, June 2, 1996.

6. Chiang Bi-ling, interview, Taipei, June 5, 1996.

7. Carl Goldstein, *FEER*, Feb. 14, 1985, p. 21.

8. Goldstein, *FEER*, Dec. 26, 1985, p. 30.

9. *Los Angeles Times*, Dec. 7, 1985.

10. *Christian Science Monitor*, Nov. 15, 1985.

11. Shaw Yu-ming, interview, Taipei, March 12, 1998.

12. *BBC Summary of World Broadcasts*, June 8, 1985, citing a Kyodo News Service report of June 7 from Peking.

13. Wang, *Hao Pei-ts'un*, p. 278.

14. Ma Shu-li, interview, May 30, 1996. Pro-KMT newspapers and other government-controlled media employed the term "bandit" until 1991.

15. Goldstein, *FEER*, May 9, 1985, p. 79.

16. Thomas B. Gold, "Go with Your Feelings: Hong Kong and Taiwan Popular Culture in Greater China," *China Quarterly*, 136 (Dec. 1993), pp. 907–925.

17. Goldstein, *FEER*, May 9, 1985, p. 79.

18. Robert F. Ash and Y. Y. Kueh, "Economic Integration within Greater China: Trade and Investment Flows," *China Quarterly*, 136 (Dec. 1993), p. 731.

19. Chiang Bi-ling, interview, June 5, 1996. Contrary to rumors, there was never an amputation.

20. Ma Shu-li, interview, May 30, 1996.

21. Wang, *Hao Pei-ts'un*, pp. 225, 230.

22. James C. Hsiung, "Taiwan in 1985: Scandals and Setbacks," *Asian Survey*, 26/1 (1986), p. 97.

23. James E. Lilley, interview, Washington, August 15, 1996.

24. *Los Angeles Times*, Dec. 7, 1985.

25. *Christian Science Monitor*, April 15, 1985.

26. Wang Mei-yu, *Chiang Fang-liang chuan chi* (Anecdotes of Chiang Fang-liang) (Taipei: China Times Publishing Company, 1997), p. 91.

27. *FBIS*, China, Taiwan, August 27, 1985, p. vi.

28. Lee Huan and Lin Yin-ting, *Chiu shui pan shih, Lee Huan yu Ching-kuo hsien sheng* (*Lee Huan: A Half Century of Following Chiang Ching-kuo*) (Taipei: Commonwealth Press, 1998), p. 268.

29. *New York Times*, Dec. 26, 1985.

30. Jay Taylor, *The Rise and Fall of Totalitarianism* (New York: Paragon, 1993), pp. 129–130.

31. Shaw Yu-ming, interview, March 19, 1998.

32. Shaw Yu-ming, "Taiwan: A View from Taipei," *Foreign Affairs* (summer 1985), p. 1063.

33. Ma Shu-li, interview, May 30, 1996.

34. Richard Baum, "China in 1985: The Greening of the Revolution," *Asian Survey,* 26/1 (Jan. 1986), p. 31.

35. Stanley Rosen, "China in 1986: A Year of Consolidation," *Asian Survey,* 27/1 (Jan. 1987), p. 38.

36. Hsin-Huang Michael Hsiao, "Emerging Social Movements and the Rise of a Demanding Civil Society in Taiwan," *The Australian Journal of Chinese Affairs,* 24 (July 1990), pp. 1264–72.

37. Wang, *Hao Pei-ts'un,* pp. 310–320.

38. Chiang Bi-ling, interview, June 5, 1996.

39. Wang, *Hao Pei-ts'un,* p. 299.

40. Chiang Bi-ling, interview, June 5, 1996.

41. Central News Agency, April 26, 1986. Harry E. T. Thayer, interview, Washington, Dec. 6, 1995.

42. James Soong, interview, Sept. 15, 1995.

43. Ma Shu-li, interview, Taipei, June 1, 1996.

44. Ma Ying-jeou, interview, May 25, 1996.

45. Fred Chien, interview, May 16, 1996.

46. Lee Huan, interview, May 18, 1996. Wan Tao-yuan, interview, Taipei, May 17, 1996.

47. Wang Chia-hua, interview, Taipei, August 25, 1998.

48. Ma Shu-li, interview, June 1, 1996.

25. BREAKTHROUGH

1. Wan Tao-yuan, interview, Taipei, May 17, 1996.

2. Wang Chia-hua, interview, Taipei, August 25, 1995.

3. James Soong, interview, Taipei, September 13, 1995. Yu Chi-chung, interview, Taipei, September 26, 1995.

4. Wang Li-hsing, *Hao Pei-ts'un jih chi: Chiang Ts'ung T'ung de tsui hou sui yueh* (President Chiang Ching-kuo's Late Years: Hao Pei-ts'un Diary) (Taipei: Tien Hsia Literary Press, 1995), pp. 313–314.

5. Yu Chi-chung, interview, May 24, 1986. Wang, *Hao Pei-ts'un,* pp. 313–314.

6. Yu Chi-chung, interview, May 24, 1996.

7. Ibid.

8. *Financial Times,* London, Oct. 14, 1986.

9. James Soong, interview, Taipei, Sept. 13, 1995.

10. Wang Shao-yu, interview, Taipei, May 11, 1996.

11. Ruan Ming, *Deng Xiaoping: Chronicle of an Empire* (Boulder, Co.: Westview Press, 1992), pp. 15–169.

12. David S. G. Goodman, *China in the Nineties: Crisis Management & Beyond,* Gerald Segal and David S. Goodman, eds. (New York: Oxford University Press, 1992), p. 106.

13. Ruan, *Deng*, p. 162.

14. Ibid., p. 164.

15. Goodman, *China in the Nineties*, pp. 48–49. The speech was on July 28.

16. Central News Agency, Oct. 9, 1986.

17. *BBC Summary of World Broadcasts*, Part 3, The Far East, citing CNA, Oct. 16, 1986.

18. Ma Ying-jeou, interview, Taipei, May 25, 1996, James Soong, interview, Sept. 15, 1995.

19. Fred Chien, interview, Taipei, May 16, 1996.

20. *Los Angeles Times*, Nov. 1, 1986. *New York Times*, Nov. 30, 1986.

21. *Christian Science Monitor*, Dec. 8, 1986.

22. Reuters North European Service, Dec. 5, 1986.

23. The Economist Publications, *Country Report, Taiwan* London, Feb. 3, 1987.

24. Ibid.

25. Central News Agency, Taipei, Dec. 31, 1986.

26. Chi Hsin, "Hsueh sheng yun tung chia k'uai min chu kai ke de chin ch'eng" (Student Movement Speeds Up Democratic Reform), *Chiu shih nien tai*, Taipei, Jan. 1987, p. 17. Central News Agency, Taipei, Jan. 25, 1987.

27. Shaw Yu-ming, interview, Taipei, March 12, 1998.

28. Goodman, *China in the Nineties*, p. 106.

29. Ruan, *Deng*, p. 166.

30. Robert Delfs, *FEER*, Jan. 15, 1987, p. 8, Jan. 22, 1987, p. 10.

31. *The Economist*, April 23, 1987.

32. Chiang Bi-ling, interview, Taipei, June 5, 1996. Hsiung Yuan, interview, Taipei, May 31, 1991.

33. Ma Shu-li, interview, March 13, 1998.

34. Ibid.

35. David Dean, interview, Virginia, August 26, 1996.

36. Yu Kuo-hua, interview, Taipei, August 28, 1995.

37. Wang, *Hao Pei-tsun*, pp. 260, 276, 293, 301, 313, 368, 379.

38. Goldstein, *FEER*, July 2, 1987, p. 15.

39. Ma Shu-li, June 1, 1996.

40. This section is based on interviews with Lee Huan on Sept. 2, 11, 1995; May 18, 1996; and March 9, 1998.

41. *State Department Bulletin*, May 1987, pp. 10–11.

42. Senior State Department official involved with East Asian affairs, interview, Washington, Feb. 2000.

43. Lee Huan, interview, March 9, 1998.

44. Shaw Yu-ming, interview, May 20, 1996.

45. James D. Seymour, "Taiwan in 1987: A Year of Political Bombshells," *Asian Survey*, 28/1 (Jan. 1988), p. 75.

46. Goldstein, *FEER*, Sept. 3, 1987, p. 15.

47. Lee Huan, interview, March 9, 1998.

48. Ma Ying-jeou, interview, March 10, 1998.

49. Ibid.

50. Lee Huan, May 18, 1996.

51. Seymour, "Taiwan in 1987," p. 74.

52. *FBIS, Daily Report*, China, Sept. 9, 1987, p. 43, citing Agence France Presse report.

53. Lee Huan, interview, March 9, 1998.

54. Ma Ying-jeou, interview, March 10, 1998.

55. Goodman, *China in the Nineties*, pp. 106–107.

56. Lee Huan, interview, March 9, 1998. Zbigniew Brzezinski, *The Grand Failure* (New York: Macmillan, 1989), p. 176. Taylor, *The Rise and Fall*, pp. 158–159.

57. Lee Huan, interview, March 9, 1998.

58. Hsiung Yuan, interview, May 16, 1996.

59. Lee Huan and Lin Yin-ting, *Chiu shui pan shih, Lee Huan yu Ching-kuo hsien sheng* (*Lee Huan: A Half Century of Following Chiang Ching-kuo*) (Taipei: Commonwealth Press, 1998), p. 255.

60. *Los Angeles Times*, Dec. 26, 1987, p. 36. Reuters Library Report, Dec. 25, 1987.

61. James Soong, Sept. 13, 1995.

62. Seymour, "Taiwan in 1987," p. 73.

26. A CHINESE DEMOCRACY

1. Shaw Yu-ming, interview, Taipei, May 20, 1996. James D. Seymour, "Taiwan in 1988: No More Bandits," *Asian Survey*, 29/1 (Jan. 1989), pp. 59–60. Shim Jae Hoon, *FEER*, Jan. 7, 1988, p. 22.

2. Hsiung Yuan, interview, Taipei, May 16, 1996. Chiang Bi-ling, interview, Taipei, June 5, 1996. A family member, notes to the author, Feb. 10, 1999. The official announcement said he died of heart failure caused by chronic inflammation of the pancreas. *Min Chung erh pao*, Mar. 16, 1988, *AIT Media Summary*, Mar. 16, 1988.

3. This section is based on Taipei interviews with Lee Huan, May 18, 1996; Ma Ying-jeou, May 22, 1996; James Soong, Sept. 13, 1995; Shaw Yu-ming, May 20, 1996; Yu Chi-chung, May 24, 1996.

4. Shim Jae Hoon, *FEER*, Jan. 28, 1988, p. 19.

5. March 10, 1998, interview with a KMT Executive Standing Committee member who "witnessed" the fake "will and testament." For the official "text" see Shim Jae Hoon, *FEER*, Jan. 28, 1988.

6. CNA in English, Jan. 21, 1988, FBIS-CHI-88-013, Jan. 21, 1988. David W. Jones, United Press International file, Taipei, Jan. 16, 1988. *FEER,* Jan. 28, 1988, p. 22.

7. Carl Goldstein, *FEER,* Jan. 28, 1988, p. 22.

8. Hao Pei-ts'un, interview, *Hsin hsin wen pao,* Feb. 16, 1997.

9. Various Taipei interviews with Lee Huan, James Soong, Yu Chi-chung, Hao Pei-ts'un, Ma Ying-jeou, Ma Shu-li, and other senior KMT members, 1995–1998.

10. Tzuhu and Touliao, only one or two miles apart, are in the township of Tahsi in T'aoyuan county.

11. Lo Ping, *Zheng ming,* Hong Kong, February 1, 1988, pp. 9–10.

12. Ibid.

13. Tai Ch'ing, "Lin Tse hsu tao Chiang Ching-kuo," in *New Authoritarianism,* eds. Liu Chun and Li Lin, p. 86, translated in Geremie Barmé and Linda Javin, *New Ghosts, Old Dreams: Chinese Rebel Voices* (New York: 1992), pp. 188–189.

14. Ma Ying-jeou, interview, May 22, 1996. Ma also believed Ching-kuo had specific plans in mind.

15. Interview in *Commonwealth* magazine, Taipei, Dec. 1987.

16. Liang Shuo-hua, interview with Fang Li-chih, *Ming pao yueh kan,* Hong Kong, 23 /7, July 7, 1988.

17. Barmé and Javin, *New Ghosts,* p. 141.

18. Ibid., p. 46.

Index

ABC of Communism, 28, 29
Aborigine Human Rights Movement, 401
Acheson, Dean, 171, 174, 199, 200, 285
Afghanistan, invasion of, 355; Soviet withdrawal from, 408
Africa, Communist governments in, 335
Agency for International Development (AID), 257, 283
Agnew, Spiro, 295–296
agriculture, reforms in, 314
Air America, 207
Air Asia, 207
air reconnaissance, success of, 258
Allen, Richard, 368
American Heritage Foundation, 341
American Institute in Taiwan (AIT), 341, 342
American Military Advisory Group (MAAG), 202, 207, 215, 216, 221; competition of with CIA, 227–229
Amin, Hafizullah, 355
Amnesty International, 359
Anikeyev, Fyodor, 63, 76
Anikeyeva, Maria Semyonovna, 63, 66, 76
Anti-Communist Heroes, 219, 349
Anti-Communist Patriotic Front (AFP), 413
Anti-Japanese Peoples United Front, proposed, 67, 71, 77–78
armed forces: political officers in, 214–216; Taiwanese in, 282; contemporary, 434
Asian, The (magazine), 361–362
Atkinson, Brooks, 109
Averbach, Leopold, 66, 69

Bamboo Gang, 357, 358, 377, 385
Barber, Charles H., 224
Barr, David, 152
Battle of Huaihai, 164
Bay of Pigs, 263
Blue Shirts, 85, 86, 99
Blyucher, Vasili K., 18, 25, 34, 70
Bolshevik revolution, 10, 11
Bordan, Maria, 278
Borodin, Michael, 18, 25, 34, 70
Boxer Rebellion, 5–6
Bridges, Styles, 174
Brzezinski, Zbigniew, 332–333
budget, publication of national, 311
Bukharin, Nikolai, 28, 29, 43
Bundy, McGeorge, 263, 264, 268
Burma: invasion plan from, 209–210; KMT influence in, 221–22; Nationalist defeat in, 262–263

Burma road, 104
Bush, George, 370, 371

Caldero, Adolfo, 392
Cambodia: American incursions into, 299–300; invasion of, 338
Canton, fall of, 183
Canton Uprising, 7
Carter, Jimmy, 324, 328, 335, 428
CC Clique, 9, 85–86, 140–141, 149
censorship, 322–323; end of, 421
Central Intelligence Agency (CIA): in Korean war, 206–207; competition with MAAG, 227–229; covert operations in Tibet of, 252–253, 267; cut back in Taiwan, 286; strong ties with Ching-kuo, 370
Central Political Institute, 149
Central Reform Committee, 202
Central Tolmatchev Military and Political Institute, 49
Ch'angch'un, *see* Manchuria
Ch'en Ch'eng, 86, 121, 152, 171, 172, 175–177, 232; as Premier, 194; as proposed Gimo successor, 249; rivalry with Ching-kuo, 249–250, 257; and party competition, 259; resignation of, 270; death of, 272
Ch'en Ch'i-li, 357, 358, 385–386, 387, 390, 392, 431
Ch'en Chieh-ju, 15–16, 25, 50, 280
Ch'en Chih-ching, 170
Ch'en Chiung-ming (Hakka General), 17
Ch'en Chu, 338
Ch'en Hu-men, 388
Ch'en Kuo-fu, 9, 19, 25, 35
Ch'en Li-fu, 9, 26, 33, 86, 132, 141, 194, 433
Ch'en Shao-yu. *See* Wang Ming
Ch'en Shou-shan, 366
Ch'en Shui-bian, 433–434
Ch'en Tu-hsiu, 11
Ch'en Wen-ch'eng, murder of, 374
Ch'en Yi (governor), 148–149, 167, 169, 173
Ch'eng Tzu-ts'ai, 299
Ch'iao Shih, 247
Ch'u Wu, 90
Chang, John, 107, 145, 226–227, 280, 292, 295, 319, 370, 381–382, 388, 433
Chang, Winston, 107, 145, 226–227, 280, 292, 295, 319, 382, 432
Chang Ch'un, 375
Chang Chih-chung, 152; defection of, 173
Chang Ching-hua, 167
Chang Feng-hsu, 309

Chang Hsi-yuan, 27, 33, 57

Chang Hsien-yi, 276, 301, 318, 431

Chang Hsueh-liang (Young Marshal), 53–54, 57, 64, 67–68, 71–73, 82–83, 137, 225–226, 431

Chang Kia-ngao, 131, 132, 142–143

Chang Tso-lin, 24, 41, 51

Chang Ya-juo, 98, 106–108

Chao Chih-hua, 270–271, 355, 368, 378, 384, 411, 418, 428

Chao, Irene, 319

Chase, William C., 215

Cheng Chieh-min, 191

Chennault, Claire, 74, 103, 104, 110, 151, 206

Chennault, Anna, 382

Chia Yi-pin, 170

Chiang, Alan, 67, 145, 225, 277–278, 294–295, 318, 421–422, 431

Chiang, Alex, 279, 295, 318–319, 381–382, 386, 390, 399, 431

Chiang, Amy, 278–279

Chiang, Antonio, 349–349, 361–362, 409

Chiang, Eddy, 295, 318, 399, 424, 432

Chiang, Faina, 80, 108–109, 145–146, 168, 174, 302, 381, 432

Chiang, Yomei, 278, 318, 432

Chiang Bi-ling, 333

Chiang Ch'ing, 285, 324

Chiang Ching-Kuo: early life of, 7, 9–10, 12–13, 16–17, 20–21; education of in USSR, 22–23, 25, 27–28, 31–32, 36, 53, 61–63; social life of, 37–38, 46, 106–108, 157, 226, 276–277, 346; relationship with Chiang Kai-shek, 43, 68–69, 78–80, 112, 115; leftist leanings of, 43–44, 45, 86–88, 90–93, 100, 158; health of, 56, 120, 333, 374, 398, 402, 404; meetings with Stalin, 58, 66, 75, 126–127, 137–139; repatriation of, 65–66, 70, 74–77; family life of, 66–67, 80–81, 112, 120–121, 145–146, 225, 277–280, 294–295, 318–319, 381, 418, 424–425; colleagues of, 82–83, 249–250, 325, 409–410; career trajectory of, 105–106, 113, 116–117, 154–61, 272, 309, 322; relations of with U.S., 110–111, 219–21, 268–269, 273–275, 297–299; and clandestine operations, 194–196, 207–209, 212–213, 239–241, 390–391, 394, 413; personal characteristics of, 210–211, 213, 223–225, 310–311, 331–333; death of, 421–422

Chiang Hsi-hou, 5

Chiang Jui-ch'ing, 5

Chiang Kai-shek: birth of, 4; marriages of, 5, 16, 49–50, 57; education of, 6; as revolutionary military leader, 8; key relationships of, 9; as father, 12–13, 14–15, 16, 58–59, 78–80, 111–112, 115; temperament of, 12; to Moscow, 18; as Commandant of Whampoa Academy, 18–19; pro-Soviet stance of, 20, 34; appointed Generalissimo, 35–36; retreats of, 48, 59–61, 163, 164–169, 174–179; kidnapping of, 71–73; personality cult of, 97, 117; to Burma, 104–105; meets with Mao, 130–131; and U.S. demarche, 183–184; as elder statesman, 223; and mainland attack, 253–254, 261–263, 264, 268, 273; declining health and death of, 294, 310, 320–321

Chiang Soong Mei-ling (Madame Chiang), 70, 73, 160, 186, 433; and Faina, 80; and Ching-kuo, 115; return to Taiwan, 192, 194, 409, 418; as Gimo's principal adviser, 207, 221; as hostess of holiday dinners, 279; political maneuvering of, 310, 326–327, 340, 341, 423, 424; contracts breast cancer, 318

Chiang Su-an, 4, 5

Chiang Wei-kuo, 13, 14–15, 68, 101–102, 167, 177, 215, 232, 250, 270, 280, 321, 386, 402

Chiang You-piao, 4

Chien, Fred, 292, 309, 322, 325, 338, 363, 391, 403, 433

China Democratic Party, 259, 260

China Lobby, 186–187, 219, 296

China News, 225

China Times, 406

China: temporarily united, 51–53; air war in, 110, travel ban to lifted, 416–441. *See also* mainland; People's Republic of China

Chinese Communist Party (CCP): formation of, 18; rising power of, 24–25; coalition with KMT, 34; purged from KMT, 46; united front strategy of, 77–78; Russian strategy on, 122–123; in Manchuria, 129, 136–137; capture of Manchuria, 152–153, 162; victory in civil war, 162–164, 167, 168, 173–174, 186; enters Korean War, 204

Chinese Communist Youth Corps, 31, 35

Chinese culture, loss of supremacy of, 3

Chinese unity, 213

Chiu, Ellen, 250

Cho Lin, 284

Chou Chih-jou, 195

Chou Lien-hua, 282

Chou Pai-chieh, 90

Chou Sheng-lien, 91

Chou Shu-kai, 309

Chou Tung, 10

Christopher, Warren, attack on, 338

Chu Te, 53, 57

Chung Shan Institute, 323
Chungking, fall of, 184–185
Civil Air Transport (CAT), 151, 206–207
civil war, 149–150, 154
Cline, Marjorie, 239
Cline, Ray S., 239, 240, 263, 264, 266, 273, 382
Cold War: early stages of, 142; Communist
    upsurge in, 153; end of, 416, 429
Consumers Foundation, 401
containment policy, 229, 286
Coordination Council for North American
    Affairs (CCNAA), 341, 342
Council for Economic Planning and
    Development (CEPD), 330
Council for International Economic
    Cooperation (CIEC), 292
criminal gangs, 357, 358; crackdown on, 387
Cross, Charles T. ("Chuck"), 354, 363
Cuban missile crisis, 267
currency reforms, collapse of, 161–162
Czechoslovakia, Soviet invasion of, 287

Dalai Lama, 252
Davies, Joseph E., 77
Dean, David, 289, 354, 370
Declaration on National Affairs, 306–307
defections, to communists, 68, 173
Democracy Wall, 339–340, 354, 355
Democratic Progressive Party (DPP):
    established, 405–407, 410; demonstrations,
    419, 421, 423
Deng Xiaoping, 11, 40, 270; as student, 27,
    32–33; on Long March, 65; and CCP, 284,
    315, 320, 325; and relations with U.S.,
    332–333, 340; and informal talks with
    Taiwan, 382–384; and Hong Kong
    settlement, 384–385; health of, 397–398;
    reaction to democratization, 407–408, 411,
    428–430; reaction to Ching-kuo's death, 425;
    and waning of liberalism in PRC, 428–430;
    death of, 432–433
depression, worldwide, 54–55
Der Spiegel, 378, 384
development, reforms to hasten, 257
Dien Bien Phu, 229–230
Dimitrov, Georgi, 76
Dirksen, Everett, 237
Drumright, Everett, 238, 240–241, 260–261,
    262, 264
Dulles, Allen, 217, 220, 252
Dulles, John Foster, 198, 199, 217, 220, 221,
    229, 230–231; on Sukarno, 240; ultimatum
    of to Taipei, 244–247
Duong Van Minh, 270

Educated Youth Expeditionary Army (Youth
    Army), 118–120; demobilization of,
    144–145; veterans of, 144, 150–151
Eighties, The (journal), 348–349, 388
Eisenhower, Dwight David, 217; meets Ching-
    kuo, 220; visit to Taipei, 253
El Salvador, 335
elections: (1972), 311–312; (1976), 328–330;
    National Assembly (1978), 331; (1978), 334,
    337, 360; (1980), 362; local (1981), 366;
    (1983), 377–378; (1986), 409–410; (1996),
    432; (2000), 433
evacuation priorities, 166, 168–169

family planning, 292–293
Fang Chih-yi, 318
Fang Li-chih, 429
Far Eastern Economic Review, 363
fascism, rise of, 55
Federal Bureau of Investigation (FBI), and Liu
    murder, 388, 389, 393
Feldman, Harvey, 336
Feng Fu-neng, 37–38, 46, 51
Feng Hao Fang house, see Hsikou
Feng Hung-kuo, 51
Feng Yu-hsiang, 22, 24, 32, 45, 51, 52
Financial, Economic, and Monetary
    Conference (FEMC), 292
Flying Tigers, 103–104
Foot, Rosemary, 218
Ford, Gerald, 315
Forman, Harrison, 92–93, 109
Formosa group, 349, 350–353
Formosa (journal), 349
Formosa Resolution in Congress, 233
Four Cardinal Principles, 354
four-point program to strengthen Taiwan, 370
Fourth Red Army, creation of, 53
Free China (magazine), 259
FX aircraft, 363, 367–369

Germany, Gimo's connections to, 68
Goldwater, Barry, 340, 367, 371–372
Gorbachev, Mikhail, 399, 401, 408
Government Information Office (GIO), 292,
    322
Graham, Katherine, 408
Great Leap Forward, 242, 253, 261
Great Proletarian Cultural Revolution, 284
Great Terror, 69–70
Green, Marshall, 308
Green Gang, 8, 9, 19, 33, 42
Grenada, 335
Guam Doctrine, 290

Haig, Alexander, 368, 369, 371–372

Hao Pei-ts'un, 389, 393, 398

Harriman, Averill, 264–265

Helms, Jesse, 367, 371

Hiroshima, 127

Holbrooke, Richard, 326

Holdridge, John, 308

Hole-in-the-Snow monastery, 9, 10, 60, 435

Hole-in-the-Snow Mountain, 170

Hong Kong Declaration, 384–385, 428

Hsieh Ts'ung-min, 306

Hsieh Tung-min, 309–319, 331

Hsikou, 3–4; family compound in, 60; bombing of, 96; evacuation of, 174–175

Hsiung Shih-hui, 131, 141

Hsiung Yuan, 418

Hsu Ch'ing-chung, 309

Hsu Chi-yuan, 90

Hsu Hsi-lin, 277–278

Hsu Hsin-liang, 410, 433, birthday celebration for, 347–348

Hsu Li-nung, 375

Hsu Tao-lin, 81–82

Hu Han-min, 23

Hu Kui, 90, 163, 170

Hu Shih, 197, 259

Hu Ts'ung-nan, 181, 209

Hu Yao-pang, 355, 366, 384, 400, 411, 428, 429

Hua Kuo-feng, 324

Huang Chung-mei, 90, 99, 108

Huang Hsi-ling, 377

Huang Hsin-chieh, 293–294, 322, 349, 353, 356–359, 362

Huang Shao-ku, 245

Huang Wen-hsiung, 299, 432

Huang, Helen, 295

human rights: and Carter administration, 328; in China, 401

Hundred Flowers Campaign, 241

Hurley, Patrick, 121–122, 126, 130

Ichigo offensive, 113, 118, 121, 122

Inchon, U.S. invasion at, 203

Indigenous Defense Fighter (IDF), 391, 393

Indochina: escalation of war in, 273; proposed use of Nationalist troops in, 275

Indonesian affair, 239–240

Industrial Technology Research Institute, 313

inflation, in civil war, 154

Institute of International Affairs, 258

Intellectual, The (journal), 306–307, 311, 312

Intelligence Bureau of the Ministry of National Defense (IBMND), 377, 386, 387–388, 393

International Monetary Fund, 365

Iron Blood Patriots Society, 349, 407, 413

Japan: modernization of, 6; imperialist ambitions of, 55, 94; war with, 83–84, 88–89

Jen Hsien-ch'un, 276–277

Joffe, Adolph, 17

Johnson, Louis, 187, 197

Johnson, Lyndon Baines, 274

Johnson, U. Alexis, 234

Joint Commission on Rural Reconstruction (JCRR), 256–257

K'ang Ning-hsiang, 311, 312, 322, 334, 343, 348, 361, 362, 364, 373, 422–423

K'ang Sheng, 76–77, 258

Kanchow, 89–90, 109

Kannan, reforms in, 90–93, 100, 109, 113–114

Kao Ming-hui, 412

Kao Ying-mao, 367

Kao, Henry, 251, 271, 281, 309

Kaohsiung riot, 351–353

Kaplan, David, 358, 385–386

Kennan, George, 197, 198

Kennedy, John F., 260, 270

Kennedy, Robert, 287

Kennedy, Ted, 340

Khabarovsk Protocol, 54

Khrushchev, Nikita, to Peking, 242

Kiangsi: soviet republic in, 57; abandoned by CCP, 64–65

Kim Il-sung, 153; invades South Korea, 193–194; visit to Moscow, 197

King, Martin Luther, Jr., 287

Kirk, Alan G., 265–266, 267

Kissinger, Henry, 290; and China initiative, 296–298, 303

Knowland, William F., 174

Koo, Wellington, 231

Korean peace negotiations, nuclear ultimatum in, 218

Korean war, 200–201, 204–205; Communist POWs issue, 217–219

Ku Ch'ing-lien, 12

Ku Cheng-ch'iu, 276–277, 331

Kung, David, 155, 160–161, 340

Kung, H. H., 50, 87

Kuo Kuo-chi ("Big Gun"), 293–294

Kuomintang (KMT), 9; leadership change in, 23–24; coalition with CCP, 34; drift to right, 40; purge of Communists in, 41–43, 45–46; corruption and factionalism in, 85, 88, 114–115, 149, 150; strategy toward Russia,

124–128; strategy in Manchuria, 133–135, 142–143; administration on Taiwan, 185–186; reform of, 202–203; democratization of, 281, 291, 293; Taiwanese in, 346, 347; fundamental changes in, 403–404, 413–414, 415–416. *See also* Republic of China, Taiwan

Kuo T'ing-liang, 231

Lai Ming-t'ang, 262
Laird, Melvin, 298
land reform: in Kannan, 92; on Taiwan, 181–182, 255–256
Lee Huan, 236, 291, 328–330, 414, 417, 433
Lee Kuan-yew, 368, 382–384, 397, 399, 405, 418
Lee Teng-hui, 257, 299, 326, 359, 365, 379–380, 398, 432; as president, 422, 423–425
leftist leaders, in 1919, 11
Lei Chen, 259–261, 274
Leng Shao-chuan, 415
Li Ao, 306
Li Mi, 209, 210
Li Ta-chao, 11, 41
Li Tsung-jen, 88, 164, 167, 171, 173, 175, 180–181
Li, K.T., 292–293, 309
Liao Cheng-chih, 343, 373
Liao Chung-k'ai, 23
Liao Wen-yi, 281
Lien Chan, 292, 412, 433
Lilley, James R., 369–370, 375, 398
Lin Piao, 65, 136, 149, 152, 299, 304–305
Lin Yang-kang, 326
Lin Yi-hsiung, 433; murder of family of, 357
Little League World Series, 307
Liu hsiao-k'ang (LSK), 345; authority of, 374, 375
Liu Shao-ch'i, as president of PRC, 253, 270
Liu, Henry, 327–328; murder of, 386–394; public relations crisis about, 389–390; impact of murder of, 393–394
Long March, 65
Louis, Victor, 287–289, 301–302

Ma Shu-li, 393, 395–396, 398
Ma Ying-jeou, 306, 366, 369, 412, 417
Macao, to China, 428
MacArthur, Douglas, 172, 187, 197–198, 201–202; removal of, 209–210
McCarthy, Joseph, 197, 219
MacConaughy, Walter, 304

McNamara, Robert, 274
mainland attack: plans for 253–254, 261–263, 264; Kennedy administration reaction to, 263–267; Secret Dragon plan for, 268
mainland: indirect Taiwan trade with, 364, 378, 397; political reform on, 369; pro-democratic protest on, 410–411; , inflation on, 429. *See also* China, People's Republic of China
Malinovsky, Rodion Y., 131–136
Manchuria, 6, 51–52, 53–54, 124, 127, 129–143; Japanese takeover of, 57–58
Manchus, 3
Mao Fu-mei: married Kai-shek, 5, 6–7; and Yao Yeh-ch'eng, 13; divorced, 15, 60; death of, 96–97
Mao Jen-feng, 191
Mao Zedong, 9, 11; as youthful organizer, 21; forms Fourth Red Army, 53, 57; meets with Chiang Kai-shek, 130–131; pact with Russia, 169–170; Russian strategy, 179; proposes Sino-American renunciation of force agreement, 234–235; and Cultural Revolution, 284; anti-Soviet stance of, 285; deification of, 285; on Chiang Kai-shek, 308; ill health and death of, 315, 324–325
Marshall, George C., 133, 136, 137
martial law, end of, 403, 404, 407–408
Martin, Robert, 224
Massachusetts Institute of Technology (MIT), 323
Matsu Island, 196, 230, 233, 242–244, 244–247
McCarthy, Joseph, 197, 219
McNamara, Robert, 274
Merchant, Livingston T., 171
Mikoyan, Anastas, 169
military hardware, sales of to Taiwan, 187, 204–205, 363, 371–373
Ming dynasty, 3
Molotov, Vyacheslav M., 121; on Ching-kuo, 138
Molotov-Ribbentrop Pact, 94, 95
Morse, Wayne, 219
Mutual Security Treaty, 230–231, 326, 339

Nanking, rape of, 84
National Development Seminars, 350
National Revolutionary Army, 35, 37, 38–40
National Security Bureau (NSB), 377, 387
National Security Law, 408–409, 415
Naulen, Hilaire, 58, 64
Naval Auxiliary Communications Center (NACC), 239
New Generation, 377

New Life Institute, 192
New Taiwan Dollar (NT$), 194
New York Times, 109, 191, 210, 315
Ngo Dinh Diem, 269
Ngo Dinh Nhu, 269
Nguyen Cao Ky, 275
Nguyen Loc Hua, 275
Nguyen Van Thieu, 275
Nicaragua, 335; ROC aid to, 391–392
Nitze, Paul, 198, 199
Nixon, Richard M., 287, 428; plans for
    rapprochement with Peking, 296–298; visit
    of to Peking, 307; resignation of, 315
NKVD (Soviet security), 69–70, 77
Nonparty Public Policy Association, 385, 396
North Korean Army, 153
North, Oliver, 391–392, 393
Nuclear Non-proliferation Treaty, 324
nuclear weapons project, 275–276, 301,
    317–318, 323–324, 431
nuclear weapons, threat of, 243, 245–246

one-China principle, 371, 384, 414–415
Operation Clean Sweep, 387
opposition, factions in, 377
Outer Mongolia, 126, 264
outreach programs, in U.S., 316–317, 326–327

P'an Ch'en-ch'iu, 330
P'eng Meng-chi, 177, 262, 250
P'eng Ming-min, 271, 280–281, 432
P'eng Te-huai, 65, 204
Pacific Corporation, 207
Pai Ch'ung-hsi, 148
Panama Canal Treaty, 335
Paoting Military Academy, 6
Park Chung Hee, 353–354
parliamentary reform, 417–418, 421, 433
party competition, rise of, 259–261
Peking, anti-Soviet protests in, 140–141
People's Daily, 303
People's Liberation Army (PLA), 147, 153
People's Republic of China (PRC): formed,
    182; offensive against India, 267; campaign
    for reunification, 343–345, 366–367,
    383–384, 426–427; democratization trend in,
    354–355, 407–408; waning of liberalism in,
    428–430. *See also* China; mainland
Petrov, A. A., 125
Phoenix Mountain Academy, 13
Pol Pot, 335
Political Action Committee, 191–192
political activism, in Hunan, 21
Political Monitor (journal), 362

Political Staff College, 213–214, 215
Pratt, Mark, 336
Provincial Peace Preservation Corps, 85–87
psychological warfare, emphasis on, 98–100
publications, political, 349, 361, 362
Pudong High School, 20–21

Quemoy Island (Chinmen), 196; expected
    invasion of, 230, 233; attack on, 242–244;
    American response to attack on, 244–247, as
    key to Chinese unity, 247
Quirino, Elpidio, 180

Radek, Karl, 29, 36, 40, 53, 69
Radford, Arthur W., 215, 232, 233
Reagan, Ronald: election of, 362; assurances to
    PRC leaders, 370–371, 372
Red Army, 84–85
Reporter, The (magazine), 219
Republic of China (ROC), recognition of, 53.
    See also Kuomintang; Taiwan
Republic of China Patriotic Society (PS), 413
Revolutionary Alliance, 6, 7–8
Reynolds, Robert, 236
Rhee, Syngman, 181, 259
Ridgway, Matthew, 210
Ringwalt, Arthur, 111
riot, anti-American, 236–238
Robertson, Walter, 238
Rogers, William, 298, 300
Roosevelt, Franklin Delano, 102–103, 122
Roy, M. N., 45
rule-of-law, transition to, 404
Rusk, Dean, 198–199, 200, 262
Russian revolution, progress of, 28–29. *See also*
    Bolshevik revolution
Russian strategy: re CCP, 122–123; re
    Manchuria, 131–136, 141–142
Russo-Japanese War, 6

Saigon, fall of, 322
Seagrave, Sterling, 396
security priorities, shift away in Taiwan from
    CCP, 211–212
Service, Robert, 109, 110–111
Shah, Konsin, 170, 174–175, 177, 195
Shanghai Communique, 308
Shanghai: Ching-kuo in, 154–162, 176; fall of,
    83; student unrest in, 146–147; evacuation
    of, 175–178
Shao Chih-kang, 27
Shao Li-tzu, 22, 40; defection of, 173
Shaw Yu-ming, 400, 411, 412, 415
Shen Ch'ang-huan, 337, 375, 389

Shen, Samson, 219, 220
Sheng Shih-ts'ai, 105, 106
Shih Ching-yi, 250
Shih Ming-te, 351, 353, 356–359, 413
Shimbu Gakko, 6, 7
Shultz, George, 391, 414–415
Siegur, Gaston, 391–392
signal intercepts, success of, 258
Singapore, 382, 384
Singlaub, John, 392
Sinkiang province, 124–125; Ching-kuo as
    proposed governor of, 105–106
Sino-British Joint Declaration of the Future of
    Hong Kong. *See* Hong Kong Declaration
Sino-Soviet relations, 241–242, 273; policy of
    peaceful coexistence, 230, 234, 241
Sino-Soviet Treaty of Friendship and Alliance,
    127, 200
Sino-Vietnamese war, undeclared, 340
Smith, Walter Bedell, 209, 210
"soft authoritarianism," 427–428
Solarz, Steven, 388, 391, 393
Soong, Charlie, 49–50
Soong, James, 325, 336, 348, 369, 402, 412, 433
Soong, T. V., 51, 87, 125–127, 140, 141
Soong Ch'ing-ling, 47, 49, 58, 61
Soong Dynasty, The, 396
Soong Mei-ling, marries Gimo, 49–50, 57. *See
    also* Chiang Soong Mei-ling
South Korea, invasion of, 199, 200–201
Soviet-Japanese Neutrality Pact, 103
Special Administrative Regions (SAR), Hong
    Kong and Taiwan as, 367
Special Warfare Center, 251
Sputnik, 241
Stalin, Joseph, 29, 42, 43, 121; on Chinese
    revolution, 39–40; meets with Ching-kuo, 58,
    66, 75, 126, 137–139; and threat of nuclear
    war, 204; death of, 217; criticism of, 241
State Compensation Act, 362
Stilwell, Joseph W., 86, 103, 104–105, 110, 118
Streams in the Desert, 112, 164
Su Shao-chih, 400–401
succession, to Ching-kuo, 365, 375, 379–381,
    398–399, 402
Sukarno, 239–240
Sun Li-jen, 136, 171–172, 182, 195, 197–199,
    185–186, 192, 199–200, 216, 386, 431; under
    house arrest, 231–232
Sun Yat-sen, 5–6, 11; pro-Soviet stance, 17–18;
    death of, 20
Sun Yat-sen University of the Toilers of China
    (Sunovka), 22, 29–31
Sun, Y. S., 278, 291, 309 , 331, 380

Sung Hsin-lien, 413
Sung Ts'ang-chih, 404

T'ang Chung-po, 276
table-tennis team, 303
Tai Ch'ing, 425–426
Tai Chi-t'ao, 9, 11, 13, 41, 185
Tainan Giants baseball team, 307
Taipei, rebellion in, 148
Taiwan: nationalist takeover of, 147–149; and
    U.S., 170–173, 206–207, 229, 316; leaders,
    American training of, 194, 195–196; defense
    against expected invasion, 196, 199; economic
    expansion in, 270, 283, 292, 302, 313–314, 330,
    365, 400, 419–420, 434; local politics in,
    280–281; social changes in, 307, 401, 434;
    democratization in, 334, 346, 425–428; liber-
    alized relations with PRC, 364, 367, 373, 382–
    384; as political reform model for mainland,
    369. *See also* Kuomintang; Republic of China
Taiwan Daily News, 334
Taiwan Greenpeace Organization, 401
Taiwan Independence Alliance, 298
Taiwan Political Review, The (journal), 322
Taiwan Relations Act (TRA), 342, 371
Taiwanese: subversive anti-KMT, 211–212;
    political position of, 255–257; into military,
    282; in KMT, 291, 346; in Ching-kuo's
    government, 309; on KMT Central
    Committee, 326
Ten Major Development Projects, 313–314
Tenth Credit Cooperative, collapse of, 395
Tet offensive, 287
Thayer, Harry, 388
"three nos" policy, 364, 367
Thurmond, Strom, 371
Tiaoyut'ai islets issue, 306
Tibet, resistance in, 252–253, 254
Tienanmen Square, 429–430
torpedo purchase plan, 317
Treaty of Friendship and Cooperation,
    USSR/North Vietnam, 335
Trotsky, Leon, 29, 30, 36, 40, 43, 47, 53
Truman, Harry S., 133, 162–163, 175, 209, 210;
    policy of disengagement, 192–193; and
    Korean war, 200–201, 204–205
Ts'ai Hui-mei, 381
Ts'u Sung-ch'iu, 360
Tsiang T'ing-fu, 70, 75
Tsiang, Y. S., 256, 291, 375, 378, 395
Tu Chang-ch'eng, 184
Tu Wei-p'ing, 156
Tu Yu-ming, 132
Tu Yueh-sheng, 155, 160

Tucker, Nancy, 229
Tukhachevsky, Mikhail, 49, 70, 75
Two Chinas solution, 245, 247, 260, 300, 301, 305
Tyazheloye Mashinostroyenie (Heavy Machinery), 65

U-2 spy planes, 239
U.S. News and World Report (magazine), 224
Unger, Leonard, 317, 322, 336–337
Union of Soviet Socialist Republics (USSR): non-aggression pact with China, 83–84; pact with Mao, 169–170; partnership with Communist China, 179–180, 193; first missile test by, 241; contacts with ROC, 288–290
United Nations, 221, 264; expulsion of Republic of China from, 305
United States: disagreement on Taiwan policy, 197–199, 199–200; Mutual Security treaty with Republic of China, 230–231, 326, 339; negotiations with People's Republic of China, 301–302, 303–304, 308–309; trade with Taiwan, 316; buttressing relations with Taiwan, 326–328; normalization of relations with Peoples Republic of China, 332–333, 335; Recognition of Peoples Republic of China, 335–341

Vahaleva, Faina Epatcheva, 63. *See also* Chiang, Faina
Vance, Cyrus, 326
Versailles Peace Treaty, 10–11
veterans, 282–283
Vietnam: American military aid program in 1954, 229; French defeat in, 229–230; Americans in, 284; coup in, 269–270; impact of in U.S., 296
Vocational Assistance Commission for Retired Servicemen (VACRS), 248–249

Wang Chang-shih, 295, 318–319
Wang Cheng-yi, 311
Wang Chi, 247
Wang Ching-hsu, 377, 387
Wang Ching-wei, 21, 23, 41, 47, 61
Wang Hsi-ling, 317, 327, 385, 386, 388–389, 390, 392, 431
Wang Hsin-heng, 225
Wang Ming, 27, 53; return to China of, 56–57; CCP representative to Comintern, 62
Wang Ou-sheng, 13
Wang Shao-yu, 389
Wang Sheng, 97–98, 99–100, 163, 191, 211–212, 213, 269, 295, 344–345, 375; and succession, 375–376, 386, 432
Wang Shu-ming ("Tiger"), 250

Wang Ts'ai-yu (grandmother), 4–5, 9, 14
Ward, Robert S., 125
Warm Currents (magazine), 362
Washington Post, 323, 389, 408
Wedemeyer, Albert C., 118, 130
Wei Ching-sheng, 355
Wei Li-huang, 162
Wei Ting-chiao, 306
Wei Yung, 325, 426
Wei, Jimmy, 225, 288–290, 301–302, 309
Wen Ch'ang, 87–88, 140
Weng Wen-hao, 163
White Terror, 177, 211–213
Whiting, Allen, 224–225
Winkler, Edwin, 427
Wolfowitz, Paul, 391, 414
Woodcock, Leonard, 335–336
World War I, 10–11
World War II, 93–95, 102–104, 117–118, 121, 124, 128
Wright, Gerald, 267
Wu Chih-hui, 9, 22–23, 35, 41
Wu P'ei-fu, 24
Wu Shao-shu, 178
Wu Tun, 392
Wu, K. C., 185, 186, 194, 216–217
Wuhan uprising, 8
Wushan Grammar School, 10, 19

Yagoda, Genrikh, 69
Yalta summit meeting, 122–123
Yang Kuo-shu, 306, 311
Yang, H. K., 340–341
Yangtze river, Communist advance across, 173–174
Yao Yeh-ch'eng, 8, 13, 15, 280
Yeh, George, 151, 194, 201, 228, 22, 236, 238
Yen, C. K., 270, 272, 331, 404; as president, 322
Yin, K. Y., 194
Young Cadre School, 97
Youth Army, *see* Educated Youth Expeditionary Army
Youth Cadre School, 113, 116–117
Youth Corps, 85, 86, 112–113, 124, 150, 237
Yu Chi-chung, 309, 406
Yu Chi-yu, 90
Yu Kuo-hua, 330, 380, 393, 423–424
Yu Yang-ho, 278–279
Yuan, opposition in, 311

Zhou Enlai, 11, 23, 25, 34; in Moscow, 52–53; on Long March, 65; cancer diagnosis, 315; death of, 324
Zi, Nancy, 277

19. Donald W. Treadgold, *Twentieth Century Russia* (Boulder, Co.: Westview Press, 1995), pp. 202–203.

20. CCK 1934 autobiography gives the date as 1930. Cline, *CCK Remembered*, p. 165, states that in December 1929 "under pressure of the Chinese Communist delegation, I became listed as alternate member of the Russian Communist Party."

21. Robert C. North, *Moscow and Chinese Communists*, 2d ed. (Stanford: Stanford University Press, 1963), p. 123.

22. Ch'in Sh'iao-i, *Chung hua min kuo chin chi fa chan shih* (History of Economic Development in the Republic of China) (Taipei: 1983), vol. 1, p. 459.

23. Jay Taylor, *The Rise and Fall of Totalitarianism* (New York: Paragon Press, 1993), p. 32.

24. Ibid., p. 34.

25. Cline, *CCK Remembered*, p. 167.

26. Chiang Ching-kuo, *Chiang Ching-kuo hsien sheng chuan chi* (Chiang Ching-kuo, *Collected Works*) (Taipei: Government Information Office, 1989), hereafter *CCKHSCC*, p. 39. 1994 RTR documentary.

27. Yu Min-ling, fax to author, June 26, 1998. Yang Tien-shih and Li Yu-chen, interview, Peking, Sept. 26, 1995.

28. Cline, *CCK Remembered*, p. 167.

29. CCK 1934 autobiography, pp. 52–55.

30. Cline, *CCK Remembered*, pp. 168–169.

31. Richard Evans, *Deng Xiaoping and the Making of Modern China* (New York: Penguin Books, 1993), p. 48.

32. North, *Moscow and Chinese*, p. 160.

33. While doing research at the Archives of the President's Office in Moscow, a Russian-speaking scholar from Peking was briefly shown the file cover of the 1931 Stalin/Chiang Ching-kuo meeting, entitled "The Political Situation in China after the September 18 Incident and the Soviet Union's Attitude toward Chiang Kai-shek," but was not allowed to read the contents. The person who showed her the file was former Soviet ambassador to China, Redolfsky. Li Yuzhen, interview, Peking, Sept. 9, 1995.

34. Yang Tianshih, former director of the Institute of Modern Chinese History and a specialist on the Republican period, written notes provided the author, Oct. 1996.

35. Chiang Kai-shek, *Nanking Diaries*, #2 Nat. Archives, Nanking, entry Jan. 25, 1931.

36. Ibid., entry Nov. 28, 1931.

37. *CCKHSCC*, vol. 1, chronology, p. 40.

38. *Nanking Diaries*, entries Dec.15 and 16, 1931.

39. Interviews with researchers and caretakers at Chiang residence in Hsikou, Oct. 1995 and June 1996.

40. *Nanking Diaries*, entry Dec. 27, 1931.

41. Ibid., entry Dec. 31, 1931.

42. Cline, *CCK Remembered*, p. 171. Ching-kuo gives the village name as "Shekov." In the chronology in CCK 1934 autobiography he identified the village as Korovino.

Zhukova was the small village where he actually lived, and Korovino was the capital of the region of Korovinsky.

43. Cline, *CCK Remembered*, pp. 171–173.

44. 1994 RTR documentary.

45. Cline, *CCK Remembered*, pp. 174–175.

46. Ibid., pp. 175–176.

47. Alexander Larin, e-mail message from Moscow to the author, Jan. 5, 1996. Ching-kuo's letter to his mother cited by *New York Times*, Feb. 12, 1936, p. 12, states that he managed 4,000 workers.

48. 1994 RTR documentary. In the documentary the woman is identified as Maria Semyonovna Anikeev and her husband as Fyodor Anikeev.

49. Ibid.

50. Cline, *CCK Remembered*, p. 178.

51. *Nanking Diaries*, entries Feb. 13, July 7, and August 15, 1934.

52. North, *Moscow and Chinese*, p. 164.

53. *Nanking Diaries*, entry Sept. 2, 1934.

54. North, *Moscow and Chinese*, p. 164.

55. Cline, *CCK Remembered*, p. 179.

56. Ibid.

57. *Nanking Diaries*, entry Dec. 14, 1996.

58. Cline, *CCK Remembered*, p. 179.

59. 1994 RTR documentary,

60. Ching-kuo's letter to his mother cited by the *New York Times*, Feb. 12, 1936, p. 12.

61. Alexander Larin, "President Jiang Jingguo," *Asia and Africa Today*, Moscow, Jan. 5, 1991, p. 62.

62. 1994 RTR documentary.

63. Larin, "Jiang," p. 62.

64. 1994 RTR documentary.

65. Letter to the author from a close family member, Feb. 22, 1999.

66. *New York Times*, Feb. 12, 1936, p. 12.

67. Ibid.

68. Ching-kuo erroneously gives the date of this meeting as Jan. 1935 rather than 1936. Conceivably he wrote the letter in early 1935, but it was not published in *Pravda* until Feb. 1936. More likely he simply got the year wrong.

69. Cline, *CCK Remembered*, p. 180.

70. Lerner, *Karl Radek*, pp. 165–171.

71. Valentin M. Berezhkov, *At Stalin's Side* (Secaucus, N.J.: Carol Publishing Group, 1994), p. 364.

72. Zbigniew Brzezinski, *The Grand Failure* (New York: Macmillan, 1989), p. 24.

73. The date of his completed questionnaire submitted to local Party headquarters.

74. Tsiang T'ing-fu, *The Reminiscences of Tsiang T'ing-fu (1895–1965)*, with Crystal Lorch Seidman, Chinese Oral History Project, East Asian Institute of Columbia University (New York: 1974), pp. 213–214.

75. Ch'en, *Storm Clouds,* p. 118–120.

76. Crozier, *Man Who Lost,* pp. 182–183.

77. Tsiang, *Reminiscences,* p. 208.

78. Spence, *The Search,* p. 423.

79. Berezhkov, *Stalin's Side,* pp. 364, 367.

80. 1994 RTR documentary shows a document titled "Resolution of Dec. 15, 1936 to admit Chiang Ching-kuo as a member of the Bolshevik Party in the 4th category." This category referred to children of the "people's enemies."

81. Han Suyin, *Eldest Son: Chou En-lai and the Making of Modern China, 1898–1976* (New York: Hill and Wang, 1994), p. 154, citing Wang Pingnan's account of the meeting.

82. Wang Chi, interview, Washington, Dec. 9, 1995, citing Chang Hsueh-liang.

83. Ch'en, *Storm Clouds,* p. 126.

5. REUNION AND WAR

1. Ray S. Cline, *Chiang Ching-kuo Remembered* (Washington, D.C.: United States Global Strategic Council, 1989), p. 183. Alexander Larin, "President Jiang Jingguo," *Asia and Africa Today,* Moscow, Jan. 5, 1991, p. 63.

2. Chiang Ching-kuo, *Chiang Ching-kuo hsien sheng chuan chi* (Chiang Ching-kuo, *Collected Works*) (Taipei: 1989), chronology, vol. 1, pp. 56–55. Henceforth *CCKHSCC*.

3. 1994 Russian Tele-Radio (RTR) TV documentary, *Cheloviek meniayet kozhu, ili zhizn i nieobichainiye prevrashchieniya gospodina Dzian Dzingo* (The Man Changes the Skin, or the Life and Extraordinary Metamorphoses of Mr. Chiang Ching-kuo). Producer Samariy Zelikin. Henceforth 1994 RTR documentary. Larin, *President Jiang,* p. 64, quotes Maria Anikeyeva as reporting the presence of the Party officials.

4. Larin, *President Jiang,* p. 64.

5. Cline, *CCK Remembered,* pp. 184–185.

6. Ching-kuo's tutor in Hsikou after his return, Hsu Tao-lin, told an American embassy officer in Taipei in 1953 that Ching-kuo had told him he had seen Stalin before his departure in March 1937. State Department Foreign Service dispatch, March 31, 1953, American Embassy in Taipei, in National Archives, RG 59, China 1950–1954, State Dept. Decimal File 1950–1954, Box 4223 (henceforth AmEmb Taipei, State-Dept, NatArch). A friendly biographer in Taiwan, Han Shan-p'i, *Chiang Ching kuo ping chuan* (The Life of Chiang Ching-kuo) (Hong Kong: Tianyuan Chubanshe, 1988), p. 79, also recounts a meeting with Stalin before Ching-kuo's return.

7. Tsiang T'ing-fu, *The Reminiscences of Tsiang T'ing-fu (1895–1965)*, with Crystal Lorch Seidman, Chinese Oral History Project, East Asian Institute of Columbia University (New York: 1974), p. 214.

8. Ibid. A photo of the couple with the embassy staff depicts their new outfits.

9. Yu Min-ling, "E kuo tang an chung te liu su hsueh sheng Chiang Ching kuo" (Chiang Ching-kuo's Student Years in the Soviet Union as Reflected in Russian Archives), Modern History Research Institute, Academia Sinica, Taipei, June 1998, p. 128.

10. *Ya chou chou k'an (Asian Week)*, "KGB Files Portray the Young Ching-kuo: Politics and Marriage," Jan. 26–Feb. 8, 1998, pp. 30–35. The article cites the research of a Russian scholar, Vladimir Prohorovich Galitsky, based on documents in the Asian African Institute at Moscow University.

11. 1994 RTR documentary.

12. Ibid. Also see *Asian Weekly,* Hong Kong, Jan. 26–Feb. 8, 1998, pp. 30–35.

13. According to some reports, at this time Ching-kuo also signed a letter to the editor of his old paper at Uralmash, *Heavy Machinery.* The letter charged that Director of Uralmash Vladimirov had known and supported the Trotskyite activities of his brother. The first question is, why did Ching-kuo not send the letter when he was in Moscow or during the Sverdlovsk stop? If it is genuine, the letter was perhaps requested by K'ang, with Stalin's approval, to test Ching-kuo, and if he passed the test, to initiate him as a participant in the Great Terror. Vladimirov, who had attended parties at the Chiang flat, was already accused of high crimes, and Ching-kuo may have reasoned that nothing could save him now. He certainly knew of K'ang Sheng's ruthlessness and assumed that if he refused to cooperate, neither he nor his family would be on the ship when it pulled out of the harbor. Valentin Zaitsev in an article in *The Journalist,* 1996, Moscow, also cites this letter, giving the date as July 1, 1937, two and a half months after Ching-kuo's return to China—a discrepancy which suggests the NKVD may have fabricated the letter and put it in the files some years later.

14. Joseph E. Davies, *Mission to Moscow* (New York: V. Gollancz, 1941), p. 134.

15. Ch'en Li-fu and Sidney H. Chang, *The Storm Clouds Clear Over China* (Stanford: Hoover Institution Press, 1994), pp. 126–127.

16. Fenghua group, interview, Sept. 27, 1995.

17. *CCKHSCC*, chronology, vol. 1, p. 57.

18. Ch'en Li-fu, interview, May 29, 1996.

19. *CCKHSCC*, vol. 2, p. 533.

20. Fenghua group, interview, Sept. 27, 1995.

21. Ch'i P'eng-fei, *Chiang Chieh-shih,* p. 118.

22. Harrison Forman, "Gissimo Junior," *Collier's,* July 31, 1943. Forman visited Kannan in 1943 and interviewed Ching-kuo.

23. Fenghua group, interview, Sept. 25, 1995.

24. Ibid.

25. Sterling Seagrave quotes as fact several stories about displays of open animosity between Ching-kuo and his stepmother, in Seagrave, *The Soong Dynasty* (New York: Harper & Row, 1985), pp. 380, 450. Chiang Ching-kuo's relationship with his father and his emotional, intellectual, and political temperament at the time make these stories unlikely.

26. *New York Times*, April 4, 1937.

27. Fenghua group, interview, Sept. 25, 1995.